TRAINING & REFERENCE

murach's C# 2008

Joel Murach

MIKE MURACH & ASSOCIATES, INC.

1-800-221-5528 • (559) 440-9071 • Fax: (559) 440-0963

murachbooks@murach.com • www.murach.com

Authors: Joel Murach
Editor: Anne Boehm
Cover Design: Zylka Design
Production: Tom Murach
Cynthia Vasquez

Books for .NET 3.5 developers

Murach's C# 2008
Murach's ASP.NET 3.5 Web Programming with C# 2008
Murach's Visual Basic 2008
Murach's ASP.NET 3.5 Web Programming with VB 2008

Books for application developers using SQL

Murach's SQL Server 2008 for Developers
Murach's Oracle SQL and PL/SQL

Books for Java developers

Murach's Java SE 6
Murach's Java Servlets and JSP (Second Edition)

Books for IBM mainframe programmers

Murach's OS/390 and z/OS JCL
Murach's Mainframe COBOL
Murach's CICS for the COBOL Programmer
DB2 for the COBOL Programmer, Part 1

For more on Murach books,
please visit us at www.murach.com

Printed in the United States of America

10 9 8 7 6 5 4 3 2
ISBN-13: 978-1-890774-46-2

Contents

Expanded contents

Section 1 An introduction to Visual Studio

Chapter 1 How to get started with Visual Studio

Chapter 2 How to design a Windows Forms application

Chapter 3 How to code and test a Windows Forms application

Chapter 8 How to work with arrays and collections

Chapter 9 How to work with dates and strings

Chapter 10 More skills for working with Windows forms and controls

Chapter 18 How to work with data sources and datasets

Chapter 19 How to work with bound controls and parameterized queries

Chapter 20 How to use ADO.NET to write your own data access code

Section 5 Other skills for C# developers

Chapter 21 How to work with files and data streams

Chapter 22 How to work with XML files

Chapter 25 How to deploy an application

Appendix A How to install and use the software and files for this book

Introduction

C# is an elegant, object-oriented language that uses syntax that's similar to C++ and Java. As a result, it provides an easy migration path for C++ and Java developers who want to leverage the power of the .NET Framework. In addition, C# provides an opportunity for Visual Basic developers to learn a powerful language that's in the C++ family without leaving the comfort of the Visual Studio development environment.

Murach's C# 2008 is an updated edition of *Murach's C# 2005*, a book that helped thousands of programmers learn the C# language. This 2008 edition carefully integrates new features like object and collection initializers, automatically implemented properties, and LINQ with the features presented in the 2005 edition of the book. The result is a book that helps you learn as quickly and easily as possible.

Who this book is for

This book is for anyone who wants to learn how to use C# 2008 for developing professional Windows Forms applications using Visual Studio 2008 and the .NET Framework. That includes the entire range of developers from complete beginners to experienced Java, C++, and Visual Basic programmers.

To be able to work equally well for beginners, professionals, and everyone in between, this book uses a unique, modular instructional method that lets you set your own pace through the material. For example, section 1 guides you through the basics of using the Visual Studio IDE and the .NET Framework. Whether you're a Java or C++ programmer or a complete beginner, you can get up to speed quickly with this development environment by reading this section and doing the exercises at the end of each chapter. On the other hand, if you're a Visual Basic programmer who is already comfortable with this IDE and Framework, you can skip or skim this section.

Sections 2 and 3 use the same modular, self-paced approach to teach the skills that you need to become productive with the C# language. If you're familiar with another language in the C++ family, such as Java, you should be able to move through this section quickly, focusing on the classes and methods that are available from the .NET Framework. Conversely, if you're already familiar with .NET, you can focus on the details of the C# syntax. Either way, you're going to learn C# at a pace that's right for you.

What software you need

To develop Windows applications with C# 2008, you can use any of the full editions of Visual Studio 2008, including the Standard Edition, Professional Edition, or Team System. All of these come with everything you need to develop the Windows applications presented in this book, including the Visual Studio development environment, version 3.5 of the Microsoft .NET Framework, C# 2008, and a scaled-back version of SQL Server called SQL Server 2005 Express Edition.

You can also use the Visual C# 2008 Express Edition to develop Windows applications. And you can use it with the SQL Server 2005 Express Edition to develop database applications. Together, these two products provide everything you need to use this book, and both can be downloaded from Microsoft's web site for free!

If you use the Express Edition with this book, you'll find that some of its menus and dialog boxes are simpler than the ones shown in this book, which are all based on the Professional Edition. You'll also find that a few features aren't available from the Express Edition. To make sure that these variations don't interfere with your learning, this book carefully notes any differences between the Express Edition and the full editions of Visual Studio 2008. Later, if you should upgrade to one of the full editions, you'll find that all the skills that you've learned and all the applications that you've developed will still work.

What this book teaches

- Section 1 tours the .NET Framework and teaches the basics of working with Microsoft's development environment, Visual Studio 2008. In this section, you'll learn how to develop a simple Windows application. To do that, you'll use the Form Designer to design a Windows form, and you'll use the Code Editor to add and edit the code for the form.
- Section 2 presents the data types, control structures, and other essential elements of the C# language as well as the core .NET classes that you'll use to develop Windows applications. Along the way, you'll also learn how to handle the tasks that are required in most business applications. In chapter 7, for example, you'll learn professional data validation techniques that you won't find in competing books, even though everyone should know them.
- Section 3 teaches the powerful object-oriented programming features of the C# language. Here, you'll learn how to create your own business and database classes, and you'll learn how to use the database classes to populate the business objects with data from files or a database. That, of course, is how applications work in the real world, even though most C# books don't show you that. You'll also learn how to use inheritance, polymorphism, interfaces, and much more.

- Section 4 teaches you the basic skills for developing database applications. To start, you'll learn how to use data sources to build database applications quicker than ever, with minimal code and without using any ADO.NET code. This is particularly useful for developing small, relatively simple applications and for prototyping larger applications. Then, you'll learn how to write ADO.NET code that directly accesses the database. You'll use these skills as your applications get more complicated.
- Finally, section 5 shows you how to work with text, binary, and XML files. It also shows you the basic skills for working with LINQ, an exciting new feature that lets you query most any data source using the C# language. Then, you'll learn how to enhance a Windows interface with a multiple-document interface (MDI), menus, toolbars, and help, all the finishing touches that make your applications thoroughly professional. Last, to complete your training, you'll learn three ways to deploy your applications.

Why you'll learn faster and better with this book

Like all our books, this one has features that you won't find in competing books. That's why we believe that you'll learn faster and better with our book than with any other. Here are five of those features.

- Unlike most C# books, this book shows you how to get the most from Visual Studio 2008 as you develop your applications. Since using the features of this IDE is one of the keys to development productivity, we illustrate the best use of Visual Studio throughout this book.
- The exercises for each chapter guide you through the development of the book applications and challenge you to apply what you've learned in new ways. Because you can download the starting points for these exercises, you get the maximum amount of practice in a minimum of time.
- Unlike most C# books, all of the examples presented in this book are drawn from business applications. This difference becomes especially apparent in the object-oriented programming section, where most C# books resort to silly examples, like animal classes for mammals, cats, and dogs. In contrast, we present the use of business classes like customers, invoices, and products so you can see how object-oriented programming is used in the real world.
- To help you develop applications at a professional level, this book presents complete, non-trivial applications. That way, you can see the relationships between the C# code, objects, properties, methods, and events that an application requires, which is essential to your understanding. In contrast, most competing books present trivial applications that have little resemblance to applications in the real world, and that limits your learning potential.

- All of the information in this book is presented in our unique paired-page format with the essential syntax, guidelines, and examples on the right page and the perspective and extra explanation on the left page. Programmers tell us that they love this format because they can learn new skills whenever they have a few minutes and because they can quickly get the information that they need when they use our books for reference.

Downloadable files that can help you learn

If you go to our web site at www.murach.com, you can download all the files that you need for getting the most from this book. These files include:

- all of the applications presented in this book
- the starting points for all of the exercises
- the solutions for all of the exercises
- the database and files that are used by the applications and exercises

The code for the book applications is especially valuable because it lets you run the applications on your own PC, view all of the source code, experiment with the code, and copy and paste any of the source code into your own applications.

Please let us know how this book works for you

When we started this book, our main goal was to teach you the new features of C# 2008 along with all the old features that you still need to know to master C# programming. Whenever possible, we've integrated the new features with the old to make it easier for you to learn the new features. The main exception is the material on LINQ, which is covered in a separate chapter in section 5. Even so, some of the features that were added to support LINQ are covered earlier in the book since they can be used outside of LINQ.

Now that we're done, we hope that we've succeeded. So, if you have any comments about our book, we would appreciate hearing from you. If you like our book, please tell a friend. And good luck with your C# programming.

Joel Murach, Author
joelmurach@yahoo.com

Anne Boehm, Editor
anne@murach.com

Section 1

An introduction to Visual Studio

This section gets you started right by introducing you to the Visual Studio 2008 components that support C# programming. To start, chapter 1 introduces you to the .NET Framework, the languages that work with the .NET Framework, and the Visual Studio development environment. Then, chapter 2 shows you how to use Visual Studio to design a form for a Windows Forms application. Finally, chapter 3 shows you how to use Visual Studio to enter and edit the code that determines how the form works.

When you complete this section, you should have a general understanding of how to use Visual Studio to develop a Windows application. You should also have the skills that you need for designing a Windows form and entering the code for it. Then, the next section of this book will teach you the essentials of the C# language.

1

How to get started with Visual Studio

This chapter gets you started with Visual Studio 2008 by introducing the .NET Framework, the languages that work with the .NET Framework, and the Visual Studio development environment. It also provides a quick tour of this development environment. Along the way, you'll learn all of the concepts and terms that you need for developing .NET applications.

An introduction to .NET development

This section presents some of the concepts and terms that you need before you begin developing .NET applications. Although this section focuses on the C# programming language, most of these concepts and terms also apply to the other .NET programming languages.

Windows Forms and Web Forms applications

You can use Visual Studio for developing the two types of applications shown in figure 1-1. A *Windows Forms application* (or *WinForms app*) is a typical *Windows application* that runs on the user's PC. Each *Windows form* (or just *form*) in the application provides a user interface that lets the user interact with the application. In the example in this figure, the application consists of a single form that lets the user perform either of two calculations: a future value or a monthly investment calculation. Many applications, though, require more than one form.

As part of the user interface, a Windows Forms application uses *Windows Forms controls*. For instance, the form in this figure uses radio buttons, labels, text boxes, and buttons. In the next chapter, you'll start learning how to develop Windows Forms applications.

Another type of application that you can develop with C# is a *Web Forms application* (or just *web application*). Like a Windows Forms application, a web application consists of one or more *web forms* that can contain controls. Unlike Windows forms, web forms are accessed by and displayed in a *web browser*. For instance, the web form in this figure is displayed in Microsoft's web browser, which is called the Internet Explorer.

As part of the user interface, a web form uses *Web Forms controls*. These controls are similar to the Windows Forms controls, but they work only with web forms.

In contrast to a Windows Forms application, which runs on the user's PC, the code for a Web Forms application runs on a web server. As this code is executed, it passes the visual portion of the application to the browser running on the client in the form of HTML (Hypertext Markup Language). The browser then interprets the HTML and displays the form.

A Windows Forms application running on the Windows desktop

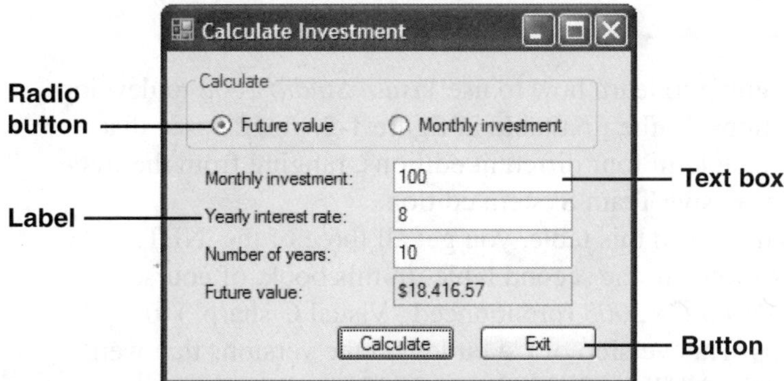

A Web Forms application running in a Web browser

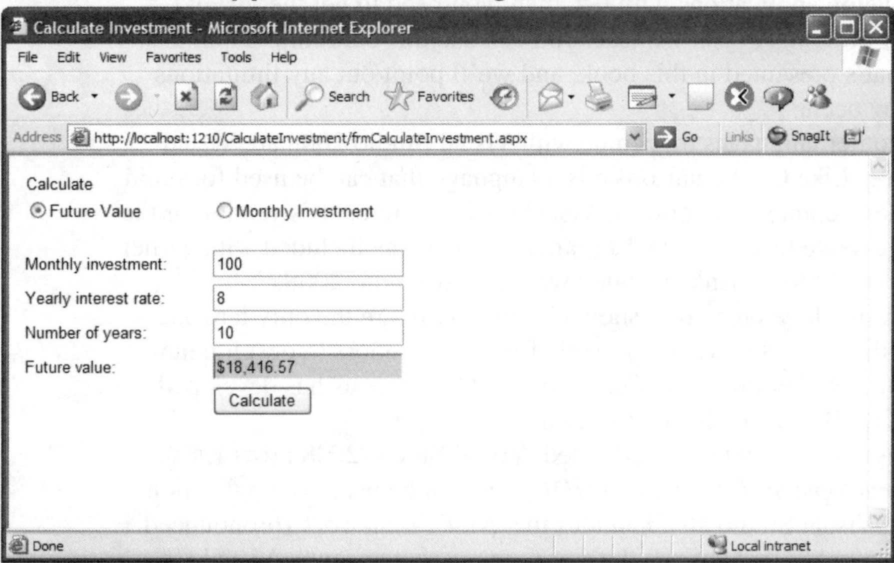

Description

- A *Windows Forms application* (or *Windows application*) runs in its own window and consists of one or more *Windows forms* that provide the user interface.
- Each Windows form contains *Windows Forms controls* like labels, text boxes, buttons, and radio buttons. These controls let the user interact with the application.
- A *Web Forms application* (or *web application*) runs on a web server, but its user interface is displayed in a *web browser* on the client machine. A Web Forms application consists of one or more *web forms* that provide the user interface for the application.
- Each web form contains *Web Forms controls* like labels, text boxes, buttons, and radio buttons.

Figure 1-1 Windows Forms and Web Forms applications

Visual Studio and the .NET programming languages

In this book, you're going to learn how to use *Visual Studio 2008* to develop Windows Forms applications. In the first table in figure 1-2, you can see that Visual Studio 2008 is available in four different editions, ranging from the free Express Edition to the expensive Team System edition.

With the last three editions in this table, you get all three of the .NET programming languages shown in the second table. In this book, of course, you'll learn how to use *Visual C# 2008* (pronounced "Visual C sharp") to develop your applications. This version of C# builds on the versions that were included with Visual Studio .NET 2002, 2003, and 2005.

In contrast, each Express Edition of Visual Studio provides only one language. To develop applications with C#, then, you need to get the *Visual C# 2008 Express Edition*. As you will see, you can use this edition to do almost everything that's presented in this book, and we'll point out any limitations whenever they occur.

The two other languages that come with Visual Studio 2008 are Visual Basic and C++. Like C#, Visual Basic is a language that can be used for rapid application development. In contrast, Visual C++ is Microsoft's version of the C++ language. Note that the Visual J# language that was included with earlier versions of Visual Studio isn't included with Visual Studio 2008.

Although the three languages shown in this figure are the only languages that come with Visual Studio, it's possible for other vendors to develop languages for the .NET Framework. For example, Micro Focus has developed a version of COBOL for the .NET Framework.

Regardless of the language that's used, Visual Studio 2008 provides an *Integrated Development Environment* (*IDE*) that can be used for application development. Visual Studio also includes the *.NET Framework* (pronounced "dot net framework") that defines the environment that executes Visual C# applications. You'll learn more about both as you progress through this chapter.

All but the Express editions of Visual Studio also include *SQL Server 2005 Express*. Otherwise, you can download SQL Server Express from the Microsoft web site for free. SQL Server Express is a lightweight version of the Microsoft SQL Server 2005 database management system, and it's ideal for testing database applications on your own PC.

In this figure, you can see that Visual Studio can be used on any PC that runs Windows XP or later. Then, the applications that are developed with Visual Studio can be run on any PC that runs Windows 2000 or later, depending on which .NET components are used by the application.

Visual Studio 2008 Editions

Edition	Description
Express Edition	A free, downloadable edition that supports just one of the Visual Studio programming languages shown below. It is appropriate for students and hobbyists. There is also an Express Edition of SQL Server called SQL Server 2005 Express.
Standard Edition	Designed for individual developers who want to build Windows and web applications
Professional Edition	Designed for individual developers who want to build a wide variety of Windows, web, mobile, and Office-based solutions
Team System	Intended for teams of developers working on large projects

Programming languages supported by Visual Studio 2008

Language	Description
Visual Basic	Designed for rapid application development
Visual C#	Combines the features of Java and C++ and is suitable for rapid application development
Visual C++	Microsoft's version of C++

Platforms that can run Visual Studio 2008

- Windows XP, Windows Vista, or later releases of Windows

Platforms that can run applications created with Visual Studio 2008

- Windows 2000 and later releases of Windows, depending on which .NET components the application uses

Description

- *Visual Studio 2008* is a suite of products that includes the .NET Framework and an *Integrated Development Environment* (*IDE*).
- The *.NET Framework* provides a library of code that supports all three programming languages shown above.
- The *Visual Studio IDE* can be used to develop applications with any of the three programming languages.
- *SQL Server 2005 Express* is a lightweight version of the Microsoft SQL Server 2005 database management system.

Notes

- Visual J#, which was included with earlier versions of Visual Studio, isn't included with Visual Studio 2008.
- A new release of SQL Server, called SQL Server 2008, is currently under development and is expected to become available in the second quarter of 2008.

Figure 1-2 Visual Studio and the .NET programming languages

The .NET Framework

To give you a more detailed view of the .NET Framework, figure 1-3 presents its main components. As you can see, the .NET Framework provides a common set of services that application programs written in a .NET language such as C# can use to run on various operating systems and hardware platforms. The .NET Framework is divided into two main components: the .NET Framework Class Library and the Common Language Runtime.

The *.NET Framework Class Library* consists of segments of pre-written code called *classes* that provide many of the functions that you need for developing .NET applications. For instance, the Windows Forms classes are used for developing Windows Forms applications. The ASP.NET classes are used for developing Web Forms applications. And other classes let you work with databases, manage security, access files, and perform many other functions.

Although it's not apparent in this figure, the classes in the .NET Framework Class Library are organized in a hierarchical structure. Within this structure, related classes are organized into groups called *namespaces*. Each namespace contains the classes used to support a particular function. For example, the System.Windows.Forms namespace contains the classes used to create forms and the System.Data namespace contains the classes you use to access data.

The *Common Language Runtime* (*CLR*) provides the services that are needed for executing any application that's developed with one of the .NET languages. This is possible because all of the .NET languages compile to a common intermediate language, which you'll learn more about in figure 1-5. The CLR also provides the *Common Type System* that defines the data types that are used by all .NET languages. Because all of the .NET applications are managed by the CLR, they are sometimes referred to as *managed applications.*

If you're new to programming, you might not understand this diagram completely, but that's all right. For now, all you need to understand is the general structure of the .NET Framework and the terms that have been presented so far. As you progress through this book, this diagram will make more sense, and you will become more familiar with each of the terms.

The .NET Framework

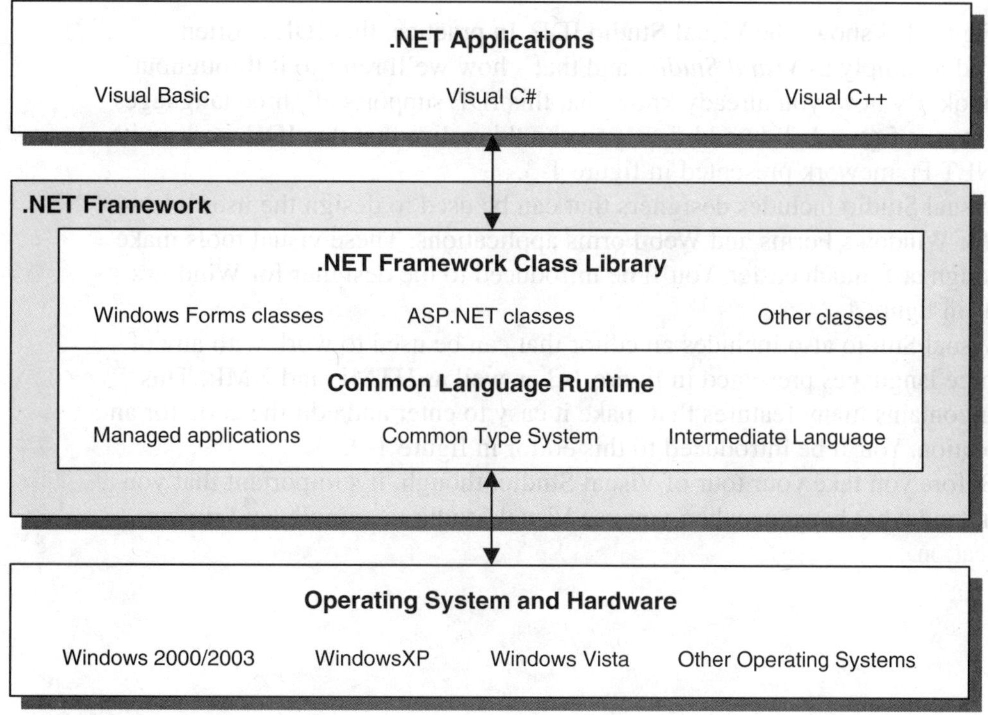

Description

- Windows Forms applications do not access the operating system or computer hardware directly. Instead, they use services of the .NET Framework, which in turn access the operating system and hardware.
- The .NET Framework consists of two main components: the .NET Framework Class Library and the Common Language Runtime.
- The *.NET Framework Class Library* provides files that contain pre-written code known as *classes* that are available to all of the .NET programming languages. This class library consists of thousands of classes, but you can create simple .NET applications once you learn how to use just a few of them.
- The *Common Language Runtime*, or *CLR*, manages the execution of .NET programs by coordinating essential functions such as memory management, code execution, security, and other services. Because .NET applications are managed by the CLR, they are called *managed applications.*
- The *Common Type System* is a component of the CLR that ensures that all .NET applications use the same basic data types no matter what programming languages are used to develop the applications.

Figure 1-3 The .NET Framework

The Visual Studio IDE

Figure 1-4 shows the Visual Studio IDE. In practice, this IDE is often referred to simply as *Visual Studio*, and that's how we'll refer to it throughout this book. By now, you already know that this IDE supports all three languages presented in figure 1-2. In addition, you should realize that this IDE works with the .NET Framework presented in figure 1-3.

Visual Studio includes designers that can be used to design the user interface for Windows Forms and Web Forms applications. These visual tools make this tough task much easier. You'll be introduced to the designer for Windows Forms in figure 1-8.

Visual Studio also includes an editor that can be used to work with any of the three languages presented in figure 1-2 as well as HTML and XML. This editor contains many features that make it easy to enter and edit the code for an application. You'll be introduced to this editor in figure 1-9.

Before you take your tour of Visual Studio, though, it's important that you understand what happens when you use Visual Studio to compile and run an application.

The Visual Studio IDE

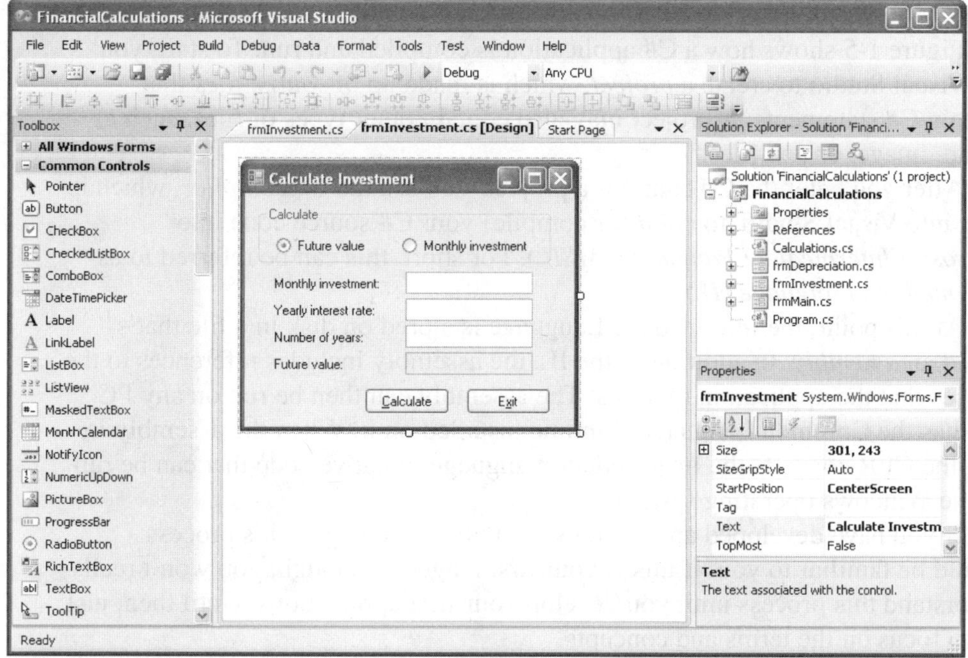

Description

- The Visual Studio IDE is often referred to as *Visual Studio*, even though that name is also used to refer to the entire suite of products, including the .NET Framework.
- Visual Studio supports all three languages presented in figure 1-2.
- Visual Studio includes designers that can be used to develop Windows Forms applications and Web Forms applications.
- Visual Studio includes a code editor that can be used to work with any of the three languages presented in figure 1-2 as well as HTML and XML.

Figure 1-4 The Visual Studio IDE

How a C# application is compiled and run

Figure 1-5 shows how a C# application is compiled and run. To start, you use Visual Studio to create a *project*, which is made up of *source files* that contain C# statements. A project may also contain other types of files, such as sound, image, or text files.

After you enter the C# code for a project, you use the *C# compiler*, which is built into Visual Studio, to *build* (or compile) your C# source code into *Microsoft Intermediate Language* (*MSIL*). For short, this can be referred to as *Intermediate Language* (*IL*).

At this point, the Intermediate Language is stored on disk in a file that's called an *assembly*. In addition to the IL, the assembly includes references to the classes that the application requires. The assembly can then be run on any PC that has the Common Language Runtime installed on it. When the assembly is run, the CLR converts the Intermediate Language to native code that can be run by the Windows operating system.

If you have developed applications with other languages, this process should be familiar to you. If this is your first language, though, you won't really understand this process until you develop your first applications. Until then, just try to focus on the terms and concepts.

Incidentally, a *solution* is a container that can hold one or more projects. Although a solution can contain more than one project, the solution for a simple application usually contains just one project. In that case, the solution and the project are essentially the same thing.

How C# differs from the other .NET languages

C# uses the same .NET Framework classes as the other .NET programming languages. These classes affect almost every aspect of programming, including creating and working with forms and controls, using databases, and working with basic language features such as arrays and strings. In addition, C# works with the same Visual Studio IDE as the other .NET languages. As a result, C# has many similarities to the other .NET languages. The main difference is the syntax of the language.

How C# differs from Java

The C# language uses a syntax that's similar to the syntax for the Java language. However, Java relies on a different framework of supporting classes, and the development environments for working with Java are different than Visual Studio. As a result, if you have experience with Java, it should be easy for you to learn the C# language. However, if Visual Studio and the .NET Framework classes are new to you, it may take some time for you to learn how they work.

How a C# application is compiled and run

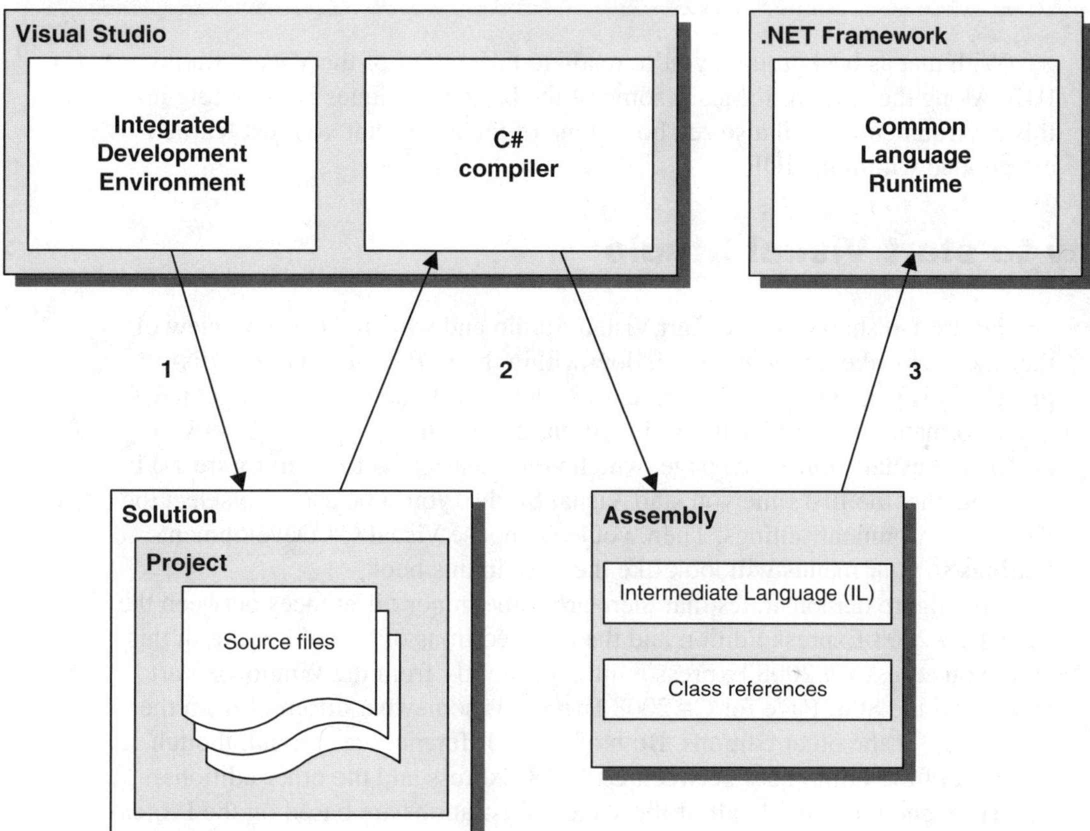

Operation

1. The programmer uses Visual Studio to create a *project*, which includes C# *source files*. In some cases, a project will also contain other types of files, such as graphic image or sound files.
2. The C# *compiler builds* (translates) the C# source code for a project into *Microsoft Intermediate Language* (*MSIL*), or just *Intermediate Language* (*IL*). This language is stored on disk in an *assembly* that also contains references to the required classes. An assembly is an executable file that has an *.exe* or *.dll* extension.
3. The assembly is run by the .NET Framework's Common Language Runtime. The CLR manages all aspects of how the assembly is run, including converting the Intermediate Language to native code that can be run by the operating system, managing memory for the assembly, and enforcing security.

About projects and solutions

- A *solution* is a container that can hold one or more projects.

Figure 1-5 How a C# application is compiled and run

A tour of the Visual Studio IDE

With that as background, you're ready to take a tour of the Visual Studio IDE. Along the way, you'll learn some of the basic techniques for working in this environment. You'll also see how some of the terms that you just learned are applied within the IDE.

How to start Visual Studio

Figure 1-6 shows how to start Visual Studio and what the opening view of the IDE looks like. In the main window within the IDE, a Start Page is displayed. This page lets you open recent projects, create new ones, and get news and information about Visual Studio. Often, though, this page just slows you down, so I usually close this page, which you'll learn how to do in figure 1-11.

Note that the first time you start Visual Studio, you'll be asked to select the default environment settings. Then, you can choose Visual C# Development Settings so your menus will look like the ones in this book.

This figure demonstrates that there are some minor differences between the Visual C# 2008 Express Edition and the other editions of Visual Studio. In this case, you access C# 2008 Express a little differently from the Windows Start menu, and the Start Page for C# 2008 Express is somewhat different from the Start Page for the other editions. Both of these differences are trivial, though, as are most of the differences between C# 2008 Express and the other editions.

Throughout this book, all of the screen illustrations are based on the Professional Edition of Visual Studio 2008. Whenever the Express Edition varies in any way that is likely to confuse someone who's using it, though, we will carefully detail the differences. As you would expect, the Professional Edition also has some features that aren't available with the Express Edition, and we will of course point out those limitations too.

In general, though, using the C# 2008 Express Edition is an excellent way to get started with Visual Studio 2008. As you will see, you can develop professional applications with that edition. And both the skills that you learn and the applications that you develop will work whenever you want to upgrade to one of the other editions.

The Start Page that's displayed when you start Visual Studio

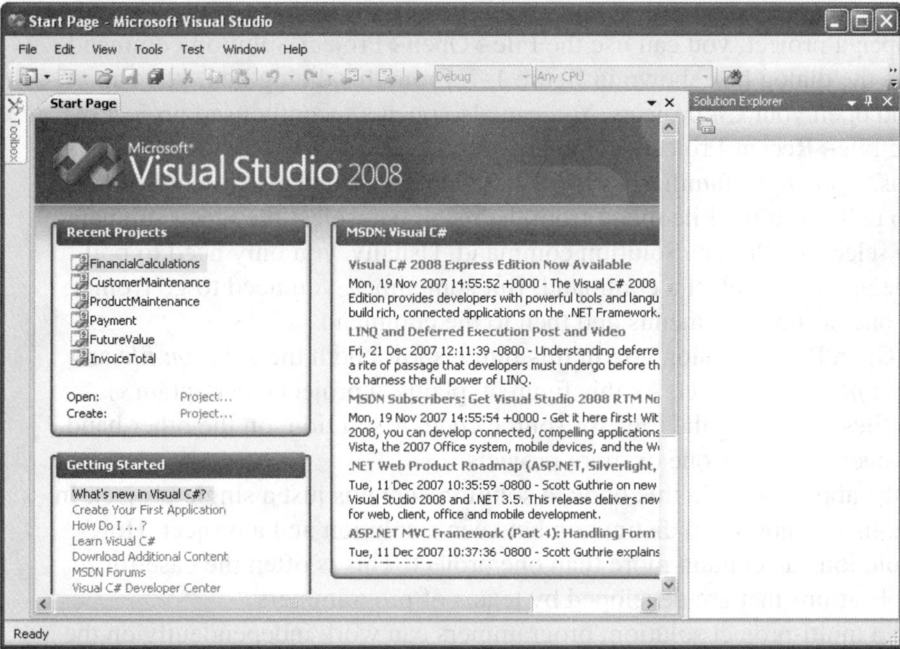

Description

- To start Visual Studio, open the Windows Start menu, then locate and select Microsoft Visual Studio 2008. Typically, this item is in the Microsoft Visual Studio 2008 submenu of the All Programs menu.
- To make it easier to start Visual Studio, you may want to create a shortcut for Microsoft Visual Studio 2008 or Microsoft Visual C# 2008 Express Edition and place it on the desktop.
- When Visual Studio starts, a Start Page is displayed in the Visual Studio IDE. You can use this page to open recent projects, create new ones, start tutorials, and so on.

Variations between the Professional and Express Editions

- In this book, all of the screen illustrations are from the Professional Edition of Visual Studio 2008. In general, these illustrations are the same for both the Professional Edition and the Visual C# 2008 Express Edition.
- Whenever the Express Edition differs significantly from the Professional Edition, we'll point out the differences.

Express Edition difference

- To start Visual Studio, open the Windows Start menu and select Microsoft Visual C# 2008 Express Edition. Typically, this item is in the All Programs menu.

Figure 1-6 How to start Visual Studio

How to open or close an existing project

To open a project, you can use the File→Open→Project/Solution command to display the dialog box shown in figure 1-7. From this dialog box, you can locate and open your C# projects. You can also open a recently used project by using the File→Recent Projects command.

In case you aren't familiar with this notation, File→Open→Project/Solution means to pull down the File menu from the menu bar, select the Open submenu, and then select the Project/Solution command. Usually, you only need to pull down one menu and select a command. But sometimes, you need to go from a menu to one or more submenus and then to the command.

The Open Project dialog box in this figure shows both the *solution file* and the *project file* for a project. As this figure explains, a project can contain multiple files, including the files for source code. A solution, on the other hand, is a container that holds one or more projects.

For the applications in this book, a solution contains just a single project. In that case, there's not much distinction between a solution and a project. However, a solution can contain more than one project. This is often the case for large applications that are developed by teams of programmers.

With a multi-project solution, programmers can work independently on the projects that make up the solution. In fact, the projects don't even have to be written in the same language. For example, a solution can contain two projects, one written in C#, the other in Visual Basic.

At this point, you might wonder whether you should open a project or a solution. In this figure, for example, FinancialCalculations.sln is a solution and FinancialCalculations.csproj is a C# project. In most cases, though, it doesn't matter whether you open the solution or the project. Either way, both the solution and the project files will be opened. And when you use the File→Close Solution command, both the solution and the project files will be closed.

Some possible menu variations

Curiously, some of the menus vary slightly based on the import and export settings that are set the first time you run Visual Studio 2008. So don't be surprised if you find that you use the File→Open Project command to open a project on your system instead of the File→Open→Project/Solution command. In this book, we specify the menus that you get when you use the Visual C# Development Settings, and we'll show you how to change your settings in the next chapter. Since these menu variations are trivial, though, you shouldn't have any trouble using menus even if the ones on your system are slightly different than the ones we specify.

The Open Project dialog box

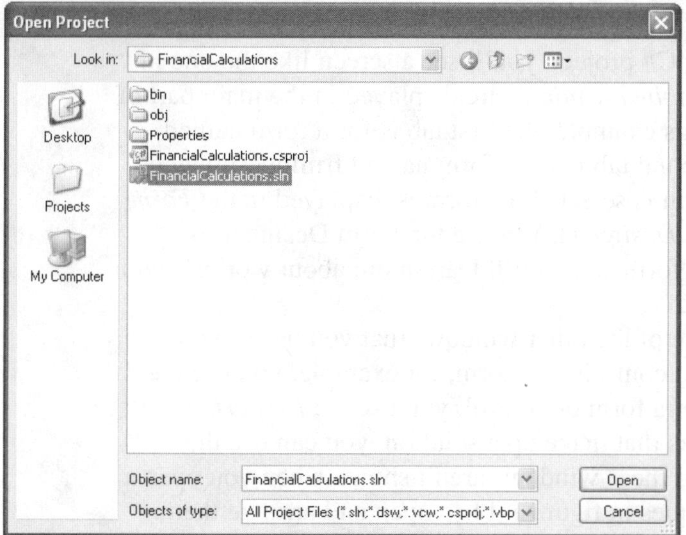

Project and solution concepts

- Every C# project has a *project file* with an extension of *csproj* that keeps track of the files that make up the project and records various settings for the project. In this figure, the project file is just above the highlighted file.
- Every solution has a *solution file* with an extension of *sln* that keeps track of the projects that make up the solution. In this figure, the solution file is highlighted.
- When you open a project file, Visual Studio opens the solution that contains the project. And when you open a solution file, Visual Studio automatically opens all the projects contained in the solution. So either way, both the project and the solution are opened.
- Sometimes the project and solution files are stored in the same directory. Sometimes the project file is stored in a subdirectory of the directory that contains the solution file.

How to open a project

- To open an existing project, use the File→Open→Project/Solution command. Then, use the controls in the Open dialog box to locate and select the project or solution you want to open.
- After you've worked on one or more projects, their names will be listed in the File→Recent Projects submenu. Then, you can click on a project name to open it.
- You can also use the links on the Start Page to open a project.

How to close a project

- Use the File→Close Solution command.

Express Edition difference

- To open an existing project, use the File→Open Project command.

Figure 1-7 How to open or close an existing project

How to use the Form Designer

When you open an existing C# project, you'll see a screen like the one in figure 1-8. Here, one or more *tabbed windows* are displayed in the main part of the Visual Studio window. In this example, the first tab is for a form named frmDepreciation.cs, and the second tab is for a form named frmInvestment.cs. Since the tab for the second form is selected, its form is displayed in the *Form Designer window* (or just *Form Designer*). You use the Form Designer to develop the user interface for a form, and you'll learn more about working with the Form Designer in chapter 2.

This figure also shows some of the other windows that you use as you develop C# applications. To add controls to a form, for example, you use the *Toolbox*. To set the properties of a form or control, you use the *Properties window*. And to manage the files that make up a solution, you can use the *Solution Explorer*. If all three of these windows aren't shown when you open a project, you can use the techniques in figure 1-11 to open and arrange them.

This figure also points out two of the toolbars that are available from Visual Studio. You can use these toolbars to perform a variety of operations, and the toolbars change depending on what you're doing. Of course, you can also perform any operation by using the menus at the top of Visual Studio. And you can perform some operations by using the context-sensitive shortcut menu that's displayed when you right-click on an object within Visual Studio.

Visual Studio with the Form Designer window displayed

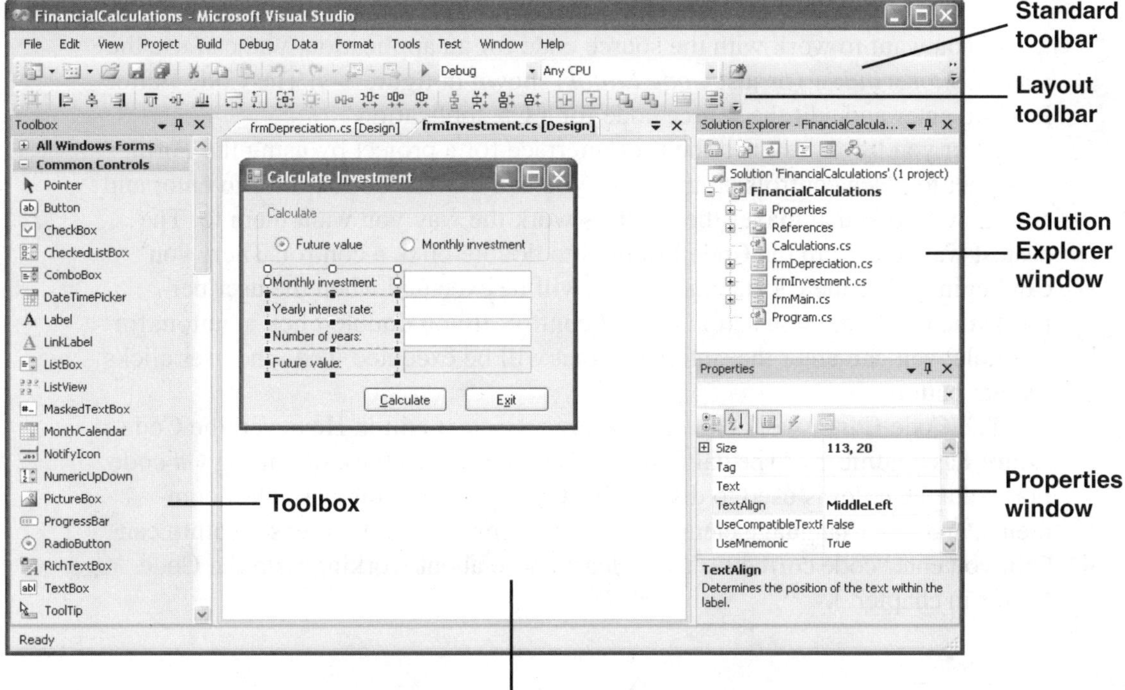

Description

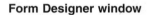

- The main Visual Studio workspace contains one or more *tabbed windows*. To develop a form, you use the *Form Designer window* (or just *Form Designer*). To develop code, you use the Code Editor window that's shown in figure 1-9.
- To add controls and other items to a form, you use the *Toolbox*. The Toolbox contains a variety of items organized into categories such as Common Controls, Containers, Menus & Toolbars, Data, and so on.
- To change the way a form or control looks or operates, you use the *Properties window*. This window displays the properties of the item that's selected in the Form Designer.
- You use the Solution Explorer window to manage project files. You'll learn more about the Solution Explorer in figure 1-10.
- Several toolbars are available from Visual Studio. The Standard toolbar includes standard Windows toolbar buttons such as Open, Save, Cut, Copy, and Paste, plus other buttons that you'll learn about as you progress through this book.
- As you work with Visual Studio, you'll find that other toolbars are displayed, depending on what you're doing.

How to use the Code Editor

If you want to work with the source code for an application, you can use the *Code Editor window* (or just *Code Editor*) shown in figure 1-9. The Code Editor lets you enter and edit the source code for a C# application.

After you have designed the user interface for a project by using the Form Designer to place controls on the form, you can use the Code Editor to enter and edit the C# code that makes the controls work the way you want them to. The easiest way to call up the Code Editor is to double-click a control. Then, you can begin typing the C# statements that will be executed when the user performs the most common action on that control. If you double-click a button, for example, you can enter the statements that will be executed when the user clicks on that button.

The Code Editor works much like any other text editor. However, the Code Editor has a number of special features that simplify the task of editing C# code. For example, color is used to distinguish C# keywords from variables, comments, and other language elements. And the improved IntelliSense feature can help you enter code correctly. You'll learn more about working with the Code Editor in chapter 3.

Visual Studio with the Code Editor window displayed

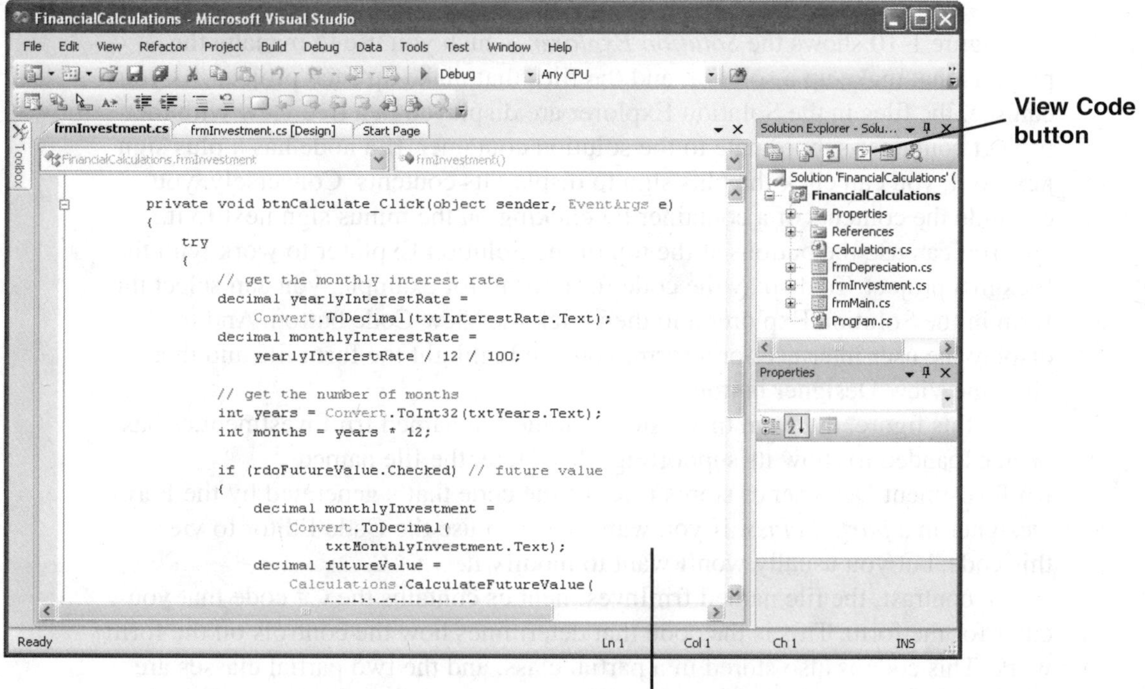

Description

- The *Code Editor window* (or just *Code Editor*) is where you create and edit the C# code that your application requires. The Code Editor works much like any other text editor, so you shouldn't have much trouble learning how to use it.
- You can display the Code Editor by double-clicking the form or one of the controls in the Form Designer window. Or, you can select the form in the Solution Explorer and click the View Code button.
- Once you've opened the Code Editor, you can return to the Form Designer by clicking the [Design] tab for that window or the View Designer button in the Solution Explorer (to the right of the View Code button). You can also move among these windows by pressing Ctrl+Tab or Shift+Ctrl+Tab, or by selecting a form from the Active Files drop-down list that's available to the right of the tabs.
- It's important to realize that the Form Designer and the Code Editor give you two different views of a form. The Form Designer gives you a visual representation of the form. The Code Editor shows you the C# code that makes the form work the way you want it to.

Figure 1-9 How to use the Code Editor

How to use the Solution Explorer

Figure 1-10 shows the *Solution Explorer*, which you use to manage the projects that make up a solution and the files that make up each project. As you can see, the files in the Solution Explorer are displayed in a tree view with the project container subordinate to the solution container. If a node has a plus sign next to it, you can click the plus sign to display its contents. Conversely, you can hide the contents of a container by clicking on the minus sign next to it.

You can use the buttons at the top of the Solution Explorer to work with the files in a project. To display the code for a form, for example, you can select the form in the Solution Explorer and then click the View Code button. And to display the user interface for a form, you can highlight the form file and then click the View Designer button.

In this figure, the form that's stored in the file named frmInvestment.cs has been expanded to show its supporting files. Here, the file named frmInvestment.Designer.cs stores most of the code that's generated by the Form Designer in a *partial class*. If you want, you can use the Code Editor to view this code, but you usually won't want to modify it.

In contrast, the file named frmInvestment.cs contains the C# code that you enter for the form. This is the code that determines how the controls on the form work. This code is also stored in a partial class, and the two partial classes are combined into a single class for the Investment form when the project is built. You'll learn a lot more about both classes and partial classes as you progress through this book.

As you develop a project, you can also create classes that contain C# code but don't define forms. In this figure, for example, the file named Calculations.cs is a source file that contains a class that isn't for a form. In this case, you can use the View Code button to display the code for the class, but the View Designer button isn't available.

To identify the files that make up a project, you can look at the icon that's displayed to the left of the file name. The icon for a form file, for example, is a form, and the icon for a C# class file that isn't for a form has a C# icon on it. As you can see, this project consists of three form files and two class files that contain C# code.

Note, however, that all of the files have the file extension cs regardless of their contents. Because of that, we recommend that you name your files in a way that identifies their contents. For example, we add the prefix frm to the names of our form files. That way, it's easy to identify the form files when you work with them outside of the Solution Explorer.

This project also includes a folder named References. This folder contains references to the assemblies that contain the namespaces that are available to the project. Remember that the namespaces contain the .NET Framework classes that the application requires. In this case, all of the assemblies were added to the project automatically when this project was created.

The Solution Explorer

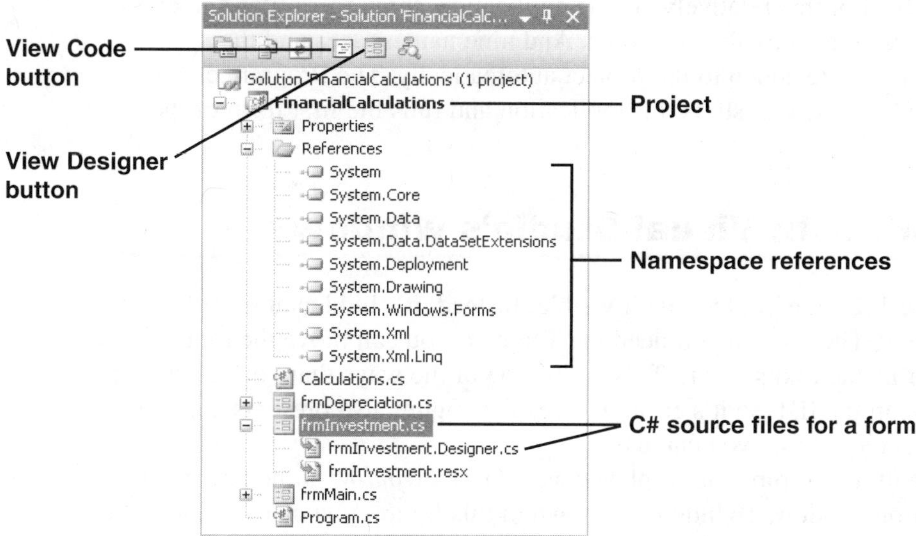

Description

- You use the *Solution Explorer* to manage and display the files and projects in a solution. The Solution Explorer lists all of the projects for the current solution, as well as all of the files that make up each project.
- Plus (+) and minus (-) signs in the Solution Explorer indicate groups of files. You can click these signs to expand and collapse the groups.
- You can perform most of the functions you need by using the buttons at the top of the Solution Explorer window. The buttons you'll use most are the View Code and View Designer buttons, which open or switch to the Code Editor and Form Designer windows.

Project files

- The Solution Explorer uses different icons to distinguish between source code files that define forms and source code files that don't define forms.
- Each form is defined by two C# source files where each file contains a *partial class*. The file with the cs extension contains the code that's entered by the programmer, and the file with the Designer.cs extension contains the code that's generated when the programmer works with the Form Designer. When the project is compiled, these partial classes are combined into a single class that determines the appearance and operation of the form.
- A source code file that doesn't define a form is usually stored in a single C# source file that contains a single class.
- The Program.cs file is created automatically when a Windows application is created. It contains the C# code that starts the application and runs the first form in the application.
- The References folder contains references to the assemblies for the namespaces that the application can use. These namespaces contain the classes that the project requires. In most cases, all the references that you need are included when the project is created.

Figure 1-10 How to use the Solution Explorer

This should give you some idea of how complicated the file structure for a project can be. For this relatively simple application, three form files and one class file were created by the developer. And nine namespaces and the Program.cs file were added to the project automatically. The Program.cs file contains the C# code that starts the application and runs the first form of the application.

How to work with Visual Studio's windows

In figure 1-11, the Toolbox isn't visible. Instead, it's hidden at the left side of the window. Then, when you need the Toolbox, you can move the mouse pointer over its tab to display it. This is just one of the ways that you can adjust the windows in the IDE so it's easier to use. This figure also presents many of the other techniques that you can use.

By default, the Toolbox is displayed as a *docked window* at the left side of the application window. To hide it as shown in this figure, you can click its Auto Hide button. The Auto Hide button looks like a pushpin, as illustrated by the button near the upper right corner of the Properties window. When a docked window is hidden, it appears as a tab at the edge of the application window.

You can also undock a docked window so it floats in the middle of the IDE. To do that, you drag its title bar away from the edge of the IDE or double-click its title bar. In this figure, for example, you can see that the Solution Explorer window that was docked at the right side of the IDE is now floating in the middle of the IDE. In addition, the Class View window is grouped with the Solution Explorer window as a tabbed window. Although we don't recommend this arrangement of windows, it should give you an idea of the many ways that you can arrange them.

As you review the information in this figure, notice that you can't hide, separate, or undock the windows in Visual Studio's main area. For the most part, you'll just move between these windows by clicking on their tabs or by using one of the other techniques.

If you experiment with these techniques for a few minutes, you'll see that they're easy to master. Then, as you get more comfortable with Visual Studio, you can adjust the windows so they work best for you.

Visual Studio with two floating windows and a hidden window

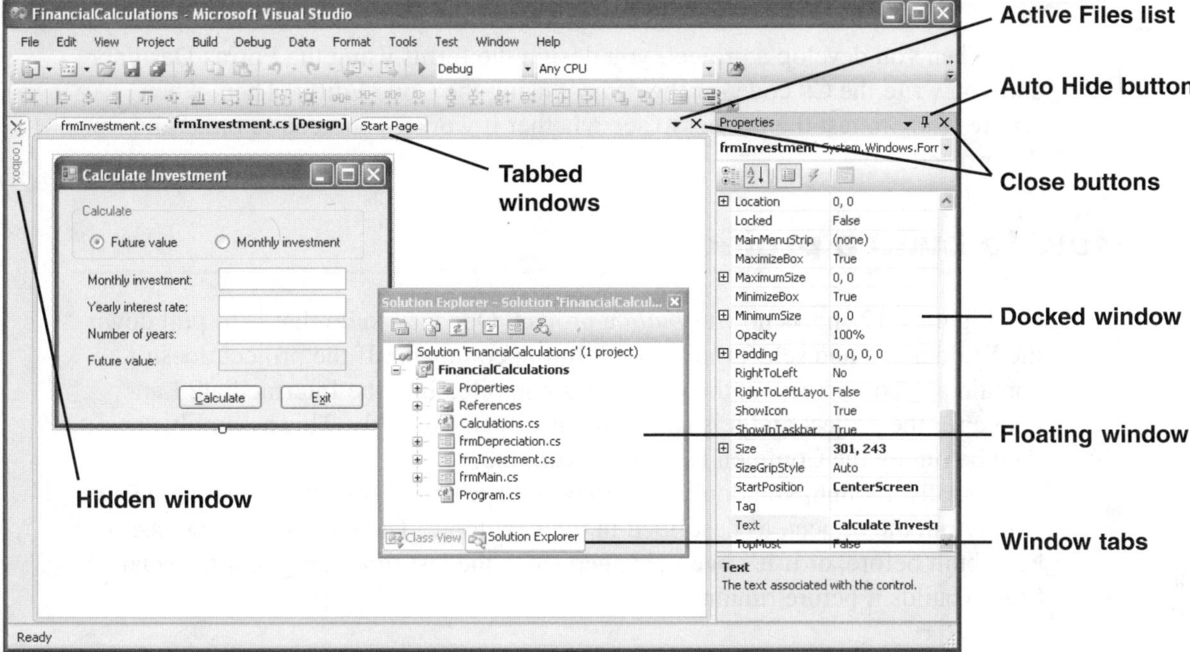

How to rearrange windows

- To close a window, click its Close button. To redisplay it, click its button in the Standard toolbar (if one is available) or select it from the View menu.
- To undock a *docked window* so it floats on the screen, drag it by its title bar away from the edge of the application window or double-click its title bar.
- To dock a floating window, drag it by its title bar onto one of the positioning arrows that become available. Or, double-click its title bar to return it to its default location.
- To hide a docked window, click its Auto Hide button. Then, the window is displayed as a tab at the edge of the screen, and you can display it by placing the mouse pointer over the tab. To change it back, display it and then click the Auto Hide button.
- To size a window, place the mouse pointer over an edge or a corner of the window, and drag it.
- If two or more windows are grouped into tabbed windows, you can display any window in the group by clicking on its tab. To close a tabbed window, you can click on its Close button or right-click on its tab and select the Close command.
- If you dock, undock, hide, or unhide a tabbed window, all the windows in the group are docked, undocked, hidden, or unhidden.

Warning

- Be careful when modifying the window layout. Although it's easy to rearrange your windows, it can be hard to get them back the way they were.

Figure 1-11 How to work with Visual Studio's windows

How to test a project

When you develop a project, you design the forms using the Forms Designer and you write the C# code for the project using the Code Editor. Then, when you're ready to test the project to see whether it works, you need to build and run the project.

How to build a project

Figure 1-12 shows how to *build* a project. One way to do that is to pull down the Build menu and select the Build Solution command. If the project doesn't contain any coding errors, the C# code is compiled into the Intermediate Language for the project and it is saved on disk in an assembly. This assembly can then be run by the Common Language Runtime.

Usually, though, you don't need to build a project this way. Instead, you can simply run the project, as described in the next topic. Then, if the project hasn't been built before, or if it's been changed since the last time it was built, Visual Studio builds it before running it.

How to run a project

The easiest way to *run* a project is to click the Start Debugging button that's identified in figure 1-12. Then, the project is built if necessary, the Intermediate Language is executed by the Common Language Runtime, and the first (or only) form of the project is displayed. In this figure, for example, you can see the first form that's displayed when the Financial Calculations project is run. This form contains two buttons that let you display the other forms of the project.

To test the project, you try everything that the application is intended to do. When data entries are required, you try ranges of data that test the limits of the application. When you're satisfied that the application works under all conditions, you can exit from it by clicking on the Close button in the upper right corner of the form or on a button control that has been designed for that purpose. If the application doesn't work, of course, you need to fix it, but you'll learn more about that in chapter 3.

The form that's displayed when the Financial Calculations project is run

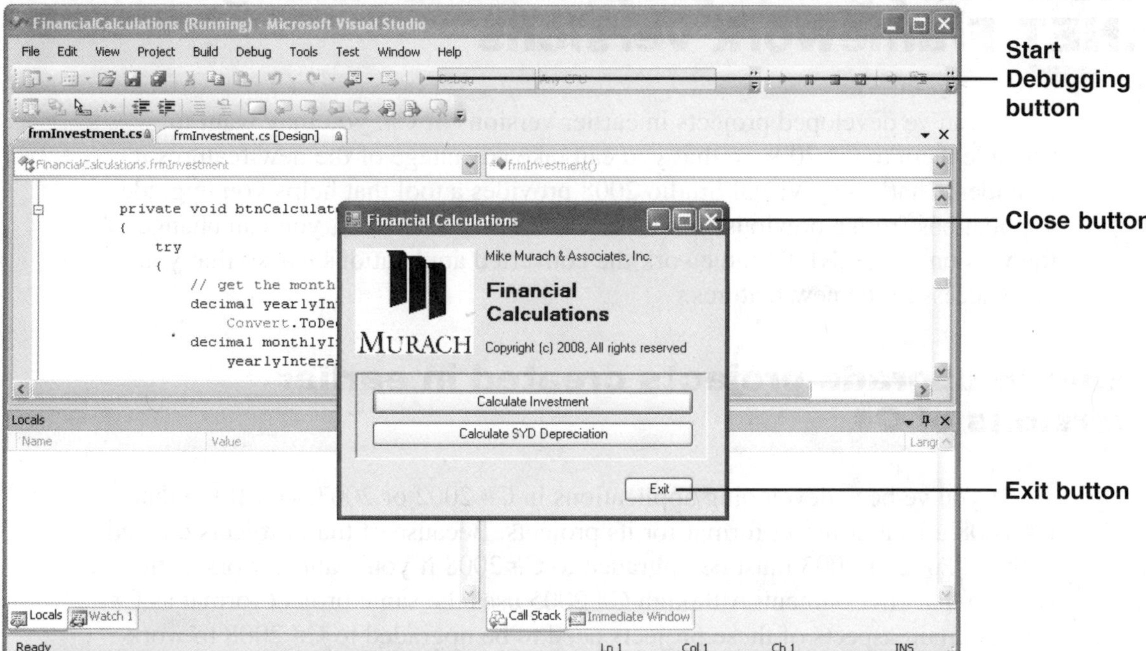

How to build a project without running it

- Use the Build→Build Solution command. Or, right-click the project in the Solution Explorer and select the Build command from the shortcut menu. This *builds* the Intermediate Language for the project and saves it in an assembly.

How to run a project

- You can *run* a project by clicking on the Start Debugging button in the Standard toolbar or by pressing F5. Then, the first form of the project is displayed on top of the Visual Studio window.
- If the project hasn't already been built, the project is first built and then run. As a result, it isn't necessary to use the Build command before you run the program.

Two ways to exit from a project that is running

- Click the Close button in the upper right corner of the startup form.
- Click the button control that's designed for exiting from the application. This is typically a button that is labeled Exit, Close, or Cancel.

How to upgrade projects and change .NET Framework versions

If you've developed projects in earlier versions of C#, you may want to upgrade them to C# 2008 so that you can take advantage of the new features it provides. That's why Visual Studio 2008 provides a tool that helps you upgrade applications from a previous version of C#. Once you do that, you can change the version of the .NET Framework the converted applications use so that you have access to the new features.

How to upgrade projects created in earlier versions of C#

If you've been developing applications in C# 2002 or 2003, you'll see that C# 2008 uses a different format for its projects. Because of that, projects created with C# 2002 or 2003 must be upgraded to C# 2008 if you want to work with them in that environment. Although C# 2005 uses the same project format as C# 2008, certain aspects of these projects need to be upgraded to C# 2008 to work with them in that environment.

Figure 1-13 presents a basic procedure for upgrading C# 2002, 2003, or 2005 projects. When you open one of these projects, Visual Studio automatically starts the Conversion Wizard. You can see the first page of this wizard in this figure. To upgrade the project, just click the Next button and follow the instructions. When the wizard is done, you can usually run the project without any further changes.

The starting page for the Visual Studio Conversion Wizard

Description

- To upgrade a project to Visual Studio 2008, use the File→Open Project command to select the project or solution. The Visual Studio Conversion Wizard starts automatically, and you can respond to its pages. If the wizard indicates that errors occurred during the conversion, you should select the option to view the conversion log.
- The conversion log indicates if a solution and each of its projects were converted successfully. If not, you can click the plus sign next to the solution or project to display additional information about the problems that were encountered.
- If Visual Studio is unable to convert a project, the project is unloaded and marked as unavailable. This typically happens due to problems such as trying to convert a solution whose projects have been moved or that is read-only.

Figure 1-13 How to upgrade projects created in earlier versions of C#

How to change the .NET Framework version used by a project

When you convert a C# project that was created in an earlier version of C# to C# 2008, the features that are provided by version 3.5 of the .NET Framework aren't automatically made available to the converted project. If you want to use any of these features, then, you'll need to change the version of the .NET Framework that's used by the project. Figure 1-14 shows you how to do that.

Here, you can see that you can select from one of three versions of the .NET Framework. When you upgrade a project from C# 2002, 2003, or 2005, the current .NET Framework, called the *target framework*, is .NET Framework 2.0. This version of the .NET Framework is the one that was made available with Visual Studio 2005. If you want to use the features of version 3.5 of the .NET Framework that are presented in this book, you can set the target framework to .NET Framework 3.5.

To understand how this works, you need to know that, unlike previous versions of the .NET Framework, .NET Framework 3.0 and .NET Framework 3.5 don't replace .NET Framework 2.0. Instead, .NET Framework 2.0 is a subset of .NET Framework 3.0, and .NET Framework 3.0 is a subset of .NET Framework 3.5. By the way, .NET Framework 3.0 is the framework that was originally included with the Windows Vista operating system.

The Advanced Compiler Settings for a project

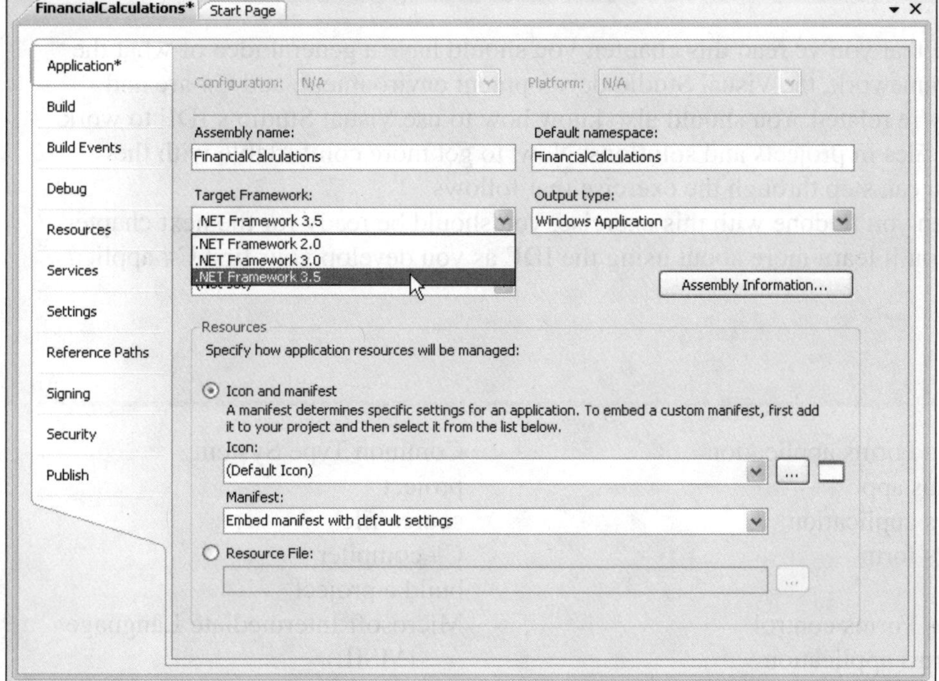

Description

- To change the version of the .NET Framework that's used by a project that you convert from an earlier version of C#, select the version you want to use from the Application tab of the Project Properties window for the project.
- To display the Project Properties window, use the Project→Properties command.
- The .NET Framework version you choose determines the features you can use in the project.

Figure 1-14 How to change the .NET Framework version used by a project

Perspective

Now that you've read this chapter, you should have a general idea of what the .NET Framework, the Visual Studio development environment, and C# are and how they're related. You should also know how to use Visual Studio's IDE to work with the files in projects and solutions. Now, to get more comfortable with the IDE, you can step through the exercise that follows.

When you're done with this exercise, you should be ready for the next chapter. There, you'll learn more about using the IDE as you develop your first C# application.

Terms

Windows Forms application
WinForms app
Windows application
Windows form
form
Windows Forms control
Web Forms application
web application
web form
web browser
Web Forms control
Visual Studio 2008
Visual C# 2008
Integrated Development Environment (IDE)
.NET Framework
Visual Studio IDE
SQL Server 2005 Express
.NET Framework Class Library
class
namespace
Common Language Runtime (CLR)
managed applications
Common Type System
project
source file
C# compiler
build a project
Microsoft Intermediate Language (MSIL)
Intermediate Language (IL)
assembly
solution
project file
solution file
tabbed window
Form Designer
Toolbox
Properties window
Code Editor
Solution Explorer
partial class
docked window
run a project
target framework

Before you do the exercises in this book

Before you do any of the exercises in this book, you need to have Visual Studio 2008 or Visual C# 2008 Express installed on your system. You also need to download the folders and files for this book from our web site and install them on your PC in the C:\C# 2008 folder. For complete instructions, please refer to appendix A.

Exercise 1-1 Tour the Visual Studio IDE

This exercise guides you through the process of opening an existing C# project, working with the windows in the IDE, and building and running a project. When you're done, you should have a better feel for some of the techniques that you will use as you develop C# applications.

Start Visual Studio and open an existing project

1. Start Visual Studio as described in figure 1-6. If a dialog box that lets you select the default environment settings is displayed, select the Visual C# Development Settings option.
2. Review the Start Page to see what it offers. When you're done, right-click on the tab of the Start Page and select the Close command to close this page. To redisplay the Start Page, you can click on the Start Page button in the Standard toolbar if it has that button, or you can use the View→Other Windows→Start Page command.
3. Use the File menu to display the Open Project dialog box as described in figure 1-7. Next, locate the project file named FinancialCalculations.csproj in the C:\C# 2008\Chapter 01\ FinancialCalculations folder. Then, double-click the project file to open the project.

Experiment with the IDE

4. If the Form Designer window for the Calculate Investment form isn't displayed as shown in figure 1-8, use the Solution Explorer to highlight the cs file for this form (frmInvestment.cs). Then, click the View Designer button.
5. Highlight the file for the Calculate Investment form (frmInvestment.cs) in the Solution Explorer and click the View Code button. A Code Editor window like the one shown in figure 1-9 should be displayed. This is the C# code that I developed for this form.
6. Click the tab for frmInvestment.cs [Design] to display the Form Designer again. Then, press Ctrl+Tab to move back to the Code Editor window, and do it again to move back to the Designer.
7. If the Toolbox is displayed, locate the pushpin near its upper right corner and click it. The Toolbox should now be displayed as a tab along the left side of the window. Place the mouse pointer over the tab to display the Toolbox, and then move the pointer outside the Toolbox to see that it's hidden again.

8. Undock the Solution Explorer window by dragging its title bar to the center of the screen. Notice that the Properties window expands to fill the space that was occupied by the docked Solution Explorer window. Double-click the title bar of the Solution Explorer window to return the window to its docked position.
9. Click the plus sign next to the References folder in the Solution Explorer window to see the namespaces that are included in the project. When you're done, click the minus sign next to the References folder to close it.
10. Click the plus sign next to the frmInvestment.cs file to display the subordinate files. Then, double-click on the frmInvestment.Designer.cs file to display its code in the Code Editor. This is the code that was generated by the Form Designer when the form was designed and you usually don't need to change it. Now, close the tabbed window for this code by clicking on its Close button.
11. Click on the Calculations.cs file in the Solution Explorer. Note that there isn't a View Designer button for this file. Then, click the View Code button to show the code. This is the code that I developed to do the calculations that are required by this application. Now, close the tabbed window for this code.

Close and reopen the project

12. Select the File→Close Solution command to close the project. If a dialog box is displayed that asks whether you want to save changes, click the No button.
13. Reopen the solution by using the File→Recent Projects submenu to select the appropriate project file.

Build and run the application

14. Build the project by pulling down the Build menu and selecting the Build Solution command. This assembles the project into Intermediate Language. It may also open another window, but you don't need to be concerned with that until the next chapter.
15. Run the application by clicking on the Start Debugging button in the Standard toolbar. When the first form is displayed, click the Calculate Investment button to go to the next form. Then, experiment with this form until you understand what it does. When you're through experimenting, exit from this form so you return to the first form.
16. Click the Calculate SYD Depreciation button to go to another form. Then, experiment with that form to see what it does. When you exit from it, you will return to the first form.
17. Exit from the first form by clicking on either the Exit button or the Close button in the upper right corner of the form.

Close the project and exit from Visual Studio

18. Close the project the way you did in step 12.
19. Exit from Visual Studio by clicking on the Close button in the Visual Studio window or by using the File→Exit command.

2

How to design a Windows Forms application

In the last chapter, you learned the basic skills for working with Visual Studio, you toured a Windows Forms application, and you tested an application with three Windows forms. Now, in this chapter, you'll learn how to use Visual Studio to design the user interface for a Windows Forms application.

How to set options and create a new project

Before you start your first Windows Forms application with Visual Studio 2008, you probably should set at least one of the Visual Studio options. That will make it easier for you to create a new project. You may also want to change the import and export settings.

How to set the options for projects and solutions

To set the options for a project, you use the Options dialog box shown in figure 2-1. Once this dialog box is open, you can expand the Projects and Solutions group by clicking on the plus sign to the left of that group, and you can click on the General option to display the options shown in this figure.

You can set the default project location by typing a path directly into the text box, or you can click the button to the right of the text box to display a dialog box that lets you navigate to the folder you want to use. This will set the default location for new projects, but you can always override the default when you create a new project.

By default, most of the options available from this dialog box are set the way you want. However, it's worth taking a few minutes to familiarize yourself with the options that are available in this dialog box. That way, you'll know what options are available, and you can change them if Visual Studio isn't working the way you want it to. For instance, you may want to use the Startup group within the Environment group to stop the display of the Start Page.

How to change the import and export settings

The first time you start Visual Studio 2008, you're asked what default environment settings you want to use. You can choose from five options including Visual Basic, Visual C#, and Web. Among other things, your choice affects what items are available from some menus and what buttons are available from the Standard toolbar. If, for example, you choose the Visual C# settings, you open a project with the File→Open→Project/Solution command. But if you choose the Visual Basic settings, you open a project with the File→Open Project command.

To change these settings, you use the Import and Export Settings Wizard as described in this figure. In the first step of the wizard, choose the Reset All Settings option. In the second step, choose the Yes, Save My Current Settings option. And in the last step, if you want your menus to work as described in this book, choose the Visual C# Development Settings option. Later, if you switch to Visual Basic or web development, you can change the settings again.

The Options dialog box for setting the project options

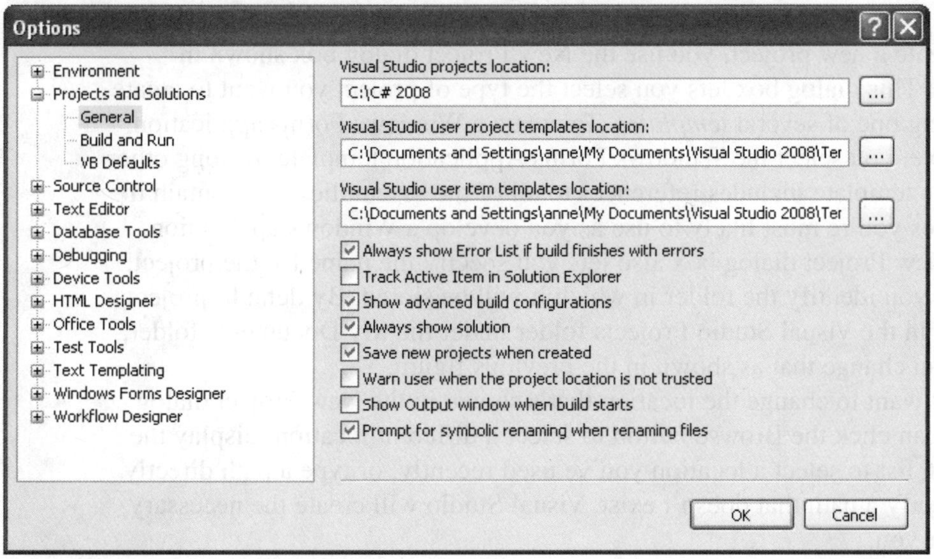

How to use the Options dialog box

- To display the Options dialog box, select the Tools→Options command.
- To expand and collapse a group of options, you can use the plus (+) and minus (-) signs to the left of each group of options. To display the options for a group, click on the group.
- To set the default location for all projects that you start from Visual Studio, you can change the Visual Studio Projects Location as shown above.
- Although most of the options should be set the way you want them, you may want to familiarize yourself with the options in each category so you know what's available.

How to set the Import and Export Settings

- The first time you start Visual Studio 2008, you are asked to choose the default environment settings. These settings affect how the menus work and what buttons are displayed on the Standard toolbar.
- To change the settings to the ones used for this book, use the Tools→Import and Export Settings command to start the Settings Wizard. Then, choose the Reset All Settings option, the Save My Current Settings option, and the Visual C# Development Settings option as you step through the wizard.

Express Edition notes

- If you want the Visual C# 2008 Express Edition to work as described in the next figure, be sure to check the Save New Projects When Created box in the Options dialog box.
- With the Express Edition, there is no third step to the Import and Export Settings Wizard because this wizard assumes that you want to use the Visual C# development settings.

Figure 2-1 How to set the options for projects and solutions

How to create a new project

To create a new project, you use the New Project dialog box shown in figure 2-2. This dialog box lets you select the type of project you want to create by choosing one of several *templates*. To create a Windows Forms application, for example, you select the Windows Forms Application template. Among other things, this template includes references to all of the assemblies that contain the namespaces you're most likely to use as you develop a Windows application.

The New Project dialog box also lets you specify the name for the project, and it lets you identify the folder in which it will be stored. By default, projects are stored in the Visual Studio Projects folder under the My Documents folder, but you can change that as shown in the previous figure.

If you want to change the location that's shown in the New Project dialog box, you can click the Browse button to select a different location; display the drop-down list to select a location you've used recently; or type a path directly. If you specify a path that doesn't exist, Visual Studio will create the necessary folders for you.

When you click the OK button, Visual Studio automatically creates a new folder for the project, using the project name you specify. In the dialog box in this figure, for example, InvoiceTotal is the project name and C:\C# 2008 is the location. By default, Visual Studio also creates a new folder for the solution, using the same name as the project. As a result, Visual Studio will create one folder for the solution, and a subfolder for the project.

If that's not what you want, you can deselect the Create Directory For Solution check box. Then, the solution is given the same name as the project and is stored in the same folder.

Incidentally, the terms *folder* and *directory* are used as synonyms throughout this book. With the introduction of Windows 95, Microsoft started referring to directories as folders. But most of the Visual Studio documentation still uses the term *directory*. That's why this book uses whichever term seems more appropriate at the time.

By default, the new projects you create target .NET Framework 3.5 so that you can use the features it provides. If you use any of these features, however, any computer that you want to run the application on must also have .NET Framework 3.5. If that's not the case, you can change the target framework using the drop-down list in the upper right corner of the New Project dialog box. You can select .NET Framework 2.0, 3.0, or 3.5 from this list. Note that if you set the target framework to 3.0 or 3.5, you can still run the application on a computer that doesn't have the specified framework as long as the application doesn't use any features of that framework. However, it's best to set the target framework appropriately for the computers where the application will run so that you don't accidentally use a feature that isn't supported.

The New Project dialog box

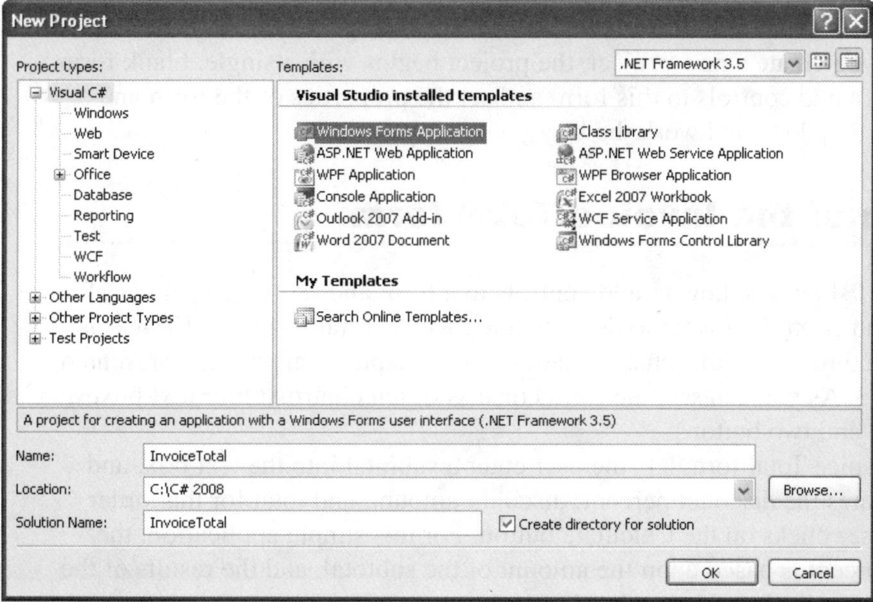

How to create a new C# project

1. Use the File→New→Project command to open the New Project dialog box.
2. Choose Visual C# as the Project Type, and choose the Windows Forms Application template for a Windows Forms application.
3. Enter a name for the project, which will enter the same name for the solution. Then, enter the location (folder) for the project (and solution).
4. Click the OK button to create the new project.

Description

- The project *template* that you select determines the initial files, assembly references, code, and property settings that are added to the project.
- If the Create Directory For Solution box is checked, Visual Studio creates one folder for the solution and a subfolder for the project. Otherwise, these files are stored in the same folder.
- If the Save New Projects When Created option is on as shown in the previous figure, the project is saved right after it's created. Otherwise, the New Project dialog box asks only that you select a template and enter a name for the project. Then, when you save the project, the Save Project dialog box asks for the other information shown above.
- If you want to target a version of the .NET Framework other than version 3.5, you can select the version from the drop-down list in the upper right corner of the dialog box.

Express Edition difference

- Use the File→New Project command to open the New Project dialog box.

Figure 2-2 How to create a new project

How to design a form

When you create a new project, the project begins with a single, blank form. You can then add controls to this form and set the properties of the form and controls so they look and work the way you want.

The design of the Invoice Total form

Before I show you how to add controls to a form and set the properties of the form and controls, I want to describe the Invoice Total form that I'll use as an example throughout this chapter and the next chapter. This form is presented in figure 2-3. As you can see, the form consists of ten controls: four text boxes, four labels, and two buttons.

The Invoice Total form lets the user enter a subtotal into the text box, and then calculates the discount percent, discount amount, and total for that order when the user clicks on the Calculate button. For this simple application, the discount percent is based upon the amount of the subtotal, and the results of the calculation are displayed in read-only text box controls.

After the results of the calculation are displayed, the user can enter a different subtotal and click the Calculate button again to perform another calculation. This cycle continues until the user clicks on the Close button in the upper right corner of the form or clicks on the Exit button. Then, the form is closed and the application ends.

This application also provides keystroke options for users who prefer using the keyboard to the mouse. In particular, the user can activate the Calculate button by pressing the Enter key and the Exit button by pressing the Esc key. The user can also activate the Calculate button by pressing Alt+C and the Exit button by pressing Alt+X.

In the early days of computing, it was a common practice to sketch the user interface for an application on paper before developing the application. That's because a programmer had to enter the code that defined the user interface, and the task of writing this code would have been error prone if the interface wasn't planned out first. As you'll see in this chapter, however, the Form Designer makes it easy to design a form at the same time that you implement it. Because of that, you usually don't need to sketch the layout of a form before you design it in Visual Studio.

As you use the Form Designer, Visual Studio automatically generates the C# code that's needed to define the form and its controls. In other words, the form that you see in the Form Designer is just a visual representation of the form that the C# code is going to display later on. Then, all you have to do is write the C# code that gives the form its functionality, and you'll learn how to do that in the next chapter.

The Invoice Total form

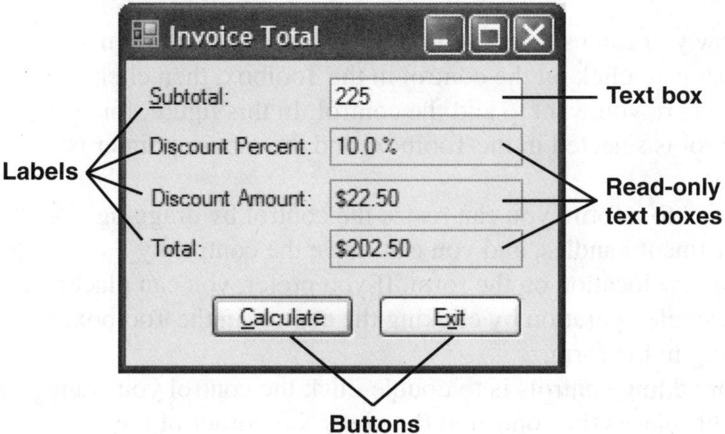

Description

- A text box is used to get the subtotal from the user. Read-only text boxes are used to display the discount percent, discount amount, and total. And label controls are used to identify the values that are in the text boxes on the form.
- After entering a subtotal, the user can click the Calculate button to calculate the discount percent, discount amount, and total. Alternatively, the user can press the Enter key to perform the calculation.
- To calculate another invoice total, the user can enter another subtotal and then click the Calculate button or press the Enter key again.
- To close the form and end the application, the user can click the Close button in the upper right corner of the form or on the Exit button. Alternatively, the user can press the Esc key to exit from the form.
- The user can press Alt+C to access the Calculate button or Alt+X to access the Exit button. On most systems, the letters that provide the access to these buttons aren't underlined until the user presses the Alt key.

Three types of controls

- A *label* displays text on a form.
- A *text box* lets the user enter text on a form.
- A *button* initiates form processing when clicked.

Figure 2-3 The design of the Invoice Total form

How to add controls to a form

Figure 2-4 shows how you can use the Toolbox to add controls to a form. The easiest way to do that is to click on the control in the Toolbox, then click the form at the location where you want to add the control. In this figure, for example, the button control is selected in the Toolbox, and the mouse pointer is positioned over the form.

Once you add a control to a form, you can resize the control by dragging one of the control's adjustment handles, and you can move the control by dragging the control to a new location on the form. If you prefer, you can place and size the control in a single operation by clicking the control in the Toolbox, then clicking and dragging in the form.

A second method for adding controls is to double-click the control you want to add in the Toolbox. This places the control in the upper left corner of the form. You can then move and resize the control.

A third way to add a control is to drag the control from the Toolbox to the form. The control is placed wherever you drop it. You can then resize the control.

If the AutoHide feature is activated for the Toolbox and you move the mouse pointer over the Toolbox tab to display it, the display frequently obscures some or all of the form. This makes it difficult to add controls. As a result, it's a good idea to turn off the AutoHide feature when you're adding controls. To do that, just click the pushpin button in the upper right corner of the Toolbox.

After you have added controls to the form, you can work with several controls at once. For example, let's say that you have four text box controls on your form and you want to make them all the same size with the same alignment. To do that, first select all four controls by holding down the Ctrl or Shift key as you click on them or by using the mouse pointer to drag a dotted rectangular line around the controls. Then, use the commands in the Format menu or the buttons in the Layout toolbar to move, size, and align the controls relative to the *primary control*. If you select the controls one at a time, the primary control will be the first control you select. If you select the controls by dragging around them, the primary control will be the last control in the group. To change the primary control, just click on it. (The primary control will have different color handles so you can identify it.)

Although these techniques may be hard to visualize as you read about them, you'll find that they're relatively easy to use. All you need is a little practice, which you'll get in the exercise for this chapter.

A form after some controls have been added to it

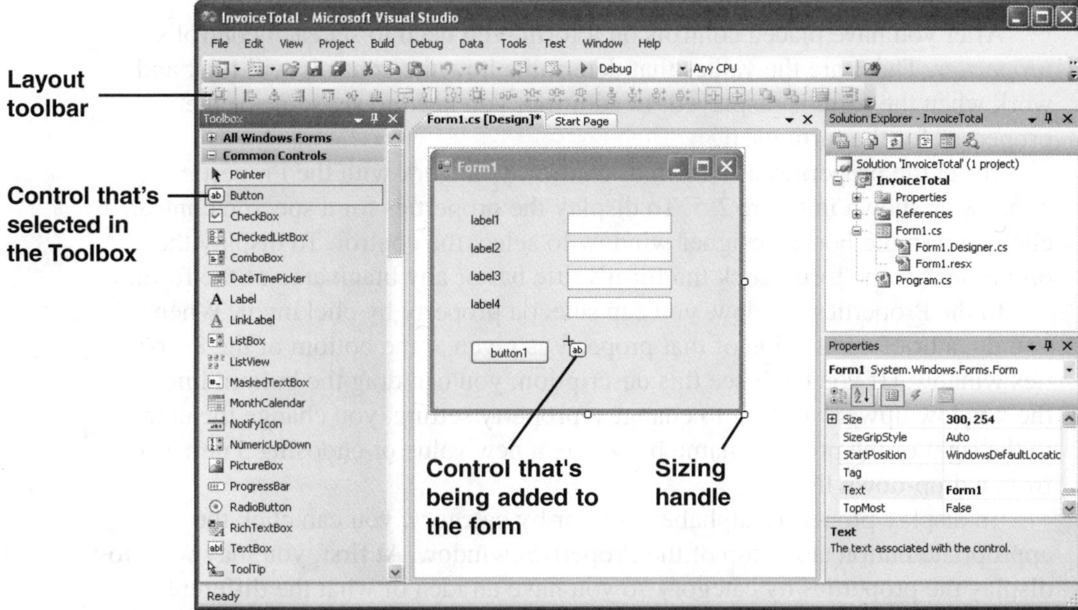

Three ways to add a control to a form

- Select the control in the Toolbox. Then, click in the form where you want to place the control. Or, drag the pointer on the form to place the control and size it at the same time.
- Double-click the control in the Toolbox. Then, the control is placed in the upper left corner of the form.
- Drag the control from the Toolbox and drop it on the form. Then, the control is placed wherever you drop it.

How to select and work with controls

- To select a control on the form, click it. To move a control, drag it.
- To size a selected control, drag one of its handles. Note, however, that a label is sized automatically based on the amount of text that it contains. As a result, you can't size a label by dragging its handles unless you change its AutoSize property.
- To select more than one control, hold down the Shift or Ctrl key as you click on each control. You can also select a group of controls by clicking on a blank spot in the form and then dragging around the controls.
- To align, size, or space a group of selected controls, click on a control to make it the *primary control*. Then, use the commands in the Format menu or the buttons on the Layout toolbar to align, size, or space the controls relative to the primary control.
- You can also size all of the controls in a group by sizing the primary control in the group. And you can drag any of the selected controls to move all the controls.
- To change the size of a form, click the form and drag one of its sizing handles.

Figure 2-4 How to add controls to a form

How to set properties

After you have placed controls on a form, you need to set each control's *properties*. These are the values that determine how the controls will look and work when the form is displayed. In addition, you need to set some of the properties for the form itself.

To set the properties of a form or control, you work with the Properties window as shown in figure 2-5. To display the properties for a specific control, click on it in the Form Designer window to select the control. To display the properties for the form, click the form's title bar or any blank area of the form.

In the Properties window, you can select a property by clicking it. When you do, a brief description of that property is given at the bottom of the Properties window. (If you can't see this description, you can drag the bottom line of the window upward.) Then, to change a property setting, you change the entry to the right of the property name by typing a new value or choosing a new value from a drop-down list.

To display properties alphabetically or by category, you can click the appropriate button at the top of the Properties window. At first, you may want to display the properties by category so you have an idea of what the different properties do. Once you become more familiar with the properties, though, you may be able to find the ones you're looking for faster if you display them alphabetically.

As you work with properties, you'll find that most are set the way you want them by default. In addition, some properties such as Height and Width are set interactively as you size and position the form and its controls in the Form Designer window. As a result, you usually only need to change a few properties for each object.

A form after the properties have been set

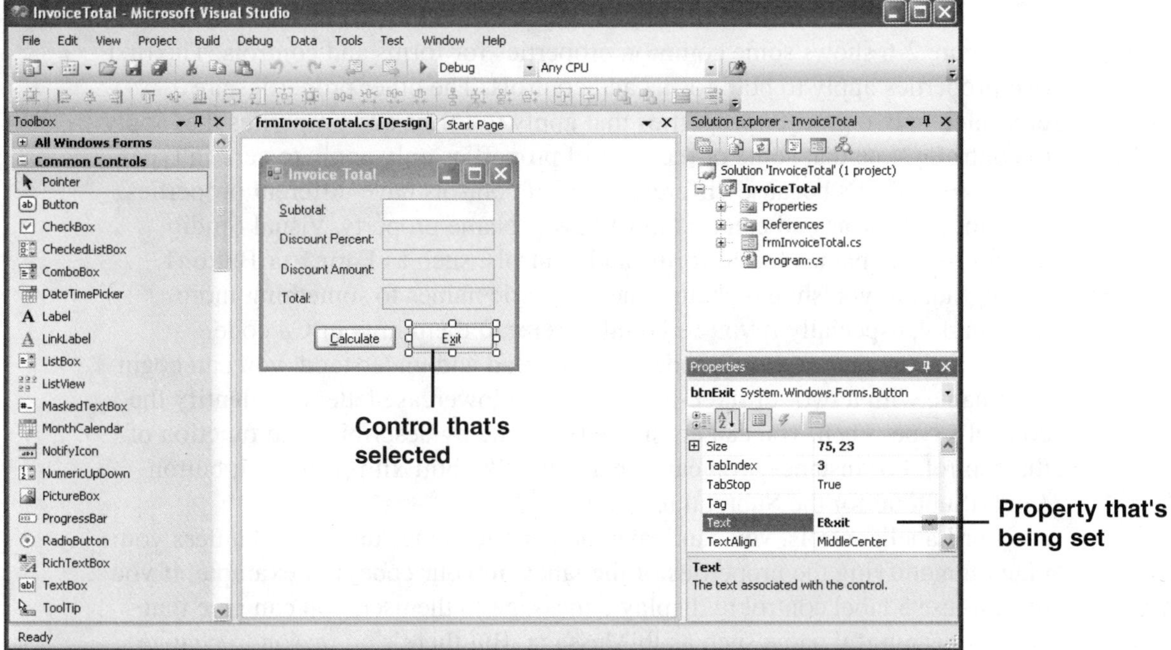

Description

- The Properties window displays the *properties* for the object that's currently selected in the Form Designer window. To display the properties for another object, click on that object or select the object from the drop-down list at the top of the Properties window.
- To change a property, enter a value into the text box or select a value from its drop-down list if it has one. If a button with an ellipsis (…) appears at the right side of a property's text box, you can click on the ellipsis to display a dialog box that lets you set options for the property.
- To change the properties for two or more controls at the same time, select the controls. Then, the common properties of the controls are displayed in the Properties window.
- When you click on a property in the Properties window, a brief explanation of the property appears in a pane at the bottom of the window. For more information, press F1 to display the help information for the property.
- You can use the first two buttons at the top of the Properties window to sort the properties by category or alphabetically.
- You can use the plus (+) and minus (-) signs displayed to the left of some of the properties and categories in the Properties window to expand and collapse the list of properties.

Note

- If a description isn't displayed when you click on a property in the Properties window, right-click on the window and select Description from the shortcut menu.

Figure 2-5 How to set properties

Common properties for forms and controls

Figure 2-6 shows some common properties for forms and controls. The first two properties apply to both forms and controls. The other properties are presented in two groups: properties that apply to forms and properties that apply to controls. Note that some of the control properties only apply to certain types of controls. That's because different types of controls have different properties.

Since all forms and controls must have a Name property, Visual Studio creates generic names for all forms and controls, such as Form1 or Button1. Often, though, you should change these generic names to something more meaningful, especially if you're going to refer to them in your C# code.

To make your program's code easier to read and understand, you can begin each name with a two- or three-letter prefix in lowercase letters to identify the control's type. Then, you can complete the name by describing the function of the control. For instance, you can use a name like btnExit for the Exit button and txtSubtotal for the Subtotal text box.

For Label controls, you can leave the generic names unchanged unless you plan on modifying the properties of the labels in your code. For example, if you want to use a label control to display a message to the user, you can give that label a meaningful name such as lblMessage. But there's no reason to change the names for label controls that display text that won't be changed by the program.

Forms and most controls also have a Text property that is visible when the form is displayed. A form's Text property is displayed in the form's title bar. For a control, the Text property is usually displayed somewhere within the control. The Text property of a button, for example, is displayed on the button, and the Text property of a text box is displayed in the text box.

As you work with properties, you'll find that you can set some of them by selecting a value from a drop-down list. For example, you can select a true or false value for the TabStop property of a control. For other properties, you have to enter a number or text value. And for some properties, a button with an ellipsis (...) is displayed. Then, when you click this button, a dialog box appears that lets you set the property.

The Name property

- Sets the name you use to identify a control in your C# code.
- Can be changed to provide a more descriptive and memorable name for forms and controls that you will refer to when you write your code (such as text boxes and buttons).
- Doesn't need to be changed for controls that you won't refer to when you write your code (such as most labels).
- Can use a three-letter prefix to indicate whether the name refers to a form (frm), button (btn), label (lbl), or text box (txt).

The Text property

- Sets the text that's displayed on the form or control. Some controls such as forms and labels display the generic form or control name that's generated by Visual Studio, which you'll almost always want to change.
- For a form, the Text value is displayed in the title bar. For controls, the Text value is displayed directly on the control.
- For a text box, the Text value changes when the user types text into the control, and you can write code that uses the Text property to get the text that was entered by the user.

Other properties for forms

Property	Description
AcceptButton	Identifies the button that will be activated when the user presses the Enter key.
CancelButton	Identifies the button that will be activated when the user presses the Esc key.
StartPosition	Sets the position at which the form is displayed. To center the form, set this property to CenterScreen.

Other properties for controls

Property	Description
Enabled	Determines whether the control will be enabled or disabled.
ReadOnly	Determines whether the text in some controls like text boxes can be edited.
TabIndex	Indicates the control's position in the tab order, which determines the order in which the controls will receive the focus when the user presses the Tab key.
TabStop	Determines whether the control will accept the focus when the user presses the Tab key to move from one control to another. Some controls, like labels, don't have the TabStop property because they can't receive the focus.
TextAlign	Sets the alignment for the text displayed on a control.

Figure 2-6 Common properties for forms and controls

How to add navigation features

Windows forms have features that make it easier for users to move around in the forms without using the mouse. These navigation features are described in figure 2-7.

The *tab order* is the order in which the controls on a form receive the *focus* when the user presses the Tab key. The tab order should usually be set so the focus moves left-to-right and top-to-bottom, beginning at the top left of the form and ending at the bottom right. However, in some cases you'll want to deviate from that order. For example, if you have controls arranged in columns, you may want the tab order to move down each column.

The tab order is initially set based on the order in which you add controls to the form. So if you add the controls in the right order, you won't need to alter the tab order. But if you do need to change the tab order, you can do so by adjusting the TabIndex property settings. The TabIndex property is simply a number that represents the control's position in the tab order, beginning with zero. So, the first control in the tab order has a TabIndex of 0, the second control's TabIndex is 1, and so on.

Incidentally, chapter 10 will show you another way to set the tab order of the controls for a form. You can do that by using Tab Order view. When a form consists of more than a few controls, it is easier to use this view than to set the tab order for one control at a time.

Access keys are shortcut keys that let the user move directly to a control. You set a control's access key by using the Text property. Just precede the letter in the Text property value that you want to use as the access key with an ampersand (&). Then, the user can activate the control by pressing Alt plus the access key.

If you assign an access key to a control that can't receive the focus, such as a label control, pressing the access key causes the focus to move to the next control in the tab order. As a result, you can use an access key with a label control to create a shortcut for a text box control, which can't have an access key.

Finally, you usually should set the AcceptButton and CancelButton properties for a form. These properties specify the buttons that are activated when the user presses the Enter and Esc keys. That can make it easier for a user to work with a form. If, for example, the AcceptButton property of the Invoice Total form in figure 2-3 is set to the Calculate button, the user can press the Enter key after entering a subtotal instead of using the mouse to click the Calculate button.

How to adjust the tab order

- *Tab order* refers to the sequence in which the controls receive the *focus* when the user presses the Tab key. You should adjust the tab order so the Tab key moves the focus from one control to the next in a logical sequence.
- Each control has a TabIndex property that indicates the control's position in the tab order. You can change this property to change a control's tab order position.
- If you don't want a control to receive the focus when the user presses the Tab key, change that control's TabStop property to False.
- Label controls don't have a TabStop property so they can't receive the focus.

How to set access keys

- *Access keys* are shortcut keys that the user can use in combination with the Alt key to quickly move to individual controls on the form.
- You use the Text property to set the access key for a control by placing an ampersand immediately before the letter you want to use for the access key. For example, &Invoice sets the access key to *I*, but I&nvoice sets the access key to *n*.
- Since the access keys aren't case sensitive, &N and &n set the same access key.
- When you set access keys, make sure to use a unique letter for each control. If you don't, the user may have to press the access key two or more times to select a control.
- You can't set the access key for a text box. However, if you set an access key for a label that immediately precedes the text box in the tab order, the access key will take the user to the text box.

How to set the Enter and Esc keys

- The AcceptButton property of the form sets the button that will be activated if the user presses the Enter key.
- The CancelButton property of the form sets the button that will be activated if the user presses the Esc key. This property should usually be set to the Exit button.
- You set the AcceptButton or CancelButton values by choosing the button from a drop-down list that shows all of the buttons on the form. So be sure to create and name the buttons you want to use before you attempt to set these values.

Another way to set the tab order

- In chapter 10, you'll learn how to use Tab Order view to set the tab order of the controls on the form. If the form consists of more than a few controls, that is the best way to set that order.

Figure 2-7 How to add navigation features

The property settings for the Invoice Total form

Figure 2-8 shows the property settings for the Invoice Total form. As you can see, you don't need to change many properties to finish the design of this form. You only need to set four properties for the form, and you only use six of the properties (Name, Text, TextAlign, ReadOnly, TabStop, and TabIndex) for the controls. Depending on the order in which you create the controls, though, you may not need to change the TabIndex settings.

Notice that the three text boxes that display the form's calculation have their ReadOnly property set to true. This setting gives the text boxes a shaded appearance, as you saw in figure 2-3, and it prevents the user from entering text into these controls. In addition, the TabStop property for these text boxes has been set to false so the user can't use the Tab key to move the focus onto these controls.

Finally, the settings for the TabIndex properties of the text box and the two buttons are 1, 2, and 3. Since the label controls can't receive the focus, and since the TabStop property for the three read-only text boxes has been set to false, the user can press the Tab key to move the focus from the Subtotal text box to the Calculate button to the Exit button.

In addition, the Subtotal label has a TabIndex property of 0 and a Text property that includes an access key of S. As a result, the user can press Alt+S to move the focus to the control that has the next available tab index. In this case, that control is the Subtotal text box, which has a TabIndex property of 1.

Of course, this is just one way that the TabIndex properties could be set. If, for example, the TabIndex properties for the 10 controls were set from 0 through 9, from top to bottom in this summary, the tab order would work the same.

The property settings for the form

Default name	Property	Setting
Form1	Text	Invoice Total
	AcceptButton	btnCalculate
	CancelButton	btnExit
	StartPosition	CenterScreen

The property settings for the controls

Default name	Property	Setting
Label1	Text	&Subtotal:
	TextAlign	MiddleLeft
	TabIndex	0
Label2	Text	Discount percent:
	TextAlign	MiddleLeft
Label3	Text	Discount amount:
	TextAlign	MiddleLeft
Label4	Text	Total:
	TextAlign	MiddleLeft
TextBox1	Name	txtSubtotal
	TabIndex	1
TextBox2	Name	txtDiscountPercent
	ReadOnly	True
	TabStop	False
TextBox3	Name	txtDiscountAmount
	ReadOnly	True
	TabStop	False
TextBox4	Name	txtTotal
	ReadOnly	True
	TabStop	False
Button1	Name	btnCalculate
	Text	&Calculate
	TabIndex	2
Button2	Name	btnExit
	Text	E&xit
	TabIndex	3

Note

- To provide an access key for the Subtotal text box, you can set the TabIndex and Text properties for the Subtotal label as shown above.

Figure 2-8 The property settings for the Invoice Total form

How to name and save the files of a project

When you're working on a project, you may want to change the names of some of the files from their defaults. Then, you'll want to save the files with their new names.

How to name the files of a project

You may have noticed throughout this chapter that I didn't change the default name of the form (Form1.cs) that was added to the Invoice Total project when the project was created. In practice, though, you usually change the name of this form so that it's more descriptive. For example, figure 2-9 shows how to use the Solution Explorer to change the name of the form file to frmInvoiceTotal.cs. When you do that, Visual Studio will also change the Name property for the form from Form1 to frmInvoiceTotal and modify any of the code that's been generated for the form accordingly.

You may also want to change the name of the project or solution. For example, if you accepted the default project name when you started the project (WindowsApplication1.proj), you many want to change it to something more meaningful. Or, you may want to change the name of the solution so it's different from the project name. If so, you can use the technique presented in this figure to do that too.

How to save the files of a project

Figure 2-9 also describes how to save the files of a project. Because Visual Studio saves any changes you make to the files in a project when you build the project, you won't usually need to save them explicitly. However, it's easy to do if you need to.

Notice in this figure that two factors determine which files are saved: what's selected in the Solution Explorer and the command you use to perform the save operation. If, for example, a single file is selected, you can use the Save command to save just that file, and you can use the Save All command to save the file along with the project and solution that contain the file. In contrast, if a project is selected in the Solution Explorer, the Save command causes the entire project to be saved, and the Save All command causes the entire solution to be saved.

If you haven't saved all of your recent changes when you close a project, Visual Studio will ask whether you want to save them. As a result, you don't need to worry that your changes will be lost.

The Solution Explorer as a form file is being renamed

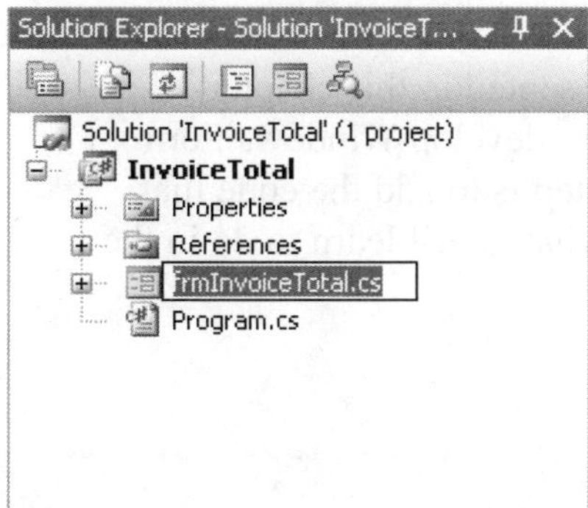

How to rename a file, project, or solution

- You can rename a file, project, or solution by right-clicking on it in the Solution Explorer window and selecting the Rename command from the shortcut menu. Or, you can select the file, project, or solution in the Solution Explorer and then press F2. Then, you can enter the new name for the file, project, or solution.
- Be sure not to change or omit the file extension when you rename a file. Remember too that using a three-letter prefix to indicate the contents of the file (like *frm* for a form file) makes it easier to tell what each file represents.
- When you change the name of a form file, Visual Studio will also change the Name property for the form and update any references within the existing code for the form, which is usually what you want.

How to save a file, project, or solution

- You can use the Save All button in the Standard toolbar or the Save All command in the File menu to save all files and projects in the solution.
- You can use the Save button in the Standard toolbar or the Save command in the File menu to save a file, project, or solution. The files that are saved depend on what's selected in the Solution Explorer window. If a single file is selected, just that file is saved. If a project is selected, the entire project and its solution are saved. And if a solution is selected, the entire solution and all its projects are saved.
- If you try to close a solution that contains modified files, a dialog box is displayed that asks you if you want to save those files.

Figure 2-9 How to name and save the files of a project

Perspective

If you can design the Invoice Total form that's presented in this chapter, you've taken a critical first step toward learning how to develop Windows Forms applications with Visual Studio 2008. Now, the next step is to add the code that makes the form work the way you want it to. That's what you'll learn to do in the next chapter.

Terms

template
label
text box
button
primary control
property
tab order
focus
access key

Exercise 2-1 Design the Invoice Total form

This exercise will guide you through the process of starting a new project and developing the user interface for the Invoice Total form shown in this chapter.

Set the default path and start a new project

1. Start Visual Studio. If you want to change the import and export settings to make sure your menus are the same as the ones in this book, use the Tools→Import and Export Settings command that's described in figure 2-1 to specify the default Visual C# development settings.
2. Use the Tools→Options command to display the Options dialog box as shown in figure 2-1. Then, expand the Projects and Solutions group, select the General category, and change the Visual Studio projects location setting to C:\C# 2008.
3. If the Save New Projects When Created box isn't checked, check it.
4. If you want to stop the Start Page from being displayed each time you start Visual Studio, click on Startup within the Environment group. Then, select another option from the At Startup drop-down list.
5. If you're interested, take a few minutes to review the other options that are available in this dialog box. Then, close the dialog box.
6. Start a new project as shown in figure 2-2. The project should be named InvoiceTotal; it should be stored in the C:\C# 2008\Chapter 02 folder; and the solution should be stored in its own folder.

Add controls to the new form and set the properties

7. Use the techniques in figure 2-4 to add controls to the form so they have approximately the same sizes and locations as in figure 2-5. But don't worry about the size of the labels, just their locations.
8. Select groups of controls and use the buttons in the Layout toolbar to size and align the controls. But here again, let the labels automatically size themselves. Then, size the form so it looks like the one in figure 2-4.
9. Use the Properties window to set the properties for the form and its controls so it looks like the form in figure 2-3. These properties are summarized in figure 2-8.

Test the user interface

10. Press F5 to build and run the project. That should display the form in the center of the screen, and it should look like the one in figure 2-3.
11. Experiment with the form to see what it can do. When you press the Tab key, notice how the focus moves from one control to another. When you click a button, notice how it indents and then pops back out just like any other Windows button control. Nothing else happens in response to these button clicks, though, because you haven't written the code for them yet.

    Notice that the Calculate button has a dark outline around it to indicate that its function will be executed if you press the Enter key. (If it doesn't have a dark outline, you haven't set the AcceptButton property of the form to the button.)

    When you press the Alt key, notice that an underline appears under the s in Subtotal, the first c in Calculate, and the x in Exit to indicate that you can use an access key to work with these controls. (If the underlines don't show, you haven't entered the Text properties correctly.)
12. If you notice that some of the properties are set incorrectly, click the Close button in the upper right corner of the form to close the form. Then, make the necessary changes and run the project again. When you're satisfied that the form is working right, close the form to return to the Form Designer.

Experiment with the properties for the form and its controls

13. In the Form Designer, click on the form so it is selected. Then, if necessary, adjust the Properties window so you can see the description for each property. To do that, drag the bottom boundary of the window up.
14. Click on the Categorized button at the top of the Properties window to display the properties by category. Then, review the properties in the Appearance, Behavior, Layout, and Window Style categories. Although you won't understand all of the descriptions, you should understand some of them.
15. In the Window Style category, change the settings for the MaximizeBox and MinimizeBox to false to see how that changes the form. Then, to undo that change, click on the Undo button in the Standard toolbar or press Ctrl+Z.

16. Click on the first text box and review the Appearance, Behavior, and Layout properties for that control. Then, repeat this process for one of the labels and one of the buttons. Here again, you won't understand all of the descriptions, but you should understand some of them.
17. Select all four of the labels, click on the plus sign before the Font property in the Appearance group, and change the Bold setting to true to see how that changes the form. Then, undo that change.

Change the name of the form files

18. Use one of the techniques presented in figure 2-9 to change the name of the form file from Form1.cs to frmInvoiceTotal.cs. When you do that, a dialog box is displayed that asks whether you want to change all of the references to the form name too. Click on Yes to close that dialog box, and Visual Studio changes all references to Form1 in the C# code that has been generated to frmInvoiceTotal.
19. Note in the Solution Explorer that this also changes the name of the two subordinate files to frmInvoiceTotal.Designer.cs and frmInvoiceTotal.resx.

Close the project and exit from Visual Studio

20. Use the File→Close Solution command to close the project. If you've made any changes to the project since the last time you tested it, a dialog box is displayed that asks whether you want to save the changes that you made. If you want to save those changes, click Yes.
21. Use the File→Exit command to exit from Visual Studio.

3

How to code and test a Windows Forms application

In the last chapter, you learned how to design a form for a Windows Forms application. In this chapter, you'll learn how to code and test a Windows Forms application. When you're done, you'll be able to develop simple applications of your own.

An introduction to coding

Before you learn the mechanics of adding code to a form, it's important to understand some of the concepts behind object-oriented programming.

Introduction to object-oriented programming

Whether you know it or not, you are using *object-oriented programming* as you design a Windows form with Visual Studio's Form Designer. That's because each control on a form is an object, and the form itself is an object. These objects are derived from classes that are part of the .NET Class Library.

When you start a new project from the Windows Application template, you are actually creating a new *class* that inherits the characteristics of the Form class that's part of the .NET Class Library. Later, when you run the form, you are actually creating an *instance* of your form class, and this instance is known as an *object*.

Similarly, when you add a control to a form, you are actually adding a control object to the form. Each control is an instance of a specific class. For example, a text box control is an object that is an instance of the TextBox class. Similarly, a label control is an object that is an instance of the Label class. This process of creating an object from a class can be called *instantiation*.

As you progress through this book, you will learn much more about classes and objects because C# is an *object-oriented language*. In chapter 12, for example, you'll learn how to use the C# language to create your own classes. At that point, you'll start to understand what's actually happening as you work with classes and objects. For now, though, you just need to get comfortable with the terms and accept the fact that a lot is going on behind the scenes as you design a form and its controls.

Figure 3-1 summarizes what I've just said about classes and objects. It also introduces you to the properties, methods, and events that are defined by classes and used by objects. As you've already seen, the *properties* of an object define the object's characteristics and data. For instance, the Name property gives a name to a control, and the Text property determines the text that is displayed within the control. In contrast, the *methods* of an object determine the operations that can be performed by the object.

An object's *events* are signals sent by the object to your application that something has happened that can be responded to. For example, a Button control object generates an event called Click if the user clicks the button. Then, your application can respond by running a C# method to handle the Click event.

By the way, the properties, methods, and events of an object or class are called the *members* of the object or class. You'll learn more about properties, methods, and events in the next three figures.

A form object and its ten control objects

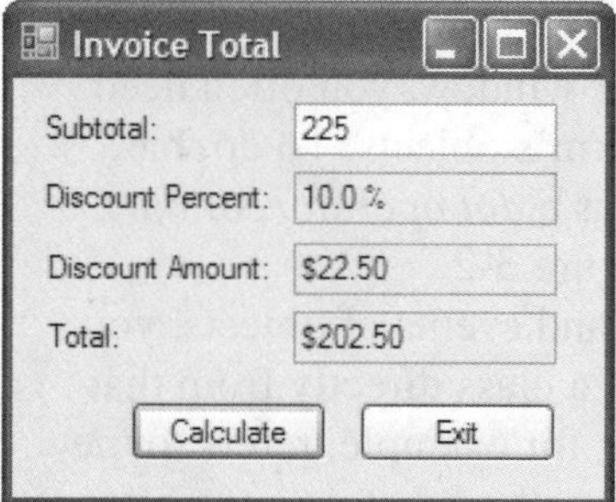

Class and object concepts

- An *object* is a self-contained unit that combines code and data. Two examples of objects you have already worked with are forms and controls.
- A *class* is the code that defines the characteristics of an object. You can think of a class as a template for an object.
- An object is an *instance* of a class, and the process of creating an object from a class is called *instantiation*.
- More than one object instance can be created from a single class. For example, a form can have several button objects, all instantiated from the same Button class. Each is a separate object, but all share the characteristics of the Button class.

Property, method, and event concepts

- *Properties* define the characteristics of an object and the data associated with an object.
- *Methods* are the operations that an object can perform.
- *Events* are signals sent by an object to the application telling it that something has happened that can be responded to.
- Properties, methods, and events can be referred to as *members* of an object.
- If you instantiate two or more instances of the same class, all of the objects have the same properties, methods, and events. However, the values assigned to the properties can vary from one instance to another.

Objects and forms

- When you use the Form Designer, Visual Studio automatically generates C# code that creates a new class based on the Form class. Then, when you run the project, a form object is instantiated from the new class.
- When you add a control to a form, Visual Studio automatically generates C# code in the class for the form that instantiates a control object from the appropriate class and sets the control's default properties. When you move and size a control, Visual Studio automatically sets the properties that specify the location and size of the control.

Figure 3-1 Introduction to object-oriented programming

How to refer to properties, methods, and events

As you enter the code for a form in the Code Editor window, you often need to refer to the properties, methods, and events of the form's objects. To do that, you type the name of the object, a period (also known as a *dot operator*, or *dot*), and the name of the member. This is summarized in figure 3-2.

In addition to referring to the properties, methods, and events of objects, you can also refer to some of the properties and methods of a class directly from that class. The code shown in the Code Editor in this figure, for example, refers to the ToDecimal method of the Convert class. A property or method that you can refer to directly from a class like this is called a *static member*. You'll learn more about static members in chapter 4. For now, you just need to realize that you can refer to static properties and methods using the same techniques that you use to refer to the properties and methods of an object.

To make it easier for you to refer to the members of an object or class, Visual Studio's IntelliSense feature displays a list of the members that are available for that class or object after you type a class or object name and a period. Then, you can highlight the entry you want by clicking on it, typing one or more letters of its name, or using the arrow keys to scroll through the list. In most cases, you can then complete the entry by pressing the Tab or Enter key.

To give you an idea of how properties, methods, and events are used in code, this figure shows examples of each. In the first example for properties, code is used to set the value that's displayed for a text box to 10. In the second example, code is used to set a text box's ReadOnly property to true. Although you can also use the Properties window to set these values, that just sets the properties at the start of the application. By using code, you can change the properties as an application is running.

In the first example for methods, the Focus method of a text box is used to move the focus to that text box. In the second example, the Close method of a form is used to close the active form. In this example, the *this* keyword is used instead of the name of the form. Here, *this* refers to the current instance of the active form. Note also that the names of the methods are followed by parentheses.

As you progress through this book, you'll learn how to use the methods for many types of objects, and you'll learn how to supply arguments within the parentheses of a method. For now, though, just try to understand that you can call a method from a class or an object and that you must code a set of parentheses after the method name.

Although you'll frequently refer to properties and methods as you code an application, you'll rarely need to refer to an event. That's because Visual Studio automatically generates the code for working with events, as you'll see later in this chapter. To help you understand the code that Visual Studio generates, however, the last example in this figure shows how you refer to an event. In this case, the code refers to the Click event of a button named btnExit.

A member list that's displayed in the Code Editor window

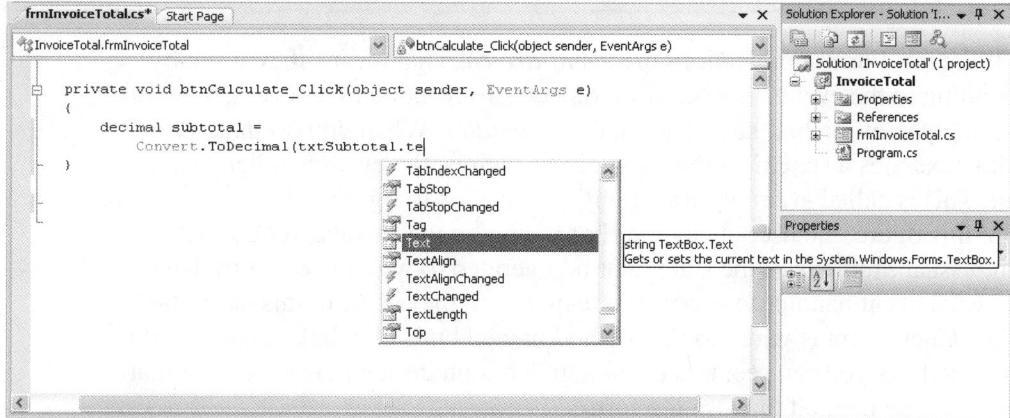

The syntax for referring to a member of a class or object

```
ClassName.MemberName
objectName.MemberName
```

Statements that refer to properties

`txtTotal.Text = "10";`	Assigns a string holding the number 10 to the Text property of the text box named txtTotal.
`txtTotal.ReadOnly = true;`	Assigns the true value to the ReadOnly property of the text box named txtTotal so the user can't change its contents.

Statements that refer to methods

`txtMonthlyInvestment.Focus();`	Uses the Focus method to move the focus to the text box named txtMonthlyInvestment.
`this.Close();`	Uses the Close method to close the form that contains the statement. In this example, *this* is a keyword that is used to refer to the current instance of the class.

Code that refers to an event

`btnExit.Click`	Refers to the Click event of a button named btnExit.

How to enter member names when working in the Code Editor

- To display a list of the available members for a class or an object, type the class or object name followed by a period (called a *dot operator*, or just *dot*). Then, you can type one or more letters of the member name, and the Code Editor will select the first entry in the list that matches those letters. Or, you can scroll down the list to select the member you want. Once it's selected, press the Tab or Enter key to insert the member into your code.
- If a member list isn't displayed, select the Tools→Options command to display the Options dialog box. Then, expand the Text Editor group, select the C# category, and check the Auto List Members and Parameters Information boxes.

Figure 3-2 How to refer to properties, methods, and events

How an application responds to events

Windows Forms applications are *event-driven*. That means they work by responding to the events that occur on objects. To respond to an event, you code a special type of method known as an *event handler*. When you do that, Visual Studio generates a statement that connects, or wires, the event handler to the event. This is called *event wiring*, and it's illustrated in figure 3-3.

In this figure, the user clicks the Exit button on the Invoice Total form. Then, Visual Studio uses the statement it generated to wire the event to determine what event handler to execute in response to the event. In this case, the btnExit.Click event is wired to the method named btnExit_Click, so this method is executed. As you can see, this event handler contains a single statement that uses the Close method to close the form.

This figure also lists some common events for controls and forms. One control event you'll respond to frequently is the Click event. This event occurs when the user clicks an object with the mouse. Similarly, the DoubleClick event occurs when the user double-clicks an object.

Although the Click and DoubleClick events are started by user actions, that's not always the case. For instance, the Enter and Leave events typically occur when the user moves the focus to or from a control, but they can also occur when code moves the focus to or from a control. Similarly, the Load event of a form occurs when a form is loaded into memory. For the first form of an application, this typically happens when the user starts the application. And the Closed event occurs when a form is closed. For the Invoice Total form presented in this figure, this happens when the user selects the Exit button or the Close button in the upper right corner of the form.

In addition to the events shown here, most objects have many more events that the application can respond to. For example, events occur when the user positions the mouse over an object or when the user presses or releases a key. However, you don't typically respond to those events.

Event: The user clicks the Exit button

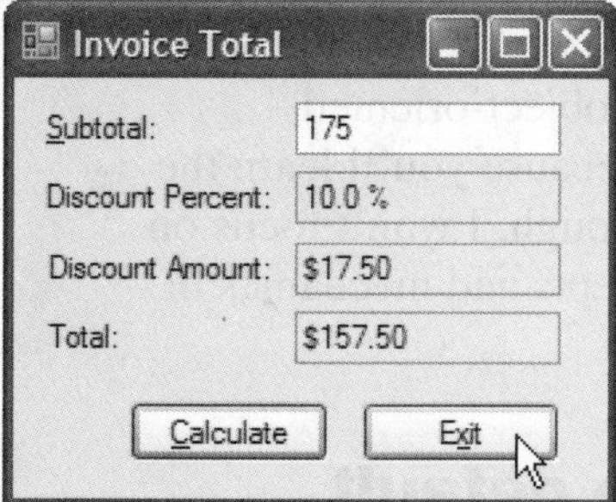

Wiring: The application determines what method to execute

```
this.btnExit.Click += new System.EventHandler(this.btnExit_Click);
```

Response: The method for the Click event of the Exit button is executed

```
private void btnExit_Click(object sender, System.EventArgs e)
{
    this.Close();
}
```

Common control events

Event	Occurs when...
Click	...the user clicks the control.
DoubleClick	...the user double-clicks the control.
Enter	...the focus is moved to the control.
Leave	...the focus is moved from the control.

Common form events

Event	Occurs when...
Load	...the form is loaded into memory.
Closing	...the form is closing.
Closed	...the form is closed.

Concepts

- Windows Forms applications work by responding to events that occur on objects.
- To indicate how an application should respond to an event, you code an *event handler*, which is a special type of method that handles the event.
- To connect the event handler to the event, Visual Studio automatically generates a statement that wires the event to the event handler. This is known as *event wiring*.
- An event can be an action that's initiated by the user like the Click event, or it can be an action initiated by program code like the Closed event.

Figure 3-3 How an application responds to events

How to add code to a form

Now that you understand some of the concepts behind object-oriented coding, you're ready to learn how to add code to a form. Because you'll learn the essentials of the C# language in the chapters that follow, though, I won't focus on the coding details right now. Instead, I'll focus on the concepts and mechanics of adding the code to a form.

How to create an event handler for the default event of a form or control

Although you can create an event handler for any event of any object, you're most likely to create event handlers for the default events of forms and controls. So that's what you'll learn to do in this chapter. Then, in chapter 6, you'll learn how to create event handlers for other events.

To create an event handler for the default event of a form or control, you double-click the object in the Form Designer. Then, Visual Studio opens the Code Editor, generates a *method declaration* for the default event of the object, and places the insertion point on a blank line between the opening and closing braces of that declaration. As a result, you can immediately start typing the C# statements that you want to include in the body of the method.

To illustrate, figure 3-4 shows the code that was generated when I double-clicked the Calculate button on the Invoice Total form. In this figure, the code for the form is stored in a file named frmInvoiceTotal.cs. In addition, the name of the method is the name of the object (btnCalculate), an underline, and the name of the event (Click). The statement that wires the Click event of this button to this event handler is stored in the file named frmInvoiceTotal.Designer.cs.

Before you start an event handler for a control, you should set the Name property of the control as described in chapter 2. That way, this name will be reflected in the *method name* of the event handler as shown in this figure. If you change the control name after starting an event handler for it, Visual Studio will change the name of the object in the event wiring, but it won't change the name of the object in the method name. And that can be confusing when you're first learning C#.

You should also avoid modifying the method declaration that's generated for you when you create an event handler. In chapter 6, you'll learn how to modify the method declaration. But for now, you should leave the method declaration alone and focus on adding code within the body of the method.

How to delete an event handler

If you add an event handler by mistake, you can't just delete it. If you do, you'll get an error when you try to run the application. This error will be displayed in an Error List window as shown in figure 3-7, and it will indicate that the event handler is missing.

The method that handles the Click event of the Calculate button

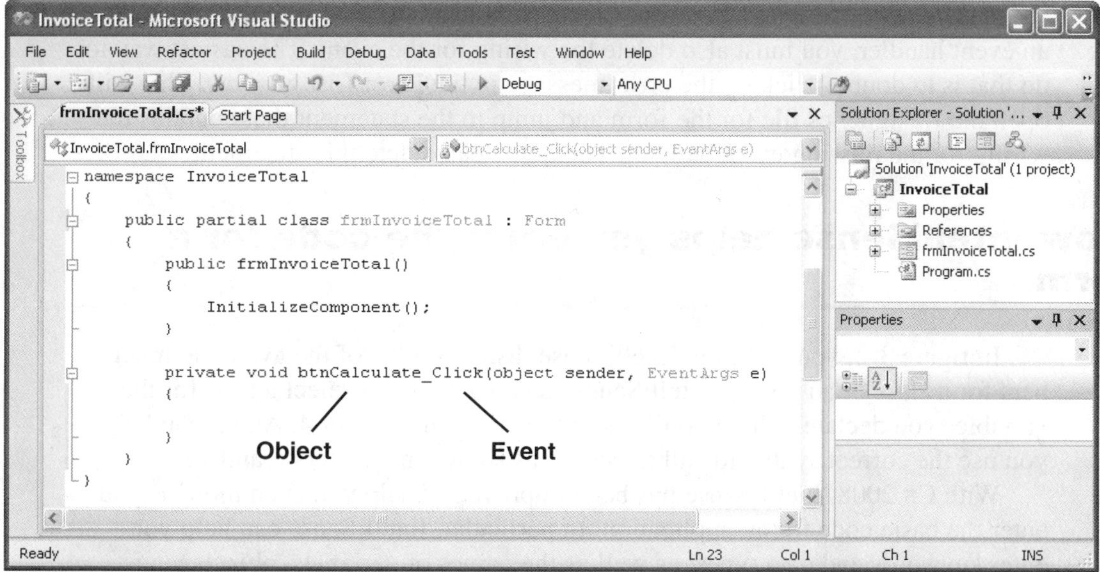

How to handle the Click event of a button

1. In the Form Designer, double-click the control. This opens the Code Editor, generates the declaration for the method that handles the event, and places the cursor within this declaration.
2. Type the C# code between the opening brace ({) and the closing brace (}) of the method declaration.
3. When you are finished writing code, you can return to the Form Designer by clicking the View Designer button in the Solution Explorer window.

How to handle the Load event for a form

- Follow the procedure shown above, but double-click the form itself.

Description

- The *method declaration* for the event handler that's generated when you double-click on an object in the Form Designer includes a *method name* that consists of the object name, an underscore, and the event name.
- The event handler is stored in the cs file for the form.
- Most of the code that's generated when you design a form, including the statement that wires the event to the event handler, is stored in the Designer.cs file for the form. If necessary, you can open this file to view or delete the event wiring.
- In chapter 6, you'll learn how to handle events other than the default event.

Figure 3-4 How to create an event handler for the default event of a form or control

That's because when you create an event handler, Visual Studio also generates a statement that wires the event to the event handler. As a result, if you delete an event handler, you must also delete the wiring for the event. The easiest way to do that is to double-click on the error message in the Error List window. This will open the Designer.cs file for the form and jump to the statement that contains the wiring for the missing event handler. Then, you can delete this statement.

How IntelliSense helps you enter the code for a form

In figure 3-2, you saw how IntelliSense displays a list of the available members for a class or an object. IntelliSense can also help you select a type for the variables you declare, which you'll learn how to do in chapter 4. And it can help you use the correct syntax to call a method as shown in chapters 6 and 12.

With C# 2008, IntelliSense has been improved to help you even more as you enter the basic code for an application. In particular, IntelliSense can help you enter keywords and data types, as well as the names of variables, objects, and classes. Figure 3-5 illustrates how this works.

The first example in this figure shows the *completion list* that IntelliSense displays when you start to enter a new line of code. Here, because I entered the letter *i*, the list is positioned on the last item I used that begins with that letter. In this case, it's positioned on the if keyword. As described earlier in this chapter, you can enter as many letters as you want, and Visual Studio will select the appropriate item based on your entry. You can also scroll through the list to select an item, and you can press the Tab or Enter key to insert the item into your code.

When you select an item in a list, Visual Studio displays information about that item in a *tool tip*. For example, the tool tip for the if keyword indicates that there is a code snippet available for the if statement. Then, if you want to insert the code snippet, you can press the Tab key twice. You'll learn more about using code snippets later in this chapter.

The second example in this figure shows the completion list that was displayed after I inserted the if keyword and then typed a space, an opening parenthesis, and the letter *s*. Here, the variable named subtotal is selected since that's the last item I entered that begins with the letter S. That made it easy to enter this item into the code.

If you've used previous versions of C#, you'll appreciate these expanded IntelliSense features. For example, it's easy to forget the names you've given to items such as controls and variables, so the list that's displayed can help you locate the appropriate name. And that can help you avoid introducing errors into your code.

Although it's not shown here, C# 2008 IntelliSense also lets you see the code that's behind a list while the list is still displayed. To do that, you simply press the Ctrl key and the list becomes semi-transparent. This eliminates the frustration a lot of programmers felt when code was hidden by a completion list in previous versions of Visual Studio.

The completion list that's displayed when you enter a letter at the beginning of a line of code

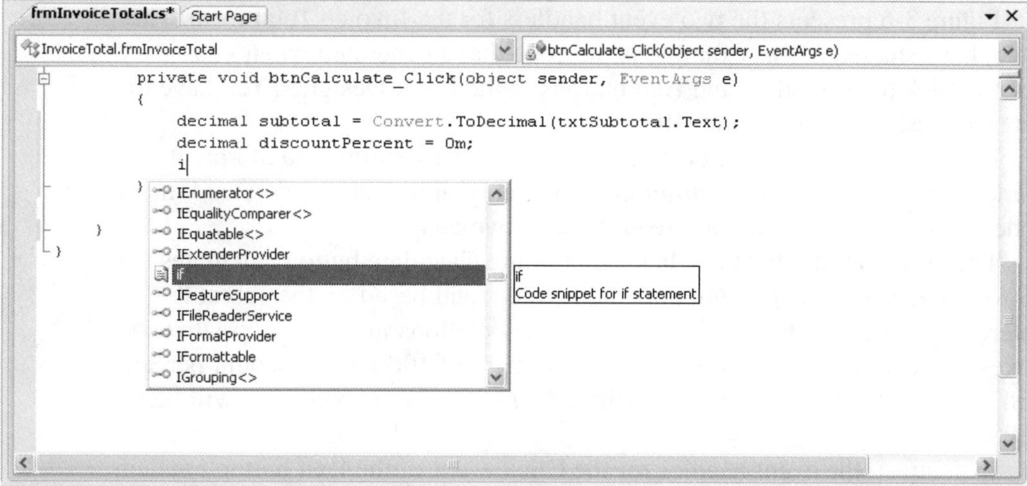

The completion list that's displayed as you enter code within a statement

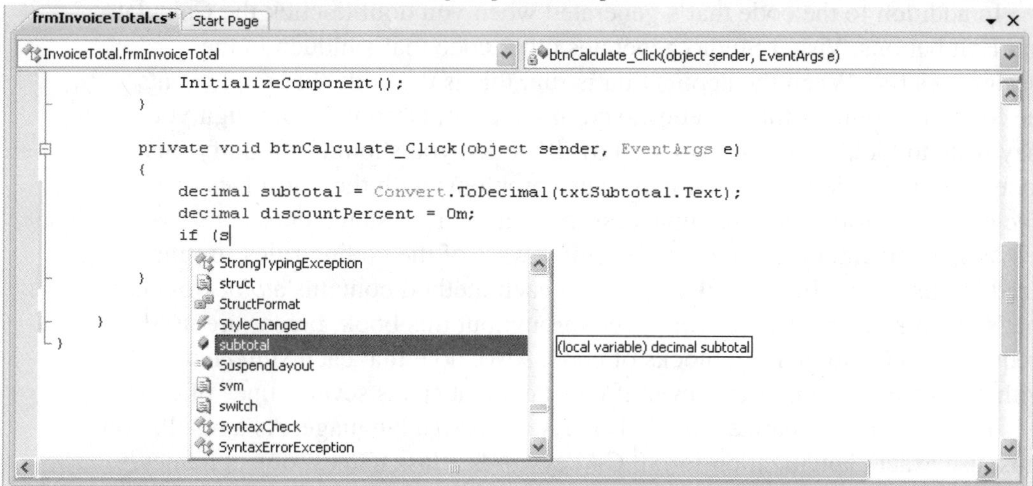

Description

- The IntelliSense that's provided for C# 2008 lists keywords, data types, variables, objects, and classes as you type so you can enter them correctly.
- When you highlight an item in a *completion list*, a tool tip is displayed with information about the item.
- If you need to see the code behind a completion list without closing the list, press the Ctrl key. Then, the list becomes semi-transparent.

Figure 3-5 How IntelliSense helps you enter the code for a form

The event handlers for the Invoice Total form

Figure 3-6 presents the two event handlers for the Invoice Total form. The code that's shaded in this example is the code that's generated when you double-click the Calculate and Exit buttons in the Form Designer. You have to enter the rest of the code yourself.

I'll describe this code briefly here so you have a general idea of how it works. If you're new to programming, however, you may not understand the code completely until after you read the next two chapters.

The event handler for the Click event of the Calculate button calculates the discount percent, discount amount, and invoice total based on the subtotal entered by the user. Then, it displays those calculations in the appropriate text boxes. For example, if the user enters a subtotal of $1000, the discount percent will be 20%, the discount amount will be $200, and the invoice total will be $800.

In contrast, the event handler for the Click event of the Exit button contains just one statement that executes the Close method of the form. As a result, when the user clicks this button, the form is closed, and the application ends.

In addition to the code that's generated when you double-click the Calculate and Exit buttons, Visual Studio generates other code that's hidden in the Designer.cs file. When the application is run, this is the code that implements the form and controls that you designed in the Form Designer. Although you may want to look at this code to see how it works, you shouldn't modify this code with the Code Editor as it may cause problems with the Form Designer. The one exception is deleting unnecessary event wiring statements.

When you enter C# code, you must be aware of the coding rules summarized in this figure. In particular, note that each method contains a *block* of code that's enclosed in braces. As you'll see throughout this book, braces are used frequently in C# to identify blocks of code. Also, note that each *statement* ends with a semicolon. This is true even if the statement spans several lines of code.

You should also realize that C# is a case-sensitive language. As a result, you must use exact capitalization for all C# keywords, class names, object names, variable names, and so on. If you use IntelliSense to help enter your code, this shouldn't be a problem.

The event handlers for the Invoice Total form

```
private void btnCalculate_Click(object sender, System.EventArgs e)
{
    decimal subtotal = Convert.ToDecimal(txtSubtotal.Text);
    decimal discountPercent = 0m;
    if (subtotal >= 500)
    {
        discountPercent = .2m;
    }
    else if (subtotal >= 250 && subtotal < 500)
    {
        discountPercent = .15m;
    }
    else if (subtotal >= 100 && subtotal < 250)
    {
        discountPercent = .1m;
    }

    decimal discountAmount = subtotal * discountPercent;
    decimal invoiceTotal = subtotal - discountAmount;

    txtDiscountPercent.Text = discountPercent.ToString("p1");
    txtDiscountAmount.Text = discountAmount.ToString("c");
    txtTotal.Text = invoiceTotal.ToString("c");

    txtSubtotal.Focus();
}

private void btnExit_Click(object sender, System.EventArgs e)
{
    this.Close();
}
```

Coding rules

- Use spaces to separate the words in each statement.
- Use exact capitalization for all keywords, class names, object names, variable names, etc.
- End each *statement* with a semicolon.
- Each *block* of code must be enclosed in braces ({}). That includes the block of code that defines the body of a method.

Description

- When you double-click the Calculate and Exit buttons in the Form Designer, it generates the shaded code shown above. Then, you can enter the rest of the code within the event handlers.
- The first event handler for the Invoice Total form is executed when the user clicks the Calculate button. This method calculates and displays the discount percent, discount amount, and total based on the subtotal entered by the user.
- The second event handler for the Invoice Total form is executed when the user clicks the Exit button. This method closes the form, which ends the application.

Figure 3-6 The event handlers for the Invoice Total form

How to detect and correct syntax errors

As you enter code, Visual Studio checks the syntax of each statement. If a *syntax error*, or *build error*, is detected, Visual Studio displays a wavy line under the code in the Code Editor. In the Code Editor in figure 3-7, for example, you can see the lines under txtPercent and txtAmount.

If you place the mouse pointer over the code in error, a brief description of the error is displayed. In this case, the error message indicates that the name does not exist. That's because the names entered in the Code Editor don't match the names used by the Form Designer. If the names are correct in the Form Designer, you can easily correct these errors by editing the names in the Code Editor. In this figure, for example, the names of the text boxes should be txtDiscountPercent and txtDiscountAmount.

If the Error List window is open as shown in this figure, any errors that Visual Studio detects will also be displayed in that window. If the Error List window isn't open, you can display it using the View→Error List command. Then, you can jump to the error in the Code Editor by double-clicking on it in the Error List window.

When you're first getting started with C#, you will inevitably encounter a lot of errors. As a result, you may want to keep the Error List window open all the time. This makes it easy to see errors as soon as they occur. Then, once you get the hang of working with C#, you can conserve screen space by using the Auto Hide button so this window is only displayed when you point to the Error List tab at the lower edge of the screen.

By the way, Visual Studio isn't able to detect all syntax errors as you enter code. Instead, some syntax errors aren't detected until the project is built. You'll learn more about building projects later in this chapter.

The Code Editor and Error List windows with syntax errors displayed

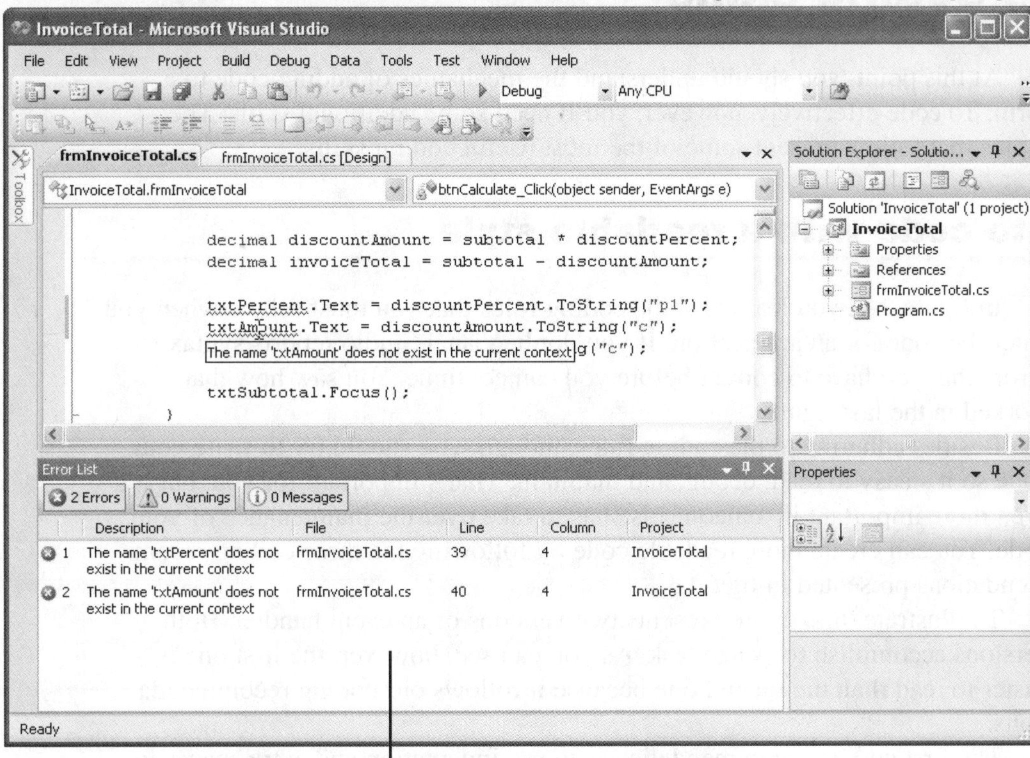

Description

- Visual Studio checks the syntax of your C# code as you enter it. If a *syntax error* (or *build error*) is detected, it's highlighted with a wavy underline in the Code Editor, and you can place the mouse pointer over it to display a description of the error.
- If the Error List window is open, all of the build errors are listed in that window. Then, you can double-click on any error in the list to take you to its location in the Code Editor. When you correct the error, it's removed from the error list.
- If the Error List window isn't open, you can display it by selecting the Error List command from the View menu. Then, if you want to hide this window, you can click its Auto Hide button.
- Visual Studio doesn't detect some syntax errors until the project is built. As a result, you may encounter more syntax errors when you build and run the project.

Figure 3-7 How to detect and correct syntax errors

More coding skills

At this point, you should understand the mechanics of adding code to a form. To code effectively, however, you'll need some additional skills. The topics that follow present some of the most useful coding skills.

How to code with a readable style

In figure 3-6, you learned some coding rules that you must follow when you enter the code for an application. If you don't, Visual Studio reports syntax errors that you have to correct before you can continue. You saw how that worked in the last figure.

Besides adhering to the coding rules, though, you should try to write your code so it's easy to read, debug, and maintain. That's important for you, but it's even more important if someone else has to take over the maintenance of your code. You can create more readable code by following the three coding recommendations presented in figure 3-8.

To illustrate, this figure presents two versions of an event handler. Both versions accomplish the same task. As you can see, however, the first one is easier to read than the second one because it follows our coding recommendations.

The first coding recommendation is to use indentation and extra spaces to align related elements in your code. This is possible because you can use one or more spaces, tabs, or returns to separate the elements in a C# statement. In this example, all of the statements within the event handler are indented. In addition, the if-else statements are indented and aligned so you can easily identify the parts of this statement.

The second recommendation is to separate the words, values, and operators in each statement with spaces. In the unreadable code in this figure, for example, you can see that each line of code except for the method declaration includes at least one operator. Because the operators aren't separated from the word or value on each side of the operator, the code is difficult to read. In contrast, the readable code includes a space on both sides of each operator.

The third recommendation is to use blank lines before and after groups of related statements to set them off from the rest of the code. This too is illustrated by the first method in this figure. Here, the code is separated into five groups of statements. In a short method like this one, this isn't too important, but it can make a long method much easier to follow.

Throughout this chapter and book, you'll see code that illustrates the use of these recommendations. You will also receive other coding recommendations that will help you write code that is easy to read, debug, and maintain.

As you enter code, the Code Editor will automatically assist you in formatting your code. When you press the Enter key at the end of a statement, for example, the Editor will indent the next statement to the same level. Although you can change how this works using the Options dialog box, you probably won't want to do that.

A method written in a readable style

```
private void btnCalculate_Click(object sender, System.EventArgs e)
{
    decimal subtotal = Convert.ToDecimal(txtSubtotal.Text);

    decimal discountPercent = 0m;
    if (subtotal >= 500)
    {
        discountPercent = .2m;
    }
    else if (subtotal >= 250 && subtotal < 500)
    {
        discountPercent = .15m;
    }
    else if (subtotal >= 100 && subtotal < 250)
    {
        discountPercent = .1m;
    }

    decimal discountAmount = subtotal * discountPercent;
    decimal invoiceTotal = subtotal - discountAmount;

    txtDiscountPercent.Text = discountPercent.ToString("p1");
    txtDiscountAmount.Text = discountAmount.ToString("c");
    txtTotal.Text = invoiceTotal.ToString("c");

    txtSubtotal.Focus();
}
```

A method written in an unreadable style

```
private void btnCalculate_Click(object sender, System.EventArgs e){
decimal subtotal=Convert.ToDecimal(txtSubtotal.Text);
decimal discountPercent=0m;
if (subtotal>=500) discountPercent=.2m;
else if (subtotal>=250&&subtotal<500) discountPercent=.15m;
else if (subtotal>=100&&subtotal<250) discountPercent=.1m;
decimal discountAmount=subtotal*discountPercent;
decimal invoiceTotal=subtotal-discountAmount;
txtDiscountPercent.Text=discountPercent.ToString("p1");
txtDiscountAmount.Text=discountAmount.ToString("c");
txtTotal.Text=invoiceTotal.ToString("c");txtSubtotal.Focus();}
```

Coding recommendations

- Use indentation and extra spaces to align statements and blocks of code so they reflect the structure of the program.
- Use spaces to separate the words, operators, and values in each statement.
- Use blank lines before and after groups of related statements.

Note

- As you enter code in the Code Editor, Visual Studio automatically adjusts its formatting by default.

Figure 3-8 How to code with a readable style

How to code comments

Comments are used to document what the program does and what specific blocks and lines of code do. Since the C# compiler ignores comments, you can include them anywhere in a program without affecting your code. Figure 3-9 shows you how to code two types of comments.

First, this figure shows a *delimited comment* at the start of a method. This type of comment is typically used to document information that applies to an entire method or to any other large block of code. You can include any useful or helpful information in a delimited comment such as a general description of the block, the author's name, the completion date, the files used by the block, and so on.

To document the purpose of a single line of code or a block of code, you can use *single-line comments*. Once the compiler reads the slashes (//) that start this type of comment, it ignores all characters until the end of the current line. In this figure, single-line comments have been used to describe each group of statements. In addition, single-line comments have been used at the end of some lines of code to clarify the code.

Although many programmers sprinkle their code with comments, that shouldn't be necessary if you write your code so it's easy to read and understand. Instead, you should use comments only to clarify code that's difficult to understand. The trick, of course, is to provide comments for the code that needs explanation without cluttering the code with unnecessary comments. For example, an experienced C# programmer wouldn't need any of the comments shown in this figure.

One problem with comments is that they may not accurately represent what the code does. This often happens when a programmer changes the code, but doesn't change the comments that go along with it. Then, it's even harder to understand the code, because the comments are misleading. So if you change the code that has comments, be sure to change the comments too.

Incidentally, all comments are displayed in the Code Editor in green by default, which is different from the color of the words in the C# statements. That makes it easy to identify the comments.

A method with comments

```
private void btnCalculate_Click(object sender, System.EventArgs e)
{
    /*************************************
    * this method calculates the total
    * for an invoice depending on a
    * discount that's based on the subtotal
    ****************************************/

    // get the subtotal amount from the Subtotal text box
    decimal subtotal = Convert.ToDecimal(txtSubtotal.Text);

    // set the discountPercent variable based
    // on the value of the subtotal variable
    decimal discountPercent = 0m;       // the m indicates a decimal value
    if (subtotal >= 500)
    {
        discountPercent = .2m;
    }
    else if (subtotal >= 250 && subtotal < 500)
    {
        discountPercent = .15m;
    }
    else if (subtotal >= 100 && subtotal < 250)
    {
        discountPercent = .1m;
    }

    // calculate and assign the values for the
    // discountAmount and invoiceTotal variables
    decimal discountAmount = subtotal * discountPercent;
    decimal invoiceTotal = subtotal - discountAmount;

    // format the values and display them in their text boxes
    txtDiscountPercent.Text =           // percent format
        discountPercent.ToString("p1"); // with 1 decimal place
    txtDiscountAmount.Text =
        discountAmount.ToString("c");   // currency format
    txtTotal.Text =
        invoiceTotal.ToString("c");

    // move the focus to the Subtotal text box
    txtSubtotal.Focus();
}
```

Description

- *Comments* are used to help document what a program does and what the code within it does.
- To code a *single-line comment*, type // before the comment. You can use this technique to add a comment on its own line or to add a comment at the end of a line.
- To code a *delimited comment*, type /* at the start of the comment and */ at the end. You can also code asterisks to identify the lines in the comment, but that isn't necessary.

Figure 3-9 How to code comments

How to work with the Text Editor toolbar

Figure 3-10 shows how you can use the Text Editor toolbar to work with code. If you experiment with this toolbar, you'll find that its buttons provide some useful functions for working with comments and indentation and for moving from one place to another.

In particular, you can use the Text Editor toolbar to modify several lines of code at once. For example, during testing, you can use this toolbar to *comment out* several lines of code by selecting the lines of code and then clicking on the Comment button. Then, you can test the program without those lines of code. If necessary, you can use the Uncomment button to restore those lines of code. Similarly, you can use the Increase Indent and Decrease Indent buttons to adjust the indentation for selected lines of code.

You can also use the Text Editor toolbar to work with *bookmarks*. After you use the Toggle Bookmark button to mark lines of code, you can easily move between the marked lines of code by using the Next and Previous buttons. Although you usually don't need bookmarks when you're working with simple applications like the one shown here, bookmarks can be helpful when you're working with applications that contain more than a few pages of code.

If you experiment with the other buttons on the Text Editor toolbar, you'll find that they provide IntelliSense features like the ones you learned about earlier in this chapter for referring to properties, methods, and events. You can use these buttons to force Visual Studio to display a member list or information about a member that's displayed in the Code Editor.

How to collapse or expand blocks of code

As you write the code for an application, you may want to *collapse* or *expand* some of the regions, comments, and methods to make it easier to scroll through the code and locate specific sections of code. To do that, you can use the techniques described in figure 3-10. In this figure, for example, the frmInvoiceTotal method has been collapsed so all you can see is its method declaration.

You may also want to collapse or expand code before you print it. Then, in the dialog box for the File→Print command, you can check or uncheck the Hide Collapsed Regions box. If this box is checked, Visual Studio will only print the code that's displayed in the Code Editor.

The Code Editor and the Text Editor toolbar

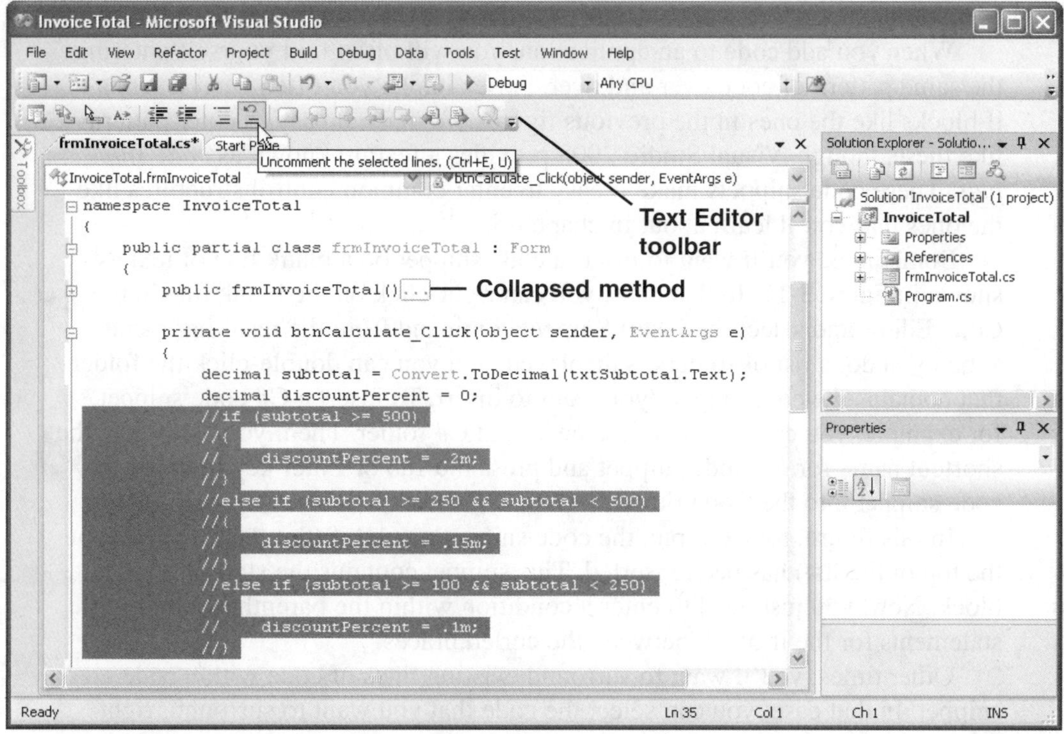

How to use the buttons of the Text Editor toolbar

- To display or hide the Text Editor toolbar, right-click in the toolbar area and choose Text Editor from the shortcut menu.
- To comment or uncomment several lines of code, select the lines and click the Comment or Uncomment button. During testing, you can *comment out* coding lines so they won't be executed. That way, you can test new statements without deleting the old statements.
- To increase or decrease the indentation of several lines of code, select the lines and click the Increase Indent or Decrease Indent button. Or, press the Tab and Shift+Tab keys.
- To move quickly between lines of code, you can use the last eight buttons on the Text Editor toolbar to set and move between *bookmarks*.

How to collapse or expand regions of code

- If a region of code appears in the Code Editor with a minus sign (-) next to it, you can click the minus sign to *collapse* the region so just the first line is displayed.
- If a region of code appears in the Code Editor with a plus sign (+) next to it, you can click the plus sign to *expand* the region so all of it is displayed.

Figure 3-10 How to use the Text Editor toolbar and collapse or expand code

How to use code snippets

When you add code to an application, you will often find yourself entering the same pattern of code over and over. For example, you often enter a series of if blocks like the ones in the previous figures. To make it easy to enter patterns like these, though, Visual Studio 2008 provides a feature known as *code snippets*. These code snippets make it easy to enter common control structures like the ones that you'll learn about in chapter 5.

Sometimes, you'll want to insert a code snippet on a blank line of text as shown in figure 3-11. In that case, you can right-click on the blank line in the Code Editor and select the Insert Snippet command from the resulting menu. When you do, a list of folders is displayed, and you can double-click the folder that contains the code snippet you want to insert. To insert a C# code snippet, for example, you can double-click the Visual C# folder. Then, you can select the shortcut name for the code snippet and press the Tab or Enter key to insert the code snippet into the Code Editor.

In this figure, for example, the code snippet named if (not the #if snippet at the top of the list) has been inserted. This snippet contains the start of an if block. Now, you just need to enter a condition within the parentheses and some statements for the if block between the curled braces.

Other times, you'll want to surround existing lines of code with a code snippet. In that case, you can select the code that you want to surround, right-click on that code, and select the Surround With command from the resulting menu. Then, you can select the appropriate snippet. For example, you might want to add an if block around one or more existing statements.

As I mentioned earlier in this chapter, C# 2008 also lets you insert a code snippet from a completion list. If you look back at figure 3-5, for example, you'll see that the tool tip that's displayed for the if keyword in the completion list in the first example indicates that the if statement has a code snippet. Then, you can just press the Tab key twice to insert that snippet.

If you find that you like using code snippets, you should be aware that it's possible to add or remove snippets from the default list. To do that, you can choose the Code Snippets Manager command from the Tools menu. Then, you can use the resulting dialog box to remove code snippets that you don't use or to add new code snippets. Be aware, however, that writing a new code snippet requires creating an XML file that defines the code snippet. To learn how to do that, you can consult the documentation for Visual Studio.

Incidentally, if you're new to programming and don't understand the if statements in this chapter, don't worry about that. Instead, just focus on the mechanics of using code snippets. In chapter 5, you'll learn everything you need to know about coding if statements.

The default list of Visual C# code snippets

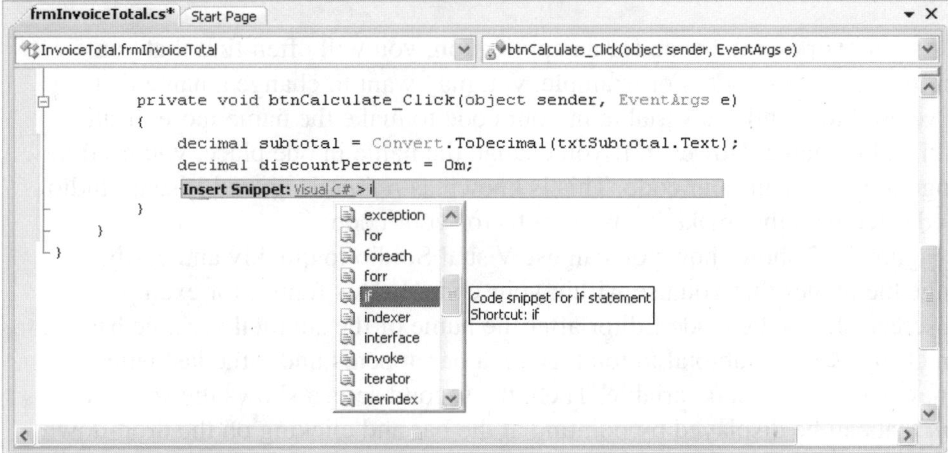

A code snippet after it has been inserted

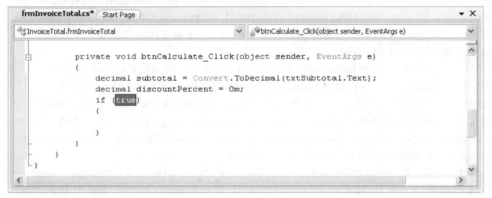

frmInvoiceTotal.cs* Start Page

InvoiceTotal.frmInvoiceTotal btnCalculate_Click(object sender, EventArgs e)

```
        private void btnCalculate_Click(object sender, EventArgs e)
        {
            decimal subtotal = Convert.ToDecimal(txtSubtotal.Text);
            decimal discountPercent = 0m;
            if (true)
            {

            }
        }
    }
}
```

Description

- To insert a code snippet, right-click in the Code Editor and select the Insert Snippet command from the resulting menu. Then, double-click the folder that contains the code snippet you want to insert (in most cases, the Visual C# folder), select the code snippet, and press the Tab or Enter key.
- You can also insert a code snippet by selecting an item from a completion list that has a code snippet and then pressing the Tab key twice.
- To surround existing code with a code snippet, select the code, right-click on it, and select the Surround With command from the resulting menu. Then, select the appropriate snippet.
- You can use the Tools→Code Snippets Manager command to display a dialog box that you can use to edit the list of available code snippets and to add custom code snippets.

Figure 3-11 How to use code snippets

How to refactor code

As you work on the code for an application, you will often find that you want to revise your code. For example, you may want to change a name that you've used to identify a variable in your code to make the name more meaningful and readable. However, if you change the name in one place, you need to change it throughout your code. This is known as *refactoring*, and Visual Studio includes features that make it easy to refactor your code.

Figure 3-12 shows how you can use Visual Studio to quickly and easily change the names that you use within your code. In this figure, for example, the first screen shows the Code Editor after the name of the subtotal variable has been changed from subtotal to total. Here, a bar appears under the last letter of the newly renamed total variable. Then, the second screen shows the *smart tag menu* that can be displayed by pointing at the bar and clicking on the drop-down arrow that becomes available.

At this point, you can select the first command to rename the variable throughout the application. Or, you can select the second command to preview the changes. If you select the second command, a Preview Changes dialog box will be displayed. Then, you can preview the changes and deselect any changes that you don't want to make.

Although this figure just shows how to change a name that's used by the code, you can also use Visual Studio's refactoring features to modify the structure of your code by extracting methods, encapsulating fields, and so on. To do that, you often begin by selecting a block of code. Then, you can right-click on the code and select the appropriate refactoring command. Or, you can select the appropriate command from the Refactor menu.

If you already have experience with another object-oriented language, these refactoring features should make sense to you. If not, don't worry. You'll learn more about these features as you progress through this book.

The bar that appears under a renamed variable

```
decimal total = Convert.ToDecimal(txtSubtotal.Text);
```

The menu that's available from the bar

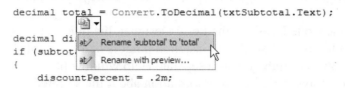

```
decimal total = Convert.ToDecimal(txtSubtotal.Text);

decimal di
if (subtot
{
    discountPercent = .2m;
```

Rename 'subtotal' to 'total'

Rename with preview...

The Preview Changes dialog box

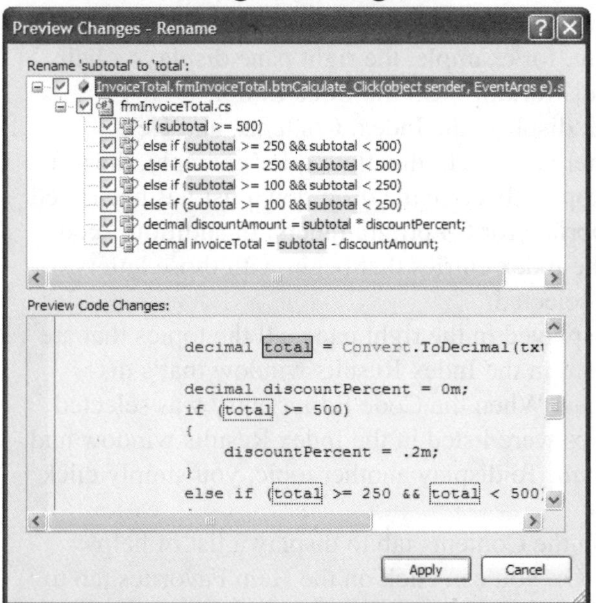

Description

- The process of revising and restructuring existing code is known as *refactoring*. Visual Studio provides many features that make it easy to refactor your code.
- When you change a name that's used in your code, Visual Studio displays a bar beneath the modified name. Then, you can display a *smart tag menu* by moving the mouse pointer over the bar, and you can click on the drop-down list to display a menu that contains the appropriate refactoring commands.
- You can also use Visual Studio's refactoring features to modify the structure of your code by extracting methods, encapsulating fields, and so on. To do that, you often begin by selecting a block of code. Then, you can right-click on the code and select the appropriate command, or you can select the command from the Refactor menu.
- Some refactoring commands display a dialog box that lets you preview the changes before you make them. Then, you can deselect any changes that you don't want to make.

Figure 3-12 How to refactor code

How to get help information

As you develop applications in C#, it's likely that you'll need some additional information about the IDE, the C# language, an object, property, method, or event, or some other aspect of C# programming. Figure 3-13 shows several ways you can get that information.

When you're working in the Code Editor or the Form Designer, the quickest way to get help information is to press F1 while the insertion point is in a keyword or an object is selected. Then, Visual Studio opens a separate Help window like the one shown in this figure and displays the available information about the selected keyword or object. Another way to launch a Help window is to select a command from Visual Studio's Help menu such as the Search, Contents, or Index command.

The Help window is split into two panes. The right pane shows the last help topic that you accessed. In this figure, for example, the right pane displays a help topic that provides information about working with the Code Editor.

The left pane, on the other hand, displays the Index, Contents, and Help Favorites tabs that help you locate help topics. In this figure, for example, the left pane displays the Index tab. At the top of this tab, the drop-down list has been used to filter help topics so they're appropriate for C# programmers. In addition, "code e" has been entered to navigate to the index entries that begin with those letters, and the Code Editor entry has been selected.

In addition to the topic that's displayed in the right pane, all the topics that are available for a selected entry are listed in the Index Results window that's displayed across the bottom of the screen. When the Code Editor entry was selected in this figure, for example, four topics were listed in the Index Results window and the first topic was displayed by default. To display another topic, you simply click on it.

In the left pane, you can click on the Contents tab to display a list of help topics that are grouped by category. Or, you can click on the Help Favorites tab to view a list of your favorite help topics. At first, the Help Favorites tab won't contain any help topics. However, you can add topics to this tab by displaying a topic and clicking on the Add To Help Favorites button that's available from the toolbar.

You can display a Search tab in the right pane by clicking on the Search button in the toolbar. From this tab, you can enter a word or phrase to search for, along with the languages, technologies, and content you want to search. Then, when you click the Search button, the results are displayed in the tab and you can click a topic to display it.

When you display information in the Help window, you should realize that the Help window uses a built-in web browser to display help topics that are available from your computer and from the Internet. In addition, the Help window works much like a web browser. To jump to a related topic, you can click on a hyperlink. To move forward and backward through previously displayed topics, you can use the Forward and Back buttons. As a result, with a little practice, you shouldn't have much trouble using this window.

The Help window

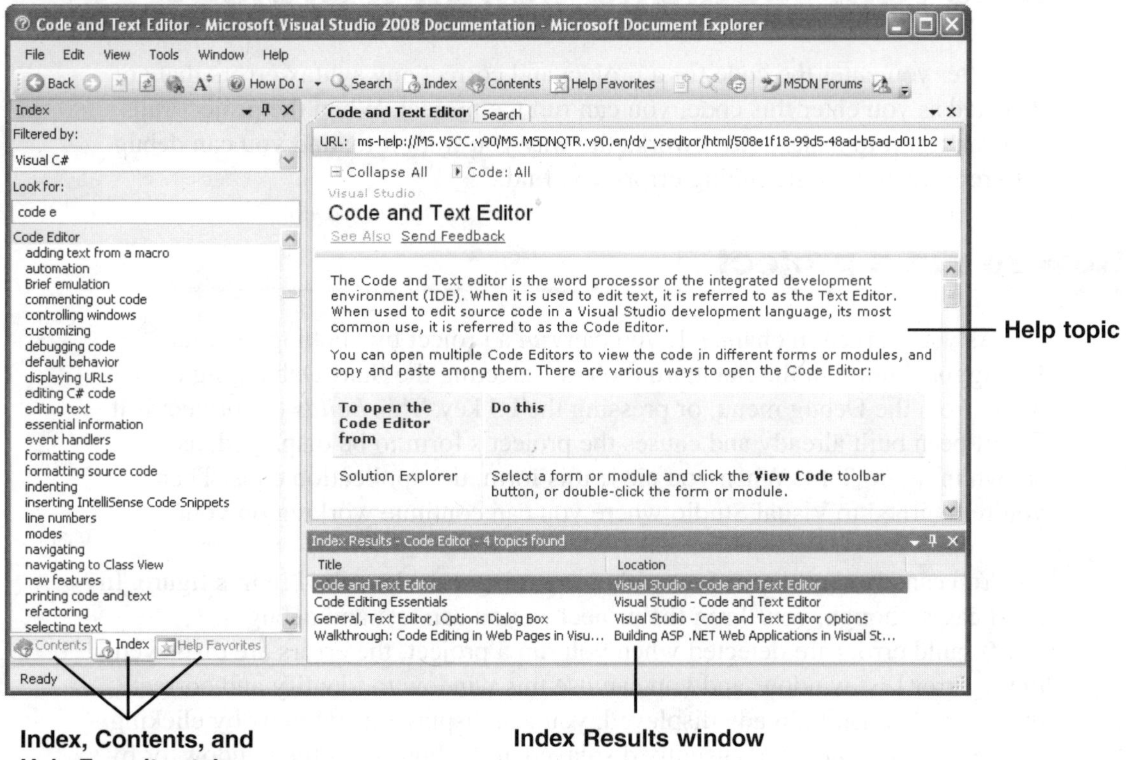

Description

- You can display a Help window by selecting an object in the Form Designer or positioning the insertion point in a keyword in the Code Editor and pressing F1.
- You can also display a Help window by selecting a command (such as Index, Contents, or Search) from Visual Studio's Help menu.
- The Help window works like a web browser and can display help topics that are available from your computer or from the Internet. You can use the buttons in its toolbar to navigate between help topics or to add topics to your list of favorite topics.
- The Help window is divided into two panes. The left pane displays the Index, Content, and Help Favorites tabs that let you locate the help topics you want to display. The right pane displays each help topic in a separate window.
- If you click on the Search button, the right pane will display a Search tab that lets you search for help topics by entering a word or phrase.
- If you click on the How Do I button, the right pane will display a How Do I tab that lets you go to a topic by clicking on a link.
- To close a tab, click on the Close button when the tab is active. To display a tab, click the tab or select it from the Active Files drop-down list that's next to the Close button.

Figure 3-13 How to get help information

How to run, test, and debug a project

After you enter the code for a project and correct any syntax errors that are detected as you enter this code, you can run the project. When the project runs, you can test it to make sure it works the way you want it to, and you can debug it to remove any programming errors you find.

How to run a project

As you learned in chapter 1, you can *run* a project by clicking the Start Debugging button in the Standard toolbar, selecting the Start Debugging command from the Debug menu, or pressing the F5 key. This *builds* the project if it hasn't been built already and causes the project's form to be displayed, as shown in figure 3-14. When you close this form, the application ends. Then, you're returned to Visual Studio where you can continue working on your program.

You can also build a project without running it as described in this figure. In most cases, though, you'll run the project so you can test and debug it.

If build errors are detected when you run a project, the errors are displayed in the Error List window, and you can use this window to identify and correct the errors. If it isn't already displayed, you can display this window by clicking on the Error List tab that's usually displayed at the bottom of the window, or by using the View→Error List command. When you do that, you should realize that the errors will still be listed in the Error List window and highlighted in the Code Editor even after you've corrected them. The errors aren't cleared until you build the project again.

The form that's displayed when you run the Invoice Total project

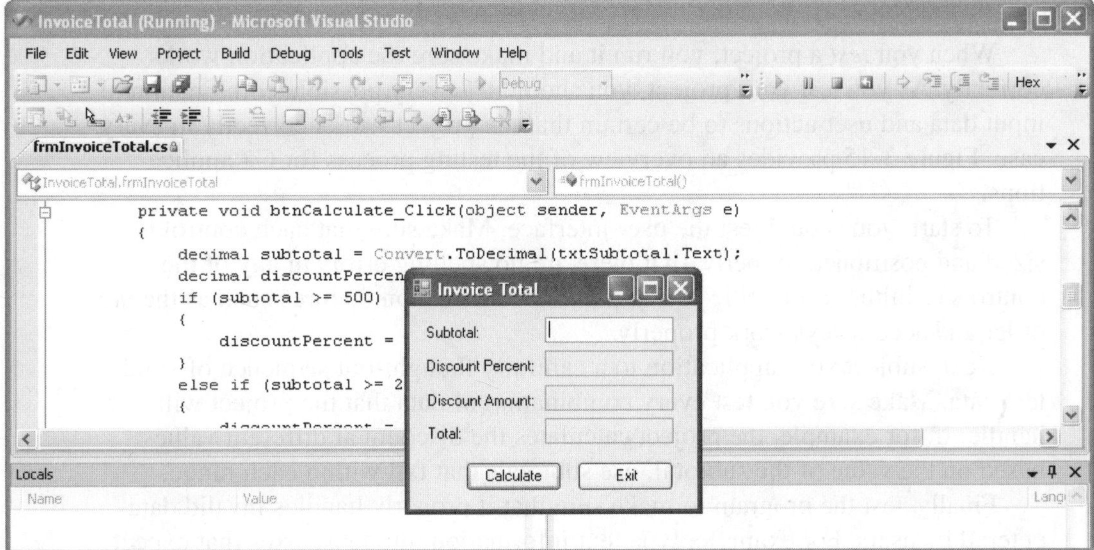

Description

- To *run* a project, click the Start Debugging button in the Standard toolbar, select the Debug→Start Debugging menu command, or press the F5 key. This causes Visual Studio to *build* the project and create an assembly. Then, assuming that there are no build errors, the assembly is run so the project's form is displayed as shown above.
- If syntax errors are detected when a project is built, they're listed in the Error List window and the project does not run.
- To locate the statement that contains the error, you can double-click on the error description in the Error List window. After you've corrected all the errors, run the project again to rebuild it and clear the errors.
- You can build a project without running it by selecting the Build→Build Solution command.
- When you build a project for the first time, all of the components of the project are built. After that, only the components that have changed are rebuilt. To rebuild all components whether or not they've changed, use the Build→Rebuild Solution command.

Figure 3-14 How to run a project

How to test a project

When you *test* a project, you run it and make sure the application works correctly. As you test your project, you should try every possible combination of input data and user actions to be certain that the project works correctly in every case. Figure 3-15 provides an overview of the testing process for C# applications.

To start, you should test the user interface. Make sure that each control is sized and positioned properly, that there are no spelling errors in any of the controls or in the form's title bar, and that the navigation features such as the tab order and access keys work properly.

Next, subject your application to a carefully thought-out sequence of valid test data. Make sure you test every combination of data that the project will handle. If, for example, the project calculates the discount at different values based on the value of the subtotal, use subtotals that fall within each range.

Finally, test the program to make sure that it properly handles invalid data entered by users. For example, type text information into text boxes that expect numeric data. Leave fields blank. Use negative numbers where they shouldn't be allowed. Remember that the goal of testing is to find all of the problems.

As you test your projects, you'll eventually encounter *runtime errors*. These errors, also known as *exceptions*, occur when C# encounters a problem that prevents a statement from being executed. If, for example, a user enters "ABC" into the Subtotal text box on the Invoice Total form, a runtime error will occur when the program tries to assign that value to a decimal variable.

When a runtime error occurs, Visual Studio breaks into the debugger and displays an Exception Assistant window like the one in this figure. Then, you can use the debugging tools that you'll be introduced to in the next figure to debug the error.

Runtime errors, though, should only occur when you're testing a program. Before an application is put into production, it should be coded and tested so all runtime errors are caught by the application and appropriate messages are displayed to the user. You'll learn how to do that in chapter 7 of this book.

The message that's displayed when a runtime error occurs

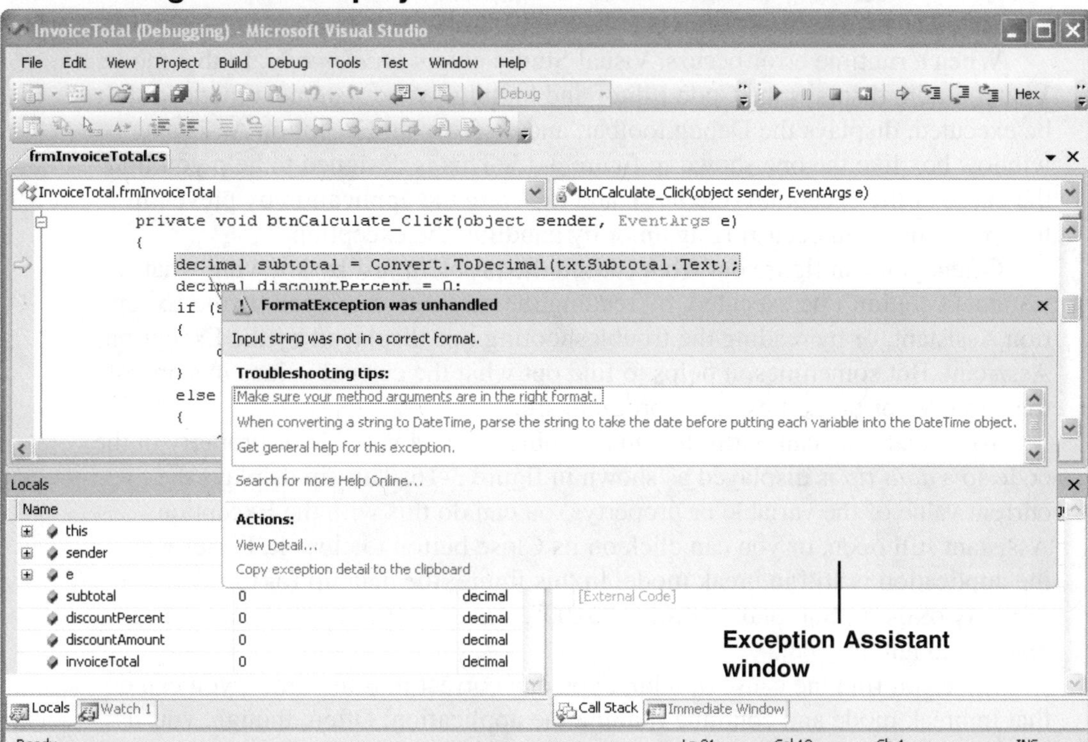

How to test a project

1. Test the user interface. Visually check all the controls to make sure they are displayed properly with the correct text. Use the Tab key to make sure the tab order is set correctly, verify that the access keys work right, and make sure that the Enter and Esc keys work properly.
2. Test valid input data. For example, enter data that you would expect a user to enter.
3. Test invalid data or unexpected user actions. For example, leave required fields blank, enter text data into numeric input fields, and use negative numbers where they are not appropriate. Try everything you can think of to make the program fail.

Description

- To *test* a project, you run the project to make sure it works properly no matter what combinations of valid or invalid data you enter or what sequence of controls you use.
- If a statement in your application can't be executed, a *runtime error*, or *exception*, occurs. Then, if the exception isn't handled by your application, the statement that caused the exception is highlighted and an Exception Assistant window like the one above is displayed. At that point, you need to debug the application as explained in the next figure.

Figure 3-15 How to test a project

How to debug runtime errors

When a runtime error occurs, Visual Studio enters *break mode*. In that mode, Visual Studio displays the Code Editor and highlights the statement that couldn't be executed, displays the Debug toolbar, and displays an Exception Assistant window box like the one shown in figure 3-15. This is designed to help you find the cause of the exception (the *bug*), and to *debug* the application by preventing the exception from occurring again or by handling the exception.

Often, you can figure out what caused the problem just by knowing what statement couldn't be executed, by reading the message displayed by the Exception Assistant, or by reading the troubleshooting tips displayed by the Exception Assistant. But sometimes, it helps to find out what the current values in some of the variables or properties in the program are.

To do that, you can place the mouse pointer over a variable or property in the code so a *data tip* is displayed as shown in figure 3-16. This tip displays the current value of the variable or property. You can do this with the Exception Assistant still open, or you can click on its Close button to close it. Either way, the application is still in break mode. In this figure, the data tip for the Text property of the txtSubtotal control is "$100", which shows that the user didn't enter valid numeric data.

Once you find the cause of a bug, you can correct it. Sometimes, you can do that in break mode and continue running the application. Often, though, you'll exit from break mode before fixing the code. To exit, you can click the Stop Debugging button in the Debug toolbar. Then, you can correct the code and test the application again.

For now, don't worry if you don't know how to correct the problem in this example. Instead, you can assume that the user will enter valid data. In chapter 7, though, you'll learn how to catch exceptions and validate all user entries for an application because that's what a professional application has to do. And in chapter 11, you'll learn a lot more about debugging.

How a project looks in break mode

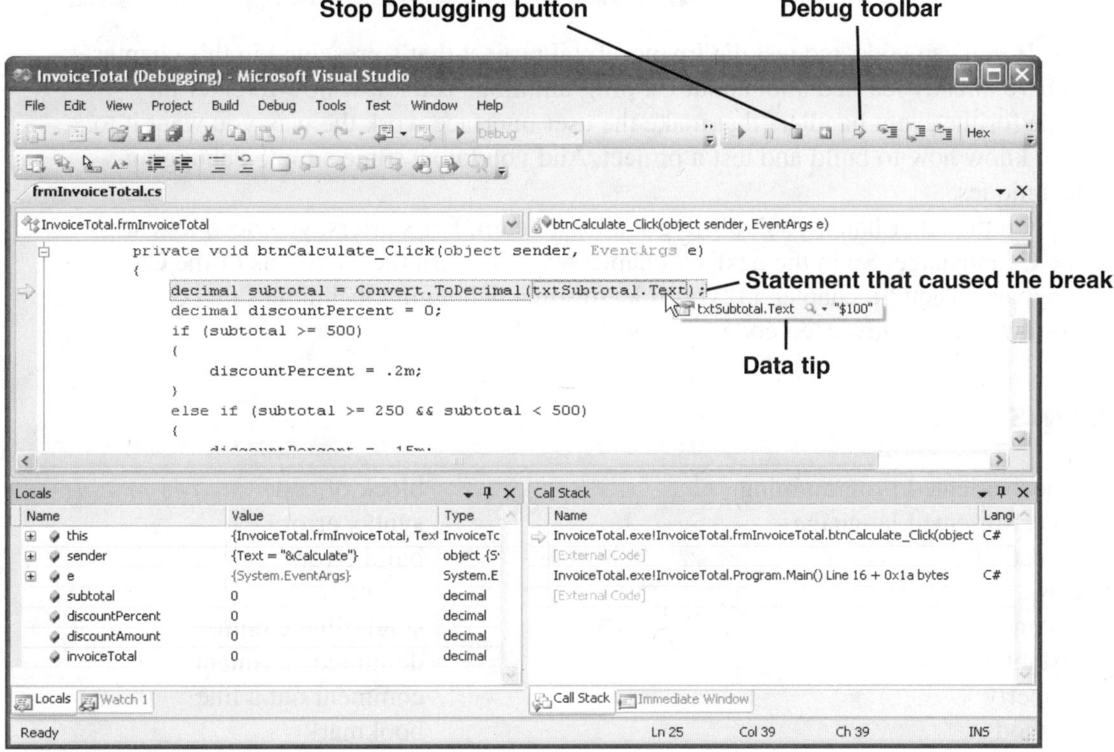

Description

- When an application encounters a runtime error, you need to fix the error. This is commonly referred to as *debugging*, and the error is commonly referred to as a *bug*.
- When an application encounters a runtime error, it enters *break mode*. In break mode, the Debug toolbar is displayed along with other windows that provide debugging features.
- The information in the Exception Assistant window should give you an idea of what the error might be. You can also click on the links in the Troubleshooting Tips list to display more information in a Help window.
- If you close the Exception Assistant window, the application remains in break mode.
- To display a *data tip* for a property or variable, move the mouse pointer over it in the C# code.
- To exit break mode and end the application, click the Stop Debugging button in the Debug toolbar or press Shift+F5. Then, you can attempt to fix the error and run the application again.
- You'll learn more about debugging and the Exception Assistant window in chapter 11.

Figure 3-16 How to debug runtime errors

Perspective

If you can code and test the Invoice Total project that's presented in this chapter, you've already learned a lot about C# programming. You know how to enter the code for the event handlers that make the user interface work the way you want it to. You know how to build and test a project. And you know some simple debugging techniques.

On the other hand, you've still got a lot to learn. For starters, you need to learn the C# language. So in the next six chapters, you'll learn the essentials of the C# language. Then, in chapter 11, you'll learn some debugging techniques that can be used with more advanced code.

Terms

object-oriented programming
object-oriented language
object
class
instance
instantiation
property
method
event
member
dot operator
dot
static member
event-driven application
event handler
event wiring
method declaration
method name
completion list
tooltip
statement
block of code
syntax error
build error
comment
single-line comment
delimited comment
comment out a line
bookmark
collapse
expand
code snippet
refactoring
build a project
run a project
test a project
runtime error
exception
bug
debug
break mode
data tip

Exercise 3-1 Code and test the Invoice Total form

In this exercise, you'll add code to the Invoice Total form that you designed in exercise 2-1. Then, you'll build and test the project to be sure it works correctly. You'll also experiment with debugging and review some help information.

Copy and open the Invoice Total application

1. Use the Windows Explorer to copy the Invoice Total project that you created for chapter 2 from the C:\C# 2008\Chapter 02 directory to the C:\C# 2008\Chapter 03 directory.

2. Open the Invoice Total solution (InvoiceTotal.sln) that's now in the C:\C# 2008\Chapter 03\InvoiceTotal directory.

Add code to the form and correct syntax errors

3. Display the Invoice Total form in the Form Designer, and double-click on the Calculate button to open the Code Editor and generate the method declaration for the Click event of this object. Then, enter the code for this method as shown in figure 3-6. As you enter the code, be sure to take advantage of all of the Visual Studio features for coding including snippets.
4. Return to the Form Designer, and double-click the Exit button to generate the method declaration for the Click event of this object. Enter the statement shown in figure 3-6 for this event handler.
5. Open the Error List window as described in figure 3-7. If any syntax errors are listed in this window, double-click on each error to move to the error in the Code Editor. Then, correct the error.

Test the application

6. Press F5 to build and run the project. If you corrected all the syntax errors in step 5, the build should succeed and the Invoice Total form should appear. If not, you'll need to correct the errors and press F5 again.
7. Enter a valid numeric value in the first text box and click the Calculate button or press the Enter key to activate this button. Assuming that the calculation works, click the Exit button or press the Esc key to end the application. If either of these methods doesn't work right, of course, you need to debug the problems and test the application again.

Enter invalid data and display data tips in break mode

8. Start the application again. This time, enter "xx" for the subtotal. Then, click the Calculate button. This will cause Visual Studio to enter break mode and display the Exception Assistant as shown in figure 3-15.
9. Note the highlighted statement and read the message that's displayed in the Exception Assistant. Then, move the mouse pointer over the variable and property in this statement to display their data tips. This shows that the code for this application needs to be enhanced so it checks for invalid data. You'll learn how to do that in chapter 7. For now, though, click the Stop Debugging button in the Debug toolbar to end the application.

Create a syntax error and see how it affects the IDE

10. When you return to the Code Editor, hide the Error List window by clicking on its Auto Hide button. Next, change the name of the Subtotal text box from txtSubtotal to txtSubTotal. This creates an error since the capitalization doesn't match the capitalization used by the Name property of the text box.
11. Try to run the application, and click No when Visual Studio tells you the build had errors and asks whether you want to continue with the last successful build. Then, double-click on the error in the Error List, correct the error, and run the application again to make sure the problem is fixed.

Use refactoring

12. Change the name of the subtotal variable from subtotal to invoiceSubtotal. When you do a bar will appear under the last letter of the variable. Point at this bar to display a drop-down arrow. Then, click on this arrow and select the Rename command. This should rename the subtotal variable throughout the form, but run the form to make sure it's working correctly.

Generate and delete an event handler

13. Display the Form Designer for the Invoice Total form and double-click a blank area on the form. This should generate an event handler for the Load event of the form.
14. Delete the event handler for the Load event of the form. Then, run the application. When you do, you'll get a build error that indicates that the form does not contain a definition for this event handler.
15. Double-click on the error. This opens the Designer.cs file for the form and jumps to the statement that wires the event handler. Delete this statement to correct the error.
16. If you're curious, review the generated code that's stored in the Designer.cs file for this simple form. Then, click the minus sign to the left of the region named "Windows Form Designer generated code" to collapse this region.
17. Run the form to make sure it's working correctly. When you return to the Code Editor, close the Designer.cs file for the form.

Experiment with the Help feature

18. To see how context-sensitive help works, place the insertion point in the Focus method in the last statement of the first event handler and press F1. This should open a Help window that tells you more about this method.
19. In the left pane, select the Index tab to display the Index window. Type "snippets" into the Look For box in this window to see the entries that are listed under this topic. Next, if Visual C# (or Visual C# Express Edition) isn't selected in the Filter By drop-down list, select it to show just the topics for C#. Then, click on one or more topics to display them.
20. Continue experimenting with the Index, Contents, Help Favorites, and Search features to see how they work, and try using some of the buttons in the Web toolbar to see how they work. Then, close the Help window.

Exit from Visual Studio

21. Click the Close button for the Visual Studio window to exit from this application. If you did everything and got your application to work right, you've come a long way!

Section 2

The C# language essentials

In section 1, you were introduced to C# programming. In particular, you learned how to use Visual Studio to design a Windows form, to enter the code for that form, and to test that code. However, you didn't actually learn the details for coding C# statements.

Now, in this section, you'll learn the C# language essentials. In chapter 4, for example, you'll learn how to code arithmetic operations. In chapter 5, you'll learn how to code selection and iteration statements. In chapter 6, you'll learn how to code your own methods. In chapter 7, you'll learn how to check the user's entries to make sure they're valid. In chapter 8, you'll learn how to use arrays and collections. And in chapter 9, you'll learn how to work with dates and strings. This gets you off to a great start.

After that, chapter 10 presents some more skills for developing Windows Forms applications. These expand upon the skills you learned in chapters 2 and 3 and require many of the language skills that you've learned in chapters 4 through 9. To conclude your mastery of these essentials, chapter 11 presents more of the Visual Studio features for debugging that you were introduced to in chapter 3.

4

How to work with numeric and string data

To start your mastery of the C# language, this chapter shows you how to work with the various types of data that C# offers. In particular, you'll learn how to perform arithmetic operations on numeric data, how to work with string data, and how to convert one type of data to another.

How to work with the built-in value types

To start, this chapter shows you how to work with the *built-in data types* that the .NET Framework provides. As you will see, these consist of value types and reference types. To start, you'll learn about the value types.

The built-in value types

Figure 4-1 summarizes the *value types* that the .NET Framework provides. To refer to each of these data types, C# provides a keyword. You can use the first eleven data types to store numbers, and you can use the last two data types to store characters and true or false values.

The first eight data types are used to store *integers*, which are numbers that don't contain decimal places (whole numbers). When you use one of the integer types, you should select an appropriate size. Most of the time, you can use the *int* type. However, you may need to use the *long* type if the value is too large for the int type. On the other hand, if you're working with smaller numbers and you need to save system resources, you can use the *short* or *byte* type. If you're working with positive numbers, you can also use the unsigned versions of these types.

You can use the next three data types to store numbers that contain decimal places. Since the *decimal* type is more accurate than the *double* and *float* types, it's commonly used for monetary values. If you need to save system resources, however, the double and float types are adequate for most situations.

You can use the *char* type to store a single character. Since C# supports the two-byte *Unicode character set*, it can store practically any character from any language around the world. As a result, you can use C# to create programs that read and print Greek or Chinese characters. In practice, though, you'll usually work with the characters that are stored in the older one-byte *ASCII character set*. These characters are the first 256 characters of the Unicode character set.

Last, you can use the *bool* type to store a true value or false value. This type of value is known as a *Boolean value*.

The built-in value types

C# Keyword	Bytes	.NET type	Description
byte	1	Byte	A positive integer value from 0 to 255
sbyte	1	SByte	A signed integer value from -128 to 127
short	2	Int16	An integer from –32,768 to +32,767
ushort	2	UInt16	An unsigned integer from 0 to 65,535
int	4	Int32	An integer from –2,147,483,648 to +2,147,483,647
uint	4	UInt32	An unsigned integer from 0 to 4,294,967,295
long	8	Int64	An integer from –9,223,372,036,854,775,808 to +9,223,372,036,854,775,807
ulong	8	UInt64	An unsigned integer from 0 to +18,446,744,073,709,551,615
float	4	Single	A non-integer number with approximately 7 significant digits
double	8	Double	A non-integer number with approximately 14 significant digits
decimal	16	Decimal	A non-integer number with up to 28 significant digits (integer and fraction) that can represent values up to 79,228 x 10^{24}
char	2	Char	A single Unicode character
bool	1	Boolean	A true or false value

Description

- The *built-in data types* are actually aliases for the data types defined by the Common Type System of the .NET Framework.
- All of the data types shown in this figure are *value types*, which means that they store their own data. In contrast, *reference types* store a reference to the area of memory where the data is stored. See figure 4-10 for more information on value types and reference types.
- A *bit* is a binary digit that can have a value of one or zero. A *byte* is a group of eight bits. As a result, the number of bits for each data type is the number of bytes multiplied by 8.
- *Integers* are whole numbers, and the first eight data types above provide for signed and unsigned integers of various sizes.
- Since the decimal type is the most accurate non-integer data type, it's typically used to store monetary values.
- The *Unicode character set* provides for over 65,000 characters, with two bytes used for each character. Each character maps to an integer value.
- The older *ASCII character set* that's used by most operating systems provides for 256 characters with one byte used for each character. In the Unicode character set, the first 256 characters correspond to the 256 ASCII characters.
- A *bool* data type stores a *Boolean value* that's either true or false.

Figure 4-1 The built-in value types

How to declare and initialize variables

A *variable* stores a value that can change as the program executes. Before you can use a variable, you must declare its data type and name and then initialize it by assigning a value to it. Figure 4-2 shows two ways you can do that.

First, you can use separate statements to *declare* and *initialize* a variable as shown in the first example in this figure. Second, you can use a single statement that declares the variable and assigns a value to it. This figure presents several examples that use this technique. Notice that the last example declares and initializes two variables with the same data type.

Although you can declare a variable without assigning a value to it, you must assign a value to the variable before you can use it in your code. Otherwise, you'll get a build error when you try to run the project. As a result, it's a good coding practice to declare and initialize a variable in one statement or to assign a value to a variable immediately after you declare it.

With C# 2008, you can also let the type of some variables be inferred from the values that are assigned to them. To do that, you code the *var* keyword instead of a type. This is most useful when you're working with LINQ, as you'll see in chapter 23.

You should also notice in the examples in this figure that the first word of each variable name starts with a lowercase letter, and the remaining words start with an uppercase letter. This is known as *camel notation*, and it's a common coding convention in C#.

When you work with variables, you can assign a *literal value*, or *literal*, to the variable. For example, you can assign a literal value of 1 to an int variable. When you code a number that has a decimal point, such as 8.125, the C# compiler assumes that you want that literal value to be a double value. As a result, if you want it to be interpreted as a decimal value, you need to code the letter *m* or *M* after the value (think *m* for *money*). Similarly, for a float type, you code the letter *f* or *F* after the value. If you omit the letter, you'll get a build error when you try to run the project.

You can use *scientific notation* to express the value of extremely large or small non-integer numbers. To use this notation, you code the letter *e* or *E* followed by a power of 10. For instance, 3.65e+9 is equal to 3.65 times 10^9 (or 3,650,000,000), and 3.65e-9 is equal to 3.65 times 10-9 (or .00000000365). If you have a scientific or mathematical background, you're already familiar with this notation. Otherwise, you probably won't ever use this notation.

You can also assign a literal value to a variable with the char data type. To do that, you enclose the value in single quotes. To assign a literal value to a variable with the bool type, you can use the *true* and *false* keywords.

How to declare and initialize constants

A *constant* stores a value that can't be changed as the program executes. Many of the skills for declaring and initializing variables also apply to declaring and initializing constants. However, you always use a single statement to declare

How to declare and initialize a variable in two statements

Syntax

```
type variableName;
variableName = value;
```

Example

```
int counter;                    // declaration statement
counter = 1;                    // assignment statement
```

How to declare and initialize a variable in one statement

Syntax

```
type variableName = value;
```

Examples

```
int counter = 1;
long numberOfBytes = 20000;
float interestRate = 8.125f;    // f or F indicates a float value
double price = 14.95;
decimal total = 24218.1928m;    // m or M indicates a decimal value
double starCount = 3.65e+9;     // scientific notation
char letter = 'A';              // enclose a character value in single quotes
bool valid = false;
int x = 0, y = 0;               // initialize 2 variables with 1 statement
```

How to declare and initialize a constant

Syntax

```
const type ConstantName = value;
```

Examples

```
const int DaysInNovember = 30;
const decimal SalesTax = .075m;
```

Description

- A *variable* stores a value that can change as a program executes, while a *constant* stores a value that can't be changed. Before you can use a variable or constant, you must declare its type and assign an initial value to it.
- Common initial values are 0 for variables that store integer values, 0.0 for variables that store decimal values, and false for variables that store Boolean values.
- To declare or initialize more than one variable for a single data type in a single statement, use commas to separate the variable names or assignments.
- To identify *literal values* as float values, you must type the letter *f* or *F* after the number. To identify decimal values, you must type the letter *m* or *M* after the number.
- The keywords for data types must be coded with all lowercase letters.

Naming conventions

- Start the names of variables with a lowercase letter, and capitalize the first letter of each word after the first word. This is known as *camel notation.*
- Capitalize the first letter of each word of a constant name.

Figure 4-2 How to declare and initialize variables and constants

and initialize a constant, and that statement must begin with the *const* keyword. In addition, it's a common coding convention to capitalize the first letter in each word of a constant, including the first word.

How to code arithmetic expressions

Figure 4-3 shows how to code *arithmetic expressions*. To create an arithmetic expression, you use the *arithmetic operators* to indicate what operations are to be performed on the *operands* in the expression. An operand can be a literal or a variable.

The first five operators listed in this figure work on two operands. As a result, they're referred to as *binary operators*. For example, when you use the subtraction operator (-), you subtract one operand from the other. In contrast, the last four operators work on one operand. As a result, they're referred to as *unary operators*. For example, you can code the negative sign operator (-) in front of an operand to reverse the value of the operand. You can also code a positive sign operator (+) in front of an operand to return the value of the operand. Since that doesn't change the value of the operand, however, the positive sign is rarely used as a unary operator.

While the addition (+), subtraction (-), and multiplication (*) operators are self-explanatory, the division (/) and modulus (%) operators require some additional explanation. If you're working with integer data types, the division operator returns an integer value that represents the number of times the right operand goes into the left operand. Then, the modulus operator returns an integer value that represents the remainder (which is the amount that's left over after dividing the left operand by the right operand). If you're working with non-integer data types, the division operator returns a value that uses decimal places to indicate the result of the division, which is usually what you want.

When you code an increment (++) or decrement (--) operator, you can *prefix* the operand by coding the operator before the operand. This is illustrated by the last two examples in the first two groups. Then, the operand is incremented or decremented before the result is assigned.

You should realize, though, that you can also *postfix* the operand by coding the operator after the operand. Then, the result is assigned before the operand is incremented or decremented. When an entire statement does nothing more than increment a variable, as in

```
counter++;
```

both the prefix and postfix forms yield the same result.

Since each char variable holds a Unicode character that maps to an integer, you can perform some integer operations on char variables. For instance, this figure shows an example of how you can use the increment operator to change the numeric value of a char variable from 67 to 68. This changes the character from the letter *C* to the letter *D*.

Arithmetic operators

Operator	Name	Description
+	Addition	Adds two operands.
-	Subtraction	Subtracts the right operand from the left operand.
*	Multiplication	Multiplies the right operand and the left operand.
/	Division	Divides the right operand into the left operand. If both operands are integers, then the result is an integer.
%	Modulus	Returns the value that is left over after dividing the right operand into the left operand.
+	Positive sign	Returns the value of the operand.
-	Negative sign	Changes a positive value to negative, and vice versa.
++	Increment	Adds 1 to the operand (x = x + 1).
--	Decrement	Subtracts 1 from the operand (x = x - 1).

Examples of arithmetic expressions

```
// integer arithmetic
int x = 14;
int y = 8;
int result1 = x + y;          // result1 = 22
int result2 = x - y;          // result2 = 6
int result3 = x * y;          // result3 = 112
int result4 = x / y;          // result4 = 1
int result5 = x % y;          // result5 = 6
int result6 = -y + x;         // result6 = 6
int result7 = --y;            // result7 = 7, y = 7
int result8 = ++x;            // result8 = 15, x = 15

// decimal arithmetic
decimal a = 8.5m;
decimal b = 3.4m;
decimal result11 = a + b;      // result11 = 11.9
decimal result12 = a - b;      // result12 = 5.1
decimal result13 = a / b;      // result13 = 2.5
decimal result14 = a * b;      // result14 = 28.90
decimal result15 = a % b;      // result15 = 1.7
decimal result16 = -a;         // result16 = -8.5
decimal result17 = --a;        // result17 = 7.5, a = 7.5
decimal result18 = ++b;        // result18 = 4.4, b = 4.4

// character arithmetic
char letter1 = 'C';            // letter1 = 'C'  Unicode integer is 67
char letter2 = ++letter1;      // letter2 = 'D'  Unicode integer is 68
```

Description

- An *arithmetic expression* consists of one or more *operands* and *arithmetic operators*.
- The first five operators above are called *binary operators* because they operate on two operands. The next four are called *unary operators* because they operate on just one operand.

Figure 4-3 How to code arithmetic expressions

How to code assignment statements

Figure 4-4 shows how you can code an *assignment statement* to assign a new value to a variable. In a simple assignment statement, you code the variable name, an equals sign, and an expression. This is illustrated by the first group of assignment statements in this figure. Notice that the expression can be a literal value, the name of another variable, or any other type of expression, such as an arithmetic expression. After the expression is evaluated, the result is assigned to the variable.

When you code assignment statements, you sometimes need to code the same variable on both sides of the equals sign as shown in the second group of statements. That way, you use the current value of the variable in an expression and then update the variable by assigning the result of the expression to it. For example, you can easily add 100 to the value of a variable and store the new value in the same variable.

Since it's common to use a variable on both sides of an assignment statement, C# provides the five shorthand *assignment operators* shown in this figure. These operators are illustrated in the third group of statements. Notice that these statements perform the same functions as the second group of statements. However, the statements that use the shorthand operators are more compact.

If you need to increment or decrement a variable by a value of 1, you can use the increment or decrement operator instead of an assignment statement. For example:

```
month = month + 1;
```

is equivalent to

```
month += 1;
```

which is equivalent to

```
month++;
```

The technique you use is mostly a matter of preference. Of course, the last technique requires the least amount of typing and is most commonly used.

Assignment operators

Operator	Name	Description
=	Assignment	Assigns a new value to the variable.
+=	Addition	Adds the right operand to the value stored in the variable and assigns the result to the variable.
-=	Subtraction	Subtracts the right operand from the value stored in the variable and assigns the result to the variable.
*=	Multiplication	Multiplies the variable by the right operand and assigns the result to the variable.
/=	Division	Divides the variable by the right operand and assigns the result to the variable. If the variable and the operand are both integers, then the result is an integer.
%=	Modulus	Divides the variable by the right operand and assigns the remainder to the variable.

The syntax for a simple assignment statement

```
variableName = expression;
```

Typical assignment statements

```
counter = 7;
newCounter = counter;
discountAmount = subtotal * .2m;
total = subtotal - discountAmount;
```

Statements that use the same variable on both sides of the equals sign

```
total = total + 100m;
total = total - 100m;
price = price * .8m;
```

Statements that use the shortcut assignment operators

```
total += 100m;
total -= 100m;
price *= .8m;
```

Description

- A simple *assignment statement* consists of a variable, an equals sign, and an expression. When the assignment statement is executed, the expression is evaluated and the result is stored in the variable.
- Besides the equals sign, C# provides the five other *assignment operators* shown above. These operators provide a shorthand way to code common assignment operations.

Figure 4-4 How to code assignment statements

How to work with the order of precedence

Figure 4-5 gives more information for coding arithmetic expressions. Specifically, it gives the *order of precedence* of the arithmetic operations. This means that all of the prefixed increment and decrement operations in an expression are done first, followed by all of the positive and negative operations, and so on. If there are two or more operations at each order of precedence, the operations are done from left to right.

Because this sequence of operations doesn't always work the way you want it to, you may need to override the sequence by using parentheses. Then, the expressions in the innermost sets of parentheses are done first, followed by the expressions in the next sets of parentheses, and so on. Within each set of parentheses, though, the operations are done from left to right in the order of precedence.

The need for parentheses is illustrated by the two examples in this figure. Because parentheses aren't used in the first example, the multiplication operation is done before the subtraction operation, which gives an incorrect result. In contrast, because the subtraction operation is enclosed in parentheses in the second example, this operation is performed before the multiplication operation, which gives a correct result.

In practice, you should use parentheses to dictate the sequence of operations whenever there's any doubt about it. That way, you don't have to worry about the order of precedence.

This figure also summarizes the information on prefixed and postfixed increment and decrement operations that I mentioned earlier, and the last set of examples shows the differences in these operations. Because this can get confusing, it's best to limit these operators to simple expressions and to use the prefix form whenever there's any doubt about how an expression will be evaluated.

The order of precedence for arithmetic operations

1. Increment and decrement
2. Positive and negative
3. Multiplication, division, and modulus
4. Addition and subtraction

A calculation that uses the default order of precedence

```
decimal discountPercent = .2m;          // 20% discount
decimal price = 100m;                   // $100 price
price = price * 1 - discountPercent;    // price = $99.8
```

A calculation that uses parentheses to specify the order of precedence

```
decimal discountPercent = .2m;          // 20% discount
decimal price = 100m;                   // $100 price
price = price * (1 - discountPercent);  // price = $80
```

The use of prefixed and postfixed increment and decrement operators

```
int a = 5;
int b = 5
int y = ++a;        // a = 6, y = 6
int z = b++;        // b = 6, z = 5
```

Description

- Unless parentheses are used, the operations in an expression take place from left to right in the *order of precedence*.
- To specify the sequence of operations, you can use parentheses. Then, the operations in the innermost sets of parentheses are done first, followed by the operations in the next sets, and so on.
- When you use an increment or decrement operator as a *prefix* to a variable, the variable is incremented or decremented and then the result is assigned. But when you use an increment or decrement operator as a *postfix* to a variable, the result is assigned and then the variable is incremented or decremented.

Figure 4-5 How to work with the order of precedence

How to work with casting

As you develop C# programs, you'll frequently need to convert data from one data type to another. To do that, you can sometimes use a technique called *casting*. Figure 4-6 illustrates how casting works.

As you can see, C# provides for two types of casting. *Implicit casts* are performed automatically and can be used to convert data with a less precise type to a more precise type. This is called a *widening conversion* because the resulting value is always wider than the original value. The first statement in this figure, for example, causes an int value to be converted to a double value. Similarly, the second statement causes a char value to be converted to an int value.

C# will also perform an implicit cast on the values in an arithmetic expression if some of the values have more precise data types than other values. This is illustrated by the next three statements in this figure. Here, the variables a, b, and c are used in an arithmetic expression. Notice that a is declared with the double data type, while b and c are declared with the int data type. Because of that, both b and c will be converted to double values when this expression is evaluated.

A *narrowing conversion* is one that casts data from a more precise data type to a less precise data type. With this type of conversion, the less precise data type may not be wide enough to hold the original value. Because C# uses *strict type semantics*, you must use an *explicit cast* to perform narrowing conversions.

To perform an explicit cast, you code the data type in parentheses before the variable that you want to convert. When you do this, you should realize that you may lose some information. This is illustrated by the first example in this figure that performs an explicit cast. Here, a double value of 93.75 is cast to an int value of 93. An explicit cast is required in this example because C# won't automatically cast a double value to an integer value since an integer value is less precise. Notice here that the double value is truncated rather than rounded.

When you use explicit casting in an arithmetic expression, the casting is done before the arithmetic operations. This is illustrated by the last two examples of explicit casts. In the last example, two integer types are cast to decimal types before the division is done so the result will have decimal places if they are needed. Without explicit casting, the expression would return an integer value that would then be cast to a decimal.

When you code an explicit cast, an exception may occur at runtime if the new data type isn't wide enough to hold the result of the expression. As a result, you should use an explicit cast only when you're sure that the new data type can hold the value.

Although you typically cast between numeric data types, you should know that you can also cast between the int and char types. That's because every char type corresponds to an int value that identifies it in the Unicode character set.

How implicit casting works

Casting from less precise to more precise data types

byte→short→int→long→float→double→decimal

char→int

Example

```
double grade = 93;                // convert int to double

int letter = 'A';                 // convert char to int

double a = 95.0;
int b = 86, c = 91;
double average = (a+b+c)/3;       // convert b and c to double values
                                  // (average = 90.666666...)
```

How to code an explicit cast

The syntax for coding an explicit cast

```
(type) expression
```

Examples

```
int grade = (int) 93.75;            // convert double to int (grade = 93)

char letter = (char) 65;            // convert int to char (letter = 'A')

double a = 95.0;
int b = 86, c = 91;
int average = ((int)a+b+c)/3;       // convert a to int value (average = 90)

decimal result = (decimal) b / (decimal) c;      // result has decimal places
```

Description

- If you code an assignment statement that assigns a value with a less precise data type to a variable with a more precise data type, C# automatically converts the less precise data type to the more precise data type. This can be referred to as an *implicit cast* or a *widening conversion.*
- When you code an arithmetic expression, C# implicitly casts operands with less precise data types to the most precise data type used in the expression.
- To code an assignment statement that assigns a value with a more precise data type to a variable with a less precise data type, you must code the less precise data type in parentheses preceding the value to be assigned. This can be referred to as an *explicit cast* or a *narrowing conversion.*
- You can also use an explicit cast in an arithmetic expression. Then, the casting is done before the arithmetic operations.

Figure 4-6 How to work with casting

How to use the Math class

Figure 4-7 presents five methods of the Math class that you can use to work with numeric data. Although this class provides a variety of methods for performing mathematical operations, these are the ones you're most likely to use. Note in the syntax summaries that square brackets indicate that a clause is optional, braces indicate a choice between two or more elements, and bold type indicates language elements that must be entered exactly as shown.

The five methods shown in this figure are *static methods*. As a result, you can call these methods directly from the Math class by coding the name of the class, a dot, the name of the method, and one or more *arguments* enclosed in parentheses. For example, the Round method requires at least one argument that represents the value to be rounded, plus an optional second argument. The Sqrt method requires just one argument. And the Pow, Min, and Max methods require two arguments.

You use the Round method to round a decimal, double, or float value to a specified number of decimal digits, called the *precision*. For instance, the first statement in this figure rounds the value in the shipWeightDouble variable to a whole number, because that's the default. In contrast, the second statement specifies two decimal places.

If you use the Round method of the Math class, you should know that it uses a special type of rounding called *banker's rounding*. With this type of rounding, if a number that's midway between two whole numbers is being rounded to a whole number, it's always rounded to the even number. This is illustrated by the second and third statements in the second set of examples in this figure. Here, you can see that both the numbers 23.5 and 24.5 are rounded to 24. That can help eliminate the errors that can occur from always rounding a decimal value of .5 up to the nearest whole number, which is how standard rounding techniques work.

You use the Pow method to raise a number to the specified power. The third statement in this figure, for example, raises the variable named radius to the second power. In other words, it calculates the square of this variable, which is used to calculate the area of a circle. Note that C# doesn't provide an arithmetic operator for raising a number to a power like some other languages do. Because of that, you'll want to use the Pow method any time you need to perform this operation.

This figure also presents three other static methods of the Math class: Sqrt, Min, and Max. The Sqrt method calculates the square root of a number. The Min and Max methods return the minimum or maximum of two numeric values that you specify. These three methods can be used with any of the numeric data types. However, when you use the Min or Max method, the two values you specify must be of the same type.

Four static methods of the Math class

The syntax of the Round method

```
Math.Round(decimalNumber[, precision])
```

The syntax of the Pow method

```
Math.Pow(number, power)
```

The syntax of the Sqrt method

```
Math.Sqrt(number)
```

The syntax of the Min and Max methods

```
Math.{Min|Max}(number1, number2)
```

Statements that use static methods of the Math class

```
int shipWeight = Math.Round(shipWeightDouble);  // round to a whole number
double orderTotal = Math.Round(orderTotal, 2);  // round to 2 decimal places
double area = Math.Pow(radius, 2) * 3.1416
double sqrtX = Math.Sqrt(x);
double maxSales = Math.Max(lastYearSales, thisYearSales);
int minQty = Math.Min(lastYearQty, thisYearQty);
```

Results from static methods of the Math class

Statement	Result	Statement	Result
Math.Round(23.75)	24	Math.Pow(5, 2)	25
Math.Round(23.5)	24	Math.Sqrt(20.25)	4.5
Math.Round(24.5)	24	Math.Max(23.75, 20.25)	23.75
Math.Round(23.754, 2)	23.75	Math.Min(23.75, 20.25)	20.25
Math.Round(23.755, 2)	23.76		

Description

- To use one of the *static methods* of the Math class, code the class name, a dot, the method name, and one or more *arguments* in parentheses. The arguments provide the values that are used by the method.
- The Round method rounds a decimal argument to the specified *precision*, which is the number of significant decimal digits. If the precision is omitted, the number is rounded to the nearest whole number.
- If you round a number with a decimal value of .5 to a whole number, the number is rounded to the nearest even number. This is referred to as *banker's rounding*.
- The Pow method raises the first argument to the power of the second argument. Both arguments must have the double data type.
- The Sqrt method returns the square root of the specified argument, which can have any numeric data type.
- The Min and Max methods return the minimum and maximum of two numeric arguments. The two arguments must have the same data type.

Figure 4-7 How to use the Math class

How to work with strings

In the topics that follow, you'll learn some basic skills for working with the string data type. These skills should be all you need for many of your applications. Then, in chapter 9, you'll learn the skills you need for advanced string operations.

Basic skills for working with strings

A *string* can consist of any letters, numbers, and characters. Figure 4-8 summarizes the techniques that you can use to work with string variables. To start, you use the *string* keyword to declare a string. Then, you can assign a *string literal* to a string by enclosing the characters within double quotes.

To assign an *empty string* to a variable, you can code a set of double quotes with nothing between them. You do that when you want the string to have a value, but you don't want it to contain any characters. A third alternative is to assign a *null value* to a string by using the *null* keyword, which usually indicates that the value of the string is unknown.

If you want to join, or *concatenate*, two or more strings into one string, you use the + operator as shown in the second example in this figure. Here, two string variables are concatenated with a string literal that consists of one space. The result is then stored in another string variable.

You can also join a string with a value data type. This is illustrated in the third example in this figure. Here, a variable that's defined with the double data type is appended to a string. When you use this technique, C# automatically converts the value to a string.

You can also use the + and += operators to *append* a string to the value of a string variable. This is illustrated in the last two examples in this figure. Notice that when you use the + operator, you include the string variable in the expression that you're assigning to this variable. In contrast, when you use the += operator, you can omit the string variable from the expression. Because of that, it's common to use this operator to simplify your code.

How to declare and initialize a string

```
string message1 = "Invalid data entry.";
string message2 = "";
string message3 = null;
```

How to join strings

```
string firstName = "Bob";                     //firstName is "Bob"
string lastName = "Smith";                    //lastName is "Smith"
string name = firstName + " " + lastName;     //name is "Bob Smith"
```

How to join a string and a number

```
double price = 14.95;
String priceString = "Price: " + price;
```

How to append one string to another string

```
string firstName = "Bob";                     //firstName is "Bob"
string lastName = "Smith";                    //lastName is "Smith"
string name = firstName + " ";                //name is "Bob "
name = name + lastName;                       //name is "Bob Smith"
```

How to append one string to another with the += operator

```
string firstName = "Bob";                     //firstName is "Bob"
string lastName = "Smith";                    //lastName is "Smith"
string name = firstName + " ";                //name is "Bob "
name += lastName;                             //name is "Bob Smith"
```

Description

- A *string* can consist of any characters in the character set including letters, numbers, and special characters like *, &, and #.
- To specify the value of a string, you can enclose text in double quotes. This is known as a *string literal*.
- To assign a *null value* to a string, you can use the *null* keyword. This means that the value of the string is unknown.
- To assign an *empty string* to a string, you can code a set of double quotes with nothing between them. This usually indicates that the value of the string is known, but the string doesn't contain any characters.
- To join, or *concatenate*, a string with another string or a value data type, use a plus sign. If you concatenate a value data type to a string, C# will automatically convert the value to a string so it can be used as part of the string.
- When you *append* one string to another, you add one string to the end of another. To do that, you can use assignment statements.
- The += operator is a shortcut for appending a string expression to a string variable.

Figure 4-8 Basic skills for working with strings

How to include special characters in strings

Figure 4-9 shows two techniques that you can use to include certain types of special characters within a string. In particular, this figure shows how to include backslashes, quotation marks, and control characters such as new lines, tabs, and returns.

One technique you can use to include these characters in a string is to use the *escape sequences* shown in this figure. Although these escape sequences are the ones you'll use most often, C# provides other escape sequences for hexadecimal and Unicode characters.

If you're assigning a string literal to a string, you may prefer to use a *verbatim string literal* instead of escape sequences. To use a verbatim string literal, you code an @ sign before the opening quote for the string. Then, you can enter backslashes, tabs, and new line characters between the opening and closing quotes. For example, you can use the Enter key to enter one or more new line characters. Then, the verbatim string literal will span two or more lines.

Although verbatim string literals work well for literals that include backslashes and single quotes, a complication occurs when you need to include a double quote in the literal. That's because double quotes are used to indicate the beginning and end of the literal. To include a double quote in a verbatim string literal, then, you must enter two double quotes.

At this point, you may be wondering when you should use escape sequences to include special characters in a string and when you should use verbatim string literals. The answer is that each technique is appropriate for certain types of coding situations. For example, verbatim string literals work well for coding file locations. On the other hand, it's often easier to use escape sequences to include new line characters and tabs in a string. Because of that, you'll want to become familiar with both techniques. Then, you can decide which technique works best for a given situation.

Common escape sequences

Key	Description
`\n`	New line
`\t`	Tab
`\r`	Return
`\\`	Backslash
`\"`	Quotation

Examples that use escape sequences

Code	Result

`string code = "JSPS";`
`decimal price = 49.50m;`
`string result =`
`    "Code: " + code + "\n" +`
`    "Price: $" + price + "\n";`
	`Code: JSPS`
	`Price: $49.50`

`string names =` `    "Joe\tSmith\rKate\tLewis\r";`	`Joe    Smith` `Kate   Lewis`
`string path = "c:\\c#.net\\files";`	`c:\c#.net\files`
`string message =` `    "Type \"x\" to exit";`	`Type "x" to exit`

Examples that use verbatim string literals

Code	Result
`string names = @"Joe    Smith` `Kate   Lewis";`	`Joe    Smith` `Kate   Lewis`
`string path = @"c:\c#.net\files";`	`c:\c#.net\files`
`string message =` `    @"Type ""x"" to exit";`	`Type "x" to exit`

Description

- Within a string, you can use *escape sequences* to include certain types of special characters.
- To code a *verbatim string literal*, you can code an @ sign, followed by an opening double quote, followed by the string, followed by a closing double quote. Within the string, you can enter backslashes, tabs, new line characters, and other special characters without using escape sequences. However, to enter a double quote within a verbatim string literal, you must enter two double quotes.

Figure 4-9 How to include special characters in strings

How to convert data types

In chapter 3, you were introduced to the use of classes, which provide properties and methods for the objects that are instantiated from the classes. Now, you'll be introduced to *structures*, which are similar to classes. Then, you'll learn how you can use these structures and classes to convert data from one type to another.

The .NET structures and classes that define data types

Figure 4-10 summarizes the structures and classes that define the data types, along with the C# keywords that you can use to work with these structures. To work with the Decimal structure, for example, you use the decimal keyword. To work with the Int32 structure, you use the int keyword. And to work with the String class, you use the string keyword.

When you declare a variable as one of the data types that's supported by a structure, that variable is a *value type*. That means that the variable stores its own data. If, for example, you declare a variable as a decimal type, that variable stores the decimal value. In addition, if you assign that variable to another decimal variable, the new variable will store a separate copy of the value.

In contrast, when you declare a variable as one of the data types that's supported by a class, an object is created from the class. Then, the variable stores a reference to the object, not the object itself. Because of that, object data types are called *reference types*.

In this figure, the two reference types defined by the .NET Framework are string and object. So when you declare a variable as a string, that variable holds a reference to a String object, which contains the data for the string. As a result, it's possible for two or more variables to refer to the same String object.

In addition to the String class, the .NET Framework also provides a generic Object class. You can use a variable created from this class to hold a reference to any type of object. You'll learn more about working with the Object class in chapter 14.

Common .NET structures that define value types

Structure	C# keyword	What the value type holds
Byte	byte	An 8-bit unsigned integer
Int16	short	A 16-bit signed integer
Int32	int	A 32-bit signed integer
Int64	long	A 64-bit signed integer
Single	float	A single-precision floating-point number
Double	double	A double-precision floating-point number
Decimal	decimal	A 96-bit decimal value
Boolean	bool	A true or false value
Char	char	A single character

Common .NET classes that define reference types

Class name	C# keyword	What the reference type holds
String	string	A reference to a String object
Object	object	A reference to any type of object

Description

- Each built-in data type is supported by a structure or a class within the .NET Framework. When you use a C# keyword to refer to a data type, you're actually using an alias for the associated structure or class.
- A *structure* defines a *value type*, which stores its own data.
- A class defines a *reference type*. A reference type doesn't store the data itself. Instead, it stores a reference to the area of memory where the data is stored.
- All of the structures and classes shown in this figure are in the System namespace of the .NET Framework.

Note

- The .NET Framework also provides structures for the other built-in data types that were listed in figure 4-1.

Figure 4-10 The .NET structures and classes that define data types

How to use methods to convert data types

Figure 4-11 presents two ways you can use methods to convert data from one type to another. First, you can use the ToString and Parse methods, which are available from any of the data structures defined by the .NET Framework. Second, you can use the static methods of the Convert class to convert a value to any of the data structures defined by the .NET Framework.

The ToString method lets you convert any value to a string. In the first group of statements in this figure, for example, the ToString method is used to convert a decimal value to a string value. Notice in this example that no arguments are provided on the ToString method. In the next figure, you'll learn how to code an argument that formats the resulting string.

Before I go on, you should realize that C# calls the ToString method implicitly in certain situations. You learned about one of those situations earlier in this chapter, and that example is repeated here. In this case, a double value is automatically converted to a string when it's joined with another string.

The Parse method is a static method that performs the reverse operation of the ToString method. In other words, it converts a string value to another data type. In the last statement in the first group of statements, for example, the Parse method of the Decimal structure is used to convert the value of a string variable to a decimal value. Note that this method only recognizes standard numeric characters. As a result, an exception will occur if you try to convert a string that includes characters such as a dollar sign, a percent sign, or a letter.

The Convert class provides static methods that you can use to convert a value with any data type to any other data type. This is illustrated by the last group of statements in this figure. Here, the first statement uses the ToDecimal method to convert a string that's entered in a text box to a decimal value. The second statement uses the ToInt32 method to convert a string that's entered in a text box to an integer value. The third statement uses the ToString method to convert a decimal value to a string value. And the fourth statement uses the ToInt32 method to convert a decimal value to an integer value.

When you use the Convert class, you should realize that the results of the conversion will vary depending on the type of conversion that you perform. If, for example, you convert a decimal to an integer as illustrated in the last statement in this figure, the conversion will round the decimal digits using banker's rounding. In other cases, C# won't be able to perform the conversion, and an exception will occur.

Common methods for data conversion

Method	Description
`ToString([format])`	A method that converts the value to its equivalent string representation using the specified format. If the format is omitted, the value isn't formatted.
`Parse(string)`	A static method that converts the specified string to an equivalent data value.

Some of the static methods of the Convert class

Method	Description
`ToDecimal(value)`	Converts the value to the decimal data type.
`ToDouble(value)`	Converts the value to the double data type.
`ToInt32(value)`	Converts the value to the int data type.
`ToChar(value)`	Converts the value to the char data type.
`ToBool(value)`	Converts the value to the bool data type.
`ToString(value)`	Converts the value to the string data type.

Conversion statements that use the ToString and Parse methods

```
decimal sales = 2574.98m;
string salesString = sales.ToString();       // decimal to string
sales = Decimal.Parse(salesString);          // string to decimal
```

An implicit call of the ToString method

```
double price = 49.50;
string priceString = "Price: $" + price;     // automatic ToString call
```

Conversion statements that use the Convert class

```
decimal subtotal = Convert.ToDecimal(txtSubtotal.Text); // string to decimal
int years = Convert.ToInt32(txtYears.Text);             // string to int
txtSubtotal.Text = Convert.ToString(subtotal);          // decimal to string
int subtotalInt = Convert.ToInt32(subtotal);            // decimal to int
```

Description

- The ToString and Parse methods are included in all of the data structures.
- In some situations where a string is expected, the compiler will automatically call the ToString method.
- The Convert class contains static methods for converting all of the built-in types. To see all of the methods of this class, you can use Visual Studio's online help to look up the Convert class.

Figure 4-11 How to use methods to convert data types

How to convert numbers to formatted strings

Figure 4-12 shows the standard codes that you can use to format a number when you convert it to a string. To use any of these codes with the ToString method, you simply code it as an argument of this method as illustrated in the first group of statements in this figure. Notice in these examples that the formatting code must be enclosed in double quotes.

You can also include an integer after any of the numeric formatting codes. In most cases, this integer indicates the number of decimal places in the resulting string. For example, if you specify the code "c0" for the value 19.95, that number will be converted to $20. Note that if you don't specify the number of decimal places, two decimal places are assumed.

If you specify a number on the D or d formatting code, it indicates the minimum number of digits in the result. Since these formatting codes are used with integers, that means that the value is padded on the left with zeros if the number you specify is greater than the number of digits in the integer. If, for example, you specify the code "d3" for the number 28, it will be converted to 028.

Another way to format numbers is to use the Format method of the String class. Since this is a static method, you access it directly from the String class rather than from an instance of this class. You must also provide two arguments.

The first argument is a string literal that contains the format specification for the value to be formatted, and the second argument is the value to be formatted. The syntax for the format specification is shown in this figure. Here, the index indicates the value to be formatted, and the format code specifies how the value is to be formatted. Although you can format up to three values using the Format method, you'll typically use it to format a single value. In that case, the index value will be 0. In chapter 9, you'll learn how to use this method to format two or three values.

The second group of statements in this figure shows how to use the Format method. As you can see, these statements perform the same functions as the statements that use the ToString method. In this case, though, these statements use literal values so you can see what the values look like before they're formatted. Notice in these statements that the format specification is enclosed in braces. In addition, the entire argument is enclosed in double quotes.

Standard numeric formatting codes

Code	Format	Description
C or c	Currency	Formats the number as currency with the specified number of decimal places.
P or p	Percent	Formats the number as a percent with the specified number of decimal places.
N or n	Number	Formats the number with thousands separators and the specified number of decimal places.
F or f	Float	Formats the number as a decimal with the specified number of decimal places.
D or d	Digits	Formats an integer with the specified number of digits.
E or e	Exponential	Formats the number in scientific (exponential) notation with the specified number of decimal places.
G or g	General	Formats the number as a decimal or in scientific notation depending on which is more compact.

How to use the ToString method to format a number

Statement	Example
`string monthlyAmount = amount.ToString("c");`	`$1,547.20`
`string interestRate = interest.ToString("p1");`	`2.3%`
`string quantityString = quantity.ToString("n0");`	`15,000`
`string paymentString = payment.ToString("f3");`	`432.818`

How to use the Format method of the String class to format a number

Statement	Result
`string monthlyAmount = String.Format("{0:c}", 1547.2m);`	`$1,547.20`
`string interestRate = String.Format("{0:p1}", .023m);`	`2.3%`
`string quantityString = String.Format("{0:n0}", 15000);`	`15,000`
`string paymentString =  String.Format("{0:f3}", 432.8175);`	`432.818`

The syntax of the format specification used by the Format method

```
{index:formatCode}
```

Description

- You can include a number after some of the numeric formatting codes to specify the number of decimal places in the result. If the numeric value contains more decimal places than are specified, the result will be rounded using standard rounding. If you don't specify the number of decimal places, the default is 2.
- You can include a number after the D or d formatting code to specify the minimum number of digits in the result. If the integer has fewer digits than are specified, zeros are added to the beginning of the integer.
- You can use the Format method of the String class to format two or more values. For more information, see chapter 9.

Figure 4-12 How to convert numbers to formatted strings

Three other skills for working with data

To complete the subject of working with data, the next three figures present three more useful skills: how to work with scope, how to work with enumerations, and how to allow value types to store null values.

How to work with scope

When you work with C#, the *scope* of a variable is determined by where you declare it, and the scope determines what code can access the variable. If, for example, you declare a variable within an event handler, the variable has *method scope* because an event handler is a method. In that case, the variable can only be referred to by statements within that method.

Often, though, you want all of the methods of a form to have access to a variable. Then, you must declare the variable within the class for the form, but outside all of the methods. In that case, the variable has *class scope* and can be called a *class variable*.

This is illustrated and summarized in figure 4-13. Here, you can see that two variables are declared after the last of the generated code for the form class, but before the first event handler for the form. As a result, these variables have class scope. In contrast, the four variables that are declared at the start of the first event handler have method scope. Note that the variables with class scope are used by both of the event handlers in this example, which is one reason for using class scope.

The other reason for using variables with class scope is to retain data after a method finishes executing. This has to do with the *lifetime* of a variable. In particular, a method variable is available only while the method is executing. When the event handler finishes, the variable is no longer available and the data is lost. Then, when the event handler is executed the next time, the method variables are declared and initialized again.

In contrast, a class variable lasts until the instance of the class is terminated. For a form, that happens when you exit the form and the form is closed. As a result, class variables can be used for accumulating values like invoice totals. You'll see this illustrated by the last application in this chapter.

Code that declares and uses variables with class scope

```
public frmInvoiceTotal()
{
    InitializeComponent();
}                                                    - Last generated method

decimal numberOfInvoices = 0m;
decimal totalOfInvoices = 0m;                        - Class scope

private void btnCalculate_Click(object sender, System.EventArgs e)
{
    decimal subtotal = Convert.ToDecimal(txtEnterSubtotal.Text);
    decimal discountPercent = .25m;
    decimal discountAmount = subtotal * discountPercent;
    decimal invoiceTotal = subtotal - discountAmount;   - Method scope

    numberOfInvoices++;
    totalOfInvoices += invoiceTotal;                 - Class scope

    // the rest of the code for the method
}

private void btnClearTotals_Click(object sender, System.EventArgs e)
{
    numberOfInvoices = 0m;
    totalOfInvoices = 0m;
}
```

Description

- The *scope* of a variable determines what code has access to it. If you try to refer to a variable outside of its scope, it will cause a build error.
- The scope of a variable is determined by where you declare it. If you declare a variable within a method, it has *method scope*. If you declare a variable within a class but not within a method, it has *class scope*.
- A variable with method scope can only be referred to by statements within that method. A variable with class scope can be referred to by all of the methods in a class.
- The *lifetime* of a variable is the period of time that it's available for use. A variable with method scope is only available while the method is executing. A variable with class scope is available while the class is instantiated.
- You can declare *class variables* right after the code that is generated for a form.

Figure 4-13 How to work with scope

How to declare and use enumerations

An *enumeration* is a set of related constants that define a value type where each constant is known as a *member* of the enumeration. The enumerations provided by the .NET Framework are generally used to set object properties and to specify the values that are passed to methods. For example, the FormBorderStyle enumeration includes a group of constants that you can use to specify the settings for the FormBorderStyle property of a form.

The table in figure 4-14 summarizes three of the constants within the FormBorderStyle enumeration, and the first example shows how you can use code to set this form property. Normally, though, you'll use the Properties window to choose the constant from the enumeration for this form property.

When writing code, you often need to select one option from a group of related options. For example, you may need to let a user choose the payment terms for an invoice. In that case, it often makes sense to define an enumeration that contains each option.

To define an enumeration, you can use the syntax shown in this figure. After you provide a name for an enumeration, you code the constant names within braces. In the first example, the enumeration is named Terms, and the constants are named Net30Days, Net60Days, and Net90Days. In this case, because values aren't provided for these constants, the default values of 0, 1, and 2 are assigned to the constants.

If you want to assign other values to the constants, you can provide a value for each constant as shown in the second example. Here, the values 30, 60, and 90 are assigned to the constants for the TermValues enumeration. In this case, these values are stored as short data types because a colon and the data type are coded after the enumeration name. If the data type is omitted, the constant values are stored as integers.

To refer to a constant value in an enumeration, you code the name of the enumeration followed by a dot and the name of the constant. This is illustrated by the first three statements in the third group of examples. Here, the first statement returns a value of the Terms type, the second statement returns the int type that corresponds with the member of the Terms enumeration, and the third statement returns the int type that corresponds to the member in the TermValues enumeration. If you want to refer the name of the constant instead of its value, you can use the ToString method as in the last example in this group.

For now, when you code an enumeration, you can code it with class scope. In other words, you can code the enumeration after the generated code for a class as shown in the previous figure. That way, it will be available to all of the methods in the class. Later, when you learn how to add classes to a project, you can store an enumeration in its own file, so it's easily accessible from all classes in the project.

Some of the constants in the FormBorderStyle enumeration

Constant	Description
FormBorderStyle.FixedDialog	A fixed, thick border typically used for dialog boxes.
FormBorderStyle.FixedSingle	A single-line border that isn't resizable.
FormBorderStyle.Sizable	A resizable border

A statement that uses the FormBorderStyle enumeration

```
this.FormBorderStyle = FormBorderStyle.FixedSingle;
```

The syntax for declaring an enumeration

```
enum EnumerationName [: type]
{
    ConstantName1 [= value][,
    ConstantName2 [= value]]...
}
```

An enumeration that sets the constant values to 0, 1, and 2

```
enum Terms
{
    Net30Days,
    Net60Days,
    Net90Days
}
```

An enumeration that sets the constant values to 30, 60, and 90

```
enum TermValues : short
{
    Net30Days = 30,
    Net60Days = 60,
    Net90Days = 90
}
```

Statements that use the constants in these enumerations

```
Terms t = Terms.Net30Days;
int i = (int) Terms.Net30Days;               // i is 0
int i = (int) TermValues.Net60Days;          // i is 60
string s = Terms.Net30Days.ToString();       // s is Net30Days
```

Description

- An *enumeration* defines a set of related constants. Each constant is known as a *member* of the enumeration.
- By default, an enumeration uses the int type and sets the first constant to 0, the second to 1, and so on.
- To use one of the other integer data types, you can code a colon after the enumeration name followed by the data type.
- To specify other values for the constants, you can code an equals sign after the constant name followed by the integer value.

Figure 4-14 How to declare and use enumerations

How to work with nullable types

By default, value types (such as the int, decimal, and bool types) can't store null values. In contrast, reference types (such as the string type) can store null values. Most of the time, you won't need to use a value type to store null values. However, a feature of C# known as *nullable types* allows you to store a null value in a value type, and figure 4-15 shows how this feature works.

To declare a nullable type, you type a question mark (?) immediately after the type in the declaration of a value type. Except for the question mark, this works just as it does for any other value type variable. In this figure, for example, the first statement declares an int variable as a nullable type. Then, the second statement uses the null keyword to assign a null value to this type.

Typically, you use a null value to indicate that the value of the variable is unknown. For example, if a user didn't enter a quantity, you might want to assign a null value to the quantity variable to indicate that the user didn't enter a value. However, when working with value types, it's more common to assign a default value such as zero to indicate that the user didn't enter a value. As a result, unless you're working with a database that returns null values, you probably won't need to use nullable types.

Note that you can only use the question mark to declare nullable types when you're working with value types. This figure, for example, shows how to declare nullable types for the int, decimal, and bool types. In addition, this figure shows that you can declare the Terms enumeration shown in figure 4-14 as a nullable type, which is what you would expect since enumerations define value types. However, you can't declare a string type as a nullable type because the string type is a reference type and can store null values by default.

Once you declare a value type as nullable, you can use the HasValue property to check if the type stores a value or if it contains a null value. This property returns a true value if the variable contains a value. Otherwise, it returns false. In the example in this figure, the value of the HasValue property is assigned to a variable. In the next chapter, though, you'll learn how to use if statements to execute different sets of statements depending on the value of this property.

If a nullable type stores a value, you may want to get that value so you can use it in your application as a non-nullable type. To do that, you use the Value property. The example in this figure, for instance, assigns the value of a nullable int variable to a regular int variable.

You can also use nullable types in arithmetic expressions. In that case, if the value of the nullable type is null, the result of the arithmetic expression is always null. This is illustrated in the last example in this figure.

How to declare a value type that can contain null values

```
int? quantity;
quantity = null;
quantity = 0;
quantity = 20;

decimal? salesTotal = null;

bool? isValid = null;

Terms? paymentTerm = null;

// string? message = null;  // not necessary or allowed
```

Two properties that work with nullable types

Property	Description
`HasValue`	Returns a true value if the nullable type contains a value. Returns a false value if the nullable type is null.
`Value`	Returns the value of the nullable type.

How to check if a nullable value type contains a value

```
bool hasValue = quantity.HasValue;
```

How to get the value of a nullable type

```
int qty = quantity.Value;
```

How to use nullable types in arithmetic expressions

```
decimal? sales1 = 3267.58m;
decimal? sales2 = null;
decimal? salesTotal = sales1 + sales2;  // result = null
```

Description

- A *nullable type* is a value type that can store a null value. Null values are typically used to indicate that the value of the variable is unknown.
- To declare a nullable type, code a question mark (?) immediately after the keyword for the value type.
- If you use a variable with a nullable type in an arithmetic expression and the value of the variable is null, the result of the arithmetic expression is always null.
- You can only declare value types as nullable types. However, because reference types (such as strings) can store null values by default, there's no need to declare reference types as nullable, and your code won't compile if you try to do that.

Figure 4-15 How to work with nullable types

Two versions of the Invoice Total application

To give you a better idea of how you can use data, arithmetic, data conversion, and scope, this chapter concludes by presenting two illustrative applications.

The basic Invoice Total application

Figure 4-16 presents a simple version of the Invoice Total application that's similar to the one presented in chapter 3. Now that you have learned how to work with data, you should be able to understand all of the code in this application.

To start, this figure shows the user interface for this application, which is the same as it was in the last chapter. Then, this figure lists the six controls that the code refers to so you can see how the code relates to those controls.

This figure also presents the code for the two event handlers of the Invoice Total application. If you study the code for the Click event of the Calculate button, you'll see that it begins by converting the string value that's entered by the user to a decimal value. Then, it sets the discount percent to .25, or 25%. This percent is then used to calculate the discount for the invoice, and the discount is subtracted from the subtotal to get the invoice total. Finally, the calculated values are formatted and displayed on the form.

If rounding is necessary when the values are displayed, the formatting statements in this application will do the rounding. Note, however, that the values stored in discountAmount and invoiceTotal aren't rounded. To round these values, you would need to use the Round method of the Math class. You often need to do that when you work with values that are going to be stored in a file or database.

You also should realize that this application will work only if the user enters a numeric value into the Subtotal text box. If the user enters any non-numeric characters, an exception will occur when the application tries to convert that value to a decimal. In chapter 7, you'll learn how to prevent this type of error.

The Invoice Total form

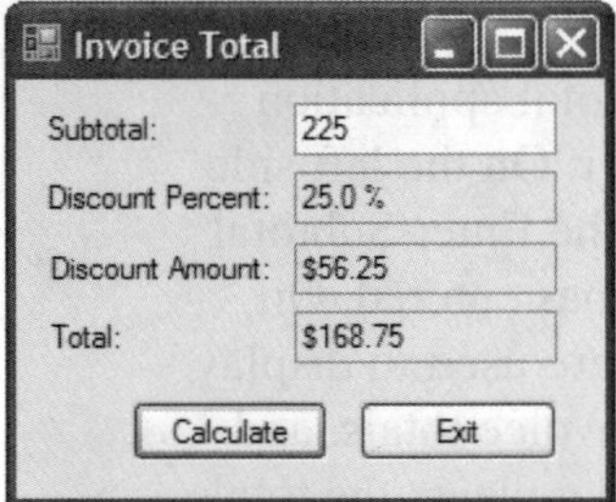

The controls that are referred to in the code

Object type	Name	Description
TextBox	txtSubtotal	A text box that accepts a subtotal amount
TextBox	txtDiscountPercent	A read-only text box that displays the discount percent
TextBox	txtDiscountAmount	A read-only text box that displays the discount amount
TextBox	txtTotal	A read-only text box that displays the invoice total
Button	btnCalculate	Calculates the discount amount and invoice total when clicked
Button	btnExit	Closes the form when clicked

The event handlers for the Invoice Total form

```
private void btnCalculate_Click(object sender, System.EventArgs e)
{
    decimal subtotal = Convert.ToDecimal(txtSubtotal.Text);
    decimal discountPercent = .25m;
    decimal discountAmount = subtotal * discountPercent;
    decimal invoiceTotal = subtotal - discountAmount;

    txtDiscountPercent.Text = discountPercent.ToString("p1");
    txtDiscountAmount.Text = discountAmount.ToString("c");
    txtTotal.Text = invoiceTotal.ToString("c");

    txtSubtotal.Focus();
}

private void btnExit_Click(object sender, System.EventArgs e)
{
    this.Close();
}
```

Figure 4-16 The basic Invoice Total application

The enhanced Invoice Total application

Figure 4-17 presents an enhanced version of the Invoice Total application that illustrates some of the other skills presented in this chapter. On the left side of the form, a new label and text box have been added below the Enter Subtotal text box. These controls display the last subtotal that the user has entered. On the right side of the form, three pairs of labels and text boxes are used to display the number of invoices that have been entered, a total of the invoice totals, and the invoice average. The form also has a Clear Totals button that clears the totals on the right side of the form so the user can enter another batch of invoices.

The controls that have been added to this form are named with our standard naming conventions, which are based on the names that are used to identify text boxes and labels. For instance, txtEnterSubtotal is used for the text box that lets the user enter a subtotal, txtSubtotal is used for the text box that displays the last subtotal that the user has entered, txtNumberOfInvoices is used for the text box that displays the number of invoices, txtTotalOfInvoices is used for the text box that displays the total of the invoice totals, txtInvoiceAverage is used for the text box that displays the invoice average, and btnClearTotals is used for the Clear Totals button.

In the code for this form, the enhancements are shaded so they're easy to review. This code starts with the declarations of the three class variables: numberOfInvoices, totalOfInvoices, and invoiceAverage. These are the variables whose values need to be retained from one execution of an event handler to another. They are initialized with zero values.

In the event handler for the Click event of the Calculate button, the first shaded line adds rounding to the calculation for the discount amount. That's necessary so only the exact amount of the invoice is added to the total for the invoices. Otherwise, the total for the invoices may become incorrect. Then, the next shaded statement displays the subtotal entered by the user in the Subtotal text box. That way, all of the data for the last invoice is shown in the text boxes on the left side of the form while the user enters the subtotal for the next invoice.

The next set of shaded statements shows how the class variables are used after each subtotal entry has been processed. The first three statements add 1 to the number of invoices, add the invoice total to the total of invoices, and calculate the invoice average. Then, the next three shaded lines assign the new values of the class variables to the text boxes that will display them. The last shaded line in this event handler assigns an empty string to the subtotal text box so the user can enter the subtotal for the next invoice.

In the event handler for the Click event of the Clear Totals button, the first three statements reset the class variables to zeros so the user can enter the subtotals for another batch of invoices. Then, the next three statements set the text boxes that display these variables to empty strings. The last statement moves the focus to the Enter Subtotal text box so the user can start the first entry of another batch of invoices.

The enhanced Invoice Total form

Enter Subtotal:	225.5		
Subtotal:	$225.50	Number of invoices:	3
Discount Percent:	25.0 %	Total of invoices:	$1,294.12
Discount Amount:	$56.38	Invoice average:	$431.37
Total:	$169.12		

Invoice Total — Calculate | Clear Totals | Exit

The code for the class variables and two event handlers

```
int numberOfInvoices = 0;
decimal totalOfInvoices = 0m;
decimal invoiceAverage = 0m;

private void btnCalculate_Click(object sender, EventArgs e)
{
    decimal subtotal = Convert.ToDecimal(txtEnterSubtotal.Text);
    decimal discountPercent = .25m;
    decimal discountAmount = Math.Round(subtotal * discountPercent, 2);
    decimal invoiceTotal = subtotal - discountAmount;

    txtSubtotal.Text = subtotal.ToString("c");
    txtDiscountPercent.Text = discountPercent.ToString("p1");
    txtDiscountAmount.Text = discountAmount.ToString("c");
    txtTotal.Text = invoiceTotal.ToString("c");

    numberOfInvoices++;
    totalOfInvoices += invoiceTotal;
    invoiceAverage = totalOfInvoices / numberOfInvoices;

    txtNumberOfInvoices.Text = numberOfInvoices.ToString();
    txtTotalOfInvoices.Text = totalOfInvoices.ToString("c");
    txtInvoiceAverage.Text = invoiceAverage.ToString("c");

    txtEnterSubtotal.Text = "";
    txtEnterSubtotal.Focus();
}

private void btnClearTotals_Click(object sender, System.EventArgs e)
{
    numberOfInvoices = 0;
    totalOfInvoices = 0m;
    invoiceAverage = 0m;

    txtNumberOfInvoices.Text = "";
    txtTotalOfInvoices.Text = "";
    txtInvoiceAverage.Text = "";

    txtEnterSubtotal.Focus();
}
```

Figure 4-17 The enhanced Invoice Total application

Perspective

If you understand the code in the enhanced Invoice Total application, you've come a long way. If not, you should get a better understanding for how this application works when you do the exercises for this chapter. Once you understand it, you'll be ready to learn how to code selection and iteration statements so you can add logical operations to your applications.

Terms

built-in data type
bit
byte
integer
Unicode character set
ASCII character set
Boolean value
variable
constant
declare
initialize
camel notation
literal
scientific notation
arithmetic expression
arithmetic operator
operand
binary operator
unary operator
prefix an operand
postfix an operand
assignment statement
assignment operator
order of precedence
casting
implicit cast
widening conversion
explicit cast
narrowing conversion
strict type semantics
static method
argument
precision
banker's rounding
string
string literal
null value
empty string
concatenate
append
escape sequence
verbatim string literal
structure
value type
reference type
scope
class scope
class variable
method scope
lifetime
enumeration
member
nullable type

Exercise 4-1 Modify the Invoice Total application

In this exercise, you'll modify the Invoice Total application that's presented in this chapter.

Open the Invoice Total application

1. Open the application that's in the C:\C# 2008\Chapter 04\InvoiceTotal directory. This is the application that's presented in figure 4-16.

Modify and test the code for the Invoice Total application

2. Build and run the application, and enter a valid subtotal to verify that the correct discount is being taken. Then, enter a valid subtotal like 225.50 that will yield a discount amount that has more than two decimal places, and make sure that only two decimal places are displayed for the discount amount and total.
3. Enter "$1000" for the subtotal and click the Calculate button. This time, an exception should occur, Visual Studio should enter break mode, and the Exception Assistant should display a message that indicates that the input string was not in a correct format.
4. Note the highlighted statement. This shows that the assignment statement can't convert the string that was entered to the decimal data type. Next, move the mouse pointer over txtSubtotal.Text so you can see the data tip that shows that the current value is $1000. Then, click the Stop Debugging button in the Debug toolbar to end the application.

Experiment with the code

5. Modify the first statement in the btnCalculate_Click method so it uses the Parse method of the Decimal class instead of the ToDecimal method of the Convert class. Then, test the application to verify that it works the same as it did before.
6. Round the values that are stored in the discountAmount and invoiceTotal variables to two decimal places, and delete the formatting codes for the statements that convert these variables to strings. Then, test the application to make sure that only two decimal places are displayed for the discount amount and total.

Save and close the project

7. Save the solution and close it.

Exercise 4-2 Enhance the Invoice Total application

This exercise will guide you through the process of enhancing the Invoice Total application of exercise 4-1 so it works like the application in figure 4-17. This will give you more practice in developing forms and working with data.

Open the Invoice Total application and enhance the form

1. Open the application in the C:\C# 2008\Chapter 04\InvoiceTotalEnhanced directory.
2. Use the techniques that you learned in chapter 2 to enlarge the form and to add the new controls that are shown in figure 4-17 to the form.
3. Set the properties for each of the controls. You should be able to do this without any guidance, but try to name each control that's going to be referred to by code with the proper prefix followed by the name that identifies it in the form (like txtNumberOfInvoices).

Add the code for the enhancements

4. Switch to the Code Editor and enter the three class variables in figure 4-17. These are the variables that will accumulate the data for all the invoices.
5. Enhance the code for the Click event of the Calculate button so it calculates and displays the new data. Try to do this without referring to figure 4-17.
6. Use the techniques you learned in chapter 3 to start the event handler for the Click event of the Clear Totals button. Then, add the code for this event. Here again, try to do this without referring to the code in figure 4-17.
7. Test the application and fix any errors until the application works properly. Be sure that it restarts properly when you click the Clear Totals button and enter another batch of invoices.

Add more controls and code

8. Add three more labels and three more text boxes below the two columns of text boxes and labels on the right side of the form. The three labels should say "Largest invoice", "Smallest invoice", and "Mid point". The text boxes to the right of the labels should display the values for the largest invoice total, the smallest invoice total, and the invoice total that's halfway between these totals.
9. Add the code that makes this work. If you're new to programming, this may challenge you. (Hint: To find the smallest invoice total, use the Math.Min method to compare each invoice total to a variable that contains the smallest invoice total to that point. Then, replace the variable value with the smaller of the two invoice totals. To make this work for the first invoice, you can initialize this variable to a large number like the MaxValue member of the Decimal class.)
10. Test the application and fix any errors until the application works properly. Then, close the project.

5

How to code control structures

In the last chapter, you learned how to write code that works with the most common data types. Now, you'll learn how to code the three types of control structures that are common to all modern programming languages: the selection, case, and iteration structures. When you finish this chapter, you'll be able to write applications that perform a wide range of logical operations.

How to code Boolean expressions

When you code an expression that evaluates to a true or false value, that expression can be called a *Boolean expression*. Because you use Boolean expressions within the control structures you code, you need to learn how to code Boolean expressions before you learn how to code control structures.

How to use the relational operators

Figure 5-1 shows how to use six *relational operators* to code a Boolean expression. These operators let you compare two operands, as illustrated by the examples in this figure. An operand can be any expression, including a variable, a literal, an arithmetic expression, or a keyword such as null, true, or false.

The first six expressions in this figure use the equality operator (==) to test if the two operands are equal. To use this operator, you must code two equals signs instead of one. That's because a single equals sign is used for assignment statements. As a result, if you try to code a Boolean expression with a single equals sign, your code won't compile.

The next expression uses the inequality operator (!=) to test if a variable is not equal to a string literal. The two expressions after that use the greater than operator (>) to test if a variable is greater than a numeric literal and the less than operator (<) to test if one variable is less than another. The last two expressions are similar, except they use the greater than or equal operator (>=) and less than or equal operator (<=) to compare operands.

If you want to include a Boolean variable in an expression, you often don't need to include the == or != operator. That's because a Boolean variable evaluates to a Boolean value by definition. So if isValid is a Boolean variable,

```
isValid
```

works the same as

```
isValid == true
```

When comparing numeric values, you usually compare values with the same data type. However, if you compare different types of numeric values, C# will automatically cast the value with the less precise type to the more precise type. For example, if you compare an int value to a decimal value, the int value will be cast to a decimal value before the comparison is performed.

If you're coming from another programming language such as Java, you may be surprised to find that you can also use some of these operators on strings, which are actually String objects. This is possible because the C# language allows classes and structures to define operators. In this case, since the String class defines the == and != operators, you can use these operators on strings.

Relational operators

Operator	Name	Description
==	Equality	Returns a true value if the left and right operands are equal.
!=	Inequality	Returns a true value if the left and right operands are not equal.
>	Greater than	Returns a true value if the left operand is greater than the right operand.
<	Less than	Returns a true value if the left operand is less than the right operand.
>=	Greater than or equal	Returns a true value if the left operand is greater than or equal to the right operand.
<=	Less than or equal	Returns a true value if the left operand is less than or equal to the right operand.

Examples

```
firstName == "Frank"       // equal to a string literal
txtYears.Text == ""        // equal to an empty string
message == null            // equal to a null value
discountPercent == 2.3     // equal to a numeric literal
isValid == false           // equal to the false value
code == productCode        // equal to another variable

lastName != "Jones"        // not equal to a string literal

years > 0                  // greater than a numeric literal
i < months                 // less than a variable

subtotal >= 500            // greater than or equal to a literal value
quantity <= reorderPoint   // less than or equal to a variable
```

Description

- You can use the *relational operators* to create a *Boolean expression* that compares two operands and returns a Boolean value.
- To compare two operands for equality, make sure you use two equals signs. If you use a single equals sign, the compiler will interpret it as an assignment statement, and your code won't compile.
- When comparing strings, you can only use the equality and inequality operators.
- If you compare two numeric operands with different data types, C# will cast the less precise operand to the type of the more precise operand.

Figure 5-1 How to use the relational operators

How to use the logical operators

Figure 5-2 shows how to use the *logical operators* to code a compound Boolean expression that consists of two or more Boolean expressions. For example, the first compound expression in this figure uses the && operator. As a result, it evaluates to true if both the expression before the && operator *and* the expression after the && operator evaluate to true. Conversely, the second compound expression uses the || operator. As a result, it evaluates to true if either the expression before the || operator *or* the expression after the || operator evaluates to true.

When you use the && and || operators, the second expression is only evaluated if necessary. Because of that, these operators are sometimes referred to as the *short-circuit operators*. To illustrate, suppose that the value of subtotal in the first example is less than 250. Then, the first expression evaluates to false. That means that the entire expression evaluates to false regardless of the value of the second expression. As a result, the second expression isn't evaluated. Since this is more efficient than always evaluating both expressions, you'll want to use these short-cut operators most of the time.

However, there may be times when you want to evaluate the second expression regardless of the value that's returned by the first expression. For example, the second expression may increment a variable, as illustrated by the third and fourth examples in this figure. In these cases, you can use the & and | operators to make sure that the second expression is evaluated.

You can also use two or more logical operators in the same expression, as illustrated by the fifth and sixth examples. When you do, you should know that And operations are performed before Or operations. In addition, both arithmetic and relational operations are performed before logical operations. If you need to change this sequence or if there's any doubt about how an expression will be evaluated, you can use parentheses to control or clarify the sequence.

If necessary, you can use the Not operator (!) to reverse the value of an expression as illustrated by the last example in this figure. Because this can create code that's difficult to read, however, you should avoid using this operator whenever possible. For example, instead of coding

```
!(subtotal < 100)
```

you can code

```
subtotal >= 100
```

Although both expressions return the same result, the second expression is easier to read.

Logical operators

Operator	Name	Description
&&	Conditional-And	Returns a true value if both expressions are true. This operator only evaluates the second expression if necessary.
||	Conditional-Or	Returns a true value if either expression is true. This operator only evaluates the second expression if necessary.
&	And	Returns a true value if both expressions are true. This operator always evaluates both expressions.
|	Or	Returns a true value if either expression is true. This operator always evaluates both expressions.
!	Not	Reverses the value of the expression.

Examples

```
subtotal >= 250 && subtotal < 500
timeInService <= 4 || timeInService >= 12

isValid == true & counter++ < years
isValid == true | counter++ < years

date > startDate && date < expirationDate || isValid == true
((thisYTD > lastYTD) || empType=="Part time") && startYear < currentYear

!(counter++ >= years)
```

Description

- You can use the *logical operators* to create a Boolean expression that combines two or more Boolean expressions.
- Since the && and || operators only evaluate the second expression if necessary, they're sometimes referred to as *short-circuit operators*. These operators are slightly more efficient than the & and | operators.
- By default, Not operations are performed first, followed by And operations, and then Or operations. These operations are performed after arithmetic operations and relational operations.
- You can use parentheses to change the sequence in which the operations will be performed or to clarify the sequence of operations.

Figure 5-2 How to use the logical operators

How to code conditional statements

Now that you know how to code Boolean expressions, you're ready to learn how to code conditional statements. These statements include the if-else statement and the switch statement.

How to code if-else statements

Figure 5-3 shows how to use the *if-else statement* (or just *if statement*) to control the logic of your programs. This type of statement is the primary logical statement of all programming languages. It is the C# implementation of a control structure know as the *selection structure* because it lets you select different actions based on the results of Boolean expressions.

In the syntax summary in this figure, the brackets [ ] indicate that a clause is optional, and the ellipsis (...) indicates that the preceding element can be repeated as many times as needed. In other words, this syntax shows that you can code an *if* clause with or without *else if* clauses or an *else* clause. It also shows that you can code as many else if clauses as you need.

When an if statement is executed, C# begins by evaluating the Boolean expression in the if clause. If it's true, the statements within this clause are executed and the rest of the clauses in the if-else statement are skipped. If it's false, C# evaluates the first else if clause (if there is one). If its Boolean expression is true, the statements within this else if clause are executed and the rest of the if-else statement is skipped. Otherwise, C# evaluates the next else if clause. This continues with any remaining else if clauses. Finally, if none of the clauses contains a Boolean expression that evaluates to true, C# executes the statements in the else clause. If the statement doesn't include an else clause, C# doesn't execute any statements.

When coding if-else statements, it's often a good coding practice to code a set of braces for each clause. However, if a clause only contains a single statement, you can omit the braces. Although omitting the braces saves you some typing and takes up less vertical space, coding the braces makes it easier to identify the statements for each clause, and it makes it easier for you to add more statements later.

In C#, whenever you use braces, you define a block of code. If you declare a variable within a block, that variable is available only to the other statements in the block. This can be referred to as *block scope*. As a result, if you need to access a variable outside of an if statement, you should declare it before the if statement.

When coding if statements, it's a common practice to code one if statement within another if statement. This is known as *nested if statements*. When you code nested if statements, it's a good practice to indent the nested statements and their clauses. This clearly identifies where the nested statement begins and ends. In the last example in this figure, you can see that C# will execute the nested if statement only if the customer type is "R". Otherwise, it executes the statements in the outer else clause.

The syntax of the if-else statement

```
if (booleanExpression) { statements }
[else if (booleanExpression) { statements }] ...
[else { statements }]
```

If statements without else if or else clauses

With a single statement

```
if (subtotal >= 100)
   discountPercent = .2m;
```

With a block of statements

```
if (subtotal >= 100)
{
   discountPercent = .2m;
   status = "Bulk rate";
}
```

An if statement with an else clause

```
if (subtotal >= 100)
   discountPercent = .2m;
else
   discountPercent = .1m;
```

An if statement with else if and else clauses

```
if (subtotal >= 100 && subtotal < 200)
   discountPercent = .2m;
else if (subtotal >= 200 && subtotal < 300)
   discountPercent = .3m;
else if (subtotal >= 300)
   discountPercent = .4m;
else
   discountPercent = .1m;
```

Nested if statements

```
if (customerType == "R")
{                                            // begin nested if
   if (subtotal >= 100)
      discountPercent = .2m;
   else
      discountPercent = .1m;
}                                            // end nested if
else    // customerType isn't "R"
{
   discountPercent = .4m;
}
```

Description

- An *if-else statement*, or just *if statement*, always contains an *if* clause. In addition, it can contain one or more *else if* clauses and a final *else* clause.
- If a clause requires just one statement, you don't have to enclose the statement in braces. You can just end the clause with a semicolon.
- If a clause requires more than one statement, you enclose the block of statements in braces.

Figure 5-3 How to code if-else statements

How to code switch statements

Figure 5-4 shows how to use the *switch statement*. This is the C# implementation of a control structure known as the *case structure*, which lets you code different actions for different cases. The switch statement can sometimes be used in place of an if statement with else if clauses.

To code a switch statement, you start by coding the switch keyword followed by a switch expression. This expression must evaluate to one of the data types listed in this figure. After the switch expression, you can code one or more *case labels* that represent the possible values of the switch expression. Then, when the switch expression matches the value specified by a case label, the statements that follow the label are executed. A switch statement can also contain a *default label* that identifies the statements that are executed if none of the values specified by the case labels match the switch expression. All of these labels are coded within braces.

When you code a case label or a default label, you must be sure to code a colon after it. Then, if the label contains one or more statements, you must code a *break statement* to exit the switch statement. Later in this chapter, you'll see that you can also use break statements to exit loops.

A break statement is required for each label within a switch statement because C# doesn't allow execution to *fall through* to the next label. This is known as the *no fall through rule*. The only exception to this rule is a case label that doesn't contain any statements. In that case, the statements within the following label are executed.

The first example in this figure shows how to code a switch statement that sets the discount percent based on the values in a string variable named customerType. If the customer type is "R", the discount percent is sent to .1. If the customer type is "C", the discount percent is set to .2. And otherwise, the discount percent is set to the default value of 0.

Please note in this example that even though the default label is the last label, it must still end with a break statement. You should also realize that you can code the case and default labels in any sequence. However, it's a common practice to code the default label last.

The second example is similar but it doesn't include a default label. Because of that, no code will be executed if none of the values in the case labels match the switch expression. The other difference is that the first case label doesn't include any statements. Because of that, if the customer type is "R", execution with fall through to the next case label. That means that the discount percent will be set to .2 if the customer type is either "R" or "C".

When you use a switch statement, you can code if statements within the cases of the statement. You can also code switch statements within the cases of another switch statement. That can make switch statements more useful. In general, though, most programmers prefer to use if-else statements instead of switch statements because if-else statements aren't as limited.

The syntax of the switch statement

```
switch (switchExpression)
{
   case constantExpression:
      statements
      break;
   [case constantExpression:
      statements
      break;]...
   [default:
      statements
      break;]
}
```

A switch statement with a default label

```
switch (customerType)
{
    case "R":
        discountPercent = .1m;
        break;
    case "C":
        discountPercent = .2m;
        break;
    default:
        discountPercent = .0m;
        break;
}
```

A switch statement that falls through the first case label

```
switch (customerType)
{
    case "R":
    case "C":
        discountPercent = .2m;
        break;
    case "T":
        discountPercent = .4m;
        break;
}
```

Description

- A *switch statement* begins by evaluating its switch expression. This expression must evaluate to a string, char, long, sbyte, byte, short, ushort, int, uint, long, or ulong type.
- After evaluating the switch expression, the switch statement transfers control to the appropriate *case label*. If control isn't transferred to one of the case labels, the optional *default label* is executed.
- The *break statement* exits the switch statement. If a label contains one or more statements, the label must end with a break statement.
- If a label doesn't contain any statements, code execution will *fall through* to the next label. That means that the statements contained by the next label will be executed.

Figure 5-4 How to code switch statements

An enhanced version of the Invoice Total application

To give you a better idea of how if-else statements can be used, figure 5-5 presents an enhanced version of the Invoice Total application that was presented in chapter 3. This time, the form for the application provides for two user entries: customer type and subtotal.

If you look at the event handler in this figure, you can see that the discount percent is determined by nested if statements. If, for example, the customer type is "R" and the subtotal is greater than or equal to 250, the discount percent is .25. Or, if the customer type is "C" and the subtotal is less than 250, the discount percent is .2.

When you code if statements like this, it's a good practice to code the conditions in a logical order. For instance, the expressions in the nested if statement for customer type "R", go from a subtotal that's less than 100, to a subtotal that's greater than or equal to 100 and less than 250, to a subtotal that's greater than or equal to 250. That covers all of the possible subtotals from the smallest to the largest. Although you could code these conditions in other sequences, that would make it harder to tell whether all possibilities have been covered.

For efficiency, it's also good to code the conditions from the one that occurs the most to the one that occurs the least. If, for example, most customers are type "R", that condition should be treated first so it will be processed first. In some cases, though, the most efficient sequence isn't logical so you have to decide whether it's worth sacrificing the readability of the code for efficiency. Typically, the performance gain isn't significant, so you may as well code the statements in the most logical sequence.

If you prefer, you can use a switch statement that contains if statements to get the same result as the nested if statements in this figure. That might even make the code easier to read. On the other hand, if you use indentation properly, an extensive series of nested if statements should be easy to read and understand.

When you enter if and switch statements into the Code Editor, remember that you can use code snippets to enter the basic if, else, and switch structures that you need, including the braces for the coding blocks. To refresh your memory about how to use code snippets, you can refer back to figure 3-11.

The enhanced Invoice Total form

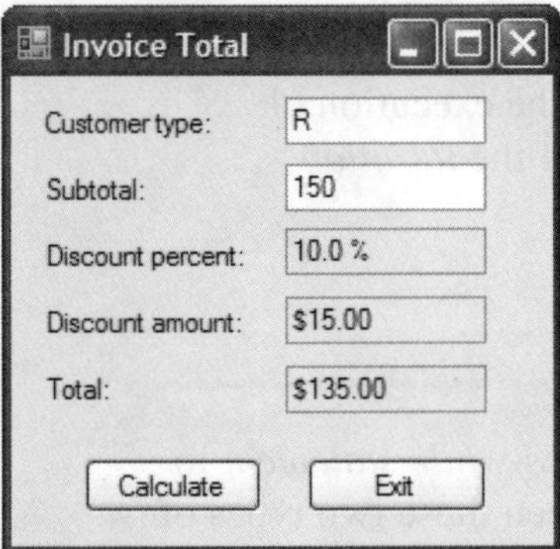

The event handler for the Click event of the Calculate button

```
private void btnCalculate_Click(object sender, System.EventArgs e)
{
    string customerType = txtCustomerType.Text;
    decimal subtotal = Convert.ToDecimal(txtSubtotal.Text);
    decimal discountPercent = .0m;

    if (customerType == "R")
    {
        if (subtotal < 100)
            discountPercent = .0m;
        else if (subtotal >= 100 && subtotal < 250)
            discountPercent = .1m;
        else if (subtotal >= 250)
            discountPercent =.25m;
    }
    else if (customerType == "C")
    {
        if (subtotal < 250)
            discountPercent = .2m;
        else
            discountPercent = .3m;
    }
    else
    {
        discountPercent = .4m;
    }

    decimal discountAmount = subtotal * discountPercent;
    decimal invoiceTotal = subtotal - discountAmount;

    txtDiscountPercent.Text = discountPercent.ToString("p1");
    txtDiscountAmount.Text = discountAmount.ToString("c");
    txtTotal.Text = invoiceTotal.ToString("c");

    txtCustomerType.Focus();
}
```

Figure 5-5 An enhanced version of the Invoice Total application

How to code loops

C# provides three different statements for controlling the execution of loops. These statements provide the C# implementations of the *iteration structure*.

How to code while and do-while loops

Figure 5-6 shows how to use the *while statement* and *do-while statement* to code *while loops* and *do-while loops*. The difference between these two types of loops is that the Boolean expression is evaluated at the beginning of a while loop and at the end of a do-while loop. As a result, the statements in a while loop are executed zero or more times, while the statements in a do-while loop are always executed at least once.

When coding while loops, it's common to use a counter variable to execute the statements in a loop a certain number of times. This is illustrated in the first example in this figure. Here, the counter variable is an int type named i, and this counter is initialized to 1. Notice that the last statement in the loop increments the counter with each iteration of the loop. As a result, the first statement in this loop will be executed as long as the counter variable is less than 5. Incidentally, it is a common coding practice to name counter variables with single letters like *i*, *j*, and *k*.

Most of the time, you can use either of these two types of loops to accomplish the same task. For instance, the second example in this figure uses a while loop to calculate the future value of a series of monthly payments at a specified interest rate, and the third example uses a do-while loop to perform the same calculation.

When you code loops, it's important to remember that any variables that you declare within the loop have block scope so they can't be used outside of the loop. That's why all of the variables used in the loops shown here have been declared outside of the loops. That way, you can use these variables after the loops have finished executing.

When you code loops, it's possible to code an *infinite loop*, which is a loop that never ends. That can happen, for example, if you forget to code a statement that increments the counter variable so the condition in the while or do-while loop never becomes false. Then, you can use the Break All command in the Debug toolbar to enter break mode and debug the program as shown later in this chapter. Or, you can use the Stop Debugging command to end the application.

The syntax of the while statement

```
while (booleanExpression)
{
   statements
}
```

A while loop that adds the numbers 1 through 4

```
int i = 1, sum = 0;
while (i < 5)
{
    sum += i;
    i++;
}
```

A while loop that calculates a future value

```
int i = 1;
while (i <= months)
{
    futureValue = (futureValue + monthlyPayment) *
        (1 + monthlyInterestRate);
    i++;
}
```

The syntax of the do-while statement

```
do
{
   statements
}
while (booleanExpression);
```

A do-while loop that calculates a future value

```
int i = 1;
do
{
    futureValue = (futureValue + monthlyPayment) *
        (1 + monthlyInterestRate);
    i++;
}
while (i <= months);
```

Description

- When you use a *while statement*, the condition is tested before the *while loop* is executed. When you use a *do-while statement*, the condition is tested after the *do-while loop* is executed.
- A while or do-while loop executes the block of statements within its braces as long as its Boolean expression is true.
- If a loop requires more than one statement, you must enclose the statements in braces. Then, any variables or constants that are declared in the block have block scope. If a loop requires just one statement, you don't have to enclose the statement in braces.
- If the conditional expression never becomes false, the statement never ends. Then, the program goes into an *infinite loop* that you can cancel by using the Break All or Stop Debugging commands from the Debug toolbar.

Figure 5-6 How to code while and do-while loops

How to code for loops

Figure 5-7 shows how to use a *for statement* to code a *for loop*. This type of loop is useful when you need to increment or decrement a counter variable that determines how many times the loop is going to be executed.

To code a for loop, you start by coding the *for* keyword followed by three expressions enclosed in parentheses and separated by semicolons. The first expression is an initialization expression that typically declares a counter variable and assigns a starting value to it. The second expression is a Boolean expression that specifies the condition under which the loop executes. And the third expression is an increment expression that determines how the counter variable is incremented or decremented each time the loop is executed.

The first example in this figure illustrates how to use these expressions. Here, the initialization expression declares a counter variable named i with the int type and assigns an initial value of 0 to it. Next, the Boolean expression specifies that the loop will be repeated as long as the counter is less than 5. Then, the increment expression adds 1 to the counter at the end of each repetition of the loop. When this loop is executed, the numbers 0 through 4 will be stored as a string variable like this:

```
0 1 2 3 4
```

This figure shows how to code this loop using a single statement or a block of statements. If you code more than one statement within the loop, you must enclose the statements in braces. But if you code only a single statement, the braces are optional.

The next example calculates the sum of the numbers 8, 6, 4, and 2. In this example, the sum variable is declared before the loop so it will be available outside the block of statements that are executed by the loop. Then, the initialization expression initializes the counter variable to 8, the Boolean expression specifies that the loop will execute as long as the counter is greater than zero, and the increment expression uses an assignment operator to subtract 2 from the counter variable with each repetition of the loop. Within the loop, the value of the counter variable is added to the value that's already stored in the sum variable. As a result, the final value for the sum variable is 20.

The last example shows how to code a for loop that calculates the future value of a series of monthly payments. Here, the loop executes one time for each month. If you compare this example with the last example in figure 5-6, you can see how a for loop improves upon a while loop when a counter variable is required.

Although it isn't shown in this figure, it's possible to declare a counter variable before the for loop. Then, this variable can be accessed outside the loop. However, if you need to access a counter variable outside of a loop, it's usually easier to use a while or do-while loop as described in figure 5-6.

You can also declare a counter variable within a for loop without specifying a type. To do that, you code the var keyword in place of the type. Then, the type is inferred from the value that's assigned to the variable. In most cases, though, you'll specify a type instead of using the var keyword.

The syntax of the for statement

```
for(initializationExpression; booleanExpression; incrementExpression)
{
    statements
}
```

A for loop that stores the numbers 0 through 4 in a string

With a single statement

```
string numbers = null;
for (int i = 0; i < 5; i++)
    numbers += i + " ";
```

With a block of statements

```
string numbers = null;
for (int i = 0; i < 5; i++)
{
    numbers += i;
    numbers += " ";
}
```

A for loop that adds the numbers 8, 6, 4, and 2

```
int sum = 0;
for (int j = 8; j > 0; j-=2)
{
   sum += j;
}
```

A for loop that calculates a future value

```
for (int i = 1; i <= months; i++)
{
    futureValue = (futureValue + monthlyPayment) *
        (1 + monthlyInterestRate);
}
```

Description

- The *for statement* is useful when you need to increment or decrement a counter that determines how many times the *for loop* is executed.
- Within the parentheses of a for loop, you code an initialization expression that declares a counter variable and assigns a starting value to it, a Boolean expression that specifies the condition under which the loop executes, and an increment expression that indicates how the counter variable should be incremented or decremented each time the loop is executed.

Figure 5-7 How to code for loops

Loops that use break and continue statements

In most cases, the statements within the loop are executed in the order that they're coded, and the loop ends when the Boolean expression for the loop evaluates to false. However, for some loops, you may need to use *jump statements* to control the order in which the statements are executed. Figure 5-8 presents two of those statements. You can use the break statement to jump to the end of a loop, and you can use the *continue statement* to jump to the start of a loop.

The first example in this figure shows how the break statement works. Here, a while loop calculates a future value as described in figure 5-6. If the future value becomes greater than 100,000, however, this loop assigns a string literal to the message variable, and it executes a break statement to end the loop.

The second example shows how to use the continue statement to jump to the beginning of a loop. When control is transferred to the beginning of the loop, the expressions that control the loop's operation are executed again. As a result, this will cause the counter variable to be incremented, and it will cause the Boolean expression to be evaluated again.

In addition to the break and continue statements, C# provides other jump statements you can code within loops. You'll learn about most of these statements as you progress through this book. One statement you won't learn about, however, is the *goto statement*. That's because goto statements often result in code that's difficult to read and maintain. As a result, it's generally considered a good coding practice to avoid using them.

A loop with a break statement

```
string message = null;
int i = 1;
while (i <= months)
{
    futureValue = (futureValue + monthlyPayment) *
        (1 + monthlyInterestRate);
    if (futureValue > 100000)
    {
        message = "Future value is too large.";
        break;
    }
    i++;
}
```

A loop with a continue statement

```
string numbers = null;
for (int i = 1; i < 6; i++)
{
    numbers += i;
    numbers += "\n";
    if (i < 4)
        continue;
    numbers += "Big\n";
}
```

The result of the previous loop

```
1
2
3
4
Big
5
Big
```

Description

- You can code a break statement to jump out of a loop.
- You can code a *continue statement* to jump to the start of a loop.

Figure 5-8 Loops that use break and continue statements

Debugging techniques for programs with loops

When you code programs that use loops, debugging often becomes more difficult because it's sometimes hard to tell how the loop is operating. As a result, you may want to use the debugging techniques that are summarized in figure 5-9. These techniques let you stop the execution of a program and enter break mode when a loop starts. Then, you can observe the operation of the loop one statement at a time.

To stop the execution of a program and enter break mode, you set a *breakpoint*. To do that, you can click the *margin indicator bar* at the left-hand side of the Code Editor window. The breakpoint is then marked by a red dot. Later, when the application is run, execution will stop just prior to the statement at the breakpoint.

Once in break mode, a yellow arrowhead marks the next statement that will be executed, which is called the *execution point*. At this point, you can use the debugging windows to display the current values of the variables used by the loop and to watch how these variables change each time through the loop. For example, you can use the Locals window to display the current values of the variables within the scope of the current method. If this window isn't displayed by default, you can display it by selecting the Locals item from the Windows submenu of the Debug menu.

While in break mode, you can also *step through* the statements in the loop one statement at a time. To do that, you repeatedly press the F11 key or click the Step Into button on the Debug toolbar. This lets you observe exactly how and when the variable values change as the loop executes. Once you understand how the loop works, you can remove the breakpoint and press the F5 key to continue normal execution.

Of course, these techniques are also useful for debugging problems that don't involve loops. If, for example, you can't figure out what's wrong with a complex set of nested if statements, you can set a breakpoint at the start of the statement. Then, when the program enters break mode, you can step through the clauses in the statement to see exactly how the expressions are being evaluated.

A for loop with a breakpoint and an execution point

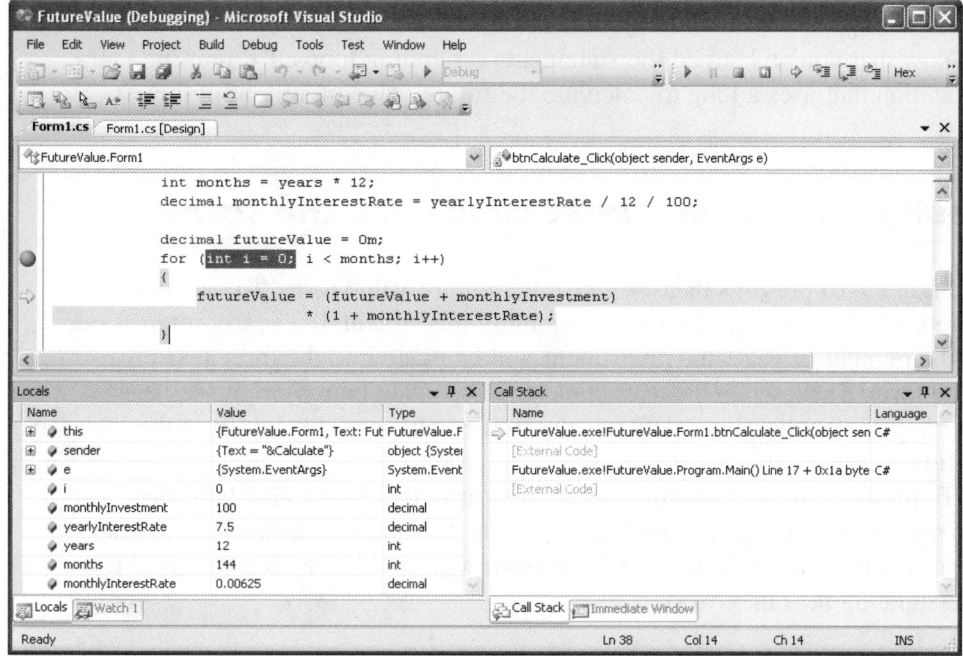

How to set and clear breakpoints

- To set a breakpoint, click in the *margin indicator bar* to the left of a statement. Or, press the F9 key to set a breakpoint at the cursor insertion point. Then, a red dot will mark the breakpoint.
- To remove a breakpoint, use either technique for setting a breakpoint. To remove all breakpoints at once, use the Clear All Breakpoints command in the Debug menu.

How to work in break mode

- In break mode, a yellow arrowhead marks the current *execution point*, which points to the next statement that will be executed.
- To *step through* your code one statement at a time, press the F11 key or click the Step Into button on the Debug toolbar.
- To continue normal processing until the next breakpoint is reached, press the F5 key.

Description

- When you set a *breakpoint* at a specific statement, the program stops before executing that statement and enters break mode. Then, you can step through the execution of the program one statement at a time.
- In break mode, the Locals window displays the current values of the variables in the scope of the current method. If this window isn't displayed, you can display it by selecting the Locals item from the Windows submenu of the Debug menu.

Figure 5-9 Debugging techniques for programs with loops

The Future Value application

Now that you've learned the statements for coding loops, I'll present a new application that uses a loop to calculate the future value of a monthly investment.

The design and property settings for the form

Figure 5-10 presents the design for the Future Value form. To calculate a future value, the user must enter the monthly investment, the yearly interest rate, and the number of years the investment will be made into the three text boxes on the form. Then, when the user clicks the Calculate button or presses the Enter key, the application calculates the future value and displays it in the last text box on the form.

To make it easy for you to develop this form, this figure also lists the property settings for the form and its controls. Since these settings are similar to the ones you used for the Invoice Total form, you shouldn't have any trouble understanding how they work.

The Future Value form

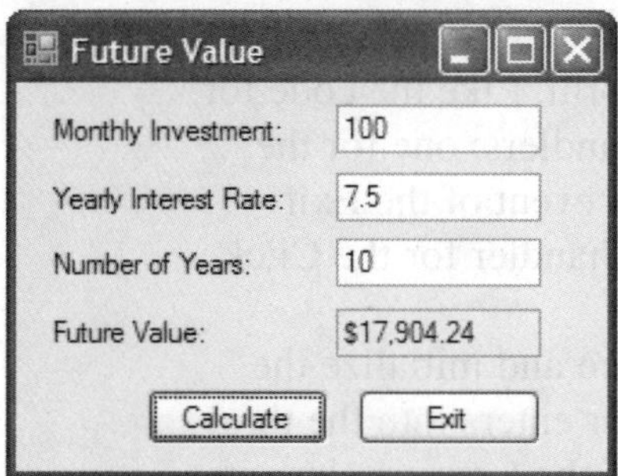

The property settings for the form

Default name	Property	Setting
Form1	Text	Future Value
	AcceptButton	btnCalculate
	CancelButton	btnExit

The property settings for the controls

Default name	Property	Setting
Label1	Text	Monthly Investment:
Label2	Text	Yearly Interest Rate:
Label3	Text	Number of Years:
Label4	Text	Future Value:
TextBox1	Name	txtMonthlyInvestment
TextBox2	Name	txtInterestRate
TextBox3	Name	txtYears
TextBox4	Name	txtFutureValue
	ReadOnly	True
	TabStop	False
Button1	Name	btnCalculate
	Text	&Calculate
Button2	Name	btnExit
	Text	E&xit

Additional property settings

- The TextAlign property of each of the labels is set to MiddleLeft.
- The TabIndex properties of the controls are set so the focus moves from top to bottom and left to right.

Figure 5-10 The form design and property settings for the Future Value application

The code for the form

Figure 5-11 presents the code for the Future Value form. Like the code for the Invoice Total form, this code consists of two event handlers: one for the Click event of the Calculate button and one for the Click event of the Exit button. Here, most of the processing occurs in the event handler for the Click event of the Calculate button.

The first three statements in this event handler declare and initialize the variables that will be used to store the values that the user enters into the three text boxes. Here, the ToDecimal and ToInt32 methods of the Convert class are used to convert the string values that are returned from the Text property of the text boxes to the appropriate numeric data types.

The next two statements perform calculations that convert the yearly values entered by the user to monthly values. That way, all of the variables used in the future value calculation will be in terms of months. The first statement converts the number of years to months by multiplying the years by 12. The second statement divides the yearly interest rate by 12 to get a monthly interest rate, and then divides that result by 100 to convert the number to a percentage.

The next group of statements uses a for loop to calculate a new future value for each month of the investment. Here, the variable that stores the future value is declared before the loop so it can be used after the loop finishes its processing. Then, within the loop, the single assignment statement that calculates the future value is executed once for each month. Since this loop contains a single statement, it doesn't require braces. However, to clearly identify the start and end of the loop, I decided to include these braces anyway.

Within the loop, the arithmetic expression adds the monthly investment amount to the future value, which has an initial value of zero. Then, the expression multiplies that sum by 1 plus the monthly interest rate. If, for example, the monthly investment amount is $100 and the monthly interest rate is 1% (or .01), future value is $101 after the expression is executed the first time through the loop:

```
(0 + 100) * (1 +.01) = 100 * 1.01 = 101
```

And future value is $203.01 after the expression is executed the second time:

```
(101 + 100) * (1 + .01) = 201 * 1.01 = 203.01
```

Continue this process for as many months as the user indicates, and future value will contain the correct result for a series of equal monthly investments.

After the loop ends, the next statement formats the future value and displays it on the form. To do that, the ToString method converts a decimal value to a string that uses the currency format. Then, this string value is assigned to the Text property of the Future Value text box. Finally, the last statement moves the focus to the Monthly Investment text box to prepare for the next calculation.

To keep this program simple, it doesn't validate the data that's entered by the user. As a result, an exception will occur if the user enters nonnumeric data in one of the text boxes. In chapter 7, you'll learn how to add data validation to this program to prevent exceptions like this.

The code for the event handlers in the Future Value application

```
private void btnCalculate_Click(object sender, System.EventArgs e)
{
    decimal monthlyInvestment =
        Convert.ToDecimal(txtMonthlyInvestment.Text);
    decimal yearlyInterestRate = Convert.ToDecimal(txtInterestRate.Text);
    int years = Convert.ToInt32(txtYears.Text);

    int months = years * 12;
    decimal monthlyInterestRate = yearlyInterestRate / 12 / 100;

    decimal futureValue = 0m;
    for (int i = 0; i < months; i++)
    {
        futureValue = (futureValue + monthlyInvestment)
                    * (1 + monthlyInterestRate);
    }

    txtFutureValue.Text = futureValue.ToString("c");
    txtMonthlyInvestment.Focus();
}

private void btnExit_Click(object sender, System.EventArgs e)
{
    this.Close();
}
```

Description

- This application uses a for loop to calculate the future value of a monthly investment amount. For this calculation to work correctly, all of the variables that it uses must be converted to the same time period. In this case, that time period is months.
- Each time through the for loop, the assignment statement adds the monthly investment amount to the future value, which starts at zero. Then, this sum is multiplied by 1 plus the monthly interest rate. The result is stored in the futureValue variable so it can be used the next time through the loop.
- Since this application doesn't provide data validation, the user will be able to enter invalid data, which will cause an exception to occur.

Figure 5-11 The code for the Future Value application

Perspective

Now that you've finished this chapter, you should know how to code if statements, switch statements, while statements, do-while statements, and for statements. These are the C# statements that implement the selection, case, and iteration structures, and they provide the logic of an application. Once you master them, you'll be able to develop significant C# applications.

Terms

Boolean expression
relational operator
logical operator
short-circuit operator
if-else statement
if statement
selection structure
block scope
nested if statement
switch statement
case structure
case label
default label
break statement
fall through
no fall through rule
iteration structure
while statement
while loop
do-while statement
do-while loop
infinite loop
for statement
for loop
jump statement
continue statement
breakpoint
margin indicator bar
execution point
step through

Exercise 5-1 Enhance the Invoice Total application

In this exercise, you'll use if-else and switch statements to determine the discount percent for the Invoice Total application that's in figure 5-5.

Open the application and change the if-else statement

1. Open the application that's in the C:\C# 2008\Chapter 05\InvoiceTotal directory.
2. Change the if-else statement so customers of type "R" with a subtotal that is greater than or equal to $250 but less than $500 get a 25% discount and those with a subtotal of $500 or more get a 30% discount. Next, change the if-else statement so customers of type "C" always get a 20% discount. Then, test the application to make sure this works.
3. Use code snippets to add another customer type to the if-else statement so customers of type "T" get a 40% discount for subtotals of less than $500, and a 50% discount for subtotals of $500 or more. Also, make sure that customer types that aren't "R", "C", or "T" get a 10% discount. Then, test the application.
4. Test the application again, but use lowercase letters for the customer types. Note that these letters aren't evaluated as capital letters. Now, stop the debugging and modify the code so the users can enter either capital or lowercase letters for the customer types. Then, test the application to make sure it works correctly.

Use a switch statement with if-else statements to get the same results

5. Use a code snippet to enter the start of a switch statement right after the if-else statement. Next, enhance this code so the switch statement provides the structure for handling the three cases for customer types: R, C, and T (but not r, c, and t). Then, within each of these cases, you can copy the related code from the if-else statement above to provide for the discounts that are based on subtotal variations. In other words, the if-else statements will be nested within the switch cases.
6. Comment out the entire if-else statement above the switch statement. Then, test to make sure the switch statement works correctly. Is this code easier to read and understand?
7. When you're through experimenting, close the application.

Exercise 5-2 Develop the Future Value application

In this exercise, you'll develop and test the Future Value application that was presented in this chapter. You'll also step through its loop.

Develop the form, write the code, and test the application

1. Open the New Project dialog box by selecting the File→New→Project command. Then, enter "FutureValue" for the name of the project, enter "C:\C# 2008\Chapter 05" for the location, and click the OK button.
2. Add the controls to the form and set the properties of the form and its controls as shown in figure 5-10. Then, generate the event handlers for the Click event of the two buttons, and add the code for these handlers. If necessary, you can refer to the code in figure 5-11, but try to write the code without doing that.
3. Test the application by entering valid data in each of the three text boxes. To start, enter simple values like 100 for the monthly investment, 12 for the yearly interest rate (which is 1% per month), and 1 for the number of years. (The result should be $1,280.93).
4. After you're sure that the application works for valid data, test it with nonnumeric entries and with large values like 100 for the interest rate and 1000 for the number of years. In either case, the application will end with a runtime error, which you'll learn how to prevent in chapter 7. Then, stop the debugging.

Set breakpoints and step through the loop

5. In the Code Editor, set a breakpoint at the for statement by clicking in the Margin Indicator Bar to the left of the statement as shown in figure 5-9. A red dot will indicate that you have set the breakpoint.
6. Run the application, and enter 100 as the monthly investment, 12 as the yearly interest rate, and 1 as the number of years. Then, click the Calculate button. This will cause the program to enter break mode. If the Locals window isn't displayed, use the Debug menu to display it.
7. Press F11 repeatedly to step through the loop. As you do this, the Locals window will display the values for i, futureValue, monthlyInvestment, and monthlyInterestRate. That way, you'll be able to see exactly how these values change as the loop is executed.
8. Press F11 to continue stepping through the application or press F5 to run the application until another breakpoint is reached.
9. Remove the old breakpoint and set a new breakpoint on the statement within the for loop. Then, run the application and note that the new breakpoint causes the application to enter break mode for each iteration of the loop. As a result, you can press F5 to move from one iteration to the next.
10. When you're through experimenting, remove the breakpoint and close the project.

6

How to code methods and event handlers

So far, you've been writing methods called event handlers for the Click events of button controls. Now, in this chapter, you'll learn how to code methods that can be called from other methods. That will help you logically divide the code for an application into manageable parts. You'll also learn how to code event handlers for events other than the Click event.

How to code and call methods

In chapter 3, you learned how to code methods that are executed automatically when a Click event occurs. Now, you'll learn how to code methods that you call explicitly from other methods in the application.

How to code methods

Figure 6-1 shows how to code a *method*. To start, you code an *access modifier* that indicates whether the method can be called from other classes. In most cases, you'll use the *private* access modifier so the method can only be called from within the class where it's coded. If you need to call the method from another class, however, you can use the *public* access modifier.

After the access modifier, you code the return type for the method, which identifies the type of data that the method returns. To specify a return type, you can use the keyword for any of the built-in data types, or you can specify the name of any class, structure, or enumeration. Then, within the method, you must code a *return statement* that identifies the value to be returned. This value must correspond to the data type that's specified as the return type.

If the method doesn't return any data, though, you code the *void* keyword as the return type. Then, you don't code a return statement.

After the return type, you code the name of the method. In most cases, you'll give the method a name that indicates the action it performs. A common coding convention is to start each method name with a verb. This convention is used in the names for the methods in this figure: DisableButtons, GetDiscountPercent, and CalculateFutureValue.

After the method name, you code a set of parentheses. Within the parentheses, you declare the *parameters* that are required by the method. This is known as the *parameter list*. Later, when you call the method, you pass arguments that correspond to these parameters. You'll learn more about that in the next figure.

If a method doesn't require any parameters, you can code an empty set of parentheses as shown in the first example in this figure. Here, a method named DisableButtons simply assigns a false value to the Enabled properties of two buttons. However, if a method does require parameters, you can code them within the parenthesis as shown in the second and third examples. Here, the second method calculates and returns a decimal discount percent based on a subtotal, and the third method calculates and returns a decimal future value based on a monthly investment, a monthly interest rate, and a number of months.

When you code the name and parameter list of a method, you form the *signature* of the method. Later in this book, you'll learn how to code two or more methods with the same name but with different parameters. This is known as *overloading* a method.

Incidentally, Visual Studio doesn't provide an easy way to start the code for a new method. So you just start the method by typing the code into the class and using the IntelliSense feature whenever it's available.

The basic syntax for coding a method

```
{public|private} returnType MethodName([parameterList])
{
   statements
}
```

A method with no parameters and no return type

```
private void DisableButtons()
{
    btnCalculate.Enabled = false;
    btnExit.Enabled = false;
}
```

A method with one parameter that returns a decimal value

```
private decimal GetDiscountPercent(decimal subtotal)
{
    decimal discountPercent = 0m;
    if (subtotal >= 500)
        discountPercent = .2m;
    else
        discountPercent = .1m;
    return discountPercent;
}
```

A method with three parameters that returns a decimal value

```
private decimal CalculateFutureValue(decimal monthlyInvestment,
    decimal monthlyInterestRate, int months)
{
    decimal futureValue = 0m;
    for (int i = 0; i < months; i++)
    {
        futureValue = (futureValue + monthlyInvestment)
                    * (1 + monthlyInterestRate);
    }
    return futureValue;
}
```

Description

- To allow other classes to access a *method*, use the *public* access modifier. To prevent other classes from accessing a method, use the *private* modifier.
- To code a method that doesn't return data, use the *void* keyword for the return type. To code a method that returns data, code a return type in the method declaration and code a *return statement* in the body of the method. The return statement ends the execution of the current method and returns the specified value to the calling method.
- Within the parentheses of a method, you can code an optional *parameter list* that contains one or more *parameters*, with the parameters separated by commas. When you code a parameter, you must code a data type and you must provide a name for the parameter.
- The name of a method plus its parameter list form the *signature* of the method, which must be unique.

Figure 6-1 How to code methods

How to call methods

Figure 6-2 shows how to *call* a method that's coded within a form class. By now, you should be familiar with the basic syntax for calling a method, so most of this figure should be review. To start, you can type the optional *this* keyword to specify that the method that's being called is in the current class, followed by the dot operator and the method name. Otherwise, you just code the method name and the current class is assumed.

If the method requires *arguments*, you code the *argument list* within parentheses right after the method name. Otherwise, you code an empty set of parentheses. Before I go on, you should realize that the terms *parameter* and *argument* are often used interchangeably. In this book, however, we'll use the term *parameter* to refer to the variables of a method declaration, and we'll use the term *argument* to refer to the values that are passed to a method.

The three examples in this figure show how you would call the three methods you saw in figure 6-1. The first example calls the DisableButtons method, which has no parameters. Because of that, the statement call doesn't include any arguments. In addition, the method doesn't return any data, so the statement simply calls the method.

The second example calls the GetDiscountPercent method. Since this method is defined with one parameter, the statement that calls it passes one argument. In this case, the argument is a variable named subtotal. However, you could also code the argument as a literal value, such as 49.50m. In addition, because this method returns a value, the method call is coded as part of an assignment statement. When this statement is executed, the return value from the method, which is declared with the decimal type, is assigned to the discountPercent variable, which is also declared as a decimal.

The third example shows how to call a method that requires three arguments. When you call a method like this, you must be sure to pass the correct number of arguments with the correct data types. If you don't, your code won't compile. In addition, you must be sure to pass the arguments in the same order that the corresponding parameters are declared in the method. Otherwise, the method won't work correctly.

In this figure, the names of the arguments are the same as the names of the corresponding parameters presented in figure 6-1. This is a common practice that makes code easier to read and write. However, this isn't required. As a result, you can use whatever names you like when you code arguments.

When you call a method that returns a value, you can assign that value to a variable as shown in the second and third examples in this figure. However, you can also code a method call within an expression. For example, you could use the GetDiscountPercent method in an expression like this:

```
total = subtotal * (1 - this.GetDiscountPercent(subtotal));
```

In this case, the decimal value that's returned by the method will be used to perform a calculation.

The syntax for calling a method

```
[this.]MethodName([argumentList])
```

A statement that calls a method that has no parameters

```
this.DisableButtons();
```

A statement that passes one argument

```
decimal discountPercent = this.GetDiscountPercent(subtotal);
```

A statement that passes three arguments

```
decimal futureValue = CalculateFutureValue(
    monthlyInvestment, monthlyInterestRate, months);
```

The IntelliSense feature for calling a method

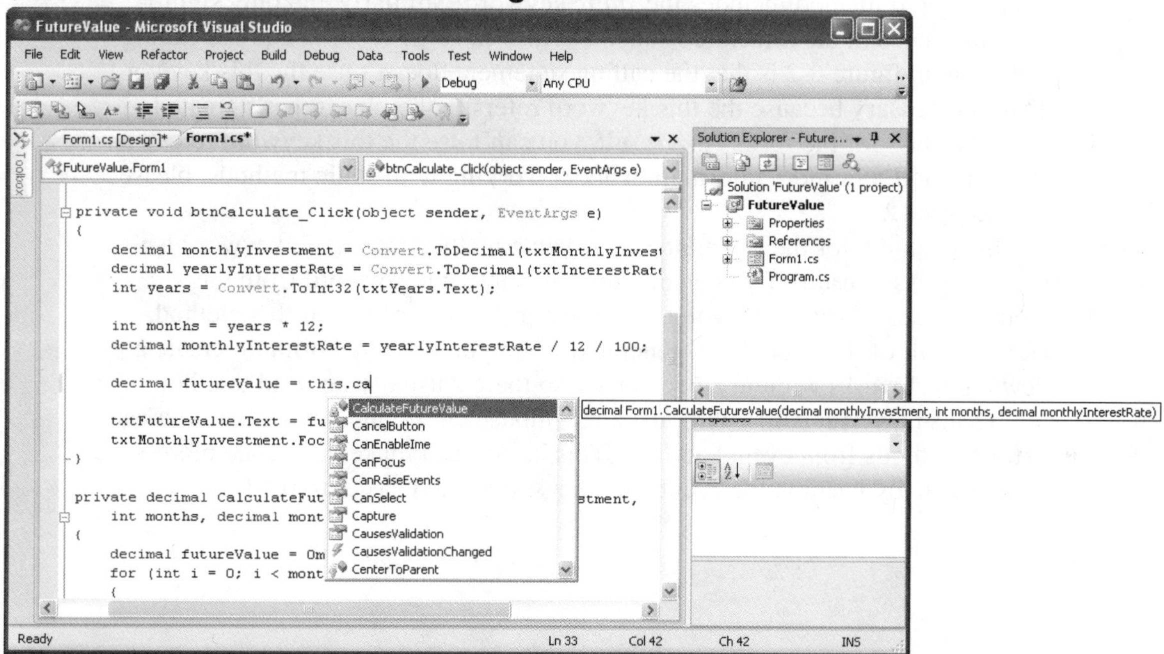

Description

- When you *call* a method, the *arguments* that you code in the *argument list* that's passed to the method must be in the same order as the parameters in the parameter list defined by the method, and they must have compatible data types. However, the names of the arguments don't need to match the names of the parameters.
- When you call a method, Visual Studio's IntelliSense feature helps you enter the name of the method and the arguments of the method.

Figure 6-2 How to call methods

How to use refactoring to create a new method and its calling statement

In chapter 3, you were introduced to *refactoring*, which refers to the process of revising and restructuring existing code. This can be especially helpful when you want to create a new method from some code that's in an event handler. This process is illustrated in figure 6-3. To refactor the code, you just select the code you want to create a method from, right-click on the selected code, choose the Extract Method command from the Refactor submenu, and enter a name for the new method.

In this figure, you can see that refactoring creates both a call statement and a new method named CalculateFutureValue. The only significant difference between this method and the CalculateFutureValue method in figure 6-1 is that the refactored method includes the *static* keyword. Similarly, the only significant difference in the refactored statement that calls the method and the calling statement in figure 6-2 is that the calling statement doesn't use the this keyword. This is necessary because the this keyword refers to the object that's created from the class for the form. As a result, you can't use the this keyword to call a static method. For more information about working with static methods, please see chapter 12.

Incidentally, for the CalculateFutureValue method, the static keyword isn't necessary. As a result, if you want, you can delete this keyword from the method. Then, if you want, you can use the this keyword to call this method. However, all of the code that's generated when you use refactoring to create a new method works without any changes, so there's usually no need to edit it.

That's powerful stuff! With just a few mouse clicks and keystrokes, you can extract methods from event handlers. This in turn can make your code more manageable by keeping the event handlers shorter and easier to read.

The btnCalculate_Click method with selected statements

```
private void btnCalculate_Click(object sender, EventArgs e)
{
    decimal monthlyInvestment = Convert.ToDecimal(txtMonthlyInvestment.Text);
    decimal yearlyInterestRate = Convert.ToDecimal(txtInterestRate.Text);
    int years = Convert.ToInt32(txtYears.Text);

    int months = years * 12;
    decimal monthlyInterestRate = yearlyInterestRate / 12 / 100;

    decimal futureValue = 0m;
    for (int i = 0; i < months; i++)
    {
        futureValue = (futureValue + monthlyInvestment)
                    * (1 + monthlyInterestRate);
    }

    txtFutureValue.Text = futureValue.ToString("c");
    txtMonthlyInvestment.Focus();
}
```

The method call that replaces the selected code

```
decimal futureValue = CalculateFutureValue(monthlyInvestment, months,
    monthlyInterestRate);
```

The method that's added to the class

```
private static decimal CalculateFutureValue(decimal monthlyInvestment,
    int months, decimal monthlyInterestRate)
{
    decimal futureValue = 0m;
    for (int i = 0; i < months; i++)
    {
        futureValue = (futureValue + monthlyInvestment)
                    * (1 + monthlyInterestRate);
    }
    return futureValue;
}
```

How to use refactoring to create a new method from existing code

1. Select the code you want to create a new method from. Then, right-click on the selection, and choose Refactor→Extract Method from the shortcut menu.
2. In the Extract Method dialog box, enter the name that you want to use for the new method and click OK. This adds a new method to the class and replaces the selected code with a call statement that calls the method.

Description

- If you want to extract a method from existing code, refactoring makes that easy with its Extract Method command.
- Note in the code above that the refactored code doesn't use the this keyword in the method call and does include the static keyword in the method declaration. You'll learn more about the static keyword in chapter 12.

Figure 6-3 How to use refactoring to create a new method and its method call

When and how to pass arguments by reference and by value

By default, the arguments that are passed to a method are passed *by value*. That means that the value of each passed variable is assigned to the corresponding parameter in the method. Because of that, the method can change the value of the parameter without affecting the value of the variable in the calling method.

In some cases, though, you'll want to be able to change the value of the variable in the calling method from the called method. To do that, you can pass the argument *by reference* as shown in figure 6-4. Here, the *ref* keyword is coded before the argument and before the parameter declaration. Then, when you call the method, a reference to the variable that you specify for the corresponding argument is passed to the method. As a result, if the method changes the value of the parameter, it also changes the value of the variable in the calling method.

In this figure, the first three arguments are passed by value, but the fourth is passed by reference. Then, when the method changes the fourth parameter, the variable in the calling method is also changed. As a result, there's no need for the method to return the value of the futureValue variable.

In general, though, it's better to pass arguments by value instead of by reference. That way, the data in the calling method can't be changed by the called method. What if you want the method to return two or more values instead of just one? The best way to do that is to return one object that contains those values, and you'll learn how to do that in section 3.

The syntax of the parameters in a parameter list

```
[ref] type variableName
```

A method named CalculateFutureValue that requires four parameters

```
private void CalculateFutureValue(decimal monthlyInvestment,
    decimal monthlyInterestRate, int months, ref decimal futureValue)
{
    for (int i = 0; i < months; i++)
    {
        futureValue = (futureValue + monthlyInvestment)
            * (1 + monthlyInterestRate);
    }
}
```

Three statements that work with the CalculateFutureValue method

```
decimal futureValue = 0m;
this.CalculateFutureValue(monthlyInvestment,
    monthlyInterestRate, months, ref futureValue);
txtFutureValue.Text = futureValue.ToString("c");
```

Description

- When you call a method, each argument can be passed to the method *by value* or *by reference.*
- If you pass an argument by value, the value of the variable in the calling method can't be changed by the called method. That's because the value of the variable is passed, not the variable itself.
- If you pass an argument by reference and the called method changes the value of the corresponding parameter, the value of the variable in the calling method is changed. That's because the passed argument provides a reference that points to the variable in the calling method.
- By default, arguments are passed by value. To pass an argument by reference, you use the *ref* keyword as shown above.
- When you pass an argument by reference and update the argument in the called method, you don't have to use the return statement to return the value of the argument.

Figure 6-4 When and how to pass arguments by reference and by value

How to work with events and delegates

In chapter 3, you learned how to generate the event handler for the default event of a control by double-clicking on the control in the Form Designer. Now, you'll learn how to create an event handler for any form or control event. In addition, you'll learn more about how event wiring works, and you'll learn how to handle two or more events with the same event handler.

How to generate an event handler for any event

Figure 6-5 shows how to generate an event handler for any event of a form or control. To do that, you select the form or control in the Form Designer and then click the Events button in the Properties window. When you do, a list of events for that form or control is displayed. In this figure, for example, you can see a list of the events for the first text box on the Future Value form. Below the list of events, you can see a short description of the highlighted event.

To generate a handler for any of these events, you can double-click on the event in this list. Then, Visual Studio will generate the method declaration for the event handler along with a statement that *wires* the event to the event handler (as you'll see in the next figure). When you use this technique, Visual Studio will give the event handler a name that combines the name of the control and the name of the event. For example, if you double-click the Validating event for the Monthly Investment text box, Visual Studio will generate an event handler with this name:

```
txtMonthlyInvestment_Validating
```

If you want to generate an event handler with a name other than the default, you can do that by entering the name next to the event in the Properties window. Then, when you press the Enter key, Visual Studio will create an event handler with that name. In most cases, you'll use this technique only when you generate an event handler that will be used to handle more than one event. You'll learn more about that in figure 6-7.

If you look through the list of events for a form or a control, you'll see that there are many events for each one. For instance, there are more than 50 events for a text box and more than 70 events for a form. In practice, though, you'll use just a few events for each form or control. As you go through this book, you'll be introduced to the ones that are commonly used.

The Events list for a text box control

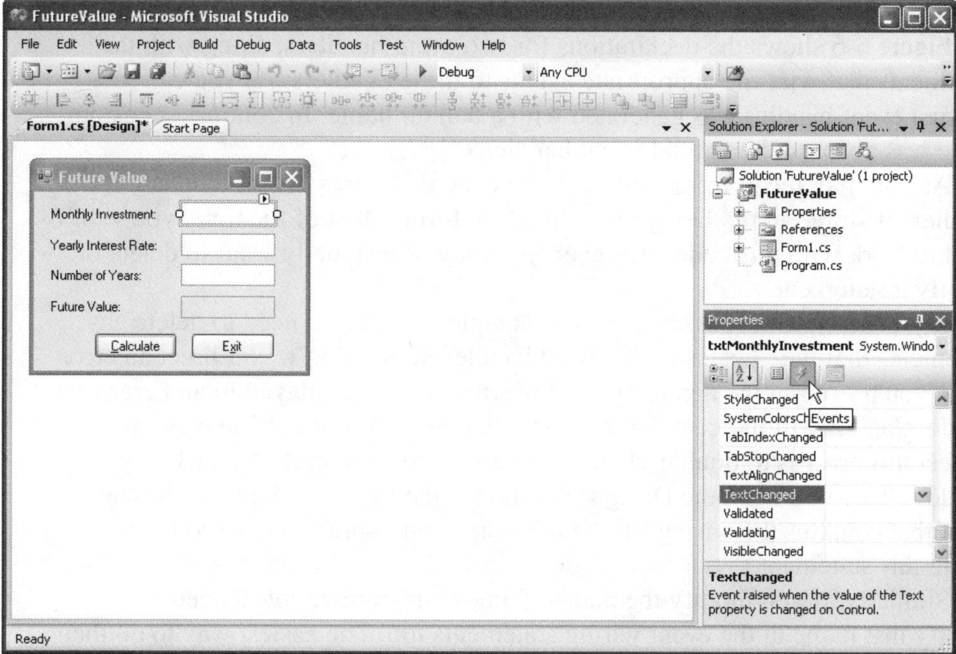

Description

- To generate the event handler for the default event of a form or control, you can double-click the form or control in the Form Designer.
- To view a list of all events for a form or control, you can select the form or control and click the Events button in the Properties window to display the Events list. Then, you can double-click on any event to generate an event handler for that event.
- By default, an event handler is given a name that consists of the form or control name, an underline, and the event name. To generate an event handler with a custom name, you can type the name of the event handler to the right of the event in the Events list and then press Enter to generate the event handler.
- When you generate an event handler for a control, Visual Studio generates the method declaration for the event handler and it connects, or *wires*, the event to the event handler as shown in the next figure.

Figure 6-5 How to generate an event handler for any event

How event wiring works

Figure 6-6 shows the declarations for two event handlers, along with the statements that wire the appropriate events to these handlers. As you can see, the first event handler was generated with a default name. In contrast, a custom name was given to the second event handler.

As you may recall from chapter 3, the code that wires events to event handlers is stored in the Designer.cs file for a form. Most of the time, you won't need to work with this code. However, you may occasionally want to delete or modify a statement.

If you delete an event handler, for example, you'll also need to delete any statements that wire events to the event handler. If you don't, you'll get an error when you try to run the application. This error will be displayed in an Error List window, and it will indicate that the event handler is missing. One way to correct this error is to double-click on the error message in the Error List window. This will open the Designer.cs file for the form and jump to the statement that contains the wiring for the missing event handler. Then, you can delete this statement.

Similarly, if you modify the name of an event handler, you'll need to modify that name in the event wiring statements too. The easiest way to do that is to use refactoring as described in chapter 3 when you rename the event handler. This automatically updates the name of the event handler in the corresponding event wiring statements. However, if you forget to use refactoring when you rename the event handler, you can use the technique presented in this figure to wire the corresponding events to the newly renamed event handler.

To wire an event to an event handler, Visual Studio uses a *delegate*, which is an object that represents a method. In this figure, the code uses the EventHandler delegate that's provided by the .NET Framework. This delegate defines the return type and parameter list for a method that can handle an event. Then, the code uses the *new* keyword to create an EventHandler delegate. When this delegate is created, the name of the method is passed to the delegate. Finally, to wire the TextChanged event of a text box to the method specified by the delegate, Visual Studio uses the += operator.

Although you can use the C# language to define your own delegates, you rarely need to do that. As a result, at least for now, you can focus on working with the delegates that are provided by the .NET Framework. Most of the time, that means using the System.EventHandler delegate as shown in this figure.

For C# to recognize a method as an event handler, the method must include the two parameters defined by the EventHandler delegate as shown in the examples. The first parameter is an object named sender. When an event handler is executed, this parameter receives the object that the event occurred on. The second parameter identifies an EventArgs object named e that contains information about the event. The exact content of this object depends on the event that occurred.

The default event handler for a text box

The method declaration for the event handler

```
private void txtMonthlyInvestment_TextChanged(object sender,
    System.EventArgs e)
{

}
```

The generated statement that wires the event to the event handler

```
this.txtMonthlyInvestment.TextChanged +=
    new System.EventHandler(this.txtMonthlyInvestment_TextChanged);
```

A custom event handler for a text box

The method declaration for the event handler

```
private void ClearFutureValue(object sender, System.EventArgs e)
{
}
```

The generated statement that wires the event to the event handler

```
this.txtMonthlyInvestment.TextChanged +=
    new System.EventHandler(this.ClearFutureValue);
```

Description

- When you use the Form Designer to generate an event handler, a statement is also generated in the Designer.cs file for the form. This statement uses a delegate to wire the event to a method.
- A *delegate* is an object that represents a method. C# uses the EventHandler delegate that's defined by the .NET Framework to wire events to methods.
- The EventHandler delegate specifies the return type and the parameters that are required for a method that can handle an event. These objects are passed to the event handler when the event occurs. The first parameter (sender) identifies the object that the event occurred on, and the second parameter identifies an EventArgs object that contains additional information about the event.
- The *new* keyword is used to create an instance of a delegate, and the argument must be the name of the method. This method must have the return type and parameters specified by the delegate.
- After the delegate is created, the += operator is used to wire the method specified by the EventHandler delegate to the event.

Figure 6-6 How event wiring works

How to handle multiple events with one event handler

In some cases, you'll want to use the same event handler to handle two or more events. For example, it's common to use one event handler for the TextChanged event of multiple text boxes on a form. To do that, you can use the procedure shown in figure 6-7.

To start, you must generate the event handler as described in figure 6-5. Typically, you will want to give this event handler a name that's not specific to any one control. Suppose, for example, that any time the user changes the value in one of the first three text boxes on the Future Value form, you want to clear the future value that's currently displayed. Then, when you create the event handler for the first text box, you might give this event handler the name ClearFutureValue.

Once you've created this event handler, it will appear in the drop-down list of the event handlers that are available. In this figure, for example, you can see that the ClearFutureValue event handler is included in the drop-down list for the TextChanged event of the Yearly Interest Rate text box. Then, you can select this event handler to generate a statement that wires the event to the event handler.

How to select an existing event handler for an event

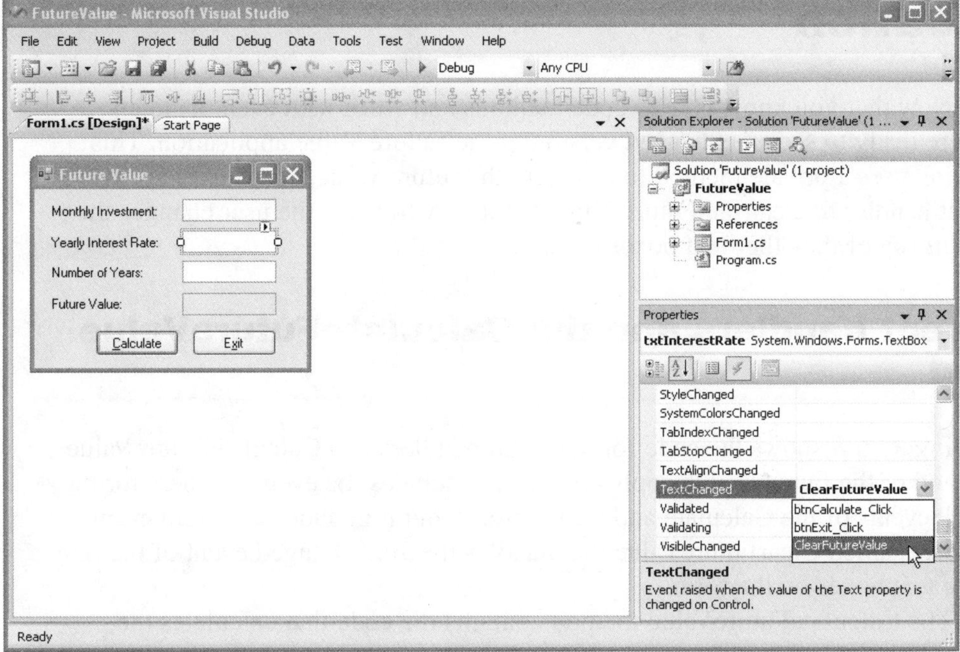

How to wire an event to an existing event handler

1. Select the control in the Form Designer.
2. If necessary, click the Events button in the Properties window to display a list of the events for the control.
3. Click to the right of the event you want to handle and display the drop-down list.
4. Select the event handler you want to use for that event.

Description

- The drop-down list that's available for each event includes all of the existing event handlers for the current form.
- When you select an event handler from the drop-down list, Visual Studio generates a statement that wires the event to the event handler.

Figure 6-7 How to handle multiple events with one event handler

Another version of the Future Value application

Now that you know how to code methods and work with event handlers, you're ready to see an enhanced version of the Future Value application. This version uses a private method to calculate the future value, and it uses a single event handler to clear the Future Value text box whenever the user changes the text in any of the other text boxes on the form.

The event handlers and the CalculateFutureValue method

Figure 6-8 shows the code for the event handlers and CalculateFutureValue method of the Future Value application. This includes the event handlers for the Click events of the Calculate and Exit buttons, and it includes a custom event handler named ClearFutureValue that handles the TextChanged event of the first three text boxes on the form.

The CalculateFutureValue method contains the code that calculates the future value. It's called by the shaded code in the event handler for the Click event of the Calculate button. This separates the calculation from the other code for the event. In a lengthy event handler, using methods like this can make it easier to code, test, and debug an application. You'll see more of this in the next chapter.

The ClearFutureValue event handler contains a single statement that sets the Text property of the Future Value text box to an empty string. In other words, it clears the future value that's displayed on the form. Since this event handler is wired to the TextChanged event of the first three text boxes on this form, this code clears the Future Value text box every time the user changes a value in any of the other text boxes. Then, the future value isn't displayed until the user clicks the Calculate button again. As a result, this code prevents the Future Value text box from displaying a value that isn't accurate for the values that are displayed in the other text boxes.

The code for the methods for the Future Value application

```
private void btnCalculate_Click(object sender, EventArgs e)
{
    decimal monthlyInvestment = Convert.ToDecimal(txtMonthlyInvestment.Text);
    decimal yearlyInterestRate = Convert.ToDecimal(txtInterestRate.Text);
    int years = Convert.ToInt32(txtYears.Text);

    int months = years * 12;
    decimal monthlyInterestRate = yearlyInterestRate / 12 / 100;

    decimal futureValue = this.CalculateFutureValue(
        monthlyInvestment, monthlyInterestRate, months);
    txtFutureValue.Text = futureValue.ToString("c");
    txtMonthlyInvestment.Focus();
}

private decimal CalculateFutureValue(decimal monthlyInvestment,
    decimal monthlyInterestRate, int months)
{
    decimal futureValue = 0m;
    for (int i = 0; i < months; i++)
    {
        futureValue = (futureValue + monthlyInvestment)
                    * (1 + monthlyInterestRate);
    }
    return futureValue;
}

private void btnExit_Click(object sender, EventArgs e)
{
    this.Close();
}

private void ClearFutureValue(object sender, EventArgs e)
{
    txtFutureValue.Text = "";
}
```

Description

- The CalculateFutureValue method separates the calculation from the rest of the code for the event handler for the Click event of the Calculate button.
- The TextChanged event of the Monthly Investment, Yearly Interest Rate, and Number of Years text boxes is wired to the ClearFutureValue event handler. As a result, the Future Value text box will be cleared every time the user changes the data in one of those text boxes.

Figure 6-8 The event handlers and the other method of the Future Value application

Some of the generated code

Figure 6-9 shows a partial listing of the generated code for the Future Value application. This code is stored in the Designer.cs file for the form within the Windows Form Designer generated code region. In this figure, you can see the code that's generated for three controls: one button and two text boxes.

To start, the InitializeComponent method creates objects from the appropriate control classes and assigns those objects to the appropriate variables, which have already been declared. Next, the InitializeComponent method includes a group of statements for each control. Most of these statements set the starting properties for these controls.

However, the last statement in each group wires an event to an event handler. Here, the TextChanged events of the two text boxes are wired to an event handler named ClearFutureValue, and the Click event of the Calculate button is wired to an event handler named btnCalculate_Click. (Although it isn't shown in this listing, the TextChanged event of the third text box on this form is also wired to the ClearFutureValue event handler.)

As the warning at the top of this listing suggests, you should avoid modifying this code with a code editor. However, you should also be aware that this generated code exists and that it is essential to the proper operation of your application. In addition, there are times when using the Code Editor to directly modify this code may be easier than using the Form Designer to indirectly modify this code. If, for example, you start an event handler and decide to delete it, you may want to use the Code Editor to delete the wiring statement. Fortunately, this doesn't cause any problems for the Form Designer.

Some of the generated code in the Designer.cs file for the form

```
#region Windows Form Designer generated code

/// <summary>
/// Required method for Designer support - do not modify
/// the contents of this method with the code editor.
/// </summary>
private void InitializeComponent()
{
    this.btnCalculate = new System.Windows.Forms.Button();
    this.txtInterestRate = new System.Windows.Forms.TextBox();
    this.txtMonthlyInvestment = new System.Windows.Forms.TextBox();
    ...
    //
    // btnCalculate
    //
    this.btnCalculate.Location = new System.Drawing.Point(54, 126);
    this.btnCalculate.Name = "btnCalculate";
    this.btnCalculate.Size = new System.Drawing.Size(75, 23);
    this.btnCalculate.TabIndex = 18;
    this.btnCalculate.Text = "&Calculate";
    this.btnCalculate.Click +=
        new System.EventHandler(this.btnCalculate_Click);
    //
    // txtInterestRate
    //
    this.txtInterestRate.Location = new System.Drawing.Point(132, 37);
    this.txtInterestRate.Name = "txtInterestRate";
    this.txtInterestRate.Size = new System.Drawing.Size(84, 20);
    this.txtInterestRate.TabIndex = 16;
    this.txtInterestRate.TextChanged +=
        new System.EventHandler(this.ClearFutureValue);
    //
    // txtMonthlyInvestment
    //
    this.txtMonthlyInvestment.Location = new System.Drawing.Point(132, 9);
    this.txtMonthlyInvestment.Name = "txtMonthlyInvestment";
    this.txtMonthlyInvestment.Size = new System.Drawing.Size(84, 20);
    this.txtMonthlyInvestment.TabIndex = 15;
    this.txtMonthlyInvestment.TextChanged +=
        new System.EventHandler(this.ClearFutureValue);
    ...
}

#endregion

private System.Windows.Forms.Button btnCalculate;
private System.Windows.Forms.TextBox txtInterestRate;
private System.Windows.Forms.TextBox txtMonthlyInvestment;
...
```

Description

- The InitializeComponent method creates an instance of each control on the form, assigns each control to a variable, sets the properties of each control, and wires control events to the appropriate event handlers.

Figure 6-9 Some of the generated code for the Future Value application

Perspective

Now that you have finished this chapter, you should be able to code and call methods. You should also be able to code event handlers for any event of a form or control. With those skills, you are well on your way toward developing programs at a professional level.

Terms

method
access modifier
return statement
parameter
parameter list
signature
overloading a method
call a method
argument
argument list
pass by value
pass by reference
event wiring
delegate

Exercise 6-1 Enhance the Future Value application

In this exercise, you'll enhance the Future Value application that you created in chapter 5 so it works like the one in figure 6-8.

Use refactoring to create the CalculateFutureValue method

1. Open the application that's in the in the C:\C# 2008\Chapter 06\FutureValue directory.
2. Use refactoring as shown in figure 6-3 to refactor the calculation in the event handler and create a new method named CalculateFutureValue.
3. Test the application to make sure the new method works correctly.

Add the CalculateFutureValue method without using refactoring

4. Press Cntl-Z several times to return the code to the way it was before you refactored it.
5. Add a method named CalculateFutureValue that works like the one in figure 6-8. To do that, type the start of the new method including its starting and ending braces. Then, move the related code from the btnCalculate_Click method to the block within the new method and modify it where necessary.
6. Modify the code in the btnCalculate_Click method so it calls the CalculateFutureValue method. As you enter the call to the method, note how the IntelliSense feature helps you enter the arguments.
7. Test the application to make sure this new method works correctly.

Add an event handler for the TextChanged events

8. In the Form Designer, select the first text box. Then, click the Events button in the Properties Window to display the Events list for that text box. Review the events that are available.
9. Enter "ClearFutureValue" to the right of the TextChanged event and press Enter. When you do, the Code Editor will open and an event handler named ClearFutureValue will be created. Enter a statement that clears the Future Value text box as shown in figure 6-8.
10. Open the Designer.cs file for the form, expand the Windows Form Designer generated code region, and locate the statements that set the properties of the Monthly Investment text box. At the end of those statements, you'll find a statement that wires the TextChanged event of this control to the ClearFutureValue event handler.
11. Return to the Form Designer and select the Yearly Interest Rate text box. Drop down the list for the TextChanged event of this control, and notice that the ClearFutureValue event handler is included in this list. Select this event handler to wire the event to it. Repeat this process for the Number of Years text box.

12. Run the application and perform a calculation. Then, change the value that's displayed in one of the text boxes. When you do that, the value that's displayed for the Future Value text box should be cleared.
13. When you're sure the enhancements are working correctly, close the application.

Exercise 6-2 Experiment with events

This exercise will give you a chance to experiment with events and the event wiring for the Future Value application.

Generate and delete an event handler

1. Open the Future Value application that you enhanced in exercise 6-1.
2. In the Form Designer, double-click on the form to generate the handler for the default event of a form, which is the Load event. Then, delete this event handler in the Code Editor, and try to build and run the application. This should lead to one build error.
3. Double-click on the error message, which will lead you to the event wiring for the event handler. Then, delete that wiring, and try to build and run the application again. This time, it should work.

Use a form event and two more control events

4. In the Form Designer, select the form, click the Events button in the Properties window, and double-click on the DoubleClick event to generate its event handler. Next, write the code for this handler so it sets the Text property for all four text boxes to an empty string. Then, test the application to make sure this works. (Be sure to double-click on the form, not on a control or the form's title bar.)
5. In the Form Designer, select the Monthly Investment text box. Next, select the MouseHover event, read its description, drop down its list, and select the ClearFutureValue event handler so it will be executed whenever the user lets the mouse hover over this text box. Then, test the application to make sure this works.
6. In the Form Designer, select the Yearly Interest Rate text box, and double-click on the DoubleClick event to generate its event handler. Next, write the code for this handler so it sets the value in the Yearly Interest Rate text box to 12. Then, test this enhancement.
7. Use your own imagination to work with other events. When you're through experimenting with events, close the application.

How to handle exceptions and validate data

In the last two chapters, you learned how to code a Future Value application that calculates the future value of a series of monthly payments. However, if the user enters data that can't be handled by this application, an exception will occur and the application will crash. In this chapter, you'll learn how to prevent that from happening by handling any exceptions that occur and by validating data to prevent exceptions.

An introduction to exceptions

Before you learn how to handle exceptions, it's helpful to know more about how exceptions work. In addition, it's helpful to know how to display a dialog box that contains a message about an exception that has occurred. So that's what you'll learn in the two topics that follow.

How exceptions work

It's inevitable that your applications will encounter exceptions. For example, a user may enter data that's not appropriate for the application. Then, if the application doesn't check to be sure that the data is valid, the .NET runtime environment will *throw* an *exception* when it tries to work with that data. An exception is an object that's created from the Exception class or one of its subclasses like the ones shown in figure 7-1. Exception objects represent errors that have occurred, and they contain information about those errors.

A well-coded application will *catch* any exceptions that might be thrown and handle them. This is known as *exception handling*. Exception handling can be as simple as notifying users that they must enter valid data. However, for more serious exceptions, exception handling may involve notifying users that the application is being shut down, saving as much data as possible, cleaning up resources, and exiting the application as smoothly as possible.

When you're testing an application, it's common to encounter exceptions that haven't been handled. In that case, Visual Studio will enter break mode and display an Exception Assistant dialog box like the one shown in this figure. This dialog box includes the name of the class for the exception, a brief message that describes the cause of the exception, and some troubleshooting tips to help you fix the problem that caused the exception to be thrown.

All exceptions are *subclasses* of the Exception class. For example, the FormatException class is a subclass of the Exception class that represents a specific type of exception that occurs when a value of one data type can't be converted to another data type. This exception can be thrown by the To methods of the Convert class or the Parse method of any class.

The ArithmeticException class is also a subclass of the Exception class. It represents an exception that occurs during an arithmetic, casting, or conversion operation. This class contains other subclasses, including the OverflowException and DivideByZeroException classes shown here. An overflow exception occurs when the result of an arithmetic, casting, or conversion operation is too large for the receiving variable. A divide-by-zero exception occurs if an application attempts to divide a number by zero.

For now, that's all you need to know about the Exception hierarchy. As you progress through this book, though, you'll learn about other types of exceptions. In section 4, for example, you'll learn how to work with the exceptions that can occur when you're working with databases. You'll also learn more about subclasses and how they work in chapter 14.

The dialog box for an unhandled exception

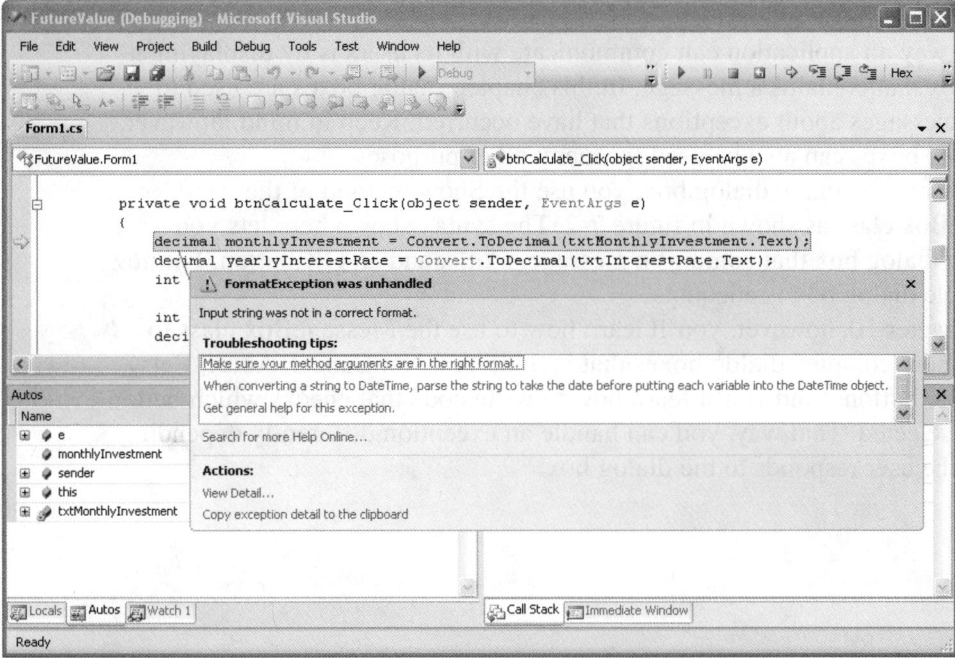
FutureValue (Debugging) - Microsoft Visual Studio
File Edit View Project Build Debug Tools Test Window Help
Form1.cs
FutureValue.Form1
btnCalculate_Click(object sender, EventArgs e)
private void btnCalculate_Click(object sender, EventArgs e)
decimal monthlyInvestment = Convert.ToDecimal(txtMonthlyInvestment.Text);
decimal yearlyInterestRate = Convert.ToDecimal(txtInterestRate.Text);
FormatException was unhandled
Input string was not in a correct format.
Troubleshooting tips:
Make sure your method arguments are in the right format.
When converting a string to DateTime, parse the string to take the date before putting each variable into the DateTime object.
Get general help for this exception.
Search for more Help Online...
Actions:
View Detail...
Copy exception detail to the clipboard
Autos
Name
e
monthlyInvestment
sender
this
txtMonthlyInvestment
Locals Autos Watch 1
Call Stack Immediate Window
Ready

The Exception hierarchy for five common exceptions

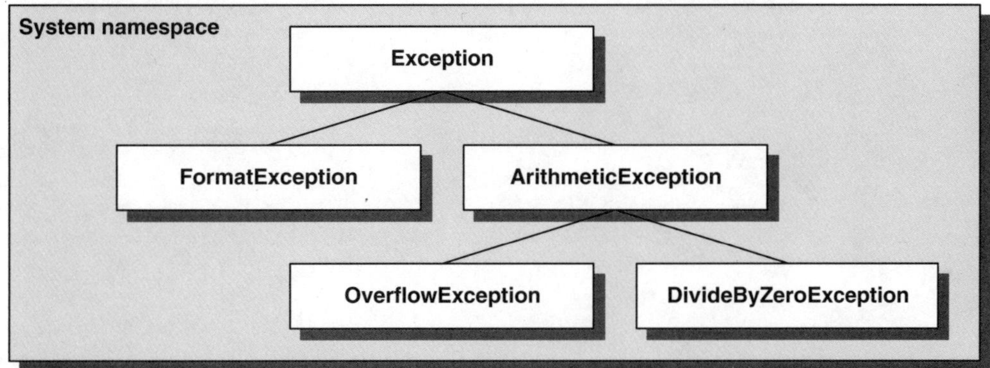
System namespace
Exception
FormatException
ArithmeticException
OverflowException
DivideByZeroException

Methods that might throw exceptions

Class	Method	Exception
`Convert`	`ToDecimal(string)`	`FormatException`
`Convert`	`ToInt32(string)`	`FormatException`
`Decimal`	`Parse(string)`	`FormatException`
`DateTime`	`Parse(string)`	`FormatException`

How to display a dialog box

One way an application can communicate with its users is by displaying a dialog box that contains a message. In this chapter, dialog boxes are used to display messages about exceptions that have occurred. Keep in mind, however, that dialog boxes can also be used for many other purposes.

To display a simple dialog box, you use the Show method of the MessageBox class as shown in figure 7-2. The syntax shown here lets you display a dialog box that contains a message, a title, and an OK button. For now, this simple dialog box is adequate.

In chapter 10, however, you'll learn how to use the MessageBox class to display more complex dialog boxes that include Yes, No, Cancel, Abort, Retry, and Ignore buttons, and you'll learn how to write code that checks which button the user selected. That way, you can handle an exception differently depending on how the user responds to the dialog box.

The syntax to display a dialog box with an OK button

```
MessageBox.Show(text[, caption]);
```

A dialog box with an OK button

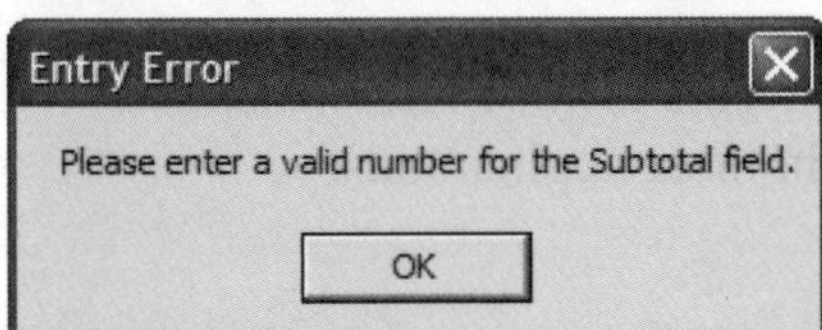

The statement that displays this dialog box

```
MessageBox.Show(
    "Please enter a valid number for the Subtotal field.",
    "Entry Error");
```

Description

- You can use the static Show method of the MessageBox class to display a dialog box. Dialog boxes are commonly used to display information about an exception to the user.
- If you omit the caption argument, the dialog box will be displayed without a caption in its title bar.

Note

- In chapter 10, you'll learn how to use the MessageBox class to display more complex dialog boxes that contain Yes, No, Cancel, Abort, Retry, and Ignore buttons and accept a response from the user.

Figure 7-2 How to display a dialog box

How to use structured exception handling

To prevent your applications from crashing due to runtime errors, you can write code that handles exceptions when they occur. This is known as *structured exception handling*, and it plays an important role in most applications.

How to catch an exception

Figure 7-3 shows how to use *try-catch statements* to catch and handle exceptions. First, you code a *try block* around the statement or statements that may throw an exception. Then, immediately after the try block, you code a *catch block* that contains the statements that will be executed if an exception is thrown by a statement in the try block. This is known as an *exception handler*.

The try-catch statement in this figure shows how you might catch any exceptions thrown by four of the statements in the Invoice Total application. For example, if the user enters a non-numeric value into the Subtotal text box, the ToDecimal method of the Convert class will throw an exception. Then, the application will jump into the catch block, skipping all the remaining statements in the try block. In this case, the catch block simply displays a dialog box that notifies the user of the problem. Then, the user can click the OK button and enter a valid number.

The syntax for a simple try-catch statement

```
try { statements }
catch { statements }
```

A try-catch statement

```
try
{
    decimal subtotal = Convert.ToDecimal(txtSubtotal.Text);
    decimal discountPercent = .2m;
    decimal discountAmount = subtotal * discountPercent;
    decimal invoiceTotal = subtotal - discountAmount;
}
catch
{
    MessageBox.Show(
        "Please enter a valid number for the Subtotal field.",
        "Entry Error");
}
```

The dialog box that's displayed if an exception occurs

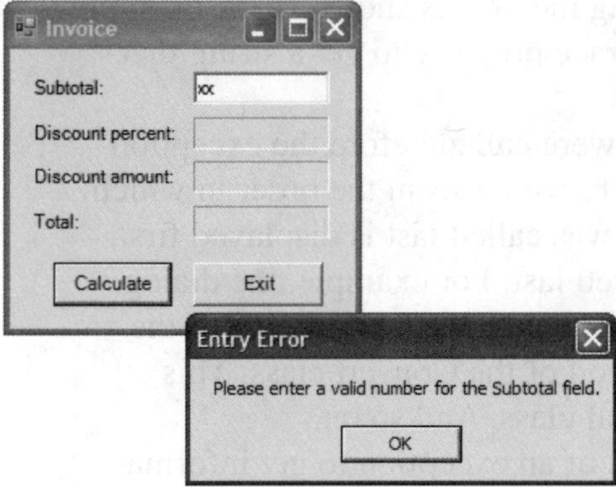

Description

- You can use a *try-catch statement* to code an *exception handler* that catches and handles any exceptions that are thrown.
- You can code a *try block* around any statements that may throw an exception. Then, you can code a *catch block* that contains the statements to be executed when an exception is thrown in the try block.

How to use the properties and methods of an exception

Since an exception is an object, it has properties and methods. If you want to use the properties or methods of an exception in the catch block that catches the exception, you must supply a name for the exception as shown in figure 7-4. To do that, you code a set of parentheses after the catch keyword. Within those parentheses, you code the name of the exception class, followed by a name for the exception.

If you're coding the try-catch statement within an event handler, you can't use e as the name of the exception. That's because, by default, the event handler already uses this name for its EventArgs parameter. As a result, you must specify another name such as x or ex. Or, you must change the name of the EventArgs parameter from e to another name.

Once you specify a name for an exception, you can use the Message property to get a brief description of the error. You can also use the GetType method to get the type of class that was used to create the exception object. Then, to get the name of that type, you can use the ToString method as shown in the example in this figure. Finally, you can use the StackTrace property to get a string that represents the *stack trace*.

A stack trace is a list of the methods that were called before the exception occurred. These methods are listed in the reverse order from the order in which they were called. As a result, the method that was called last is displayed first, and the method that was called first is displayed last. For example, the dialog box in this figure shows that line 24 of the btnCalculate_Click method of the Invoice Total form called the ToDecimal method of the Convert class. This method called the Parse method of the Decimal class. And so on.

When you use the properties and methods of an exception to get information about the exception, you can display that information in a dialog box. That way, if an exception is thrown, your users will be able to give you information about the exception so you can fix the problem. Or, if a serious exception occurs that prevents the application from continuing, you can write information about the exception to a log file so you can monitor and review these exceptions. You'll learn how to write data to files in chapter 21.

The syntax for a try-catch statement that accesses the exception

```
try { statements }
catch(ExceptionClass exceptionName) { statements }
```

Two common properties for all exceptions

Property	Description
`Message`	Gets a message that briefly describes the current exception.
`StackTrace`	Gets a string that lists the methods that were called before the exception occurred.

A common method for all exceptions

Method	Description
`GetType()`	Gets the type of the current exception.

A try-catch statement that accesses the exception

```
try
{
    decimal subtotal = Convert.ToDecimal(txtSubtotal.Text);
}
catch(Exception ex)
{
    MessageBox.Show(
        ex.Message + "\n\n" +
        ex.GetType().ToString() + "\n" +
        ex.StackTrace,
        "Exception");
}
```

The dialog box that's displayed if an exception occurs

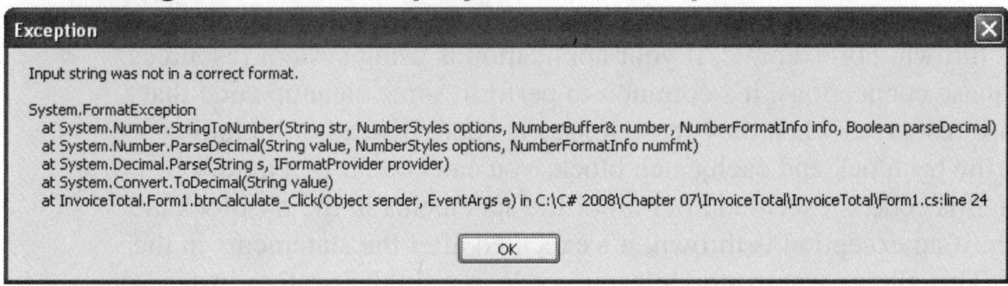
Exception
Input string was not in a correct format.
System.FormatException
at System.Number.StringToNumber(String str, NumberStyles options, NumberBuffer& number, NumberFormatInfo info, Boolean parseDecimal)
at System.Number.ParseDecimal(String value, NumberStyles options, NumberFormatInfo numfmt)
at System.Decimal.Parse(String s, IFormatProvider provider)
at System.Convert.ToDecimal(String value)
at InvoiceTotal.Form1.btnCalculate_Click(Object sender, EventArgs e) in C:\C# 2008\Chapter 07\InvoiceTotal\InvoiceTotal\Form1.cs:line 24
OK

Description

- If you want to use the properties or methods of the exception in the catch block, you must supply a name for the exception.
- The *stack trace* is a list of the methods that were called before the exception occurred. The list appears in reverse order, from the last method called to the first method called.

Note

- If you're coding the try-catch statement within an event handler, you can't use e for the name of the exception because it's used as the name of a parameter for the handler.

Figure 7-4 How to use the properties and methods of an exception

How to catch specific types of exceptions

In some cases, the statements in the try block of a try-catch statement can throw more than one type of exception. Then, you may want to handle each exception differently. To do that, you can code catch blocks like the ones shown in figure 7-5. Here, the first catch block catches a FormatException, the second catch block catches an OverflowException, and the third catch block catches any other exceptions.

When you catch specific exceptions, you should realize that you must code the catch blocks for the most specific exceptions in a class hierarchy first, and you must code the catch blocks for the least specific exceptions last. In this figure, for example, the FormatException type and the OverflowException type are both more specific than the Exception type. As a result, their catch blocks must be coded before the catch block for the Exception type. If they were coded after the Exception type, you would get a build error when you tried to compile the project. That's because the catch blocks are evaluated in sequence, which means that the catch block for the Exception type would catch any exception that occurred. In other words, the other catch blocks would never be executed.

Although you have to code the catch blocks for the FormatException and OverflowException types before the catch block for the Exception type, you don't have to code the catch block for the OverflowException type before the FormatException type. That's because the OverflowException class is a subclass of the ArithmeticException class, not the FormatException class. In other words, the least specific exception to most specific exception rule applies only within subclasses that are based on the same class.

When you code try-catch statements, you may find that you have some code that should run regardless of whether an exception is thrown or what type of exception is thrown. For example, if your application is using system resources such as database connections, it's common to perform some cleanup code that releases those resources when they're no longer needed. Instead of including this code in the try block and each catch block, you can code it in a *finally block*. Then, this code is executed after all of the statements in the try block are executed. Or, if an exception is thrown, it's executed after the statements in the catch block. This allows you to store cleanup code in a single location instead of multiple locations, which results in code that's easier to read and maintain.

The complete syntax for the try-catch statement

```
try { statements }
[catch(MostSpecificException [exceptionName]) { statements }]...
catch([LeastSpecificException [exceptionName]]) { statements }
[finally { statements }]
```

A try-catch statement that catches two specific exceptions

```
try
{
    decimal monthlyInvestment =
        Convert.ToDecimal(txtMonthlyInvestment.Text);
    decimal yearlyInterestRate =
        Convert.ToDecimal(txtInterestRate.Text);
    int years = Convert.ToInt32(txtYears.Text);
}
catch(FormatException)    // a specific exception
{
    MessageBox.Show(
        "A format exception has occurred. Please check all entries.",
        "Entry Error");
}
catch(OverflowException) // another specific exception
{
    MessageBox.Show(
        "An overflow exception has occurred. Please enter smaller values.",
        "Entry Error");
}
catch(Exception ex)       // all other exceptions
{
    MessageBox.Show(ex.Message, ex.GetType().ToString());
}
finally       // this code runs whether or not an exception occurs
{
    PerformCleanup();
}
```

Description

- You can code one catch block for each type of exception that may occur in the try block. If you code more than one catch block, you must code the catch blocks for the most specific types of exceptions first.
- Since all exceptions are subclasses of the Exception class, a catch block for the Exception class will catch all types of exceptions.
- You can code a *finally block* after all the catch blocks. The code in this block is executed whether or not an exception occurs. It's often used to free any system resources.

Figure 7-5 How to catch specific types of exceptions

How to throw an exception

Now that you've learned how to catch exceptions, you're ready to learn how to throw exceptions from the methods that you code. To do that, you can use the *throw statement* as shown in figure 7-6. As you can see, you can use this statement either to throw a new exception or to throw an existing exception.

To throw a new exception, you code the throw keyword followed by the *new* keyword and the name of the exception class you want to create the exception from. (As you'll see later in this book, the new keyword is the keyword that's used to create an object from a class.) When you do that, you can also supply a string argument that provides a brief description of the exception. This argument is assigned to the Message property of the exception. Then, when you handle the exception, you can use the Message property to get this string.

This use of the throw statement is illustrated in the first example in this figure. Here, before performing its calculation, the CalculateFutureValue method checks if the values used in the calculation are less than or equal to zero. If so, an exception that's created from the Exception class is thrown. Both of the throw statements shown here include a string that briefly describes the cause of the exception.

In general, you should throw an exception only when a truly exceptional condition occurs. In the first example, the CalculateFutureValue method can't perform the calculation when it receives a negative number. As a result, this is an exceptional condition, and it makes sense to throw an exception. Another way to handle this situation would be to return a negative decimal value (such as -1.0m) to indicate that the calculation can't be performed. However, throwing an exception allows you to provide a description of the exceptional condition, which is often helpful to other programmers who might want to use this method.

You can also use the throw statement to test an exception handling routine as shown in the second example. Here, the throw statement is coded within the try block of a try-catch statement. Then, when this statement is executed, the code within the catch block is executed so you can be sure that it works properly.

The third example in this figure shows how to throw an existing exception. This technique is useful if you need to catch an exception, perform some processing that partially handles the exception, and then throw the exception again so that another exception handler can finish handling the exception. In this case, the ToDecimal method is used within a try block to convert the value the user enters into a text box to a decimal. If the user enters a value that's not a valid decimal, a FormatException is thrown. Then, the catch block catches this exception, moves the focus to the text box, and rethrows the exception. That way, the calling method can also catch the exception and perform some additional processing.

The syntax for throwing a new exception

```
throw new ExceptionClass([message]);
```

The syntax for throwing an existing exception

```
throw exceptionName;
```

A method that throws an exception when an exceptional condition occurs

```
private decimal CalculateFutureValue(decimal monthlyInvestment,
    decimal monthlyInterestRate, int months)
{
    if (monthlyInvestment <= 0)
        throw new Exception("Monthly Investment must be greater than 0.");
    if (monthlyInterestRate <= 0)
        throw new Exception("Interest Rate must be greater than 0.");
        .
        .
}
```

Code that throws an exception for testing purposes

```
try
{
    decimal subtotal = Convert.ToDecimal(txtSubtotal.Text);
    throw new Exception("An unknown exception occurred.");
}
catch (Exception ex)
{
    MessageBox.Show(ex.Message + "\n\n"
        + ex.GetType().ToString() + "\n"
        + ex.StackTrace, "Exception");
}
```

Code that rethrows an exception

```
try
{
    Convert.ToDecimal(txtSubtotal.Text);
}
catch (FormatException fe)
{
    txtSubtotal.Focus();
    throw fe;
}
```

When to throw an exception

- When a method encounters a situation where it isn't able to complete its task.
- When you want to generate an exception to test an exception handler.
- When you want to catch the exception, perform some processing, and then throw the exception again.

Description

- You can use the *throw statement* to throw a new or existing exception. When you create a new exception, you can specify a string that's assigned to the Message property.

Figure 7-6 How to throw an exception

The Future Value application with exception handling

Figure 7-7 presents an improved version of the Future Value application you saw in the last chapter. As you can see, this version uses structured exception handling to catch any exceptions that might be thrown when the user clicks the Calculate button on the form.

To catch exceptions, all of the statements in the btnCalculate_Click method are coded within a try block. Then, the first catch block handles any format exceptions that are thrown if the user enters data with an invalid numeric format in one of the text boxes. Next, the second catch block handles any overflow exceptions that are thrown if the user enters numbers that are too large. If either of these exceptions are thrown, the code in the catch block displays a dialog box that describes the exception and indicates a corrective action that the user can take.

While the first two catch blocks catch specific exceptions, the third catch block catches all other exceptions. Since the cause of these exceptions isn't known, the application uses the properties and methods of the exception to display some information about the exception in a dialog box. In this case, the name of the exception class is displayed in the title bar of the dialog box, and a brief description of the exception is displayed in the body of the dialog box. That way, the user will be able to provide some information about the exception to the person who is going to fix this bug.

Note that this third catch block can't use e as the name of the exception because e is used for the System.EventArgs parameter. Instead, this catch block uses ex as the name of the Exception object.

Note also that if an exception occurs in the CalculateFutureValue method, the exception isn't caught by that method. As a result, the exception is passed back to the calling method, in this case, btnCalculate_Click. Then, the appropriate catch block in that method handles the exception.

The code for the Future Value application with exception handling

```
private void btnCalculate_Click(object sender, System.EventArgs e)
{
    try
    {
        decimal monthlyInvestment =
            Convert.ToDecimal(txtMonthlyInvestment.Text);
        decimal yearlyInterestRate =
            Convert.ToDecimal(txtInterestRate.Text);
        int years = Convert.ToInt32(txtYears.Text);

        decimal monthlyInterestRate = yearlyInterestRate / 12 / 100;
        int months = years * 12;

        decimal futureValue = this.CalculateFutureValue(
            monthlyInvestment, monthlyInterestRate, months);
        txtFutureValue.Text = futureValue.ToString("c");
        txtMonthlyInvestment.Focus();
    }
    catch(FormatException)
    {
        MessageBox.Show(
            "Invalid numeric format. Please check all entries.",
            "Entry Error");
    }
    catch(OverflowException)
    {
        MessageBox.Show(
            "Overflow error. Please enter smaller values.",
            "Entry Error");
    }
    catch(Exception ex)
    {
        MessageBox.Show(
            ex.Message,
            ex.GetType().ToString());
    }
}

private decimal CalculateFutureValue(decimal monthlyInvestment,
    decimal monthlyInterestRate, int months)
{
    decimal futureValue = 0m;
    for (int i = 0; i < months; i++)
    {
        futureValue = (futureValue + monthlyInvestment)
            * (1 + monthlyInterestRate);
    }

    return futureValue;
}
```

Figure 7-7 The Future Value application with exception handling

How to validate data

Whenever a user enters data, that data usually needs to be checked to make sure that it's valid. This is known as *data validation*. When an entry is invalid, the application needs to display an error message and give the user another chance to enter valid data. This needs to be repeated until all the entries on the form are valid.

How to validate a single entry

When a user enters text into a text box, you may want to perform several types of data validation. In particular, it's common to perform the three types of data validation shown in figure 7-8.

First, if the application requires that the user enters a value into a text box, you can check the Text property of the text box to make sure the user has entered one or more characters. Second, if the application requires that the user enters a number in the text box, you can use the appropriate To method of the Convert class within a try-catch statement to check that the Text property of the text box can be converted to the appropriate numeric data type. Third, if the application requires that the user enters a number within a specified range, you can use if-else statements to check that the number falls within that range. This is known as *range checking*.

Although this figure only shows how to check data that the user has entered into a text box, the same principles apply to other types of controls. In chapter 10, you'll learn more about validating entries made in other types of controls. In addition, although this figure only shows how to check the range of a number, you can also check strings and dates to make sure that they fall within certain ranges. You'll learn more about working with dates and strings in chapter 9.

Often, the code that performs the data validation prevents exceptions from being thrown. For example, if the user doesn't enter a value in the Monthly Investment text box, the code in this figure displays a dialog box and moves the focus to the Monthly Investment text box. If you didn't include this code, an exception would occur when the application tried to convert the empty string to a numeric data type.

Since code that validates data without using exception handling runs faster than code that uses exception handling, you should avoid using exception handling to validate data whenever possible. Of course, this isn't always practical or possible. For example, it's difficult to parse a string to check whether it contains a valid numeric format without using the ToDecimal method. That's why the second example uses a try-catch statement to check whether converting a string to a decimal throws an exception. In chapter 9, though, you'll learn how to write code that performs the same function without catching an exception.

Code that checks that an entry has been made

```
if (txtMonthlyInvestment.Text == "")
{
    MessageBox.Show(
        "Monthly Investment is a required field.", "Entry Error");
    txtMonthlyInvestment.Focus();
}
```

Code that checks an entry for a valid decimal format

```
try
{
    Convert.ToDecimal(txtMonthlyInvestment.Text);
}
catch (FormatException)
{
    MessageBox.Show(
        "Monthly Investment must be a numeric value.", "Entry Error");
    txtMonthlyInvestment.Focus();
}
```

Code that checks an entry for a valid range

```
decimal monthlyInvestment = Convert.ToDecimal(txtMonthlyInvestment.Text);
if (monthlyInvestment <= 0)
{
    MessageBox.Show(
        "Monthly Investment must be greater than 0.", "Entry Error");
    txtMonthlyInvestment.Focus();
}
else if (monthlyInvestment >= 1000)
{
    MessageBox.Show(
        "Monthly Investment must be less than 1,000.", "Entry Error");
    txtMonthlyInvestment.Focus();
}
```

Description

- When a user enters data, that data usually needs to be checked to make sure that it is valid. This is known as *data validation*.
- When an entry is invalid, the program needs to display an error message and give the user another chance to enter valid data.
- Three common types of validity checking are (1) to make sure that a required entry has been made, (2) to make sure that an entry has a valid numeric format, and (3) to make sure that an entry is within a valid range (known as *range checking*).
- To test whether a value has been entered into a text box, you can check whether the Text property of the box is equal to an empty string.
- To test whether a text box contains valid numeric data, you can code the statement that converts the data in a try block and use a catch block to catch a format exception.
- To test whether a value is within an acceptable range, you can use if-else statements.

Figure 7-8 How to validate a single entry

How to use generic methods to validate an entry

Since it's common to check text boxes for valid data, it often makes sense to create generic methods like the ones shown in figure 7-9 for data validation. These methods perform the same types of validation described in the previous figure, but they work for any text box instead of a specific text box.

In this figure, the IsPresent method checks to make sure the user has entered data in a text box. This method accepts two parameters and returns a Boolean value. The first parameter is a variable that refers to the text box, and the second parameter is a string that contains a name that describes the text box. If the user hasn't entered any characters into the text box, this method displays a dialog box with a message that includes the name parameter. Then, it moves the focus to the text box. Finally, it returns a false value. However, if the user has entered one or more characters, the method returns a true value.

The IsDecimal method accepts the same parameters as the IsPresent method, but it uses a try-catch statement to check if the value entered by the user is a decimal value. If it isn't, the ToDecimal method of the Convert class will throw an exception and the statements in the catch block will be executed. These statements display a dialog box with an appropriate message, move the focus to the text box, and return a false value.

Once you understand how the IsDecimal method works, you can code methods for other numeric types. For example, you can code an IsInt32 method that uses the ToInt32 method to check if the user has entered a valid int value.

The IsWithinRange method begins with the same two parameters as the IsPresent and IsDecimal methods, but it includes two additional parameters: min and max. These parameters contain the minimum and maximum values that can be entered into the text box.

The IsWithinRange method begins by converting the value the user entered into the text box to a decimal value. Then, it uses an if statement to check if the decimal value is within the range specified by the min and max parameters. If not, this method displays a dialog box with an appropriate message, moves the focus to the text box, and returns a false value.

Since the IsWithinRange method uses the decimal type, which is the widest (most accurate) numeric data type, this method works with all numeric types. This works because all numeric types can be automatically cast to the decimal type. If, for example, you pass arguments of the int type to the min and max parameters, they will be cast to the decimal type.

The code at the bottom of this figure shows how to call these three methods to make sure a valid decimal value has been entered in the Monthly Investment text box. First, this code calls the IsPresent method to make sure the user has entered one or more characters. Then, it calls the IsDecimal method to make sure the user has entered a string that can be successfully converted to a decimal value. Finally, it calls the IsWithinRange method to make sure that this decimal value is greater than or equal to 1 and less than or equal to 1000. If all three methods return a true value, this code displays a dialog box that indicates that the entry is valid.

A method that checks for a required field

```
public bool IsPresent(TextBox textBox, string name)
{
    if (textBox.Text == "")
    {
        MessageBox.Show(name + " is a required field.", "Entry Error");
        textBox.Focus();
        return false;
    }
    return true;
}
```

A method that checks for a valid numeric format

```
public bool IsDecimal(TextBox textBox, string name)
{
    try
    {
        Convert.ToDecimal(textBox.Text);
        return true;
    }
    catch(FormatException)
    {
        MessageBox.Show(name + " must be a decimal value.", "Entry Error");
        textBox.Focus();
        return false;
    }
}
```

A method that checks for a valid numeric range

```
public bool IsWithinRange(TextBox textBox, string name,
    decimal min, decimal max)
{
    decimal number = Convert.ToDecimal(textBox.Text);
    if (number < min || number > max)
    {
        MessageBox.Show(name + " must be between " + min.ToString()
            + " and " + max.ToString() + ".", "Entry Error");
        textBox.Focus();
        return false;
    }
    return true;
}
```

Code that uses these methods to check the validity of one entry

```
if (IsPresent(txtMonthlyInvestment, "Monthly Investment") &&
    IsDecimal(txtMonthlyInvestment, "Monthly Investment") &&
    IsWithinRange(txtMonthlyInvestment, "Monthly Investment", 1, 1000))
{
    MessageBox.Show("Monthly Investment is valid.", "Test");
}
```

Description

- Since it's common to need to check text boxes for valid data, it often makes sense to create generic methods like these for data validation.

Figure 7-9 How to use generic methods to validate an entry

How to validate multiple entries

Figure 7-10 shows two ways to code a method named IsValidData that validates multiple entries on a form. The methods shown here validate the Monthly Investment and Interest Rate text boxes on the Future Value form using the three methods you saw in figure 7-9. Although these methods only check two text boxes, you can use methods like this to check every entry on a form for validity. That way, all the data validation for the form is coded in one location, which makes the code easy to read and maintain.

The first method in this figure uses a series of if statements to check each of the three conditions. Within each if statement, the Not (!) operator is used to reverse the Boolean value that's returned by each method. For example, if an entry for the Monthly Investment text box is *not* present, the IsPresent method displays a dialog box and returns a false value. As a result, the rest of the if statements in the method aren't executed.

The second method uses a single return statement to check all the validation conditions. To do this, it returns the result of all the validation conditions, connected with the conditional-And operator (&&). Since this operator is a short-circuit operator, the next condition is evaluated only if the previous condition returns a true value. As a result, the validation methods will only be called until the first one returns a false value. Then, that method will display the appropriate dialog box, and the entire IsValidData method will return a false value.

Note that both of these methods call the IsPresent method first, followed by the IsDecimal method, followed by the IsWithinRange method. In this case, IsDecimal must be called before IsWithinRange because IsWithinRange assumes that the text box that's being passed to it contains a valid numeric value. If you pass a text box that contains an invalid numeric value, this method will throw a FormatException. If you use the IsDecimal method to check the text box for a decimal value first, however, the IsWithinRange method should never throw a FormatException.

Code that uses a series of simple if statements

```
public bool IsValidData()
{
    // Validate the Monthly Investment text box
    if (!IsPresent(txtMonthlyInvestment, "Monthly Investment"))
        return false;
    if (!IsDecimal(txtMonthlyInvestment, "Monthly Investment"))
        return false;
    if (!IsWithinRange(txtMonthlyInvestment, "Monthly Investment", 1, 1000))
        return false;

    // Validate the Interest Rate text box
    if (!IsPresent(txtInterestRate, "Interest Rate"))
        return false;
    if (!IsDecimal(txtInterestRate, "Interest Rate"))
        return false;
    if (!IsWithinRange(txtInterestRate, "Interest Rate", 1, 20))
        return false;

    return true;
}
```

Code that uses compound conditions in a single return statement

```
public bool IsValidData()
{
    return

        // Validate the Monthly Investment text box
        IsPresent(txtMonthlyInvestment, "Monthly Investment") &&
        IsDecimal(txtMonthlyInvestment, "Monthly Investment") &&
        IsWithinRange(txtMonthlyInvestment, "Monthly Investment",
           1, 1000) &&

        // Validate the Interest Rate text box
        IsPresent(txtInterestRate, "Yearly Interest Rate") &&
        IsDecimal(txtInterestRate, "Yearly Interest Rate") &&
        IsWithinRange(txtInterestRate, "Yearly Interest Rate", 1, 20);

}
```

Description

- Both of these methods use the methods shown in the previous figure to check multiple entries on a form. Methods like these let you code all of the data validation for an entire form in one location.

Figure 7-10 How to validate multiple entries

The Future Value application with data validation

In figure 7-7, you saw a version of the Future Value application that used structured exception handling to catch all exceptions that might be thrown. Now, you'll see an improved version of this application that includes code that validates the user entries. This code prevents format and overflow exceptions from being thrown, and it provides more descriptive messages to the user.

The dialog boxes

Figure 7-11 shows the dialog boxes that are displayed when the user enters invalid data. For example, the first dialog box is displayed if the user doesn't enter a value for the Yearly Interest Rate text box. In contrast, the last dialog box is displayed if an exception that hasn't been anticipated is thrown. To test this dialog box, you can code a throw statement within the code for the Future Value application as shown in figure 7-6.

The code

Figure 7-12 shows the code for this version of the Future Value application. To start, the btnCalculate_Click method contains an exception handler that catches and handles any unanticipated exceptions. Within the try block, an if statement checks whether the IsValidData method returns a true value. If so, the future value is calculated and displayed. Otherwise, none of the statements within the if block are executed. However, the data validation method that detected the error will display a dialog box with an appropriate message and move the focus to the appropriate text box.

The IsValidData method checks all three of the text boxes on the form to make sure that they contain valid numeric entries. Within this method, a method named IsInt32 is called to check that the user entered a valid int value into the Number of Years text box. This method works much like the IsDecimal method.

Each method in this application performs a specific task. For example, the btnCalculate_Click method contains the code that gets the values from the form and displays values on the form. The IsValidData, IsPresent, IsDecimal, IsInt32, and IsWithinRange methods contain the code that validates the data that's entered by the user. And the CalculateFutureValue method contains the code that performs the calculation. This is a good design because it leads to code that's reusable and easy to maintain.

However, this code could be more efficient. For example, if the user enters a valid decimal value in the Monthly Investment text box, the ToDecimal method is called three times: once by the IsDecimal method, once by the IsWithinRange method, and once by the btnCalculate_Click method. For most applications, however, the benefits that result from being able to reuse and easily maintain this code far outweigh any performance issues.

The Future Value form with a dialog box for required fields

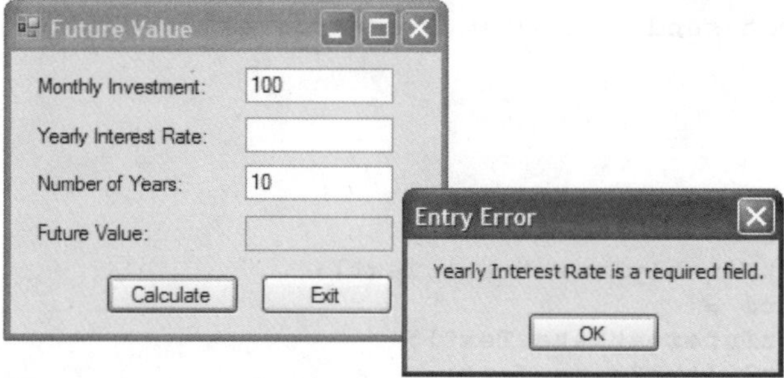

The dialog box for invalid decimals

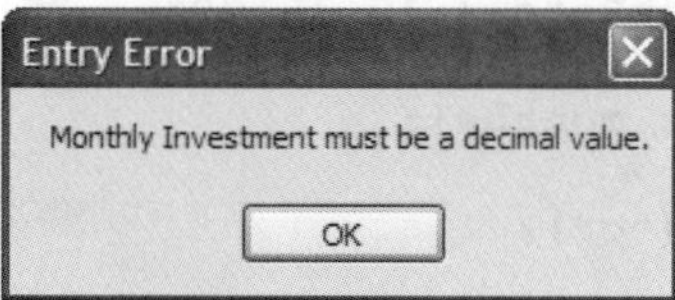

The dialog box for invalid ranges

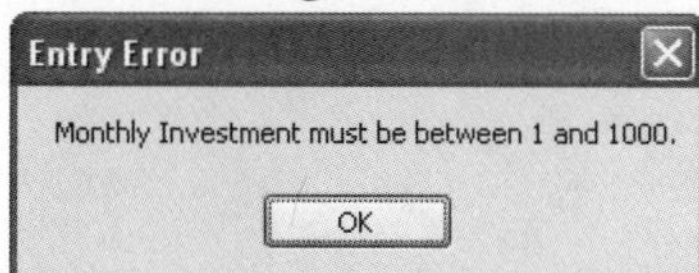

The dialog box for an unanticipated exception

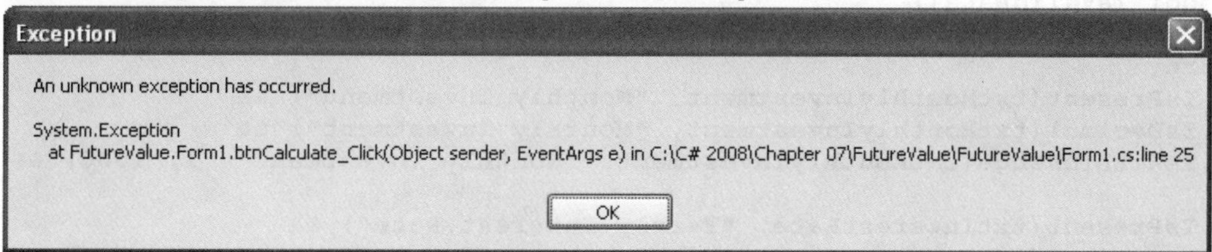

Description

- The first dialog box is displayed if the user doesn't enter a required field.
- The second dialog box is displayed if the user enters a value for the monthly investment or yearly interest rate that isn't in a valid decimal format.
- The third dialog box is displayed if the user enters a number that isn't within the range specified by the application.
- The fourth dialog box is displayed if any other type of exception occurs that hasn't been provided for in the validation code.

Figure 7-11 The dialog boxes of the Future Value application

The code for the Future Value application

```
private void btnCalculate_Click(object sender, System.EventArgs e)
{
    try
    {
        if (IsValidData())
        {
            decimal monthlyInvestment =
                Convert.ToDecimal(txtMonthlyInvestment.Text);
            decimal yearlyInterestRate =
                Convert.ToDecimal(txtInterestRate.Text);
            int years = Convert.ToInt32(txtYears.Text);

            int months = years * 12;
            decimal monthlyInterestRate = yearlyInterestRate / 12 / 100;
            decimal futureValue = CalculateFutureValue(
                monthlyInvestment, monthlyInterestRate, months);

            txtFutureValue.Text = futureValue.ToString("c");
            txtMonthlyInvestment.Focus();
        }
    }
    catch(Exception ex)
    {
        MessageBox.Show(ex.Message + "\n\n" +
            ex.GetType().ToString() + "\n" +
            ex.StackTrace, "Exception");
    }
}

public bool IsValidData()
{
    return
        IsPresent(txtMonthlyInvestment, "Monthly Investment") &&
        IsDecimal(txtMonthlyInvestment, "Monthly Investment") &&
        IsWithinRange(txtMonthlyInvestment, "Monthly Investment", 1, 1000) &&

        IsPresent(txtInterestRate, "Yearly Interest Rate") &&
        IsDecimal(txtInterestRate, "Yearly Interest Rate") &&
        IsWithinRange(txtInterestRate, "Yearly Interest Rate", 1, 20) &&

        IsPresent(txtYears, "Number of Years") &&
        IsInt32(txtYears, "Number of Years") &&
        IsWithinRange(txtYears, "Number of Years", 1, 40);
}

public bool IsPresent(TextBox textBox, string name)
{
    if (textBox.Text == "")
    {
        MessageBox.Show(name + " is a required field.", "Entry Error");
        textBox.Focus();
        return false;
    }
    return true;
}
```

Figure 7-12 The code for the Future Value application (part 1 of 2)

The code for the Future Value application

```
public bool IsDecimal(TextBox textBox, string name)
{
    try
    {
        Convert.ToDecimal(textBox.Text);
        return true;
    }
    catch(FormatException)
    {
        MessageBox.Show(name + " must be a decimal value.", "Entry Error");
        textBox.Focus();
        return false;
    }
}

public bool IsInt32(TextBox textBox, string name)
{
    try
    {
        Convert.ToInt32(textBox.Text);
        return true;
    }
    catch(FormatException)
    {
        MessageBox.Show(name + " must be an integer.", "Entry Error");
        textBox.Focus();
        return false;
    }
}

public bool IsWithinRange(TextBox textBox, string name,
    decimal min, decimal max)
{
    decimal number = Convert.ToDecimal(textBox.Text);
    if (number < min || number > max)
    {
        MessageBox.Show(name + " must be between " + min
            + " and " + max + ".", "Entry Error");
        textBox.Focus();
        return false;
    }
    return true;
}

private decimal CalculateFutureValue(decimal monthlyInvestment,
    decimal monthlyInterestRate, int months)
{
    decimal futureValue = 0m;
    for (int i = 0; i < months; i++)
    {
        futureValue = (futureValue + monthlyInvestment)
            * (1 + monthlyInterestRate);
    }
    return futureValue;
}
```

Figure 7-12 The code for the Future Value application (part 2 of 2)

Perspective

In this chapter, you learned how to handle exceptions and validate data so you can code applications that are "bulletproof." This means that your applications won't throw unhandled exceptions no matter what data the user enters or how the user works with the user interface. This is an essential feature of any professional application.

But there's still a lot more for you to learn about the C# language. So in chapter 8, you'll learn how to work with arrays and collections. In chapter 9, you'll learn how to work with dates, and you'll learn more about working with strings. And in chapter 10, you'll learn how to develop forms that use other types of controls. When you finish these chapters, you'll be able to develop applications of considerable complexity.

Terms

exception
throw an exception
catch an exception
exception handling
subclass
structured exception handling
try-catch statement
exception handler
try block
catch block
stack trace
finally block
throw statement
data validation
range checking

Exercise 7-1 Enhance the Invoice Total application

This exercise guides you through the process of enhancing the Invoice Total application so it catches any runtime errors and validates the Subtotal entry.

1. Open the application that's in the C:\C# 2008\Chapter 07\InvoiceTotal directory. This is the version that you worked on in chapter 4.
2. Add a try-catch statement to the btnCalculate_Click method so it catches any exception that the ToDecimal method of the Convert class might throw. The catch block should display a dialog box like the one in figure 7-2. Then, test the application to make sure this works correctly.
3. Add code to the try block that checks that the user enters a value in the Subtotal text box. If a value isn't entered, a dialog box should be displayed with a message indicating that Subtotal is a required field. Then, test this enhancement.
4. Add code to the try block that range checks the user entry so it's greater than zero and less than 10,000. If it isn't, a dialog box should be displayed that specifies the acceptable range. Then, test this enhancement. When you're satisfied that the application works correctly, close it.

Exercise 7-2 Enhance the Future Value application

This exercise guides you through the process of enhancing the Future Value application that you worked on in chapter 6.

1. Open the application that's in the C:\C# 2008\Chapter 07\FutureValue directory.
2. Add a try-catch statement to the btnCalculate_Click method that catches and handles any FormatException or OverflowException that might occur. These catch blocks should display dialog boxes with appropriate messages. Then, test these enhancements.
3. Add another catch block to the try-catch statement that will catch any other exception that might occur. This catch block should display a dialog box that displays the message contained in the exception object, along with the exception type and the stack trace.
4. Add a throw statement to the CalculateFutureValue method that throws a new exception of the Exception class regardless of the result of the calculation. This statement will be used to test the enhancements of step 3, and it should specify a generic message that indicates an unknown error. Then, test the application by entering valid values in the three text boxes and clicking the Calculate button. If the exception is thrown and the last catch block works correctly, end the application and comment out the throw statement.
5. Code four generic validation methods named IsPresent, IsDecimal, IsInt32, and IsWithinRange that test whether a text box contains an entry, a valid decimal value, a valid int value, and a value within a given range. If the validation is unsuccessful, each method should display a dialog box with a message that includes the name of the text box that's being validated. If you need help in coding these methods, you can refer to figure 7-9.
6. Code an IsValidData method that calls the four generic methods you created in step 5 to validate the data the user enters into the three text boxes. Each text box should be tested for three types of invalid data: (1) nothing entered, (2) invalid format, and (3) invalid range. You can use either of the two techniques presented in figure 7-10 to do this.
7. Modify the code in the event handler for the Calculate button so it uses the IsValidData method to validate the data before it processes it. Then, test the application to be sure it works correctly. If it does, end the application and comment out the FormatException and OverflowException catch blocks since these exceptions are now prevented by the data validation.
8. Do a final test of the application, and close it.

8

How to work with arrays and collections

Arrays and collections are objects that act as containers. As you develop C# applications, you'll find many uses for arrays and collections. For example, you can use a sales array or a sales collection to hold the sales amounts for each of the 12 months of the year. Then, you can use that array or collection to perform calculations on those amounts. In this chapter, you'll learn the basic concepts and techniques for working with arrays and collections.

How to work with one-dimensional arrays

You can use an *array* to store a set of related data. Since a one-dimensional array is the simplest type of array, you'll start by learning how to create and use one-dimensional arrays.

How to create an array

To create a *one-dimensional array*, you use the syntax shown in figure 8-1. As you can see, you can create an array using either one or two statements. This is similar to the techniques you use to declare variables, except that you code square brackets after the data type to indicate that the variable refers to an array. Within the second set of brackets, you code a number that indicates the *length*, or *size*, of the array. This specifies the number of elements that the array can hold.

Notice that you also use the new keyword to create an array. That's because, as you'll learn later in this chapter, arrays are created from the Array class that's provided by the .NET Framework. So when you create an array, you're creating an instance of this class.

When you create an array, each *element* in the array is initialized to a default value. This value depends on the data type of the array as indicated by the table in this figure. Specifically, numeric types are set to zero, char types are set to the null character, Boolean types are set to false, DateTime types are set to 12:00:00 AM on January 1, 0001, and reference types are set to nulls. In the next figure, you'll learn how to assign new values to the elements of an array.

In most cases, all of the elements in an array will contain the same type of data, and you'll declare the array with that data type. However, if you don't know what type of data an array will contain, you can declare it with the object data type. Then, each element can contain data of any type.

The syntax for creating a one-dimensional array

With two statements

```
type[] arrayName;                          // declaration statement
arrayName = new type[arrayLength];         // assignment statement
```

With one statement

```
type[] arrayName = new type[arrayLength];
```

How to create an array of decimal types

With two statements

```
decimal[] totals;
totals = new decimal[4];
```

With one statement

```
decimal[] totals = new decimal[4];
```

Other examples

An array of strings

```
string[] description = new string[3];
```

Two arrays in one statement

```
const int MaxCount = 100;
decimal[] prices = new decimal[MaxCount],
          discountPercentages = new decimal[MaxCount];
```

Default values for array elements

Data type	Default value
numeric	0 (zero)
char	'\0' (the null character)
Boolean	false
DateTime	01/01/0001 00:00:00
reference types	null

Description

- An *array* can store one or more *elements*. The *length*, or *size*, of an array is the number of elements in the array.
- When you create an array, each element of the array is set to a default value. If the array contains value types, each element is set to the value shown above. If the array contains reference types, each element is set to null.

Figure 8-1 How to create an array

How to assign values to the elements of an array

Figure 8-2 shows how to assign values to the elements of an array. As the syntax at the top of this figure indicates, you refer to an element in an array by coding the array name followed by its *index* in brackets. The index that you specify must be from 0, which refers to the first element in the array, to the *upper bound* of the array, which is one less than the length of the array.

To understand how this works, take a look at the first example in this figure. This example declares an array of decimals that contains four elements. Then, it uses indexes 0 through 3 to assign values to those four elements. Here, the length of the array is 4, and the upper bound of the array is 3. Note that if you use an index that's greater than the upper bound, an IndexOutOfRangeException will be thrown.

The syntax and examples at the bottom of this figure show how to declare an array and assign values to its elements in a single statement. Here, you start the array declaration as before, but you code a list of values in braces after the declaration. Notice that when you use this technique, you can omit the new keyword and the type and length specification. Then, C# automatically sets the length of the array to the number of elements within the braces. If you include the data type and length specification, however, they must match the list of values you provide.

The next three statements show how this works. The first statement creates the same array as the first example in this figure. Notice that this statement specifies the data type and length of the array. The second statement creates the same array, but the data type and length are omitted. Finally, the third statement creates the same array of strings that was created by the second example in this figure. Like the second statement, the data type and length are omitted from this statement.

You may remember from chapter 4 that you can use the var keyword to declare a variable that infers its type from the value that's assigned to it. You can also use the var keyword with an array, as illustrated in the last statement in this figure. This statement creates an array that contains four int values.

Although we recommend that you specify the type of an array whenever possible, you should notice three differences in how this statement is coded in case you ever want to use this technique. First, you don't code square brackets following the var keyword like you do when you specify a type. Second, you must include the new keyword followed by square brackets on the assignment statement. And third, you must not specify the length of the array within the square brackets.

The syntax for referring to an element of an array

```
arrayName[index]
```

Examples that assign values by accessing each element

Code that assigns values to an array of decimal types

```
decimal[] totals = new decimal[4];
totals[0] = 14.95m;
totals[1] = 12.95m;
totals[2] = 11.95m;
totals[3] = 9.95m;
//totals[4] = 8.95m;    this would throw an IndexOutOfRangeException
```

Code that assigns objects to an array of strings

```
string[] names = new string[3];
names[0] = "Ted Lewis";
names[1] = "Sue Jones";
names[2] = "Ray Thomas";
```

The syntax for creating an array and assigning values in one statement

```
type[] arrayName = [new type[length]] {value1[, value2][, value3]...};
```

Examples that create an array and assign values in one statement

```
decimal[] totals = new decimal[4] {14.95m, 12.95m, 11.95m, 9.95m};
decimal[] totals = {14.95m, 12.95m, 11.95m, 9.95m};
string[] names = {"Ted Lewis", "Sue Jones", "Ray Thomas"};
```

A statement that creates an array whose type is inferred from its values

```
var grades = new[] {95, 89, 91, 98};
```

Description

- To refer to the elements in an array, you use an *index* where 0 is the first element, 1 is the second element, 2 is the third element, and so on. The index of the last element in an array is known as the *upper bound.*
- If you list the values to be assigned to an array without using the new keyword to create the array, an array is created with a length equal to the number of values in the list. If you use the new keyword with a list of values, the length you specify for the array must match the number of values in the list, and the values must match the type you specify.
- You can also create an array without specifying a data type. To do that, you use the var keyword. Then, the data type is inferred from the values that are assigned to the array. When you use this technique, you must not code square brackets following the var keyword, you must code the new keyword followed by square brackets, and you must not specify a length.
- If you specify an index that's less than zero or greater than the upper bound of an array, an IndexOutOfRangeException will be thrown when the statement is executed.

Figure 8-2 How to assign values to the elements of an array

How to work with arrays

Now that you understand how to declare an array and assign values to its elements, you're ready to learn how to work with the values in an array. Figure 8-3 presents some of the basic techniques for doing that.

This figure starts by presenting the Length property of an array, which gets the number of elements in the array. You'll use this property frequently as you work with arrays.

The first example in this figure shows how to get the values from an array and calculate the average value of the elements. Here, the first statement declares a totals array that contains four decimal values. Then, the second statement sets the sum variable equal to the sum of the four elements in the array. Finally, the third statement computes the average value of these elements by dividing the sum by four.

The second example uses a for loop to put the numbers 0 through 9 into an array. Here, the first statement declares an array named numbers that contains 10 int values. Then, the for loop assigns the value of the loop's counter to each of the elements in the array.

The third example uses a for loop to display the elements of the numbers array in a message box. Here, the first statement declares a string variable. Then, the for loop accesses each element of the numbers array and appends the string and a space to the string variable. When the for loop finishes, the next statement displays the string that contains the numbers in a message box.

The fourth example shows how to use a loop to calculate the average value of the elements in the totals array. Here, the first statement declares the sum variable. Then, the for loop gets the value of each element of the array and adds that value to the current value of the sum variable. After the loop, the next statement uses the sum variable and the Length property of the array to calculate the average. If you compare this code to the code in the first example, you'll see that they both accomplish the same task. However, the code in this example will work equally well whether the totals array contains 4 or 400 values. As a result, it usually makes sense to use loops when working with arrays.

The last example shows how to display the elements of the totals array, along with the sum and average for the array, in a message box. Like the third example, this one uses a for loop to format the values in the array as a string. Then, it displays the string and the sum and average values in a message box.

The syntax for using the Length property of an array

```
arrayName.Length
```

Code that computes the average of an array of totals

```
decimal[] totals = {14.95m, 12.95m, 11.95m, 9.95m};
decimal sum = totals[0] + totals[1] + totals[2] + totals[3];
decimal average = sum/4;
```

Code that puts the numbers 0 through 9 into an array

```
int[] numbers = new int[10];
for (int i = 0; i < numbers.Length; i++)
    numbers[i] = i;
```

Code that displays the numbers array in a message box

```
string numbersString = "";
for (int i = 0; i < numbers.Length; i++)
    numbersString += numbers[i] + " ";
MessageBox.Show(numbersString, "Numbers Test");
```

The message box that's displayed

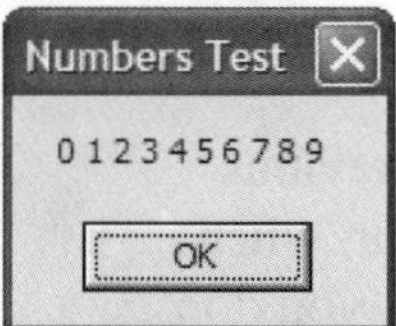

Code that uses a for loop to compute the average of the totals array

```
decimal sum = 0.0m;
for (int i = 0; i < totals.Length; i++)
    sum += totals[i];
decimal average = sum/totals.Length;
```

Code that displays the totals array in a message box

```
string totalsString = "";
for (int i = 0; i < totals.Length; i++)
    totalsString += totals[i] + "\n";
MessageBox.Show("The totals are:\n" +
    totalsString + "\n" +
    "Sum: " + sum + "\n" +
    "Average: " + average, "Totals Test");
```

The message box that's displayed

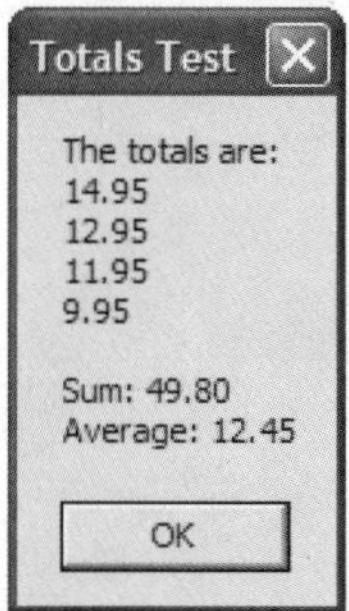

Figure 8-3 How to work with arrays

How to use foreach loops to work with arrays

Although you can use for loops to work with the elements of an array, it's often easier to use a *foreach statement* to code a *foreach loop*. Figure 8-4 shows how to do that.

To code a foreach loop, you begin by coding the *foreach* keyword followed by a set of parentheses. Within the parentheses, you code the data type of the elements in the array, the name you want to use to access the elements, the in keyword, and the name of the array. You can also code the var keyword in place of the data type, in which case the type is inferred from the type of the array.

Next, you can code one or more statements that use the element name to work with the element. If the foreach loop contains two or more statements, you must code braces around them. Otherwise, you can omit the braces.

When a foreach loop is executed, its statements are executed once for each element in the array. For example, the first example in this figure shows how you can use a foreach loop to display the elements in the numbers array that you saw in the previous figure. Similarly, the second example computes the average of the totals array, and the third example displays the elements in the totals array.

If you compare these examples to the for loop examples in the previous figure, you'll see that foreach loops are less complicated. In particular, when you use a foreach loop, you don't need to use a counter variable, and you don't need to use an index to get an element from the array. As a result, it's often easier to use a foreach loop than a for loop.

You should realize, however, that there are still times when you'll need to use a for loop to work with an array. For example, if you only want to access some of the elements in an array, you'll need to use a for loop. You'll also need to use a for loop if you want to use a counter variable to assign values to the elements of the array as shown in the second example in figure 8-3.

The syntax of a foreach loop

```
foreach (type elementName in arrayName)
{
   statements
}
```

Code that displays the numbers array in a message box

```
string numbersString = "";
foreach (int number in numbers)
{
    numbersString += number + " ";
}
MessageBox.Show(numbersString, "Numbers Test");
```

The message box that's displayed

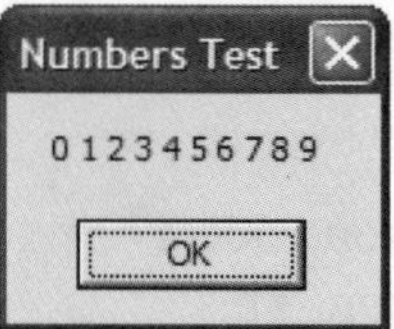

Code that computes the average of the totals array

```
decimal sum = 0.0m;
foreach (decimal total in totals)
    sum += total;
decimal average = sum/totals.Length;
```

Code that displays the totals array in a message box

```
string totalsString = "";
foreach (decimal total in totals)
    totalsString += total + "\n";
MessageBox.Show("The totals are:\n" +
    totalsString + "\n" +
    "Sum: " + sum + "\n" +
    "Average: " + average,
    "Totals Test");
```

The message box that's displayed

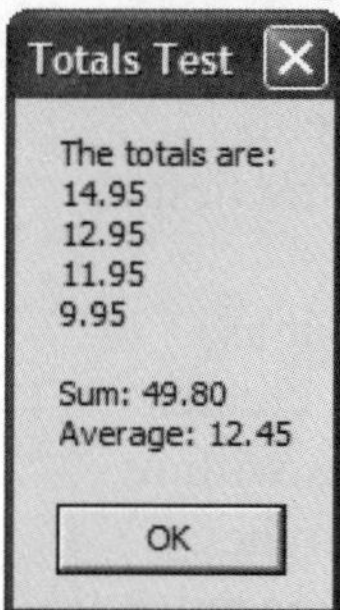

Description

- You can use a *foreach loop* to access each element of an array. You can also use foreach loops to work with collections like the ones you'll learn about later in this chapter.

How to work with rectangular arrays

So far, this chapter has shown how to use an array that uses one index to store elements in a one-dimensional array. Now, you'll learn how to work with rectangular arrays that use two indexes. You can think of a *rectangular array* as a table that has rows and columns. Since rectangular arrays store data in two dimensions, they're also known as *two-dimensional arrays*.

Although it's possible to create arrays that contain more than two dimensions, that's rarely necessary. However, if you do need to use an array that has three or more dimensions, you can extend the two-dimensional techniques that you'll learn next.

How to create a rectangular array

Figure 8-5 shows how to create a rectangular array. To do that, you code a comma within the set of brackets that follows the data type declaration. This indicates that the array will have two dimensions. Then, when you use the new keyword to create the array, you specify the number of rows in the array, followed by a comma, followed by the number of columns in the array.

The first statement in this figure creates a rectangular array of integers. In this case, the array has three rows and two columns. After this statement executes, each element in the array will be assigned the default value of 0 as described in figure 8-1.

How to assign values to a rectangular array

After you create an array, you can assign values to it. To do that, you refer to each element of the array using its row and column index. This is illustrated by the table of index values shown in figure 8-5. Because this array consists of four rows and four columns, the index values range from 0,0 to 3,3.

To assign values to the elements of a rectangular array, you can code one statement for each element as shown in the first example. These statements assign values to the elements of the numbers array that was created by the first statement in this figure.

You can also assign values to a rectangular array when you declare it as illustrated by the second and third examples. Here, the second example creates the numbers array and assigns values to it by coding three sets of braces within an outer set of braces. The three inner braces represent the three rows in the array, and the values in these braces are assigned to the two columns in each row. The third example works the same except that it uses string objects instead of int values.

How to create a rectangular array

The syntax for creating a rectangular array

```
type[,] arrayName = new type[rowCount,columnCount];
```

A statement that creates a 3x2 array

```
int[,] numbers = new int[3,2];
```

How to assign values to a rectangular array

The syntax for referring to an element of a rectangular array

```
arrayName[rowIndex, columnIndex]
```

The index values for the elements of a 4x4 rectangular array

```
0,0    0,1    0,2    0,3
1,0    1,1    1,2    1,3
2,0    2,1    2,2    2,3
3,0    3,1    3,2    3,3
```

Code that assigns values to the numbers array

```
numbers[0,0] = 1;
numbers[0,1] = 2;
numbers[1,0] = 3;
numbers[1,1] = 4;
numbers[2,0] = 5;
numbers[2,1] = 6;
```

Code that creates a 3x2 array and assigns values with one statement

```
int[,] numbers = { {1,2}, {3,4}, {5,6} };
```

Code that creates and assigns values to a 3x2 array of strings

```
string[,] products = { {"CS08", "Murach's C# 2008"},
                       {"JSE6", "Murach's Java SE 6"},
                       {"A3CS", "Murach's ASP.NET 3.5 with C# 2008"} };
```

Description

- A *rectangular array* uses two indexes to store data. You can think of this type of array as a table that has rows and columns. Rectangular arrays are sometimes referred to as *two-dimensional arrays*.
- Although it's rarely necessary, you can extend this two-dimensional syntax to work with arrays that have more than two dimensions.

Figure 8-5 How to create a rectangular array and assign values to its elements

How to work with rectangular arrays

Figure 8-6 presents some examples that show how to work with rectangular arrays. The first example shows how to use the GetLength method to get the number of elements in a dimension of an array. Here, the first statement gets the number of rows in the numbers array by calling the GetLength method and specifying 0 to get the length of the first dimension. Then, the second statement gets the number of columns in the array by calling the GetLength method and specifying 1 to get the length of the second dimension. Finally, the third statement uses indexes to get the values from both of the elements in the first row of the array and add them together.

The second example shows how to use nested for loops to display the elements of a rectangular array in a message box. In this case, the elements of the numbers array you saw in figure 8-5 are displayed. As you can see, the outer for loop uses a counter variable to cycle through the rows in the array. To determine the number of rows in the array, this loop uses the GetLength method. Then, the inner for loop uses another counter variable to cycle through each column of each row in the array. Just like the outer for loop, the inner for loop uses the GetLength method to determine the number of columns in the array.

To display the value of each element, the statement within the inner for loop uses both counter variables to get the value of the element and append it to a string. Each element is also separated from the next element by a space. Then, after each row is processed by the inner loop, a new line character is appended to the string so the elements in each row will appear on a separate line. When the outer loop ends, the string is displayed in a message box as shown in this figure.

The third example is similar, except that it displays the array of products you saw in figure 8-5. If you compare this code with the code in the second example, you'll see the only difference is that the elements in the two columns are separated by tab characters so that they're aligned as shown here.

The syntax for using the GetLength method of a rectangular array

```
arrayName.GetLength(dimensionIndex)
```

Code that works with the numbers array

```
int numberOfRows = numbers.GetLength(0);
int numberOfColumns = numbers.GetLength(1);
int sumOfFirstRow = numbers[0,0] + numbers[0,1];
```

Code that displays the numbers array in a message box

```
string numbersString = "";
for (int i = 0; i < numbers.GetLength(0); i++)
{
    for (int j = 0; j < numbers.GetLength(1); j++)
        numbersString += numbers[i,j] + " ";

    numbersString += "\n";
}
MessageBox.Show(numbersString, "Numbers Test");
```

The message box that's displayed

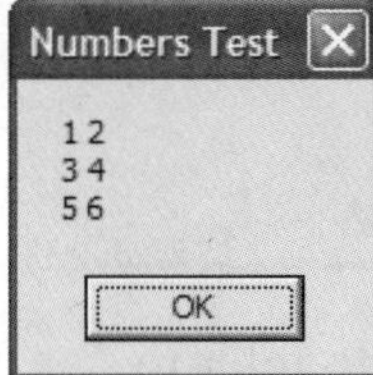

Code that displays the products array in a message box

```
string productsString = "";
for (int i = 0; i < products.GetLength(0); i++)
{
    for (int j = 0; j < products.GetLength(1); j++)
        productsString += products[i,j] + "\t";

    productsString += "\n";
}
MessageBox.Show(productsString, "Products Test");
```

The message box that's displayed

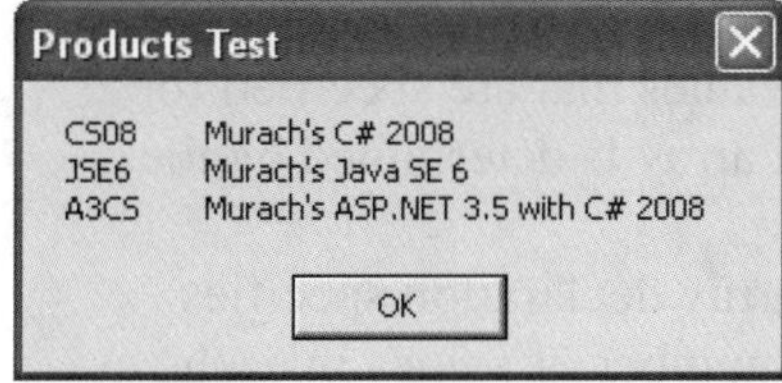

Description

- You use the GetLength method to get the number of rows or columns in a rectangular array. To get the number of rows, specify 0 for the dimensionIndex argument. To get the number of columns, specify 1 for this argument.
- You use nested for loops to iterate through the rows and columns of a rectangular array.

Figure 8-6 How to work with rectangular arrays

How to work with jagged arrays

Jagged arrays let you store data in a table that can have rows of unequal lengths. Since each row in a jagged array is stored as a separate array, a jagged array is also known as an *array of arrays*.

How to create a jagged array

Figure 8-7 shows how to create a jagged array. To start, you code the data type followed by two sets of brackets. This indicates that each row of the array will contain another array. Then, when you use the new keyword to create the jagged array, you specify the number of rows that the array will contain. For example, the first statement in the first example creates a jagged array named numbers that contains three rows. Finally, when you declare the array for each row, you specify the number of columns in that row. The first row of the numbers array, for example, has three columns, the second row has four columns, and the third row has two columns.

How to assign values to a jagged array

Once you create a jagged array, you use row and column indexes to refer to the elements in the array just as you do for a rectangular array. When you refer to an element in a jagged array, however, you code each index within a separate set of brackets as illustrated in figure 8-7. To assign values to the numbers array, for example, you can use the statements shown in the second example in this figure.

You can also create a jagged array and assign values to its elements in one statement. The third and fourth examples illustrate how this works. The third example creates the same array as the first example. Here, you can see that a set of braces is used to enclose a list of array declarations. Each declaration in this list defines an array for one row in the jagged array. Notice in this example that the declarations don't specify the number of columns in each row. Instead, the number of columns is determined by the number of values that are specified for that row. Similarly, the number of rows in the jagged array is determined by the number of arrays in the list of arrays.

The fourth example is similar, except that each array declaration specifies the number of columns in the array. In that case, the number of values in each list of values must match the number you specify.

How to create a jagged array

The syntax for creating a jagged array

```
type[][] arrayName = new type[rowCount][];
```

Code that creates a jagged array with three rows of different lengths

```
int[][] numbers = new int[3][];    // the number of rows
numbers[0] = new int[3];           // the number of columns for row 1
numbers[1] = new int[4];           // the number of columns for row 2
numbers[2] = new int[2];           // the number of columns for row 3
```

How to refer to the elements of a jagged array

The syntax for referring to an element of a jagged array

```
arrayName[rowIndex][columnIndex]
```

The index values for the elements of a jagged array

```
0,0    0,1    0,2
1,0    1,1    1,2    1,3
2,0    2,1
```

Code that assigns values to the numbers array

```
numbers[0][0] = 1;
numbers[0][1] = 2;
numbers[0][2] = 3;
numbers[1][0] = 4;
numbers[1][1] = 5;
numbers[1][2] = 6;
numbers[1][3] = 7;
numbers[2][0] = 8;
numbers[2][1] = 9;
```

Code that creates the numbers array with one statement

```
int[][] numbers = { new int [] {1, 2, 3},
                    new int [] {4, 5, 6, 7},
                    new int [] {8, 9} };
```

Code that creates a jagged array of strings

```
string[][] titles = {
   new string [3] {"War and Peace", "Wuthering Heights", "1984"},
   new string [4] {"Casablanca", "Wizard of Oz", "Star Wars", "Birdy"},
   new string [2] {"Blue Suede Shoes", "Yellow Submarine"} };
```

Description

- You can use a *jagged array* to store data in a table that has rows of unequal lengths. Each row in a jagged array is stored as a separate array. Because of that, a jagged array is also known as an *array of arrays*.
- If you don't assign values to the elements of a jagged array when you declare the array, the declaration statement must specify the number of rows in the array. Then, you must declare the number of columns in each row before you assign values to the elements in that row.
- To assign values to the elements of a jagged array when you declare the array, you create a list of arrays that defines one array for each row. Then, the jagged array is created with one row for each array in that list.

Figure 8-7 How to create a jagged array and assign values to its elements

How to work with jagged arrays

Figure 8-8 shows how to work with jagged arrays. Since the examples in this figure are similar to the examples for working with rectangular arrays shown in figure 8-6, you shouldn't have much trouble understanding how they work. However, you should notice two differences in these examples.

First, two sets of brackets are used within the inner for loop to refer to each element in the array. Second, the inner loop uses the Length property to get the number of columns in each row. That makes sense if you remember that each row in a jagged array is an array. You must use the Length property because each row can have a different length. As a result, you can't use the GetLength method to return the number of columns in a row as you do with rectangular arrays.

Code that displays the numbers array in a message box

```
string numbersString = "";
for (int i = 0; i < numbers.GetLength(0); i++)
{
    for (int j = 0; j < numbers[i].Length; j++)
        numbersString += numbers[i][j] + " ";
    numbersString += "\n";
}
MessageBox.Show(numbersString, "Jagged Numbers Test");
```

The message box that's displayed

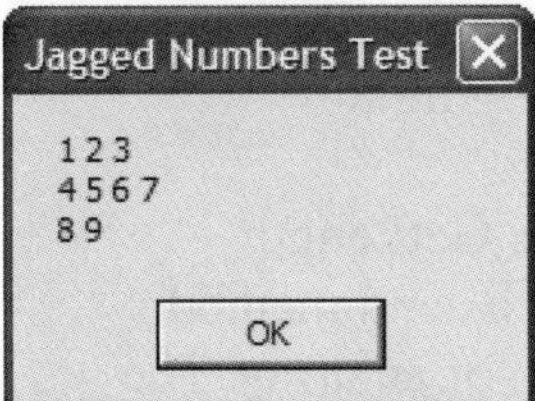

Code that displays the titles array in a message box

```
string titlesString = "";
for (int i = 0; i < titles.GetLength(0); i++)
{
    for (int j = 0; j < titles[i].Length; j++)
        titlesString += titles[i][j] + "|";

    titlesString += "\n";
}
MessageBox.Show(titlesString, "Jagged Titles Test");
```

The message box that's displayed

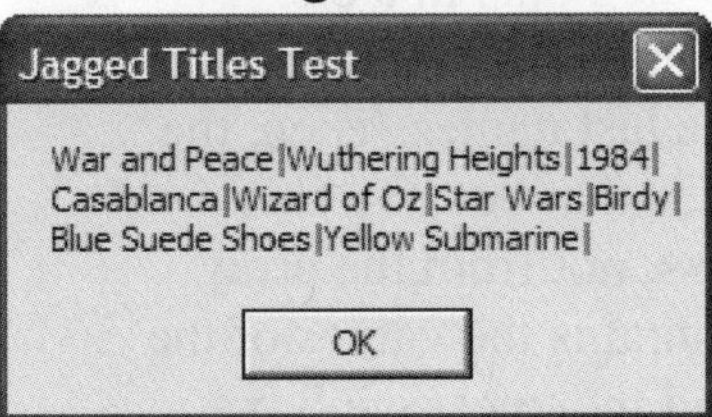

Description

- Since the number of columns in each row of a jagged array varies, you can't use the GetLength method to get the length of a row. Instead, you have to use the Length property of the array for that row.

More skills for working with arrays

Now that you know how to work with one-dimensional, rectangular, and jagged arrays, you're ready to learn some additional skills for working with arrays.

How to use the Array class

Because an array is actually an instance of the Array class, you can use the properties and methods of this class to work with your arrays. Figure 8-9 presents the properties and methods you're most likely to use.

You've already seen how to use the Length property and the GetLength method. Another property you may want to use is the GetUpperBound method, which returns the index of the last element in a given dimension of an array. The first example in this figure illustrates the difference between the GetLength and GetUpperBound methods. Here, you can see that the GetLength method returns a value of 4 for a one-dimensional array that contains four elements. In contrast, the GetUpperBound method returns a value of 3 because the four elements are referred to with the index values of 0 through 3.

Although values have been assigned to the elements of the array that's used in this example, you should realize that the GetLength and GetUpperBound methods return the same values whether or not values have been assigned to the array. In other words, these methods depend only on the number of elements that were declared for the array. That's true of the Length property as well.

The Sort method of the Array class lets you sort the elements in a one-dimensional array. This is illustrated by the second example in this figure. Here, the first statement declares an array that consists of three last names. Then, the Sort method is used to sort the names in that array. Notice that because this method is a static method, it's called from the Array class, not from the array itself. After the array is sorted, a string is created that contains the values of the elements in ascending order. Then, the string is displayed in a message box.

The third example shows how you can use the BinarySearch method to locate a value in a one-dimensional array. This code uses the BinarySearch method to get the index of the specified employee in an employees array. Then, this index is used to get the corresponding sales amount from a salesAmounts array.

For the BinarySearch method to work properly, the array must be sorted in ascending sequence. If it's not, this method usually won't be able to find the specified value, even if it exists in the array. When the BinarySearch method can't find the specified value, it returns a value of -1. Then, if you try to use this value to access an element of an array, an IndexOutOfRangeException will be thrown.

Common properties and methods of the Array class

Property	Description
`Length`	Gets the number of elements in all of the dimensions of an array.
Instance method	**Description**
`GetLength(dimension)`	Gets the number of elements in the specified dimension of an array.
`GetUpperBound(dimension)`	Gets the index of the last element in the specified dimension of an array.
Static method	**Description**
`Copy(array1, array2, length)`	Copies some or all of the values in one array to another array. For more information, see figure 8-10.
`BinarySearch(array, value)`	Searches a one-dimensional array that's in ascending order for an element with a specified value and returns the index for that element.
`Sort(array)`	Sorts the elements in a one-dimensional array into ascending order.

Code that uses the GetLength and GetUpperBound methods

```
int[] numbers = new int[4] {1, 2, 3, 4};
int length = numbers.GetLength(0);                    // length = 4
int upperBound = numbers.GetUpperBound(0);            // upperBound = 3
```

Code that uses the Sort method

```
string[] lastNames = {"Boehm", "Taylor", "Murach"};
Array.Sort(lastNames);
string message = "";
foreach (string lastName in lastNames)
    message += lastName + "\n";
MessageBox.Show(message, "Sorted Last Names");
```

The message box that's displayed

Code that uses the BinarySearch method

```
string[] employees = {"AdamsA", "FinkleP", "LewisJ", "PotterE"};
decimal[] salesAmounts = {3275.68m, 4298.55m, 5289.57m, 1933.98m};
int index = Array.BinarySearch(employees, "FinkleP");
decimal salesAmount = salesAmounts[index];            // salesAmount = 4298.55
```

Note

- The BinarySearch method only works on arrays whose elements are in ascending order. If the array isn't in ascending order, you must use the Sort method to sort the array before using the BinarySearch method.

How to refer to and copy arrays

Because arrays are created from a class, they are reference types. That means that an array variable contains a reference to an array object and not the actual values in the array. Because of that, you can use two or more variables to refer to the same array. This is illustrated in the first example in figure 8-10.

The first statement in this example declares an array variable named inches1, creates an array with three elements, and assigns values to those elements. Then, the second statement declares another array variable named inches2 and assigns the value of the inches1 variable to it. Because the inches1 variable contains a reference to the array, that means that the inches2 variable now contains a reference to the same array. As a result, if you use the inches2 variable to change any of the elements in the array as shown in the third statement, those changes will be reflected if you use the inches1 variable to refer to the array.

Once you declare the length of an array, it can't grow or shrink. In other words, arrays are *immutable*. However, you can use an existing array variable to refer to another array with a larger or smaller number of elements. To do that, you simply create the new array and assign it to the existing variable as shown in the second example in this figure. Here, an array that contains 20 elements is assigned to the inches1 variable, which originally contained only three elements. Note that when this statement is executed, the original array is discarded unless another array variable refers to it. In this case, the inches2 variable refers to the original array, so the array is maintained.

If you want to create a copy of an array, you can use the Copy method of the Array class as shown in this figure. Then, each array variable will point to its own copy of the elements of the array, and any changes that are made to one array won't affect the other array.

You can use two techniques to copy the elements of an array. First, you can copy one or more elements of the array starting with the first element by specifying the source array, the target array, and the number of elements to be copied. This is illustrated by the third example in this figure. Here, all of the elements of an array named inches are copied to an array named centimeters. Notice that the Length property of the inches array is used to specify the number of elements to be copied.

You can also copy one or more elements of an array starting with an element other than the first. To do that, you specify the index of the first element you want to copy. In addition, you specify the index of the element in the target array where you want to store the first element from the source array.

This is illustrated in the last example in this figure. Here, the first statement creates an array that contains three string values, and the second statement creates an array that can hold two string values. Then, the third statement copies the second and third strings from the first array into the second array. To do that, the first two arguments specify the source array and a starting index of 1 (the second element). Then, the next two arguments specify the target array and a starting index of 0 (the first element). Finally, the last argument specifies that two elements should be copied.

Code that creates a reference to another array

```
double[] inches1 = new double[3] {1,2,3};
double[] inches2 = inches1;
inches2[2] = 4;      // changes the third element
```

Code that reuses an array variable

```
inches1 = new double[20];   // make a new array with 20 elements
```

How to copy elements of one array to another array

The syntax for copying elements of an array

```
Array.Copy(fromArray, toArray, length);
```

Another way to copy elements from one array to another

```
Array.Copy(fromArray, fromIndex, toArray, toIndex, length);
```

Code that copies all the elements of an array

```
double[] inches = new double[3] {1,2,3};
double[] centimeters = new double[3];
Array.Copy(inches, centimeters, inches.Length);
for (int i = 0; i < centimeters.Length; i++)
    centimeters[i] *= 2.54;    // set the new values for this array
```

Code that copies some of the elements of an array

```
string[] names = {"Vasquez", "Murach", "Boehm"};
string[] lastTwoNames = new string[2];
Array.Copy(names, 1, lastTwoNames, 0, 2);
```

Description

- An array is a reference type, which means that an array variable contains a reference to an array object. To create another reference to an existing array, you assign the array to another array variable. Then, both array variables point to the same array in memory.
- To reuse an array variable so it refers to an array with a larger or smaller number of elements, you create a new array and assign it to that variable. When you do, the original array is discarded unless another array variable refers to it.
- To copy the elements of one array to another array, you use the Copy method of the Array class.
- To copy a specified number of elements from an array beginning with the first element, you can use the first syntax shown above. Then, you use the length argument to specify the number of elements to copy.
- To specify the first element in an array that you want to copy, you use the second syntax shown above. Then, the fromIndex argument specifies the index of the first element that's copied, the toIndex argument specifies the index where the first element is copied to, and the length argument specifies the number of elements that are copied.
- When you copy an array, the target array must be the same type as the sending array and it must be large enough to receive all of the elements that are copied to it.

Figure 8-10 How to refer to and copy arrays

How to code methods that work with arrays

Figure 8-11 presents the techniques you can use to code methods that return and accept arrays. To return an array from a method, you follow the return type for the method with brackets as shown in the first example. Then, you define an array within the code for the method and use the return statement to return that array.

To call a method that returns an array, you use the same techniques that you use for calling any other method. In this figure, the statement that calls the GetRateArray method declares an array variable and assigns the return value of the method to this variable. In this case, the method requires an argument that supplies the number of elements that the array should contain.

The second example shows how to code a method that accepts an array as an argument. To do that, you follow the data type of the parameter that accepts the argument with brackets to indicate that it's an array. Then, within the method, you can use all the techniques that you've learned for working with arrays to work with this parameter. In this case, a method named ToCentimeters is used to convert the inch measurements in an array to centimeters.

To call a method that's defined with an array parameter, you just pass an array argument as shown here. Note, however, that unlike other arguments, arrays are automatically passed by reference. As a result, any changes that you make to the values stored in the array parameter will be reflected in any array variables in the calling method that refer to the array. In this figure, for example, the values in the measurements array are updated after the ToCentimeters method is called.

The third example shows how to use the params keyword with an array parameter. When you use this keyword, the statement that calls the method can pass an array to the method, or it can pass a list of values. This is illustrated in the third example in this figure. Here, the statement that calls the method passes three values, which are then stored in the array parameter. Then, after these values are converted to centimeters, the array is passed back to the calling method.

Because the ToCentimeters method that uses the params keyword can accept either an array or a list of values, it's more flexible than the first ToCentimeters method. However, you should be aware of some restrictions when you use the params keyword. First, you can only use this keyword on one parameter within a method. Second, if a method is defined with two or more parameters, this keyword must be coded on the last parameter.

How to return an array from a method

The code for a method that returns an array

```
private decimal[] GetRateArray(int elementCount)
{
    decimal[] rates = new decimal[elementCount];
    for (int i = 0; i < rates.Length; i++)
        rates[i] = (decimal) (i + 1) / 100;
    return rates;
}
```

A statement that calls the method

```
decimal[] rates = this.GetRateArray(4);
```

How to code a method that accepts an array argument

A method that converts inches to centimeters

```
private void ToCentimeters(double[] measurements)
{
    for (int i = 0; i < measurements.Length; i++)
        measurements[i] *= 2.54;
}
```

Statements that declare the array and call the method

```
double[] measurements = {1,2,3};
this.ToCentimeters(measurements);
```

How to code a method that uses the params keyword

A method that converts inches to centimeters

```
private double[] ToCentimeters(params double[] measurements)
{
    for (int i = 0; i < measurements.Length; i++)
        measurements[i] *= 2.54;
    return measurements;
}
```

A statement that calls the method

```
double[] measurements = this.ToCentimeters(1,2,3);
```

Description

- To return an array from a method, you code a set of brackets after the return type declaration to indicate that the return type is an array.
- To accept an array as a parameter of a method, you code a set of brackets after the parameter type to indicate that the parameter is an array. By default, arrays are passed by reference.
- If you want to pass two or more arguments that haven't been grouped in an array to a method and have the method store the values in an array, you can include the *params* keyword on the parameter declaration. You code this keyword before the array type and name, you can code it on a single parameter, and you must code it on the last parameter.

Figure 8-11 How to code methods that work with arrays

How to work with collections

Like an array, a *collection* can hold one or more elements. Unlike arrays, collections don't have a fixed size. Instead, the size of a collection is increased automatically when elements are added to it. In addition, most types of collections provide methods you can use to change the capacity of a collection. In other words, collections are *mutable*. As a result, collections are usually more appropriate and can usually manage system resources better than arrays when you need to work with a varying number of elements.

In the topics that follow, you'll learn how to use four types of collections: lists, sorted lists, queues, and stacks. Although the .NET Framework provides for other collections, these are the ones you'll use most often.

Commonly used collection classes

Prior to .NET 2.0, the collection classes in the .NET Framework could store any type of object. As a result, the collections created from these classes are sometimes referred to as *untyped collections*. In fact, you can store different types of objects in the same collection, even though that's usually not a good idea. However, if you accidentally write code that adds the wrong type of object to an untyped collection, it will result in an error that won't be discovered until you run the application.

That's why the collection classes in the .NET 2.0 Framework use a feature known as *generics* to allow you to create *typed collections*. With a typed collection, you specify the data type in angle brackets (<>) after the name of the collection class. Then, you can only store objects of the specified data type in that collection, and any errors will be discovered when you attempt to compile the application.

Figure 8-12 shows four of the most commonly used typed collections that were introduced with .NET 2.0. The classes for these collections are stored in the System.Collections.Generic namespace.

In addition, this figure shows the four corresponding untyped collections that were commonly used prior to .NET 2.0. The classes for these collections are stored in the System.Collections namespace and are included in the .NET 2.0 Framework. As a result, they're still available to C# 2008 applications. (Remember that the .NET 2.0 Framework is a subset of the .NET 3.0 Framework, and the .NET 3.0 Framework is a subset of the .NET 3.5 Framework. So these collections are available when you use the .NET 3.0 or 3.5 Framework as well.)

As you'll see in the next figure, typed collections have several advantages over untyped collections. As a result, you'll typically want to use typed collections for most new development. However, you may need to use untyped collections when working with legacy applications.

How arrays and collections are similar

- Both can store multiple elements, which can be value types or reference types.

How arrays and collections are different

- An array is a feature of the C# language. Collections are classes in the .NET Framework.
- Collection classes provide methods to perform operations that arrays don't provide.
- Arrays are fixed in size. Collections are variable in size.

Commonly used collection classes

.NET 2.0 to 3.5	.NET 1.x	Description
List<T>	ArrayList	Uses an index to access each element. Is very efficient for accessing elements sequentially. Can be inefficient when inserting elements in the middle of a list.
SortedList<K, V>	SortedList	Uses a key to access a value, which can be any type of object. Can be inefficient for accessing elements sequentially. Is very efficient for inserting elements into the middle of a list.
Queue<T>	Queue	Uses methods to add and remove elements.
Stack<T>	Stack	Uses methods to add and remove elements.

Description

- A *collection* is an object that can hold one or more *elements*.
- The collection classes in the System.Collections.Generic namespace use a feature known as *generics* to allow you to create *typed collections* that can only store the specified data type. With a typed collection, you specify the data type in angle brackets (<>) after the name of the collection class.
- The collection classes in the System.Collections namespace allow you to create *untyped collections*. With an untyped collection, you can store any type of object in the collection.

Figure 8-12 Commonly used collection classes

Typed vs. untyped collections

Figure 8-13 shows the differences between typed and untyped collections. In particular, it shows that typed collections have two advantages over untyped collections. First, they check the type of each element at compile-time and thus prevent runtime errors from occuring. Second, they reduce the amount of casting that's needed when retrieving objects.

The first example shows how to use the ArrayList class from the System.Collections namespace to create an untyped collection. To start, the statement that creates the ArrayList object doesn't specify a data type. As a result, the Add method can be used to add elements of any type to the collection. In this figure, for example, the code adds two int types and a string type to the collection. This is possible because each element in the array is stored as an object type.

Once the elements have been added to the untyped list, a for loop is used to calculate the sum of the elements. To accomplish this, the first statement in the loop casts each element to the int type. This is necessary, because each element is an object data type. However, since a string type has been added to the collection, this will cause a runtime error when the loop reaches the string type.

The second example shows how to use the new List<> class from the System.Collections.Generic namespace to create a typed collection. To start, the statement that creates the list uses angle brackets (<>) to specify the int type. As a result, the Add method can only be used to add int values to the collection. In this figure, for example, the code adds two int types to the collection. If you tried to add another type such as a string type to the collection, you would get a compile-time error.

Once the elements have been added to the typed list, a for loop is used to calculate the sum of the elements. To accomplish this, the first statement in the loop retrieves each element and stores it in an int variable. Since this is a typed collection, no casting is necessary.

Since typed collections have several advantages over untyped collections, Visual Studio includes the *using statement* for the System.Collections.Generic namespace in most new applications. That way, by default, you will usually work with typed collections such as the four typed collections described in the previous figure. However, if you're upgrading a .NET 1.x application, the using statement will probably refer to the System.Collections namespace. In that case, you'll be working with untyped collections such as the four untyped collections described in the previous figure.

If you want to switch from untyped to typed collections or vice versa, you can begin by editing the using statement so it refers to the correct namespace. Then, you can edit the statements that work with the collection. That usually means editing the statement that creates the collection, and adding or removing any casting as necessary.

Untyped collections

The using statement

```
using System.Collections;
```

An example

```
ArrayList numbers = new ArrayList();
numbers.Add(3);
numbers.Add(7);
numbers.Add("Test");    // will compile - causes runtime error
int sum = 0;
for (int i = 0; i < numbers.Count; i++)
{
    int number = (int)numbers[i];  // cast is required
    sum += number;
}
```

Typed collections

The using statement

```
using System.Collections.Generic;
```

An example

```
List<int> numbers = new List<int>();
numbers.Add(3);
numbers.Add(7);
//numbers.Add("Test");    // won't compile - prevents runtime error
int sum = 0;
for (int i = 0; i < numbers.Count; i++)
{
    int number = numbers[i];  // no cast needed
    sum += number;
}
```

Description

- Typed collections have two advantages over untyped collections. First, they check the type of each element at compile-time and prevent runtime errors from occuring. Second, they reduce the amount of casting that's needed when retrieving objects.
- If you want to use untyped collections, you can edit the *using statement* so it refers to the System.Collections namespace instead of the System.Collections.Generic namespace that's often included by default in new applications. Then, you need to make sure to cast the elements to the appropriate type when you retrieve them from the collection.

Figure 8-13 Typed vs. untyped collections

How to work with a list

Now that you understand the difference between typed and untyped collections, you're ready to learn how to use the List<> class to create and work with a *list*, the most common of the typed collections. To create a list, you use the new keyword to create an object from the List<> class as shown in part 1 of figure 8-14. When you do this, you must specify the data type for each element within angle brackets (<>) immediately after the class name. In this figure, for example, the first example specifies the string type, and the second example specifies the decimal type. However, you could also specify any other data types from the .NET framework (such as DateTime types) or custom data types (such as a Product type like the one you'll learn about in chapter 12).

When you create a list, you can specify its initial capacity by coding it within parentheses after the class name. In this figure, for example, the third statement sets the initial capacity to 3. If you omit the initial capacity, though, it's set to 16 as illustrated by the first two statements.

Part 1 of figure 8-14 also lists some common properties and methods of the List<> class. You'll see how to use some of these properties and methods in part 2 of this figure. For now, you should notice that some of these properties and methods provide functions that aren't available with arrays. For example, you can use the Insert method to insert an element into the middle of a list, and you can use the RemoveAt method to remove an element from a list.

You should also realize that when you use the Add or Insert method to add elements to a list, the capacity of the list is doubled each time its capacity is exceeded. This is illustrated by the last eight statements in part 1 of this figure. Each of these statements adds another element to the lastNames array that was created with an initial capacity of three elements. Then, when the fourth element is added, the capacity is increased to six elements. Similarly, when you add the seventh element, the capacity is doubled again to 12.

A statement that creates a list of string elements

```
List<string> titles = new List<string>();
```

A statement that creates a list of decimal elements

```
List<decimal> prices = new List<decimal>();
```

A statement that creates a list of strings with a capacity of 3

```
List<string> lastNames = new List<string>(3);
```

Common properties and methods of the List<> class

Indexer	Description
[index]	Gets or sets the element at the specified index. The index for the first item in a list is 0.
Property	**Description**
Capacity	Gets or sets the number of elements the list can hold.
Count	Gets the number of elements in the list.
Method	**Description**
Add(object)	Adds an element to the end of a list and returns the element's index.
Clear()	Removes all elements from the list and sets its Count property to zero.
Contains(object)	Returns a Boolean value that indicates if the list contains the specified object.
Insert(index, object)	Inserts an element into a list at the specified index.
Remove(object)	Removes the first occurrence of the specified object from the list.
RemoveAt(index)	Removes the element at the specified index of a list.
BinarySearch(object)	Searches a list for a specified object and returns the index for that object.
Sort()	Sorts the elements in a list into ascending order.

Code that causes the size of the list of names to be increased

```
List<string> lastNames = new List<string>(3);
lastNames.Add("Boehm");
lastNames.Add("Vasquez");
lastNames.Add("Murach");
lastNames.Add("Taylor");              //Capacity is doubled to 6 elements
lastNames.Add("Holland");
lastNames.Add("Steelman");
lastNames.Add("Slivkoff");            //Capacity is doubled to 12 elements
```

Description

- A *list* is a collection that automatically adjusts its capacity to accommodate new elements.
- The default capacity of a list is 16 elements, but you can specify a different capacity when you create a list. When the number of elements in a list exceeds its capacity, the capacity is automatically doubled.
- The List<> class is in the System.Collections.Generic namespace.

Figure 8-14 How to work with a list (part 1 of 2)

Part 2 of figure 8-14 shows how to use some of the methods of the List class to work with the elements in a list. Here, the first example creates a list of decimal values. Unlike the statements you saw in part 1 of this figure, this example uses a *collection initializer* to assign values to the list. When you use a collection initializer, you don't have to use the Add method to add elements to the list. Instead, you code the elements within braces as shown here.

The second example shows how to use an index to refer to an element in a list. The syntax for doing that is the same as the syntax for referring to an element in an array. You just specify the index in square brackets after the name of the list and the element is returned.

The third example shows how to insert and remove elements from a list. Here, a new element with a decimal value of 2745.73 is inserted at the beginning of the list named salesTotals. As a result, the other four values in the list are pushed down one index. Then, the second element of the list is removed, and the other three values are moved back up one index. The final result is that the first element is replaced with a new element.

The fourth example uses a foreach loop to display the elements in the salesTotals list in a message box. As you can see, this works the same as it does for an array.

The fifth example shows how to use the Contains method to check if the salesTotals list contains an object. If it does, the Remove method is used to remove the object from the list. In this case, the object contains a decimal value of 2745.73. However, this would work regardless of the data type the object contained.

The sixth example shows how you can sort and search the elements in a list. Here, the first statement uses the Sort method to sort the elements in the salesTotals list. Then, the second statement uses the BinarySearch method to search for an element that contains a decimal value of 4398.55.

You should notice in this example that, unlike the Sort method of the Array class, the Sort method of the List<> class is an instance method. Because of that, you call it from the list object. That's true for the BinarySearch method too. Otherwise, these methods work similarly.

The syntax for retrieving a value from a list

```
listName[index]
```

Code that creates a list that holds decimal values

```
List<decimal> salesTotals = new List<decimal>
    { 3275.68m, 4398.55m, 5289.75m, 1933.98m };
```

Code that retrieves the first value from the list

```
decimal sales1 = salesTotals[0];            // sales1 = 3275.68
```

Code that inserts and removes an element from the list

```
salesTotals.Insert(0, 2745.73m);            // insert a new first element
sales1 = salesTotals[0];                    // sales1 = 2745.73
decimal sales2 = salesTotals[1];            // sales2 = 3275.68
salesTotals.RemoveAt(1);                    // remove the second element
sales2 = salesTotals[1];                    // sales2 = 4398.55
```

Code that displays the list in a message box

```
string salesTotalsString = "";
foreach (decimal d in salesTotals)
    salesTotalsString += d.ToString() + "\n";
MessageBox.Show(salesTotalsString, "Sales Totals");
```

The message box that's displayed

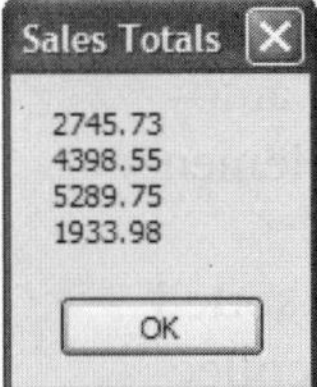

Code that checks for an element in the list and removes it if it exists

```
decimal x = 2745.73m;
if (salesTotals.Contains(x))
    salesTotals.Remove(x);
```

Code that sorts and searches the list

```
salesTotals.Sort();
int sales2Index = salesTotals.BinarySearch(sales2);
```

A message box that displays the results of the sort and search operation

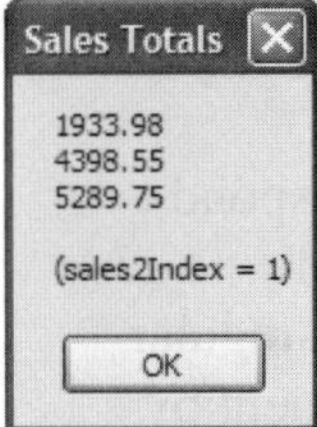

How to work with a sorted list

You can also implement a collection by using the SortedList<> class that's described in figure 8-15. Since the SortedList class exists in both the System.Collections and System.Collections.Generic namespaces, you need to make sure to code the correct using statement when working with the SortedList<> class. The examples in this figure work with the SortedList<> class from the System.Collections.Generic namespace.

A *sorted list* is useful when you need to look up values in the list based on a key value. If, for example, a sorted list consists of item numbers and unit prices, the keys are the item numbers. Then, the list can be used to look up the unit price for any item number. Each item in a sorted list is actually a KeyValuePair<> structure that consists of two properties: Key and Value. Here, the Value property can store value types or reference types.

Like a list, you can set the initial capacity of a sorted list by specifying the number of elements in parentheses when the list is created. Then, if the number of elements in the list exceeds the capacity as the program executes, the capacity is automatically doubled.

The first example in this figure shows one way to create and load a sorted list. When you add an element to a sorted list, you specify the key along with the value associated with that key. In this example, the keys are the names of employees, and the values are the sales totals for those employees. Note that although the keys in this list are added in alphabetical order, a sorted list automatically sorts itself by key values regardless of the order in which the elements are added.

The second example shows another way to create and load the same sorted list. Here, instead of using the Add method to add elements to the list, a collection initializer is used. Notice that because each element of a sorted list consists of two values, each element is enclosed in braces within the outer braces.

The third example shows how to look up a value in a sorted list based on a key. Here, a value of "LewisJ" is specified as the key for the element. As a result, this key returns a decimal value of 5289.75.

The fourth example creates a string that contains the keys and values in a sorted list. To start, it declares and initializes the string. Then, it uses a foreach loop to retrieve each KeyValuePair value in the sorted list. Within the foreach loop, it uses the Key and Value properties of the KeyValuePair structure to access each element's key and value. In this example, a tab character is placed between the key and the value and a new line character is placed after the key/value pair.

Since a sorted list makes it easy to look up a key and return its corresponding value, it's the ideal collection to use when you need to do this type of lookup. It would be much more difficult to perform the same task with a regular list. However, a regular list works fine when you need to look up an element by an index.

Common properties and methods of the SortedList<> class

Indexer	Description
[key]	Gets or sets the value of the element with the specified key.
Property	**Description**
Keys	Gets a collection that contains the keys in the list.
Values	Gets a collection that contains the values in the list.
Capacity	Gets or sets the number of elements the list can hold.
Count	Gets the number of elements in the list.
Method	**Description**
Add(key, value)	Adds an element with the specified key and value to the sorted list.
Clear()	Removes all elements from the sorted list.
ContainsKey(key)	Returns a Boolean value that indicates whether or not the sorted list contains the specified key.
ContainsValue(value)	Returns a Boolean value that indicates whether or not the sorted list contains the specified value.
Remove(key)	Removes the element with the specified key from the sorted list.
RemoveAt(index)	Removes the element at the specified index from the sorted list.

Properties of the KeyValuePair<K, V> structure

Property	Description
Key	The key for the SortedList item.
Value	The value associated with the key.

Code that creates and loads a sorted list

```
SortedList<string, decimal> salesList = new SortedList<string, decimal>(4);
salesList.Add("AdamsA", 3275.68m);
salesList.Add("FinkleP", 4398.55m);
salesList.Add("LewisJ", 5289.75m);
salesList.Add("PotterE", 1933.98m);
```

Another way to create and load the sorted list

```
SortedList<string, decimal> salesList = new SortedList<string, decimal>
    { { "AdamsA", 3275.68m }, { "FinkleP", 4398.55m },
      { "LewisJ", 5289.75m }, { "PotterE", 1933.98m } };
```

Code that looks up a value in the sorted list based on a key

```
string employeeKey = "LewisJ";
decimal salesTotal = salesList[employeeKey];
```

Code that converts the sorted list to a tab-delimited string

```
string salesTableString = "";
foreach (KeyValuePair<string, decimal> employeeSalesEntry in salesList)
{
    salesTableString += employeeSalesEntry.Key + "\t"
                      + employeeSalesEntry.Value + "\n";
}
MessageBox.Show(salesTableString, "Employee Sales Totals");
```

Figure 8-15 How to work with a sorted list

How to work with queues and stacks

Figure 8-16 shows the properties and methods of the Queue<> and Stack<> classes that you can use to create queues and stacks. Like the SortedList class, both of these classes come in typed and untyped varieties. As a result, you need to make sure to specify the correct namespace when using these classes. In this figure, the examples use the System.Collections.Generic namespace.

Unlike other collections, queues and stacks do not use the Add method to add items or an index to retrieve items. Instead, queues use the Enqueue and Dequeue methods to add and retrieve items, and stacks use the Push and Pop methods. This also means that you can't use collection initializers with stacks and queues. That's because collection initializers are implemented using the Add method.

You can think of a *queue* (pronounced cue) as a line of items waiting to be processed. When you use the Enqueue method to add an item to the queue, the item is placed at the end of the queue. When you use the Dequeue method to retrieve an item from the queue, the item is taken from the front of the queue. Because items are retrieved from a queue in the same order in which they were added, a queue can be referred to as a *first-in, first-out* (*FIFO*) collection.

In contrast, a *stack* is a *last-in, first-out* (*LIFO*) collection. When you use the Push method to place an item on a stack, that item is placed on the top of the stack. If you then push another item onto the stack, the new item is placed on the top of the stack and the item that was previously on the top of the stack moves to second from the top. In contrast, the Pop method retrieves the top item and removes it, so the item that was second from the top moves to the top position. If it helps you, you can think of a stack as a stack of dishes. The last dish that you put on the stack is also the first dish that you take off the stack.

The two examples in this figure illustrate the differences between queues and stacks. Each example begins by defining a new queue or stack, and then adding three names. Next, a while loop is used to build a string that contains the names in the order that they are retrieved from the queue or stack, and the resulting list is displayed in a message box. If you compare the message boxes for these examples, you can see that the queue names are displayed in the same order that they were added to the queue. But in the stack example, the names are retrieved in the opposite order.

In both examples, the while loop repeats as long as the Count property is greater than zero. This works because the Dequeue and Pop methods remove the item from the queue or stack, so the Count property is automatically decreased by one each time through the loop. When all of the items have been read from the queue or stack, the Count property reaches zero and the while loop terminates.

Compared to lists, queues and stacks don't provide as many properties and methods. However, if you need to implement a strictly FIFO or LIFO collection, you won't need any of those extra properties and methods. In that case, it makes sense to use a queue or stack as described in this figure.

Properties and methods of the Queue<> class

Property	Description
`Count`	Gets the number of items in the queue.
Method	**Description**
`Enqueue(object)`	Adds the specified object to the end of the queue.
`Dequeue()`	Gets the object at the front of the queue and removes it from the queue.
`Clear()`	Removes all items from the queue.
`Peek()`	Retrieves the next item in the queue without deleting it.

Code that uses a queue

```
Queue<string> nameQueue = new Queue<string>();
nameQueue.Enqueue("Boehm");
nameQueue.Enqueue("Vasquez");
nameQueue.Enqueue("Murach");
string nameQueueString = "";
while (nameQueue.Count > 0)
    nameQueueString += nameQueue.Dequeue() + "\n";
MessageBox.Show(nameQueueString, "Queue");
```

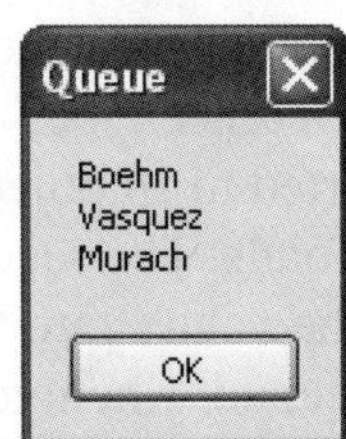

Properties and methods of the Stack<> class

Property	Description
`Count`	Gets the number of items in the stack.
Method	**Description**
`Push(object)`	Adds the specified object to the top of the stack.
`Pop()`	Gets the object at the top of the stack and removes it from the stack.
`Clear()`	Removes all items from the stack.
`Peek()`	Retrieves the next item in the stack without deleting it.

Code that uses a stack

```
Stack<string> nameStack = new Stack<string>();
nameStack.Push("Boehm");
nameStack.Push("Vasquez");
nameStack.Push("Murach");
string nameStackString = "";
while (nameStack.Count > 0)
    nameStackString += nameStack.Pop() + "\n";
MessageBox.Show(nameStackString, "Stack");
```

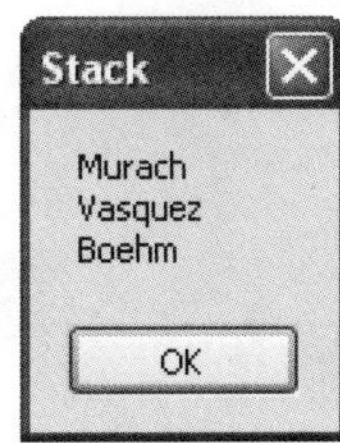

Description

- *Queues* and *stacks* provide distinct features that let you process them like lists.
- A queue is sometimes called a *first-in, first-out* (*FIFO*) collection because its items are retrieved in the same order in which they were added.
- A stack is sometimes called a *last-in, first-out* (*LIFO*) collection because its items are retrieved in the reverse order from the order in which they were added.

Figure 8-16 How to work with queues and stacks

How to work with an array list

Although you'll probably want to use typed lists whenever possible, figure 8-17 shows how to work with an *array list*, the most common untyped collection. This should illustrate both the similarities and differences between typed and untyped lists. For the most part, an array list works like a list. However, since an array list defines an untyped collection, there are a few differences.

First, when you create an object from the ArrayList class, you don't define the type within angle brackets (<>). Instead, each element in an array list is stored as an object type. As a result, any value type you store in an array list must be converted to a reference type. To do that, an object is created and then the value is stored in that object. The process of putting a value in an object is known as *boxing*, and it's done automatically whenever a value type needs to be converted to a reference type. In the first example, for instance, the decimal value type is converted to an object reference type before it is stored in the array list named salesTotals. The second example is similar except it uses a collection initializer to load the values into the list.

Second, when you retrieve an element from an array, you must cast the object type to the appropriate data type. In the third example, for instance, the first element in the array list named salesTotal is cast from the object type to the decimal type. The process of getting a value out of the object is known as *unboxing*, and you must write code like this whenever you need to unbox a value.

The rest of the examples work the same as the examples for the List<> class shown in figure 8-14. The only difference is that you must cast an object to the appropriate data type when you retrieve it from an array list. If you compare the examples in this figure to the ones for the List<> class, you'll see that they're very similar. As a result, it's easy to convert code that uses the ArrayList class to code that uses the List<> class and vice versa. Once you understand how to do that, you should be able convert code from any untyped collection to any typed collection and vice versa.

The syntax for retrieving a value from an array list

```
(type) arrayName[index]
```

Code that creates an array list that holds decimal values

```
decimal[] newSalesTotals = {3275.68m, 4398.55m, 5289.75m, 1933.98m};
ArrayList salesTotals = new ArrayList();
foreach (decimal d in newSalesTotals)
    salesTotals.Add(d);
```

Another way to create the array list

```
ArrayList salesTotals = new ArrayList
    { 3275.68m, 4398.55m, 5289.75m, 1933.98m };
```

Code that retrieves the first value from the array list

```
decimal sales1 = (decimal) salesTotals[0];  // sales1 = 3275.68
```

Code that inserts and removes an element from the array list

```
salesTotals.Insert(0, 2745.73m);             // insert a new first element
sales1 = (decimal) salesTotals[0];           // sales1 = 2745.73
decimal sales2 = (decimal) salesTotals[1];   // sales2 = 3275.68
salesTotals.RemoveAt(1);                     // remove the second element
sales2 = (decimal) salesTotals[1];           // sales2 = 4398.55
```

Code that displays the array list in a message box

```
string salesTotalsString = "";
foreach (decimal d in salesTotals)
    salesTotalsString += d + "\n";
MessageBox.Show(salesTotalsString, "Sales Totals");
```

The message box that's displayed

Code that checks for an element in the array list and removes it if it exists

```
decimal x = 2745.73m;
if (salesTotals.Contains(x))
    salesTotals.Remove(x);
```

Code that sorts and searches the array list

```
salesTotals.Sort();
int sales2Index = salesTotals.BinarySearch(sales2);
```

Description

- The ArrayList class is part of the System.Collections namespace.
- The ArrayList class has the same properties and methods as the List<> class in the System.Collections.Generic namespace. As a result, it's easy to convert code that uses the ArrayList class to code that uses the List<> class and vice versa.

Figure 8-17 How to work with an array list

Perspective

In this chapter, you've learned how to use both arrays and collections for working with groups of related data. You've also learned that the .NET Framework provides several different classes that offer useful properties and methods for working with arrays and collections. These include the Array, List<>, SortedList<>, Queue<>, Stack<>, and ArrayList classes.

As you develop your own applications, you need to decide between the use of an array or collection. Then, if you decide to use a collection, you need to choose the most appropriate type of collection. If you make the right decisions, your code will be easier to write, debug, and maintain.

Terms

array
element
length
size
one-dimensional array
index
upper bound
foreach statement
foreach loop
rectangular array
two-dimensional array
jagged array
array of arrays
immutable
collection
mutable
typed collection
generics
untyped collection
using statement
list
collection initializer
sorted list
queue
stack
first-in first-out
FIFO
last-in first-out
LIFO
array list
boxing
unboxing

Exercise 8-1 Use an array and a list

This exercise will guide you through the process of adding an array and a list to the Invoice Total application that you enhanced in the last chapter.

Open the Invoice Total application

1. Open the Invoice Total application that's in the C:\C# 2008\Chapter 08\InvoiceTotal directory.

Use an array to store invoice totals

2. Declare two class variables: (1) an array that can hold up to five invoice totals and (2) an index that you can use to work with that array.
3. Add code that adds the invoice total to the next element in the array each time the user clicks the Calculate button.
4. Add code that displays all the invoice totals in the array in a message box when the user clicks the Exit button. To do that, use a foreach loop to loop through the totals and format the message for the message box. Within this loop, you should include an if statement so that you only display totals that are not equal to zero.
5. Test the program by entering subtotals for up to five invoices and then clicking the Exit button. This should display a dialog box like this one:

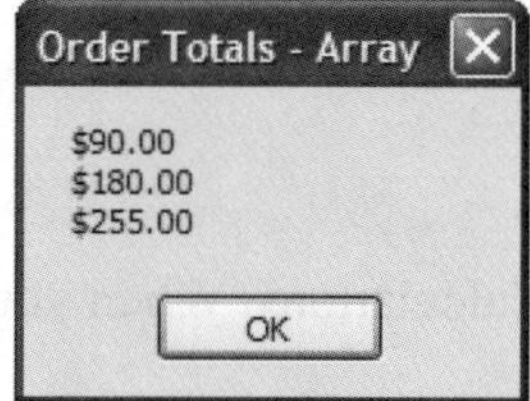

6. Test the program by entering more than five invoices. When you do, an IndexOutOfRangeException should be thrown. Then, modify the try-catch statement so it handles this exception.

Sort the invoice totals

7. Add code to sort the invoice totals in the array.
8. Test the program again to be sure that the message box displays the invoice totals in the correct sequence.

Modify the program so it uses a list

9. Without changing any of the current code, repeat steps 2-8 but use a list to hold the totals and add a second foreach loop to format and display the totals stored in the list in a second message box. In other words, display two message boxes: one for the array and one for the list.
10. When you've got this working right, close the solution.

Exercise 8-2 Use a rectangular array

This exercise will guide you through the process of adding a rectangular array to the Future Value application. This array will store the values for each calculation that's performed.

Open the Future Value application

1. Open the Future Value application that's in the C:\C# 2008\Chapter 08\FutureValue directory.

Use a rectangular array to store future value calculations

2. Declare class variables for a row counter and a rectangular array of strings that provides for 10 rows and 4 columns.
3. Add code that stores the values for each calculation in the next row of the array when the user clicks the Calculate button. Store the monthly investment and future value in currency format, and store the interest rate in percent format.
4. Add code to display the elements in the array in a message box when the user clicks the Exit button. Use tab characters to format the message box so it looks like this:

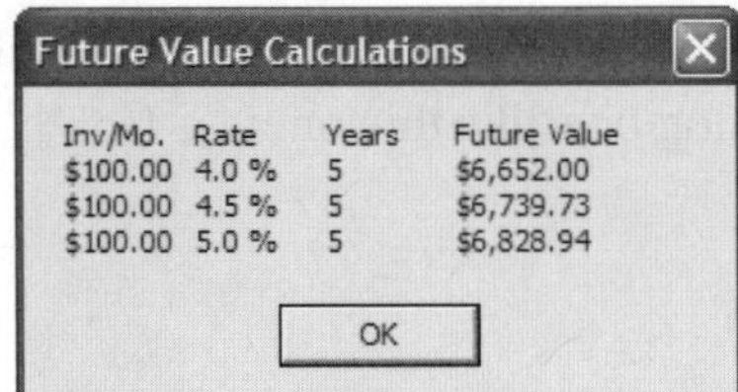

Future Value Calculations
Inv/Mo. Rate Years Future Value
$100.00 4.0 % 5 $6,652.00
$100.00 4.5 % 5 $6,739.73
$100.00 5.0 % 5 $6,828.94
OK

5. Test the program by making up to 10 future value calculations. When you've got this working right, close the solution.

9

How to work with dates and strings

In chapter 4, you learned some basic skills for working with strings. In this chapter, you'll learn more about working with strings, and you'll learn how to work with dates. Because you'll use dates and strings in many of the applications you develop, you'll want to be sure you know how to use the skills presented in this chapter.

How to work with dates and times

To work with dates and times in C#, you use the DateTime structure. As you'll see, this structure provides a variety of properties and methods for getting information about dates and times, formatting DateTime values, and performing operations on dates and times.

How to create a DateTime value

Figure 9-1 presents two ways that you can create a DateTime value. First, you can use the new keyword to create a DateTime value from the DateTime structure. This is different from the way you create other built-in value types. That's because C# doesn't provide a keyword for working with this structure like it does for the other value types.

When you create a DateTime value using the new keyword, you must always specify the year, month, and day. In addition, you can optionally specify the time in hours, minutes, seconds, and milliseconds. If you don't specify the time, it's set to 12:00 AM. This is illustrated by the first two statements in this figure.

You can also create a DateTime value using the static Parse method of the DateTime structure. When you use the Parse method, you specify the date and time as a string as illustrated by the third, fourth, and fifth statements in this figure. Here, the third statement specifies just a date. Because of that, the time portion of the DateTime value is set to 12:00 AM. The fourth statement specifies both a date and time. The fifth statement illustrates that you can create a DateTime value from a property or variable that contains a date/time string. In this case, a DateTime value is created from the Text property of a text box.

When you use the Parse method to create a DateTime value, the date and time you specify must be in a valid format. Some of the most common formats are listed in this figure. Later in this chapter, you'll learn more about the acceptable date and time formats.

Although the statements in this figure indicate the DateTime values that are created, you should realize that these aren't the actual values that are stored in the variables. Instead, they show what happens when a DateTime value is converted to a string. The date and time are actually stored as the number of *ticks* (100 nanosecond units) that have elapsed since 12:00:00 AM, January 1, 0001. That makes it easy to perform arithmetic operations on dates and times, as you'll see later in this chapter.

The syntax for creating a DateTime value

```
DateTime variableName = new DateTime(year, month, day
    [, hour, minute, second[, millisecond]]);
```

Another way to create a DateTime value

```
DateTime variableName = DateTime.Parse(string);
```

Statements that create DateTime values

```
DateTime startDate = new DateTime(08, 01, 30);     // 1/30/2008 12:00 AM
DateTime startDateAndTime =
    new DateTime(2008, 1, 30, 14, 15, 0);          // 1/30/2008 2:15 PM

DateTime startDate = DateTime.Parse("01/30/08");   // 1/30/2008 12:00 AM
DateTime startDateAndTime
    = DateTime.Parse("Jan 30, 2008 2:15 PM");      // 1/30/2008 2:15 PM
DateTime invoiceDate = DateTime.Parse(txtInvoiceDate.Text);
```

Valid date formats

```
01/30/2008
1/30/08
01-01-2008
1-1-08
2008-01-01
Jan 30 2008
January 30, 2008
```

Valid time formats

```
2:15 PM
14:15
02:15:30 AM
```

Description

- You can use the DateTime structure of the .NET Framework to create and work with dates and times.
- To create a DateTime value, you can use the new keyword and then specify the date and time values you want to use to create the date.
- You can also use the static Parse method of the DateTime structure to create a DateTime value from a string.
- If you omit the time specification when you create a DateTime value, the time is set to 12:00 AM. You can also omit the date specification when you create a DateTime value using the Parse method. Then, the date is set to the current date.
- If the Parse method can't parse the string you specify, a format exception occurs.
- A date is stored as a 64-bit signed integer that represents the number of *ticks* (100 nanosecond units) that have elapsed since 12:00 AM, January 1, 0001.

Figure 9-1 How to create a DateTime value

How to get the current date and time

Figure 9-2 presents two static properties of the DateTime structure that you can use to get the current date and time. If you use the Now property, both the date and time are returned. If you use the Today property, only the date is returned, and the time is set to 12:00:00 AM. The first two statements in this figure illustrate how this works.

How to format DateTime values

To format dates and times, you can use the four methods of the DateTime structure that are shown in figure 9-2. Note, however, that these formats may vary somewhat from the formats that are used on your system. The exact formats depend on your computer's regional settings. If these methods don't provide the format you need, you can use the formatting techniques you'll learn about later in this chapter to format the date and time the way you want them.

DateTime properties for getting the current date and time

Property	Description
`Now`	Returns the current date and time.
`Today`	Returns the current date.

Statements that get the current date and time

```
DateTime currentDateTime = DateTime.Now;       // 1/30/2008 4:24:59 AM
DateTime currentDate = DateTime.Today;         // 1/30/2008 12:00:00 AM
```

DateTime methods for formatting a date or time

Method	Description
`ToLongDateString()`	Converts the DateTime value to a string that includes the name for the day of the week, the name for the month, the day of the month, and the year.
`ToShortDateString()`	Converts the DateTime value to a string that includes the numbers for the month, day, and year.
`ToLongTimeString()`	Converts the DateTime value to a string that includes the hours, minutes, and seconds.
`ToShortTimeString()`	Converts the DateTime value to a string that includes the hours and minutes.

Statements that format dates and times

```
string longDate =
    currentDateTime.ToLongDateString();        // Wednesday, January 30, 2008
string shortDate =
    currentDateTime.ToShortDateString();       // 1/30/2008
string longTime =
    currentDateTime.ToLongTimeString();        // 4:24:59 AM
string ShortTime =
    currentDateTime.ToShortTimeString();       // 4:24 AM
```

Description

- The Now and Today properties are static properties of the DateTime structure.
- The format that's used for a date or time depends on your computer's regional settings.

Figure 9-2 How to get the current date and format DateTime values

How to get information about dates and times

The DateTime structure provides a variety of properties and methods for getting information about dates and times. These properties and methods are listed in figure 9-3, and the statements presented here show how to work with most of them.

The first statement uses the Now property to get the current date and time. Then, the second statement uses the Month property to get the month of that date, the third statement uses the Hour property to get the hour of that time, and the fourth statement uses the DayOfYear property to get an int value from 1 to 366 that represents the day of the year.

The next two statements show how to use the two methods for getting information about a date. Since both of these methods are static, they're accessed through the DateTime structure. The first method, DaysInMonth, returns the number of days in a given month and year. In this example, since 2008 is a leap year, there are 29 days in February. However, if you specified 2007, which isn't a leap year, there would be 28 days in February. The second method, IsLeapYear, returns a true or false value that indicates whether the specified year is a leap year.

The last code example in this figure shows how to use the DayOfWeek property. Note that this property returns a member of the DayOfWeek enumeration. In this case, the first statement gets the day of the week for the current date. Then, an if statement checks if the current date is a Saturday or a Sunday. If so, a string variable named message is set to "Weekend". Otherwise, it's set to "Weekday".

Properties and methods for working with dates and times

Property	Description
`Date`	Returns the DateTime value with the time portion set to 12:00:00 AM.
`Month`	Returns an integer for the month portion of the DateTime value.
`Day`	Returns an integer for the day portion of the DateTime value.
`Year`	Returns an integer for the year portion of the DateTime value.
`Hour`	Returns an integer for the hour portion of the DateTime value.
`Minute`	Returns an integer for the minute portion of the DateTime value.
`Second`	Returns an integer for the second portion of the DateTime value.
`TimeOfDay`	Returns a TimeSpan value that represents the amount of time that has elapsed since 12:00:00 AM. For more information about the TimeSpan structure, see figure 9-4.
`DayOfWeek`	Returns a member of the DayOfWeek enumeration that represents the day of the week of a DateTime value.
`DayOfYear`	Returns an integer for the numeric day of the year.
Method	**Description**
`DaysInMonth(year, month)`	Returns the number of days in a specified month and year.
`IsLeapYear(year)`	Returns a Boolean value that indicates whether or not a specified year is a leap year.

Statements that get information about a date or time

```
DateTime currentDateTime = DateTime.Now;            // 1/30/2008 10:26:35 AM
int month = currentDateTime.Month;                  // 1
int hour = currentDateTime.Hour;                    // 10
int dayOfYear = currentDateTime.DayOfYear;          // 30
int daysInMonth = DateTime.DaysInMonth(2008, 2);    // 29
bool isLeapYear = DateTime.IsLeapYear(2008);        // true
```

Code that uses the DayOfWeek property and enumeration

```
DayOfWeek dayOfWeek = currentDateTime.DayOfWeek;
string message = "";
if (dayOfWeek == DayOfWeek.Saturday ||
    dayOfWeek == DayOfWeek.Sunday)
{
    message = "Weekend";
}
else
{
    message = "Weekday";
}
```

Figure 9-3 How to get information about dates and times

How to perform operations on dates and times

Figure 9-4 presents some of the methods of the DateTime structure that you can use to perform operations on dates and times. Most of these methods let you add a specific number of intervals, like hours, days, or months, to a DateTime value. However, you can use the Add method to add a TimeSpan value to a date, and you can use the Subtract method to determine the time span between two dates, which is often required in business applications.

Like DateTime values, TimeSpan values are based on a structure defined by the .NET Framework. TimeSpan values also hold a number of ticks, just like DateTime values. However, a TimeSpan value represents a time interval. In contrast, a DateTime value represents a specific point in time.

The first group of statements in this figure show how some of the Add methods work. For example, the second statement shows how to add two months to a DateTime value, and the third statement shows how to add 60 days. Similarly, the fourth statement shows how to add 30 minutes, and the fifth statement shows how to add 12 hours.

The second group of statements show how you can use a TimeSpan variable to determine the number of days between two DateTime values. Here, the first statement retrieves the current date, and the second statement assigns a date to another DateTime variable. Next, the third statement uses the Subtract method to subtract the two date values and assign the result to a TimeSpan variable, which represents the number of days, minutes, hours, and seconds between the two dates. Finally, the last statement uses the Days property of the TimeSpan structure to extract the number of days from the TimeSpan value. This is one of several properties of this structure that let you extract the data from a TimeSpan value.

In addition to the properties and methods provided by the DateTime structure for working with dates, you can use some of the standard operators to work with dates. For instance, the third example in this figure shows how to use the subtraction operator to calculate the time between two dates instead of using the Subtract method. The last example shows that you can also use DateTime values in a conditional expression. Here, the conditional expression tests if one DateTime value is greater than another.

Methods for performing operations on dates and times

Method	Description
`AddDays(days)`	Adds the specified numbers of days to a DateTime value and returns another DateTime value.
`AddMonths(months)`	Adds the specified number of months to a DateTime value and returns another DateTime value.
`AddYears(years)`	Adds the specified number of years to a DateTime value and returns another DateTime value.
`AddHours(hours)`	Adds the specified number of hours to a DateTime value and returns another DateTime value.
`AddMinutes(minutes)`	Adds the specified number of minutes to a DateTime value and returns another DateTime value.
`AddSeconds(seconds)`	Adds the specified number of seconds to a DateTime value and returns another DateTime value.
`Add(timespan)`	Adds the specified TimeSpan value to a DateTime value and returns another DateTime value.
`Subtract(datetime)`	Subtracts the specified DateTime value from a DateTime value and returns a TimeSpan value.

Statements that perform operations on dates and times

```
DateTime dateTime =
    DateTime.Parse("3/1/2008 13:28");              // 3/1/2008 1:28:00 PM
DateTime dueDate = dateTime.AddMonths(2);          // 5/1/2008 1:28:00 PM
dueDate = dateTime.AddDays(60);                    // 4/30/2008 1:28:00 PM
DateTime runTime = dateTime.AddMinutes(30);        // 3/1/2008 1:58:00 PM
runTime = dateTime.AddHours(12);                   // 3/2/2008 1:28:00 AM
```

Code that results in a TimeSpan value

```
DateTime currentDate = DateTime.Today;                  // 1/30/2008
dueDate = DateTime.Parse("2/15/2008");                  // 2/15/2008
TimeSpan timeTillDue = dueDate.Subtract(currentDate);   // 16:00:00:00
int daysTillDue = timeTillDue.Days;                     // 16
```

A statement that uses the – operator to subtract two dates

```
TimeSpan timeTillDue = dueDate - currentDate;    // 16:00:00:00
```

An if statement that uses the > operator on DateTime values

```
bool pastDue = false;
if (currentDate > dueDate)
    pastDue = true;
```

Description

- A TimeSpan value represents a period of time stored as ticks. You can use the Days, Hours, Minutes, and Seconds properties of a TimeSpan value to get portions of that value.
- In addition to the DateTime methods, you can use the +, -, ==, !=, >, >=, <, and <= operators to work with DateTime values.

Figure 9-4 How to perform operations on dates and times

How to work with strings

Many types of programs require that you work with the characters within strings. If, for example, a user enters the city, state, and zip code of an address as a single entry, your program may need to divide (or parse) that single string into city, state, and zip code variables. Or, if a user enters a telephone number that includes parentheses and hyphens, you may need to remove those characters so the number can be stored as a 10-digit integer.

When you create a string, you are actually creating a String object from the String class. Then, you can use the properties and methods of the String class to work with the String object. Another alternative, though, is to create StringBuilder objects from the StringBuilder class so you can use the properties and methods of that class to work with strings. In the topics that follow, you'll learn both ways of working with strings.

The properties and methods of the String class

Figure 9-5 summarizes some of the properties and methods of the String class that you can use as you work with String objects. When you use these properties and methods, you often need to use an index to refer to a specific character within a string. To do that, you use 0 to refer to the first character, 1 to refer to the second character, and so on. When you refer to a character in a string, you code the index for a string character within brackets. This is the same technique that you use to refer to an element of an array. In fact, it sometimes helps to think of a string as an array of characters.

One method that's particularly useful for parsing strings is Split. This method returns an array where each element contains a substring of the original string. The argument that you specify for this method identifies the character that's used to delimit each substring. You'll see examples of this method in figure 9-7.

Common properties and methods of the String class

Indexer	Description
`[index]`	Gets the character at the specified position.

Property	Description
`Length`	Gets the number of characters in the string.

Method	Description
`StartsWith``(string)`	Returns a Boolean value that indicates whether or not the string starts with the specified string.
`EndsWith``(string)`	Returns a Boolean value that indicates whether or not the string ends with the specified string.
`IndexOf``(string[, startIndex])`	Returns an integer that represents the position of the first occurrence of the specified string starting at the specified position. If the starting position isn't specified, the search starts at the beginning of the string. If the string isn't found, -1 is returned.
`LastIndexOf``(string[, startIndex])`	Returns an integer that represents the position of the last occurrence of the specified string starting at the specified position. If the starting position isn't specified, the search starts at the end of the string. If the string isn't found, -1 is returned.
`Insert``(startIndex, string)`	Returns a string with the specified string inserted beginning at the specified position.
`PadLeft``(totalWidth)`	Returns a string that's right-aligned and padded on the left with spaces so it's the specified width.
`PadRight``(totalWidth)`	Returns a string that's left-aligned and padded on the right with spaces so it's the specified width.
`Remove``(startIndex, count)`	Returns a string with the specified number of characters removed starting at the specified position.
`Replace``(oldString, newString)`	Returns a string with all occurrences of the old string replaced with the new string.
`Substring``(startIndex[, length])`	Returns the string that starts at the specified position and has the specified length. If the length isn't specified, all of the characters to the end of the string are returned.
`ToLower``()`	Returns a string in lowercase.
`ToUpper``()`	Returns a string in uppercase.
`Trim``()`	Returns a string with leading and trailing spaces removed.
`Split``(splitCharacters)`	Returns an array of strings where each element is a substring that's delimited by the specified character or characters.

Description

- You can use an index to access each character in a string, where 0 is the index for the first character, 1 is the index for the second character, and so on.

Figure 9-5 The properties and methods of the String class

Code examples that work with strings

Figure 9-6 shows how to use most of the properties and methods summarized in the last figure. The first example shows how you can use an index to return a character from a string. Then, the second example shows how you can use an index and the Length property in a for loop to insert a space character between each character in the string. The third example performs the same operation as the second example, but it uses a foreach loop instead of a for loop.

The fourth example shows how you can use the StartsWith and EndsWith methods. Here, the first statement checks if the string named chars that was created in the first example starts with the string "abc", and the second statement checks if this string ends with "abc". As you can see, the result of the first statement is true, and the result of the second statement is false.

The fifth example shows how to use the IndexOf and LastIndexOf methods. Here, the first statement sets the value of the string. Then, the second and third statements use the IndexOf method to retrieve the index of the first space in the string. The fourth statement uses the same method to return the index of a string of characters. Since the characters don't exist in the string, this method returns a value of -1. The last statement uses the LastIndexOf method to return the index of the last space in the string.

The sixth example shows how to use the Remove, Insert, and Replace methods to work with the string in the fifth example. Here, the first statement removes the first five characters of the string. In this statement, the first argument specifies the starting index, and the second argument specifies the number of characters to remove. In this case, the number of characters to remove is calculated by adding 1 to the index of the first space, which is 4. Then, the second statement uses the Insert method to insert ", Inc." at the end of the string. Here, the first argument uses the Length method to set the starting index at the end of the string, and the second argument specifies the string to be inserted. Finally, the third statement uses the Replace method to replace all occurrences of "and" with "And".

The seventh example shows how to use the Substring, ToUpper, and ToLower methods to make sure a string is lowercase with an initial cap. Here, the second statement returns a substring that contains the first character in the string. To do that, the first argument specifies a starting index of 0 and the second argument specifies a length of 1. Then, to convert the returned substring to uppercase, this statement calls the ToUpper method. The third statement is similar, but it uses the ToLower method to return the remaining characters in the string and convert them to lowercase. The last statement combines the two strings into a single string.

The eighth example shows how to use the = operator to copy one string to another string. Because a string is a reference type, you might think that the second statement would copy the reference to the string object created by the first statement to the second string variable. In this case, however, a new string object is created and the value in the original string is copied to that object. Then, a reference to the new object is assigned to the new string variable.

Code that uses an index to access a character in a string

```
string chars = "abcdefg";
char a = chars[0];                    // 'a'
char b = chars[1];                    // 'b'
```

Code that uses a for loop to access each character in the string

```
string charsAndSpaces = "";
for (int i = 0; i < chars.Length; i++)
    charsAndSpaces += chars[i] + " ";
MessageBox.Show(charsAndSpaces, "String Test");
```

The message box that's displayed

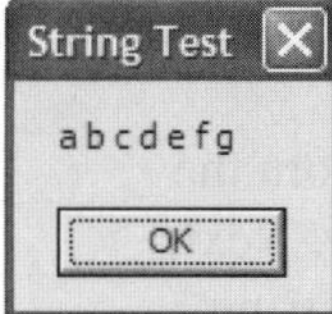

Code that uses a foreach loop to access each character in the string

```
string charsAndSpaces = "";
foreach (char c in chars)
    charsAndSpaces += c + " ";
MessageBox.Show(charsAndSpaces, "String Test");
```

Code that uses the StartsWith and EndsWith methods

```
bool startsWithABC = chars.StartsWith("abc");  // true
bool endsWithABC = chars.EndsWith("abc");      // false
```

Code that uses the IndexOf method

```
string companyName = "Mike Murach and Associates";
int index1 = companyName.IndexOf(" ");       // 4
int index2 = companyName.IndexOf(' ');       // 4
int index3 = companyName.IndexOf("Inc.");    // -1
int index4 = companyName.LastIndexOf(" ");   // 15
```

Code that uses the Remove, Insert, and Replace methods

```
companyName = companyName.Remove(0, index1 + 1);
companyName = companyName.Insert(companyName.Length, ", Inc.");
companyName
   = companyName.Replace("and", "And");     // Murach And Associates, Inc.
```

Code that uses the Substring, ToUpper, and ToLower methods

```
string firstName = "anne";
string firstLetter = firstName.Substring(0, 1).ToUpper();
string otherLetters = firstName.Substring(1).ToLower();
firstName = firstLetter + otherLetters;       // Anne
```

Code that copies one string to another string

```
string s1 = "abc";
string s2 = s1;     // this copies the value stored in s1 to s2
s2 = "def";         // this doesn't change the value stored in s1
```

Figure 9-6 Code examples that work with strings

More code examples that work with strings

Figure 9-7 presents some additional string-handling routines. The first four parse the data in strings. The fifth one adds characters to a string. And the sixth one replaces some of the characters in a string with other characters. If you can understand the code in these routines, you should be able to write your own routines whenever needed.

The first routine shows how to parse the first name from a string that contains a full name. Here, the full name is assigned to the fullName variable so you can visualize how the statements that follow work with that name. In practice, though, the name would be entered by a user or read from a file so you wouldn't know what it was.

To start, this routine uses the Trim method to remove any spaces from the beginning and end of the string that a user may have typed accidentally. Next, the IndexOf method is used to get the position of the first space in the string, which should be between the first name and the middle name or last name. If this method doesn't find a space in the string, though, it returns a -1. In that case, the if-else statement that follows assigns the entire string to the first name variable. Otherwise, it uses the Substring method to set the first name variable equal to the string that begins at the first character of the string and that has a length that's equal to the position of the first space.

The second routine in this figure shows how to parse a string that contains an address into the components of the address. In this case, a pipe character (|) separates each component of the address. In addition, the string may begin with one or more spaces followed by a pipe character, and it may end with a pipe character followed by one or more spaces.

To remove the spaces from the beginning and end of the string, this routine also uses the Trim method. Then, it uses the StartsWith and EndsWith methods to determine whether the first or last character in the string is a pipe character. If it is, the Remove method removes that character from the string.

The next three statements use the IndexOf method to determine the index values of the first character for each substring other than the first. (The first substring will start at index 0.) To do that, it determines the index of the next pipe character and then adds 1. After that, the next four statements use these index variables as arguments of the Substring method to return the street, city, state, and zip code substrings. To calculate the length of each substring, this code subtracts the starting index from the ending index and then subtracts 1 from that value. This results in the length of the substring without the pipe character.

The third and fourth routines use the Split method to perform the same operations as the first and second routines. As you can see, the Split method can simplify your code significantly, particularly if the string you're parsing consists of several elements.

The fifth and sixth routines show how to add hyphens to a phone number and change the hyphens in a date to slashes. To add hyphens, you simply use the Insert method to insert the hyphens at the appropriate index. And to change hyphens to slashes, you use the Replace method.

Code that parses a first name from a name string

```
string fullName = " Edward C Koop    ";                // " Edward C Koop    "
fullName = fullName.Trim();                             // "Edward C Koop"
int firstSpace = fullName.IndexOf(" ");                 // 6
string firstName = "";
if (firstSpace == -1)
    firstName = fullName;
else
    firstName = fullName.Substring(0, firstSpace);      // Edward
```

Code that parses a string that contains an address

```
string address = " |805 Main Street|Dallas|TX|12345| ";
address = address.Trim();
if (address.StartsWith("|"))
    address = address.Remove(0, 1);
if (address.EndsWith("|"))
    address = address.Remove(address.Length - 1, 1);
int cityIndex = address.IndexOf("|") + 1;
int stateIndex = address.IndexOf("|", cityIndex) + 1;
int zipIndex = address.IndexOf("|", stateIndex) + 1;
string street = address.Substring(0, cityIndex - 1);
string city = address.Substring(cityIndex, stateIndex - cityIndex - 1);
string state = address.Substring(stateIndex, zipIndex - stateIndex - 1);
string zipCode = address.Substring(zipIndex);
```

Code that uses the Split method to parse the name string

```
string fullName = " Edward C Koop    ";
fullName = fullName.Trim();
string[] names = fullName.Split(' ');
string firstName = names[0];                            // Edward
```

Code that uses the Split method to parse the address string

```
address = address.Trim();
if (address.StartsWith("|"))
    address = address.Remove(0, 1);
string[] columns = address.Split('|');
string street = columns[0];                 // 805 Main Street
string city = columns[1];                   // Dallas
string state = columns[2];                  // TX
string zipCode = columns[3];                // 12345
```

Code that adds hyphens to a phone number

```
string phoneNumber = "9775551212";
phoneNumber = phoneNumber.Insert(3, "-");
phoneNumber = phoneNumber.Insert(7, "-");  // 977-555-1212
```

Code that replaces the hyphens in a date with slashes

```
string date = "12-27-2007";
date = date.Replace("-", "/");              // 12/27/2007
```

Figure 9-7 More code examples that work with strings

Two methods for validating user entries

In chapter 7, you learned how to code a data validation method named IsDecimal that checked whether a user entry contained a valid decimal value. To do that, this method used the ToDecimal method to try to convert the entry string to a decimal. Then, an exception was thrown if the user entered any non-numeric characters, including dollar signs, percent signs, and commas. Since these characters are used frequently to format numeric values, however, it makes sense to allow them in numeric entries. To do that, you can use methods like the ones shown in figure 9-8.

The first method in this figure is another version of the IsDecimal method that can be used to validate decimal entries. This method has two advantages over the IsDecimal method presented in chapter 7. First, it runs more quickly when the user enters an invalid decimal value because it doesn't rely on the ToDecimal method of the Convert class to throw an exception. Second, it lets the user enter numeric formatting characters, including dollar signs, percentage signs, commas, and white space. As a result, the user can enter these characters and this method will still recognize the entry as a valid decimal value.

The IsDecimal method works by using a foreach loop to check each character in the entry string to be sure it contains a number from 0 through 9, a decimal point, or a valid formatting character ($, %, comma, or space). If an invalid character is encountered, a Boolean variable named validDecimal is set to false and a break statement ends the foreach loop. If all the characters are valid, however, the loop continues by checking if the character is a decimal point. If so, a variable named decimalCount is incremented by 1.

The if statement that follows the foreach loop checks that all of the characters are valid and that the entry contains no more than one decimal point. If both conditions are true, the method returns a true value to the calling method. Otherwise, it displays an error message, moves the focus to the appropriate text box, and returns a false value.

Because the IsDecimal method allows the user to enter formatting characters, you'll need to remove these characters before attempting to convert the string to a decimal. To do that, you can use the Strip method shown in this figure. Like the IsDecimal method, this method uses a foreach loop to check each character in the entry string. Then, if a character is one of the valid formatting characters, it uses the Remove method to remove that character from the string.

The code at the bottom of this figure shows how you might call these two methods to validate the monthly investment that the user enters into the Future Value application. As you can see, the IsDecimal method is specified as the condition on an if statement. Then, if this method returns a true value, the Strip method is called to remove any formatting characters, and the resulting string is converted to a decimal.

A method that checks if a string contains a decimal value

```
public bool IsDecimal(TextBox textBox, string name)
{
    string s = textBox.Text;
    int decimalCount = 0;
    bool validDecimal = true;
    foreach (char c in s)
    {
        if (!(
            c == '0' || c == '1' || c == '2' ||   // numeric chars
            c == '3' || c == '4' || c == '5' ||
            c == '6' || c == '7' || c == '8' ||
            c == '9' || c == '.' ||
            c == '$' || c == '%' || c == ',' ||   // formatting chars
            c == ' '
            ))
        {
            validDecimal = false;
            break;
        }
        if (c == '.')
        {
            decimalCount++;
        }
    }
    if (validDecimal && decimalCount <= 1)
    {
        return true;
    }
    else
    {
        MessageBox.Show(name + " must be a decimal value.",
            "Entry Error");
        textBox.Focus();
        return false;
    }
}
```

A method that strips formatting characters from a numeric string

```
public string Strip(string s)
{
    foreach (char c in s)
    {
        if (c == '$' || c == '%' || c == ',' || c == ' ')
        {
            int i = s.IndexOf(c);
            s = s.Remove(i, 1);
        }
    }
    return s;
}
```

Code that calls the two methods shown above

```
decimal monthlyInvestment = 0;
if (IsDecimal(txtMonthlyInvestment, "Monthly Investment")
{
    monthlyInvestment = Convert.ToDecimal(
        Strip(txtMonthlyInvestment.Text));
}
```

Figure 9-8 Two methods for validating user entries

How to use the StringBuilder class

When you use the String class to create a string, the string has a fixed length and value. In other words, the String class creates strings that are *immutable*. Then, when you assign a new value to a string variable, the original String object is deleted and it's replaced with a new String object that contains the new value.

Another way to work with strings, though, is to use the StringBuilder class. Then, you create StringBuilder objects that are *mutable* so you can add, delete, or replace characters in the objects. This makes it easier to write some types of string-handling routines, and these routines run more efficiently. As a result, you should use the StringBuilder class for string handling routines that append, insert, remove, or replace characters in strings, especially if you're working with long strings that use significant system resources.

In figure 9-9, you can see some of the most useful properties and methods for working with a string that's created from the StringBuilder class. As you can see, you can use an index to refer to a character in a StringBuilder object, and you can use the Length property to get the number of characters in a string just as you can with a String object. You can also use the Insert, Remove, and Replace methods with StringBuilder objects. However, instead of returning a new string, these methods change the existing string.

When you use the StringBuilder class, you'll want to include a using statement for the System.Text namespace that contains it. You code this statement at the start of the class, along with the using statements that are added to the class by default. That way, you can refer to the StringBuilder class without qualifying it with the name of this namespace.

When you create a StringBuilder object, you can code one or two arguments that assign an initial value, an initial capacity, or both. The statements in the second example illustrate how this works. Here, the first statement doesn't include any arguments, so the StringBuilder object is created with a default capacity of 16 characters and an initial value of an empty string. The second statement creates a StringBuilder object with an initial capacity of 10. The third and fourth statements are similar, but they specify an initial value for the object.

The last example in this figure shows how you can use five methods of the StringBuilder class. Here, the first statement creates a StringBuilder object with an initial capacity of 10, and the second statement appends a 10-character phone number to the object. The third and fourth statements insert periods into the string to format the number. The fifth statement removes the area code and the period that follows it. The sixth statement replaces the remaining period with a hyphen. And the last statement converts the characters stored in the StringBuilder object to a string.

This example also shows how a StringBuilder object automatically increases its capacity when necessary. Here, the StringBuilder object has a capacity of 10 when it's created, and this capacity remains at 10 until the first period is inserted. Then, to be able to store the 11 characters, the StringBuilder object automatically doubles its capacity to 20.

The syntax for creating a StringBuilder object

```
StringBuilder variableName = new StringBuilder([value][,][capacity]);
```

Common properties and methods of the StringBuilder class

Indexer	Description
`[index]`	Gets the character at the specified position.
Property	**Description**
`Length`	Gets the number of characters in the string.
`Capacity`	Gets or sets the number of characters the string can hold.
Method	**Description**
`Append(string)`	Adds the specified string to the end of the string.
`Insert(index, string)`	Inserts the specified string at the specified index in the string.
`Remove(startIndex, count)`	Removes the specified number of characters from the string starting at the specified index.
`Replace(oldString, newString)`	Replaces all occurrences of the old string with the new string.
`ToString()`	Converts the StringBuilder object to a string.

A statement that simplifies references to the StringBuilder class

```
using System.Text;
```

Statements that create and initialize StringBuilder objects

```
StringBuilder address1 = new StringBuilder();            // Capacity is 16
StringBuilder address2 = new StringBuilder(10);          // Capacity is 10
StringBuilder phoneNumber1 =
    new StringBuilder("9775551212");                     // Capacity is 16
StringBuilder phoneNumber2 =
    new StringBuilder("9775551212", 10);                 // Capacity is 10
```

Code that creates a phone number and inserts dashes

```
StringBuilder phoneNumber = new StringBuilder(10);       // Capacity is 10
phoneNumber.Append("9775551212");                        // Capacity is 10
phoneNumber.Insert(3, ".");                              // Capacity is 20
phoneNumber.Insert(7, ".");                              // 977.555.1212
phoneNumber.Remove(0, 4);                                // 555.1212
phoneNumber.Replace(".", "-");                           // 555-1212
lblPhoneNumber.Text = phoneNumber.ToString();            // 555-1212
```

Description

- Unlike string objects, StringBuilder objects are *mutable*, which means that they can be changed.
- To refer to the StringBuilder class, you must either qualify it with System.Text or include a using statement for this namespace at the start of the class that uses it.
- The capacity of a StringBuilder object is the amount of memory that's allocated to it. That capacity is increased automatically whenever necessary. If you don't set an initial capacity when you create a StringBuilder object, the default is 16 characters.

Figure 9-9 How to use the StringBuilder class

How to format numbers, dates, and times

In chapter 4, you learned how to apply standard numeric formats to numbers. Then, earlier in this chapter, you learned how to apply standard formats to dates and times. However, you can also apply custom formatting to numbers, dates, and times.

How to format numbers

Figure 9-10 shows how to use the Format method of the String class to format numbers. Because this is a static method, you access it directly from the String class rather than from an instance of this class. The result of this method is a string that contains the formatted number.

As you can see in the syntax for this method, the first argument is a string. This string contains the format specifications for the value or values to be formatted. Following this string, you specify one or more values that you want to format. In most cases, you'll use this method to format a single value.

For each value to be formatted, you code a format specification within the string argument. This specification is divided into three parts. The first part indicates the value to be formatted. Because the values are numbered from zero, you'll usually code a zero to indicate that the first value is to be formatted. The next part indicates the width of the formatted value along with its alignment. In most cases, you'll omit this part of the specification.

The third part of the format specification contains the actual format string. This string can contain multiple formats. If only one format is specified, it's used for all numbers. If two formats are specified, the first is used for positive numbers and zero values, and the second is used for negative values. If all three formats are specified, the first is used for positive numbers, the second is used for negative numbers, and the third is used for zero values.

Each format can consist of one of the standard numeric formatting codes listed in this figure. If, for example, you want to format a number as currency, you can code a statement like the first statement in this figure. Here, the format specification, which is enclosed in braces, indicates that the first value (0) should be formatted with the currency format (c). Then, this specification is enclosed in quotes to indicate that it is a string literal. That way, it can be passed as an argument to the Format method of the String class.

If the standard numeric formatting codes don't provide the format you want, you can create your own format using the custom codes presented in this figure. For instance, the second statement uses these codes to create a custom currency format. Here, the first format string indicates that positive numbers and the value 0 should be formatted with a decimal and thousands separators (if appropriate). In addition, the first digit to the left of the decimal point and the first two digits to the right of the decimal are always included, even if they're zero. The other digits are included only if they're non-zero.

The syntax of the Format method of the String class

```
Format(string, value1[, value2]...)
```

The syntax of a format specification within the string argument

```
{N[, M][:formatString]}
```

Explanation

N	An integer that indicates the value to be formatted.
M	An integer that indicates the width of the formatted value. If M is negative, the value will be left-justified. If it's positive, it will be right-justified.
formatString	A string of formatting codes.

The syntax of a format string

```
positiveformat[;negativeformat[;zeroformat]]
```

Standard numeric formatting codes

C or c	Formats the number as currency with the specified number of decimal places.
D or d	Formats an integer with the specified number of digits.
E or e	Formats the number in scientific (exponential) notation with the specified number of decimal places.
F or f	Formats the number as a decimal with the specified number of decimal places.
G or g	Formats the number as a decimal or in scientific notation depending on which is more compact.
N or n	Formats the number with thousands separators and the specified number of decimal places.
P or p	Formats the number as a percent with the specified number of decimal places.

Custom numeric formatting codes

0	Zero placeholder	,	Thousands separator
#	Digit placeholder	%	Percentage placeholder
.	Decimal point	;	Section separator

Statements that format a single number

```
string balance1 = String.Format("{0:c}", 1234.56);              // $1,234.56
string balance2 =
    String.Format("{0:$#,##0.00;($#,##0.00)}", -1234.56);   // ($1,234.56)
string balance3 =
    String.Format("{0:$#,##0.00;($#,##0.00);Zero}", 0);      // Zero
string quantity = String.Format("{0:d3}", 43);                 // 043
string payment =  String.Format("{0:f2}", 432.8175);           // 432.82
```

A statement that formats two numbers

```
string totalDue =
    String.Format("Invoice total: {0:c}; Amount due: {1:c}.", 354.75, 20);
// Invoice total: $354.75; Amount due: $20.00.
```

Figure 9-10 How to format numbers

The format for negative numbers is similar. However, this format includes parentheses, which means that negative numbers will be displayed with parentheses around them as shown in the result for this statement. Notice that the parentheses aren't actually formatting codes. They're simply literal values that are included in the output string. The same is true of the dollar signs.

The third statement is similar to the second one, but it includes an additional format for zero values. In this case, a zero value is displayed as the literal "Zero" as you can see in the result for this statement.

The last two statements show how to use standard formatting codes for integers and decimals. In the first statement, an integer is formatted with three digits since the number 3 is included after the formatting code. In the second statement, a decimal is formatted with two decimal places. As you can see, if the number includes more decimal places than are specified, the number is rounded.

The example at the bottom of this figure shows how you can use the Format method to format two numbers. Here, the string argument includes text in addition to the format specification for each of the two values to be formatted. In this case, the first value is formatted according to the first format specification, and the second value according to the second format specification.

How to format dates and times

You can also use the Format method of the String class to format dates and times. This method works the same way that it does for numeric formatting, but you use the standard and custom formatting codes for DateTime values that are presented in figure 9-11. The examples in this figure show how this works. If you understand how to use this method to format numbers, you shouldn't have any trouble using it to format dates and times.

Standard DateTime formatting codes

d	Short date	f	Long date, short time
D	Long date	F	Long date, long time
t	Short time	g	Short date, short time
T	Long time	G	Short date, long time

Custom DateTime formatting codes

d	Day of the month without leading zeros	h	Hour without leading zeros
dd	Day of the month with leading zeros	hh	Hour with leading zeros
ddd	Abbreviated day name	H	Hour on a 24-hour clock without leading zeros
dddd	Full day name	HH	Hour on a 24-hour clock with leading zeros
M	Month without leading zeros	m	Minutes without leading zeros
MM	Month with leading zeros	mm	Minutes with leading zeros
MMM	Abbreviated month name	s	Seconds without leading zeros
MMMM	Full month name	ss	Seconds with leading zeros
y	Two-digit year without leading zero	f	Fractions of seconds (one *f* for each decimal place)
yy	Two-digit year with leading zero	t	First character of AM/PM designator
yyyy	Four-digit year	tt	Full AM/PM designator
/	Date separator	:	Time separator

Statements that format dates and times

```
DateTime currentDate = DateTime.Now;           // 1/30/2008 10:37:32 PM
String.Format("{0:d}", currentDate)            // 1/30/2008
String.Format("{0:D}", currentDate)            // Wednesday, January 30, 2008
String.Format("{0:t}", currentDate)            // 10:37 PM
String.Format("{0:T}", currentDate)            // 10:37:32 PM
String.Format("{0:ddd, MMM d, yyyy}",
    currentDate)                               // Wed, Jan 30, 2008
String.Format("{0:M/d/yy}", currentDate)       // 1/30/08
String.Format("{0:HH:mm:ss}", currentDate)     // 22:37:32
```

Figure 9-11 How to format dates and times

Perspective

Now that you've completed this chapter, you should be able to use the DateTime structure to work with dates and times and the String and StringBuilder classes to work with strings. You should also be able to use the Format method of the String class to provide custom formatting for numbers, dates, and times, although most of the applications that you develop won't require that.

Terms

tick
immutable
mutable

Exercise 9-1 Work with dates and times

In this exercise, you'll use the DateTime and TimeSpan structures.

1. Open the application that's in the C:\C# 2008\Chapter 09\DateHandling directory. Within this project, you'll find a form that accepts a future date and a birth date from the user and provides buttons for performing the due days and age calculations.
2. Add code to calculate the due days when the user enters a future date and clicks the Calculate Due Days button. For simplicity, you can assume valid user entries. Then, display the results in a message box like this:

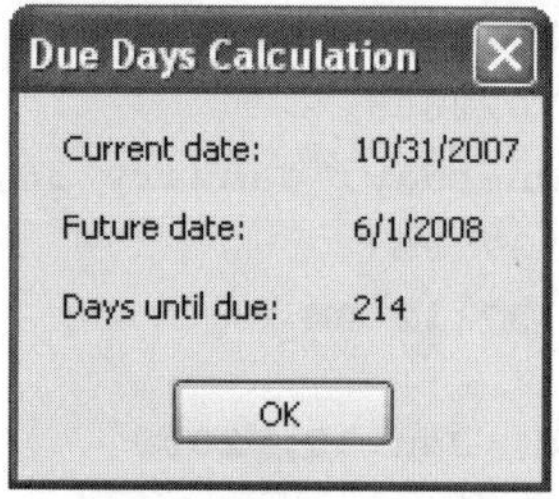

3. Test your code with a variety of date formats to see what formats can be successfully parsed. When you're done, close the form.
4. Add code to calculate the age when the user enters a birth date and clicks the Calculate Age button. Then, display the results in a message box like the one that follows. For simplicity, you can assume valid user entries.

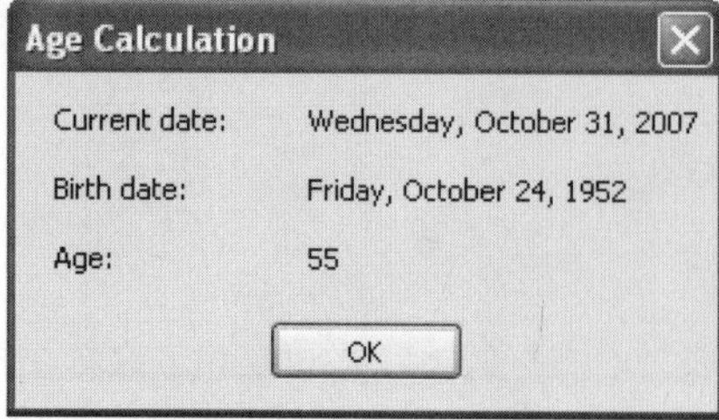

5. Run the application and test your code to make sure it works for all dates. When you're done, close the form.

Exercise 9-2 Work with strings

In this exercise, you'll use methods of the String class to work with strings.

Open the application and add code to parse a name

1. Open the application that's in the C:\C# 2008\Chapter 09\StringHandling directory. Within this project, you'll find a form that accepts a name and a phone number from the user and provides buttons for parsing the name and editing the phone number.
2. Add code to parse the name when the user enters a name and clicks the Parse Name button. This code should work whether the user enters a first, middle, and last name or just a first and last name. It should also convert the parsed name so the first letters are uppercase but the other letters are lowercase. The results should be displayed in a message box like this:

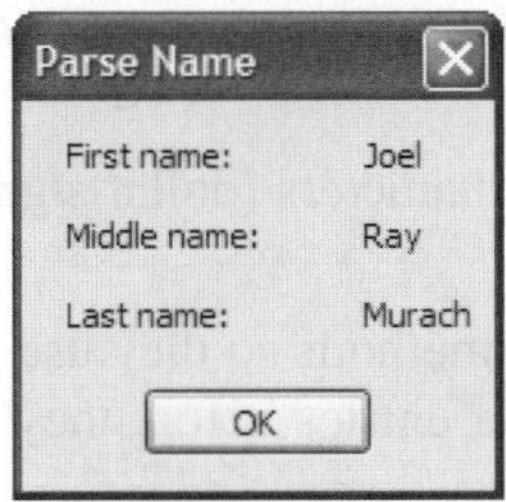

3. Test the application to see if it works. Try entering the name in all uppercase letters or all lowercase letters to make sure the parsed name is still displayed with only the first letters capitalized. When you're done, close the form.

Add code to edit a phone number

4. Add code to edit the phone number when the user enters a phone number and clicks the Edit Phone Number button. This code should remove all special characters from the user entry so the number consists of 10 digits. Then, format the phone number with hyphens. These results should be displayed in a message box like the one that follows. For simplicity, you can assume that the user enters ten digits.

5. Test the application with a variety of entry formats to make sure it works. When you're done, close the form and then close the solution.

Exercise 9-3 Enhance the Future Value application

This exercise will guide you through the process of enhancing the Future Value application so it uses an IsDecimal method like the one presented in figure 9-8.

Open the Future Value application

1. Open the application that's in the C:\C# 2008\Chapter 09\FutureValue directory.

Add the code that provides for formatted entries

2. Modify the IsDecimal method so it checks that the string value in a text box only contains numbers and numeric formatting characters (dollar signs, percent signs, commas, and spaces). If you need help, refer to figure 9-8.
3. Modify the IsDecimal method so it only allows one decimal point. Then, test that enhancement.
4. Modify the IsInt32 method so it works like the IsDecimal method, but doesn't allow a decimal point.
5. Add a Strip method that strips numeric formatting characters (dollar signs, percent signs, commas, and spaces) from a string.
6. Modify the btnCalculate_Click and IsWithinRange methods so they use the Strip method to strip invalid characters from the user entries before they're converted to the appropriate numeric format.
7. Test the application by entering numeric values that contain formatting characters.

Add code to format the displayed values

8. Add statements to the btnCalculate_Click method that format the values that are displayed in each text box like this:

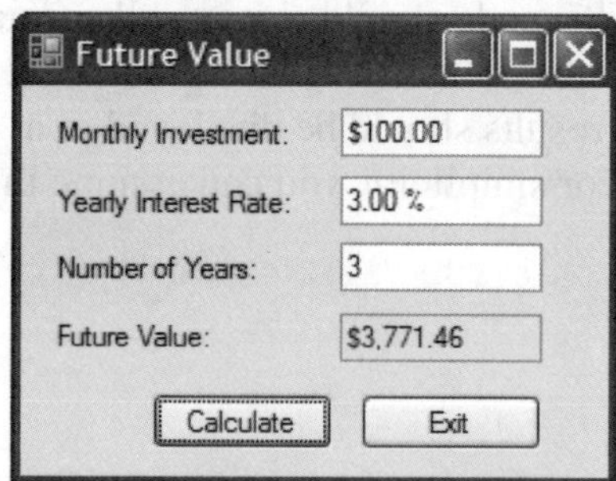

9. Test the application to make sure it works correctly. Then, close the application.

10

More skills for working with Windows forms and controls

In previous chapters, you learned how to work with a project that uses a single form that contains labels, text boxes, and buttons. In this chapter, you'll learn how to use some other common controls, such as combo boxes and check boxes, and you'll learn some basic skills for working with two or more forms in the same project. When you're done, you'll be able to develop a project that contains multiple forms and uses any of the controls presented in this chapter.

How to work with controls

Although you'll use label, text box, and button controls on almost every form you develop, their functionality is limited. As a result, you need to know how to use some of the other controls provided by the .NET Framework. In particular, you need to learn how to use the five controls presented in the topics that follow.

Five more types of controls

Figure 10-1 shows a form that contains two combo boxes, one list box, one group box, two radio buttons, and a check box. Although you've undoubtedly used these controls when working with Windows programs, take a moment to consider these controls from a programmer's point of view.

You can use a *combo box* to let the user select one item from a list of items. That reduces the amount of typing that's required by the user, and it reduces the chance that the user will enter invalid or inaccurate data. As you'll see in the next figure, you can also create combo boxes that let the user enter text that doesn't appear in the list.

Like a combo box, a *list box* lets the user select an item from a list of items. However, the list portion of a list box is always visible. In contrast, the list portion of a combo box is typically hidden until the user clicks the arrow at the right side of the control. The user can also select two or more items from a list box, but can only select a single item from a combo box.

Radio buttons provide a way to let the user select one item from a group of items. To create a group of radio buttons, you can place two or more radio buttons within a *group box*. Then, when the user selects one radio button, all the other radio buttons in the group are automatically deselected. Since the user can only select one radio button within each group, these buttons present mutually exclusive choices.

Check boxes provide a way to present the user with choices that are not mutually exclusive. That means that if the user checks or unchecks one check box, it doesn't affect the other check boxes on the form.

A form with five more types of controls

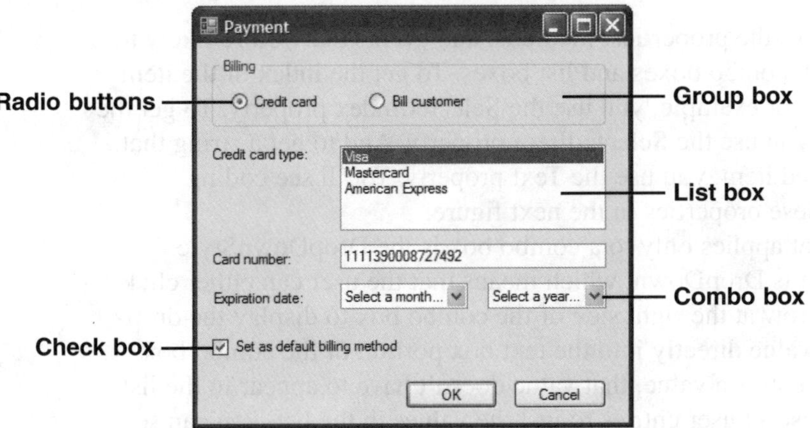

Description

- A *combo box* lets the user select one option from a drop-down list of items. A combo box can also let the user enter text into the text box portion of the combo box.
- A *list box* lets the user select one or more options from a list of items. If a list box contains more items than can be displayed at one time, a vertical scroll bar is added automatically.
- *Radio buttons* let the user select one option from a group of options.
- A *group box* can group related controls. For example, it's common to place related radio buttons within a group box. Then, the user can only select one of the radio buttons in the group.
- A *check box* lets the user select or deselect an option.

Figure 10-1 Five more types of controls

How to work with combo boxes and list boxes

Figure 10-2 shows the properties, methods, and events that you're likely to use as you work with combo boxes and list boxes. To get the index of the item that the user selects, for example, you use the SelectedIndex property. To get the selected item itself, you use the SelectedItem property. And to get a string that represents the selected item, you use the Text property. You'll see coding examples that use these properties in the next figure.

One property that applies only to a combo box is the DropDownStyle property. The default is DropDown, which means that the user can either click on the drop-down arrow at the right side of the combo box to display the drop-down list or enter a value directly into the text box portion of the combo box. Note that if the user enters a value, that value doesn't have to appear in the list.

If you want to restrict user entries to just the values in the list, you can set the DropDownStyle property to DropDownList. Then, the user can only select a value from the list or enter the first character of a value in the list to select it.

One property that applies only to a list box is the SelectionMode property. The default is One, which means that the user can only select one item from the list box. However, you can let the user select multiple items by setting this property to MultiSimple or MultiExtended. If you set it to MultiSimple, the user can only select multiple entries by clicking on them. If you set it to MultiExtended, the user can hold down the Ctrl and Shift keys to select nonadjacent and adjacent items. This works just as it does for any standard Windows application. By the way, you can also set this property to None, in which case the user can't select an entry. You might use this setting if you just want to display items.

If you allow the user to select multiple items from a list box, you can use the SelectedIndices property to return a collection of the selected indexes, and you can use the SelectedItems property to return a collection of selected items. Or, you can use the SelectedIndex and SelectedItem properties to select the first index or item in the collection of selected items.

When you work with the items in a list box or combo box, you should realize that you're actually working with the items in a collection. To refer to this collection, you use the Items property of the control. Then, you can use an index to refer to any item in the collection. Or, you can use properties and methods that the .NET Framework provides for working with collections. The most common properties and methods are summarized in this figure.

The most common event for working with combo boxes and list boxes is the SelectedIndexChanged event. This event occurs when the value of the SelectedIndex property changes, which happens when the user selects a different item from the list. For a combo box, you can also use the TextChanged event to detect when the user enters a value into the text box portion of the control. Keep in mind, though, that this event will occur each time a single character is added, changed, or deleted.

Common members of list box and combo box controls

Property	Description
`SelectedIndex`	The index of the selected item. Items are numbered from 0. If no item is selected, this property has a value of -1.
`SelectedItem`	The object of the selected item.
`Text`	The text value for the selected item.
`Sorted`	If set to true, the items in the list are sorted alphabetically in ascending order.
`Items`	Provides access to the collection of items.
`DropDownStyle`	Determines whether the user can enter text in the text box that's at the top of a combo box. If this property is set to DropDownList, the user must select an item from the list. If this property is set to DropDown, the user can enter data in the text box portion of the combo box.
`SelectionMode`	Determines whether the user can select more than one item from a list box. If this property is set to One, the user can only select one item. If it's set to MultiSimple or MultiExtended, the user can select multiple items.
Event	**Description**
`SelectedIndexChanged`	Occurs when the user selects a different item from the list.
`TextChanged`	Occurs when the user enters a value into the text box portion of a combo box.

Common members of the Items collection

Indexer	Description
`[index]`	Gets or sets the item at the specified index in the list.
Property	**Description**
`Count`	Gets the number of items in the list.
Method	**Description**
`Add(object)`	Adds the specified item to the list.
`Insert(index, object)`	Inserts an item into the list at the specified index.
`Remove(object)`	Removes the specified item from the list.
`RemoveAt(index)`	Removes the item at the specified index from the list.
`Clear()`	Removes all items from the list.

Description

- To work with the items in a list box or combo box list, you use the Items property of the control. To refer to any item in this collection, you can use an index.

Figure 10-2 Members for working with combo boxes and list boxes

After you add a combo box or list box to a form and set its properties the way you want, you can use code like that shown in figure 10-3 to work with the control. Here, the first example uses a foreach loop to load the name of each month in an array into a combo box. Each time through the loop, the Add method is used to add a month name to the Items collection for this combo box.

The first item in the array that's loaded into the list indicates that the user should select a month from the list. This is a common technique that's used to provide instructions to the user. As you'll see later in this chapter, though, you'll need to include additional code when you use this technique to be sure that the user selects an item other than the one that provides instructions.

The second example is similar, but it uses a while loop to load eight integer values into a combo box. The first value is the current year, and the next values are the seven years that follow. Like the combo box that contains the names of the months, the first entry in this combo box provides instructions for the user.

The third example shows how you can load a list box like the one shown in figure 10-1. To make sure that no items have already been loaded into this list box, this example begins by calling the Clear method to clear all the items. Then, it adds three items to the list box. Finally, it sets the SelectedIndex property to 0, which causes the first item in the list to be selected.

Although it's not shown here, it's common to put code that loads a combo box or list box in the event handler for the Load event of the form. That way, the control is loaded when the form is loaded. After that, the user can select an item from the combo box or list box and other methods can get information about that item.

The statements in the fourth example show four ways that you can get information from a combo or list box. The first statement uses the SelectedIndex property to get the index of the item that's currently selected in the Years combo box. The second statement shows how to get the value that's displayed in the text box portion of this combo box. The third statement shows how to get the value of the item that's currently selected in this combo box. Notice that because the SelectedItem property returns an object type, you must cast this object to the appropriate data type to get the value of the item. Finally, the fourth statement uses an index to get the second item in the Months combo box. Since the value of this item is a string type, the ToString method is used to get the value of this item. However, you could also cast the object to a string type like this:

```
string expMonthValue = (string) cboExpirationMonth.Items[1];
```

The fifth example shows how to use the Add, Insert, and RemoveAt methods to work with the items in a combo box list. This example begins with a foreach loop that adds three names to the list. Then, the Insert method inserts a new name at the beginning of the list, and the RemoveAt method removes the last item from the list. When you use these methods, you indicate the index where you want the item inserted or removed. Finally, the last statement shows how you can initialize a combo box so that no value is selected. To do that, you set the SelectedIndex property of the control to -1.

Code that loads the Months combo box shown in figure 10-1

```
string[] months =
    {"Select a month...",
    "January", "February", "March", "April",
    "May", "June", "July", "August",
    "September", "October", "November", "December"};

foreach (string month in months)
{
    cboExpirationMonth.Items.Add(month);
}
```

Code that loads the Years combo box shown in figure 10-1

```
int year = DateTime.Today.Year;
int endYear = year + 8;
cboExpirationYear.Items.Add("Select a year...");
while (year < endYear)
{
    cboExpirationYear.Items.Add(year);
    year++;
}
```

Code that clears and loads the list box shown in figure 10-1

```
lstCreditCardType.Items.Clear();
lstCreditCardType.Items.Add("Visa");
lstCreditCardType.Items.Add("Mastercard");
lstCreditCardType.Items.Add("American Express");
lstCreditCardType.SelectedIndex = 0;          // select the first item
```

Statements that get information from a combo box or list box

```
int expYearIndex = cboExpirationYear.SelectedIndex;

string expYearText = cboExpirationYear.Text;

int expYearValue = (int) cboExpirationYear.SelectedItem;

string expMonthValue = cboExpirationMonth.Items[1].ToString();
```

Code that works with a combo box of names

```
string[] names = {"Doug Lowe", "Anne Boehm", "Ed Koop"};
foreach (string name in names)
{
    cboNames.Items.Add(name);
}
cboNames.Items.Insert(0, "Joel Murach");
cboNames.Items.RemoveAt(3);
cboNames.SelectedIndex = -1;                  // don't select an item
```

Notes

- You can also use the String Collection Editor to load items into a combo box or list box. To display this editor, select the control in the Form Designer and select the Edit Items command from the smart tag menu.
- In chapter 19, you'll learn techniques that can be used to load combo boxes and list boxes with data that's stored in a database.

Figure 10-3 Code examples for working with combo boxes and list boxes

How to work with check boxes and radio buttons

Figure 10-4 shows you how to work with check boxes and radio buttons. The main difference between these two types of controls is that radio buttons in a group are mutually exclusive and check boxes operate independently. In other words, if the user selects one radio button in a group, all of the other buttons are automatically turned off. In contrast, when the user selects a check box, it has no effect on the other check boxes on the form, even if they appear as a group.

To group radio buttons, you typically place them in a group box control. If you place any radio buttons outside of a group, however, all of the radio buttons on the form that aren't in a group box function as a group.

The property you're most likely to use when working with radio buttons and check boxes is the Checked property. This property can have a value of either true or false to indicate whether or not the control is checked.

The two statements in the first example set the Checked properties of a radio button and a check box to true. Then, the if-else statement in the second example tests the Checked property of the radio button. If the value of this property is true, a method named EnableControls is executed. But if the value of this property is false, it indicates that another radio button is selected. In that case, a method named DisableControls is executed.

Notice that the if-else statement in this example is coded within the event handler for the CheckedChanged event of the control. This event occurs when you select or deselect a radio button or check box, and it's the event you're most likely to use. Also note that because the Checked property contains a Boolean value, you could code the if clause without the equality operator like this:

```
if (rdoCreditCard.Checked)
```

The third example in this figure simply retrieves the Checked property of the check box and stores it in a Boolean variable. If the user has checked this box, this variable will be set to true. Otherwise, it will be set to false.

How to work with group boxes

Figure 10-4 also illustrates how to use a group box. For example, the group box shown at the top of this figure contains two radio buttons. That makes it clear that these controls function as a group. You specify the name of the group, which is displayed in the upper left corner of the group box, by setting the Text property of the control.

When you use a group box, you should know that all the controls it contains will move with the group box when you move it in the Form Designer. You should also know that you can't add existing controls on a form to a group box by dragging the group box over them. Instead, you have to add the group box and then drag the controls into the group box.

A group box that contains two radio buttons

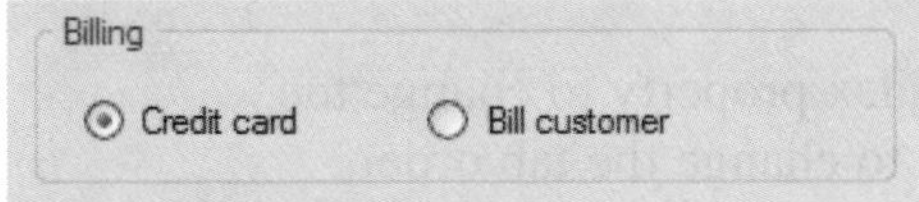

Common members of radio button and check box controls

Property	Description
`Checked`	Gets or sets a Boolean value that indicates whether the control is checked.
Event	**Description**
`CheckedChanged`	Occurs when the user checks or unchecks the control.

Code that sets the value of a radio button or check box

```
rdoCreditCard.Checked = true;
chkDefault.Checked = true;
```

Code that checks the value of a radio button

```
private void rdoCreditCard_CheckedChanged(object sender, System.EventArgs e)
{
    if (rdoCreditCard.Checked == true)
        EnableControls();
    else
        DisableControls();
}
```

Code that gets the value of a check box

```
bool isDefaultBilling = chkDefault.Checked;
```

Description

- To determine whether a radio button or check box is checked, you test its Checked property.
- You can use a group box to group controls. Group boxes are typically used to group controls like radio buttons that function as a group.
- To add controls to a group box, drag them from the Toolbox into the group box. If you've already added the controls you want to include in the group box to the form, just drag them into the group box.
- Any radio buttons that aren't placed within a group box function as a separate group.
- If you move a group box, all of the controls it contains move with it.

Figure 10-4 How to work with radio buttons, check boxes, and group boxes

How to use Tab Order view to set the tab order

In chapter 2, you learned how to use the TabIndex property to change the *tab order* of the controls on a form. An easier way to change the tab order, though, is to use Tab Order view. This view is illustrated in figure 10-5.

When you display a form in Tab Order view, an index value is displayed at the left of each control that indicates the control's position in the tab order. Notice that the index values of the two radio button controls indicate their position in the tab order relative to the group box that contains them.

To change the tab order, you click on each control in the appropriate sequence. As you click on each control, the numbers are displayed as shown in the second form in this figure. Here, I clicked on the list box, followed by the text box, followed by the two combo boxes, followed by the check box, followed by the two buttons and then the group box. That way, when the form is first displayed, the focus will be on the list box. Then, when the user presses the Tab key, the focus will move through the controls in sequence.

Notice that when I selected the group box control, the main indexes of the radio buttons within this control changed too so that they're the same as the group box. However, the sub index of each radio button didn't change. In other words, the indexes of the radio buttons relative to each other remained the same. If you wanted to change these indexes, though, you could do that by clicking on them just like any other control.

Also notice in the second form that I didn't set the tab index for any of the labels. In most cases, it isn't necessary to change the tab order of controls that can't receive the focus. One case where you will want to include a label control explicitly in the tab order is if it defines an access key. In that case, you'll want to position it in the tab order just before the control it identifies. Then, if the user presses the access key for that control, the focus will move to the control it identifies since it's next in the tab order.

A form in Tab Order view before and after the tab order is changed

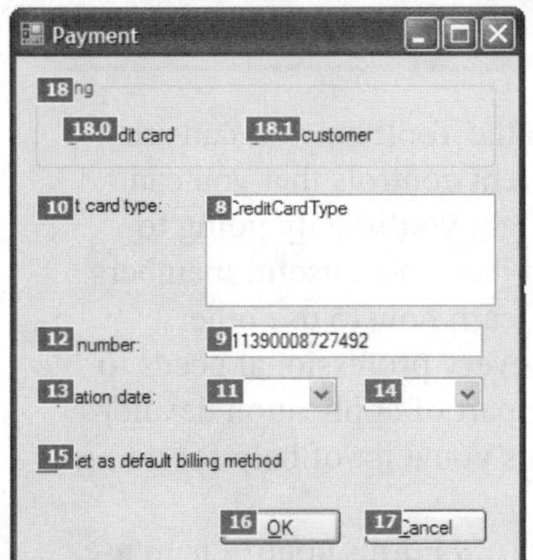

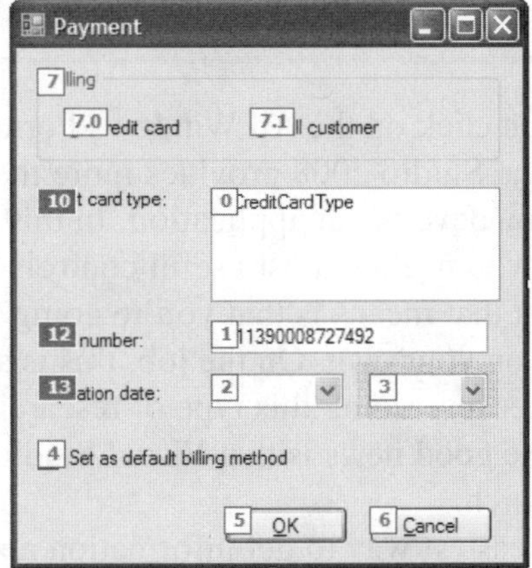

How to use Tab Order view to change the tab order

- To display a form in Tab Order view, select the form and then select the View➔Tab Order command. This displays the tab index for each control as in the first form above.
- To change the tab indexes of the controls, click on the controls in the sequence you want to use. As you click, the new tab indexes appear as in the second form above.
- If a group box contains other controls, the controls in the group box are displayed with sub indexes as illustrated by the radio buttons above. Then, you can click on the group box to change its index and the main indexes of the controls it contains. To change the sub indexes of the controls in the group box, click on them individually.

Description

- The *tab order* determines the order in which controls receive the focus when the Tab key is pressed. The TabIndex property of the controls determines this order.
- By default, the value of a control's TabIndex property is determined by the sequence in which it's added to the form. The TabIndex property is set to 0 for the first control, 1 for the second control, and so on.
- A label can't receive the focus. As a result, you typically don't need to include the labels in the tab order. However, if the label defines an access key, the TabIndex property of the label should be set to one less than its related control. That way, the related control will receive the focus when the access key for the label is activated.
- When setting the tab order, you can skip controls whose TabStop, Enabled, or Visible properties have been set to false, unless those properties will change as the form runs.

Figure 10-5 How to use Tab Order view to set the tab order

How to get the information you need for using a control

If you click on the All Windows Forms group in the Toolbox, you can see that Visual Studio 2008 provides more than 60 different controls that you can use as you develop an application. In this book, though, you're only going to learn how to use the most useful controls along with their most useful members.

What that means is that you're going to have to learn how to use other controls on your own. On the job, this is a skill that every professional needs to master because doing this type of research is a large part of application development. The good news is that Visual Studio 2008 gives you a lot of help for doing this research.

The easiest way to get information about a Windows Forms control is to use the Help documentation that comes with Visual Studio. To access this documentation, you can use the commands in the Help menu. The one I've found to be most useful is the Index command. When you select this command, a Help window like the one in figure 10-6 is displayed.

The Index tab in the left pane of this window lets you enter the text you want to look for in the Look For text box. To look for information on a control, for example, you can enter the name of the control. You can also filter the information that's displayed using the drop-down list at the top of the Index tab.

In this figure, I entered "DateTimeP" and then selected the "about" topic under the "DateTimePicker control [Windows Forms]" heading. When I did that, some basic information about the DateTimePicker control was displayed in the right pane of the window. This is usually a good place to start when you're learning how to use a control that you haven't used before.

Once you have a basic idea of how a control works, you can display other topics that describe specific features or functions of the control. You can do that by using the links that are available within a topic or by selecting topics from the Index tab.

In addition to the topics that are listed for a control, you may want to review the members of the class that defines the control. In this figure, you can see the DateTimePicker class at the top of the Index tab. You can select the "all members" topic beneath this heading to display all the members of the class. Or, you can display each type of member separately by selecting the appropriate topic. For example, you can select the "methods" topic to display all methods that are available from the DateTimePicker class.

Some of the Help documentation for the DateTimePicker control

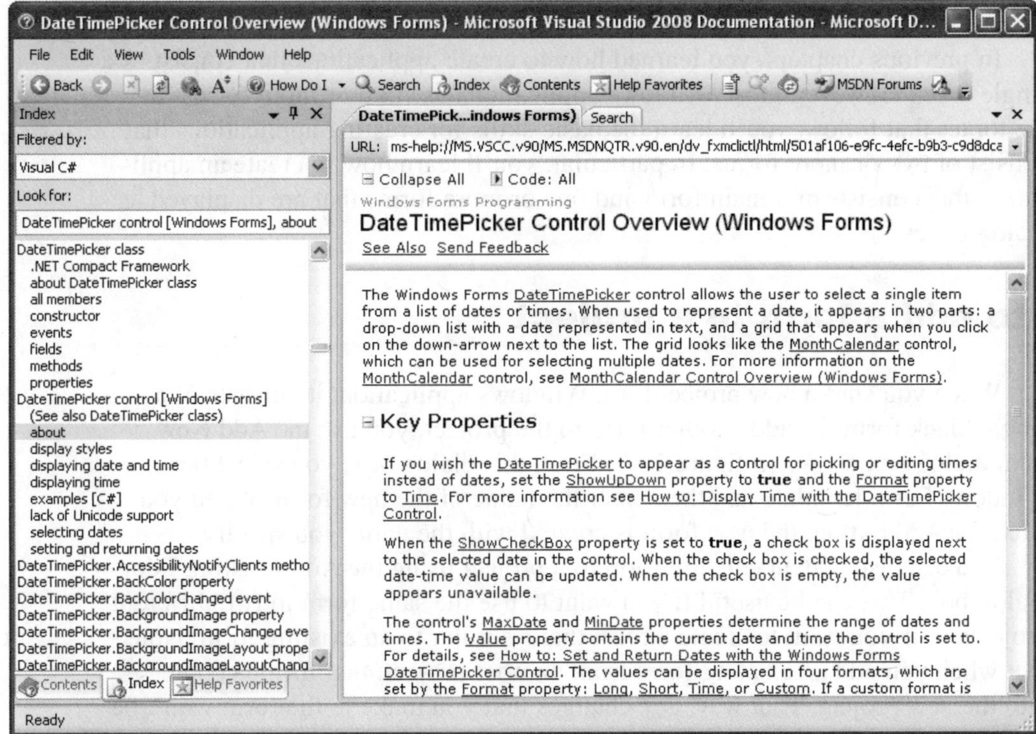

Description

- Visual Studio 2008 provides an abundance of information on the Windows Forms controls. The easiest way to display this information is to use the Help→Index command.
- To start, you can review the information about the basic function and usage of the control. To do that, just enter the name of the control in the Look For text box and then select the appropriate entries.
- Most controls include an index entry that describes the control and a separate index entry that describes the class for the control. To learn how to work with a control, you'll typically need to use both of these entries.
- The index entry for most Windows Forms controls includes an "about" topic like the one shown above that provides basic information about the control along with other related topics. Some of these topics such as "setting and returning dates" describe specific features of the control.
- The index entry for most control classes includes a topic that describes all members that are available from the control. To view this topic, you can select the "all members" topic. Or, you can select a more specific topic such as "methods" to display a specific type of member.

Figure 10-6 How to get the information you need for using a control

How to work with multi-form projects

In previous chapters, you learned how to create applications that consist of a single form. However, most Windows applications use two or more forms. In the topics that follow, you'll learn the basic skills for creating applications that consist of two or more forms. In particular, you'll learn how to create an application that consists of a main form and one or more forms that are displayed as dialog boxes.

How to add a form to a project

When you start a new project for a Windows application, it consists of a single blank form. To add another form to the project, you use the Add New Item dialog box shown in figure 10-7. From this dialog box, you select the Windows Form template and then enter the name of the new form. When you click the Add button, the new form is created with the name you specify.

You can also add an existing form to a project using the Add Existing Item dialog box. This can be useful if you want to use the same form in two different projects or if you want to create a form that's similar to an existing form. Note that when you add an existing form from another project, that form is copied into the new project. That way, any changes that you make to the form won't be applied to the original form, which is typically what you want.

The Add New Item dialog box

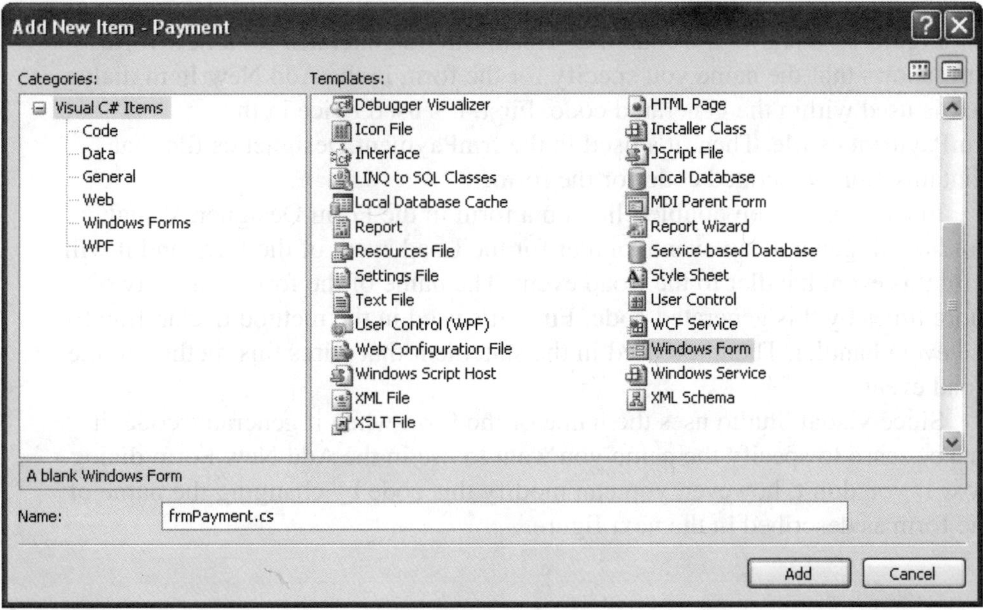

How to add a new form

- Display the Add New Item dialog box by selecting the Project→Add New Item command. Or, select the Add→Add New Item command from the shortcut menu that's displayed when you right-click on the project in the Solution Explorer.
- To add a new form, select the Windows Form template from the Add New Item dialog box, enter a name for the form, and click the Open button.

How to add an existing form

- Display the Add Existing Item dialog box by selecting the Project→Add Existing Item command. Or, select the Add→Add Existing Item command from the shortcut menu for the project.
- To add an existing form, select the cs file for the form from the Add Existing Item dialog box and then click the Open button.

Note

- When you name a form, we recommend you use the prefix *frm* so it's clear that the file contains a form.

Figure 10-7 How to add a form to a project

The code that's generated for a new form

Figure 10-8 shows the code that Visual Studio generates for a new form. This shows that the name you specify for the form in the Add New Item dialog box is used within the generated code. First, it's used twice in the frmPayment.cs file. Then, it's used in the frmPayment.Designer.cs file that contains more generated code for the form.

In addition, if you double-click on a form in the Form Designer, Visual Studio will generate an event handler for the Load event of the form and it will wire this event handler to the Load event. The name of the form is used two more times by this generated code. First, it's used in the method declaration for the event handler. Then, it's used in the statement that wires this method to the Load event.

Since Visual Studio uses the name of the form when it generates code, it makes sense to specify the name you want to use in the Add New Form dialog box. If you don't, however, you can modify this code by changing the name of the form as described in the next figure.

The generated code for a new form named frmPayment

For the frmPayment.cs file

```
namespace Payment
{
    public partial class frmPayment : Form
    {
        public frmPayment()
        {
            InitializeComponent();
        }
    }
}
```

For the frmPayment.Designer.cs file

```
namespace Payment
{
    partial class frmPayment
    {
        #region Windows Form Designer generated code
    }
}
```

The code that's generated for the Load event handler of the form

The method declaration in the frmPayment.cs file

```
private void frmPayment_Load(object sender, System.EventArgs e)
{
    // code that handles the event goes here
}
```

The wiring in the frmPayment.Designer.cs file

```
this.Load += new System.EventHandler(this.frmPayment_Load);
```

Description

- The name you specify for the form in the Add New Item dialog box is used by both files for the form class and it appears several times in the generated code.
- Visual Studio uses the name of the form when you create an event handler for one of the form's events such as the Load event.

Figure 10-8 The code that's generated for a new form

How to rename a form

Figure 10-9 shows a procedure that you can use to rename a form. To start, you can right-click the form in the Solution Explorer and select the Rename command. Or, you can select the form in the Solution Explorer and press F2. Then, you can enter the new name for the form. In the project shown in this figure, for example, I renamed the form that was originally named Form1.cs to frmCustomer.cs. This automatically changes all names necessary to get the form to run correctly.

However, if you have added event handlers for form events to the form before renaming the form, the old form name will still be used by these event handlers and their wiring. Although this code should work correctly, you may want to update it so it reflects the new form name. If so, you can edit the name of the form in the method declaration for the event handler. When you do, the refactoring bar should appear under the name of the event handler. Then, you can point at that bar, click the drop-down arrow, and select the Rename command from the resulting menu. This will rename the method declaration and update the wiring for the event handler.

A project that contains two forms

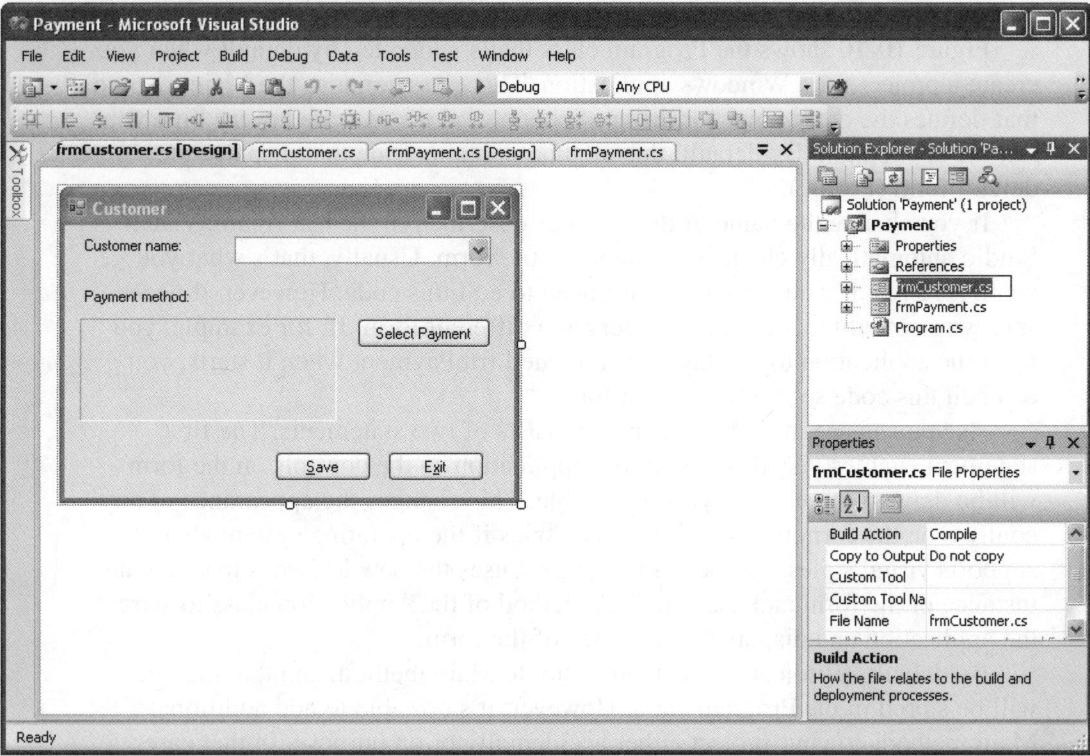

How to change the name of a form

- Right-click the form in the Solution Explorer and select the Rename command. Or, select the form in the Solution Explorer and press F2.
- Enter the new name for the form. When you do, Visual Studio uses the new refactoring feature to change the name for the form wherever it's used.

How to change the name of any event handlers for a form's events

- Edit the name of the method that's used by the event handler.
- Point at the refactoring bar that appears under the name of the method to display the smart tag menu, click on the drop-down arrow to display the refactoring menu, and select the Rename command.

Note

- Although it's possible to use the Name property of the form to change the name that's used to identify the form in code without changing the name of the form file, it's a good programming practice to use the same name for the file and the class.

Figure 10-9 How to rename a form

How to display the first form of an application

Figure 10-10 shows the Program class that's generated by default when you create a project for a Windows application. This class contains the Main method that defines the entry point for the application, and it's executed every time you run the application. By default, this method contains code that displays the default form (Form1).

If you change the name of this form as described in the last figure, Visual Studio automatically changes the name of the form. Usually, that's what you want. As a result, you typically don't need to edit this code. However, if necessary, you can edit this code so it refers to a different form. If, for example, you want the application to display a form named frmPayment when it starts, you can edit this code so it refers to that form.

As you can see, the Main method consists of two statements. The first statement enables visual styles for the application so the controls on the form will be drawn with visual styles if possible. This changes the appearance of any controls on the form that support visual styles if the operating system also supports visual styles. The second statement uses the new keyword to create an instance of the form and uses the Run method of the Application class to start the application and display that instance of the form.

By default, a project will contain a single Main method, and that method will be stored in the Program class. However, it's possible to add additional Main methods to your project either accidentally or on purpose. In that case, your application may use the wrong Main method when it starts. To solve this problem, you can delete the Main methods that you don't want to use. Or, you can display the Property Pages dialog box by selecting the Properties command from the Project menu. Then, you can use that dialog box to specify the class that contains the Main method you want to use. To do that, you click on the Application tab and select the class from the Startup Object combo box, which lists all the objects that contain Main methods.

Code that defines the main entry point for an application

```
using System;
using System.Collections.Generic;
using System.Windows.Forms;

namespace Payment
{
    static class Program
    {
        /// <summary>
        /// The main entry point for the application.
        /// </summary>
        [STAThread]
        static void Main()
        {
            Application.EnableVisualStyles();
            Application.Run(new frmCustomer());
        }
    }
}
```

Description

- When you create a Windows application, Visual Studio automatically generates a class named Program that contains a Main method that defines the main entry point for the application. This class is stored in the Program.cs file.
- The Main method uses the Run method of the Application class to display the first form for the application. If you want to change the form that's displayed when the application starts, you can change the name of the form supplied to the Run method.
- If your project contains more than one Main method, you can delete the Main methods that you don't want to use. Or, you can use the Project→*ProjectName* Properties command to display the Property Pages dialog box. Then, you can click on the Application tab and select the class that contains the Main method that you want to use from the Startup Object combo box.

Figure 10-10 How to display the first form of an application

How to display a form as a dialog box

When designing applications that contain two or more forms, it's common to display a form as a dialog box. A form that's displayed as a dialog box can also be called a *modal form*. In figure 10-11, for example, you can see a Payment form that's displayed as a dialog box. This form is displayed when the user clicks the Select Payment button in the Customer form that's also shown here.

When you create a form that will be displayed as a dialog box, you typically set the form properties as shown in this figure. These property settings prevent the user from changing the size of the form or from closing the form other than by using the controls you provide on the form. Although setting the ControlBox property to false removes the Maximize button from a form, the user can still maximize the form by double-clicking its title bar. That's why you should also set the MaximizeBox property to false.

If you want to include a standard Close button in the title bar of a dialog box, you can do that too. Just leave the ControlBox property at its default setting of true, and set the MaximizeBox and MinimizeBox properties to false. Then, the title bar will look like the one you'll see in the dialog box in figure 10-14.

To display a form as a dialog box, you use the new keyword to create a new instance of the form. Then, you call the ShowDialog method of the form object. When you use this method to display a form, the user must respond to the dialog box before the code that follows the ShowDialog method can be executed. This code typically tests the user response to determine what to do next. You'll learn more about getting the response from a dialog box in the next figure.

In addition to modal forms, an application can also contain *modeless forms*. When you use modeless forms, the user can typically move back and forth between the forms as necessary. In most cases, that gives the user a wider range of possible actions, which means that the program must include code that provides for all of those actions. While this type of form is appropriate for some applications, it can make an application more difficult to develop. That's why it's common to use dialog boxes to control the flow of the application and to limit possible user actions.

The Payment form displayed as a dialog box

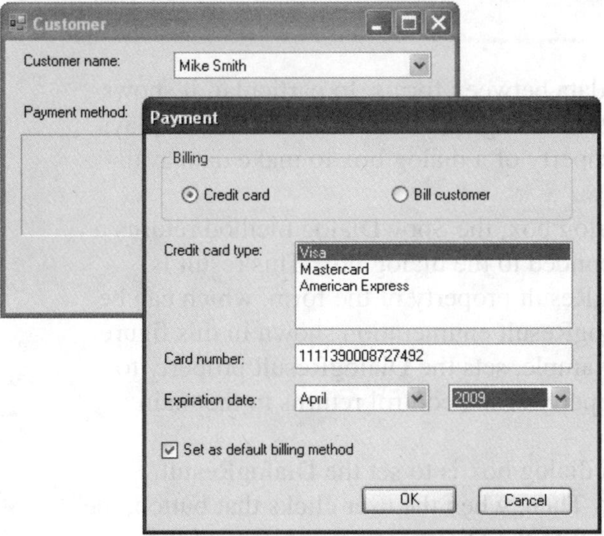

Properties for creating custom dialog boxes

Property	Description
`FormBorderStyle`	Typically set to FixedDialog to prevent the user from resizing the form by dragging its border.
`ControlBox`	Typically set to false so the control box and the Maximize, Minimize, and Close buttons don't appear in the title bar of the form.
`MaximizeBox`	Typically set to false so the user can't maximize the form by double-clicking the title bar.
`MinimizeBox`	Can be set to false to prevent the Minimize button from being displayed if the ControlBox property is set to true.

Code that creates and displays a custom dialog box

```
Form paymentForm = new frmPayment();
paymentForm.ShowDialog();
// execution continues here after the user responds to the dialog box
```

Description

- If you display a form as a dialog box, the user must respond to the form before continuing to any other forms. A form like this is sometimes referred to as a custom dialog box or a *modal form*.
- You use the ShowDialog method of a form object to display the form as a dialog box. After the user responds to the dialog box, execution continues with the statement that follows the ShowDialog method.

Figure 10-11 How to display a form as a dialog box

How to pass data between a form and a custom dialog box

Figure 10-12 shows how to pass data between forms. In particular, it shows how to get the user response to a custom dialog box from the form that displays it, and it shows how to use the Tag property of a dialog box to make data available to the form that displays it.

When you display a form as a dialog box, the ShowDialog method returns a value that indicates how the user responded to the dialog box. This result is determined by the value of the DialogResult property of the form, which can be set to any of the members of the DialogResult enumeration shown in this figure. The first statement shown here, for example, sets the DialogResult property to DialogResult.OK. As soon as this property is set, control returns to the main form.

Another way to set the result of a dialog box is to set the DialogResult property of a button in the dialog box. Then, when the user clicks that button, the DialogResult property of the form is set to the DialogResult property of the button. If, for example, you set the DialogResult property of the Cancel button on the Payment form shown in figure 10-11 to Cancel, that value is returned when the user clicks that button and the dialog box is closed. In that case, no code is required for the Click event of that button unless some additional processing is required.

You can also set the DialogResult property of a button to Cancel by setting the CancelButton property of the form. Then, the Cancel member of the DialogResult enumeration is returned when the user clicks that button. Here again, no code is required for the Click event of the button unless some additional processing is required.

After the DialogResult property is set and control returns to the form that displayed the dialog box, that form can use the DialogResult enumeration to determine how the user responded. To see how this works, take a look at the third example in this figure. Here, the first statement creates an instance of the Payment form. Then, the second statement displays that form using the ShowDialog method and stores the result of that method in a DialogResult variable named selectedButton. Next, an if statement is used to test if the result is equal to DialogResult.OK.

Another way to pass data between a dialog box and another form is to use the Tag property of the dialog box. The second statement in this figure, for example, sets the Tag property of a dialog box to a variable named msg. Note that you must set this property before control returns to the main form.

Once control returns to the main form, you can get the data that was stored in the Tag property as shown in the last statement of the third example. Here, the Text property of a label is set to the value that was stored in the Tag property of the dialog box. Notice that because the Tag property holds an object type, the object must be cast to a string type before it can be assigned to the Text property.

An enumeration that works with dialog boxes

Enumeration	Members
`DialogResult`	OK, Cancel, Yes, No, Abort, Retry, Ignore, None

The Tag property

Property	Description
`Tag`	Gets or sets data associated with the form or a control. The Tag property holds a reference to an object type, which means that it can hold any type of data.

A statement that sets the DialogResult property of a form

```
this.DialogResult = DialogResult.OK;
```

A statement that sets the Tag property of a form

```
this.Tag = msg;
```

Code that uses the result of a dialog box and the Tag property

```
Form paymentForm = new frmPayment();
DialogResult selectedButton = paymentForm.ShowDialog();
if (selectedButton == DialogResult.OK)
    lblPayment.Text = paymentForm.Tag.ToString();
```

How to use the DialogResult enumeration

- The DialogResult enumeration provides members that represent the values that a dialog box can return. The ShowDialog method returns a member of this enumeration.
- You specify the result value of a custom dialog box by setting its DialogResult property. Or, you can set the DialogResult property of a button in the dialog box. Then, when the user clicks that button, the DialogResult property of the form is set accordingly.
- If you set the CancelButton property of a form to a button on that form, the DialogResult property of that button is automatically set to Cancel.
- After you set the DialogResult property of a dialog box, the form is closed and control is returned to the form that displayed it. If you close a dialog box without setting the DialogResult property, a value of Cancel is returned to the main form.

How to use the Tag property

- The Tag property provides a convenient way to pass data between forms in a multi-form application. A dialog box can set its Tag property before it returns control to the main form. Then, the main form can get the data from this property and use it as necessary.
- Because the Tag property is an object type, you must explicitly cast it to the appropriate type to retrieve the data it contains. Or, you can use the ToString method to convert the data to a string.

Figure 10-12 How to pass data between a form and a custom dialog box

How to use the MessageBox class

Although you can create custom dialog boxes using the techniques you learned in the last two topics, it's also common to use the MessageBox class to display certain types of dialog boxes. In chapter 7, for example, you learned how to use the MessageBox class to display a simple dialog box with an error message and an OK button. Now, you'll learn how to use the MessageBox class to display more complex dialog boxes, and you'll learn how to get the user's response to these dialog boxes.

How to display a dialog box and get the user response

Figure 10-13 shows how to display a dialog box and get a response from a user. To display a dialog box, you use the Show method shown at the top of this figure. As you can see, you can specify up to five arguments for this method. The first argument is the text message that you want to display. Although this is the only argument that's required, you'll typically code the second argument too, which displays a caption in the title bar of the dialog box.

You can use the third argument to control the buttons that are displayed in the dialog box. You can use the fourth argument to control the icon that's displayed in the dialog box. And you can use the fifth argument to control the default button that's activated when the user presses the Enter key. To specify these arguments, you use the constants in the first three enumerations that are summarized in this figure.

Like the ShowDialog method, the Show method of the MessageBox class returns a value that indicates how the user responded to the dialog box. The value that's returned is one of the members of the DialogResult enumeration. These members represent the buttons that can be displayed in a dialog box, and the return value is automatically set to the appropriate member when the user clicks a button.

The first example in this figure shows how to code a Show method that specifies all five arguments. Here, the third argument indicates that only Yes and No buttons should be included in the dialog box, and the fifth argument indicates that the second button, in this case, No, should be the default button.

The second example shows how you can use the DialogResult value that's returned by the Show method to determine which button the user clicked in the dialog box. Here, an if statement tests if the DialogResult value that was returned by the Show method is equal to DialogResult.Yes. If it is, it means that the user clicked the Yes button, and the code within the if statement is executed.

The syntax for the Show method of the MessageBox class

```
MessageBox.Show(text[, caption[, buttons[, icon[, defaultButton]]]]);
```

The enumerations that work with the MessageBox class

Enumeration	Members
`MessageBoxButtons`	OK, OKCancel, YesNo, YesNoCancel, AbortRetryIgnore
`MessageBoxIcon`	None, Information, Error, Warning, Exclamation, Question, Asterisk, Hand, Stop
`MessageBoxDefaultButton`	Button1, Button2, Button3
`DialogResult`	OK, Cancel, Yes, No, Abort, Retry, Ignore

A statement that displays a dialog box and gets the user response

```
DialogResult button =
    MessageBox.Show(
        "Are you sure you want to save this data?",
        "Payment",
        MessageBoxButtons.YesNo,
        MessageBoxIcon.Question,
        MessageBoxDefaultButton.Button2);
```

The dialog box that's displayed

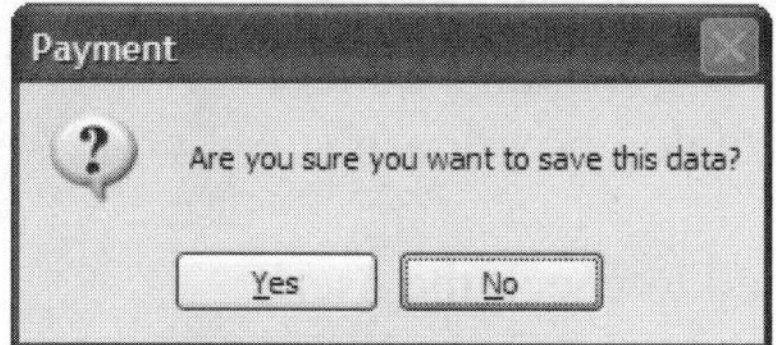

A statement that checks the user response

```
if (button == DialogResult.Yes)
{
    SaveData();
    isDataSaved = true;
}
```

Description

- You can use the Show method of the MessageBox class to display a message to a user and accept a response from the user.
- You use the first three enumerations listed above to specify the buttons and icon that will appear in the dialog box and the button that's treated as the default.
- If you omit the buttons argument, the OK button is displayed by default. If you omit the icon argument, no icon is displayed by default. If you omit the default button argument, the first button is the default.
- The Show method returns a DialogResult value that corresponds to one of the members of the DialogResult enumeration. You can use this value to determine which button the user clicked.

Figure 10-13 How to display a dialog box and get the user response

How to use the FormClosing event

Figure 10-14 shows how you can use a dialog box to cancel the FormClosing event of a form. This technique is often used when a user attempts to close a form that contains unsaved data.

To start, it's important to understand that the FormClosing event is executed when the user attempts to close the form but before the form is actually closed. This event occurs if the user clicks a button on the form that calls the Close method for the form. It also occurs if the user clicks the Close button in the upper right corner of the form.

This figure presents an event handler for the FormClosing event of a form. This event handler receives two parameters. You can use the Cancel property of the second parameter, which is named e, to determine whether or not the form is closed. By default, this property is set to false, which means that the FormClosing event will not be cancelled and the form will be closed. If you don't want to close the form, you can set this property to true to cancel the FormClosing event.

The event handler shown here starts by checking a class variable named isDataSaved to determine if the form contains unsaved data. If it doesn't, no additional processing is performed and the form is closed. If the form contains unsaved data, however, a dialog box is displayed that asks the user if the data should be saved. As you can see, this dialog box contains Yes, No, and Cancel buttons as well as a warning icon. Since the code for this dialog box doesn't specify a default button, the first button is the default.

After the dialog box is displayed, if statements are used to check the user's response and perform the appropriate action. If the user clicks the Cancel button, for example, the Cancel property of the e parameter is set to true. This cancels the FormClosing event and returns the user to the form. If the user clicks the Yes button, the code checks whether the form contains valid data. If it does, the SaveData method is called to save the data and the form is closed. If it doesn't, the Cancel property of the parameter named e is set to true and the FormClosing event is cancelled. On the other hand, if the user clicks the No button, no code is executed. As a result, the form is closed without saving the data.

The code for a dialog box that cancels the Closing event

```
private void frmCustomer_FormClosing(object sender, FormClosingEventArgs e)
{
    if (isDataSaved == false)
    {
        string message =
            "This form contains unsaved data.\n\n" +
            "Do you want to save it?";

        DialogResult button =
            MessageBox.Show(message, "Customer",
            MessageBoxButtons.YesNoCancel,
            MessageBoxIcon.Warning);

        if (button == DialogResult.Yes)
        {
            if (IsValidData())
                this.SaveData();
            else
                e.Cancel = true;
        }
        if (button == DialogResult.Cancel)
        {
            e.Cancel = true;
        }
    }
}
```

The dialog box that's displayed by the code shown above

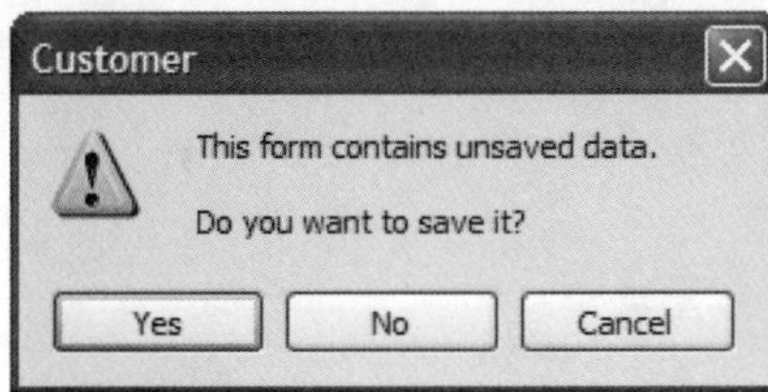

Description

- The event handler for the FormClosing event of a form receives a parameter named e that's created from the FormClosingEventArgs class. The Cancel property of this parameter lets you specify whether or not the event should be canceled. To cancel the event, set this property to true.

Figure 10-14 How to use the FormClosing event

The Payment application

This chapter closes by presenting the operation, property settings, and code for a project that contains two forms that use the controls and coding techniques that were presented in this chapter. By studying the code for this application, you will get a better idea of how you can use these controls and techniques in your own applications.

The operation

Figure 10-15 shows how the Payment application works. To start, this application displays the Customer form. On this form, the user must select a customer from the Customer Name combo box. Then, the user must click the Select Payment button to display the Payment dialog box and specify payment information for the selected customer.

Within the Payment dialog box, the user can select to charge the customer's credit card and then enter the required information. Or, the user can select to bill the customer directly. To complete the form, the user clicks the OK button. Then, control is returned to the Customer form and the payment information is displayed on that form. To save the payment information, the user clicks the Save button.

The Customer form

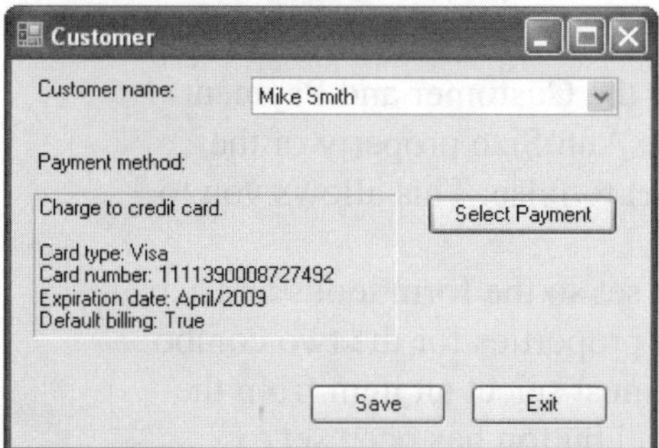

Two versions of the Payment dialog box

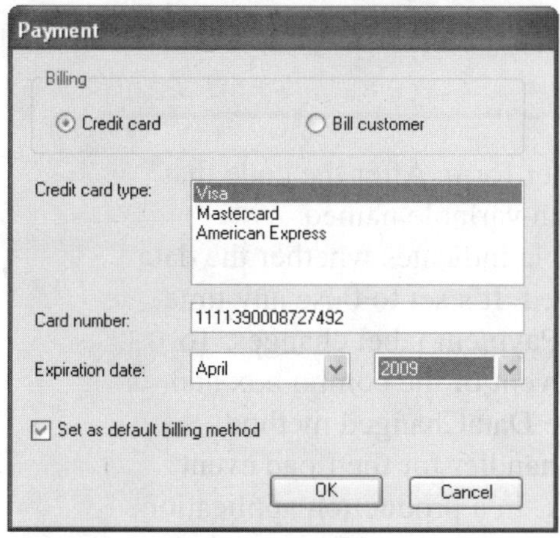

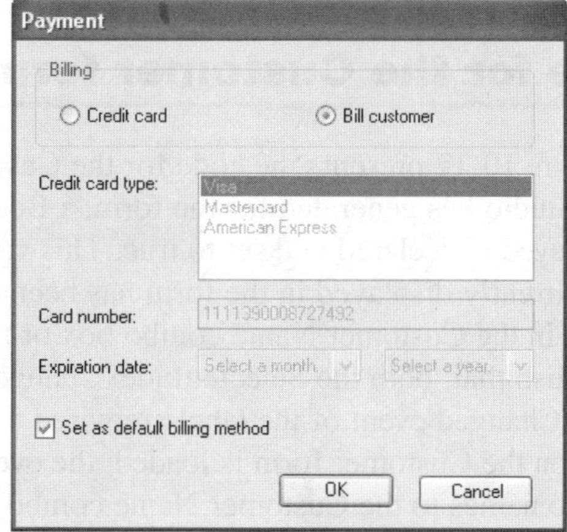

Description

- The Customer Name combo box in the Customer form lets the user select a customer.
- The Select Payment button in the Customer form displays the Payment dialog box, which lets the user specify payment information for the customer.
- If the Credit Card option is selected, the user must select a credit card type, enter a card number, and select an expiration month and year.
- If the Bill Customer option is selected, the Credit Card Type, Card Number, and Expiration Date controls are disabled.
- When the user clicks the OK button on the Payment form, control returns to the Customer form and the payment information is displayed in the Payment Method label.

Note

- This application doesn't actually save the data the user enters. In a production application, however, the data would be saved to a database or file.

Figure 10-15 The operation of the Payment application

The property settings

Figure 10-16 presents the property settings for the Customer and Payment forms and their controls. In the Customer form, the AutoSize property of the label that displays the payment method has been set to false. This allows you to use the Form Designer to size the label.

In the Payment form, the properties have been set so the form looks and acts like a dialog box. In addition, the DropDownStyle properties for the two combo boxes have been set to DropDownList so the user must select an item from the list. Finally, the DialogResult property of the Cancel button has been set to Cancel, which happens automatically when the CancelButton property of the form is set to the Cancel button.

The code for the Customer form

Figure 10-17 presents the code for the Customer form. After the code that Visual Studio has generated for the form, a Boolean variable named isDataSaved is declared and set to true. This variable indicates whether the data that's currently displayed in the form has been saved. It's set to false any time the data in the Customer Name combo box or the Payment label changes. To accomplish that, both the SelectedIndexChanged event of the combo box and the TextChanged event of the label are wired to the DataChanged method.

When the Customer form is loaded, the event handler for the Load event adds two names to the Customer Name combo box. In a production application, of course, the combo box would include many more names, and they would be loaded from a file or database. But for the purposes of this chapter, two names are sufficient.

When the user clicks the Select Payment button, the Click event handler for that button displays the Payment form as a dialog box. Then, if the user clicks the OK button in that dialog box, the payment data is displayed in the Payment Method label on the Customer form. As you can see, this data is stored in the Tag property of the Payment form.

If the user clicks the Save button, the Click event handler for that button calls the IsValidData method shown on page 2 of this listing. This method checks that the user has selected a customer and entered a payment. If so, the event handler for the Click event of the Save button calls the SaveData method. This method sets the SelectedIndex property of the Customer Name combo box to -1 so that no customer is selected, and it clears the Payment Method label. Then, it sets the isDataSaved variable to true and moves the focus to the combo box. In a production application, this data would be saved to a file or database.

The last method is executed when the user tries to close the Customer form. This is the same method you saw in figure 10-14, so you shouldn't have any trouble understanding how it works.

The property settings for the Customer form

Default name	Property	Setting
Form1	Name	frmCustomer
	Text	Customer
	CancelButton	btnExit
ComboBox1	Name	cboNames
	DropDownStyle	DropDownList
Label3	Name	lblPayment
	BorderStyle	Fixed3D
	AutoSize	False
	Text	""
Button1	Name	btnSave
Button2	Name	btnExit
Button3	Name	btnSelectPayment

The property settings for the Payment form

Default name	Property	Setting
Form2	Name	frmPayment
	Text	Payment
	AcceptButton	btnOK
	CancelButton	btnCancel
	ControlBox	False
	MaximizeBox	False
	FormBorderStyle	FixedDialog
GroupBox1	Text	Billing
RadioButton1	Name	rdoCreditCard
	Checked	True
RadioButton2	Name	rdoBillCustomer
ListBox1	Name	lstCreditCardType
TextBox1	Name	txtCardNumber
ComboBox1	Name	cboExpirationMonth
	DropDownStyle	DropDownList
ComboBox2	Name	cboExpirationYear
	DropDownStyle	DropDownList
CheckBox1	Name	chkDefault
	Checked	True
Button1	Name	btnOK
Button2	Name	btnCancel
	DialogResult	Cancel

Description

- In addition to the properties shown above, you'll want to set the text and alignment properties so the forms look like the forms shown in figure 10-15.

Figure 10-16 The property settings for the Customer and Payment forms

The code for the Customer form **Page 1**

```
public partial class frmCustomer : Form
{
    public frmCustomer()
    {
        InitializeComponent();
    }

    bool isDataSaved = true;

    private void frmCustomer_Load(object sender, System.EventArgs e)
    {
        cboNames.Items.Add("Mike Smith");
        cboNames.Items.Add("Nancy Jones");
    }

    private void DataChanged(object sender, System.EventArgs e)
    {
        isDataSaved = false;
    }

    private void btnSelectPayment_Click(object sender, System.EventArgs e)
    {
        Form paymentForm = new frmPayment();
        DialogResult selectedButton = paymentForm.ShowDialog();
        if (selectedButton == DialogResult.OK)
        {
            lblPayment.Text = (string) paymentForm.Tag;
        }
    }

    private void btnSave_Click(object sender, System.EventArgs e)
    {
        if (IsValidData())
        {
            SaveData();
        }
    }

    private void SaveData()
    {
        cboNames.SelectedIndex = -1;
        lblPayment.Text = "";
        isDataSaved = true;
        cboNames.Focus();
    }
```

Figure 10-17 The code for the Customer form (part 1 of 2)

The code for the Customer form **Page 2**

```
    private bool IsValidData()
    {
        if (cboNames.SelectedIndex == -1)
        {
            MessageBox.Show("You must select a customer.", "Entry Error");
            cboNames.Focus();
            return false;
        }
        if (lblPayment.Text == "")
        {
            MessageBox.Show("You must enter a payment.", "Entry Error");
            return false;
        }
        return true;
    }

    private void btnExit_Click(object sender, System.EventArgs e)
    {
        this.Close();
    }

    private void frmCustomer_FormClosing(object sender,
        FormClosingEventArgs e)
    {
        if (isDataSaved == false)
        {
            string message =
                "This form contains unsaved data.\n\n" +
                "Do you want to save it?";

            DialogResult button =
                MessageBox.Show(message, "Customer",
                MessageBoxButtons.YesNoCancel,
                MessageBoxIcon.Warning);

            if (button == DialogResult.Yes)
            {
                if (IsValidData())
                    this.SaveData();
                else
                    e.Cancel = true;
            }
            if (button == DialogResult.Cancel)
            {
                e.Cancel = true;
            }
        }
    }
}
```

Figure 10-17 The code for the Customer form (part 2 of 2)

The code for the Payment form

Figure 10-18 presents the code for the Payment form. After the code that Visual Studio has generated for the form, the event handler for the Load event adds the appropriate items to the list box and the two combo boxes on the form. In addition, this method sets the SelectedIndex property for these controls so the first item is selected.

When the user clicks the OK button on this form, the Click event handler starts by calling the IsValidData method shown on page 2 of this listing. If the Credit Card radio button is selected, this method checks that the user selected a credit card type and entered a credit card number. It also checks that the user selected an item other than the first one from the two combo boxes. That's necessary because the first item of these combo boxes contains user instructions ("Select a month…" and "Select a year…").

If the data is valid, the Click event handler for the OK button continues by calling the SaveData method shown on page 3 of this listing. This method creates a string that includes the payment information. Then, it stores that string in the Tag property of the Payment form. As you've already seen, the Customer form uses this property to display the payment information. Finally, the SaveData method sets the DialogResult property of the form to the OK member of the DialogResult enumeration. This is necessary to close the Payment form and allow the execution of the application to return to the Customer form.

When the user selects one of the radio buttons on this form, the CheckedChanged event occurs. For both radio buttons, this event is wired to the Billing_CheckChanged event handler. If the Credit Card radio button is selected when this event handler is executed, it calls the EnableControls method to enable the other controls on the form so the user can enter the required information. If the Credit Card button isn't selected, however, it means that the Bill Customer button is selected. Then, this event handler calls the DisableControls method to disable the other controls.

The code for the Payment form **Page 1**

```
public partial class frmPayment : Form
{
    public frmPayment()
    {
        InitializeComponent();
    }

    private void Payment_Load(object sender, EventArgs e)
    {
        lstCreditCardType.Items.Add("Visa");
        lstCreditCardType.Items.Add("Mastercard");
        lstCreditCardType.Items.Add("American Express");
        lstCreditCardType.SelectedIndex = 0;

        string[] months = {"Select a month...",
            "January", "February", "March", "April",
            "May", "June", "July", "August",
            "September", "October", "November", "December"};
        foreach (string month in months)
            cboExpirationMonth.Items.Add(month);
        cboExpirationMonth.SelectedIndex = 0;

        int year = DateTime.Today.Year;
        int endYear = year + 8;
        cboExpirationYear.Items.Add("Select a year...");
        while (year < endYear)
        {
            cboExpirationYear.Items.Add(year);
            year++;
        }
        cboExpirationYear.SelectedIndex = 0;
    }

    private void btnOK_Click(object sender, EventArgs e)
    {
        if (IsValidData())
        {
            this.SaveData();
        }
    }
```

Figure 10-18 The code for the Payment form (part 1 of 3)

The code for the Payment form — Page 2

```
    private bool IsValidData()
    {
        if (rdoCreditCard.Checked)
        {
            if (lstCreditCardType.SelectedIndex == -1)
            {
                MessageBox.Show("You must select a credit card type.",
                    "Entry Error");
                lstCreditCardType.Focus();
                return false;
            }
            if (txtCardNumber.Text == "")
            {
                MessageBox.Show("You must enter a credit card number.",
                    "Entry Error");
                txtCardNumber.Focus();
                return false;
            }
            if (cboExpirationMonth.SelectedIndex == 0)
            {
                MessageBox.Show("You must select a month.", "Entry Error");
                cboExpirationMonth.Focus();
                return false;
            }
            if (cboExpirationYear.SelectedIndex == 0)
            {
                MessageBox.Show("You must select a year.", "Entry Error");
                cboExpirationYear.Focus();
                return false;
            }
        }
        return true;
    }
```

Figure 10-18 The code for the Payment form (part 2 of 3)

The code for the Payment form **Page 3**

```
    private void SaveData()
    {
        string msg = null;
        if (rdoCreditCard.Checked == true)
        {
            msg += "Charge to credit card." + "\n";
            msg += "\n";
            msg += "Card type: " + lstCreditCardType.Text + "\n";
            msg += "Card number: " + txtCardNumber.Text + "\n";
            msg += "Expiration date: "
                + cboExpirationMonth.Text + "/"
                + cboExpirationYear.Text + "\n";
        }
        else
        {
            msg += "Send bill to customer." + "\n";
            msg += "\n";
        }

        bool isDefaultBilling = chkDefault.Checked;
        msg += "Default billing: " + isDefaultBilling;

        this.Tag = msg;
        this.DialogResult = DialogResult.OK;
    }

    private void Billing_CheckedChanged(object sender, System.EventArgs e)
    {
        if (rdoCreditCard.Checked)
            EnableControls();
        else
            DisableControls();
    }

    private void EnableControls()
    {
        lstCreditCardType.Enabled = true;
        txtCardNumber.Enabled = true;
        cboExpirationMonth.Enabled = true;
        cboExpirationYear.Enabled = true;
    }

    private void DisableControls()
    {
        lstCreditCardType.Enabled = false;
        txtCardNumber.Enabled = false;
        cboExpirationMonth.Enabled = false;
        cboExpirationYear.Enabled = false;
    }

}
```

Figure 10-18 The code for the Payment form (part 3 of 3)

Perspective

In this chapter, you learned how to use five new controls for building Windows applications. These controls are the ones you'll use most often. If you need to use any of the controls that weren't presented here, though, you should be able to figure out how to do that on your own. In most cases, it's just a matter of becoming familiar with the properties, methods, and events that are available, and you can usually do that by reviewing the documentation for the control and the class it's based on.

In addition, you learned how to work with a project that contains two or more forms. Specifically, you learned how to work with projects that use dialog boxes.

For many projects, the skills presented in this chapter are the only ones you'll need when you're working with the forms of an application. In chapter 12, though, you'll learn another technique for passing data between forms. And in chapter 24, you'll learn some additional skills for working with forms that let you enhance the user interface of an application.

Terms

combo box
list box
radio button
group box
check box
tab order
modal form
modeless form

Exercise 10-1 Create the Payment application

This exercise will guide you through the process of creating the Payment application that's described in this chapter. To make that easier for you, you'll start from an application that contains the Customer form.

Open the project and prepare the two forms

1. Open the application that's in the C:\C# 2008\Chapter 10\Payment directory. This application contains a single form named Form1.
2. Rename Form1 to frmCustomer. Make sure to change both the file name and the name that's used in the code. If necessary, modify the Main method so it displays this form when the application starts.
3. Add a second form named frmPayment to the project.

Design the Payment form

4. Add the controls to the Payment form and set the properties for this form and its controls as described in figures 10-15 and 10-16.
5. Use Tab Order view to set the tab order for the controls on the Payment form if necessary.

Add the code for the Customer form

6. Generate the event handlers for the Load event of the Customer form, for the Closing event of the form, and for the Click event of all three buttons. Then, add the global isDataSaved variable, and add the code for these events as shown in figure 10-17.
7. Generate an event handler named DataChanged for the SelectedIndexChanged event of the Customer Name combo box. Then, wire this event handler to the TextChanged event of the Payment Method label, and add the code to this event handler so it sets the isDataSaved variable to false.
8. Add the SaveData and IsValidData methods.
9. Test the Customer form to make sure that it works properly. At this point, you should be able to display the Payment form, but it won't work correctly since you haven't added any code to it.

Add the code for the Payment form

10. Generate the event handlers for the Load event of the Payment form and for the Click event of the OK button. Then, add the code for these events as shown in figure 10-18.
11. Generate an event handler named Billing_CheckChanged for the CheckChanged event of the Credit Card radio button. Then, wire this event handler to the CheckChanged event of the Bill Customer radio button, and add the code for this event handler.
12. Add the EnableControls, DisableControls, and IsValidData methods.
13. Test the program to be sure that it works as described in figure 10-15. When you're sure it does, close the project.

Exercise 10-2 Enhance the Future Value application

This exercise will guide you through the process of adding a combo box and a list box to the Future Value application.

Open the Future Value application and add two controls

1. Open the application that's in the C:\C# 2008\Chapter 10\FutureValue directory.
2. Delete the Number of Years text box and replace it with a Number of Years combo box. Then, delete the Future Value text box and replace it with a Future Values list box.

Add the code that works with the controls

3. Generate the event handler for the Load event of the form. Then, add code that loads the numbers 1 through 20 in the Number of Years combo box, and add code that selects 3 as the default number of years.
4. Delete the code in the IsValidData method that refers to the Number of Years text box since it isn't needed anymore.
5. Modify the event handler for the Click event of the Calculate button so it adds the future value for each year to the Future Values list box. For example, if you calculate the future value for three years, the Future Value form should return a result like this:

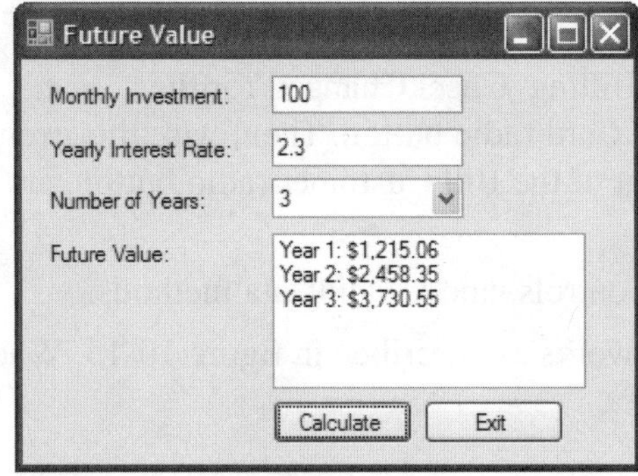

6. To get this to work correctly, you'll need to use the Clear method of the Items collection for the list box to clear the list box each time the Calculate button is clicked. In addition, you can use the modulus operator (%) to add the future value after every twelve months of the calculation. For example:

```
if (month % 12 == 0) // add the future value to the list box
```

7. Test this application to make sure it works correctly.

11

How to debug an application

In chapters 3 and 5, you learned how to work in break mode when a runtime error occurs, how to use the Exception Assistant to get information about the error, how to use data tips to find out what value a variable or property contains, how to use a breakpoint to enter break mode before a specific statement is executed, and how to step through the statements in an application from a breakpoint. These are the basic skills that you need for debugging simple applications.

As your applications get more complicated, though, debugging gets more complicated. In fact, if you've done much programming, you know that debugging is often the most difficult and time-consuming phase of programming. The good news is that Visual Studio offers many other tools for testing and debugging. In this chapter, you'll learn how to use the most useful ones, and you'll review the tools you've already been introduced to.

Basic debugging techniques

Before you begin debugging, you can set the options that control how Visual Studio handles exceptions. Then, you can use the basic debugging skills that you learned in previous chapters to find and fix most types of exceptions.

How to set the debugging options

Figure 11-1 presents the two dialog boxes you can use to set the options for debugging. Although you may never need to change any of these options, you should at least take the time to review them so you know what they do.

The Options dialog box lets you set General options like whether the Exception Assistant is displayed when an exception occurs as shown in the next figure. It also lets you enable or disable the Edit and Continue feature, which you'll learn more about in a moment.

The Exceptions dialog box lets you determine which exceptions are thrown and how they're handled. These exceptions are grouped by categories (namespaces), and you can set the options for a namespace or a specific exception within a namespace. In the dialog box in this figure, for example, the User-Unhandled option is set for most of the exceptions for the Common Language Runtime.

By default, the Thrown box is unchecked for all categories and exceptions, and the User-Unhandled box is usually checked. As a result, the application will continue when an exception is thrown instead of breaking into the debugger. This gives any exception-handling code that you have written a chance to be executed, which is usually what you want. However, if you check the Thrown box, you can enter break mode when the exception is thrown and use the debugging features described in this chapter *before* any exception-handling code is executed.

When you use the Exceptions dialog box, the options that you set cascade down to all exceptions below the specified category. As a result, the settings for the Common Language Runtime Exceptions apply to all of the namespaces and exceptions below that entry. However, you can override any of the namespaces and exceptions below an entry by checking the boxes for each namespace or exception. For example, if you want to break any time an exception in the System namespace is thrown (even if the exception is handled), you can check the Thrown box for the System namespace.

The Options dialog box

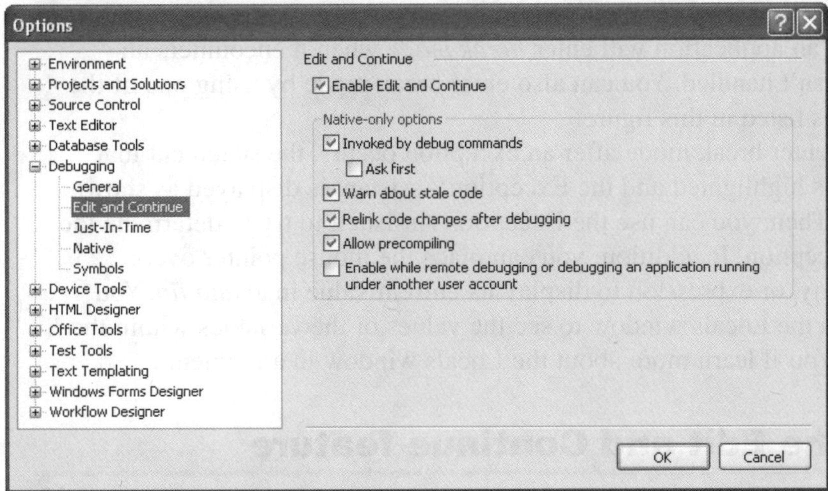

The Exceptions dialog box

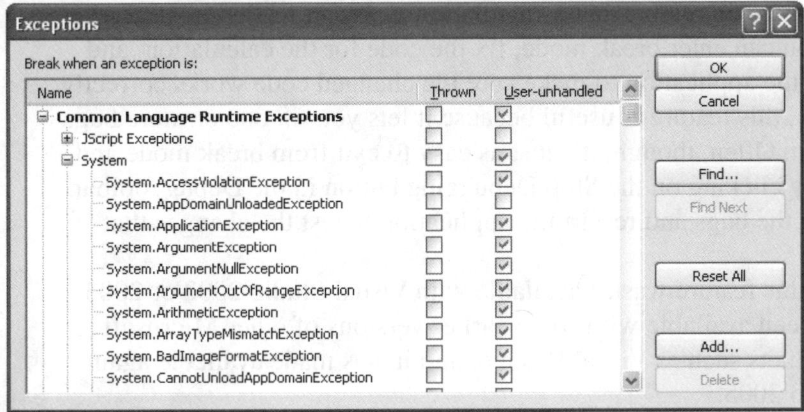

Description

- To display the Options dialog box, use the Tools→Options command.
- By default, the Edit and Continue feature is on in the Options dialog box. This feature lets you change the code while in break mode and continue running the application.
- To display the Exceptions dialog box, use the Debug→Exceptions command.
- By default, an application will enter break mode only when an exception is thrown and there is no exception-handling code for that exception. However, you can change that by checking or unchecking the boxes to the right of an exception category or a specific exception.
- Although you should be aware of the options in the Options and Exceptions dialog boxes, you usually won't need to change any of them.

Figure 11-1 How to set the debugging options

How to work in break mode

By default, an application will enter *break mode* when it encounters an exception that isn't handled. You can also enter break mode by using one of the other techniques listed in this figure.

When you enter break mode after an exception occurs, the statement that was executing is highlighted and the Exception Assistant is displayed as shown in figure 11-2. Then, you can use the Exception Assistant to try to determine the cause of the exception. In addition, you can place the mouse pointer over a variable, property, or expression to display its current value in a *data tip*. You can also look in the Locals window to see the values of the variables within the current scope. You'll learn more about the Locals window in a moment.

How to use the Edit and Continue feature

The *Edit and Continue feature* lets you make a change to the code for an application while you're in break mode and then continue running the application. If, for example, you realize that a calculation is wrong while you're testing an application, you can enter break mode, fix the code for the calculation, and continue running the application to make sure the changed code works correctly.

In some cases, this feature is useful because it lets you fix one or more bugs in a single test run. Often, though, it's just as easy to exit from break mode and end the test run by clicking on the Stop Debugging button in the Debug toolbar. Then, you can fix the bugs and restart the application to test the changes that you've made.

Incidentally, this feature wasn't available with Visual Studio 2002 or 2003. However, it had been available with some earlier versions of other Microsoft development products such as Visual Basic 6, and it was made available again with Visual Studio 2005.

The Future Value application in break mode

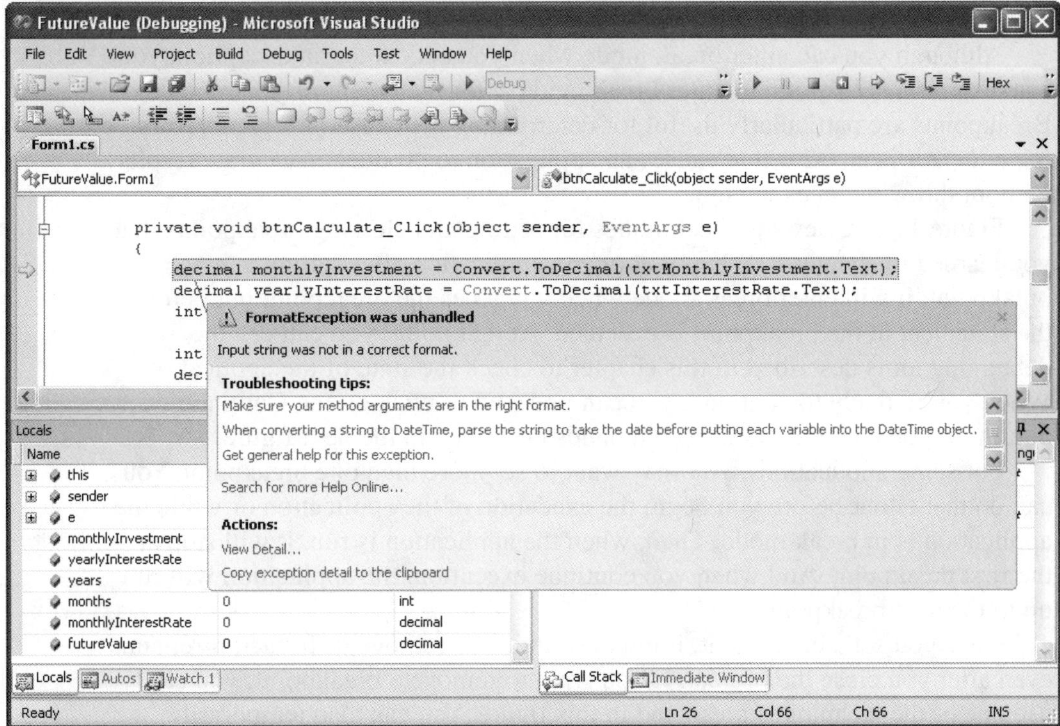

Four ways to enter break mode

- Force an unhandled exception to be thrown.
- Set a breakpoint and run the application.
- Choose the Debug→Step Into command or press F11 to begin debugging at the first line of the application.
- Choose the Debug→Break All command or press Ctrl+Alt+Break while the application is executing.

Description

- When you enter *break mode*, Visual Studio displays the Exception Assistant and highlights the statement that was executing when the exception occurred. Then, you can use the Exception Assistant and the debugging windows to determine the cause of the exception.
- To display the value of a variable or property in a *data tip*, position the mouse pointer over it in the Code Editor. To display a data tip for an expression, select the expression and then point to it. The expression must not contain a method call.
- The *Edit and Continue feature* lets you make changes to the code while in break mode and continue running the application with the changes in force.
- To exit break mode and end the application, click on the Stop Debugging button in the Debug toolbar or use the Debug→Stop Debugging command.

Figure 11-2 How to work in break mode

How to use breakpoints

Although you can enter break mode when you encounter an exception, you can also set a *breakpoint* to enter break mode at the statement of your choice. Breakpoints are particularly useful for determining the cause of logical errors. A *logical error* is an error that causes an application to produce inaccurate results without throwing an exception.

Figure 11-3 reviews the techniques for setting and clearing breakpoints that you learned in chapter 5. When you run an application after setting a breakpoint, it will enter break mode when it reaches the breakpoint but before the statement at the breakpoint is executed. At that point, you can use the debugging tools described in this chapter to check the state of the application. When you're ready to continue, you can press F5 or click on the Continue button, or you can use the Step commands described in the next figure.

For some applications, you may want to set more than one breakpoint. You can do that either before you begin the execution of the application or while the application is in break mode. Then, when the application is run, it will stop at the first breakpoint. And when you continue execution, the application will run up to the next breakpoint.

Once you set a breakpoint, it remains until you remove it. In fact, it remains even after you close the project. If you want to remove a breakpoint, you can use one of the techniques presented in this figure. You can also temporarily disable all breakpoints as described here.

You can also work with breakpoints from the Breakpoints window. For example, you can disable a breakpoint by removing the check mark in front of the breakpoint. Then, the breakpoint remains in the Breakpoints window, but it is disabled until you enable it again. To disable or enable all breakpoints, you can use the Disable All Breakpoints/Enable All Breakpoints button that's available from the Breakpoints window. Similarly, you can use the Delete All Breakpoints button to remove all breakpoints.

The Express Edition of Visual C# 2008 supports most, but not all, of the debugging features described in this chapter. For example, the Breakpoints window isn't available from the Express Edition. Fortunately, the Express Edition includes the most important debugging features presented in this chapter. In addition, if a debugging feature isn't available from the Express Edition, or if it works a little differently than the other editions, we have noted that in the figures of this chapter.

The Future Value application with a breakpoint

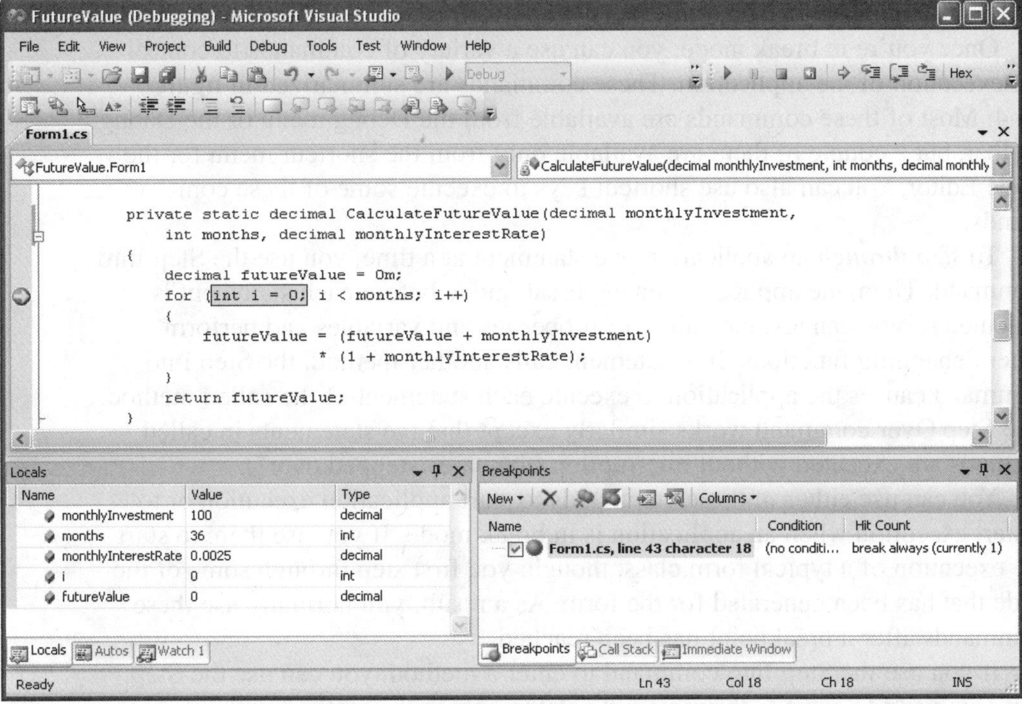

How to set and clear breakpoints

- To set a *breakpoint*, click in the margin indicator bar to the left of a statement. Or, press the F9 key to set a breakpoint at the insertion point. You can set a breakpoint before you run an application or while the application is in break mode.
- To remove a breakpoint, use either technique for setting a breakpoint. To remove all breakpoints at once, use the Debug→Delete All Breakpoints command.
- To disable all breakpoints, use the Debug→Disable All Breakpoints command. To enable all breakpoints, use the Debug→Enable All Breakpoints command.

Description

- You can set a breakpoint only on a line that contains an executable statement. You can't set breakpoints on blank lines or comments.
- When Visual Studio encounters a breakpoint, it enters break mode before it executes the statement that contains the breakpoint.
- The current breakpoints are displayed in the Breakpoints window. This window is most useful for enabling and disabling existing breakpoints, but you can also use it to add, modify, move, and delete breakpoints.

Express Edition difference

- The Breakpoints window is not available from the Visual C# 2008 Express Edition.

Figure 11-3 How to use breakpoints

How to control the execution of an application

Once you're in break mode, you can use a variety of commands to control the execution of the application. These commands are summarized in figure 11-4. Most of these commands are available from the Debug menu or the Debug toolbar, but a couple of them are available only from the shortcut menu for the Code Editor. You can also use shortcut keys to execute some of these commands.

To *step through* an application one statement at a time, you use the Step Into command. Then, the application enters break mode before each statement is executed so you can test the values of properties and variables and perform other debugging functions. If a statement calls another method, the Step Into command causes the application to execute each statement of the called method. The Step Over command works similarly except that the statements in called methods are executed without interruption (they are "stepped over").

You can use either of these commands to start application execution or to restart execution when an application is in break mode. If you use them to start the execution of a typical form class, though, you first step through some of the code that has been generated for the form. As a result, you normally use these commands after a breakpoint has been reached.

If you use the Step Into command to enter a method, you can use the Step Out command to execute the remaining statements in the method without interruption. After that, the application enters break mode before the next statement in the calling method is executed.

To skip code that you know is working properly, you can use the Run To Cursor or Set Next Statement command. You can also use the Set Next Statement command to rerun lines of code that were executed before an exception occurred. And if you've been working in the Code Editor and have forgotten where the next statement to be executed is, you can use the Show Next Statement command to move to it.

Commands in the Debug menu and toolbar

Command	Toolbar	Keyboard	Description
Start/Continue		F5	Start or continue execution of the application.
Break All		Ctrl+Alt+Break	Suspend execution of the application.
Stop Debugging		Shift+F5	Stop debugging and end execution of the application.
Restart		Ctrl+Shift+F5	Restart the entire application.
Show Next Statement			Display the next statement to be executed. Also available from the shortcut menu for the Code Editor.
Step Into		F11	Execute one statement at a time.
Step Over		F10	Execute one statement at a time except for called methods.
Step Out		Shift+F11	Execute the remaining lines in the current method.

Commands in the Code Editor's shortcut menu

Command	Description
Run to Cursor	Execute the application until it reaches the statement that contains the insertion point.
Set Next Statement	Set the statement that contains the insertion point as the next statement to be executed.

Description

- If you use the Step Into or Step Over command to start the execution of an application, Visual Studio will enter break mode before it executes the first statement in the application. If you use the Run to Cursor command, Visual Studio will enter break mode when it reaches the statement that contains the insertion point.
- Once the application enters break mode, you can use the Step Into, Step Over, Step Out, and Run To Cursor commands to execute one or more statements.
- To alter the normal execution sequence of the application, you can use the Set Next Statement command. Just place the insertion point in the statement you want to execute next, issue this command, and click on the Continue button.
- To enter break mode when you need to stop the execution of an application, you can use the Break All command.

Figure 11-4 How to control the execution of an application

How to use the debugging windows

Now that you know how to work with break mode, you're ready to learn how to use the primary debugging windows. These windows include the Locals window, the Autos window, the Watch windows, the Immediate window, the Call Stack window, and the Output window.

How to use the Locals window to monitor variables

If you need to see the values of several variables used in the same area of an application, you can do that using the Locals window as shown in figure 11-5. By default, this window is displayed in the group of windows in the lower left corner of Visual Studio when an application enters break mode. If it isn't, you can display it by selecting the Locals command from the Windows submenu of the Debug menu.

The Locals window displays information about the variables that are in the current scope. In this figure, for example, the Locals window shows the five variables that are in the scope of the for loop in the CalculateFutureValue method. In addition, it shows the this keyword that includes information about the current form.

Whenever a variable contains other variables, the Locals window displays a plus sign (+) to the left of the variable. To drill down through this information, you can click the plus sign to expand the entry. In this figure, for example, you can click the plus sign to the left of the this keyword to view information about the current form. That includes information about all of the properties for the form and all of the properties for each control on the form.

Besides displaying the values of variables, you can use the Locals windows to change these values. To do that, you double-click on the value you want to change and enter a new value. Then, you can continue the execution of the application.

How to use the Autos window to monitor variables

If you want to limit the number of variables that are displayed, you can use the Autos window instead of the Locals window. This window works similarly to the Locals window, except it only displays information about the variables used in the current statement and the previous statement. As a result, it doesn't display as many variables, especially if the current block of code has a large number of variables within scope. To display this window, you can select the Autos command from the Windows submenu of the Debug menu. However, this window isn't available from the Express Edition of C# 2008.

The Locals window

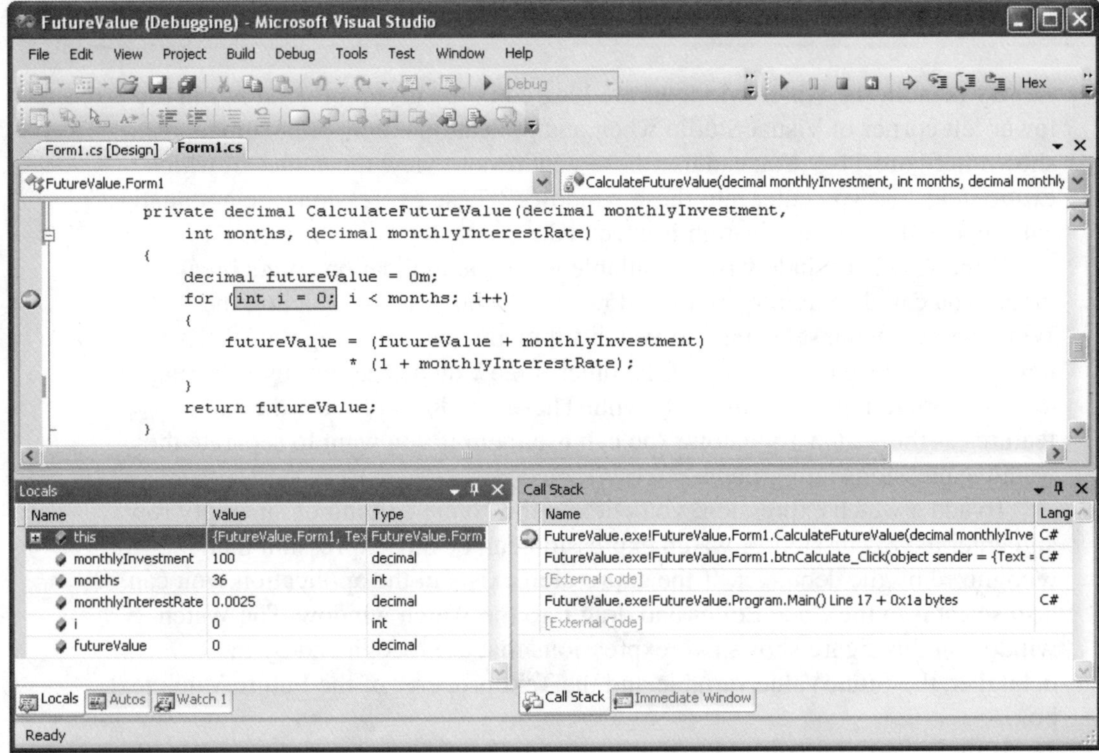

How to use the Locals window

- The Locals window displays information about the variables within the current scope.
- To display the Locals window, click on the Locals tab or use the Debug➔Windows➔Locals command.
- If you are debugging a form and you click on the plus sign to the left of the this keyword, the properties and variables of the form are displayed.
- To change the value of a property or variable, double-click on the value in the Value column, then type a new value and press the Enter key.

How to use the Autos window

- The Autos window works like the Locals window, but it only displays information about variables used by the current statement and the previous statement.
- To display the Autos window, you can use the Debug➔Windows➔Autos command.

Express Edition difference

- The Autos window is not available from the Visual C# 2008 Express Edition.

Figure 11-5 How to use the Locals and Autos windows to monitor variables

How to use Watch windows to monitor expressions

By default, the Watch windows are located in the group of windows in the lower left corner of Visual Studio when an application enters break mode, as shown in figure 11-6. You can use these windows to view the values of *watch expressions* that you enter into these windows. These expressions are automatically updated as the application is executed.

If the Watch 1 window isn't available when an application enters break mode, you can display it by pulling down the Debug menu, selecting the Windows submenu, selecting the Watch submenu, and selecting the Watch 1 item. You can also display any of the other three watch windows by selecting the appropriate item from this submenu. These windows provide the same features as the Watch 1 window. You can use them if you want to separate the watch expressions into groups.

To add a watch expression, you click in the Name column of an empty row and enter the expression. A watch expression can be any expression that's recognized by the debugger. If the expression exists in the application, you can also select it in the Code Editor and drag it to the Watch window. The Watch window in this figure shows two expressions that are recognized by the debugger, the futureValue variable and the Text property of the Future Value text box.

If the expression you add to the Watch window is the name of an object, the Watch window will display a plus sign to the left of the name. Then, you can click on the plus sign to display the properties of the object. A plus sign is also added to an expression if it's the name of an array. Then, you can click on the plus sign to display the elements in the array.

You can change the value of a watch expression by double-clicking on the value in the Value column and entering the new value. To delete a watch expression, you can use the Delete Watch command on the shortcut menu that's displayed when you right-click on an expression. To delete all watch expressions, you can use the Select All command on the shortcut menu followed by the Delete Watch command.

A Watch window

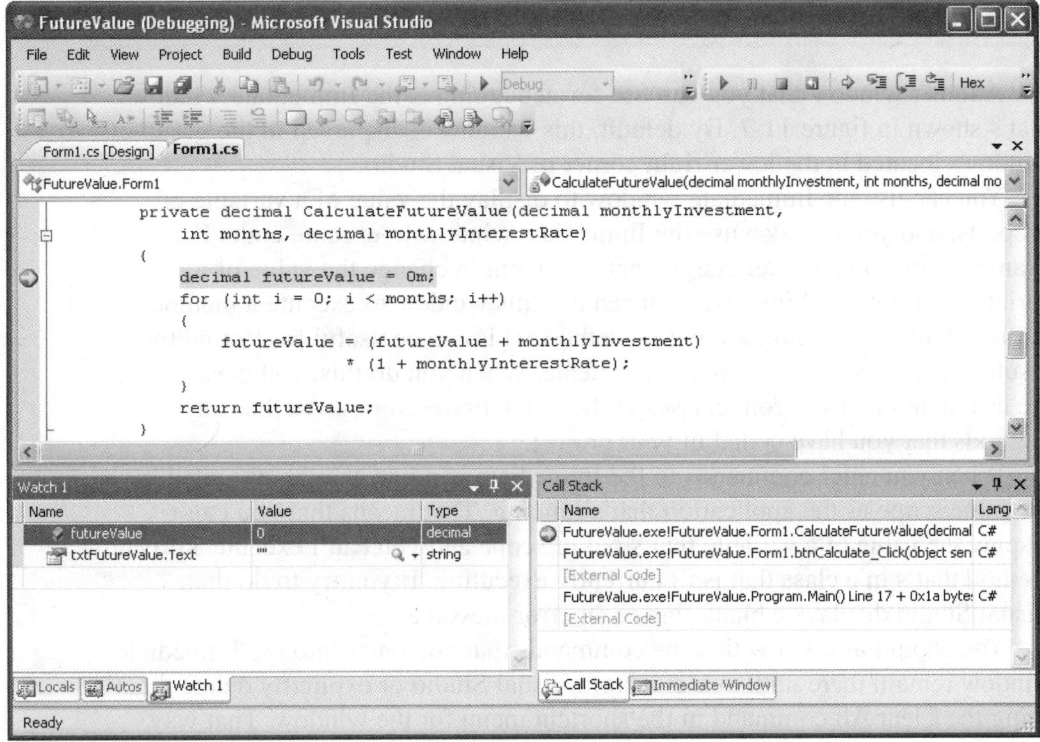
FutureValue (Debugging) - Microsoft Visual Studio
File Edit View Project Build Debug Tools Test Window Help
Form1.cs [Design] Form1.cs
FutureValue.Form1
CalculateFutureValue(decimal monthlyInvestment, int months, decimal mo
private decimal CalculateFutureValue(decimal monthlyInvestment,
int months, decimal monthlyInterestRate)
{
decimal futureValue = 0m;
for (int i = 0; i < months; i++)
{
futureValue = (futureValue + monthlyInvestment)
* (1 + monthlyInterestRate);
}
return futureValue;
}
Watch 1
Name Value Type
futureValue 0 decimal
txtFutureValue.Text "" string
Call Stack
Name Lang
FutureValue.exe!FutureValue.Form1.CalculateFutureValue(decimal C#
FutureValue.exe!FutureValue.Form1.btnCalculate_Click(object sen C#
[External Code]
FutureValue.exe!FutureValue.Program.Main() Line 17 + 0x1a byte: C#
[External Code]
Locals Autos Watch 1
Call Stack Immediate Window
Ready

Description

- The Watch windows let you view the values of *watch expressions* while an application is in break mode. To display a Watch window, click on its Watch tab. Or, select Debug→Windows→Watch and choose Watch 1, Watch 2, Watch 3, or Watch 4.
- To add an expression to a Watch window, click on an empty row in the Name column, then type the expression. You can also highlight an expression in the Code Editor and drag it into a Watch window.
- If an expression is out of scope, it will appear dimmed in the Watch window along with a message that says the expression isn't valid in the current context.
- If you enter the name of an object or an array in the Watch window, a tree control will appear next to its name. Then, you can use this control to expand or collapse this entry.
- To change the value of a watch expression, double-click on its value in the Value column, enter the new value, and press the Enter key.
- To delete a watch expression, right-click on the expression and select the Delete Watch command from the shortcut menu. To delete all watch expressions, right-click on the Watch window, select the Select All command, and select the Delete Watch command.

Express Edition difference

- The Visual C# 2008 Express Edition offers just one Watch window named Watch.

Figure 11-6 How to use Watch windows to monitor expressions

How to use the Immediate window to execute commands

Another window that you can use for debugging is the Immediate window that's shown in figure 11-7. By default, this window is displayed in the group of windows located in the lower right corner of Visual Studio.

You can use the Immediate window to display the value of a variable or property, and you can also use the Immediate window to execute code. For example, you can enter an assignment statement to change the value of a variable or property. Similarly, you can use this window to execute a method or to display the value returned by the method. This can be useful for testing the result of a method with different arguments. When you do this, you can execute the available methods from classes in the .NET Framework as well as any methods that you have coded in your project.

When you enter commands in the Immediate window, they're executed in the same scope as the application that's running. That means that you can't display the value of a variable that's out of scope and you can't execute a private method that's in a class that isn't currently executing. If you try to do that, Visual Studio displays a blank line or an error message.

You should also know that the commands that you enter into the Immediate window remain there until you exit from Visual Studio or explicitly delete them using the Clear All command in the shortcut menu for the window. That way, you can use standard Windows techniques to edit and re-use the same commands from one execution of an application to another without having to re-enter them. Unlike expressions in the Watch window, though, the command results aren't updated as the application executes.

To execute a command that you've already entered in the Immediate window, press the Up or Down arrow keys to locate the command. This displays the command at the bottom of the window. Then, if you want, you can edit the command. Or, you can press Enter to execute the command.

The Immediate window

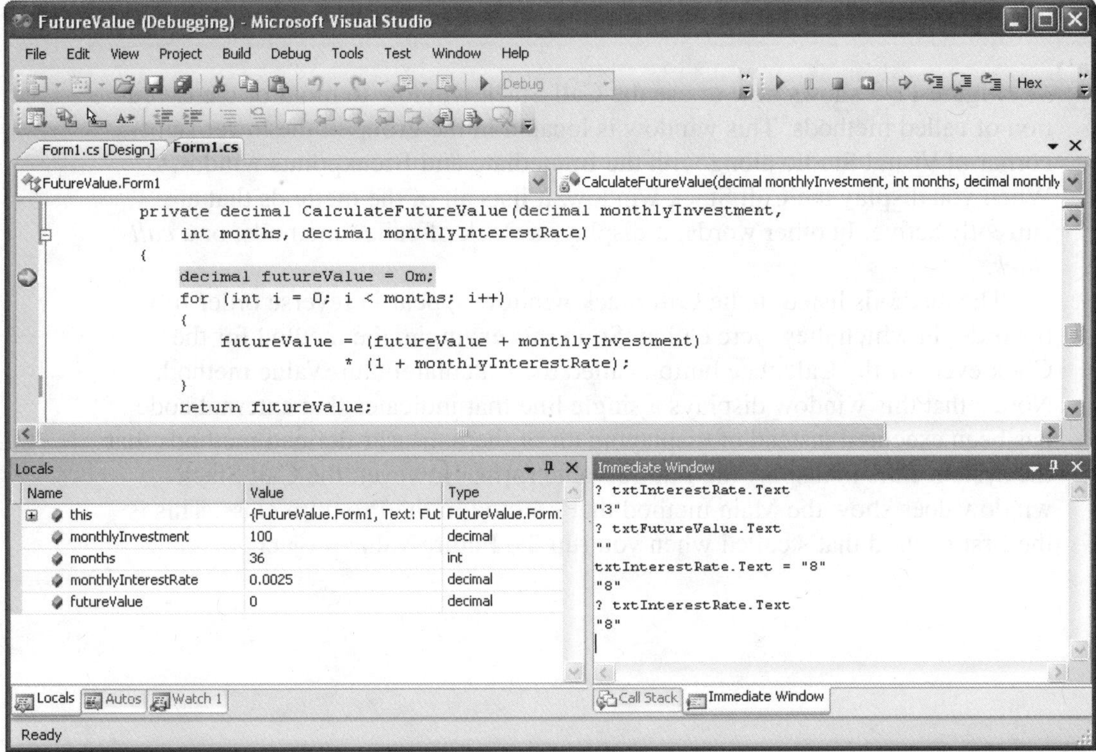

Description

- You can use the Immediate window to display and assign values from an application during execution. To display this window, click on the Immediate Window tab or use the Debug→Windows→Immediate command.
- To display a value, enter a question mark followed by the expression whose value you want to display. Then, press the Enter key.
- To assign a different value to a variable or property, enter an assignment statement. Then, press the Enter key.
- To execute a method, enter its name and any arguments it requires. Then, press the Enter key. If you want to display the result of a method, precede the method call with a question mark.
- To reissue a command, use the Up or Down arrow keys to display the command you want. Then, you can edit the command or press the Enter key to execute it.
- To remove all commands and output from the Immediate window, use the Clear All command in the shortcut menu for the window.

Figure 11-7 How to use the Immediate window to execute commands

How to use the Call Stack window to monitor called methods

Figure 11-8 shows how to use the Call Stack window to monitor the execution of called methods. This window is located in the group in the lower right corner of Visual Studio along with the Immediate and Breakpoints windows. When you display the Call Stack window, it lists all of the methods that are currently active. In other words, it displays a stack of called methods, or a *call stack*.

The methods listed in the Call Stack window appear in reverse order from the order in which they were called. So in this example, the method for the Click event of the Calculate button called the CalculateFutureValue method. Notice that this window displays a single line that indicates that external code has been executed instead of displaying all of the non-user-defined methods that the system calls to display the Future Value form. However, the Call Stack window does show the Main method that's stored in the Program class. This is the first method that's called when you run the Future Value project.

The Call Stack window

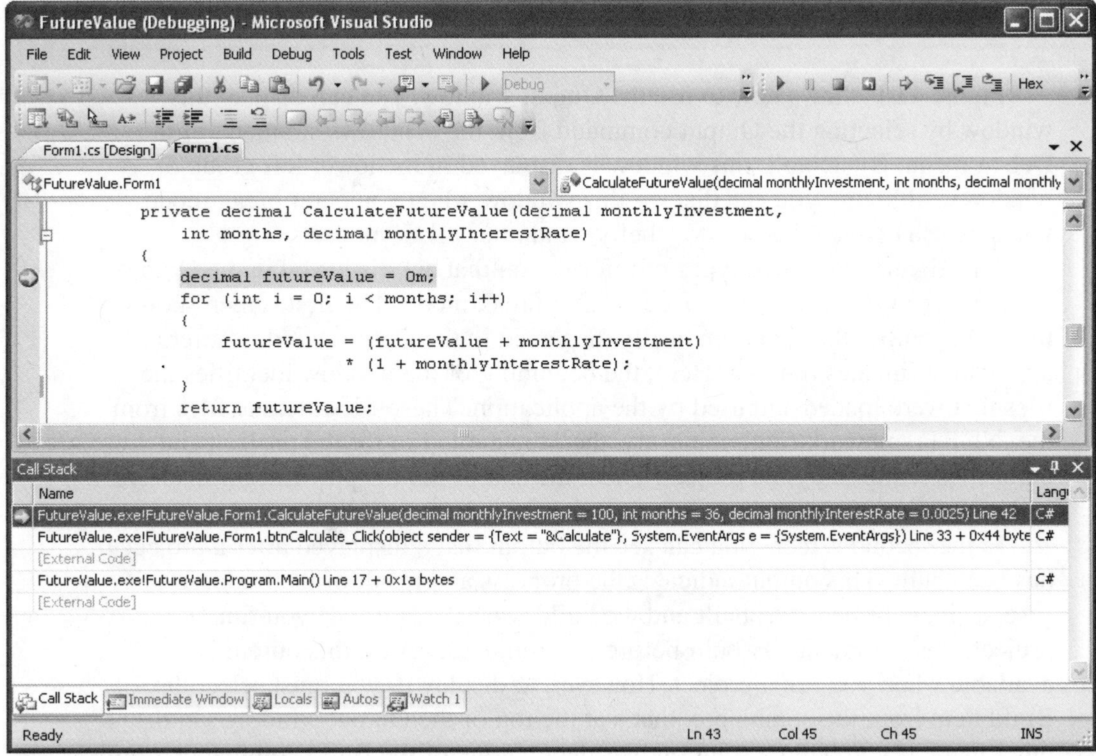
FutureValue (Debugging) - Microsoft Visual Studio
File Edit View Project Build Debug Tools Test Window Help
Debug
Hex
Form1.cs [Design]
Form1.cs
FutureValue.Form1
CalculateFutureValue(decimal monthlyInvestment, int months, decimal monthly
private decimal CalculateFutureValue(decimal monthlyInvestment,
int months, decimal monthlyInterestRate)
{
decimal futureValue = 0m;
for (int i = 0; i < months; i++)
{
futureValue = (futureValue + monthlyInvestment)
* (1 + monthlyInterestRate);
}
return futureValue;
Call Stack
Name
Langu
FutureValue.exe!FutureValue.Form1.CalculateFutureValue(decimal monthlyInvestment = 100, int months = 36, decimal monthlyInterestRate = 0.0025) Line 42
C#
FutureValue.exe!FutureValue.Form1.btnCalculate_Click(object sender = {Text = "&Calculate"}, System.EventArgs e = {System.EventArgs}) Line 33 + 0x44 byte
C#
[External Code]
FutureValue.exe!FutureValue.Program.Main() Line 17 + 0x1a bytes
C#
[External Code]
Call Stack
Immediate Window
Locals
Autos
Watch 1
Ready
Ln 43
Col 45
Ch 45
INS

Description

- The Call Stack window lists all of the methods that are active when an application enters break mode. To display this window, click on the Call Stack tab or use the Debug→Windows→Call Stack command.
- In the Call Stack window, the current method is listed at the top of the window, followed by the method that called it (if any), and so on. This list of method names is referred to as a *call stack*.
- You can use the commands in the shortcut menu for the Call Stack window to control what's displayed in this window.

Figure 11-8 How to use the Call Stack window to monitor called methods

How to use the Output window to view project information

Figure 11-9 shows how to use the Output window. You can display this window by selecting the Output command from the Windows submenu of the Debug menu. By default, this window is displayed in the lower left group of windows. Although you can display this window when you enter break mode, you can also display this window before and after break mode.

This figure shows two types of information that are displayed in the Output window when it's displayed before or after break mode. The first screen shows the debug output that's automatically displayed in the Output window after an application finishes running. Here, the beginning of the window identifies the files that were loaded and used by the application. These files include files from the .NET Framework runtime library, the executable file for the project, and other files required by the project. Then, the end of the Output window displays some information that indicates that an unhandled exception occurred.

In the second screen, you can see the output that's displayed after a project has been built. This output indicates the progress and result of the build. In this case, a single project was built and the build was successful. If you run a project, it is automatically built before it is run. As a result, this output is available when you run a project. However, to display it, you must select the Build item from the combo box that's at the top of the Output window. On the other hand, if you build a solution by selecting one of the Build commands from the Build menu, the Output window will automatically select the Build option and show this information.

Most of the time, you won't need the information that's displayed in the Output window. If a build error occurs, for example, the error is displayed in the Error List window and you can use that window to locate and correct the error. And if an unhandled exception occurs, you can use the information in the Exception Assistant window to identify the cause of the exception. Of course, once you exit break mode, the Exception Assistant is no longer available. However, some information about the exception is still available in the Output window. As a result, you can use the Output window to look up this information even after you've exited break mode.

An Output window that shows debug information

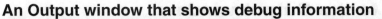

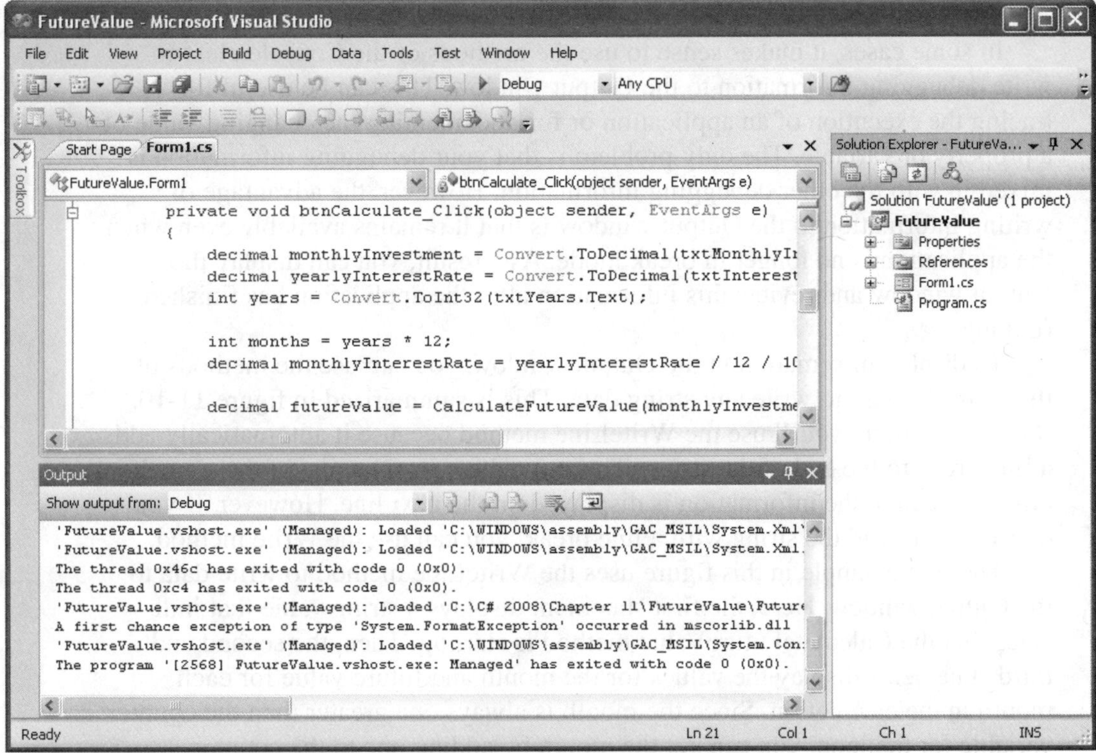

An Output window that shows build information

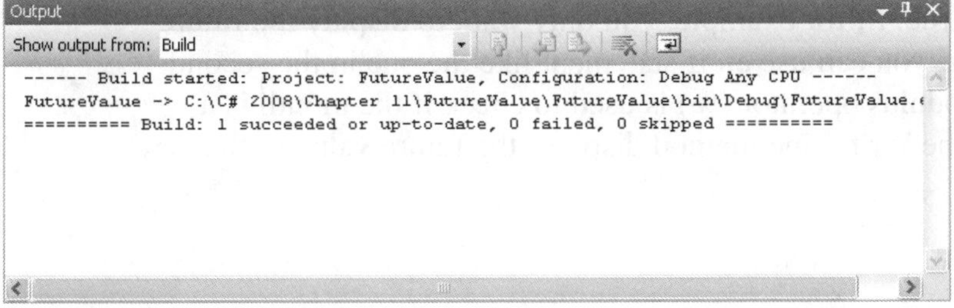

Description

- After a solution finishes running, you can use the Output window to view the debug output. This output lists the files that were loaded and used by the project, information about unhandled exceptions (if any), and a completion code.
- After you build a project or solution, you can use the Output window to view the build output. This output includes an indication of how many projects were built successfully, how many builds failed, and how many projects weren't built.
- You can use the combo box at the top of the Output window to select whether build or debug output is displayed.
- To display this window, use the Debug→Windows→Output command.

Figure 11-9 How to use the Output window to view project information

How to write data to the Output window

In some cases, it makes sense to use the methods of the Console class to write debugging information to the Output window. This can be useful for tracing the execution of an application or for documenting the changing value of a property or variable. The only problem is that your debugging information is mixed in with the other debugging information. However, the advantage of writing information to the Output window is that it remains available even when the application is no longer in break mode. As a result, you can display the Output window and review this information after the application has finished running.

To display information in the Output window, you can use the methods of the Console class to write any string data. This is summarized in figure 11-10. Most of the time, you'll use the WriteLine method because it automatically adds a line break to the end of the string. That way, the next time one of these methods is executed, the information is displayed on the next line. However, if you don't want to end the string with a line break, you can use the Write method.

The first example in this figure uses the WriteLine method to write data to the Output window. Here, the first statement displays a string value that indicates that the CalculateFutureValue method is starting. Then, the second and third statements display the values for the month and future value for each month in the calculation. Since the month is always one greater than the counter variable for the loop, you can get the month by adding one to the counter variable.

Sometimes, you may only want to display data in the Output window when a certain condition is true. If, for example, you only want to display the future value every 12 months, you can use an if statement like the one in the second example. Here, the modulus operator (%) is used to check if the month is a multiple of 12. If so, the WriteLine method displays the future value in the Output window.

An Output window that displays debugging information

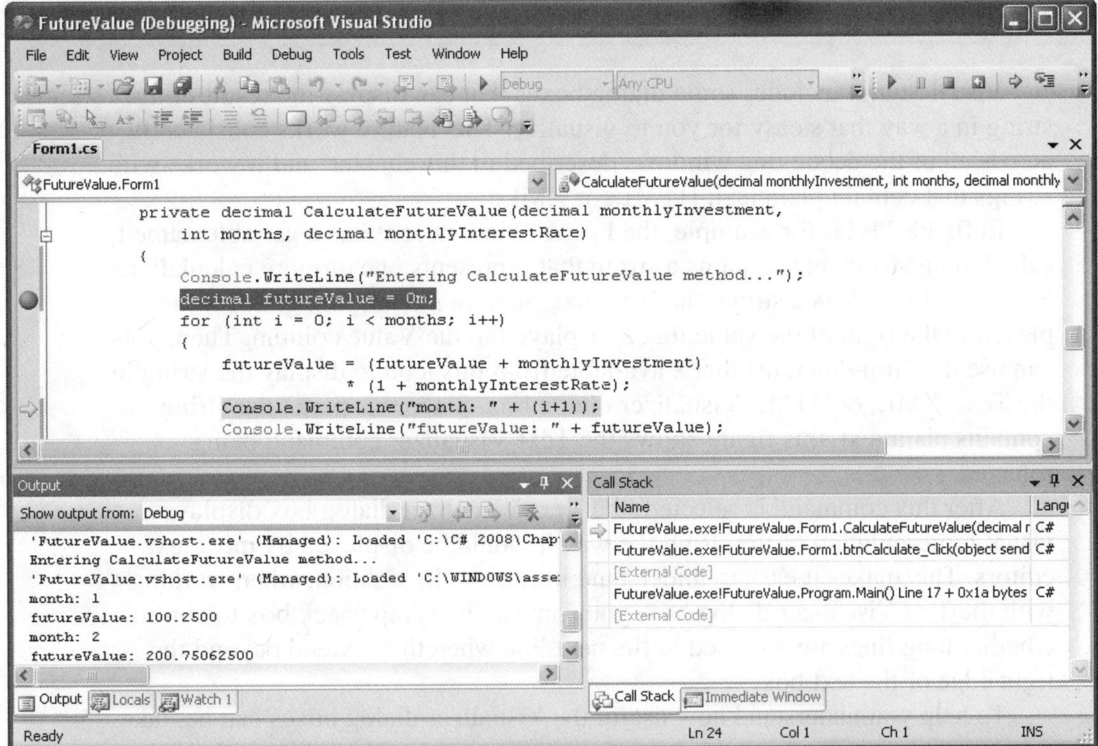

Methods of the Console class that write data to the Output window

Method	Description
`Write(string)`	Displays the value of the specified string.
`WriteLine(string)`	Displays the value of the specified string, followed by a line break.

Three statements that write data to the Output window

```
Console.WriteLine("Entering CalculateFutureValue method...");
Console.WriteLine("month: " + (i+1));
Console.WriteLine("futureValue: " + futureValue);
```

Code that uses an if statement to control when data is written

```
if ((i+1)%12 == 0) // every 12 months
    Console.WriteLine("futureValue: " + futureValue);
```

Description

- You can use the Write methods of the Console class to write data to the Output window. This can be useful for tracing application execution or for documenting changes in the values of variables.

Figure 11-10 How to write data to the Output window

How to use the Visualizer dialog boxes to view strings

Visual Studio includes some dialog boxes that can display the result of a string in a way that's easy for you to visualize. This feature works consistently across all of the debugging windows described in this chapter, and it works with strings that contain plain text, HTML, or XML.

In figure 11-11, for example, the Locals window contains a variable named calculationsString that contains a string that represents one or more calculations. Since this variable is a string, the Visualizer icon (a magnifying glass) is displayed to the right of the value that's displayed in the Value column. Then, you can use the drop-down list that's available from this icon to display the string in the Text, XML, or HTML Visualizer dialog box. Since this particular string contains plain text, this figure shows the Text Visualizer command being selected.

After this command is selected, the Text Visualizer dialog box displays a visual representation of the string the way it would be displayed by most text editors. This makes it easy to understand the string. In addition, when working with the Text Visualizer dialog box, you can use the Wrap check box to control whether long lines are wrapped to the next line when they extend beyond the right edge of the text box.

To help you understand how useful the Visualizer dialog boxes can be, take a moment to consider what the string in this figure would look like without the Text Visualizer dialog box. It would look something like this (without the word wrapping):

```
"Monthly Investment:\t$100.00\nYearly Interest
Rate:\t3.00\nYears:\t3\nFuture Value:\t$3,771.46\n\n"
```

The HTML and XML Visualizer dialog boxes work like the Text Visualizer dialog box, except that they are designed to work with HTML or XML. As a result, if a string contains an HTML or XML document, you'll probably want to use these dialog boxes. Then, the HTML or XML document will be displayed in a user-friendly format.

The Visualizer drop-down menu in the Locals window

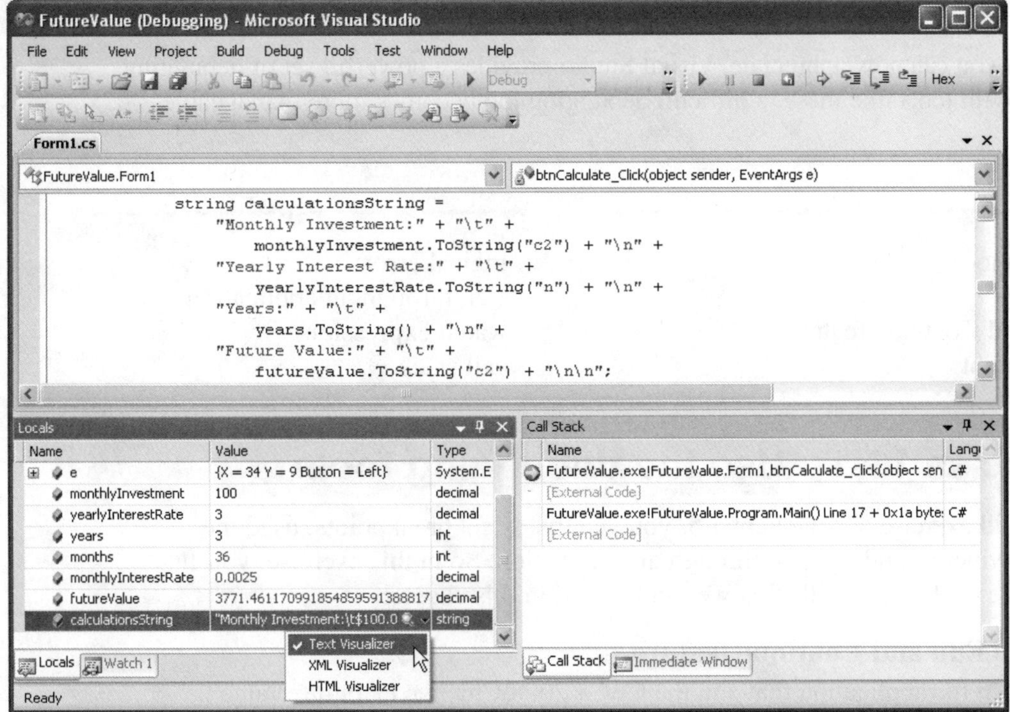

The Text Visualizer dialog box

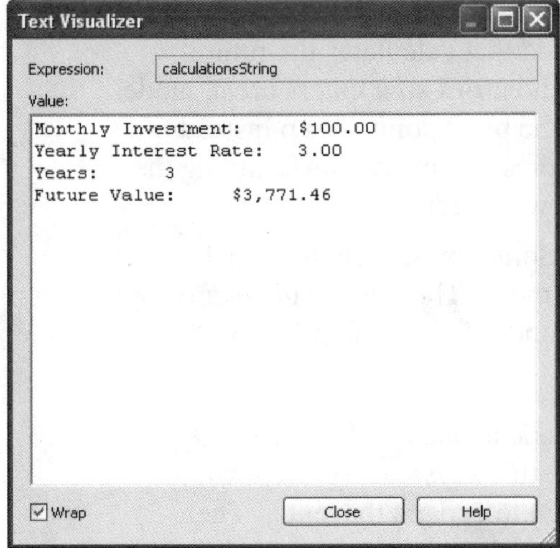

Description

- All string values that are displayed by the debugging windows have a Visualizer icon (a magnifying glass) to their right.
- To display an appropriate Visualizer dialog box for the string value, select the appropriate command from the drop-down list that's available from the Visualizer icon.

Figure 11-11 How to use the Visualizer dialog boxes to view strings

Perspective

As you can now appreciate, Visual Studio provides a powerful set of debugging tools. With tools like these, a difficult debugging job becomes more manageable.

Terms

break mode
data tip
Edit and Continue feature
breakpoint
logical error
step through an application
watch expression
call stack

Exercise 11-1 Use the debugging tools

If you did exercise 5-2 in chapter 5, you've already set breakpoints, used the Locals window, and stepped through an application. So in this exercise, you'll use some of the new skills that were presented in this chapter.

Use the Edit and Continue feature

1. Open the application that's in the C:\C# 2008\Chapter 11\FutureValue directory. Then, run the project with the default entries, and notice that the future value amount is formatted as a percent.
2. End the application and set a breakpoint on the statement in the btnCalculate_Click method that calls the method that calculates the future value. Then, run the application with the default entries so it enters break mode. In break mode, notice that the statement after the breakpoint uses p instead of c as the formatting code. Correct this code, and press F5 to continue running the application and notice that the formatting is now correct.
3. This illustrates the Edit and Continue feature. Sometimes, though, Visual Studio won't let you change the code in break mode. Then, you can click on the Stop Debugging button, make the change, and restart the application.

Use the Locals windows

4. Click on the Calculate button to enter break mode again, display the Locals window, click on the plus sign to the left of the this keyword, scroll down to txtMonthlyInvestment, and click on its plus sign to expand this entry. Then, scroll down to the Text property to see its string value and the Visualizer icon in the Value column.
5. Click on the Visualizer icon to display the value in the Text Visualizer dialog box. Then, close this dialog box, and click on the minus sign to the left of the this keyword to collapse this entry.
6. Press F11 to step through the statements, and notice the parameters and variables that are displayed in the Locals window at each step. Then, set a

second breakpoint on the last statement in the CalculateFutureValue method (the return statement), and press F5 to run the application until it enters break mode again. Now, you can see the final values for the calculation.

7. Press F5 to restart the application and display the Future Value form. Click on the Calculate button to start another calculation and enter break mode again. Next, locate the months variable in the Locals window, double-click in the Value column, enter 24, and press the Enter key to change the value. Then, press F5 to continue execution, and notice that 24 is used as the value of the months variable in the future value calculation.

Use the Breakpoints window to disable both breakpoints

If you're using C# 2008 Express, skip the next two steps.

8. Display the Breakpoints window and click the Disable All Breakpoints button at the top of the Breakpoints window. This disables both break points without removing them. Then, press F5 to continue execution. Since no breakpoints are enabled, this should display the Future Value form.
9. Click the Exit button to end the program. Then, use the Debug→Enable All Breakpoints command to enable both breakpoints, and run the application until it enters break mode at the first breakpoint.

Use the Immediate window to work with a variable and a method

10. Display the Immediate window, and display the value of the months variable in this window. Then, display the percentage format of the monthly interest rate by calling the ToString method from the monthlyInterestRate variable like this:

```
? monthlyInterestRate.ToString("p")
```

11. Assign a value of 12 to the months variable by entering an assignment statement in the Immediate window. Then, continue running the application so you can see that this value is used in the calculations.

Use a Watch window to monitor expressions

12. Run the application one more time with a value of 1 for the years entry. When the application enters break mode, display a Watch window, highlight the futureValue variable, and drag it to that window. Next, drag the i variable to that window. Then, click in the Name column of the first blank row in the Watch window and enter this expression:

```
i < months
```

13. Press F11 to step through the application and check the values in the Watch window until the value of i < months becomes false.

Use the Output window

14. Use the Console.WriteLine method in the btnCalculate_Click method to display the values of the monthlyInvestment, monthlyInterestRate, months, and futureValue variables. Then, run the application and check the Output window to see how these values are displayed.
15. When you're through experimenting, close the project.

Section 3

Object-oriented programming

In the first three sections of this book, you've learned how to use classes that are provided as part of the .NET Framework. For instance, you've learned how to use the properties, methods, and events of the form and control objects that are defined by the .NET classes, and you've learned how to use the List<> class to create collection objects that can hold other objects. Although that's one aspect of object-oriented programming, it's not the whole picture.

In addition to using the .NET classes, you can create your own classes. That's what the chapters in this section teach you to do. To start, chapter 12 shows you the basics of creating classes. Then, chapter 13 expands on those basics to show you how to create classes that include advanced features such as indexers, delegates, events, and overloaded operators.

After that, chapter 14 shows you how to use inheritance, one of the most important features of object-oriented programming. Chapter 15 shows you how to use interfaces (another important feature of object-oriented programming) and generics (a feature that became available with C# 2005). And Chapter 16 shows you how to document and organize your classes, including how to work with class libraries. When you're done, you'll not only know how to create and use your own classes, but you'll also understand how the .NET classes work.

You can read the chapters in this section any time after you complete the first 11 chapters of this book, and you should read them in sequence. However, only chapter 12 is a prerequisite for sections 4 and 5. So if you want to learn database programming before you learn more about object-oriented programming, you can skip to section 4 after you complete chapter 12. Or, if you want to learn how a database class is implemented for a text, binary, or XML file, you can skip to chapter 21 or 22 after you read chapter 12. Eventually, though, you need to master the object-oriented skills that are presented in chapters 13 through 16, so be sure to return to them.

12

How to create and use classes

This chapter presents the basics of creating and using classes in C# applications. Here, you'll learn how to create classes that include properties, methods, fields, and constructors, as well as classes that contain static members. In addition, you'll see a complete application that uses three user-defined classes, and you'll learn how to create structures, which are similar to classes.

When you complete this chapter, you'll start to see how creating your own classes can help simplify the development of an application. As a bonus, you'll have a better understanding of how the .NET classes work.

An introduction to classes

The topics that follow introduce you to the concepts you need before you create your own classes. First, you'll learn how classes are typically used in a business application to simplify the overall design of the application. Next, you'll learn about the variety of members you can add to a class. Then, you'll see a complete example of a simple class. Finally, you'll learn how classes are instantiated to create objects.

How classes can be used to structure an application

Figure 12-1 shows how you can use classes to simplify the design of a business application using a *multi-layered architecture*. In a multi-layered application, the classes that perform different functions of the application are separated into two or more layers.

A *three-layered* application architecture like the one shown in this figure consists of a presentation layer, a middle layer, and a database layer. In practice, the middle layer is sometimes eliminated and its functions split between the database and presentation layers. On the other hand, the design of some applications further develops the middle layer into additional layers.

The classes in the *presentation layer* handle the details of the application's user interface. For a Windows application, this consists of the form classes that display the user interface. One class is required for each form displayed by the application.

The classes of the *database layer* are responsible for all database access required by the application. These classes typically include methods that connect to the database and retrieve, insert, add, and delete information from the database. Then, the other layers can call these methods to access the database, leaving the details of database access to the database classes. Although we refer to this layer as the database layer, it can also contain classes that work with data that's stored in files.

The *middle layer* provides an interface between the database layer and the presentation layer. This layer often includes classes that correspond to business entities (for example, products and customers). It may also include classes that implement business rules, such as discount or credit policies. When the classes represent *business objects*, they are often called *business classes*.

One advantage of developing applications with a layered architecture is that it allows application development to be spread among members of a development team. For example, one group of developers might work on the database layer, another group on the middle layer, and still another group on the presentation layer.

Another advantage is that it allows classes to be shared among applications. In particular, the classes that make up the database and middle layers can be

The architecture of a three-layered application

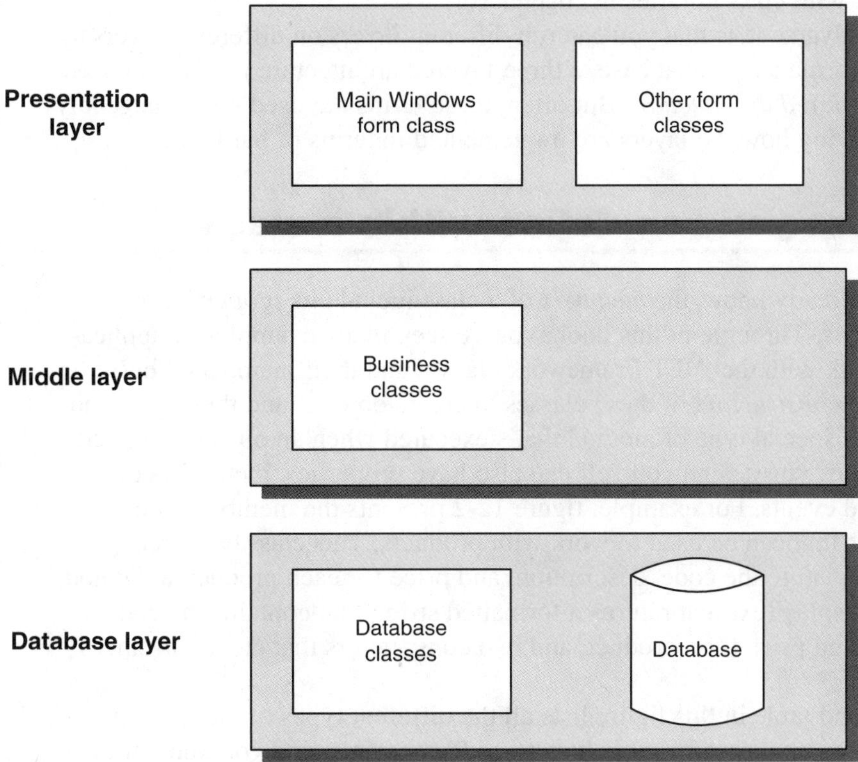

Description

- To simplify development and maintenance, many applications use a *three-layered architecture* to separate the application's user interface, business rules, and database processing. Classes are used to implement the functions performed at each layer of the architecture.
- The classes in the *presentation layer* control the application's user interface. For a Windows Forms application, the user interface consists of the various forms that make up the application.
- The classes in the *database layer* handle all of the application's data processing.
- The classes in the *middle layer*, sometimes called the *business rules layer*, act as an interface between the classes in the presentation and database layers. These classes can represent business entities, such as customers or products, or they can implement business rules, such as discount or credit policies.
- When the classes in the middle layer represent business entities, the classes can be referred to as *business classes*, and the objects that are created from these classes can be referred to as *business objects*.
- Often, the classes that make up the database layer and the middle layer are implemented in *class libraries* that can be shared among applications.

Figure 12-1 How classes can be used to structure an application

placed in *class libraries* that can be used by more than one project. You'll learn how to work with class libraries in chapter 16.

A third advantage is that you can run different layers on different servers to improve performance. In that case, a three-layered architecture is often referred to as a *three-tiered architecture*. But often, these terms are used interchangeably without implying how the layers are implemented in terms of hardware.

The members you can define within a class

As you already know, the *members* of a class include its *properties*, *methods*, and *events*. Throughout this book, you've seen many examples of applications that work with the .NET Framework classes and their members. You've also used the *constructors* of these classes to create objects, and these constructors are just a special type of method that's executed when an object is created.

The classes you design yourself can also have properties, methods, constructors, and events. For example, figure 12-2 presents the members of a Product class that can be used to work with products. This class has three properties that store the code, description, and price for each product, a method named GetDisplayText that returns a formatted string that contains the code, description, and price for a product, and two constructors that create instances of the class.

The second table in this figure lists all the different types of members a class can have. You already know how to code constants, and you know the basic skills for coding methods. By the time you finish the chapters in this section, you'll know how to create the other types of members as well.

Of course, not every class you create will contain all these types of members. In fact, most classes will have just properties, methods, and constructors. But it's important to know about all possible member types so you'll be able to decide which types are appropriate for the classes you create.

This figure also reviews the basic concepts of object-oriented programming that were first introduced in chapter 3. In addition, it presents a fundamental concept of object-oriented programming that you may not be familiar with. This is the concept of *encapsulation*.

Encapsulation lets the programmer hide, or encapsulate, some of the data and operations of a class while exposing others. For example, although a property or method of a class can be called from other classes, its implementation is hidden within the class. That way, users of the class can think of it as a black box that provides useful properties and methods. This also means that you can change the code within a class without affecting the other classes that use it. This makes it easier to enhance or change an application because you only need to change the classes that need changing. You'll get a better idea of how encapsulation works when you see the code for the Product class in the next figure.

The members of a Product class

Properties	Description
`Code`	A string that contains a code that uniquely identifies each product.
`Description`	A string that contains a description of the product.
`Price`	A decimal that contains the product's price.
Method	**Description**
`GetDisplayText(sep)`	Returns a string that contains the code, description, and price in a displayable format. The *sep* parameter is a string that's used to separate the elements. It's typically set to a tab or new line character.
Constructors	**Description**
`()`	Creates a Product object with default values.
`(code, description, price)`	Creates a Product object using the specified code, description, and price values.

Types of class members

Class member	Description
Property	Represents a data value associated with an object instance.
Method	An operation that can be performed by an object.
Constructor	A special type of method that's executed when an object is instantiated.
Delegate	A special type of object that's used to wire an event to a method.
Event	A signal that notifies other objects that something noteworthy has occurred.
Field	A variable that's declared at the class level.
Constant	A constant.
Indexer	A special type of property that allows individual items within the class to be accessed by index values. Used for classes that represent collections of objects.
Operator	A special type of method that's performed for a C# operator such as + or ==.
Class	A class that's defined within the class.

Class and object concepts

- An *object* is a self-contained unit that has *properties*, *methods*, and other *members*. A *class* contains the code that defines the members of an object.
- An object is an *instance* of a class, and the process of creating an object is called *instantiation.*
- *Encapsulation* is one of the fundamental concepts of object-oriented programming. It lets you control the data and operations within a class that are exposed to other classes.
- The data of a class is typically encapsulated within a class using *data hiding*. In addition, the code that performs operations within the class is encapsulated so it can be changed without changing the way other classes use it.
- Although a class can have many different types of members, most of the classes you create will have just properties, methods, and constructors.

Figure 12-2 The members you can define within a class

The code for the Product class

Figure 12-3 shows the complete code for the Product class whose members were described in figure 12-2. As you can see, it begins with a class statement that declares the Product class with the public access modifier. This access modifier lets other classes access the class.

The code within the class block defines the members of the Product class. In the rest of this chapter, you'll learn how to write code like the code shown here. For now, I'll just present a preview of this code so you have a general idea of how it works.

The first three statements in this class are declarations for three class variables, called *fields*. As you'll see in a minute, these fields are used to store the data for the Code, Description, and Price properties. Because these variables are defined with the private access modifier, they cannot be referred to from outside the class.

After the fields are declarations for the two constructors of the Product class. The first constructor, which accepts no arguments, creates an instance of the Product class and initializes its fields to default values. The second constructor creates an instance of the class and initializes it with values passed via the code, description, and price parameters.

Next are the declarations for the three properties of the Product class. These properties provide access to the values stored in the three fields. Within each of these property declarations are two blocks of code that get and set the value of the property.

Last is the declaration for the GetDisplayText method, which accepts a string parameter named sep. This method returns a string that concatenates the code, description, and price values, separated by the value passed via the sep parameter.

Notice that you always use the public access modifier to identify the properties and methods that can be accessed from other classes. In contrast, you use the private access modifier to declare fields that you don't want to be accessed from other classes. In this case, for example, the fields can only be accessed through the properties defined by the class. You can also use the private access modifier to code properties and methods that you don't want to be accessed from other classes.

The Product class

```
using System;

namespace ProductMaint
{
    public class Product
    {
        private string code;
        private string description;
        private decimal price;

        public Product(){}

        public Product(string code, string description, decimal price)
        {
            this.Code = code;
            this.Description = description;
            this.Price = price;
        }

        public string Code
        {
            get
            {
                return code;
            }
            set
            {
                code = value;
            }
        }

        public string Description
        {
            get
            {
                return description;
            }
            set
            {
                description = value;
            }
        }

        public decimal Price
        {
            get
            {
                return price;
            }
            set
            {
                price = value;
            }
        }

        public string GetDisplayText(string sep)
        {
            return code + sep + price.ToString("c") + sep + description;
        }
    }
}
```

Fields

An empty constructor

A custom constructor

The Code property

The Description property

The Price property

The GetDisplayText method

Figure 12-3 The code for the Product class

How instantiation works

The process of creating an object from a class is called *instantiation*. Figure 12-4 describes how instantiation works. Here, you can see two *instances* of the Product class. Each instance represents a different Product object. Because both instances were created from the same class, they both have the same properties. However, the instances have distinct values for each property. For example, the value of the Code property for the product1 object is CS08, but the value of the Code property for the product2 object is VB08.

The first code example in this figure shows how you can create these two object instances. Here, the first line of code declares two variables named product1 and product2 that have a type of Product. Then, the next two lines create Product objects. To do that, they use the new keyword, followed by the name of the class and the values that will be passed to the constructor and used to initialize the objects.

The second code example in this figure shows another way to create the same object instances. This code uses a new feature of C# 2008 called *object initializers*. Object initializers let you create an instance of an object and assign values to it without explicitly calling a constructor. To do that, you follow the class name with a list enclosed in braces that specifies the names of the properties or public fields you want to initialize and the values you want to assign to those properties or fields.

One of the advantages of object initializers is that they let you create an object and assign values to it in a single statement. To illustrate, assume that the Product class doesn't have a constructor that accepts the code, description, and price. In that case, you would have to use the following code to create an instance of the class and assign values to it without using an object initializer:

```
product1 = new Product();
product1.Code = "CS08";
product1.Description = "Murach's C# 2008";
product1.Price = 54.5m;
```

This feature is most useful, though, when you write query expressions with LINQ, which you'll learn how to do in chapter 23.

At this point, it's important to realize that a class defines a *reference type*. That means that the variable that's used to access an object contains the address of the memory location where the object is stored, not the object itself. In other words, the product1 variable holds a *reference* to a Product object, not an actual Product object.

Two Product objects that have been instantiated from the Product class

product1	product2
Code=CS08 Description=Murach's C# 2008 Price=54.50	Code=VB08 Description=Murach's Visual Basic 2008 Price=54.50

Code that creates these two object instances

```
Product product1, product2;
product1 = new Product("CS08", "Murach's C# 2008", 54.50m);
product2 = new Product("VB08", "Murach's Visual Basic 2008", 54.50m);
```

Another way to create the object instances

```
product1 = new Product { Code = "CS08",
    Description = "Murach's C# 2008", Price = 54.50m };
product2 = new Product { Code = "VB08",
    Description = "Murach's Visual Basic 2008", Price = 54.50m };
```

Description

- When an object is instantiated, a *constructor* is executed to initialize the data that makes up the object. If a class doesn't provide a constructor, a default constructor is executed. The default constructor simply initializes all the data to default values.
- The data that makes up an object is sometimes referred to as the object's *state*. Once an object has been instantiated, its state can change.
- The state of an object changes whenever you change the value of one of the object's properties or public fields. The state can also change when you call a method that affects the data stored within an object.
- An application can create two or more instances of the same class. Each instance is a separate entity with its own state. If you change the state of one object, the state of other objects created from the same class is not affected.
- *Object initializers* are a new feature of C# 2008 that let you create an instance of an object and assign values to that object in a single statement without explicitly calling a constructor.
- A class defines a *reference type*. That means that the variable that's used to access an object instantiated from a class contains the address of the object, not the actual object.

Figure 12-4 How instantiation works

How to create a class

Now that you've learned about the members that make up a class and you've seen the code for the Product class, you're ready to learn the basic skills for creating and using your own classes. The topics that follow present these skills.

How to add a class file to a project

To create a user-defined class, you start by adding a *class file* to your project. To do that, you use the dialog box shown in figure 12-5. When you complete this dialog box, the class file will appear in the Solution Explorer with the extension *cs*.

When you add a class to a project, Visual Studio automatically generates the class declaration. Then, you can complete the class by adding fields, constructors, properties, methods, and whatever other members the class may require.

The dialog box for adding a class

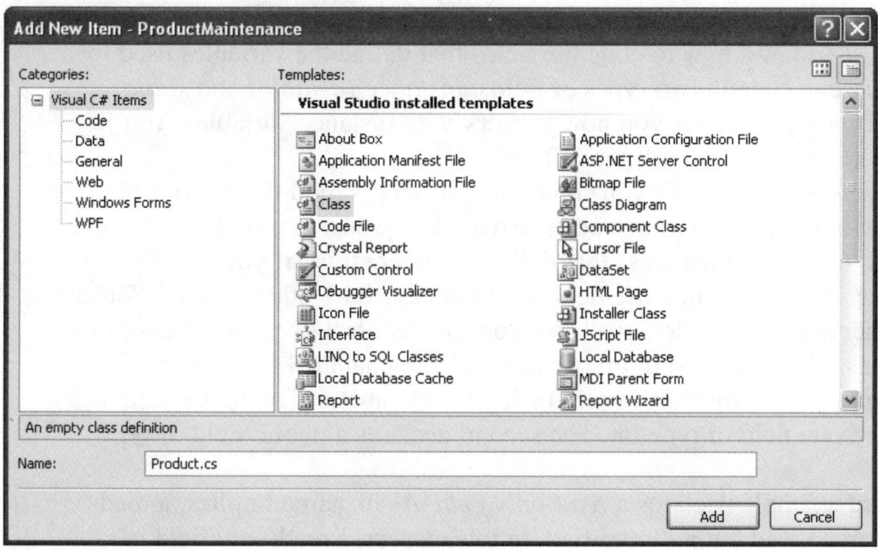

The starting code for the new class

```
using System;
using System.Collections.Generic;
using System.Linq;
using System.Text;

namespace ProductMaintenance
{
    class Product
    {
    }
}
```

Description

- To add a new class to a project, use the Project→Add Class command to display the Add New Item dialog box. Then, enter the name you want to use for the new class and click the Add button.
- When you complete the Add New Item dialog box, a *class file* is added to the project. This class file will appear in the Solution Explorer window with the extension *cs*.
- The namespace and class blocks are automatically added to the class. Then, you can enter the code for the class within the class block.

Figure 12-5 How to add a class file to a project

How to code fields

Figure 12-6 shows how to code the fields that define the variables used by a class. A class can contain two types of fields: *instance variables* and *static variables*. This figure shows you how to work with instance variables. You'll learn about static variables in figure 12-10.

When you declare a field, you should use an access modifier to control the accessibility of the field. If you specify *private* as the access modifier, the field can be used only within the class that defines it. In contrast, if you specify *public* as the access modifier, the field can be accessed by other classes. You can also use other access modifiers that give you finer control over the accessibility of your fields. You'll learn about those modifiers in chapter 14.

This figure shows three examples of field declarations. The first example declares a private field of type int. The second declares a public field of type decimal.

The third example declares a *read-only field*. As its name implies, a read-only field can be read but not modified. In this respect, a read-only field is similar to a constant. The difference is that the value of a constant is set when the class is compiled, while the value of a read-only field is set at runtime. You can assign a value to a read-only field when you declare it as shown in the third example or in the code for one of the constructors of the class.

Note that although fields work like regular variables, they must be declared within the class body, not inside properties, methods, or constructors. That way, they're available throughout the entire class. In this book, all of the fields for a class are declared at the beginning of the class. However, when you read through code from other sources, you may find that the fields are declared at the end of the class or at other locations within the class.

This figure also presents another version of the Product class that uses public fields instead of properties. This works because the properties of the Product class that was presented in figure 12-3 didn't do anything except get and set the values of private fields. Because of that, you could just provide direct access to the fields by giving them public access as shown here. In some cases, though, a property will perform additional processing. Then, you'll need to use a property instead of a public field.

By the way, you may notice that the names of the public fields in this class and in the second and third examples at the beginning of this figure begin with a capital letter. That's because these fields are used in place of properties, and the names of properties are always capitalized. In contrast, the name of the private field in the first example begins with a lowercase letter because it can only be accessed within the class.

Examples of field declarations

```
private int quantity;               // A private field.
public decimal Price;               // A public field.
public readonly int Limit = 90;     // A public read-only field.
```

A version of the Product class that uses public fields instead of properties

```
public class Product
{
    // Public fields
    public string Code;
    public string Description;
    public decimal Price;

    public Product()
    {
    }

    public Product(string code, string description, decimal price)
    {
        this.Code = code;
        this.Description = description;
        this.Price = price;
    }

    public string GetDisplayText(string sep)
    {
        return Code + sep + Price.ToString("c") + sep + Description;
    }
}
```

Description

- A variable that's defined at the class level within a class is called a *field*.
- A field can be a primitive data type, a class or structure from the .NET Framework, or a user-defined class or structure.
- You can use the *private* access modifier to prevent other classes from accessing a field. Then, the field can be accessed only from within the class.
- An *instance variable* is a field that's defined in a class and is allocated when an object is instantiated. Each object instance has a separate copy of each instance variable.
- If you initialize an instance variable, the initialization will occur before the constructor for the class is executed. As a result, the constructor may assign a new value to the variable.
- You can create a *read-only field* by specifying the *readonly* keyword in the field's declaration. Then, the field's value can be retrieved, but it can't be changed. You can set the value for a read-only field when you declare it or in the code for a constructor.
- A *public field* is a field that's declared with the *public* access modifier. Public fields can be accessed by other classes within the application, much like properties. However, properties can have additional features that make them more useful than public fields.

Figure 12-6 How to code fields

How to code properties

Figure 12-7 presents the syntax for coding a property. As you can see, a property declaration specifies both the type and name of the property. In addition, a property is typically declared with the public access modifier so it can be accessed by other classes.

Within the block that defines a property, you can include two blocks called *accessors* because they provide access to the property values. The *get accessor* is executed when a request to retrieve the property value is made, and the *set accessor* is executed when a request to set the property value is made. If both get and set accessors are included, the property is called a *read/write property*. If only a get accessor is included, the property is called a *read-only property*. You can also create a *write-only property*, which has just a set accessor, but that's uncommon.

In most cases, each property has a corresponding private instance variable that holds the property's value. In that case, the property should be declared with the same data type as the instance variable. It's also common to use the same name for the property and the instance variable, but to use Camel notation for the instance variable name (first word starts with a lowercase character, all words after that start with uppercase characters) and to use Pascal notation for the property name (each word starts with an uppercase character). For example, the name of the instance variable for the Code property is code. And a property named UnitPrice would have a corresponding instance variable named unitPrice.

Because a get accessor returns the value of the property, it typically ends with a return statement that provides that value. In the first property in this figure, for example, the return statement simply returns the value of the instance variable that holds the property value. The second property, however, illustrates that the get accessor can be more complicated than that. Here, the get accessor performs a calculation to determine the value that's returned.

The set accessor uses an implicit parameter named value to access the value to be assigned to the property. Typically, the set accessor simply assigns this value to the instance variable that stores the property's value. However, the set accessor can perform more complicated processing if necessary. For example, it could perform data validation.

If the get and set accessors for a property simply return the value of an instance variable and assign the value parameter to the instance variable, you can code the property as an *auto-implemented property*. Auto-implemented properties are a new feature of C# 2008 that provides a shorthand for coding simple properties. The auto-implemented property in the third example in this figure, for example, is equivalent to the property in the first example.

When you use an auto-implemented property, you should know that the compiler creates a private instance variable for you. Because of that, this property is only accessible through the get and set accessors. You should also know that an auto-implemented property must include both get and set accessors. However, you can create a read-only property by coding the private keyword in front of the set keyword. You can't create write-only auto-implemented properties.

The syntax for coding a public property

```
public type PropertyName
{
    [get { get accessor code }]
    [set { set accessor code }]
}
```

A read/write property

```
public string Code
{
    get { return code; }
    set { code = value; }
}
```

A read-only property

```
public decimal DiscountAmount
{
    get
    {
        discountAmount = subtotal * discountPercent;
        return discountAmount;
    }
}
```

An auto-implemented property

```
public string Code { get; set; }
```

A statement that sets a property value

```
product.Code = txtProductCode.Text;
```

A statement that gets a property value

```
string code = product.Code;
```

Description

- You use a *property* to get and set data values associated with an object. Typically, each property has a corresponding private instance variable that stores the property's value.
- It's common to use the same name for the property and the related instance variable, but to begin the property name with an uppercase letter and the instance variable name with a lowercase letter.
- You can code a *get accessor* to retrieve the value of the property. Often, the get accessor simply returns the value of the instance variable that stores the property's value.
- You can code a *set accessor* to set the value of the property. Often, the set accessor simply assigns the value passed to it via the *value* keyword to the instance variable that stores the property's value.
- If no additional code is required in the get and set accessors, you can create an *auto-implemented property*. Then, a corresponding private instance variable is created automatically, and that variable is only accessible through the property.
- A property that has both a get and a set accessor is called a *read/write property*. A property that has just a get accessor is called a *read-only property*. And a property that has just a set accessor is called a *write-only property*.

Figure 12-7 How to code properties

How to code methods

Figure 12-8 shows you how to code the methods for a class. Because the basics of coding methods were presented in chapter 6, most of the information in this figure should be review for you. In fact, this figure only introduces two new techniques. The first is the use of the public access modifier on a method declaration, which makes the method available to other classes.

The second is the concept of overloading. When you *overload* a method, you code two or more methods with the same name, but with unique combinations of parameters. In other words, you code methods with unique *signatures*.

For a method signature to be unique, the method must have a different number of parameters than the other methods with the same name, or at least one of the parameters must have a different data type. Note that the names of the parameters aren't part of the signature. So using different names isn't enough to make the signatures unique. Also, the return type isn't part of the signature. As a result, you can't create two methods with the same name and parameters but different return types.

The purpose of overloading is to provide more than one way to invoke a given method. For example, this figure shows two versions of the GetDisplayText method. The first one is the one you saw in figure 12-3 that accepts a parameter named sep. The second one doesn't accept this parameter. Instead, it uses a comma and a space to separate the code, price, and description.

When you refer to an overloaded method, the number of arguments you specify and their types determine which version of the method is executed. The two statements in this figure that call the GetDisplayText method illustrate how this works. Because the first statement specifies an argument, it will cause the version of the GetDisplayText method that accepts a parameter to be executed. In contrast, the second statement doesn't specify an argument, so it will cause the version of the GetDisplayText method that doesn't accept a parameter to be executed.

In chapter 3, you learned that if you type the name of a method followed by a left parenthesis into the Code Editor, Visual Studio's IntelliSense feature displays a list of the method's parameters. You may not have realized, though, that if up and down arrows appear to the left of the argument list, it indicates that the method is overloaded. Then, you can click the up and down arrows or press the up and down arrow keys to move from one overloaded method to another.

This works with overloaded methods in user-defined classes as well. For example, the illustration in this figure shows how the IntelliSense feature displays the overloaded GetDisplayText methods. In this case, the second of the two methods is displayed.

The syntax for coding a public method

```
public returnType MethodName([parameterList])
{
    statements
}
```

A method that accepts parameters

```
public string GetDisplayText(string sep)
{
    return code + sep + price.ToString("c") + sep + description;
}
```

An overloaded version of the GetDisplayText method

```
public string GetDisplayText()
{
    return code + ", " + price.ToString("c") + ", " + description;
}
```

Two statements that call the GetDisplayText method

```
lblProduct.Text = product.GetDisplayText("\t");
lblProduct.Text = product.GetDisplayText();
```

How the IntelliSense feature lists overloaded methods

```
Product product = newProductForm.GetNewProduct();
Console.WriteLine(product.GetDisplayText(
                        ▲2 of 2▼ string Product.GetDisplayText (string sep)
```

Description

- To provide other classes with access to a method, you declare it using the public access modifier. To prevent other classes from accessing a method, you declare it using the private access modifier.
- The name of a method combined with its parameters form the method's *signature*. Although you can use the same name for more than one method, each method must have a unique signature.
- When you create two or more methods with the same name but with different parameter lists, the methods are *overloaded*. It's common to use overloaded methods to provide two or more versions of a method that work with different data types or that supply default values for omitted parameters.
- When you type a method name followed by a left parenthesis, the IntelliSense feature of Visual Studio displays the parameters expected by the method. If up and down arrows are displayed as shown above, you can click these arrows or press the up and down arrow keys to display each of the method's overloaded parameter lists.

How to code constructors

By default, when you use the new keyword to create an instance of a user-defined class, C# assigns default values to all of the instance variables in the new object. If that's not what you want, you can code a special method called a *constructor* that's executed when an object is created from the class. Figure 12-9 shows you how to do that.

To create a constructor, you declare a public method with the same name as the class name. For example, a constructor for the Product class must be named Product. Within the constructor, you initialize the instance variables, and you include any additional statements you want to be executed when an object is created from the class. Note that a constructor must not be declared with a return type.

The first example in this figure is a constructor that doesn't provide for any parameters, so it's called when you create an instance of the class without specifying any arguments. Because this constructor has no executable statements, it simply initializes all the instance variables to their default values (excluding read-only variables). The default values for the various data types are listed in this figure.

In some cases, a class might not be defined with any constructors. For example, you could forget to code a constructor. Or, you could code a class within another class (see chapter 16) and not declare a constructor for that class. In that case, C# provides a *default constructor* that's equivalent to the constructor shown in the first example.

The second constructor in this figure shows that you can overload constructors just like you can overload methods. Here, a constructor that accepts three parameters is defined. This constructor uses the values passed to the parameters to initialize the instance variables. This technique is often used to set initial property values when an object is created.

The third constructor shows how you might provide a constructor for the Product class that accepts just a product code as a parameter. Then, it calls a method named GetProduct in a database class named ProductDB to retrieve the data for the specified product. After the data is retrieved, the constructor uses it to initialize the instance variables.

Notice that both the second and third constructors use the this keyword to refer to the properties whose values are being initialized. Although this isn't required, it makes it clear that the property that's being referred to is defined in the current class and not in another class.

This figure also presents statements that execute the three constructors shown here. The first statement executes the constructor with no parameters. The second statement executes the constructor with three parameters. And the third statement executes the constructor with one parameter. Although you've seen statements like these before, you should now have a better understanding of how they work.

A constructor with no parameters

```
public Product()
{
}
```

A constructor with three parameters

```
public Product(string code, string description, decimal price)
{
    this.Code = code;
    this.Description = description;
    this.Price = price;
}
```

A constructor with one parameter

```
public Product(string code)
{
    Product p = ProductDB.GetProduct(code);
    this.Code = p.Code;
    this.Description = p.Description;
    this.Price = p.Price;
}
```

Statements that call these constructors

```
Product product1 = new Product();
Product product2 = new Product("CS08", "Murach's C# 2008", 54.50m);
Product product3 = new Product(txtCode.Text);
```

Default values for instance variables

Data type	Default value
All numeric types	zero (0)
Boolean	false
Char	binary 0 (null)
Object	null (no value)
Date	12:00 a.m. on January 1, 0001

Description

- The name of a constructor must be the same as the name of the class. In addition, a constructor must always be declared with the public access modifier, and it can't specify a return type.
- To code a constructor that has parameters, code a data type and name for each parameter within the parentheses that follow the class name.
- The name of a class combined with its parameter list form the signature of the constructor. Each constructor must have a unique signature.
- If a constructor doesn't assign a value to an instance variable and the variable hasn't been initialized, the variable will be assigned a default value as shown above.

Figure 12-9 How to code constructors

How to code static members

As figure 12-10 shows, *static members* are members that can be accessed without creating an instance of a class. The idea of static members shouldn't be new to you because you've seen them used in several chapters in this book. In chapter 4, for example, you learned how to use static methods of the Math and Convert classes. And in chapter 9, you learned how to use static members of the DateTime structure and the String class. This figure shows how to create static members in your own classes.

To create a static member, you simply include the *static* keyword on the declaration for the member. The class shown in this figure, for example, provides static members that can be used to perform data validation. This class has a static field named title, a static property named Title, and a static method named IsPresent.

The static IsPresent method validates the Text property of a text box control to make sure the user entered a value. If the Text property is an empty string, the IsPresent method displays an error message, sets the focus to the text box, and returns false. Otherwise, it returns true. Note that this method uses the Tag property of the text box to get the name that's displayed in the dialog box. Because of that, this property must be set for any text box that's validated by this method.

The second example in this figure shows how you might call the static IsPresent method to validate three text boxes. Here, the return values from three calls to the IsPresent method are tested. If all three calls return true, a Boolean variable named isValidData is set to true. Otherwise, this variable is set to false.

Since the Validator class shown in this figure contains only static members, the static keyword has been used to declare the entire class as a *static class*. This prevents you from accidentally coding any non-static members for this class or from creating an object from this class. If you attempt to write such code, this class won't compile.

However, a class that isn't declared as a static class can include static members and non-static members. Then, when you create an instance of that class, all of the instances share the static members. Because of that, you can't access a static member from the variable that refers to the instance of the class. Instead, you can access it only by coding the name of the class.

Keep in mind, too, that a static property or method can only refer to other static members. For example, because the Title property shown in this figure is declared as static, the title field it refers to must be declared as static. Similarly, if a static property or method refers to another method, that method must be declared as static.

A class that contains static members

```
public static class Validator
{
    private static string title = "Entry Error";

    public static string Title
    {
        get
        {
            return title;
        }
        set
        {
            title = value;
        }
    }

    public static bool IsPresent(TextBox textBox)
    {
        if (textBox.Text == "")
        {
            MessageBox.Show(textBox.Tag + " is a required field.", Title);
            textBox.Focus();
            return false;
        }
        return true;
    }
```

Code that uses static members

```
if (  Validator.IsPresent(txtCode) &&
      Validator.IsPresent(txtDescription) &&
      Validator.IsPresent(txtPrice) )
    isValidData = true;
else
    isValidData = false;
```

Description

- A *static member* is a field, property, or method that can be accessed without creating an instance of the class. To define a static member, you use the *static* keyword.
- Static properties and methods can refer only to other static members or to variables declared within the property or method.
- A constant that's declared with the public keyword is implicitly static. You can't code the static keyword on a constant declaration.
- If you create an object from a class, you can't refer to a static member through the variable for the object. You can refer to a static member only through the name of the class.
- If a class only contains static members, you can use the static keyword in the class declaration to declare the class as a *static class*. This prevents programmers from accidentally adding a non-static member to the class or from creating an object from the class.

Figure 12-10 How to code static members

The Product Maintenance application

Now that you've learned the basic skills for creating classes, the topics that follow present a Product Maintenance application that maintains a simple file of products. As you'll see, this application uses three user-defined classes in addition to the two form classes and the Program class that starts the program by running the first form.

The operation of the Product Maintenance application

Figure 12-11 describes the operation of the Product Maintenance application. As you can see, this application uses two forms. The main form displays a list of the products that are stored in a file in a list box. The user can use this form to add or delete a product.

If the user clicks the Add Product button, the New Product form is displayed as a dialog box. Then, the user can enter the data for a new product and click the Save button to add the product to the file. After the product is saved, the list box in the Product Maintenance form is refreshed so it includes the new product. The user can also click the Cancel button on the New Product form to cancel the add operation.

To delete a product, the user selects the product in the list and clicks the Delete Product button. Then, a dialog box is displayed to confirm the operation. If the operation is confirmed, the product is deleted and the list box is refreshed so it no longer includes the deleted product.

This figure also shows how the Tag properties of the three text boxes on the New Product form are set. As you'll see in a minute, the methods of the data validation class use the Tag property of these text boxes to display meaningful error messages if the user enters incorrect data.

The Product Maintenance form

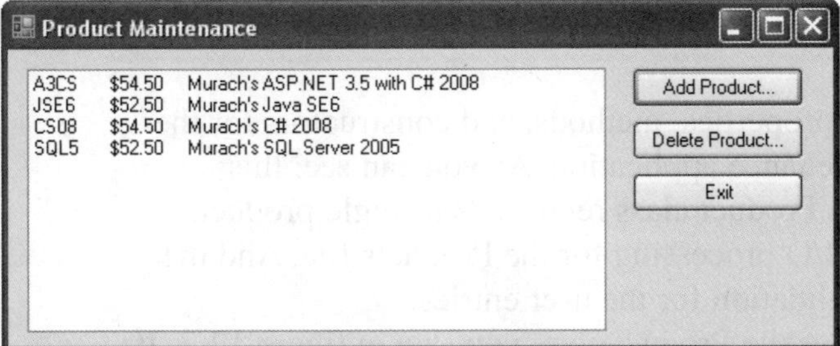

The New Product form

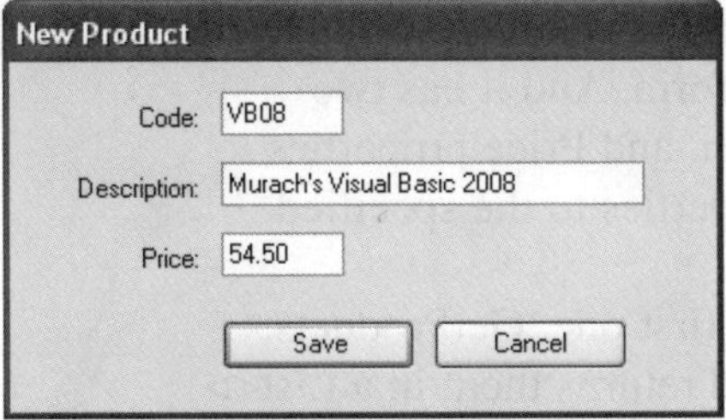

The Tag property settings for the text boxes on the New Product form

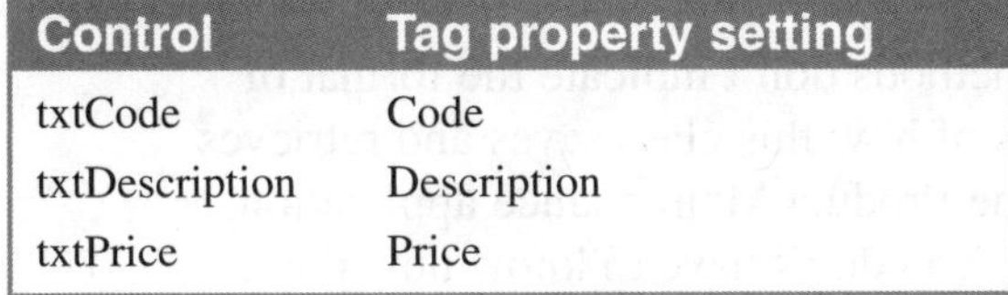

Control	Tag property setting
txtCode	Code
txtDescription	Description
txtPrice	Price

Description

- The Product Maintenance application retrieves product information from a file, displays it in a list box, and lets the user add or delete products.
- To add a product, the user clicks the Add Product button to display the New Product form. Then, the user can enter the data for the new product and click the Save button. Alternatively, the user can click the Cancel button to cancel the add operation. In either case, the user is returned to the Product Maintenance form.
- To delete a product, the user selects the product to be deleted and then clicks the Delete Product button. Before the product is deleted, the delete operation is confirmed.
- The Tag properties of the three text boxes on the New Product form are set so that the Validator class can display meaningful error messages if the user enters invalid data.

Figure 12-11 The operation of the Product Maintenance application

The classes used by the Product Maintenance application

Figure 12-12 summarizes the properties, methods, and constructors for the classes used by the Product Maintenance application. As you can see, this application uses three classes. The Product class represents a single product. The ProductDB class handles the I/O processing for the Products file. And the Validator class handles the data validation for the user entries.

The Product class is the same as the Product class you saw in figure 12-3. It has three properties named Code, Description, and Price that define the values for a Product object. It has a single method named GetDisplayText that returns a string that contains the code, description, and price in a format that can be displayed in the list box of the Product Maintenance form. And it has two constructors: one that initializes the Code, Description, and Price properties to their default values, and one that initializes these properties to the specified values.

The ProductDB class contains two methods. The first one, GetProducts, retrieves all of the products from the Products file and returns them in a List<> of Product objects. The second one, SaveProducts, accepts a List<> of Product objects and writes the products in the list to the Products file, overwriting the previous contents of the file.

Note that the specifications for these methods don't indicate the format of the Products file. That's because the details of how this class saves and retrieves product information are of no concern to the Product Maintenance application. That's one of the benefits of encapsulation: You don't have to know how the class works. You just have to know what members it contains and how you refer to them.

The Validator class contains four static methods that provide for different types of data validation. For example, the IsPresent method checks if the user entered data into a text box, and the IsDecimal method checks if the data the user entered is a valid decimal value. If one of these methods determines that the data is invalid, it displays an error message using the Title property as the title for the dialog box, it moves the focus to the text box that's being validated, and it returns false. Otherwise, it returns true.

The Product class

Property	Description
`Code`	A string that contains a code that uniquely identifies the product.
`Description`	A string that contains a description of the product.
`Price`	A decimal that contains the product's price.
Method	**Description**
`GetDisplayText(sep)`	Returns a string that contains the code, description, and price separated by the sep string.
Constructor	**Description**
`()`	Creates a Product object with default values.
`(code, description, price)`	Creates a Product object using the specified values.

The ProductDB class

Method	Description
`GetProducts()`	A static method that returns a List<> of Product objects from the Products file.
`SaveProducts(list)`	A static method that writes the products in the specified List<> of Product objects to the Products file.

The Validator class

Property	Description
`Title`	A static string that contains the text that's displayed in the title bar of a dialog box that's displayed for an error message.
Method	**Description**
`IsPresent(textBox)`	A static method that returns a Boolean value that indicates if data was entered into the specified text box.
`IsInt32(textBox)`	A static method that returns a Boolean value that indicates if an integer was entered into the specified text box.
`IsDecimal(textBox)`	A static method that returns a Boolean value that indicates if a decimal was entered into the specified text box.
`IsWithinRange(textBox, min, max)`	A static method that returns a Boolean value that indicates if the value entered into the specified text box is within the specified range.

Note: Each of these methods displays an error message in a dialog box and moves the focus to the text box if the data is invalid.

Note

- Because you don't need to know how the ProductDB class works, its code isn't shown in this chapter. Please refer to chapters 21 and 22 for three different versions of this class.

Figure 12-12 The classes used by the Product Maintenance application

The code for the Product Maintenance application

Figures 12-13 through 12-15 show the code for the Product Maintenance form, the New Product form, and the Validator class. Since you saw the code for the Product class in figure 12-3, I won't repeat it here. Also, because you don't need to know how the ProductDB class is implemented to understand how this application works, I won't present the code for that class either. If you're interested, however, you'll find three different implementations of this class in chapters 21 and 22.

The code for the Product Maintenance form, shown in figure 12-13, begins by declaring a class variable named products of the List<> type. Next, in the Load event handler for the form, the GetProducts method of the ProductsDB class is called to fill this list with Product objects created from the data in the Products file. Then, the FillProductListBox method is called. This method uses a foreach loop to add the string returned by each product's GetDisplayText method to the list box. Notice that a tab character is passed to this method so the products appear as shown in figure 12-11.

If the user clicks the Add Product button, an instance of the New Product form is created, and the GetNewProduct method of that form is called. If the Product object returned by this method isn't null, the product is added to the products list. Then, the SaveProducts method of the ProductDB class is called to update the Products file, and the FillProductListBox method is called to refresh the list box so the new product is included.

If the user selects a product in the list and clicks the Delete Product button, a confirmation dialog box is displayed. Then, if the user confirms the deletion, the product is removed from the products list, the Products file is updated, and the list box is refreshed.

The code for the New Product form is shown in figure 12-14. It declares a private Product object named product. Then, the GetNewProduct method that's called from the Product Maintenance form starts by displaying the New Product form as a dialog box. If the user clicks the Save button in this dialog box, the IsValidData method is called to validate the data. This method calls the IsPresent method of the Validator class for each text box on the form. In addition, it calls the IsDecimal method for the Price text box.

If all of the values are valid, a new Product object is created with the values entered by the user, the dialog box is closed, and the Product object is returned to the Product Maintenance form. In contrast, if the user clicks the Cancel button, the dialog box is closed and the product variable, which is initialized to null, is returned to the Product Maintenance form.

The code for the Validator class, shown in figure 12-15, should present no surprises. In fact, you saw code similar to this code back in figure 12-10. The only difference is that this version of the Validator class includes an IsDecimal method as well as an IsPresent method. Note that because the Product Maintenance application doesn't use the IsInt32 or IsWithinRange methods, I omitted those methods from this figure.

The code for the Product Maintenance form

```
public partial class frmProductMain : Form
{
    public frmProductMain()
    {
        InitializeComponent();
    }

    private List<Product> products = null;

    private void frmProductMain_Load(object sender, System.EventArgs e)
    {
        products = ProductDB.GetProducts();
        FillProductListBox();
    }

    private void FillProductListBox()
    {
        lstProducts.Items.Clear();
        foreach (Product p in products)
        {
            lstProducts.Items.Add(p.GetDisplayText("\t"));
        }
    }

    private void btnAdd_Click(object sender, System.EventArgs e)
    {
        frmNewProduct newProductForm = new frmNewProduct();
        Product product = newProductForm.GetNewProduct();
        if (product != null)
        {
            products.Add(product);
            ProductDB.SaveProducts(products);
            FillProductListBox();
        }
    }

    private void btnDelete_Click(object sender, System.EventArgs e)
    {
        int i = lstProducts.SelectedIndex;
        if (i != -1)
        {
            Product product = products[i];
            string message = "Are you sure you want to delete "
                + product.Description + "?";
            DialogResult button =
                MessageBox.Show(message, "Confirm Delete",
                MessageBoxButtons.YesNo);
            if (button == DialogResult.Yes)
            {
                products.Remove(product);
                ProductDB.SaveProducts(products);
                FillProductListBox();
            }
        }
    }

    private void btnExit_Click(object sender, EventArgs e)
    {
        this.Close();
    }
}
```

Figure 12-13 The code for the Product Maintenance form

The code for the New Product form

```
public partial class frmNewProduct : Form
{
    public frmNewProduct()
    {
        InitializeComponent();
    }

    private Product product = null;

    public Product GetNewProduct()
    {
        this.ShowDialog();
        return product;
    }

    private void btnSave_Click(object sender, System.EventArgs e)
    {
        if (IsValidData())
        {
            product = new Product(txtCode.Text,
                txtDescription.Text, Convert.ToDecimal(txtPrice.Text));
            this.Close();
        }
    }

    private bool IsValidData()
    {
        return Validator.IsPresent(txtCode) &&
               Validator.IsPresent(txtDescription) &&
               Validator.IsPresent(txtPrice) &&
               Validator.IsDecimal(txtPrice);
    }

    private void btnCancel_Click(object sender, System.EventArgs e)
    {
        this.Close();
    }
}
```

Figure 12-14 The code for the New Product form

The code for the Validator class

```
public static class Validator
{
    private static string title = "Entry Error";

    public static string Title
    {
        get
        {
            return title;
        }
        set
        {
            title = value;
        }
    }

    public static bool IsPresent(TextBox textBox)
    {
        if (textBox.Text == "")
        {
            MessageBox.Show(textBox.Tag + " is a required field.", Title);
            textBox.Focus();
            return false;
        }
        return true;
    }

    public static bool IsDecimal(TextBox textBox)
    {
        try
        {
            Convert.ToDecimal(textBox.Text);
            return true;
        }
        catch (FormatException)
        {
            MessageBox.Show(textBox.Tag + " must be a decimal number.", Title);
            textBox.Focus();
            return false;
        }
    }
}
```

Note

- The code for the IsInt32 and IsWithinRange methods isn't shown here because these methods aren't used by the Product Maintenance application.

Figure 12-15 The code for the Validator class

How to use the Class View window and class diagrams

Now that you've seen a complete application that uses classes, you're ready to learn how to use the Class View window and *class diagrams*. Although you can create applications without using these features, they often make it easier to visualize and work with the classes of a project.

How to use the Class View window

The *Class View window* is a tabbed window that's displayed in the group with the Solution Explorer window. As figure 12-16 shows, this window contains a hierarchical view of the classes in your solution as well as the members of each class. In short, class view gives you an overall view of the structure of your application.

The solution in this figure is for the Product Maintenance application that was presented in figures 12-11 through 12-15. Here, I've expanded the project in the top pane of the Class View window and clicked on the Product class to show its members in the bottom pane. As you can see, the members for this class include two signatures for the GetDisplayText method; two constructors; the Code, Description, and Price properties; and the private fields named code, description, and price. The padlocks on the icons for the private fields indicate that these fields are not accessible from outside the class.

You can also use the Class View window to display the code for any member in the Code Editor. To do that, just double-click the member in the lower pane of the Class View window. In this figure, for example, you can see the code that was displayed when I double-clicked the Price property.

The Class View window

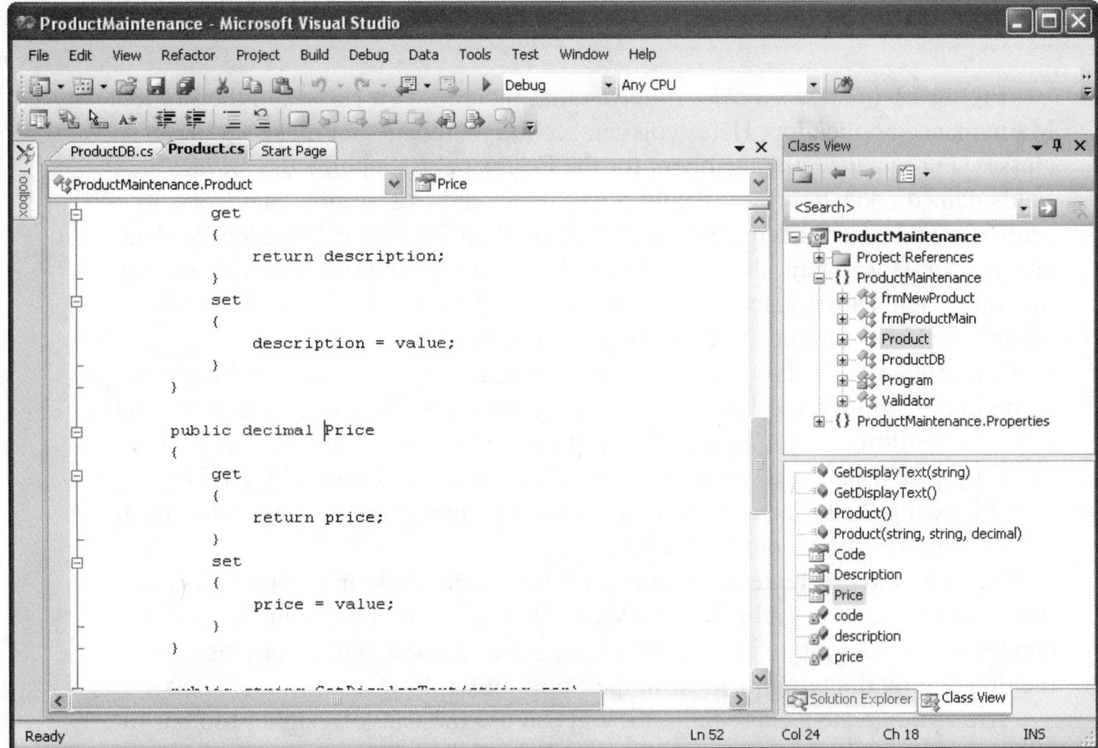

Description

- The *Class View window* lets you browse the classes in a solution.
- In the top pane, the Class View window displays the classes of a project. In the bottom pane, the Class View window displays the members of the selected class, including properties, methods, events, and fields.
- To display the Class View window, click the Class View tab that's grouped with the Solution Explorer window, or use the View→Class View command.
- To display the classes for a project, expand the project in the top pane.
- To display the members for a class in the lower pane, click on the class in the top pane.
- To display the C# code for a member in the Code Editor, double-click on the member in the Class View window.

Figure 12-16 How to use the Class View window

How to use class diagrams and the Class Details window

Figure 12-17 shows a *class diagram* that includes two classes in the Product Maintenance application. Here, you can see the members that make up these classes. For instance, the members for the Product class include the private fields named code, description, and price; the Code, Description, and Price properties; the overloaded GetDisplayText method; and the overloaded Product constructor. Here again, the padlocks on the icons for the private fields indicate that these fields are not accessible from outside the class. Also, the dotted lines around the Validator class indicate that it's a static class.

You can create a class diagram like this one by right-clicking on the project name in the Solution Explorer, and selecting the View Class Diagram command from the resulting menu. This creates a class diagram that contains every class in the project. Then, you can remove any class from the diagram by clicking on it and pressing the Delete key. And you can add a new class by dragging it from the Solution Explorer onto the diagram.

Another way to create a class diagram is to right-click on just one class in the Solution Explorer and select the View Class Diagram command. That creates a class diagram with just one class. Then, you can add other classes to the diagram by dragging them from the Solution Explorer.

After you create a class diagram, you can use the Class Designer toolbar to adjust the diagram. For instance, you can click on the a:T button to display both the name and type for each member of a class, and you can click on the a( ) button to display the name, type, and signature for each member.

When you select a class in a class diagram, you can use the *Class Details window* that's below the diagram to view the details about the members of the class or the selected member in that class. In this figure, for example, the Code property is selected in the class diagram so it is also highlighted in the Class Details window.

To navigate to the code for any member of the selected class, just double-click the icon for the member in either the class diagram or the Class Details window. Then, Visual Studio will open the class in the Code Editor window (if it isn't already open) and jump to the code for the selected member.

To generate the starting code for new properties, methods, fields, and events, click on the appropriate row or button in the Class Details window. For example, you can click on the <add property> row or the New Property button in the Class Details window to start a new property. Then, you enter the name, type, and modifier in the row. To jump to the Code Editor so you can complete the code for the property, you can double-click on the icon for the row. Using the Class Details window like this is a quick way to develop the starting code for all of the members of a class.

Finally, to delete a member from a class, you can press the Delete key when the member is selected in either the class diagram or the Class Details window. This not only deletes the member from the class diagram and Class Details window, it also deletes the code for that member in the Code Editor.

A class diagram that shows two of the classes in the project

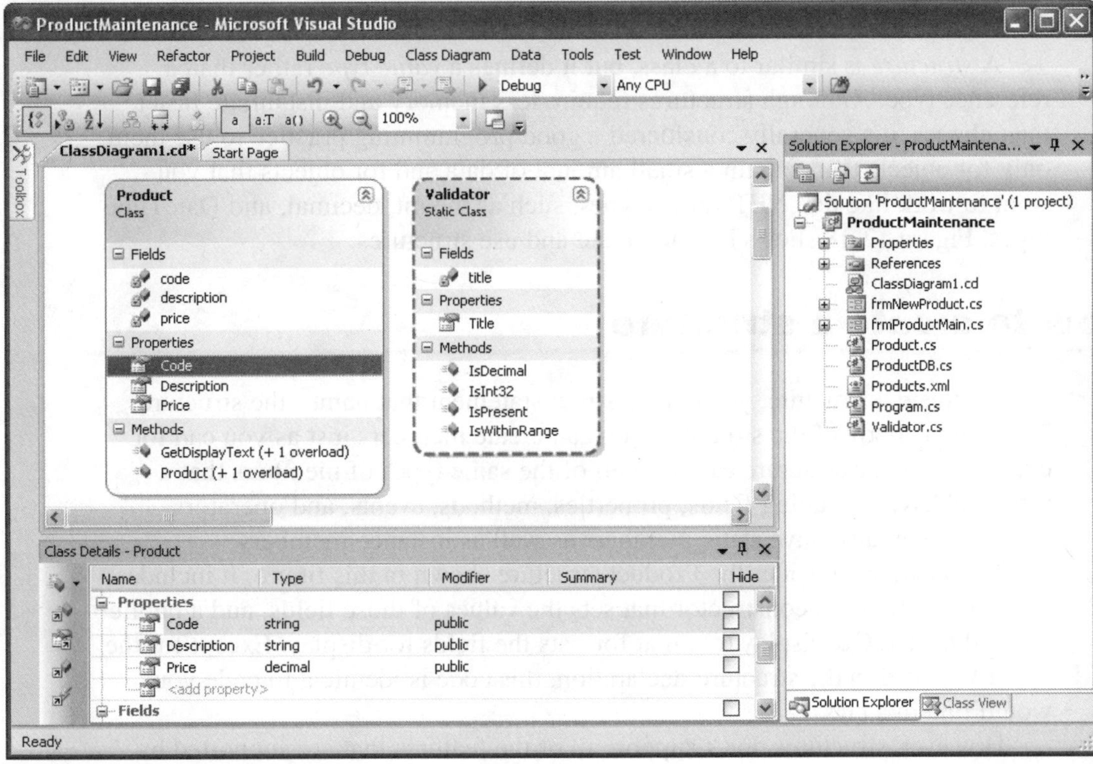

Description

- A *class diagram* is a visual representation of the methods, properties, fields, and events for one or more classes. To create a class diagram, right-click on a project or class in the Solution Explorer and select the View Class Diagram command.
- To select a class in a diagram, click on it. To expand or collapse the members of a class, click the icon in the upper right corner of the class. To delete a class, press the Delete key. To add a class, drag a class from the Solution Explorer to the diagram. To adjust the way the diagram is displayed, use the buttons in the Class Designer toolbar.
- The details for the selected class or member in the class diagram are shown in the Class Details window. To jump to the code for a member in the Code Editor window, double-click on the member's icon in the class diagram or the Class Details window.
- To generate the starting code for new properties, methods, fields, and events, click on the appropriate row or button in the Class Details window and enter the required information. Then, you can switch to the Code Editor window to complete the code.
- To delete the code for a member, select it in the class diagram or Class Details window and press the Delete key.

Express Edition limitation

- The C# 2008 Express Edition doesn't have class diagrams or the Class Details window.

Figure 12-17 How to use class diagrams and the Class Details window

How to work with structures

A *structure* is similar to a class, but it defines a *value type* rather than a reference type. Although structures require less memory and instantiate faster than classes, it's generally considered a good programming practice to use them only for objects that contain a small amount of data and for objects that you want to work like the .NET values types, such as the int, decimal, and DateTime types. Figure 12-18 shows how to create and use structures.

How to create a structure

To create a structure, you code a struct statement that names the structure. Then, in the body of the structure, you can create members just as you can for classes. In fact, a structure can have all of the same types of members that a class can have, including fields, properties, methods, events, and operators. Structures can also have static members as well as instance members.

To illustrate, consider the Product structure shown in this figure. It includes three public fields, a constructor that sets the values of those fields, and a public method named GetDisplayText that formats the fields for display. Except for the struct keyword in the structure declaration, this code is identical to code you would find in a class.

However, structures don't support all of the features that are supported by classes. For example, a structure can't contain a parameterless constructor. And if you provide a constructor that includes parameters, this constructor must initialize all instance variables in the structure. In addition, you can extend the functionality of a class by coding another class that inherits the first class (see chapter 14), but you can't do that with structures.

How to use a structure

To use a structure, you start by declaring a variable with the structure type just as you would any other data type. For example, the first statement in the first code example declares a variable named p of type Product.

When you declare a variable with a structure type, an instance of that structure is created but values aren't assigned to its instance variables. Then, you must assign values to those variables before you can call any properties or methods of the structure. That's why the three assignment statements that follow the structure declaration in this figure set the values of the Code, Description, and Price fields before the last statement calls the GetDisplayText method.

Because an instance is automatically created when you declare a structure, you don't need to use the new keyword to create an instance. If the structure defines a constructor that accepts parameters, however, you can use the new keyword just as you would for a class as shown in the last example in this figure.

The syntax for creating a structure

```
public struct StructureName
{
    structure members...
}
```

A Product structure

```
public struct Product
{
    public string Code;
    public string Description;
    public decimal Price;

    public Product(string code, string description, decimal price)
    {
        this.Code = code;                  // If you code a constructor
        this.Description = description;    // you must initialize
        this.Price = price;                // all instance variables
    }

    public string GetDisplayText(string sep)
    {
        return Code + sep + Price.ToString("c") + sep + Description;
    }
}
```

Code that declares a variable as a structure type and assigns values to it

```
Product p;              // Create an instance of the Product structure
p.Code = "CS08";        // Assign values to each instance variable
p.Description = "Murach's C# 2008";
p.Price = 54.50m;
string msg = p.GetDisplayText("\n"); // Call a method
```

Code that uses the structure's constructor

```
Product p = new Product("CS08", "Murach's C# 2008", 54.50m);
```

Description

- A *structure* is similar to a class, but it represents a *value type*, not a reference type.
- A structure can contain the same types of members as a class, including fields, properties, methods, constructors, and events.
- When you code a structure, you can't code an empty constructor. When you declare a structure, it automatically uses this constructor to initialize itself. As a result, you only need to use the new keyword to create an instance of a structure when you're passing values to a constructor that accepts parameters.
- You can't call any of the properties or methods of a structure until you initialize all of the instance variables of the structure.
- Unlike classes, structures can't be inherited by other classes. For more information about how inheritance works, please see chapter 14.

Figure 12-18 How to work with structures

Perspective

At this point, you may be wondering why you should go to the extra effort of dividing an application into classes. The answer is twofold. First, dividing the code into classes makes it easier to use the code in two or more applications. For example, any application that needs to work with the data in the Products file can use the Product and ProductDB classes. Second, using classes helps you separate the business logic and database processing of an application from the user interface. That can simplify the development of the application and make it easier to maintain and enhance later on.

Now that you've had this introduction to the use of classes, you can continue in two different ways. If you already feel comfortable with the use of classes, you can read the next four chapters in this section to learn more about object-oriented programming. That will give the background you need for understanding how the .NET classes work and for creating complex classes of your own.

On the other hand, if you're new to programming and the use of classes, you may want to skip to section 4 or 5 where you'll see how business classes are used in other applications. As you will see in those chapters, this chapter has already given you the skills that you need for developing most business classes and applications. Then, when you're more comfortable with the use of classes, you can return to the last four chapters in this section.

Terms

multi-layered architecture
three-layered architecture
presentation layer
database layer
middle layer
business rules layer
business class
business object
three-tiered architecture
object
property
method
member
class
instantiation
object initializer
encapsulation
data hiding
constructor
state
reference type
class file
field
instance variable
read-only field
public field
get accessor
set accessor
read/write property
read-only property
write-only property
auto-implemented property
signature
overloaded method
static member
Class View window
class diagram
Class Details window
structure

Exercise 12-1 Create a Customer Maintenance application that uses classes

In this exercise, you'll create a Customer Maintenance application that uses three classes. To make this application easier to develop, we'll give you the starting forms, a complete Validator class, and a complete CustomerDB class that you'll use to work with the data in a file of customers. Note that the CustomerDB class assumes that the file of customers (Customers.txt) is in the C:\C# 2008\Files directory. If you placed this file in a different directory after downloading and installing the files for this book, you will need to change the path specification in the CustomerDB class.

Open the project and add a Customer class

1. Open the application in the C:\C# 2008\Chapter 12\CustomerMaintenance directory. Then, review both of the forms in the Form Designer window so you get an idea of how this project should work.
2. Add a class named Customer to this project, and add the properties, method, and constructors that are shown in the table below.

Property	Description
`FirstName`	Gets or sets a string that contains the customer's first name.
`LastName`	Gets or sets a string that contains the customer's last name.
`Email`	Gets or sets a string that contains the customer's email address.
Method	**Description**
`GetDisplayText()`	Returns a string that contains the customer's name and email address formatted like this: Joanne Smith, jsmith@armaco.com.
Constructor	**Description**
`()`	Creates a Customer object with default values.
`(firstName, lastName, email)`	Creates a Customer object using the specified values.

3. When you complete the Customer class, use the Class View window to review the members and jump to the code for one or more of the members. Then, review the members for the Validator class. Note that one of the methods is IsValidEmail, which you can use to validate email addresses.
4. If you're not using the Express Edition of C# 2008, create a class diagram and use it to review the members and code of the Customer and Validator classes as described in step 3.

Add code to implement the Add Customer form

5. Display the code for the Add Customer form, and declare a class variable named customer of type Customer with an initial value of null.

6. Add a public method named GetNewCustomer that displays the form as a dialog box and returns a Customer object.
7. Add an event handler for the Click event of the Save button that validates the data on the form using the methods of the Validator class (all three fields are required and the email field must be a valid email address), and then creates a new Customer object and closes the form if the data is valid.
8. Add an event handler for the Click event of the Cancel button that simply closes the form.

Add code to implement the Customer Maintenance form

9. Display the code for the Customer Maintenance form, and declare a class variable named customers of type List<Customer> with an initial value of null.
10. Add an event handler for the Load event of the form that uses the GetCustomers method of the CustomerDB class to load the customers list and then adds the customers to the Customers list box. Use the GetDisplayText method of the Customer class to format the customer data.
11. Add an event handler for the Click event of the Add button that creates a new instance of the Add Customer form and executes the GetNewCustomer method of that form. If the customer object that's returned by this method is not null, this event handler should add the new customer to the list, call the SaveCustomers method of the CustomerDB class to save the list, and then refresh the Customers list box.
12. Add an event handler for the Click event of the Delete button that removes the selected customer from the list, calls the SaveCustomer method of the CustomerDB class to save the list, and refreshes the Customers list box. Be sure to confirm the delete operation.
13. Add an event handler for the Click event of the Exit button that closes the form.

Run and test the application

14. Run the application and test it to be sure that it works properly. When you're done, end the application, but leave the solution open if you're going to continue with the next exercise.

Exercise 12-2 Use a structure

In this exercise, you'll modify your solution to exercise 12-1 by converting the Customer class to a structure.

1. If it isn't open already, open the project in the C:\C# 2008\Chapter 12\CustomerMaintenance directory.
2. Modify the Customer class so it defines a structure. Be sure to omit the parameterless constructor since they're not allowed in structures.
3. Run the application, and debug any errors that you encounter. Note that you can't assign a null value to a Customer object anymore as it is now a value type. However, you can check if any of the properties of the Customer object contain a null value as those properties are of the String type.

13

How to work with indexers, delegates, events, and operators

In the last chapter, you learned some basic skills for creating and working with classes. Now, this chapter will teach you some additional skills that you can use to create more complex classes. That includes creating indexers, throwing argument exceptions, defining delegates, raising events, and overloading operators.

An introduction to the ProductList class

As you may recall, the Product Maintenance application that was presented in chapter 12 used the List<> class to store Product objects. To demonstrate the techniques that are presented in this chapter, I'll use a new class named ProductList. As you'll see, this class represents a collection of Product objects.

The code for a simple ProductList class

Figure 13-1 shows a simple version of the ProductList class. This class only uses coding techniques described in chapter 12. As a result, you shouldn't have any trouble understanding how this class works.

To start, The ProductList class defines a private List<> variable named products to store the product list. Then, it provides a constructor with no parameters that instantiates a new list, followed by a Count property that indicates how many products are in the product list.

Next, this class includes an overloaded Add method. The first version of this method accepts a single parameter: a Product object that's added to the product list. The second version accepts three parameters: code, description, and price. The Add method uses these parameters to create a Product object, which is then added to the list.

After that, the ProductList class provides a GetProductByIndex method that returns a Product object from the list based on the specified index, and a Remove method that removes a specified product from the list. The last two methods in this class are a Fill method that fills the product list with the data from a file, and a Save method that saves the product list to a file. Both of these methods call static methods in the ProductDB class.

Of these methods, only the Fill and Save methods provide functionality that isn't available from the List<> class itself. In fact, the ProductList class actually limits the functionality of the List<> class. For example, the ProductList class doesn't provide many of the properties and methods that are available from the List<> class (such as the Insert method). Still, this class works for the purposes of this chapter. In the next chapter, though, you'll learn an easy way to code a ProductList class that provides access to all of the functionality of the List<> class.

The code for a simple ProductList class

```
public class ProductList
{
    private List<Product> products;

    public ProductList()
    {
        products = new List<Product>();
    }

    public int Count
    {
        get { return products.Count; }
    }

    public void Add(Product product)
    {
        products.Add(product);
    }

    public void Add(string code, string description, decimal price)
    {
        Product p = new Product(code, description, price);
        products.Add(p);
    }

    public Product GetProductByIndex(int i)
    {
        return products[i];
    }

    public void Remove(Product product)
    {
        products.Remove(product);
    }

    public void Fill()
    {
        products = ProductDB.GetProducts();
    }

    public void Save()
    {
        ProductDB.SaveProducts(products);
    }

}
```

Figure 13-1 The code for a simple ProductList class

The specifications for the enhanced ProductList class

Figure 13-2 shows the specifications for an enhanced version of the ProductList class. To start, this class provides two indexers that let you access a product based on its index or product code (instead of using the GetProductByIndex method). Besides these indexers, the enhanced ProductList class includes a + operator that adds a product to the list and a – operator that removes a product from the list.

Finally, this class includes a delegate named ChangeHandler and an event named Changed. The delegate is designed to wire event handlers to the Changed event of the ProductList class. The ProductList class raises this event whenever the contents of the product list changes due to a product being added to or removed from the list. As you'll see, the Product Maintenance application uses this event to determine when it should save the product list and refresh the list box that displays the products.

The ProductList class

Indexer	Description
[index]	Provides access to the product at the specified position.
[code]	Provides access to the product with the specified code.
Property	**Description**
Count	An integer that indicates how many Product objects are in the list.
Method	**Description**
Add(product)	Adds the specified Product object to the list.
Add(code, description, price)	Creates a Product object with the specified code, description, and price values, and then adds the Product object to the list.
Remove(product)	Removes the specified Product object from the list.
Fill()	Fills the list with product data from a file.
Save()	Saves the products to a file.
Operator	**Description**
+	Adds a Product object to the list.
-	Removes a Product object from the list.
Delegate	**Description**
ChangeHandler	Can be used to register the method that's used to handle the Changed event.
Event	**Description**
Changed	Raised whenever a Product object is added to or removed from the list.

Figure 13-2 The specifications for the enhanced ProductList class

How to work with indexers

In the topics that follow, you'll learn two skills for working with indexers. First, you'll learn how to code an indexer. Then, you'll learn how to throw an argument exception if the argument that's passed to the indexer isn't valid.

How to create an indexer

As figure 13-3 shows, an *indexer* is a special type of property that lets you create classes that represent collections of objects. An indexer lets other classes that use the class access a specific item in the collection by specifying an index value.

The first example in this figure shows an indexer for the ProductList class. Notice that this class starts by declaring a private List<> field named products. This list will be used to store products within a ProductList object. Then, an indexer with the type Product is declared. Notice that this indexer is not given a name. Instead, it uses the this keyword to refer to the current object. This keyword is followed by a parameter that identifies the index used by the indexer. Unlike most parameters, which are coded within parentheses, the parameter for an indexer is coded with brackets.

Like any other property, an indexer can provide get and set accessors. For example, the get accessor in the first example uses an integer index to return a Product object from the products list based on its position in the list. Conversely, the set accessor allows you to assign a Product object to the products list at the specified integer index.

The second example in this figure shows another possible indexer for the ProductList class. This indexer varies from the first one in two ways. First, it doesn't include a set accessor, so it provides read-only access to the products list. Second, it uses a string index that provides for accessing the products by product code. To do that, this get accessor uses a foreach loop to search the products list, and it returns the first product whose Code property matches the index value. If no match is found, null is returned.

The third example in this figure shows how you can use these indexers. The first two statements create a new ProductList object and add a product to it using the Add method. Then, the next two statements use the two indexers in this figure to retrieve products from the list by index and by product code. Finally, the last statement in this group uses the set accessor to add a new product to the list at the index specified by the variable i.

An indexer that uses an integer as an index

```
private List<Product> products;

public Product this[int i]
{
    get
    {
        return products[i];
    }
    set
    {
        products[i] = value;
    }
}
```

A read-only indexer that uses a string as an index

```
public Product this[string code]
{
    get
    {
        foreach (Product p in products)
        {
            if (p.Code == code)
                return p;
        }
        return null;
    }
}
```

Code that uses these indexers

```
ProductList products = new ProductList();
products.Add("CS08", "Murach's C# 2008", 54.50m);
Product p1 = products[0];
Product p2 = products["CS08"];
products[i] = new Product(code, description, price);
```

Description

- An *indexer* is a special type of property that lets a user of the class access individual items within the class by specifying an index value. Indexers are used for classes that represent collections of objects.
- Before you add an indexer to a class, you should create an array or a collection as a private instance variable to hold the objects that will be accessed by the indexer.
- The declaration for an indexer includes the type of object it indexes, the this keyword, and a parameter that defines the index to be used, enclosed in brackets.
- The indexer's get accessor should return the object specified by the index value that's passed to it from the underlying collection. The indexer's set accessor should set the object in the underlying collection that's specified by the index that's passed to it to the object passed via the value keyword.
- Although the index used by an indexer is typically an int, it doesn't have to be.

Figure 13-3 How to create an indexer

How to throw an argument exception

When you code properties and methods, it's often a good idea to check the arguments that are passed to the properties or methods to make sure that they are valid. Then, if an argument isn't valid, an exception should be thrown to notify the user of the class that an error has occurred. For example, when you code indexers, you may want to check to make sure that the index argument falls within a valid range.

Figure 13-4 shows how argument exceptions should be handled. Here, the get accessor for the first indexer checks that the int value that's passed to it falls within a valid range. If the int value is less than zero or if it is greater than or equal to the number of products in the list, the indexer throws an exception. Otherwise, the int value is used to return the specified Product object from the product list.

The second indexer works similarly to the first indexer, but it accepts a string that specifies the product's code. To start, the get accessor checks if the string contains more than four characters. If so, the indexer throws an exception. Otherwise, a foreach loop compares the product code with the product code for each product in the list. If the product codes match, the get accessor returns the Product object from the list. Otherwise, the get accessor returns a null value.

As you learned in chapter 7, the throw statement specifies an exception object for the exception to be thrown. The .NET Framework defines the three exception classes listed in this figure as standard exceptions that you can use when validating arguments. If an argument is outside the range of values that are acceptable for a property, for example, you should throw an ArgumentOutOfRangeException. If an attempt is made to set a property to a null value and the property requires a value, you should throw an ArgumentNullException. For any other argument errors, you should throw an ArgumentException.

Notice that all three of these exceptions have a constructor that accepts a message parameter. You can use this parameter to provide an error message that indicates what is wrong with the data. However, since the ArgumentOutOfRangeException already contains an error message that describes the problem, you can just specify the name of the parameter that's out of range.

When you code a statement that uses a property or method that throws an argument exception, you might think that you should enclose the statement in a try-catch statement so you can catch any exception when it occurs. But I don't recommend that. Instead, you should validate the data before passing it to the property or method. The if statement in this figure, for example, checks the length of the product code that the user enters before it passes this product code to the second indexer. That way, the exception should never occur.

So why include the validation code in the class at all? Because if you design your classes so they're reusable, you can't always count on other programmers to validate the data they pass to the class. By including this validation code, you make the class completely self-contained.

An indexer that checks range and throws an argument exception

```
public Product this[int i]
{
    get
    {
        if (i < 0 || i >= products.Count)
        {
            throw new ArgumentOutOfRangeException(i.ToString());
        }
        return products[i];
    }
    ...
}
```

An indexer that validates data and throws an argument exception

```
public Product this[string code]
{
    get
    {
        if (code.Length > 4)
        {
            throw new ArgumentException(
                "Maximum length of Code is 4 characters.");
        }
        foreach (Product p in products)
        {
            if (p.Code == code)
                return p;
        }
        return null;
    }
}
```

Three argument exceptions

Exception	Description
`ArgumentOutOfRangeException(message)`	Use when the value is outside the acceptable range of values.
`ArgumentNullException(message)`	Use when the value is null and a null value is not allowed.
`ArgumentException(message)`	Use when the value is invalid for any other reason.

An if statement that validates data before setting a property value

```
Product p = null;
if (txtCode.Text.Length <= 4)
     p = products[txtCode.Text];
```

Description

- If a class detects an invalid argument, it should throw one of the three argument exceptions with a message argument that describes the error.
- All of the argument exceptions are part of the System namespace.

Figure 13-4 How to throw an argument exception

How to work with delegates and events

In addition to fields, properties, indexers, methods, and constructors, a class can also define delegates and events.

How to define and use a delegate

A *delegate* can be used to specify the signature of a method that can handle an event. For example, the .NET Framework uses the EventHandler delegate to wire an event to the method that handles the event. This delegate specifies two arguments: an object that represents the sender of the event, and an EventArgs object.

If you look in the code that's generated by the Windows Form Designer for the Product Maintenance form, you can see how this works. For example, the Click event of the Exit button uses the standard EventHandler delegate to wire the btnExit_Click method like this:

```
this.btnExit.Click +=
    new System.EventHandler(this.btnExit_Click);
```

This works because the btnExit_Click method has the same signature as the EventHandler delegate:

```
private void btnExit_Click(object sender, System.EventArgs e){}
```

Although you can use the delegates defined by the .NET Framework to handle events, you sometimes need to define your own delegates as shown in figure 13-5. To start, you can define a delegate by coding the public and delegate keywords followed by the return type, the name of the delegate, and the parameter list for the method. In this figure, for example, a delegate named ChangeHandler has been defined for a method with a void return type and a single ProductList parameter. Then, you can use that delegate with any event handler that has that signature. In this figure, the PrintToConsole method has the same signature as the ChangeHandler delegate.

To use the ChangeHandler delegate, you start by creating the delegate object. This works the same as instantiating any type of object, except that you need to qualify the name of the delegate with the ProductList class because the delegate is declared in that class. You also specify the method that's used by the delegate. In this figure, that's the PrintToConsole method. Then, you can call the delegate and pass all required arguments to the delegate, which in this case is just one ProductList object. This causes all of the products in the product list to be printed to the console along with a message that indicates that the product list has changed.

When working with delegates, you can sometimes shorten and simplify your code by using an *anonymous method*, which is simply a method that doesn't have a name. This is particularly true if the method is short and it's only called from one place. In this figure, for example, the anonymous method

The syntax for declaring a delegate

```
public delegate returnType DelegateName([parameterList]);
```

Code that declares a delegate in the ProductList class

```
public delegate void ChangeHandler(ProductList products);
```

A method with the same signature as the delegate

```
private static void PrintToConsole(ProductList products)
{
    Console.WriteLine("The products list has changed!");
    for (int i = 0; i < products.Count; i++)
    {
        Product p = products[i];
        Console.WriteLine(p.GetDisplayText("\t"));
    }
}
```

Code that uses a delegate

```
// create the argument that's required by the delegate
ProductList products = new ProductList();
products.Add("JSE6", "Murach's Java SE 6", 52.50m);
products.Add("CS08", "Murach's C# 2008", 54.50m);

// create the delegate and identify its method
ProductList.ChangeHandler myDelegate =
    new ProductList.ChangeHandler(PrintToConsole);

// call the delegate and pass the required argument
myDelegate(products);
```

Code that uses an anonymous method

```
ProductList.ChangeHandler myDelegate =
    delegate(ProductList products)
    {
        Console.WriteLine("The products list has changed!");
        for (int i = 0; i < products.Count; i++)
        {
            Product p = products[i];
            Console.WriteLine(p.GetDisplayText("\t"));
        }
    };
myDelegate(products);
```

Description

- A *delegate* can be used to specify the signature of a method that can handle an event. For example, the .NET Framework uses the EventHandler delegate to wire events to the methods that handle the event. This delegate specifies two arguments: an object that represents the sender of the event, and an EventArgs object.
- An *anonymous method* is a method without a name. When working with delegates, you can use an anonymous method instead of wiring a delegate to a named method. If the method is only called from one place, this can help simplify your code.

Figure 13-5 How to define and use a delegate

performs the same task as the PrintToConsole method, but it doesn't take as many lines of code because it doesn't require a method signature. Also, if the anonymous method doesn't require a parameter, you can cut the parameter declaration like this:

```
ProductList.ChangeHandler myDelegate =
    delegate
    {
        MessageBox.Show("The products list has changed!");
    };
```

C# 2008 introduced a new feature similar to anonymous methods called *lambda expressions*. Although lambda expressions are more flexible than anonymous methods, they're not used frequently in business applications. For more information on lambda expressions, please see Visual Studio help.

How to define and use events

An *event* is a signal that a particular action has occurred on an object that's created from the class. Then, any class that uses that object can respond to the event by wiring an event handler to it. Figure 13-6 illustrates how this works with delegates like the ones in the last figure.

To define an event, you start by declaring a delegate that will wire the event handlers for the event. This is done by the first statement in the ProductList class. Then, you code an event declaration as shown by the second statement. This declaration names the delegate followed by an event name. In this case, the event declaration specifies the ChangeHandler delegate and the Changed event.

Once you've declared an event, you can raise it by referring to it by name as shown in the Add method of the ProductList class. This method raises the Changed event after it adds a product to the list. Here, the this keyword is used as the parameter, which causes the ProductList object that raised the event to be passed to the event handler.

To respond to an event that's raised by a class, you use code like that shown in the second example. This code includes an event handler named HandleChange that will handle the event. Notice that this event handler accepts the ProductList parameter that will be passed by the Changed event.

To use this event handler, you start by creating an instance of the class that raises the event. In this case, an instance of the ProductList class named products is created. Then, you wire the event handler to the event. Here, the ChangeHandler delegate is used to wire the HandleChange event handler to the Changed event of the products list. As a result, the HandleChange method will be called whenever the Changed event is raised for this object.

In most cases, you'll code the statement that wires the event handler in the Load event of the form that uses it. However, you can also wire an event handler in the constructor of a class. The only restriction is that this statement must be executed before the event is raised. If the event is raised before you've wired the event handler to it, the event handler won't execute.

The last example in this figure shows you can use an anonymous method to handle the Changed event. As you see, this can simplify the coding requirements whenever the event-handling code is only called from one place.

The syntax for declaring an event

```
public event Delegate EventName;
```

Code that declares and raises an event in the ProductList class

```
public class ProductList

    public delegate void ChangeHandler(ProductList products);
    public event ChangeHandler Changed;  // Declare the event

    public void Add(Product product)
    {
        products.Add(product);
        Changed(this);   // Raise the event
    }
...
```

Code that uses a named method to handle an event

```
ProductList products = new ProductList();

// Wire the event to the method that handles the event
products.Changed += new ProductList.ChangeHandler(HandleChange);

// Handle the event
private void HandleChange(ProductList products)
{
    products.Save();
    FillProductListBox();
}
```

Code that uses an anonymous method to handle an event

```
// Wire the event to the anonymous method that handles the event
products.Changed += delegate(ProductList products)
    {
        products.Save();
        FillProductListBox();
    };
```

Description

- An *event* is a signal that an action has occurred on an object that was created from the class. To create an event that can be used by other classes, the event must be declared with public access at the class level. Then, the event can be called from any properties or methods that need to raise the event.
- An event declaration specifies a delegate that will handle the event along with an event name.
- To raise the event, you refer to it by its name, and you code the arguments required by the delegate.
- To handle an event from another class, you create an instance of the class that raises the event and assign it to a class variable. Then, you declare an event handler with a signature that matches the event's signature. Finally, you wire the event to the event handler in the class constructor or, if the class is a form, in the Load event handler.

Figure 13-6 How to define and use events

How to overload operators

The ProductList class in figure 13-2 uses overloaded operators. Specifically, this class overloads the + and - operators so you can add products to and remove products from the product list using these operators rather than the Add and Remove methods. The following topics explain how you implement overloaded operators like these.

An introduction to operator overloading

Figure 13-7 presents some basic information about *operator overloading*. First, you should know that you can overload both unary and binary operators. The most common operators you can overload are listed in this figure.

C# defines the meanings of these operators for built-in types such as decimal, int, string, and DateTime. However, for user-defined types such as the Product class presented in the last chapter or the ProductList class presented in this chapter, these operators are either undefined or are defined in ways that may not be appropriate for the class. For example, the + operator isn't defined for user-defined types, but the == operator is. By default, if you compare two object variables using the == operator, they're considered equal if they refer to the same object.

With operator overloading, you can create your own implementations of C# operators that are appropriate for your classes. For example, a more appropriate definition of the == operator for the Product class would be to consider two Product variables equal if they refer to objects with the same Code, Description, and Price properties.

As the syntax at the top of this figure shows, you use the operator keyword to declare an operator. In the operator declaration, you specify the return type, which indicates the type of object that's returned by the operation. In most cases, the return type is the same as the class that contains the declaration (for example, Product in the Product class). Then, you specify the operator you want to define, followed by one or two operands depending on whether the operator is a unary or a binary operator.

Notice that operators are always declared as static. That way, they can deal with null operands properly. That will make more sense when you see the code for the overloaded == operator.

Overloaded operators often depend on methods that are defined by the class. In figure 13-8, for example, you'll see that the + operator for the ProductList class uses the Add method of the class to add a product to the list. Then, in figure 13-9, you'll see that the == and != operators for the Product class are implemented by overriding the Equals method of the Object class, which is inherited by all other classes.

The syntax for overloading unary operators

```
public static returnType operator unary-operator(type operand)
```

The syntax for overloading binary operators

```
public static returnType operator
    binary-operator(type-1 operand-1, type-2 operand-2)
```

Common operators you can overload

Unary operators

```
+ - ! ++ -- true false
```

Binary operators

```
+ - * / % & | == != > < >= <=
```

The Equals method of the Object class

Method	Description
`Equals(object)`	Returns a Boolean value that indicates whether the current object refers to the same instance as the specified object. If that's not what you want, you can override this method as shown in figure 13-9.
`Equals(object1, object2)`	A static version of the Equals method that compares two objects to determine if they refer to the same instance.

The GetHashCode method of the Object class

Method	Description
`GetHashCode()`	Returns an integer value that's used to identify objects in a hash table. If you override the Equals method, you must also override the GetHashCode method.

Description

- You use the *operator* keyword to *overload an operator* within a class. For example, you might overload the + operator in the ProductList class so that it can be used to add products to the list. You might also overload the == and != operators in the Product class so you can compare two Product objects to see if they contain identical data rather than whether they refer to the same instance.
- You can overload all of the unary and binary operators shown above, as well as some that aren't presented in this book. When you overload a binary operator, *operand-1* is the operand that appears to the left of the operator, and *operand-2* is the operand that appears to the right of the operator.
- *Overloaded operators* are always static so they can deal with null operands properly.
- When you overload relational operators like == and !=, you need to provide your own versions of the Equals and GetHashCode methods. See figure 13-9 for details.

Figure 13-7 An introduction to operator overloading

How to overload arithmetic operators

Figure 13-8 shows how to overload arithmetic operators such as + and -. For instance, the code at the top of this figure shows an implementation of the + operator for the ProductList class. This operator is used to add a Product object to the product list. As you can see, the declaration for the + operator specifies ProductList as the return type, which means that it will return a ProductList object. In addition, this operator accepts two parameters: a ProductList object named pl and a Product object named p. Then, the code for the + operator calls the Add method of the pl operand, passing the p object as the argument. This method adds the p object to the products list that's stored in the p1 object. Then, the + operator returns the pl object.

The second code example shows how you might use the + operator in an application to add a Product object to a product list. First, a new ProductList object named products is created. Then, a new Product object named p is created. Finally, the + operator is used in an assignment statement to add the product to the product list.

The last statement in this figure shows another way that you can use the overloaded + operator of the ProductList class to add a Product object to a product list. As you can see, this statement uses the += shortcut assignment operator. You may remember from chapter 4 that you can use shortcut operators like these in place of the assignment operator when the expression that's being assigned involves an arithmetic operation. You can use these shortcut operators with overloaded operators as well. Note that you don't need to provide any special code to use a shortcut operator. That's because when you use a shortcut operator, the compiler automatically converts it to an equivalent assignment statement that uses the assignment operator (=) and an arithmetic operator.

Part of a ProductList class that overloads the + operator

```
public class ProductList
{
    private List<Product> products;

    public void Add(Product p)
    {
        products.Add(p);
    }

    public static ProductList operator + (ProductList pl, Product p)
    {
        pl.Add(p);
        return pl;
    }
    .
    .
}
```

Code that uses the + operator of the ProductList class

```
ProductList products = new ProductList();
Product p = new Product("CS08", "Murach's C# 2008", 54.50m);
products = products + p;
```

Another way to use the + operator

```
products += p;
```

Description

- You can overload the built-in arithmetic operators so they perform customized functions on objects created from the class that defines them.
- You should overload only those arithmetic operators that make sense for a class. For example, it's reasonable to overload the + operator for the ProductList class as a way to add products to a product list. But it doesn't make sense to overload the * or / operators for this class.
- You don't overload the += or -= operators separately. Instead, these operators are handled automatically by the overloaded + and - operators.

Note

- Although C# uses the += operator to add event handlers to an event, this is not an example of overloading operators. Instead, the use of the += operator for wiring events is a language feature that's built in to the C# compiler.

Figure 13-8 How to overload arithmetic operators

How to overload relational operators

Figure 13-9 shows that relational operators are often more difficult to overload than arithmetic operators. Here, the first example shows how to implement the == operator for the Product class so you can compare products based on their values rather than on object references. The two objects that will be compared are passed as arguments to this operator.

The operator starts by using the Equals method of the Object class to check both objects to see if they're equal to null. This implementation of the Equals method is based on reference, not value. As a result, it lets you test an object to see if it is null. This testing is necessary to prevent the overloaded == operator from throwing an exception if one of the operands is null.

If both operands are null, the == operator returns true. If the first operand is null but the second one isn't, it returns false. And if the first operand isn't null, the == operator calls the Equals method of the first operand to compare it with the second operand, and then returns the result of the comparison.

Notice that the declaration for the Equals method includes the override keyword. That means that it overrides the Equals method defined by the Object class that every class inherits. In the next chapter, you'll learn how to work with inheritance. Then, you'll be able to understand how this code works.

The Equals method starts by testing the object that's passed to it, in this case, the second operand of the == operator, for a null. If this object is null, the Equals method returns false. That makes sense, because no object should be considered equal to a null.

If the object that's passed to the Equals method isn't null, this method casts the object to a Product object named p. Then, it compares its own Code, Description, and Price values with the Code, Description, and Price values of the p object. If all three properties are equal, it returns true. Otherwise, it returns false.

When you overload a comparison operator, you must also overload the operator that performs the opposite operation. If, for example, you overload the == operator, you must also overload the != operator. Similarly, if you overload the < operator, you must also overload the > operator. The code that's used to implement the != operator in the Product class is also shown in this figure. As you can see, this operator defines itself in terms of the == operator. That way, you can be sure that these operators return consistent results.

The last method that's required when you overload the == operator is the GetHashCode method. Like the Equals method, this method overrides the GetHashCode method that's defined by the Object class. The main requirement for the GetHashCode method is that it must always return the same value for any two objects that are considered equal by the Equals method. The easiest way to accomplish that is to combine the values that are used for comparison in the Equals method to create a string, and then return the hash code of that string.

The second example in this figure shows how you can use the == operator to compare two Product objects. First, two object variables named p1 and p2 are created from the Product class with identical values. Then, the products are

Code that overloads the == operator for a Product class

```
public static bool operator == (Product p1, Product p2)
{
    if (Object.Equals(p1, null))
        if (Object.Equals(p2, null))
            return true;
        else
            return false;
    else
        return p1.Equals(p2);
}

public static bool operator != (Product p1, Product p2)
{
    return !(p1 == p2);
}

public override bool Equals(Object obj)
{
    if (obj == null)
        return false;
    Product p = (Product)obj;
    if (this.Code == p.Code &&
        this.Description == p.Description &&
        this.Price == p.Price)
        return true;
    else
        return false;
}

public override int GetHashCode()
{
    string hashString = this.Code + this.Description + this.Price;
    return hashString.GetHashCode();
}
```

Code that uses the == operator of the Product class

```
Product p1 = new Product("CS08", "Murach's C# 2008", 54.50m);
Product p2 = new Product("CS08", "Murach's C# 2008", 54.50m);
if (p1 == p2)       // This evaluates to true. Without the overloaded
                    // == operator, it would evaluate to false.
```

Description

- If you overload the == operator, you must also override the non-static Equals method. Then, the == operator should use this Equals method for its equality test.
- Before it calls the Equals method, the overloaded == operator should test the operands for null values. If both operands are null, they should be considered equal. If only the first operand is null, the operands should be considered unequal.
- Relational operators must always be implemented in pairs. For example, if you overload the == operator, you must also overload the != operator.
- When you override the Equals method, you must also override the GetHashCode method. That's because the GetHashCode method must return the same hash code for any two instances that are considered equal by the Equals method.

Figure 13-9 How to overload the == operator

compared in an if statement using the == operator. Because both products have the same Code, Description, and Price values, this comparison returns true. If the Product class didn't override the == operator, however, this comparison would return false because the p1 and p2 variables refer to different instances of the Product class, even though they both have the same values.

Before I go on, you might want to consider why it's necessary for the == operator to be static. If it weren't, you would have to call it from an instance of the Product class, for example, p1. But what if p1 was null? In other words, what if p1 didn't refer to an instance of the Product class? In that case, you couldn't use the == operator. To work with null operands, then, overloaded operators must be declared as static.

An enhanced version of the Product Maintenance application

Now that you've learned the techniques for enhancing your classes, the topics that follow present an enhanced version of the Product Maintenance application that uses those enhancements. From the user's standpoint, this application operates exactly like the one that was presented in chapter 12. The only difference is that the classes in this version of the application are implemented differently. Specifically, the ProductList class includes the additional members that are shown in figure 13-2.

Because the code for the Product class is the same as the Product class presented in chapter 12, I won't repeat it here. Similarly, the New Product form that's used in this version of the Product Maintenance application is identical to the code shown in chapter 12. As a result, I won't repeat that code either. Finally, like the application in chapter 12, you should know that this application will work with any of the three versions of the ProductDB class that are presented in chapters 21 and 22.

The code for the ProductList class

Figure 13-10 shows the code for the ProductList class, which stores a collection of Product objects. To help you follow it, I've highlighted some of the critical statements.

As you can see, this class begins by declaring a List<> object named products. This instance variable is used to store the product list. Next, the ProductList class declares a delegate named ChangeHandler, and an event named Changed that uses this delegate. This event is raised whenever the contents of the products list are changed.

The two indexers for this class let users of the class access a specific product in the list by specifying an integer value or a product code. Since these indexers are similar to the two indexers in figure 13-3, you shouldn't have any trouble understanding how they work. The main difference is that the set

The code for the ProductList class Page 1

```
public class ProductList
{
    private List<Product> products;

    public delegate void ChangeHandler(ProductList products);
    public event ChangeHandler Changed;

    public ProductList()
    {
        products = new List<Product>();
    }

    public int Count
    {
        get
        {
            return products.Count;
        }
    }

    public Product this[int i]
    {
        get
        {
            if (i < 0)
            {
                throw new ArgumentOutOfRangeException(i.ToString());
            }
            else if (i >= products.Count)
            {
                throw new ArgumentOutOfRangeException(i.ToString());
            }
            return products[i];
        }
        set
        {
            products[i] = value;
            Changed(this);
        }
    }

    public Product this[string code]
    {
        get
        {
            foreach (Product p in products)
            {
                if (p.Code == code)
                    return p;
            }
            return null;
        }
    }
```

Figure 13-10 The code for the enhanced ProductList class (part 1 of 2)

accessor for the first indexer raises the Changed event to indicate that the contents of the products list have been changed.

The Fill method of the ProductList class, shown on page 2 of this listing, calls the GetProducts method of the ProductDB class to get the products from a file. Similarly, the Save method calls the SaveProducts method of this class to save the products to a file.

The ProductList class also provides two overloads for the Add method: one that accepts a Product object and one that accepts a code, description and price. It also includes a Remove method that removes the specified Product object. As you can see, all three of these methods raise the Changed event.

Finally, this class provides an overloaded + operator and an overloaded - operator. The overloaded + operator calls the first Add method to add the specified object to the product list and then returns the updated product list. Similarly, the – operator calls the Remove method to remove the specified product from the product list and then returns the updated product list.

The code for the ProductList class **Page 2**

```
    public void Fill()
    {
        products = ProductDB.GetProducts();
    }

    public void Save()
    {
        ProductDB.SaveProducts(products);
    }

    public void Add(Product product)
    {
        products.Add(product);
        Changed(this);
    }

    public void Add(string code, string description, decimal price)
    {
        Product p = new Product(code, description, price);
        products.Add(p);
        Changed(this);
    }

    public void Remove(Product product)
    {
        products.Remove(product);
        Changed(this);
    }

    public static ProductList operator + (ProductList pl, Product p)
    {
        pl.Add(p);
        return pl;
    }

    public static ProductList operator - (ProductList pl, Product p)
    {
        pl.Remove(p);
        return pl;
    }

}
```

Figure 13-10 The code for the enhanced ProductList class (part 2 of 2)

The code for the Product Maintenance form

Figure 13-11 shows the code for the enhanced version of the Product Maintenance form. Because most of this code is the same as in chapter 12, I've highlighted the key differences here.

First, the products variable that's used by the class to store Product objects is a ProductList object, not a List<> object. As a result, this version of the application can use the features of the ProductList class, such as the indexer, the Fill and Save method, the overloaded + and - operators, and the Changed event.

In the Load event handler for the form, the ChangeHandler delegate is used to wire the HandleChange method (which appears at the end of the listing) to the Changed event of the products object. As you have seen in the ProductList class, this event is raised any time a product is added to, removed from, or changed in the product list. Then, the HandleChange method calls the Save method of the products object to save the new list, and it calls the FillProductListBox method to refresh the list box.

After it wires the Changed event, the Load event handler calls the Fill method of the products object to fill the product list. Then, it calls the FillProductListBox method to fill the list box. Notice that this method uses a for loop to retrieve each product in the product list by its index.

The Click event handler for the Add button calls the GetNewProduct method of the New Product form to get a new product. Then, if the Product object that's returned by this method isn't null, the += operator is used to add the product to the product list.

The Click event handler for the Delete button uses an indexer of the ProductList class to retrieve the selected product from the product list. Then, assuming the user confirms that the product should be deleted, it uses the -= operator to remove the product from the list.

The code for the Product Maintenance form

```
private ProductList products = new ProductList();

private void frmProductMain_Load(object sender, System.EventArgs e)
{
    products.Changed += new ProductList.ChangeHandler(HandleChange);
    products.Fill();
    FillProductListBox();
}

private void FillProductListBox()
{
    Product p;
    lstProducts.Items.Clear();
    for (int i = 0; i < products.Count; i++)
    {
        p = products[i];
        lstProducts.Items.Add(p.GetDisplayText("\t"));
    }
}

private void btnAdd_Click(object sender, System.EventArgs e)
{
    frmNewProduct newForm = new frmNewProduct();
    Product product = newForm.GetNewProduct();
    if (product != null)
    {
        products += product;
    }
}

private void btnDelete_Click(object sender, System.EventArgs e)
{
    int i = lstProducts.SelectedIndex;
    if (i != -1)
    {
        Product product = products[i];
        string message = "Are you sure you want to delete "
            + product.Description + "?";
        DialogResult button = MessageBox.Show(message, "Confirm Delete",
            MessageBoxButtons.YesNo);
        if (button == DialogResult.Yes)
        {
            products -= product;
        }
    }
}

private void btnExit_Click(object sender, System.EventArgs e)
{
    this.Close();
}

private void HandleChange(ProductList products)
{
    products.Save();
    FillProductListBox();
}
```

Figure 13-11 The code for the Product Maintenance form

Perspective

In this chapter, you've learned about a variety of features that you can include in the classes you create. You should keep in mind, however, that not all classes require these features. In fact, most classes require just the features you learned about in chapter 12. Nevertheless, it's important that you know about the features presented in this chapter so you can use them when that's appropriate.

Now that you've read this chapter, you should begin to appreciate the power and complexity of C# classes. Still, there's much more to learn about coding C# classes than what's presented here. In the next chapter, then, you'll learn about one of the most important and potentially confusing aspects of object-oriented programming in C#: inheritance.

Terms

indexer
delegate
anonymous method
lamda expression
event
overload an operator
operator overloading
hash code

Exercise 13-1 Create a Customer Maintenance application that uses classes

In this exercise, you'll create a Customer Maintenance application that uses classes with the features presented in this chapter. To make this application easier to develop, we'll give you the starting forms and classes.

Open the project and add validation code to the Customer class

1. Open the application in the C:\C# 2008\Chapter 13\CustomerMaintenance directory.
2. Open the Customer class and note how the constructor for this class sets the properties to the appropriate parameters. Then, add code to the set accessors for the FirstName, LastName, and Email properties that throws an exception if the value is longer than 30 characters.
3. Test the class by trying to add a new customer with an email address that's longer than 30 characters. Then, end the application.
4. Set the MaxLength properties of the First Name, Last Name, and Email text boxes to 30. Then, run the application again and try to add a new customer with an email address that's longer than 30 characters. This shows one way to avoid the exceptions, but your classes should still throw them in case they are used by other applications that don't avoid them.

Add a CustomerList class

5. Add a class named CustomerList to the project, and add the following members to this class:

Indexer	Description
`[index]`	Provides access to the Customer at the specified position.
Property	**Description**
`Count`	An integer that indicates how many Customer objects are in the list.
Method	**Description**
`Add(customer)`	Adds the specified Customer object to the list.
`Remove(customer)`	Removes the specified Customer object from the list.
`Fill()`	Fills the list with customer data from a file using the GetCustomers method of the CustomerDB class.
`Save()`	Saves the customers to a file using the SaveCustomers method of the CustomerDB class.

6. Modify the Customer Maintenance form to use this class. To do that, you'll need to use the Fill and Save methods of the CustomerList object instead of the methods of the CustomerDB class. In addition, you'll need to use a for loop instead of a foreach loop when you fill the list box.
7. Run the application and test it to be sure it works properly.

Add overloaded operators to the CustomerList class

8. Add overloaded + and - operators to the CustomerList class that add and remove a customer from the customer list.
9. Modify the Customer Maintenance form to use these operators instead of the Add and Remove methods. Then, run and test the application.

Add a delegate and an event to the CustomerList class

10. Add a delegate named ChangeHandler to the CustomerList class. This delegate should specify a method with a void return type and a CustomerList parameter as described in figure 13-5.
11. Add an event named Changed to the CustomerList class. This event should use the ChangeHandler delegate and should be raised any time the customer list changes as described in figure 13-6.
12. Modify the Customer Maintenance form to use the Changed event to save the customers and refresh the list box any time the list changes. To do that, you'll need to code an event handler that has the signature specified by the delegate, you'll need to wire the event to the event handler, and you'll need to remove any unnecessary code from the event handlers for the Save and Delete buttons.
13. Run and test the application.

14

How to work with inheritance

Inheritance is one of the key concepts of object-oriented programming. It lets you create a class that's based on another class. As you'll see in this chapter, inheritance is used throughout the classes of the .NET Framework. In addition, you can use it in the classes that you create.

An introduction to inheritance

Inheritance allows you to create a class that's based on another class. When used correctly, inheritance can simplify the overall design of an application. The following topics present an introduction to the basic concepts of inheritance. You need to understand these concepts before you learn how to write the code needed to implement classes that use inheritance.

How inheritance works

Figure 14-1 illustrates how inheritance works. When inheritance is used, a *derived class* inherits the properties, methods, and other members of a *base class*. Then, the objects that are created from the derived class can use these inherited members. The derived class can also provide its own members that extend the base class. In addition, the derived class can *override* properties and methods of the base class by providing replacement definitions for them.

The two classes shown in this figure illustrate how this works. Here, the base class is System.Windows.Forms.Form, the .NET Framework class that all Windows forms inherit. As this figure shows, this class has several public properties and methods, such as the Text property and the Close method. (This class has many more properties and methods. I included just a few representative ones here.)

The derived class in this figure is the class for the New Product form in the Product Maintenance application (ProductMaintenance.frmNewProduct). As you can see, two groups of members are listed for this class. The first group includes the properties and methods that the class inherits from its base class. The second group includes the members that have been added to the derived class. In this case, the derived class includes five new properties (the text box and button controls) and one new method (GetNewProduct).

Although this figure doesn't show it, a derived class can also replace an inherited property or method with its own version of the property or method. You'll learn how this works later in this chapter.

How inheritance works

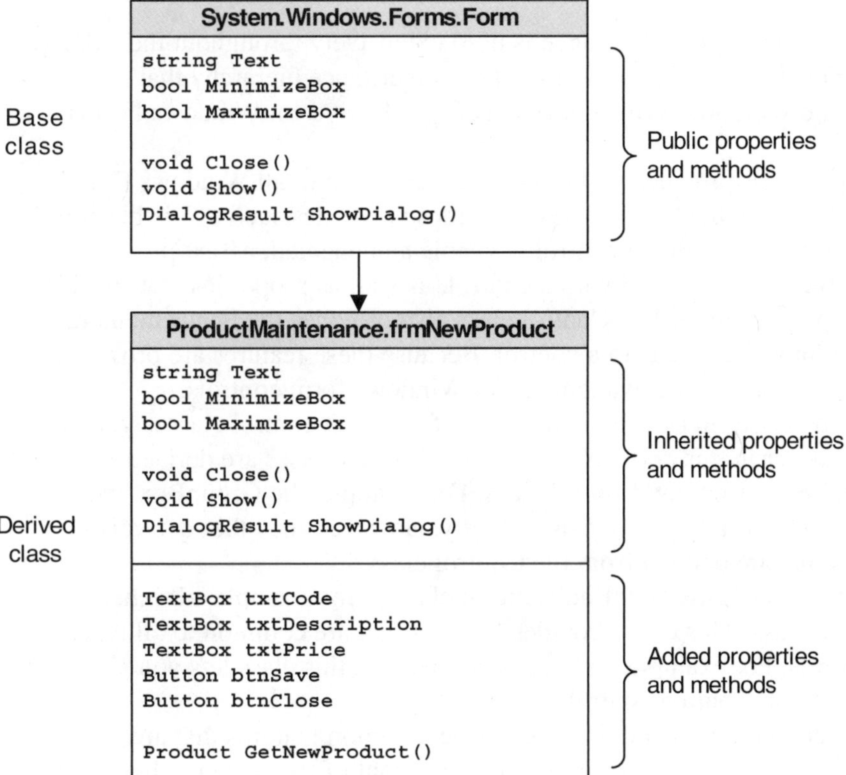

Description

- *Inheritance* lets you create a new class based on an existing class. Then, the new class *inherits* the properties, methods, and other members of the existing class.
- A class that inherits from an existing class is called a *derived class*, *child class,* or *subclass.* A class that another class inherits is called a *base class*, *parent class*, or *superclass*.
- A derived class can *extend* the base class by adding new properties, methods, or other members to the base class. It can also replace a member from the base class with its own version of the member. Depending on how that's done, this is called *hiding* or *overriding*.
- When you create a new form in C#, the form inherits the .NET Framework class named System.Windows.Forms.Form. As a result, all C# forms inherit the members defined by this base class. Then, as you add controls and code to the form, you extend the base class by creating new properties and methods.

Figure 14-1 How inheritance works

How the .NET Framework uses inheritance

Figure 14-2 shows that inheritance is used extensively throughout the .NET Framework. This figure shows a portion of the inheritance hierarchy that's used by several of the Windows form control classes in the System.Windows.Forms namespace.

The Control class provides features that are common to all Windows form controls. For example, the Control class provides properties such as Visible and Enabled that indicate whether a control is visible and enabled, a Text property that specifies the text associated with a control, as well as properties that specify a control's display location. The Control class also provides the Focus method, which lets you move the focus to a control. Because these features are provided by the Control class, they are available to all Windows form controls.

The shaded classes in this figure are nine of the form control classes you've learned about so far in this book. Note that all of these classes are derived directly or indirectly from the Control class. For example, the GroupBox and Label controls inherit the Control class directly. However, the other controls inherit classes that are derived from the Control class.

The Button, CheckBox, and RadioButton classes, for example, all inherit the ButtonBase class. This class provides features that are common to all types of button controls. For example, the Image property of this class lets you display an image on a button control.

Similarly, combo boxes and list boxes have common features that are provided by the ListControl class. The most important of these are the Items property, which provides the list that's displayed by the control, and the SelectedIndex, SelectedValue, and SelectedItem properties, which let you access the item that's selected in the list.

Likewise, the TextBoxBase class provides some features that are common to text box controls. That includes the MultiLine property that lets you display multiple lines and the ReadOnly property that lets you create read-only text boxes. By the way, if you're wondering why an intermediate TextBoxBase class is used in the TextBox hierarchy, it's because the .NET Framework provides a second type of text box, called a RichTextBox, that also inherits TextBoxBase. Because the RichTextBox control isn't covered in this book, however, I didn't include it in this figure.

You may be surprised to learn that the Form class itself is also derived from the Control class by way of two other classes: ContainerControl and ScrollableControl. A form's ability to contain other controls is provided by the ContainerControl class. And a form's ability to display scroll bars if its controls can't all be displayed at once is provided by the ScrollableControl class.

Don't be dismayed by the amount of detail presented in this figure. In fact, the actual inheritance hierarchy for the classes in the System.Windows.Forms namespace is far more complicated than indicated here. The intent of this figure is simply to illustrate that inheritance is a feature that's used extensively within the .NET Framework.

The inheritance hierarchy for form control classes

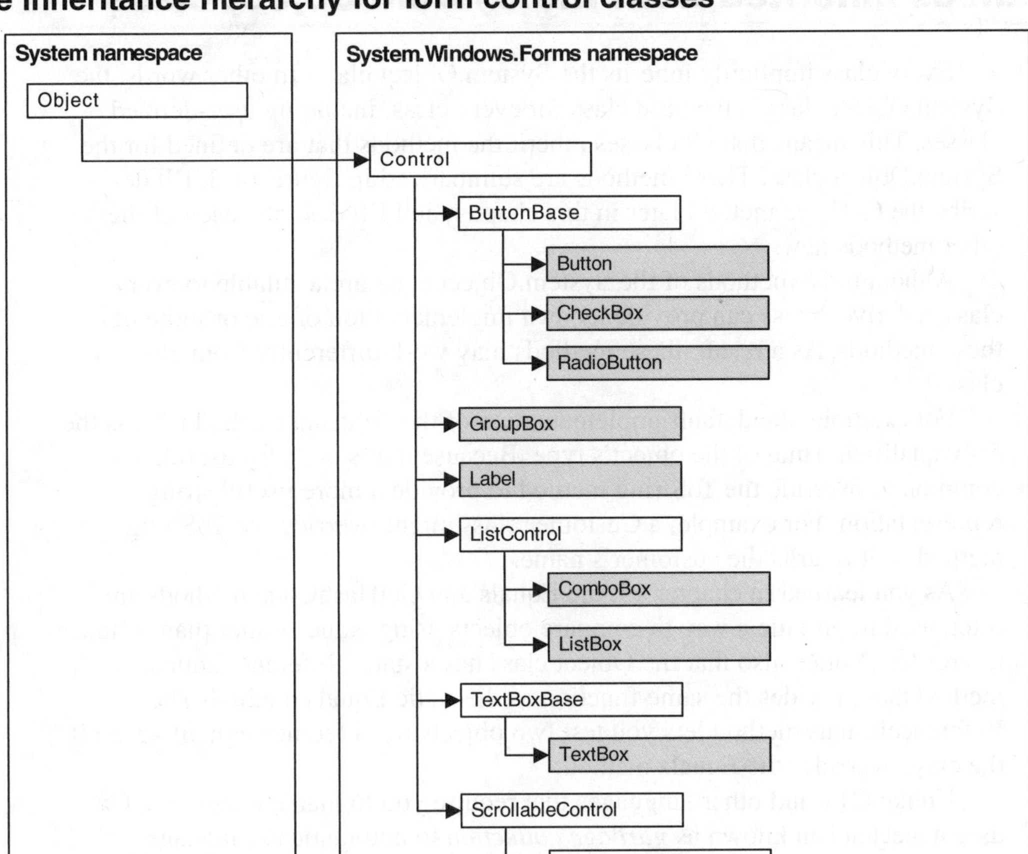

Description

- The .NET Framework uses inheritance extensively in its own classes. For example, inheritance is used throughout the System.Windows.Forms namespace.
- All of the control classes are derived from a base Control class. This class provides properties and methods that all controls have in common, such as Tag and Text. Like all classes, the Control class is ultimately derived from System.Object.
- Some controls have an additional layer of inheritance. For example, the ListControl class provides features common to ListBox and ComboBox controls, such as the SelectedValue property.
- The *fully qualified name* of a class includes the name of the namespace that the class belongs to. For example, the fully qualified name for the ComboBox control is System.Windows.Forms.ComboBox.

Figure 14-2 How the .NET Framework uses inheritance

Methods inherited from the System.Object class

Every class implicitly inherits the System.Object class. In other words, the System.Object class is the base class for every class, including user-defined classes. This means that all classes inherit the methods that are defined for the System.Object class. These methods are summarized in figure 14-3. I'll describe the GetType method later in this chapter, and I'll describe each of the other methods now.

Although the methods of the System.Object class are available to every class, a derived class can provide its own implementation of one or more of these methods. As a result, these methods may work differently from class to class.

For example, the default implementation of the ToString method returns the fully qualified name of the object's type. Because that's not very useful, it's common to override the ToString method to provide a more useful string representation. For example, a Customer class might override the ToString method so it returns the customer's name.

As you learned in chapter 13, the Equals and GetHashCode methods are often used to provide a way to compare objects using values rather than instance references. Notice also that the Object class has a static ReferenceEquals method that provides the same function as the static Equals method. The ReferenceEquals method lets you test two objects for reference equality even if the class overrides the Equals method.

Unlike C++ and other languages that require you to manage memory, C# uses a mechanism known as *garbage collection* to automatically manage memory. When the garbage collector determines that the system is running low on memory and that the system is idle, it frees the memory for any objects that don't have any more references to them. Before it does that, though, it calls the Finalize method for each of those objects, even though the default implementation of this method doesn't do anything. Although you can override the Finalize method to provide specific finalization code for an object, you rarely need do that.

The last method shown in this figure is MemberwiseClone. You can use this method to create a simple copy of an object that doesn't expose other objects as properties or fields. You'll learn more about cloning objects in the next chapter.

Methods of the System.Object class

Method	Description
`ToString()`	Returns a string that contains the fully qualified name of the object's type.
`Equals(object)`	Returns true if this object refers to the same instance as the specified object. Otherwise, it returns false, even if both objects contain the same data.
`Equals(object1, object2)`	A static version of the Equals method that compares two objects to determine if they refer to the same instance.
`ReferenceEquals(object1, object2)`	A static method that determines whether two object references refer to the same instance. This method is typically not overridden, so it can be used to test for instance equality in classes that override the Equals method.
`GetType()`	Returns a Type object that represents the type of an object.
`GetHashCode()`	Returns the integer hash code for an object.
`Finalize()`	Frees resources used by an object. This method is called by the garbage collector when it determines that there are no more references to the object.
`MemberwiseClone()`	Creates a shallow copy of an object. For more information, refer to chapter 15.

Description

- System.Object is the root base class for all classes. In other words, every class inherits either System.Object or some other class that ultimately inherits System.Object. As a result, the methods defined by System.Object are available to all classes.
- When creating classes, it's a common practice to override the ToString and Equals methods so they work appropriately for each class. For example, the ToString method might return a value that uniquely identifies an object. And the Equals method might compare two objects to see if their values are equal.
- The *hash code* for an object is an integer that uniquely identifies the object. Given the same data, each instance of an object should return the same hash code. A common way to implement the GetHashCode method is to return ToString().GetHashCode(). This returns the hash code of the object's ToString() result.
- In general, you don't need to override the Finalize method for an object, even though its default implementation doesn't do anything. That's because the .NET *garbage collector* automatically reclaims the memory of an object whenever it needs to. Before it does that, though, it calls the Finalize method of the object.

Figure 14-3 Methods inherited from the System.Object class

How to use inheritance in your applications

Figure 14-4 describes the two main ways inheritance is used in business applications. First, it can be used to simplify the task of creating classes that represent similar types of objects. For example, the first inheritance hierarchy in this figure shows how you might use inheritance to create classes for two types of products: books and software products. As you can see, the Product class is used as the base class for the Book and Software classes. These subclasses inherit the Code, Description, and Price properties as well as the GetDisplayText method from the Product class. In addition, each class adds a property that's unique to the class: The Book class adds an Author property, and the Software class adds a Version property.

The second inheritance hierarchy in this figure shows how you can use the classes of the .NET Framework as base classes for your own classes. Here, a ProductList class inherits the System.Collections.Generic.List<Product> class. That way, the ProductList class has all of the features of a List<> of Product objects (such as an indexer and a Remove method). However, the ProductList class provides its own Add method that is used instead of the Add method that's available from the List<Product> class. This lets you change any members in the base class that don't work the way you want them to. You'll learn more about how this works in figure 14-6. Finally, the ProductList class provides two more methods (the Fill and Save methods) that don't exist in the base class. These methods allow you to read and write the list to a data store.

An important aspect of inheritance is that you can use a subclass as an argument or return value for any method that is designed to work with the base class. For example, the Add method of the ProductList class accepts a parameter of type Product. However, because both the Book and Software classes are subclasses of the Product class, you can pass either a Book or a Software object to the Add method to add a book or software product to the product list. You'll learn more about how this works in figure 14-7.

Business classes for a Product Maintenance application

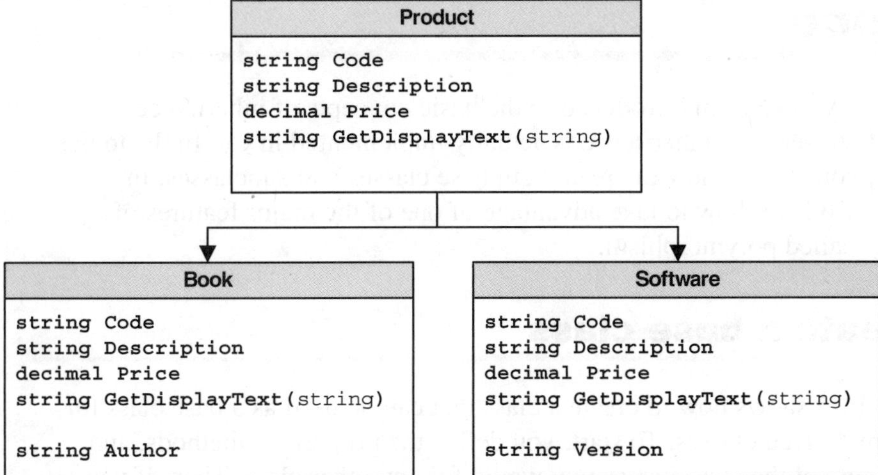

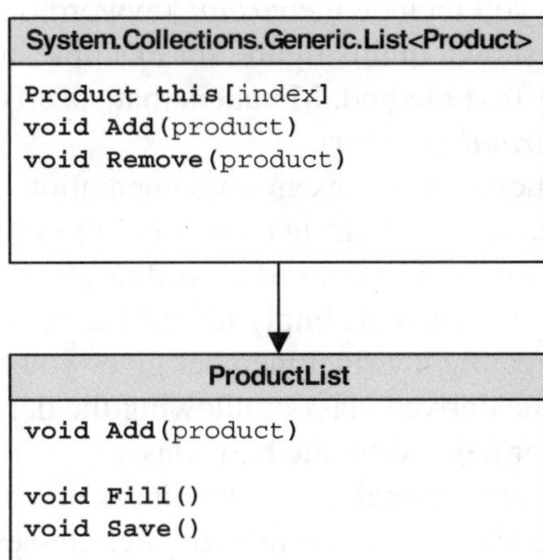

Description

- You can use inheritance in your applications to create generic base classes that implement common elements of related subclasses. For example, if you need separate classes to represent distinct types of products, you can create a Product base class, then use it to create a separate subclass for each type of product.
- It's also common to create classes that inherit from classes that are defined by the .NET Framework. For example, you might create a ProductList class that inherits the List<Product> class.
- When you inherit a class, you can use the derived class whenever an instance of the base class is called for. For example, a ProductList object based on a class that inherits List<Product> can be used whenever a List<Product> object is called for.

Figure 14-4 How to use inheritance in your applications

Basic skills for working with inheritance

Now that you've been introduced to the basic concepts of inheritance, you're ready to see how inheritance is actually implemented in C#. In the topics that follow, you'll learn how to create both base classes and subclasses. In addition, you'll learn how to take advantage of one of the major features of inheritance, called polymorphism.

How to create a base class

Figure 14-5 shows how to create a class that can be used as a base class for one or more derived classes. To start, you define the properties, methods, and other members of the class just as you would for any other class. Then, if you want a class that's derived from this class to be able to override one of the members of the base class, you include the *virtual* keyword on the declaration for that member. The code shown in this figure, for example, uses the virtual keyword on the GetDisplayText method. Members that specify the virtual keyword are often called *virtual members*.

Notice that the Product class provides an implementation of the GetDisplayText method that rcturns a string containing the values for the Code, Description, and Price properties. If a derived class doesn't override the GetDisplayText method, that class will simply inherit the version implemented by this class. As a result, creating a virtual member gives you the option of overriding the member in the derived class or allowing the derived class to defer to the version of the member defined by the base class.

The table in this figure lists several *access modifiers* you can use to indicate whether members of a base class are accessible to other classes. You already know how to use the private and public modifiers to create private and public members. When you work with inheritance, you also need to know about the protected modifier. A *protected member* is a member that can be accessed within the defining class and within any class that's derived from the defining class, but not by any other class. Protected members let derived classes access certain parts of the base class without exposing those parts to other classes.

The internal and protected internal access modifiers are sometimes useful when you work with class libraries or with solutions that have more than one project. To understand how they work, remember that when you build a project, all of the classes that make up the project are compiled into a single assembly. Members that use the internal keyword alone are accessible to all of the classes within that assembly, but not to classes in other assemblies. Similarly, members that specify protected internal are accessible to derived classes that are a part of the same assembly, but not to derived classes in other assemblies.

The code for a simplified version of the Product base class

```
public class Product
{
    public string Code;
    public string Description;
    public decimal Price;

    public virtual string GetDisplayText(string sep)
    {
        return Code + sep + Description + sep + Price.ToString("c");
    }
}
```

Access modifiers

Keyword	Description
`public`	Available to all classes.
`protected`	Available only to the current class or to derived classes.
`internal`	Available only to classes in the current assembly.
`protected internal`	Available only to the current class, derived classes, or classes in the current assembly.
`private`	Available only to the containing class.

Description

- You create a base class the same way you create any other class: by defining its properties, methods, events, and other members.
- *Access modifiers* specify the accessibility of the members declared by a class. Public members are accessible to other classes, while private members are accessible only to the class in which they're defined.
- *Protected members* are accessible within the class in which they're declared. They can also be used by any class that inherits the class in which they're declared.
- A derived class can access the public and protected members of its base class, but not the private members.
- *Internal members* are accessible by other classes in the same assembly, but not by classes in other assemblies. This can sometimes be useful to control access to members declared by classes in a class library. For more information about class libraries, see chapter 16.
- If you want to be able to override a member in a derived class, you must include the *virtual* keyword on the member declaration.
- If you don't code an access modifier, the default access is private.

How to create a subclass

Figure 14-6 shows how to create a subclass. To indicate that a class is a subclass, you follow the class name on the class declaration with a colon and the name of the base class that the subclass inherits. For example, the code for the Book class shown in this figure specifies that the Book class is a subclass of the Product class.

After you identify the base class, you can extend its functionality by coding additional properties, methods, or other members. In this figure, for example, the Book class adds a new constructor and a new public field named Author. In addition, it overrides the GetDisplayText method defined by the Product class.

The constructor for the Book subclass accepts four parameters: code, description, author, and price. A colon after the constructor name followed by the *base* keyword and a parameter list indicates that this constructor should call the constructor from the base class using the specified parameters. In this case, the base class constructor is called using the code, description, and price parameters that were passed to the constructor of the Book class. Then, the base class constructor initializes the Code, Description, and Price properties with these values. After the base class constructor is called, the code in the Book subclass constructor is executed. This code initializes the Author field with the value passed to the author parameter.

To override the GetDisplayText method, the method declaration includes the *override* keyword. Note that when you override a method, the override must have the same signature as the method it's overriding. In this case, the method must have a single string parameter. This parameter receives the separator that's used to format the Code, Description, Author, and Price properties.

Notice that this GetDisplayText method provides its own complete implementation. In contrast, the GetDisplayText method in the second code example builds on to the implementation of this method in the Product class. To do that, it starts by calling the GetDisplayText method of the base class, which returns a formatted string that contains the Code, Description, and Price properties. Then, it adds the Author property to the end of this string.

This figure also introduces the concept of *hiding*. When you use the *new* keyword on a subclass member, the member *hides* the corresponding base class member. As a result, the subclass doesn't inherit the original version of the member, but uses the new version instead. Hiding is similar to overriding, but can be used only with non-virtual methods or properties. Because hiding doesn't provide for polymorphism as described in the next topic, you should avoid hiding if possible. Instead, you should use virtual methods and properties whenever you expect to provide a different implementation of a method or property in a subclass.

The syntax for creating subclasses

To declare a subclass

```
public class SubclassName : BaseClassName
```

To create a constructor that calls a base class constructor

```
public ClassName(parameterlist) : base(parameterlist)
```

To call a base class method or property

```
base.MethodName(parameterlist)
base.PropertyName
```

To hide a non-virtual method or property

```
public new type name
```

To override a virtual method or property

```
public override type name
```

The code for a Book class

```
public class Book : Product
{
    public string Author;          // A new public field

    public Book(string code, string description, string author,
        decimal price) : base(code, description, price)
    {
        this.Author = author;      // Initializes the Author field after
    }                              // the base class constructor is called.

    public override string GetDisplayText(string sep)
    {
        return this.Code + sep + this.Description
            + "( " + this.Author + ")" + sep + this.Price.ToString("c");
    }
}
```

Another way to override a method

```
public override string GetDisplayText(string sep)
{
    return base.GetDisplayText(sep) + "( " + this.Author + ")";
}
```

Description

- A constructor of a derived class automatically calls the default constructor of the base class before the derived class constructor executes. If you want to call a non-default base class constructor, you can specify the constructor to call when you declare the constructor of the derived class. Then, you can pass parameters to the base class constructor.
- You use the *base* keyword to refer to a member of the base class.
- You use the *override* keyword to override a virtual member of the base class.
- You can use the *new* keyword to provide a new implementation for a non-virtual method or property of the base class. This is called *hiding*. But in most cases, it's better to use virtual and overridden methods and properties so you can benefit from polymorphism.

Figure 14-6 How to create a subclass

How polymorphism works

Polymorphism is one of the most important features of object-oriented programming and inheritance. As figure 14-7 shows, polymorphism lets you treat objects of different types as if they were the same type by referring to a base class that's common to both objects. For example, consider the Book and Software classes that were presented in figure 14-4. Because both of these classes inherit the Product class, objects created from these classes can be treated as if they were Product objects.

One benefit of polymorphism is that you can write generic code that's designed to work with a base class. Then, you can use that code with instances of any class that's derived from the base class. For example, the Add method for the List<Product> class described in figure 14-4 accepts a Product object as a parameter. Since the ProductList class inherits the List<Product> class, this method is also available to the ProductList class. And since the Book and Software classes are derived from the Product class, this Add method will work with Book or Software objects.

The code examples in this figure illustrate a confusing but useful aspect of polymorphism. The first example shows a virtual method named GetDisplayText that's defined in the Product base class. This method returns a string that includes the Code, Description, and Price properties. The next two examples show overridden versions of the GetDisplayText method for the Book and Software classes. The Book version of this method calls the GetDisplayText method of the base class and then adds the author's name to the end of the string that's returned by that method. Similarly, the Software version calls the GetDisplayText method of the base class and then adds the software version to the end of the string that's returned.

The last code example in this figure shows how you can use polymorphism with these classes. This code begins by creating an instance of the Book class and assigning it to a variable named b. Then, it creates an instance of the Software class and assigns it to a variable named s.

Next, a variable named p of type Product is declared, and the Book object is assigned to it. Then, the GetDisplayText method of the Product class is called. When the .NET Framework sees that the GetDisplayText method of the Product class is a virtual method, however, it checks to see what type of object the p variable refers to. In this case, the p variable refers to a Book object, so it calls the overridden version of the GetDisplayText method that's defined by the Book class.

The example then does the same thing with the Software object. First, this object is assigned to the p variable. Then, the GetDisplayText method defined by the Product class is called. This time, .NET determines that the product is a Software object, so it calls the overridden version of the GetDisplayText method that's defined by the Software class.

Note that to use this type of polymorphism, you must code the virtual keyword on the base class member. Otherwise, you can't override the member in the derived classes. Then, any call to the base class member executes that member regardless of the object type.

Three versions of the GetDisplayText method

A virtual GetDisplayText method in the Product base class

```
public virtual string GetDisplayText(string sep)
{
    return code + sep + price.ToString("c") + sep + description;
}
```

An overridden GetDisplayText method in the Book class

```
public override string GetDisplayText(string sep)
{
    return base.GetDisplayText(sep) + sep + author;
}
```

An overridden GetDisplayText method in the Software class

```
public override string GetDisplayText(string sep)
{
    return base.GetDisplayText(sep) + sep + version;
}
```

Code that uses the overridden methods

```
Book b = new Book("CS08", "Murach's C# 2008", "Joel Murach", 54.50m);
Software s = new Software("NPTK", ".NET Programmer's Toolkit",
                          "2.1", 149.50m);
Product p;
p = b;
MessageBox.Show(p.GetDisplayText("\n"));  // Calls Book.GetDisplayText
p = s;
MessageBox.Show(p.GetDisplayText("\n"));  // Calls Software.GetDisplayText
```

Description

- *Polymorphism* is a feature of inheritance that lets you treat objects of different subclasses that are derived from the same base class as if they had the type of the base class. If, for example, Book is a subclass of Product, you can treat a Book object as if it were a Product object.
- If you access a virtual member of a base class object and the member is overridden in the subclasses of that class, polymorphism determines the member that's executed based on the object's type. For example, if you call the GetDisplayText method of a Product object, the GetDisplayText method of the Book class is executed if the object is a Book object.
- Polymorphism is most useful when you have two or more derived classes that use the same base class. It allows you to write generic code that targets the base class rather than having to write specific code for each object type.

Figure 14-7 How polymorphism works

An inheritance version of the Product Maintenance application

Now that you've learned how to create base classes and subclasses, the following topics present a version of the Product Maintenance application that uses inheritance. This version of the application uses the classes that were described in figure 14-4. It works with a Products file that can hold two distinct types of products: books and software.

Note that this version of the Product Maintenance application won't work with the ProductDB classes that are presented in chapters 21 and 22, since those classes are designed to work only with Product objects. Instead, this version of the application requires a ProductDB class that can save and retrieve data for both Book and Software objects. Although this class isn't presented here, you shouldn't have any trouble figuring out how to implement it after you read chapter 21 or 22.

The operation of the Product Maintenance application

Figure 14-8 shows the operation of this version of the Product Maintenance application. As you can see, the Product Maintenance form looks just like the one you saw in chapter 12. From this form, you can click the Add Product button to display the New Product form, or you can select a product in the list and then click the Delete Product button to delete a product.

The main difference between this application and the application presented in chapter 12 is that the New Product form includes two radio buttons. These buttons let the user choose whether a book or a software product is added to the file. Note that the label that's displayed for the third text box changes depending on which of these buttons is selected. If the Book button is selected, this label is set to Author. If the Software button is selected, it's set to Version.

The Product Maintenance form

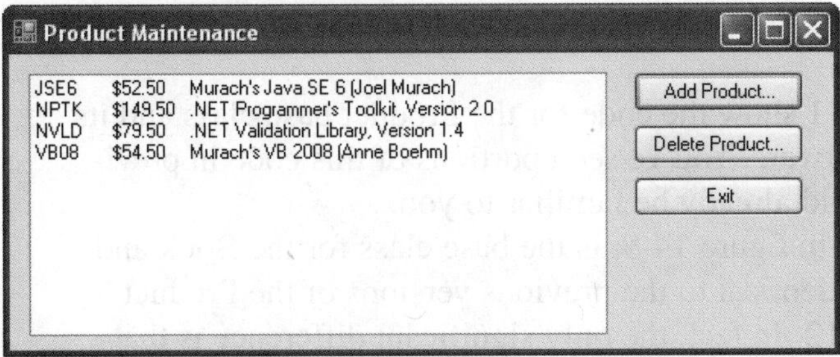

Two versions of the New Product form

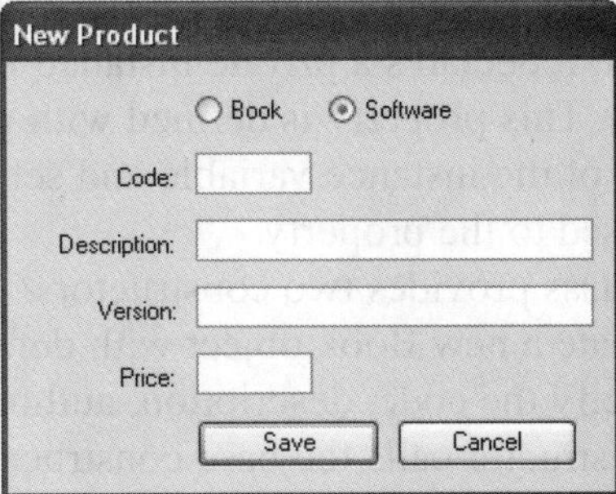

Description

- This version of the Product Maintenance application handles two types of products: books and software.
- The New Product form has a radio button that lets the user choose to create a book or a software product. The label for the third text box changes depending on which option is selected.

Figure 14-8 The operation of the Product Maintenance application

The code for the Product, Book, and Software classes

Figures 14-9 through 14-11 show the code for the Product base class and its two subclasses, Book and Software. You've seen portions of this code in previous figures, so most of it should already be familiar to you.

The Product class, shown in figure 14-9, is the base class for the Book and Software classes. It's almost identical to the previous versions of the Product class that you saw in chapter 12. In fact, the only significant difference is that the GetDisplayText method specifies the virtual keyword. That way, this method can be overridden by the Book and Software classes.

The Book class, shown in figure 14-10, specifies the Product class as its base class. Then, it declares a private instance variable to hold the value of the Author property. This property is defined with get and set accessors that simply return the value of the instance variable and set the value of this variable to the value that's passed to the property.

The Book class provides two constructors. The first is an empty constructor that lets you create a new Book object with default values. The second constructor lets you specify the code, description, author, and price for a new Book object. This constructor calls the base constructor to initialize the Code, Description, and Price properties. As a result, the body of this constructor is just a single line of code that initializes the Author property.

The overridden GetDisplayText method for the Book class calls the base GetDisplayText method to get a string that includes the code, price, and description. Then, it adds the author's name in parentheses to the end of this string.

The Software class, shown in figure 14-11, is similar to the Book class, but it adds a property named Version. It too provides a constructor that calls the base constructor to initialize the Code, Description, and Price properties before it initializes the Version property. It also overrides the GetDisplayText method by calling the base GetDisplayText method and then adding the version information to the end of the string that's returned.

The code for the Product class

```
public class Product
{
    private string code;
    private string description;
    private decimal price;

    public Product()
    {
    }

    public Product(string code, string description, decimal price)
    {
        this.Code = code;
        this.Description = description;
        this.Price = price;
    }

    public string Code
    {
        get
        {
            return code;
        }
        set
        {
            code = value;
        }
    }

    public string Description
    {
        get
        {
            return description;
        }
        set
        {
            description = value;
        }
    }

    public decimal Price
    {
        get
        {
            return price;
        }
        set
        {
            price = value;
        }
    }

    public virtual string  GetDisplayText(string sep)
    {
        return code + sep + price.ToString("c") + sep + description;
    }
}
```

Figure 14-9 The code for the Product class

The code for the Book class

```
public class Book : Product
{
    private string author;

    public Book()
    {
    }

    public Book(string code, string description, string author,
        decimal price) : base(code, description, price)
    {
        this.Author = author;
    }

    public string Author
    {
        get
        {
            return author;
        }
        set
        {
            author = value;
        }
    }

    public override string GetDisplayText(string sep)
    {
        return base.GetDisplayText(sep) + " (" + author + ")";
    }

}
```

Description

- The Book class inherits the Product class. It adds a property named Author and overrides the GetDisplayText method.

Figure 14-10 The code for the Book class

The code for the Software class

```
public class Software : Product
{
    private string version;

    public Software()
    {
    }

    public Software(string code, string description, string version,
        decimal price) : base(code, description, price)
    {
        this.Version = version;
    }

    public string Version
    {
        get
        {
            return version;
        }
        set
        {
            version = value;
        }
    }

    public override string GetDisplayText(string sep)
    {
        return base.GetDisplayText(sep) + ", Version " + version;
    }

}
```

Description

- The Software class inherits the Product class. It adds a property named Version and overrides the GetDisplayText method.

The code for the ProductList class

Figure 14-12 shows the code for the ProductList class, which is used to hold the Book and Software objects that are maintained by the Product Maintenance application. This class inherits the List<Product> class. As a result, the basic functions of the ProductList class, such as its ability to hold multiple Product objects, are provided by the base class. For example, even though the ProductList class doesn't provide code for an indexer or a Remove method, both of these members are available from the ProductList class because they are available from the base class.

However, the ProductList class does provide an implementation of an Add method that hides the Add method that's available from the List<Product> class. To start, the declaration for this Add method uses the new keyword to indicate that it hides rather than overrides the Add method from the base class. Since this method isn't declared as virtual in the base class, this is the only way to modify this method. Then, the statement within this method uses the base keyword to call the Insert method of the List<Product> class to insert the Product object that's passed to the method at the beginning of the list. As a result, the Add method for this version of the ProductList class adds products to the beginning of the list instead of adding them to the end of the list. Although this might not be the behavior you would want for most lists, it does show how you can change the functionality of a subclass by hiding a method from the base class.

The last two methods of the ProductList class (the Fill and Save methods) aren't available from the base class. These methods can be used to read or write the list of products to a data store. For example, the Fill method calls the GetProducts method of the ProductDB class to load the products in the Products file into a list of products. Then, it uses a foreach loop to add each product in the list to the base list by calling the Add method of the base class. Conversely, the Save method calls the SaveProducts method of the ProductDB class to save the current instance of the ProductList class to the Products file.

The code for the ProductList class

```
public class ProductList : List<Product>
{
    // Modify the behavior of the Add method of the List<Product> class
    public new void Add(Product p)
    {
        base.Insert(0, p);
    }

    // Provide two additional methods
    public void Fill()
    {
        List<Product> products = ProductDB.GetProducts();
        foreach (Product product in products)
            base.Add(product);
    }

    public void Save()
    {
        ProductDB.SaveProducts(this);
    }
}
```

Description

- This version of the ProductList class inherits the List<> class of the .NET Framework. As a result, it doesn't need to define a List<> instance variable because the class is itself a type of List<> class.

Figure 14-12 The code for the ProductList class

The code for the Product Maintenance form

Figure 14-13 shows the code for this version of the Product Maintenance form. The first thing you should notice here is the code for the FillProductListBox method. You may remember that the code for this method in the Product Maintenance form in chapter 13 had to use a for loop along with the indexer of the ProductList class to process the product list. In contrast, because the ProductList class in this chapter inherits the List<Product> class, I was able to use a foreach loop to process the product list. You'll learn more about the features that make it possible to process a collection this way in the next chapter.

You can also see polymorphism at work in this foreach loop. Here, the statement that adds the text to the Items collection of the list box calls the GetDisplayText method for each product. Because GetDisplayText is a virtual method that's overridden by both the Book and Software classes, this code calls the GetDisplayText method of the Book class for Book objects and the GetDisplayText method of the Software class for Software objects. To confirm that's what's happening, you can look back to figures 14-10 and 14-11 to see the differences between these two methods, and you can look back to figure 14-8 to see the differences in the resulting display.

The code for the Product Maintenance form

```
public partial class frmProductMain : Form
{
    public frmProductMain()
    {
        InitializeComponent();
    }

    private ProductList products = new ProductList();

    private void frmProductMain_Load(object sender, System.EventArgs e)
    {
        products.Fill();
        FillProductListBox();
    }

    private void FillProductListBox()
    {
        lstProducts.Items.Clear();
        foreach (Product p in products)
            lstProducts.Items.Add(p.GetDisplayText("\t"));
    }

    private void btnAdd_Click(object sender, System.EventArgs e)
    {
        frmNewProduct newForm = new frmNewProduct();
        Product product = newForm.GetNewProduct();
        if (product != null)
        {
            products.Add(product);
            products.Save();
            FillProductListBox();
        }
    }

    private void btnDelete_Click(object sender, System.EventArgs e)
    {
        int i = lstProducts.SelectedIndex;
        if (i != -1)
        {
            Product product = products[i];
            string message = "Are you sure you want to delete "
                + product.Description + "?";
            DialogResult button =
                MessageBox.Show(message, "Confirm Delete",
                MessageBoxButtons.YesNo);
            if (button == DialogResult.Yes)
            {
                products.Remove(product);
                products.Save();
                FillProductListBox();
            }
        }
    }

    private void btnExit_Click(object sender, System.EventArgs e)
    {
        this.Close();
    }
}
```

Figure 14-13 The code for the Product Maintenance form

The code for the New Product form

Figure 14-14 shows the code for the New Product form. Here, you can see that an event handler for the CheckedChanged event of the Book radio button is used to set the Text and Tag properties of the third label control to reflect the radio button that's selected. This works because the Checked property of the Book radio button changes regardless of whether the user selects the Book or Software option. Then, within the CheckedChanged event handler, the Checked property of the Book radio button is tested to determine which option is selected. The Checked property of the Book radio button is also tested in the event handler for the Click event of the Save button to determine whether it should create a Book or Software object. Last, the IsValidData method in this form uses the IsPresent method of the Validator class to validate the author or version that the user enters.

The code for the New Product form

```
public partial class frmNewProduct : Form
{
    public frmNewProduct()
    {
        InitializeComponent();
    }

    private Product product = null;

    public Product GetNewProduct()
    {
        this.ShowDialog();
        return product;
    }

    private void rbBook_CheckedChanged(object sender, System.EventArgs e)
    {
        if (rbBook.Checked)
        {
            lblAuthorOrVersion.Text = "Author: ";
            txtAuthorOrVersion.Tag = "Author";
        }
        else
        {
            lblAuthorOrVersion.Text = "Version: ";
            txtAuthorOrVersion.Tag = "Version";
        }
        txtCode.Focus();
    }

    private void btnSave_Click(object sender, System.EventArgs e)
    {
        if (IsValidData())
        {
            if (rbBook.Checked)
                product = new Book(txtCode.Text, txtDescription.Text,
                    txtAuthorOrVersion.Text, Convert.ToDecimal(txtPrice.Text));
            else
                product = new Software(txtCode.Text, txtDescription.Text,
                    txtAuthorOrVersion.Text, Convert.ToDecimal(txtPrice.Text));
            this.Close();
        }
    }

    private bool IsValidData()
    {
        return Validator.IsPresent(txtCode) &&
            Validator.IsPresent(txtDescription) &&
            Validator.IsPresent(txtAuthorOrVersion) &&
            Validator.IsPresent(txtPrice) &&
            Validator.IsDecimal(txtPrice);
    }

    private void btnCancel_Click(object sender, System.EventArgs e)
    {
        this.Close();
    }
}
```

Figure 14-14 The code for the New Product form

Object types and casting

Now that you've learned the basics of inheritance and you've seen an example of an application that uses it, you're ready to learn some additional techniques that are often required when you work with inheritance. That includes casting objects and getting information about an object's type.

How to use the Type class to get information about an object's type

As you know, the System.Object class includes a GetType method that you can use to get a Type object that represents the type of a .NET object. Figure 14-15 lists some of the members of the Type class that you can use to get information about an object. For example, you can use the Name property to get the name of a type, such as "Product" or "Book;" you can use the Namespace property to get the name of the namespace that contains a type, such as "ProductMaintenance;" and you can use the FullName property to get the fully qualified name of a type, such as "ProductMaintenance.Book." In addition, you can use the BaseType property to get a Type object that represents the type of the class that a type inherits.

The first example in this figure shows how you can use these properties to display information about an object. Here, the GetType method is used to get information about a Book object that's accessed through a variable of type Product. Notice that even though the variable has a type of Product, the Type object that's returned by the GetType method represents a Book object.

The second example shows how you can code an if statement to test an object's type. Here, I simply called the Product object's GetType method to get a Type object. Then, I compared the Name property of that object with a string to determine if the object is of type Book.

The third example shows another way to test an object's type. Here, I used the static GetType method of the Type class to get a Type object for the Book class of the ProductMaintenance namespace. Then, I compared this type object to the Type object that's returned by the GetType method of the Product. Note that when you use the GetType method of the Type class, you must supply the fully qualified name of the class you want to get a Type object for.

The Type class

Property	Description
`Name`	Returns a string that contains the name of a type.
`FullName`	Returns a string that contains the fully qualified name of a type, which includes the namespace name and the type name.
`BaseType`	Returns a Type object that represents the class that a type inherits.
`Namespace`	Returns a string that contains the name of the namespace that contains a type.
Method	**Description**
`GetType(fullname)`	A static method that returns a Type object for the specified name.

Code that uses the Type class to get information about an object

```
Product p;
p = new Book("CS08", "Murach's C# 2008", "Joel Murach", 59.50m);
Type t = p.GetType();
Console.WriteLine("Name: " + t.Name);
Console.WriteLine("Namespace: " + t.Namespace);
Console.WriteLine("FullName: " + t.FullName);
Console.WriteLine("BaseType: " + t.BaseType.Name);
```

The result that's displayed on the console

```
Name: Book
Namespace: ProductMaintenance
FullName: ProductMaintenance.Book
BaseType: Product
```

How to test an object's type

```
if (p.GetType().Name == "Book")
```

Another way to test an object's type

```
if (p.GetType() == Type.GetType("ProductMaintenance.Book"))
```

Description

- Every object has a GetType method that returns a Type object that corresponds to the object's type.
- You can use the properties of the Type class to obtain information about the type of any object, such as the type's name and the name of its base class.
- The properties and methods shown above are only some of the more than 90 properties and methods of the Type class.
- You can use the static GetType method to get a Type object for any class. This is useful when you want to check to see if an object is of a particular type.

Figure 14-15 How to use the Type class to get information about an object's type

How to use casting with inheritance

Another potentially confusing aspect of using inheritance is knowing when to cast inherited objects explicitly. The basic rule is that C# can implicitly cast a subclass to its base class, but you must use explicit casting if you want to treat a base class object as one of its subclasses. Figure 14-16 illustrates how this works.

The two methods at the top of this figure both call the GetDisplayText method to get data in a displayable format. The first method, named DisplayProduct, accepts a Product object and executes the GetDisplayText method of the Product class, so it can be used with either a Book or a Software object. In contrast, the second method, named DisplayBook, accepts a Book object and calls the GetDisplayText method of the Book class, so it can only be used with Book objects.

The second example shows code that doesn't require casting. Here, the first statement creates a new Book object and assigns it to a variable of type Book. Then, the DisplayProduct method is called to format the Book object that this variable refers to. Although the DisplayProduct method expects a Product object, it can cast the Book object to a Product object since Book is a subclass of the Product class.

The third example is similar, but it assigns the new Book object to a variable of type Product. Then, it calls the DisplayBook method. Because this method expects a Book object, however, the Product object must be explicitly cast to a Book object. If it isn't, the C# compiler will display a compiler error indicating that it can't convert a Product object to a Book object.

The fourth example shows code that results in a casting exception. Here, a Software object is assigned to a variable of type Product. Then, the DisplayBook method is called to format the object that this variable refers to. Notice that this variable is explicitly cast to a Book object since that's what the DisplayBook method expects. Because the p variable holds a Software object rather than a Book object, however, this cast results in a casting exception.

The last example shows how you can use the as operator to avoid throwing an exception if a cast is invalid. The as operator is similar to a cast, but returns null if the object can't be converted to the specified type. In the example, a null value will be passed to the DisplaySoftware method because the object referenced by the p variable is a Book object, which can't be cast to a Software object.

Two methods that display product information

```
public void DisplayProduct(Product p)
{
    MessageBox.Show(p.GetDisplayText());
}

public void DisplayBook(Book b)
{
    MessageBox.Show(b.GetDisplayText());
}
```

Code that doesn't require casting

```
Book b = new Book("CS08", "Murach's C# 2008", "Joel Murach", 54.50m);
DisplayProduct(b);          // Casting is not required because Book
                            // is a subclass of Product.
```

Code that requires casting

```
Product p = new Book("CS08", "Murach's C# 2008", "Joel Murach", 54.50m);
DisplayBook((Book)p);       // Casting is required because DisplayBook
                            // accepts a Book object.
```

Code that throws a casting exception

```
Product p = new Software("NPTK", ".NET Programmer's Toolkit",
                            "2.5", 149.50m);
DisplayBook((Book)p);       // Will throw a casting exception because p is a
                            // Software object, not a Book object.
```

Code that uses the as operator

```
Product p = new Book("CS08", "Murach's C# 2008", "Joel Murach", 54.50m);
DisplaySoftware(p as Software);  // Passes null because p isn't a Software object
```

Description

- C# can implicitly cast a subclass to its base class. As a result, you can use a subclass whenever a reference to its base class is called for. For example, you can specify a Book object whenever a Product object is expected because Book is a subclass of Product.
- You must explicitly cast a base class object when a reference to one of its subclasses is required. For example, you must explicitly cast a Product object to Book if a Book object is expected.
- If you attempt to cast a base class object to a subclass, InvalidCastException will be thrown if the object is not of the correct type. For example, if you store a Software object in a variable of type Product and then try to cast the Product variable to a Book, a casting exception will be thrown.
- You can use the as operator to cast an object to another type without throwing a casting exception if the cast is invalid. The as operator simply returns null if the cast is invalid.

Figure 14-16 How to use casting with inheritance

How to work with abstract and sealed classes

The last two topics of this chapter show how you can require or restrict the use of inheritance in the classes you create by using abstract and sealed classes.

How to work with abstract classes

An *abstract class* is a class that can't be instantiated. In other words, it can be used only as a base class that other classes can inherit. Figure 14-17 shows how to work with abstract classes.

To declare an abstract class, you include the *abstract* keyword in the class declaration as shown in the Product class at the top of this figure. Then, you can code any members you want within this class. In addition, you can code *abstract methods* and *abstract properties*. For example, the Product class shown here includes an abstract method named GetDisplayText. As you can see, the declaration for this method includes the abstract keyword, and no method body is coded. You code an abstract property using a similar technique, as illustrated by the second example.

When you include abstract properties and methods in an abstract class, you must override them in any class that inherits the abstract class. This is illustrated in the third example in this figure. Here, you can see that a class named Book that inherits the Product class overrides the abstract GetDisplayText method that's defined by that class. Although you must override abstract properties and methods, you should notice that they're not declared with the virtual keyword. That's because abstract properties and methods are implicitly virtual.

At this point, you may be wondering why you would use abstract classes. To help you understand, consider the Product Maintenance application that's presented in this chapter. This application uses two types of product objects: Book objects and Software objects. However, there's nothing to stop you from creating instances of the Product class as well. As a result, the Product class hierarchy actually allows for three types of objects: Book objects, Software objects, and Product objects.

If that's not what you want, you can declare the Product class as an abstract class. Then, you can't create instances of the Product class itself. Instead, the Product class can only be used as the base class for other classes.

Note that this doesn't mean that you can't declare variables of an abstract type. It simply means that you can't use the new keyword with an abstract type to create an instance of the type. For example, if you declared the Product class as an abstract class, you could still declare a Product variable that could hold Book or Software objects like this:

```
Product p = new Book("CS08", "Murach's C# 2008",
                     "Joel Murach", 54.50m);
```

However, you wouldn't be able to use the new keyword with the Product class to create a Product object.

An abstract Product class

```
public abstract class Product
{
    public string Code;
    public string Description;
    public decimal Price;

    public abstract string GetDisplayText(string sep);
    // No method body is coded.
}
```

An abstract read-only property

```
public abstract bool IsValid
{
    get;          // No body is coded for the get accessor.
}
```

A class that inherits the abstract Product class

```
public class Book : Product
{
    public string Author;

    public override string GetDisplayText(string sep)
    {
        return this.Code + sep + this.Description
            + "( " + this.Author + ")" + sep + this.Price.ToString("c");
    }
}
```

Description

- An *abstract class* is a class that can be inherited by other classes but that you can't use to create an object. To declare an abstract class, code the *abstract* keyword in the class declaration.
- An abstract class can contain properties, methods, and other members just like other base classes. In addition, an abstract class can contain abstract methods and properties.
- To create an *abstract method*, you code the abstract keyword in the method declaration and you omit the method body.
- To create an *abstract property*, you code the abstract keyword in the property declaration. Then, you code a get accessor, a set accessor, or both get and set accessors with no bodies.
- Abstract methods and properties are implicitly virtual, and you can't code the virtual keyword on an abstract method or property.
- When a subclass inherits an abstract class, all abstract methods and properties in the abstract class must be overridden in the subclass.
- An abstract class doesn't have to contain abstract methods or properties. However, any class that contains an abstract method or property must be declared as abstract.

Figure 14-17 How to work with abstract classes

How to work with sealed classes

In contrast to an abstract class that must be inherited, a *sealed class* is a class that can't be inherited. Because C# doesn't have to generate code that provides for inheritance and polymorphism when it compiles sealed classes, using them can result in a minor performance benefit. If you know that a class won't be used as a base class, then, you should consider creating a sealed class.

Figure 14-18 shows how to create and work with sealed classes, as well as sealed properties and methods. To create a sealed class, you include the *sealed* keyword in the class declaration as shown in the example at the top of this figure. Then, you add the members that are required by the class just as you do for any other class.

You can also seal selected properties and methods of a class by omitting the sealed keyword from the class declaration and coding it on just the properties and methods you want to seal. Then, you can use the class as a base class for other classes, but you can't override the sealed members. This is illustrated by the example in this figure.

This example uses three classes named A, B, and C. Class A is a base class that declares a virtual method named ShowMessage. Class B inherits class A and overrides the ShowMessage method. In addition, class B seals this method. Then, class C inherits class B and attempts to override the ShowMessage method. Because class B sealed the ShowMessage method, however, this results in a compiler error.

In most cases, an entire class will be sealed rather than specific methods or properties. Because of that, you won't have to worry about whether individual properties and methods of a class are sealed. If you ever encounter sealed properties or methods, however, you should now understand how they work.

Keep in mind too that it's often hard to know when someone else might want to inherit a class that you create. So you shouldn't seal a class unless you're certain that no one else will benefit by extending it.

The class declaration for a sealed Book class

```
public sealed class Book : Product
```

How sealed methods work

A base class named A that declares a virtual method

```
public class A
{
    public virtual void ShowMessage()
    {
        MessageBox.Show("Hello from class A");
    }
}
```

A class named B that inherits class A and overrides and seals its method

```
public class B : A
{
    public sealed override void ShowMessage()
    {
        MessageBox.Show("Hello from class B");
    }
}
```

A class named C that inherits class B and tries to override its sealed method

```
public class C : B
{
    public override void ShowMessage()    // Not allowed
    {
        MessageBox.Show("Hello from class C");
    }
}
```

Description

- A *sealed class* is a class that can't be inherited. To create a sealed class, you code the *sealed* keyword in the class declaration.
- Sealing a class can result in a minor performance improvement for your application because the C# compiler doesn't have to allow for inheritance and polymorphism. As a result, it can generate more efficient code.
- You can also seal individual properties and methods. To create a *sealed property* or a *sealed method*, code the sealed keyword in the property or method declaration.
- You can only seal a property or method if the property or method overrides a member of the base class. This allows you to create a virtual member in a base class, and then seal it in a derived class so that any subclasses derived from that class can't override the member. This feature is rarely used in business applications.

Figure 14-18 How to work with sealed classes

Perspective

Conceptually, this is probably the most difficult chapter in this book. Although the basic idea of inheritance isn't that difficult to understand, the complications of virtual members, overridden members, casting, and abstract and sealed classes are enough to make inheritance a difficult topic. So if you find yourself a bit confused right now, don't be disheartened. It will become clearer as you actually use the techniques you've learned here.

The good news is that you don't have to understand every nuance of how inheritance works to use it. In fact, you've used inheritance in every C# application you've written without even knowing it. Now that you've completed this chapter, though, you should have a better understanding of how the .NET Framework works, and you should have a greater appreciation for how much the Framework does on your behalf. In addition, you should have a better idea of how you can use inheritance to improve the design of your own classes.

Although it's not covered in this chapter, you may want to know about a new feature of C# 2008 called extension methods. Just like when you use inheritance, you can use extension methods to add functionality to an existing type. Unlike inheritance, however, you don't have to create a new derived type to add that functionality. The .NET Framework 3.5 includes some extension methods, such as the ones that provide for the LINQ query operators you'll learn about in chapter 23. If you want to create your own extension methods, you can refer to Visual Studio help to find out how to do that.

Terms

inheritance
derived class
child class
subclass
base class
parent class
superclass
overriding
fully qualified name
hash code
garbage collector
virtual member
access modifier
protected member
internal member
hiding
polymorphism
abstract class
abstract method
abstract property
sealed class
sealed property
sealed method

Exercise 14-1 Create a Customer Maintenance application that uses inheritance

In this exercise, you'll create a Customer Maintenance application that uses classes with the inheritance features presented in this chapter. This application works with two types of customers: retail customers and wholesale customers. Both customer types are derived from a Customer base class, both extend the Customer class by adding a property, and separate forms are used to add the two types of customers. To make this application easier to develop, we'll give you the starting forms and classes.

The design of the Customer Maintenance form

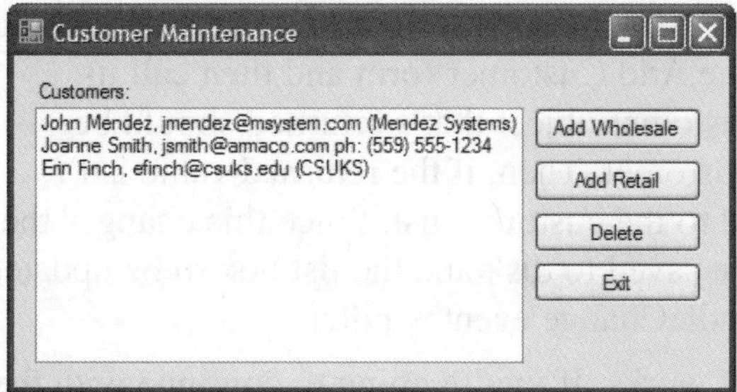

The design of the Add Customer forms

Open the project and create the derived classes

1. Open the application in the C:\C# 2008\Chapter 14\CustomerMaintenance directory.
2. Display the Customer class and modify the GetDisplayText method so it's overridable.
3. Add a class named WholesaleCustomer that inherits the Customer class. This new class should add a string property named Company. It should also provide a default constructor and a constructor that accepts four parameters (first name, last name, email, and company) to initialize the class properties. This constructor should call the base class constructor to initialize the properties defined by that class. Finally, this class should override the GetDisplayText method to add the company name in parentheses to the end of the display string, as in this example:

   John Mendez, jmendez@msystem.com (Mendez Systems)

4. Add another class named RetailCustomer that inherits the Customer class and adds a string property named HomePhone. Like the WholesaleCustomer class, the RetailCustomer class should provide a default constructor and a constructor that accepts four parameters, and it should override the GetDisplayText method so the phone number is added to the end of the string like this:

   Joanne Smith, jsmith@armaco.com ph: (559) 555-1234

Complete the code for the forms

5. Complete the event handlers for the Click events of the Save buttons on the Add Wholesale Customer and Add Retail Customer forms so they create a new customer of the appropriate type using the data entered by the user.
6. Complete the event handlers for the Click events of the Add Wholesale and Add Retail buttons on the Customer Maintenance form. These methods should create an instance of the appropriate Add Customer form and then call its GetNewCustomer method. The Customer object that's returned should be saved in a local variable of type Customer. Then, if the returned value isn't null, the customer should be added to the customer list. Since this changes the list, this should cause the data to be saved to disk and the list box to be updated, but that should be done by the HandleChange event handler.
7. Run the application to make sure it works. If you're going to continue with the next exercise, leave the solution open. Otherwise, close it.

Exercise 14-2 Modify the CustomerList class to inherit the List<> class

This exercise builds on the Customer Maintenance application you created in exercise 14-1 by modifying the CustomerList class so it inherits the .NET Framework's List<> class.

1. If it isn't already opened, open the project in the C:\C# 2008\Chapter 14\CustomerMaintenance directory.
2. Modify the CustomerList class so it inherits the List<Customer> class instead of using a private List<> variable to hold the customer list. To do that, you can delete the Count method because it's provided by the base class. You can use the new keyword to hide some of the methods in the base class so you can use the ones that are already in this CustomerList class. And you can use the base keyword to refer to the base class whenever that's necessary. As you do this step, you may want to use figure 14-12 as a guide.
3. Modify the FillCustomerListBox method of the Customer Maintenance form so it fills the list box using a foreach statement instead of a for statement.
4. Run the application and test it to be sure it works properly.

15

How to work with interfaces and generics

This chapter starts by showing you how to use interfaces. Interfaces are similar to abstract classes, but they have several advantages that make them easier to create and more flexible to use. Then, this chapter shows you how to use generics so you can code your own collections that work like the generic collections from the .NET Framework presented in chapter 8. Along the way, you'll learn how to work with the generic interfaces that are used with generic collections.

How to work with interfaces

In some object-oriented programming languages, such as C++ and Perl, a class can inherit more than one class. This is known as *multiple inheritance*. In C#, however, a class can inherit only one class.

Although C# doesn't support multiple inheritance, it does support a special type of coding element known as an *interface*. An interface provides many of the advantages of multiple inheritance without some of the problems that are associated with it. In the topics that follow, you'll learn how to work with interfaces.

An introduction to interfaces

In some ways, an interface is similar to an abstract class. That's why figure 15-1 compares interfaces to abstract classes. To start, abstract classes and interfaces can both include one or more members that aren't implemented. In the case of an abstract class, the implementation for these members must be provided by any subclass that inherits the abstract class. Similarly, the implementation for the members of an interface must be included in any class that *implements* the interface. The difference is that an interface can't include the implementation for any of its members, but an abstract class can.

An important difference between abstract classes and interfaces is that a C# class can inherit only one class (abstract or not), but it can implement more than one interface. This is how C# interfaces can be used to provide some of the features of multiple inheritance.

The examples in this figure show how a simple interface is declared and implemented by a class. The first example shows the declaration for a custom interface named IDisplayable. This interface includes a single method named GetDisplayText that allows an object to return a string that can be used to display the object. Any class that implements the IDisplayable interface must provide an implementation of the GetDisplayText method.

The second example shows a simplified version of a Product class that implements the IDisplayable interface. Here, you can see that the class statement for the Product class lists IDisplayable as an interface that's implemented by the class. Then, the class provides an implementation of the GetDisplayText method that returns a string that contains all three fields of the Product class.

The third example shows that a Product object that implements the IDisplayable interface can be stored in a variable of the IDisplayable type. In other words, an object created from a Product class that implements the IDisplayable interface is both a Product object and an IDisplayable object. As a result, you can use this object anywhere an IDisplayable object is expected.

In this figure, the interface name begins with the capital letter I. Although that's not a requirement, it's a coding convention that's followed by all the interfaces in the .NET Framework, and it helps you distinguish between interfaces and classes. So when you create your own interfaces, we recommend that you follow this coding convention.

The IDisplayable interface

```
interface IDisplayable
{
    string GetDisplayText(string sep);
}
```

A Product class that implements the IDisplayable interface

```
public class Product : IDisplayable
{
    public string Code;
    public string Description;
    public decimal Price;

    public Product(string Code, string Description, decimal Price)
    {
        this.Code = Code;
        this.Description = Description;
        this.Price = Price;
    }

    public string GetDisplayText(string sep)
    {
       return this.Code + sep + this.Description
          + sep + this.Price.ToString("c");
    }
}
```

Code that uses the IDisplayable interface

```
IDisplayable product = new Product("CS08", "Murach's C# 2008", 54.5m);
Console.WriteLine(product.GetDisplayText("\n"));
```

A comparison of interfaces and abstract classes

- Both interfaces and abstract classes provide signatures for properties and methods that a class must implement.
- All of the members of an interface are abstract. In contrast, an abstract class can implement some or all of its members.
- A class can inherit only one class (including abstract classes), but a class can implement more than one interface.
- Interfaces can't declare static members, but abstract classes can.

Description

- An *interface* consists of a set of signatures for one or more methods, properties, indexers, or events. An interface doesn't provide an implementation for any of its members. Instead, it indicates what members must be defined by any class that *implements* the interface.
- By convention, interface names begin with the letter I to distinguish them from classes.
- To implement an interface, a class must name the interface on the class declaration, and it must provide an implementation for every member of the interface.

Figure 15-1 An introduction to interfaces

Some of the interfaces defined by the .NET Framework

The .NET Framework defines hundreds of interfaces. Fortunately, most of them are intended for use by other Framework classes. As a result, you don't need to learn them all. To give you an idea of what some of these interfaces do, however, figure 15-2 lists a few of them.

The first table in this figure lists four general purpose .NET interfaces: ICloneable, IComparable, IConvertible, and IDisposeable. Of these four, the one you're most likely to implement is ICloneable. This interface lets you create objects that can produce copies of themselves. It consists of a single method (Clone) that returns a copy of the object. You'll see an example of a Product class that implements this interface in figure 15-5.

While the other three interfaces in the first table are commonly used by .NET interfaces, you typically won't need to implement any of them for the classes that you code. For example, the IComparable interface provides a standard way for an object to compare itself with another object. However, most business classes don't have any real basis for determining whether one instance of the class is greater than, equal to, or less than another. For example, how would you determine whether one product object is greater than, equal to, or less than another product object? By comparing the product codes? The price? The amount of inventory on hand?

The second table in this figure lists several interfaces that are used by collection classes in the System.Collections namespace. The most important of these are IEnumerable and IEnumerator, which provide a standard mechanism for iterating through the items of a collection. If you implement these interfaces in a class, you can then use the class in a foreach statement. In fact, this is the main benefit of implementing the IEnumerable and IEnumerator interfaces.

The other three interfaces listed in the second table provide standard ways to implement collection features. The ICollection interface defines a basic collection that maintains a count of items, can be synchronized, and can copy the collection items to an array. The IList interface adds an indexer and methods to add, clear, and remove items. And the IDictionary interface implements a dictionary, which can be used to maintain key/value pairs.

When reviewing these interfaces, keep in mind that these are the interfaces that were used by the .NET Framework prior to the introduction of generics. As a result, they aren't used by the generic collection classes in the System.Collections.Generic namespace. Instead, these collection classes use the generic interfaces presented in figure 15-8. Later in this chapter, you'll be introduced to generic interfaces, and you'll learn how to implement two of them.

Commonly used .NET interfaces

Interface	Members	Description
`ICloneable`	`object Clone()`	Creates a duplicate copy of an object.
`IComparable`	`int CompareTo(object)`	Compares objects.

`IConvertible`	`TypeCode GetTypeCode()`
	`decimal ToDecimal()`
	`int ToInt32()`
	...
		Converts an object to one of the common language runtime types, such as Int32, Decimal, or Boolean.

`IDisposeable`	`void Dispose()`	Frees unmanaged resources.

Commonly used .NET interfaces for collections

Interface	Members	Description
`IEnumerable`	`IEnumerator GetEnumerator()`	Gets an enumerator for the collection.

`IEnumerator`	`object Current`
	`bool MoveNext()`
	`void Reset()`
		Defines an enumerator that provides read-only, forward-only access to a collection.

`ICollection`	`int Count`
	`bool IsSynchronized`
	`object SyncRoot`
	`void CopyTo(array, int)`
		Provides basic properties for an enumerable collection. This interface inherits IEnumerable.

`IList`	`[int]`
	`int Add(object)`
	`void Clear()`
	`void Remove(object)`
	`void RemoveAt(int)`
		Manages a basic list of objects. This interface inherits ICollection and IEnumerable.

`IDictionary`	`[int]`
	`ICollection Keys`
	`ICollection Values`
	`int Add(object)`
	`void Remove(object)`
	`void Clear()`
		Manages a collection of key/value pairs. This interface inherits ICollection and IEnumerable.

Description

- The .NET Framework defines many interfaces that you can implement in your classes. However, many of these interfaces have been updated by the generic interfaces that are presented later in this chapter.
- The ICollection interface inherits the IEnumerable interface, which means that any class that implements ICollection must also implement IEnumerable. Similarly, the IList and IDictionary interfaces inherit ICollection and IEnumerable.
- This table only lists the most important members of each interface. For a complete description of these interfaces and a list of their members, see the online documentation.
- The interfaces for working with Collections are stored in the System.Collections namespace.

Figure 15-2 Some of the interfaces defined by the .NET Framework

How to create an interface

Figure 15-3 shows how to create an interface. As you can see in the syntax diagram at the top of this figure, you declare an interface using the *interface* keyword. This keyword is followed by the interface name.

Within the body of an interface, you can declare one or more methods, properties, and events. Although these declarations are similar to the declarations for a class, there are three important differences. First, because an interface doesn't provide the implementation for its members, method declarations and the get and set accessors within a property always end in a semi-colon. Second, you can't code access modifiers on a member declaration for an interface. Instead, all members are considered to be public and abstract. If you inadvertently code the public or abstract keyword on a member declaration, the compiler will generate an error message. Third, interfaces can't define static members, so you can't use the static keyword.

To begin coding an interface, you can add a new interface to your project by selecting the Project→Add New Item command and select the Interface item from the resulting dialog box. This will generate the code for the beginning of the interface. Then, you can modify the generated code and add members to the interface.

In the first example, the IDisplayable interface has been declared as public, so it's available to all classes in the current namespace. In addition, a GetDisplayText method has been declared. The signature for this method specifies that the method accepts a separator string as a parameter and returns a string that contains the display text for the object.

In the second example, the IPersistable interface defines two methods and a property. Here, the Read and Save methods can be used to read and write the object, and the HasChanges property can be used to determine if the object contains any unsaved changes.

If an interface inherits other interfaces, the interface name is followed by a colon and a list of the inherited interfaces. In the last example, for instance, the IDataAccessObject interface inherits the IDisplayable and IPersistable interfaces. As a result, any class that implements IDataAccessObject must implement all three of the methods and the one property defined by IDisplayable and IPersistable. Although it isn't shown in this figure, IDataAccessObject could also add additional members.

The syntax for creating an interface

```
public interface InterfaceName
{
    type MethodName(parameters);        // Declares a method

    type PropertyName                   // Declares a property
    {
       [get;]                           // Declares a get accessor
       [set;]                           // Declares a set accessor
    }
    ...
}
```

An interface that defines one method

```
public interface IDisplayable
{
    string GetDisplayText(string sep);
}
```

An interface that defines two methods and a property

```
public interface IPersistable
{
    object Read(string id);
    bool Save(object o);
    bool HasChanges
    {
        get;
        set;
    }
}
```

The syntax for creating an interface that inherits other interfaces

```
public interface InterfaceName : InterfaceName1[, InterfaceName2...]
{
    interface members...
}
```

An interface that inherits two interfaces

```
public interface IDataAccessObject : IDisplayable, IPersistable
{
    // add additional members here
}
```

Description

- The declaration for an interface is similar to the declaration for a class. The only difference is that you use the *interface* keyword instead of the class keyword.
- Methods and properties that are declared within an interface can't include implementation. As a result, method declarations and get and set accessors always end with a semicolon.
- You shouldn't include any access modifiers on interface members. All members are considered to be public and abstract, and static members aren't allowed.

Figure 15-3 How to create an interface

How to implement an interface

Figure 15-4 shows how to code a class that implements one or more interfaces. To do that, you code the class name, followed by a colon and a list of the interfaces on the class declaration. Note that if the class also inherits another class, you must list the class before the interfaces.

The three class declarations in this figure illustrate how this works. The first class declaration is for a Product class that implements the ICloneable interface. The second class declaration is for a Product class that implements two interfaces: ICloneable and IDisplayable. And the third class declaration is for a Book class that inherits the Product class and implements the ICloneable and IDisplayable interfaces.

When you enter the name of an interface on a class declaration, you can automatically generate stubs for each member of the interface. To do that, you can right-click on the name of the interface and select the Implement Interface command from the resulting menu. Then, code that's similar to the code in the second to last example in this figure is inserted into the class. At this point, you can begin entering the code that's needed to implement each member of the interface.

Notice in this example that the generated code is bracketed by #region and #endregion directives. In the Code Editor window, you can collapse regions like this by clicking on the – symbol to the left of the region name. Or, you can expand the code region by clicking the + symbol that appears next to the collapsed region. This makes it easy for you to hide or display all of the members of an interface.

If you right-click on the name of an interface and select the Explicitly Implement Interface command, this works like the regular Implement Interface command. However, it doesn't use the public keyword, and it fully qualifies each member of the interface. In this figure, for example, it specifies Cloneable.Clone instead of just specifying the Clone method. Although this can help to avoid naming conflicts in some situations, you typically won't need to use this command.

The syntax for implementing an interface

```
public class ClassName : [BaseClassName,] InterfaceName1
                         [, InterfaceName2]...
```

A Product class that implements ICloneable

```
public class Product : ICloneable
```

A Product class that implements two interfaces

```
public class Product : ICloneable, IDisplayable
```

A class that inherits a class and implements two interfaces

```
public class Book : Product, ICloneable, IDisplayable
```

The prompt that's displayed when you enter an interface name

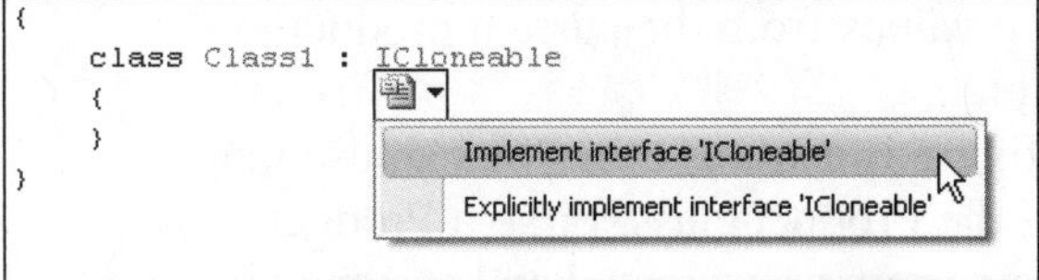

The code that's generated when you implement the interface

```
#region ICloneable Members

public object Clone()
{
    throw new Exception("The method or operation is not implemented.");
}

#endregion
```

The code that's generated when you explicitly implement the interface

```
#region ICloneable Members

object ICloneable.Clone()
{
    throw new Exception("The method or operation is not implemented.");
}

#endregion
```

Description

- To declare a class that implements one or more interfaces, type a colon after the class name, then list the interfaces that the class implements.
- If a class inherits another class, you must include the name of the inherited class before the names of any interfaces the class implements.
- After you enter the name of an interface on a class declaration, you can automatically generate stubs for the members of the interface. To do that, right-click on the name of the interface and select the Implement Interface command from the resulting menu. Then, you can add the code required to implement the members.

Figure 15-4 How to implement an interface

A Product class that implements the ICloneable interface

Now that you've seen the basic skills for creating and implementing interfaces, figure 15-5 presents an example of a Product class that implements the IDisplayable and ICloneable interfaces. This example is similar to the example that was shown in figure 15-1.

The Product class begins by declaring three public fields named Code, Description, and Price. Then, after the constructor for the class, the GetDisplayText method provides the implementation for the IDisplayable interface. This method is coded within a region that's generated by Visual Studio. As a result, when working in the Code Editor, you can collapse or expand this method. And finally, the Clone method creates a new product, copies the Code, Description, and Price values from the current product to the new product, and returns the new product.

The second code example in this figure illustrates how you can use the Clone and GetDisplayText methods of the Product class. First, a Product variable named p1 is declared and a new product is created and assigned to it. Then, a second Product variable named p2 is declared, and the Clone method of the p1 product is used to create a copy that's assigned to this variable. Notice that because the Clone method returns an object type, the return value must be cast to the Product type so it can be assigned to the p2 variable. Next, the Code and Description fields of the second object are modified. Finally, the last two statements use the GetDisplayText method to display both products on the console. As you can see, both products contain different data, which proves that the clone worked.

In this example, the data of a Product object is stored in three fields with built-in value types. But what if you wanted to clone a more complicated object with fields that represent other objects? For example, consider an Invoice class with a Customer property that returns a Customer object that's stored in a private field. In that case, you can clone the Invoice object using either a shallow copy or a deep copy.

If you use a *shallow copy*, the Customer field of the cloned Invoice object would refer to the same Customer object as the original Invoice object. In contrast, if you use a *deep copy*, the Customer field of the cloned Invoice object would refer to a clone of the Customer object. The easiest way to accomplish that would be to implement the ICloneable interface in the Customer class and then call the Clone method of this class from the Invoice object. However, you could also clone the Customer object within the Clone method of the Invoice class.

As defined by the ICloneable interface, the Clone method doesn't specify whether the returned value should be a deep copy or a shallow copy. So you can implement whichever type of copy you think is most appropriate for a class. Just be sure to specify whether the Clone method returns a deep copy or a shallow copy in the class documentation so users of the class will know what to expect when they use the Clone method.

The code for the cloneable Product class

```
public class Product : IDisplayable, ICloneable
{
    public string Code;
    public string Description;
    public decimal Price;

    public Product(string Code, string Description, decimal Price)
    {
        this.Code = Code;
        this.Description = Description;
        this.Price = Price;
    }

    #region IDisplayable Members

    public string GetDisplayText(string sep)
    {
        return this.Code + sep + this.Description
            + sep + this.Price.ToString("c");
    }

    #endregion

    #region ICloneable Members

    public object Clone()
    {
        Product p = new Product();
        p.Code = this.Code;
        p.Description = this.Description;
        p.Price = this.Price;
        return p;
    }

    #endregion
}
```

Code that creates and clones a Product object

```
Product p1 = new Product("JAV5", "Murach's Beginning Java 2, JDK 5",
                         52.50m);
Product p2 = (Product)p1.Clone();
p2.Code = "JSE6";
p2.Description = "Murach's Java SE 6";
Console.WriteLine(p1.GetDisplayText("\n") + "\n");
Console.WriteLine(p2.GetDisplayText("\n") + "\n");
```

The output that's displayed by the code shown above

```
JAV5
Murach's Beginning Java 2, JDK 5
$52.50

JSE6
Murach's Java SE 6
$52.50
```

Figure 15-5 A Product class that implements the ICloneable interface

How to use an interface as a parameter

Figure 15-6 shows how to use an interface as a parameter of a method. To do that, you code the name of the interface as the parameter type as shown in the first example. Here, a method named CreateList accepts two parameters: an object that implements ICloneable and an integer. This method returns a list that's filled with copies of the object specified by the first parameter. The number of copies to be included in the list is specified by the second parameter. To generate the copies, the CreateList method uses the Clone method of the object that's passed to it.

The second example shows how to code a method named WriteToConsole that accepts the IDisplayable interface as a parameter. This method uses the GetDisplayText method of the IDisplayable interface to return the display text for the object. Then, it uses the WriteLine method of the Console object to print this text to the console.

When you declare a method that accepts an interface as a parameter, you can pass any object that implements that interface to the method. This is illustrated in the third code example in this figure. Here, a new Product object is created and stored in a variable named product. Then, the CreateList method is used to create three copies of the Product object. And finally, the WriteToConsole method is used to write each Product object to the console. You can see the result in the dialog box that's shown in this figure.

The key point here is that the CreateList method doesn't know what type of object it's cloning. All it knows is that the object implements the ICloneable interface, which means that it has a Clone method. Similarly, the WriteToConsole method doesn't know what type of object it's writing to the console. All it knows is that the object implements the IDisplayable interface. Both of these methods work for the Product object because the Product class implements ICloneable and IDisplayable.

This example illustrates an even larger point. In short, a Product object can be thought of as an ICloneable or IDisplayable object. As a result, you can supply a Product object anywhere an ICloneable or IDisplayable object is expected. In this figure, interfaces are used to specify the type for a parameter of a method. However, interfaces can also be used to specify a type in other places too. For example, an interface can be used as a return type for a method. Similarly, an interface can be used to specify the type of a property. And anywhere an interface is used to specify a type, you can supply any object that implements that interface.

A CreateList method that uses an interface as a parameter

```
public static List<object> CreateList(ICloneable obj, int count)
{
    List<object> objects = new List<object>();
    for (int i = 0; i < count; i++)
    {
        object o = obj.Clone();
        objects.Add(o);
    }
    return objects;
}
```

A WriteToConsole method that uses an interface as a parameter

```
public static void WriteToConsole(IDisplayable d)
{
    Console.WriteLine(d.GetDisplayText("\n") + "\n");
}
```

Code that uses these methods

```
Product product = new Product("CS08", "Murach's C# 2008", 54.50m);
List<object> products = CreateList(product, 3);
foreach (Product p in products)
{
    WriteToConsole(p);
}
```

The output displayed by the code shown above

```
CS08
Murach's C# 2008
$54.50

CS08
Murach's C# 2008
$54.50

CS08
Murach's C# 2008
$54.50
```

Description

- You can declare a parameter that's used by a method as an interface type. Then, you can pass any object that implements the interface to the parameter.
- Since the Product class implements both the ICloneable and IDisplayable interfaces, it can be passed as an argument to a method that accepts an object of the ICloneable or IDisplayable type.

How to work with generics

In chapter 8, you learned how to work with generic collections such as ones defined by the List<>, SortedList<>, Stack<>, and Queue<> classes. Most of the time, you can use these or other collections from the .NET Framework whenever you need to work with a collection of objects. However, there may be times when you need to use *generics* to define your own generic collection to add some functionality that isn't available from the generic collections available from the .NET Framework. If so, the topics that follow show you how to do that. In addition, they shed some light on the inner workings of the generic collections available from the .NET Framework.

How to code a class that defines a generic collection

Part 1 of figure 15-7 shows a class named CustomList<> that defines a generic collection. Although this class is simple and doesn't provide any additional functionality that improves upon the List<> class, it illustrates all of the basic principles that are needed to define a generic collection.

To start, a data type variable named T is declared within the angle brackets immediately after the class name. This variable represents the data type that's specified for the class when an object is created from the class. For example, if you create a custom list class like this:

```
CustomList<Product> products = new CustomList<Product>();
```

the compiler substitutes the Product type wherever the T variable is coded. As a result, when you code the CustomList class, you can use the T variable to represent the data type that's specified for the class.

To start, this class declares a private List<> variable of type T. As a result, this private list can store any data type. Then, the Add method adds an object of type T to the private list. Next, the read-only indexer for this class returns an object of type T at the specified index, and the Count property returns the number of items in the list. Finally, this class declares a standard ToString method that returns a string that represents the objects of type T that are stored in the list.

Although this CustomList class uses T as the name of the type parameter for the class, you can use any parameter name here. For example, you could use a longer name such as DocumentType. However, most generic classes use T as the name of the type parameter. The main exception to this rule is the generic collections that work with dictionaries that contain keys and values. These generic collections typically use K for the key type and V for the value type like this:

```
public class CustomDictionary<K, V>
```

Incidentally, this shows how to define a generic class that accepts two type parameters, which is possible but rare.

A CustomList<> class that uses generics

```
public class CustomList<T>
{
    private List<T> list = new List<T>();

    // an Add method
    public void Add(T item)
    {
        list.Add(item);
    }

    // a read-only indexer
    public T this[int i]
    {
        get
        {
            return list[i];
        }
    }

    // a read-only property
    public int Count
    {
        get
        {
            return list.Count;
        }
    }

    // the ToString method
    public override string ToString()
    {
        string listString = "";
        for (int i = 0; i < list.Count; i++)
        {
            listString += list[i].ToString() + "\n";
        }
        return listString;
    }
}
```

Description

- You can use *generics* to define a type-safe collection that can accept elements of any type.
- To define a class for a generic collection, you code angle brackets after the name of the class, and you specify the type parameter within these brackets. Then, within the class, you can use the type parameter anywhere that a data type might be used. For example, you can use it as a return type or parameter type for a method.
- By convention, most programmers use the letter T as the type parameter for most classes. However, you can use any parameter name here.

Figure 15-7 How to code a class that uses generics (part 1 of 2)

Part 2 of figure 15-7 shows some code that uses the CustomList<> class defined in part 1. To start, the first test creates a CustomList<> class that can store int types, adds two int values to the list, and prints these values to the console. Then, the second test creates a CustomList<> class that can store Product types, adds two Product objects to the list, and prints these objects to the console.

This example shows that the CustomList<> class can store value types (such as int types) or reference types (such as Product types). More importantly, it shows that the CustomList<> class works like the other generic classes defined by the .NET Framework, although it doesn't yet provide as much functionality as any of those classes. Note that the output for this example assumes that the Product class contains a ToString method that returns a string that includes the product's code, description, and price separated by tabs.

Code that uses the CustomList<> class

```
// Test 1
Console.WriteLine("List 1 - ints");
CustomList<int> list1 = new CustomList<int>();
int i1 = 11;
int i2 = 7;
list1.Add(i1);
list1.Add(i2);
Console.WriteLine(list1.ToString());

// Test 2
Console.WriteLine("List 2 - Products");
CustomList<Product> list2 = new CustomList<Product>();
Product p1 = new Product("VB08", "Murach's Visual Basic 2008", 54.50m);
Product p2 = new Product("CS08", "Murach's C# 2008", 54.50m);
list2.Add(p1);
list2.Add(p2);
Console.Write(list2.ToString());
```

Resulting Output

```
List 1 - ints
11
7

List 2 - Products
VB08    Murach's Visual Basic 2008              $54.50
CS08    Murach's C# 2008              $54.50
```

Description

- The generic CustomList<> class works like the generic collection classes of the .NET Framework described in chapter 8.
- The resulting output shown above assumes that the Product class includes a ToString method that displays the product code, description, and price separated by tabs.

Some of the generic interfaces defined by the .NET Framework

The generic collections of the .NET Framework work with the generic interfaces described in figure 15-8. If you compare these with the interfaces presented in figure 15-2, you'll see that most of these generic interfaces have corresponding regular interfaces. However, the generic interfaces use angle brackets to specify the data type for the interface, just as generic classes use angle brackets to specify the data type for the class. In addition, the generic interfaces are stored in the System.Collections.Generic namespace and were designed to work with the generic collections stored in that namespace.

If you decide to define your own generic collection, such as the CustomList<> class shown in the previous figure, you may want to implement some of these interfaces. For example, if you want to be able to use a foreach loop to iterate through your generic collection, you'll need to implement the IEnumerable<> interface. You'll learn how to do that in figure 15-11. But first, you'll learn how to implement the IComparable<> interface in the next figure.

A commonly used generic .NET interface

Interface	Members	Description
IComparable<>	int CompareTo(T)	Compares objects of type T.

Commonly used .NET interfaces for generic collections

Interface	Members	Description
IEnumerable<>	IEnumerator<T> GetEnumerator()	Gets an enumerator of type T for the collection.
ICollection<>	int Count bool IsReadOnly T SyncRoot Add(T) void Clear() bool Contains(T) void CopyTo(array, int) bool Remove(T)	Provides basic properties for an enumerable collection. This interface inherits IEnumerable<>.
IList<>	[int] int IndexOf(T) void Insert(int, T) void RemoveAt(int)	Manages a basic list of objects. This interface inherits ICollection<> and IEnumerable<>.
IDictionary<>	[int] ICollection<K> Keys ICollection<V> Values void Add(K, V) bool ContainsKey(K) bool Remove(K) bool TryGetValue(K, V)	Manages a collection of key/value pairs. This interface inherits ICollection<> and IEnumerable<>.

Description

- The .NET Framework defines many generic interfaces. These interfaces are particularly useful for working with classes that define generic collections, and they correspond with most of the regular interfaces described in figure 15-2.
- The ICollection<> interface inherits the IEnumerable<> interface, which means that any class that implements ICollection<> must also implement IEnumerable<>. Similarly, the IList<> and IDictionary<> interfaces inherit ICollection<> and IEnumerable<>.
- The interfaces for working with generic collections are stored in the System.Collections.Generic namespace.
- This table only lists the most important members of each interface. For a complete description of these interfaces and a list of their members, see the online documentation.

Figure 15-8 Some of the generic interfaces defined by the .NET Framework

How to implement the IComparable<> interface

Figure 15-9 shows a Product class that implements the IComparable<> interface. To start, the declaration for this class indicates that it implements the IComparable interface for the Product type. Since you would typically want to compare one Product object to another Product object, this makes sense.

Then, this class implements the IComparable<> interface's only member, the CompareTo method. Since the class specifies an IComparable interface for a Product type, this method compares a parameter of the Product type against the current Product object and returns an int value. For this method to work properly, this int value should be greater than zero if the current product is greater than the compared product, less than zero if the current product is less than the compared product, and zero if the two products are equal.

To accomplish this task, this method uses the CompareTo method of the String class to compare the Code field for the two Product objects. The CompareTo method of the String class compares the two strings alphabetically and returns a 1 when the current string comes later in the alphabet than the compared string. Conversely, this method typically returns -1 when the current string comes earlier in the alphabet than the compared element. And it returns a 0 when the two strings are the same. As a result, the CompareTo method of the Product class allows you to define a generic collection of Product objects that are sorted alphabetically by their Code fields. You'll see an example of this in the next figure.

The second example shows some code that uses the CompareTo method of the Product class. To start, this code creates two Product objects. The first has a Code field of "VB08", and the second has a Code field of "CS08". Then, this example uses the CompareTo method to compare these two objects. Since the Code field for the first object comes later in the alphabet, the CompareTo method returns an int value of 1. As a result, the if statements in this example print a message to the console that indicates that the first Product object is greater than the second one.

A class that implements the IComparable<> interface

```
public class Product : IComparable<Product>
{
    public string Code;
    public string Description;
    public decimal Price;

    // other members

    #region IComparable<Product> Members

    public int CompareTo(Product other)
    {
        return this.Code.CompareTo(other.Code);
    }

    #endregion
}
```

Code that uses the class

```
Product p1 = new Product("VB08", "Murach's Visual Basic 2008", 54.50m);
Product p2 = new Product("CS08", "Murach's C# 2008", 54.50m);
int compareValue = p1.CompareTo(p2);
if (compareValue > 0)
    Console.WriteLine("p1 is greater than p2");
else if (compareValue < 0)
    Console.WriteLine("p1 is less than p2");
else if (compareValue == 0)
    Console.WriteLine("p1 is equal to p2");
```

Values that can be returned by the CompareTo method

Value	Meaning
-1	The current element is less than the compare element.
0	The current element is equal to the compare element.
1	The current element is greater than the compare element.

Description

- Since the IComparable<> interface is a generic interface, you can use angle brackets after the IComparable<> interface to identify the type of the objects that are being compared.
- To implement the IComparable<> interface, you must implement the CompareTo method. This method returns an int value that determines if the current element is less than, equal to, or greater than the element that's passed as a parameter of the method.

How to use constraints

As you work with generic classes, you may occasionally encounter situations where you need to restrict the possible data types that the generic class can accept. For example, you may need to make sure that the generic class only accepts reference types, not value types. Or, you may need to make sure that the generic class inherits another class or implements an interface. To do that, you can code a *constraint* as shown in figure 15-10.

The example at the top of the figure shows the beginning of a CustomList<> class that uses the CompareTo method of an object to insert the object at a point in the list so the list is always sorted. In other words, it implements a sorted list. To accomplish this task, this class restricts the types that can be accepted by the CustomList<> class to classes (which define reference types) that implement the IComparable<> interface.

Since any T variable in this class must be a reference type, the Add method can assign a null value to a variable of type T. Then, later in the method, the code can check if that variable is still equal to a null value. This wouldn't be possible without the constraint since you can't assign a null value to a structure (which defines a value type).

Similarly, since the T variable must implement the IComparable<> interface, the Add method can call the CompareTo method from that variable. Without the constraint, this wouldn't be possible, as there would be no guarantee that the T variable would implement the IComparable<> interface.

To declare a constraint, you begin by coding the *where* keyword after the class declaration. Then, you code the generic type parameter (usually T) followed by a colon. Finally, you code a list of the constraints, separating each constraint with a comma.

When you code these constraints, you must code them in a specific order. To start, if you want to constrain the generic type to a class or structure, you must code the class or struct keyword first. Similarly, if you want to constrain the generic type to a subclass of a particular class, you must code the name of that class first and you can't use the class or struct keywords. After that, you can code a list of the interfaces that the type must implement. Finally, if you want to constrain the generic type to a class that has a default constructor, you can code the new() keyword at the end of the list.

If you study the code in the Add method in the CustomList<> list class, you can see that this figure doesn't present all of the code for this method. That's because this code is too long to fit here, and because there are many ways that this could be coded. However, the code shown here does illustrate the main point, which is that the constraints for this class make it possible to assign a null value to a T item and to use the CompareTo method to compare two T items.

A class that uses a constraint

```
public class CustomList<T> where T: class, IComparable<T>
{
    private List<T> list = new List<T>();

    // an Add method that keeps the list sorted
    public void Add(T item)
    {
        if (list.Count == 0)
        {
            list.Add(item);
        }
        else
        {
            for (int i = 0; i < list.Count; i++)
            {
                T currentItem = list[i];
                T nextItem = null;
                if (i < list.Count - 1)
                {
                    nextItem = list[i + 1];
                }

                int currentCompare = currentItem.CompareTo(item);
                if (nextItem == null)
                {
                    if (currentCompare >= 0)
                    {
                        list.Insert(i, item);  // insert before current item
                        break;
                    }
    ...
...
```

Keywords that can be used to define constraints

Keyword	Description
class	The type argument must be a class.
struct	The type argument must be a structure.
new()	The type argument must have a default constructor. You can't use this keyword when the type argument must be a structure.

A class that uses constraints

```
public class StructList<T> where T: struct
```

Another class that uses constraints

```
public class ProductList<T> where T: Product, IComparable<T>, new()
```

Description

- When you define a generic class, you can use *constraints* to restrict the data types that your generic class accepts.

Figure 15-10 How to use constraints

How to implement the IEnumerable<> interface

The foreach loop only works on generic collections that implement the IEnumerable<> interface. As a result, if you want to use the foreach loop on a generic collection that you've defined, you must implement the IEnumerable<> interface. For example, to be able to use a foreach loop on the generic collection defined by the CustomList<> class presented in this chapter, you must implement the IEnumerable<> interface for this class as shown in figure 15-11.

In C# 2002 and 2003, allowing a foreach loop to iterate a custom collection was a confusing undertaking that involved writing a fair amount of code to implement both the IEnumerator and IEnumerable interfaces. Thankfully, C# 2005 introduced a simpler way to implement an enumerator that only involves writing a few lines of code.

To start, you can generate the method stubs for the IEnumerable<> interface. This generates method stubs for the GetEnumerator method for both the regular IEnumerable interface and the generic IEnumerable<> interface. However, you only need to implement the GetEnumerator method for the generic IEnumerable<> interface.

The easiest way to do that is to code a foreach loop that loops through each item in the list. Then, you can use the *yield* keyword together with the return keyword to return the current item to the enumerator object and to yield control.

In this figure, the enumerator object is the CustomList<Product> object named list. With each execution of the foreach loop that's shown at the end of the figure, the enumerator object (the list) returns a Product object and yields control to the foreach loop. This allows the foreach loop to call the ToString method of the Product object before yielding control back to the enumerator object. In short, this allows the two loops shown in this figure to be synchronized.

A class that implements the IEnumerable<> interface

```
public class CustomList<T> : IEnumerable<T>
{
    private List<T> list = new List<T>();

    // other members

    #region IEnumerable<T> Members

    public IEnumerator<T> GetEnumerator()
    {
        foreach (T item in list)
        {
            yield return item;
        }
    }
    #endregion

    #region IEnumerable Members

    System.Collections.IEnumerator
        System.Collections.IEnumerable.GetEnumerator()
    {
        throw new Exception("The method or operation is not implemented.");
    }

    #endregion

}
```

Code that uses the class

```
Product p1 = new Product("VB08", "Murach's Visual Basic 2008", 54.50m);
Product p2 = new Product("CS08", "Murach's C# 2008", 54.50m);
CustomList<Product> list = new CustomList<Product>();
list.Add(p1);
list.Add(p2);
foreach (Product p in list)
{
    Console.WriteLine(p.ToString());
}
```

Description

- The foreach loop only works on generic collections that implement the IEnumerable<> interface. As a result, if you want to use the foreach loop on a generic collection that you've defined, you must implement the IEnumerable<> interface.
- When implementing the GetEnumerator method, you can use the *yield* keyword with the return keyword to return the current element to the object that implements the IEnumerable<> interface and yield control.

Figure 15-11 How to implement the IEnumerable<> interface

How to code an interface that uses generics

Figure 15-12 shows how to define a generic interface. In particular, it shows how to define a generic interface named IGenericPersistable<>. The code for this interface provides a standard way for a business object to read itself from or write itself to a data source such as a database.

To give you an idea of how the IGenericPersistable<> interface might be used, this figure also shows part of a Customer class that implements this interface. Here, you can see the stubs that have been generated for the members of the interface. As a result, the Read method must return a Customer object based on the id that's passed to it. The Save method must accept a Customer object as a parameter and return a Boolean value that indicates whether the save was successful. And the HasChanges property must have accessors that get and set the property to indicate whether the Customer object has been changed since the last time it was saved.

An interface named IGenericPersistable<> that uses generics

```
interface IGenericPersistable<T>
{
    T Read(string id);
    bool Save(T obj);
    bool HasChanges
    {
        get;
        set;
    }
}
```

A class that implements the IGenericPersistable<> interface

```
class Customer : IGenericPersistable<Customer>
{

    // other members

    #region IGenericPersistable<Customer> Members

    public Customer Read(string id)
    {
        throw new Exception("The method or operation is not implemented.");
    }

    public bool Save(Customer obj)
    {
        throw new Exception("The method or operation is not implemented.");
    }

    public bool HasChanges
    {
        get
        {
            throw new Exception("The property is not implemented.");
        }
        set
        {
            throw new Exception("The property is not implemented.");
        }
    }

    #endregion
}
```

Description

- When defining an interface, you can use generics, just as you do when defining a class that uses generics.
- When implementing a generic interface that you defined, you can specify the type argument, just as you do when implementing generic interfaces from the .NET Framework.

Figure 15-12 How to code an interface that uses generics

Perspective

In this chapter, you learned how to work with interfaces. Depending on the type of programming that you're doing, you may or may not need to define your own interfaces. However, understanding interfaces is critical to working with the .NET Framework and to using an object-oriented language like C#.

You also learned how to define classes and interfaces that use generics. This allows you to create collection classes and interfaces that can accept any data type and still be type-safe. Again, depending on the type of programming that you're doing, you may never need to create these types of custom collection classes. However, understanding generics helps you understand the inner workings of the generic collection classes of the .NET Framework.

Now that you've completed this chapter, you have all of the critical skills you need for developing object-oriented programs. In the next chapter, though, you'll learn some new skills for documenting and organizing these classes. This will make it easier for you to share the classes that you develop with other programmers.

Terms

interface
implement an interface
multiple inheritance
shallow copy
deep copy
generics
constraint

Exercise 15-1 Implement the ICloneable interface

In this exercise, you'll create an application that includes a Customer class that implements the ICloneable interface. This application creates a List<> that contains clones of a pre-defined Customer object and displays the cloned customers in a list box as shown below. To make this application easier to develop, we'll give you the starting form and classes.

The design of the Clone Customer form

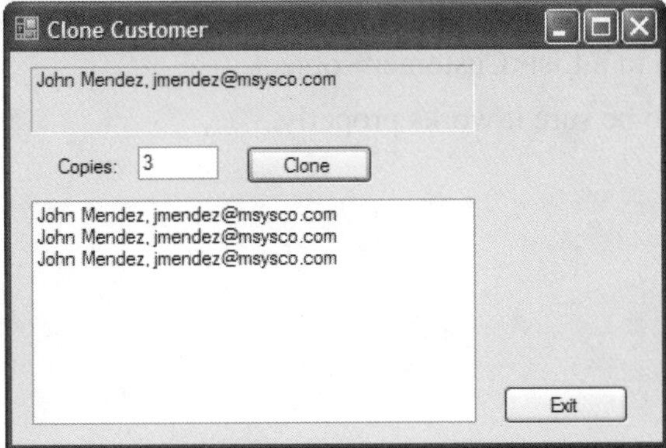

Development procedure

1. Open the application in the C:\C# 2008\Chapter 15\CloneCustomer directory.
2. Display the code for the form, and notice that the Load event handler creates a Customer object, stores it in a variable named customer, and displays the customer in the label at the top of the form.
3. Modify the Customer class so it implements the ICloneable interface.
4. Add an event handler for the Click event of the Clone button. This event handler should use the methods in the Validator class to check the value in the Copies text box to be sure it's present and also an integer. Then, it should create a List<> object that contains the required number of clones of the Customer object. Finally, it should display the cloned customers in the list box.
5. Run the application and test it to make sure it works properly.

Exercise 15-2 Implement an enumerator

In this exercise, you'll modify your solution to exercise 15-1 so the clones are stored in a CustomerList object that implements an enumerator.

1. If it isn't already open, open the application in the C:\C# 2008\Chapter 15\CloneCustomer directory.
2. Implement the IEnumerable<Customer> interface for the CustomerList class. (This class wasn't used by the previous exercise.) To do that, implement the GetEnumerator method as described in figure 15-11.
3. Modify the code in the form class so it stores the cloned Customer objects in a CustomerList object rather than in a List<Customer> object.
4. Run the application and test it to be sure it works properly.

16

How to organize and document your classes

In the last four chapters, you learned how to develop object-oriented programs that use classes. Now, you'll learn how to organize and document your classes, and you'll learn how to store your classes in class libraries. This makes it easier for other programmers to use your classes.

How to organize your classes

In this topic, you'll learn how to organize applications that use multiple classes by coding more than one class per file, by splitting a single class across multiple files, and by working with namespaces.

How to code multiple classes in a single file

In most cases, you'll code each class that's required by an application in a separate file. If two or more classes are closely related, however, you might want to consider storing them in the same file. Figure 16-1 shows two ways you can do that.

First, you can simply code the class declarations one after the other as shown in the first example. The advantage of doing that is that it makes it easier to manage the files that make up the application. If the classes are large, however, you should place them in separate files even if they are closely related. Otherwise, it may be difficult to locate the code for a specific class.

You can also code two or more classes in a single file by nesting one class within another class. *Nested classes* are useful when one class only makes sense within the context of the other class. The second example in this figure illustrates how to nest two classes. Here, the class named InnerClass is nested within a class named OuterClass.

If you want to refer to the inner class from a class other than the outer class, you have to qualify it with the name of the outer class like this:

```
OuterClass.InnerClass ic = new OuterClass.InnerClass();
```

However, you typically only need to refer to the inner class from the outer class, and you can do that without qualifying the name of the inner class.

A file with two classes coded one after the other

```
public class Class1
{
   // Body of Class1
}

public class Class2
{
   // Body of Class2
}
```

A file with nested classes

```
public class OuterClass
{
    InnerClass ic = new InnerClass();    // code that uses the inner class
    // Body of OuterClass

    public class InnerClass
    {
        // Body of InnerClass
    }
}
```

Description

- When two classes are closely related, it sometimes makes sense to code them in the same file, especially if the classes are relatively small. That way, the project consists of fewer files.
- One way to code two classes in a single file is to code them one after the other as shown in the first example above.
- Another way to code two classes in a single file is to *nest* one class within the other as shown in the second example above. This is useful when one class is used only within the context of another class.
- To refer to a nested class from another class, you must qualify it with the name of the class it's nested within like this:
  `OuterClass.InnerClass`

Figure 16-1 How to code multiple classes in a single file

How to split a single class across multiple files

Figure 16-2 shows how to use *partial classes* to split a single class across multiple files. To do that, you just code the *partial* keyword before the class keyword to indicate that the members of the class may (or may not) be split across multiple source files. Then, when you build the solution, the compiler combines all of the files that it finds for the partial classes to create the class. The resulting intermediate language produced by the compiler is the same as it would be if the entire class was coded in the same source file. One limitation is that all of the partial classes must be in the same assembly.

If a class that you're working on becomes very long, or if you want to have different programmers work on different parts of a class, you can use partial classes to split the class across two or more files. In this figure, for instance, the first code example shows how to split a Customer class across two files. In most cases, it probably makes more sense to store all of the code for a class that defines a customer in a single source file. However, if necessary, you could split a Customer class across two or more source files.

Visual Studio uses partial classes to separate the code that's generated for a Form class from the code that's entered by the programmer. In this figure, for example, the second example shows the files that Visual Studio uses for a Form class.

Here, the Form1.cs file contains the code that's added to the form by the programmer. The class declaration for this file does three things. First, it marks the Form1 class with the public access modifier. Second, it marks the class as a partial class. Third, it shows that the Form1 class inherits the Form class.

In contrast, the Form1.Designer.cs file contains the code that's generated by Visual Studio. The class declaration for this file marks the class as a partial class. However, since the declaration in the Form1.cs file has already declared the class as public and as a subclass of the Form class, that information isn't duplicated.

Finally, you should realize that a solution won't compile if partial classes contain contradictory information. For example, if one partial class is declared as public and the other as private, you'll get a compile-time error.

With C# 2008, you can also code *partial methods* within partial classes. Partial methods are used to implement methods that are similar to events. To code a partial method, you code the signature of the method in one part of the partial class, and you code the implementation of the method in another part of the class. Partial methods are typically used by developers of code generation tools to allow users of those tools to "hook in" to the generated code. Because of that, I won't show you how to code partial methods in this book.

A Customer class that's split into two files

The first file

```
public partial class Customer
{
    // Some members of the Customer class
}
```

The second file

```
public partial class Customer
{
    // The rest of the members of the Customer class
}
```

A Form class that's split into two files

The Form1.cs file

```
public partial class Form1 : Form
{
    // The code for the Form1 class that's added
    // by the programmer
}
```

The Form1.designer.cs file

```
partial class Form1
{
    // The code for the Form1 class that's generated
    //by Visual Studio
}
```

Description

- *Partial classes* can be used to split the code for a class across several files.
- To code a partial class, enter the *partial* keyword before the class keyword.
- All partial classes must belong to the same namespace and the same assembly.
- If a class that you're working on becomes very long, or if you want to have different programmers work on different parts of a class, you can use partial classes to split the class across two or more files.
- Visual Studio uses partial classes to separate the code that's generated for a Form class from the code that's entered by the programmer.

Figure 16-2 How to split a class across multiple files

How to work with namespaces

As you know, a *namespace* is a container that is used to group related classes. For example, all of the .NET Framework classes that are used for creating Windows forms are grouped in the System.Windows.Forms namespace, and all of the classes for working with collections are grouped in the System.Collections namespace.

Every C# class must belong to a namespace. This namespace is identified by a namespace statement that appears near the beginning of the C# source file. This is illustrated in all three of the examples in figure 16-3.

When you create a C# application, Visual Studio creates a namespace that has the same name as the project. Then, it stores all of the classes you create for that project in that namespace. For example, the default form for the Product Maintenance application is stored in a namespace named ProductMaintenance as shown in the first example in this figure. In addition, any other class you create as part of this project is stored in the same namespace.

You can also nest namespaces. In fact, most of the .NET Framework namespaces are nested. For example, System.Collections is actually a namespace named Collections that's nested within a namespace named System. As this figure shows, you can create nested namespaces using one of two techniques. First, you can code a namespace statement within another namespace as shown in the second example. This example creates a namespace named Murach.Validation. The more common technique, however, is to simply name all of the nested namespaces on a single namespace statement as shown in the third example.

Although all of the classes of a project are typically stored in the same namespace, those classes use classes that are stored in other namespaces. For example, all C# applications use classes that are defined by the .NET Framework. To use a class in another namespace, you typically include a using statement for that namespace at the beginning of the class. Alternatively, you can qualify any reference to the class with the name of the namespace.

For simple C# projects, you don't need to worry about namespaces because Visual Studio takes care of them for you. However, namespaces may become an issue in two situations. The first situation occurs if you copy a class from one project into another project. When you do that, you may need to change the name of the namespace in the class file to the name of the namespace for the project you copied the class into.

The second situation occurs if you want to share a class among several projects by creating a class library. In that case, you should create a separate namespace for the classes in the library. You'll learn how to do that later in this chapter.

Code that declares a namespace

```
namespace ProductMaintenance
{
    public partial class Form1 : Form
    {
        // Body of Form1 class
    }

}
```

Code that declares nested namespaces

```
namespace Murach
{
    namespace Validation
    {
        // Body of Validation namespace
    }
}
```

Another way to nest namespaces

```
namespace Murach.Validation
{
    // Body of Validation namespace
}
```

A using statement that specifies a namespace

```
using Murach.Validation;
```

Description

- A *namespace* is a container that can be used to group related classes. In most cases, all of the classes that make up a C# project are part of the same namespace.
- The namespace statement that appears near the beginning of a source file identifies the namespace that classes defined in that file belong to. By default, when you add a class to a project, it's added to a namespace with the same name as the project.
- Namespaces can be nested. One way to nest namespaces is to include a namespace statement within the body of another namespace. Another way is to code the fully-qualified name of the nested namespace in a namespace statement.
- To use a class in a namespace other than the current namespace, you must either provide a using statement that names the other namespace, or you must qualify the class with the name of the namespace.

How to document your classes

In this topic, you'll learn how to add documentation to your classes. This can make it easier for other programmers to use your classes.

How to add XML documentation to a class

As you already know, you can add general comments to any C# program by using comment statements that begin with a pair of slashes. You can also use a documentation feature called *XML documentation* to create documentation for the classes and class members you create. XML documentation can make your classes easier for other programmers to use by providing information about the function of the class and its members. Then, this information appears in screen tips that are displayed when you work with the class in Visual Studio.

Figure 16-4 shows how to add XML documentation to a class. Although XML documentation is based on XML syntax, you don't have to know much about XML to use it. As you can see, XML documentation lines begin with three slashes and appear immediately before the class or member they document.

The documentation for a class or member can contain one or more *documentation elements*. Each element begins with a *start tag*, such as <summary>, and ends with an *end tag*, such as </summary>. The contents of the element appear between the start and end tags. The table shown in this figure lists the most commonly used XML documentation elements.

The easiest way to create XML documentation is to type three slashes on the line that immediately precedes a class or class member. Then, Visual Studio automatically generates skeleton XML documentation for you. This includes whatever tags are appropriate for the class or member you're documenting. For example, if you type three slashes on the line before a member that lists parameters and has a return type, Visual Studio will generate a summary tag for the method, a param tag for each parameter passed to the method, and a returns tag for the method's return value. You can then type descriptive information between these tags to complete the documentation for the class.

Part of a Validator class that includes XML documentation

```
/// <summary>
/// Provides static methods for validating data.
/// </summary>
public class Validator
{
    public Validator()
    {
    }

    /// <summary>
    /// The title that will appear in dialog boxes.
    /// </summary>
    public static string Title = "Entry Error";

    /// <summary>
    /// Checks whether the user entered data into a text box.
    /// </summary>
    /// <param name="textBox">The text box control to be validated.</param>
    /// <returns>True if the user has entered data.</returns>
    public static bool IsPresent(TextBox textBox)
    {
        if (textBox.Text == "")
        {
            MessageBox.Show(textBox.Tag + " is a required field.", Title);
            textBox.Focus();
            return false;
        }
        return true;
    }
```

XML elements you can use for class documentation

Element	Description
`<summary>`	Provides a general description of a class, property, method, or other element.
`<value>`	Describes the value of a property.
`<returns>`	Describes the return value of a method.
`<param name="name">`	Describes a parameter of a method.

Description

- You can use special *XML tags* in C# source code to provide class documentation.
- An *XML documentation* line begins with three slashes. Each *documentation element* begins with a *start tag*, such as <summary>, and ends with an *end tag*, such as </summary>. You code the description of the element between these tags.
- If you type three slashes on the line immediately preceding a class or member declaration, Visual Studio automatically generates empty elements for you. Then, you just fill in the text that's appropriate for each element.

Figure 16-4 How to add XML documentation to a class

How to view the XML documentation

Once you add XML documentation, Visual Studio will use the XML documentation when it displays the screen tips that appear in the Visual Studio Code Editor window as shown in figure 16-5.

In the first example, when I typed the Validator class and a period, the IntelliSense feature displayed a list of the members of the Validator class. Then, I used the arrow keys to select the IsPresent method. When I did that, Visual Studio displayed a screen tip that included the signature of the IsPresent method along with the summary that's provided by the XML documentation that's shown in the previous figure.

In the second example, when I typed the opening parenthesis for the IsPresent method, Visual Studio displayed a screen tip that included the description of the TextBox parameter that's provided by the XML documentation that's shown in the previous figure.

A screen tip that displays the documentation for a method

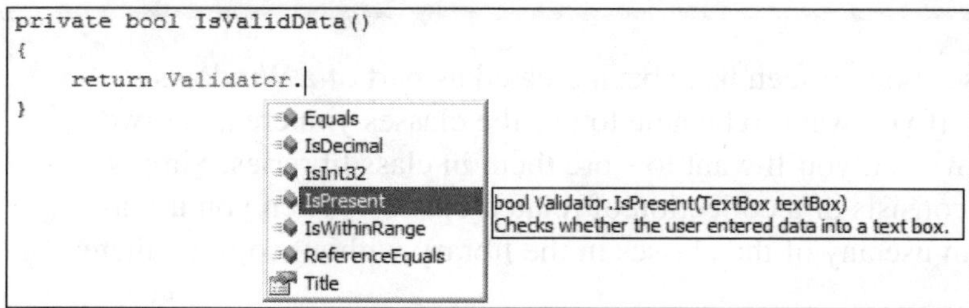

A screen tip that displays the documentation for a parameter

```
private bool IsValidData()
{
    return Validator.IsPresent(
}
```

bool Validator.IsPresent (**TextBox textBox**)
textBox:
The text box control to be validated.

Description

- The XML documentation that you add to a class is also visible in the screen tips that are displayed in the Code Editor.

Figure 16-5 How to view the XML documentation

How to create and use class libraries

So far, the classes you've seen have been created as part of a Windows Application project. If you want to be able to use the classes you create in two or more projects, however, you'll want to store them in class libraries. Simply put, a *class library* consists of a collection of related classes. When you use a class library, you can use any of the classes in the library without copying them into the project.

How class libraries work

Figure 16-6 illustrates the difference between using classes created within a Windows Application project and classes created within a class library project. As you can see, classes that are created in a Windows project must be included in every project that uses them. In contrast, classes that are created in a class library project exist separately from any project that uses them. Because of that, they are available to any project that has access to the class library.

One of the benefits of using class libraries is that the size of each project that uses them is reduced. That's because each project includes only a reference to the class library rather than the code for each class that it needs. Also, because the classes in a class library are already compiled, Visual Studio doesn't have to compile them every time you build the application. This results in faster compile times.

Another benefit of using class libraries is that they simplify maintenance. If you must make a change to a class that's in a class library, you can change the class without changing any of the applications that use the library. When you're done, the modified library is immediately available to the projects that use it.

But probably the main benefit of using class libraries is that they let you create reusable code. If you design your classes carefully and place them in a library, you can reuse them in other projects that require similar functions. In most cases, you'll use the classes directly. However, you can also use them as base classes for the new classes that you add to your projects.

Two projects that use the Validator class

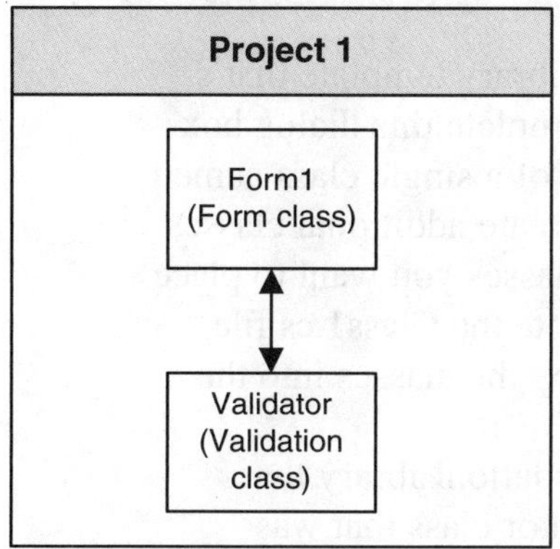

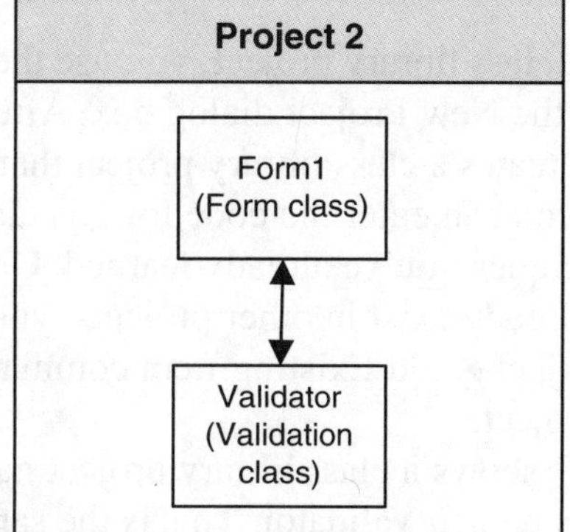

Two projects that access the Validator class via a class library

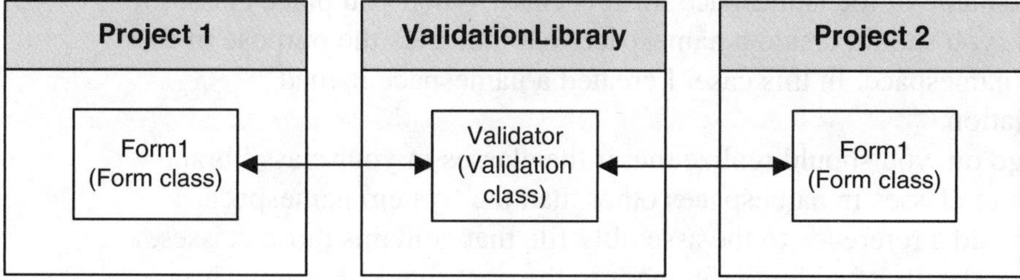

Description

- *Class libraries* provide a central location for storing classes that are used by two or more applications.
- When you store a class in a class library, you don't have to include the class in each application that uses it. Instead, you include a reference to the class library in those applications.
- When you modify a class in a class library, the changes are immediately available to all applications that use the library.
- To create a class library, you develop a class library project. Then, when you build the project, Visual Studio creates a *DLL file* for the class library. It's this *DLL* that you refer to from any application that needs to use the class library.

Figure 16-6 How class libraries work

How to create a class library project

To create a class library project, you use the Class Library template that's available from the New Project dialog box. After you complete this dialog box, Visual Studio creates a class library project that consists of a single class named Class1. Then, you can enter the code for this class and create additional classes using the techniques you've already learned. Or, if the classes you want to place in the library already exist in other projects, you can delete the Class1.cs file and use the Project→Add Existing Item command to copy the classes into the class library project.

Figure 16-7 shows a class library project named ValidationLibrary that includes a class named Validator. This is the same Validator class that was presented in chapter 12. In this case, though, the class is stored in a class library project instead of in the Windows project that uses it.

Notice the name of the namespace for this class. When you place classes in a class library, you should create a namespace that indicates the purpose of the classes in the namespace. In this case, I created a namespace named Murach.Validation.

Before I go on, you should realize that if the classes in your class library require access to classes in namespaces other than the System namespace, you'll need to add a reference to the assembly file that contains those classes. You'll learn the details of adding references in the next figure. For now, just realize that the Validator class uses the MessageBox class in the System.Windows.Forms namespace. Because of that, a reference to this namespace was added to the ValidationLibrary class library.

When you're done designing a class library, you build it to create an assembly. The assembly for a class library is a *DLL file*, or just *DLL*. This is a file with the *dll* extension that contains the executable code for the class library. This file is stored in the Bin\Debug folder beneath the project folder for the project. Then, you can include a reference to this file in other projects as described in the next topic.

As you're developing a class library, it's often useful to create the class library as a project in a solution that also has a Windows form project. That way, you can use the Windows form project to test the class library. To add a new class library project to an existing solution, right-click the solution in the Solution Explorer, then choose Add→New Project. You can also add an existing class library project to a solution by choosing Add→Existing Project.

A class library project

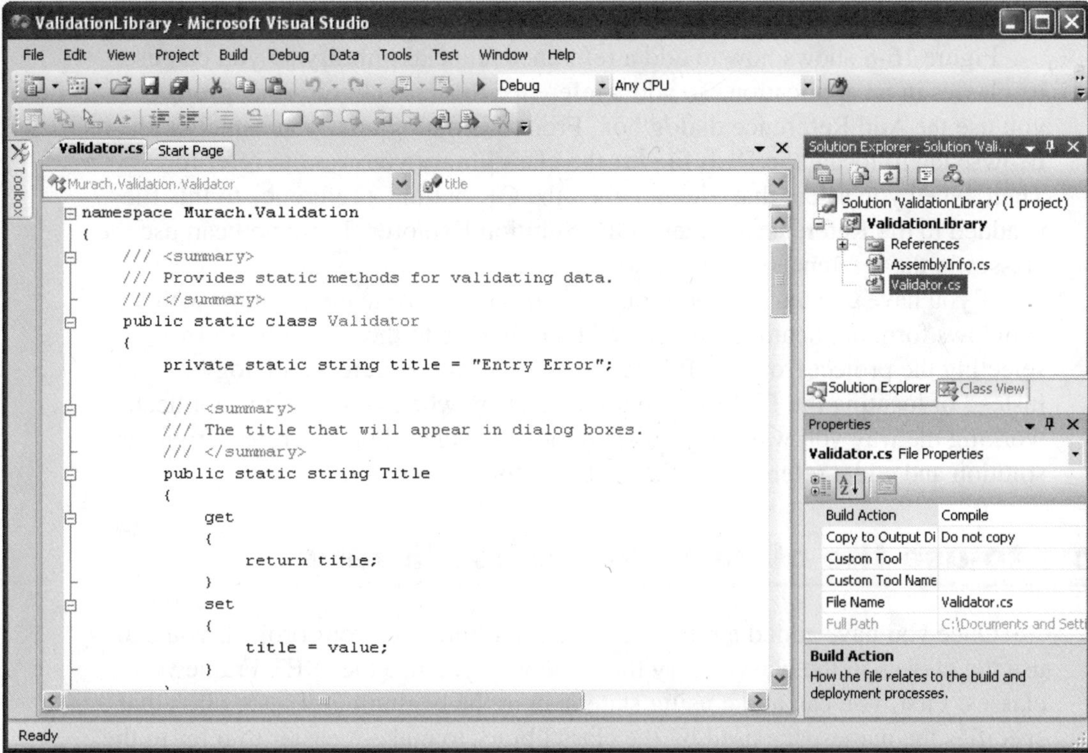
ValidationLibrary - Microsoft Visual Studio
File Edit View Project Build Debug Data Tools Test Window Help
Debug
Any CPU
Validator.cs
Start Page
Murach.Validation.Validator
title
namespace Murach.Validation
{
/// <summary>
/// Provides static methods for validating data.
/// </summary>
public static class Validator
{
private static string title = "Entry Error";
/// <summary>
/// The title that will appear in dialog boxes.
/// </summary>
public static string Title
{
get
{
return title;
}
set
{
title = value;
}
Solution Explorer - Solution 'Vali...
Solution 'ValidationLibrary' (1 project)
ValidationLibrary
References
AssemblyInfo.cs
Validator.cs
Solution Explorer
Class View
Properties
Validator.cs File Properties
Build Action
Compile
Copy to Output Di
Do not copy
Custom Tool
Custom Tool Name
File Name
Validator.cs
Full Path
C:\Documents and Setti
Build Action
How the file relates to the build and deployment processes.
Ready

Description

- To create a class library project, display the New Project dialog box. Then, select the Class Library template and enter a name and location for the project.
- By default, a class library project includes a single class named Class1. You can modify this class any way you want or delete it from the project. You can also add new classes using the Project→Add Class command or add classes from another project using the Project→Add Existing Item command.
- You should create a namespace for your class library that indicates the purpose of the classes contained in the library. In this example, the namespace is Murach.Validation.
- To compile a class library project, select the Build→Build Solution command. Then, the class library is compiled into a DLL file that's stored in the Bin\Debug folder for the project.

Note

- The Validator class shown above requires the System.Windows.Forms namespace so it can use the MessageBox class to display error messages. Because class libraries don't have access to this namespace by default, a reference to this namespace has been added to the project. See figure 16-8 for information on how to add a reference to a project.

How to add a reference to a class library

Figure 16-8 shows how to add a reference to a class library so you can use its classes in an application. To add a reference to a class library in a project, you use the Add Reference dialog box. From this dialog box, you can click the Browse tab to locate the DLL file for the class library you want to refer to. Then, when you select that file and click the OK button, a reference to this file is added to the References folder in the Solution Explorer. Then, you can use the classes in the referenced class library.

If you have created a class library as a project in the same solution with a Windows form application, you can add a reference to the class library by selecting the project from the Projects tab of the Add Reference dialog box instead of locating the DLL for the project. Then, when you have the application working the way you want it, you can remove the class library project from the solution and add a reference to the DLL file for this project.

How to use the classes in a class library

Once you have added a reference to a class library to your project, you can use the classes in the class library the same way you use the .NET Framework classes. First, you can add a using statement at the beginning of a C# class that specifies the namespace used by the class library to make it easier to refer to the classes it contains. The code example in figure 16-8, for example, shows a using statement for the Murach.Validation namespace.

After you add the using statement, you can use the classes in the library as if they were part of the same project. A complication arises, however, if the class you want to refer to in the class library has the same name as a class in another namespace in the project or has the same name as the namespace that contains the project (which is usually the same as the project name). In that case, you have to qualify the name of the class so C# knows where to look for it.

A project that includes a reference to a class library

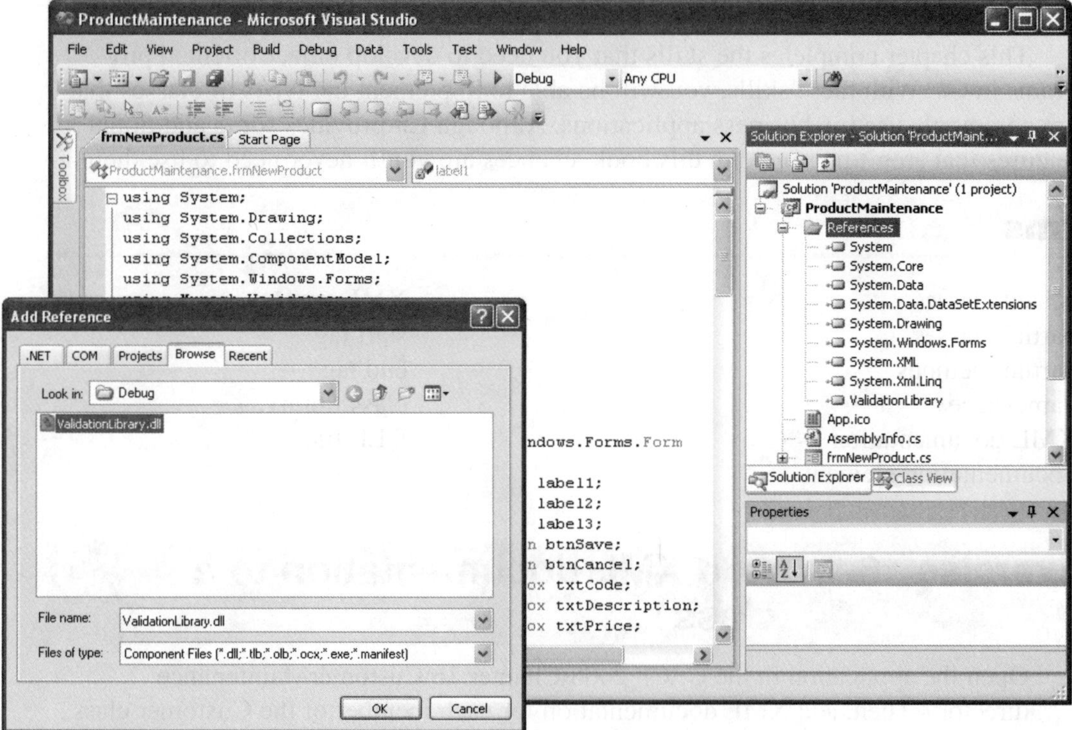

A using statement that simplifies access to the validation class library

```
using Murach.Validation;
```

How to use a class library

- Add a reference to the class library to your project by right-clicking the References folder in the Solution Explorer and selecting the Add Reference command. In the Add Reference dialog box, click the Browse tab, locate the DLL for the class library, select it, and select the OK button.
- If the class library project is included in the same solution as the client project, that project will appear in the list at the top of the Projects tab. Then, you can add a reference for the class library by double-clicking the project name.
- Once you have created a reference to the class library, you can include a using statement for the class library's namespace in any class that uses it. You can then use the classes in the class library without qualification. Alternatively, you can qualify the class names with the namespace name you assigned to the library.

Figure 16-8 How to use a class library

Perspective

This chapter completes the skills that you need to develop object-oriented programs in C#. With these skills, you will be able to implement the types of classes that are commonly used in business applications. Although C# provides some additional features that aren't presented in this book, chances are you'll never need to use them.

Terms

nested classes
partial classes
partial methods
namespace
XML documentation
documentation element
XML tag
start tag
end tag
class library
DLL file

Exercise 16-1 Add XML documentation to a class

1. Open the application in the C:\C# 2008\Chapter 16\CustomerMaintenance directory. Then, add XML documentation for each member of the Customer class.
2. Open the Add Customer form, and activate IntelliSense for each constructor, property, and method of the Customer class. Note how Visual Studio automatically displays the XML documentation in the screen tip.
3. Continue experimenting until you're comfortable with how XML documentation works. Then, close the solution.

Exercise 16-2 Create and use a class library

In this exercise, you'll create a class library that contains the Validator class. Then, you'll use that class library with the CustomerMaintenance application.

1. Create a new Class Library project named ValidationLib. Then, delete the empty Class1.cs file, and add the Validator.cs file from the CustomerMaintenance project that you worked on in the previous exercise.
2. Change the namespace in the Validator class to Murach.Validation, and add a reference to the System.Windows.Forms.dll assembly. Then, use the Build→Build Solution command to build the class library, and close the solution.
3. Open the application that you used in the previous exercise, delete the Validator.cs file, and add a reference to the ValidationLib assembly you created in step 2. Then, open the Add Customer form and add a using statement for the Murach.Validation namespace.
4. Run the project and test it to make sure the validation works correctly.

Section 4

Database programming

Most real-world applications store their data in databases. As a result, this section is devoted to teaching you the essentials of database programming in C#. When you complete the four chapters in this section, you should be able to develop substantial database applications. You should also have a solid foundation for learning other ADO.NET techniques on your own.

To start, chapter 17 introduces you to the concepts and terms you need to know when you develop database applications with ADO.NET. Then, chapters 18 and 19 show you how to use Visual Studio's data sources feature to develop database applications quickly and easily. Finally, chapter 20 shows you how to write your own ADO.NET code that uses commands to access the underlying database. When you're done with these chapters, you'll have the basic skills you need to develop database applications of your own.

Remember, though, that you don't have to read the sections in this book in sequence. So if you prefer, you can skip to section 5 before returning to this section. If you're new to programming, that makes sense because database programming is usually the most difficult aspect of application development. Then, when you have more coding experience, you can return to this section and learn the database programming skills that you're going to need.

17

An introduction to database programming

Before you can develop a database application, you need to be familiar with the concepts and terms that apply to database applications. In particular, you need to understand what a relational database is and how you work with it using SQL and ADO.NET. So that's what you'll learn in this chapter.

To illustrate these concepts and terms, this chapter presents examples that use the Microsoft *SQL Server 2005 Express* database server. This is a scaled-back version of Microsoft *SQL Server 2005* that you can run on your own PC. Because SQL Server Express is based on SQL Server 2005, though, the applications you develop with SQL Server Express will also run on SQL Server 2005. They'll also run on SQL Server 2008 or SQL Server 2008 Express when those products become available.

An introduction to client/server systems

In case you aren't familiar with client/server systems, this topic introduces you to their essential hardware and software components. Then, the rest of this chapter presents additional information on these components and on how you can use them in database applications.

The hardware components of a client/server system

Figure 17-1 presents the three hardware components of a *client/server system*: the clients, the network, and the server. The *clients* are usually the PCs that are already available on the desktops throughout a company. And the *network* is made up of the cabling, communication lines, network interface cards, hubs, routers, and other components that connect the clients and the server.

The *server*, commonly referred to as a *database server*, is a computer that has enough processor speed, internal memory (RAM), and disk storage to store the files and databases of the system and provide services to the clients of the system. This computer is usually a high-powered PC, but it can also be a midrange system like an IBM iSeries or a Unix system, or even a mainframe system. When a system consists of networks, midrange systems, and mainframe systems, often spread throughout the country or world, it is commonly referred to as an *enterprise system*.

To back up the files of a client/server system, a server usually has a tape drive or some other form of offline storage. It often has one or more printers or specialized devices that can be shared by the users of the system. And it can provide programs or services like email that can be accessed by all the users of the system. In larger networks, however, features such as backup, printing, and email are provided by separate servers. That way, the database server can be dedicated to the task of handling database requests.

In a simple client/server system, the clients and the server are part of a *local area network* (*LAN*). However, two or more LANs that reside at separate geographical locations can be connected as part of a larger network such as a *wide area network* (*WAN*). In addition, individual systems or networks can be connected over the Internet.

A simple client/server system

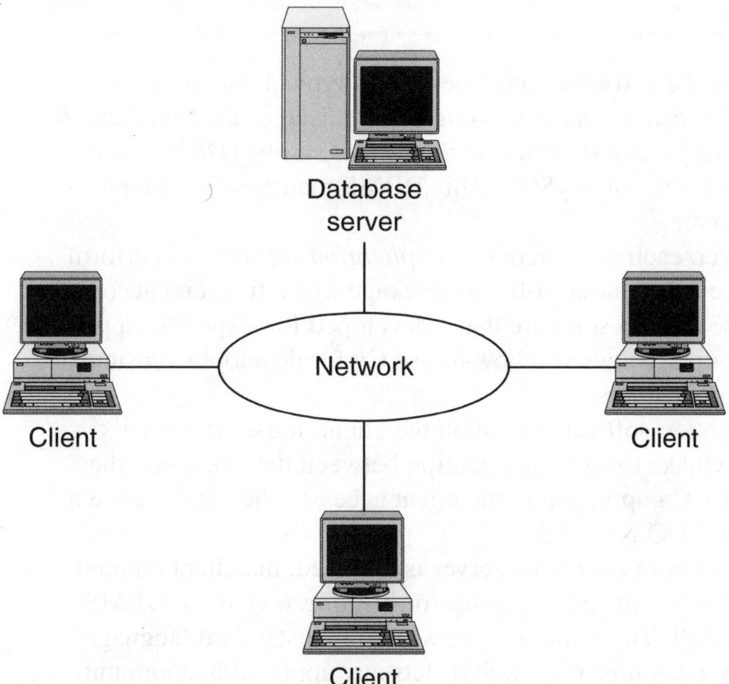

The three hardware components of a client/server system

- The *clients* are the PCs, Macintoshes, or workstations of the system.
- The *server* is a computer that stores the files and databases of the system and provides services to the clients. When it stores databases, it's often referred to as a *database server*.
- The *network* consists of the cabling, communication lines, and other components that connect the clients and the servers of the system.

Client/server system implementations

- In a simple *client/server system* like the one shown above, the server is typically a high-powered PC that communicates with the clients over a *local area network* (*LAN*).
- The server can also be a midrange system, like an IBM iSeries or a Unix system, or it can be a mainframe system. Then, special hardware and software components are required to make it possible for the clients to communicate with the midrange and mainframe systems.
- A client/server system can also consist of one or more PC-based systems, one or more midrange systems, and a mainframe system in dispersed geographical locations. This type of system is commonly referred to as an *enterprise system.*
- Individual systems and LANs can be connected and share data over larger private networks, such as a *wide area network* (*WAN*) or a public network like the Internet.

Figure 17-1 The hardware components of a client/server system

The software components of a client/server system

Figure 17-2 presents the software components of a typical client/server system. In addition to a *network operating system* that manages the functions of the network, the server requires a *database management system* (*DBMS*) like Microsoft SQL Server, Oracle, or MySQL. This DBMS manages the databases that are stored on the server.

In contrast to a server, each client requires *application software* to perform useful work. This can be a purchased software package like a financial accounting package, or it can be custom software that's developed for a specific application. This book, of course, shows you how to use C# for developing custom software for database applications.

Although the application software is run on the client, it uses data that's stored on the server. To make this communication between the client and the data source possible for a C# application, the client accesses the database via a *data access API* such as ADO.NET 3.5.

Once the software for both client and server is installed, the client communicates with the server by passing *SQL queries* (or just *queries*) to the DBMS through the data access API. These queries are written in a standard language called *Structured Query Language* (*SQL*). SQL lets any application communicate with any DBMS. After the client sends a query to the DBMS, the DBMS interprets the query and sends the results back to the client. (In conversation, SQL is pronounced as either *S-Q-L* or *sequel*.)

As you can see in this figure, the processing done by a client/server system is divided between the clients and the server. In this case, the DBMS on the server is processing requests made by the application running on the client. Theoretically, at least, this balances the workload between the clients and the server so the system works more efficiently. In contrast, in a file-handling system, the clients do all of the work because the server is used only to store the files that are used by the clients.

Client software, server software, and the SQL interface

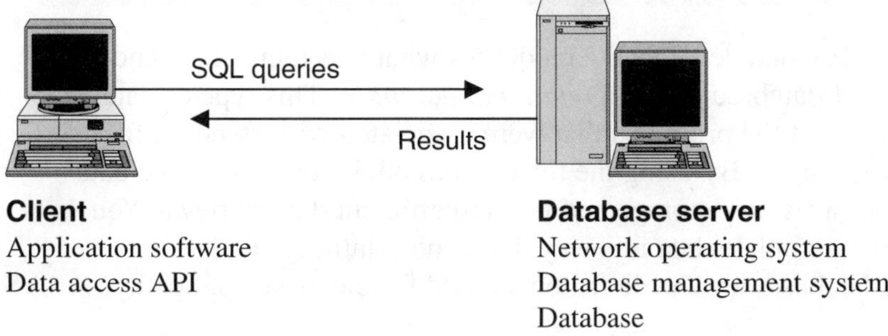

Client
Application software
Data access API

Database server
Network operating system
Database management system
Database

Server software

- To manage the network, the server runs a *network operating system* such as Windows Server 2003.
- To store and manage the databases of the client/server system, each server requires a *database management system* (*DBMS*) such as Microsoft SQL Server.
- The processing that's done by the DBMS is typically referred to as *back-end processing*, and the database server is referred to as the *back end*.

Client software

- The *application software* does the work that the user wants to do. This type of software can be purchased or developed.
- The *data access API* (*application programming interface*) provides the interface between the application and the DBMS. The newest data access API is ADO.NET 3.5, which is a part of Microsoft's .NET Framework.
- The processing that's done by the client software is typically referred to as *front-end processing*, and the client is typically referred to as the *front end*.

The SQL interface

- The application software communicates with the DBMS by sending *SQL queries* through the data access API. When the DBMS receives a query, it provides a service like returning the requested data (the *query results*) to the client.
- *SQL,* which stands for *Structured Query Language*, is the standard language for working with a relational database.

Client/server versus file-handling systems

- In a client/server system, the processing done by an application is typically divided between the client and the server.
- In a file-handling system, all of the processing is done on the clients. Although the clients may access data that's stored in files on the server, none of the processing is done by the server. As a result, a file-handling system isn't a client/server system.

Figure 17-2 The software components of a client/server system

An introduction to relational databases

In 1970, Dr. E. F. Codd developed a model for what was then a new and revolutionary type of database called a *relational database*. This type of database eliminated some of the problems that were associated with standard files and other database designs. By using the relational model, you can reduce data redundancy, which saves disk storage and leads to efficient data retrieval. You can also view and manipulate data in a way that is both intuitive and efficient. Today, relational databases are the de facto standard for database applications.

How a table is organized

The model for a relational database states that data is stored in one or more *tables*. It also states that each table can be viewed as a two-dimensional matrix consisting of *rows* and *columns*. This is illustrated by the relational table in figure 17-3. Each row in this table contains information about a single product.

In practice, the rows and columns of a relational database table are sometimes referred to by the more traditional terms, *records* and *fields*. In fact, some software packages use one set of terms, some use the other, and some use a combination.

If a table contains one or more columns that uniquely identify each row in the table, you can define these columns as the *primary key* of the table. For instance, the primary key of the Products table in this figure is the ProductCode column.

In this example, the primary key consists of a single column. However, a primary key can also consist of two or more columns, in which case it's called a *composite primary key*.

In addition to primary keys, some database management systems let you define additional keys that uniquely identify each row in a table, called *non-primary keys*. In SQL Server, these keys are also called *unique keys*, and they're implemented by defining *unique key constraints* (also known simply as *unique constraints*). The only difference between a unique key and a primary key is that a unique key can be null and a primary key can't.

Indexes provide an efficient way to access the rows in a table based on the values in one or more columns. Because applications typically access the rows in a table by referring to their key values, an index is automatically created for each key you define. However, you can define indexes for other columns as well. If, for example, you frequently need to sort the rows in the Products table by the Description column, you can set up an index for that column. Like a key, an index can include one or more columns.

The Products table in the MMABooks database

Primary key — Columns — Rows

ProductCode	Description	UnitPrice	OnHandQuantity
A2C#	Murach's ASP.NET 2.0 Web Programming with C# 2005	52.5000	4637
A2VB	Murach's ASP.NET 2.0 Web Programming with VB 2005	52.5000	3974
ADV2	Murach's ADO.NET 2.0 Database Programming VB 2005	52.5000	4538
CRFC	Murach's CICS Desk Reference	50.0000	1865
DB1R	DB2 for the COBOL Programmer, Part 1 (2nd Edition)	42.0000	4825
DB2R	DB2 for the COBOL Programmer, Part 2 (2nd Edition)	45.0000	621
JSE6	Murach's JAVA SE 6	52.5000	3455
MC#5	Murach's C# 2005	52.5000	5136
MCBL	Murach's Structured COBOL	62.5000	2386
MCCP	Murach's CICS for the COBOL Programmer	54.0000	2368
MJSP	Murach's JAVA Servlets and JSP	49.5000	4999
MVB5	Murach's Visual Basic 2005	52.5000	0
SQL5	Murach's SQL Server 2005	52.5000	2465
ZJLR	Murach's OS/390 and z/os JCL	62.5000	677

Concepts

- A *relational database* uses *tables* to store and manipulate data. Each table consists of one or more *records*, or *rows*, that contain the data for a single entry. Each row contains one or more *fields*, or *columns*, with each column representing a single item of data.
- Most tables contain a *primary key* that uniquely identifies each row in the table. The primary key often consists of a single column, but it can also consist of two or more columns. If a primary key uses two or more columns, it's called a *composite primary key*.
- In addition to primary keys, some database management systems let you define one or more *non-primary keys*. In SQL Server, these keys are called *unique keys*, and they're implemented using *unique key constraints*. Like a primary key, a non-primary key uniquely identifies each row in the table.
- A table can also be defined with one or more *indexes*. An index provides an efficient way to access data from a table based on the values in specific columns. An index is automatically created for a table's primary and non-primary keys.

Figure 17-3 How a table is organized

How the tables in a database are related

The tables in a relational database can be related to other tables by values in specific columns. The two tables shown in figure 17-4 illustrate this concept. Here, each row in an Invoices table is related to one or more rows in an InvoiceLineItems table. This is called a *one-to-many relationship*.

Typically, relationships exist between the primary key in one table and the *foreign key* in another table. The foreign key is simply one or more columns in a table that refer to a primary key in another table. In SQL Server, relationships can also exist between a unique key in one table and a foreign key in another table. For simplicity, though, I'll assume relationships are based on primary keys.

Although it isn't apparent in this figure, the InvoiceLineItems table has a composite primary key that consists of two columns: InvoiceID and ProductCode. As a result, any row in the InvoiceLineItems table can be uniquely identified by a combination of its invoice ID and product code. However, the InvoiceLineItems table can have more than one row for a given invoice ID and more than one row for a given product code.

One-to-many relationships are the most common type of database relationships. However, two tables can also have a one-to-one or many-to-many relationship. If a table has a *one-to-one relationship* with another table, the data in the two tables could be stored in a single table. Because of that, one-to-one relationships are used infrequently.

In contrast, a *many-to-many relationship* is usually implemented by using an intermediate table, called a *linking table*, that has a one-to-many relationship with the two tables in the many-to-many relationship. In other words, a many-to-many relationship can usually be broken down into two one-to-many relationships.

The relationship between the Invoices and InvoiceLineItems tables

Primary key

InvoiceID	CustomerID	InvoiceDate	ProductTotal	SalesTax	Shipping	InvoiceTotal
41	333	4/13/2007 12:0...	62.5000	4.6900	3.7500	70.9400
42	666	4/13/2007 12:0...	62.5000	4.6900	3.7500	70.9400
43	332	4/13/2007 12:0...	52.5000	3.9375	3.7500	60.1875
44	555	4/13/2007 12:0...	62.5000	4.6900	3.7500	70.9400
45	213	4/13/2007 12:0...	62.5000	4.6900	3.7500	70.9400
46	20	4/13/2007 12:0...	212.5000	15.9375	7.5000	235.9375
47	10	4/13/2007 12:0...	242.5000	18.1900	8.7500	269.4400

Foreign key

InvoiceID	ProductCode	UnitPrice	Quantity	ItemTotal
41	A2VB	62.5000	1	62.5000
42	A2VB	62.5000	1	62.5000
43	JSE6	52.5000	1	52.5000
44	A2VB	62.5000	1	62.5000
45	A2VB	62.5000	1	62.5000
46	A2VB	62.5000	1	62.5000
46	DB2R	45.0000	1	45.0000
46	MVB5	52.5000	1	52.5000
46	SQL5	52.5000	1	52.5000
47	A2VB	62.5000	1	62.5000
47	DB2R	45.0000	4	180.0000

Concepts

- The tables in a relational database are related to each other through their key columns. For example, the InvoiceID column is used to relate the Invoices and InvoiceLineItems tables above. The InvoiceID column in the InvoiceLineItems table is called a *foreign key* because it identifies a related row in the Invoices table.
- Usually, a foreign key corresponds to the primary key in the related table. In SQL Server, however, a foreign key can also correspond to a unique key in the related table.
- When two tables are related via a foreign key, the table with the foreign key is referred to as the *foreign key table* and the table with the primary key is referred to as the *primary key table.*
- The relationships between the tables in a database correspond to the relationships between the entities they represent. The most common type of relationship is a *one-to-many relationship* as illustrated by the Invoices and InvoiceLineItems table. A table can also have a *one-to-one relationship* or a *many-to-many relationship* with another table.

Figure 17-4 How the tables in a database are related

How the columns in a table are defined

When you define a column in a table, you assign properties to it as indicated by the design of the Products table in figure 17-5. The two most important properties for a column are Column Name, which provides an identifying name for the column, and Data Type, which specifies the type of information that can be stored in the column. With SQL Server, you can choose from *system data types* like the ones in this figure, and you can define your own data types that are based on the system data types. As you define each column in a table, you generally try to assign the data type that will minimize the use of disk storage because that will improve the performance of the queries later.

In addition to a data type, you must identify whether the column can be *null*. Null represents a value that's unknown, unavailable, or not applicable. It isn't the same as an empty string or a zero numeric value. Columns that allow nulls often require additional programming, so many database designers avoid columns that allow nulls unless they're absolutely necessary.

You can also assign a *default value* to each column. Then, that value is assigned to the column if another value isn't provided. If a column doesn't allow nulls and doesn't have a default value, you must supply a value for the column when you add a new row to the table. Otherwise, an error will occur.

Each table can also contain a numeric column whose value is generated automatically by the DBMS. In SQL Server, a column like this is called an *identity column*. Identity columns are often used as the primary key for a table.

A *check constraint* defines the acceptable values for a column. For example, you can define a check constraint for the Products table in this figure to make sure that the UnitPrice column is greater than zero. A check constraint like this can be defined at the column level because it refers only to the column it constrains. If the check constraint for a column needs to refer to other columns in the table, however, it can be defined at the table level.

After you define the constraints for a database, they're managed by the DBMS. If, for example, a user tries to add a row with data that violates a constraint, the DBMS sends an appropriate error code back to the application without adding the row to the database. The application can then respond to the error code.

An alternative to constraints is to validate the data that is going to be added to a database before the program tries to add it. That way, the constraints shouldn't be needed and the program should run more efficiently. In many cases, both data validation and constraints are used. That way, the programs run more efficiently if the data validation routines work, but the constraints are there in case the data validation routines don't work or aren't coded.

The Server Explorer design view window for the Products table

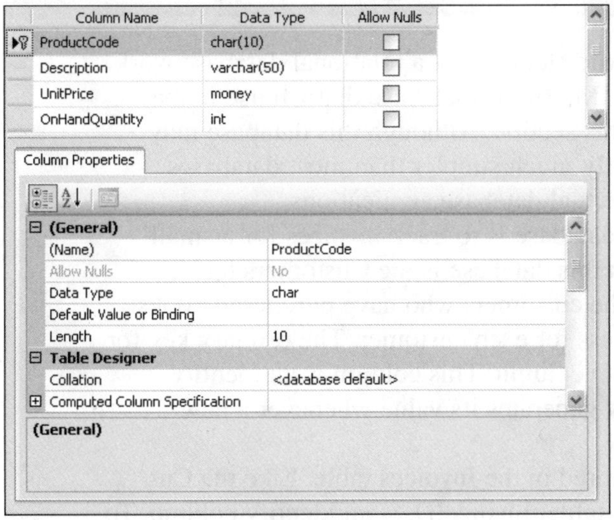

Column Name	Data Type	Allow Nulls
ProductCode	char(10)	☐
Description	varchar(50)	☐
UnitPrice	money	☐
OnHandQuantity	int	☐

Column Properties

(General)	
(Name)	ProductCode
Allow Nulls	No
Data Type	char
Default Value or Binding	
Length	10
Table Designer	
Collation	<database default>
Computed Column Specification	

(General)

Common SQL Server data types

Type	Description
bit	A value of 1 or 0 that represents a true or false value.
char, varchar, text	Any combination of letters, symbols, and numbers.
datetime, smalldatetime	Alphanumeric data that represents a date and time. Various formats are acceptable.
decimal, numeric	Numeric data that is accurate to the least significant digit. The data can contain an integer and a fractional portion.
float, real	Floating-point values that contain an approximation of a decimal value.
bigint, int, smallint, tinyint	Numeric data that contains only an integer portion.
money, smallmoney	Monetary values that are accurate to four decimal places.

Description

- The *data type* that's assigned to a column determines the type of information that can be stored in the column. Depending on the data type, the column definition can also include its length, precision, and scale.
- Each column definition also indicates whether or not the column can contain *null values*. A null value indicates that the value of the column is not known.
- A column can be defined with a *default value*. Then, that value is used for the column if another value isn't provided when a row is added to the table.
- A column can also be defined as an *identity column*. An identity column is a numeric column whose value is generated automatically when a row is added to the table.
- To restrict the values that a column can hold, you define *check constraints*. Check constraints can be defined at either the column level or the table level.

Figure 17-5 How the columns in a table are defined

The design of the MMABooks database

Now that you've seen how the basic elements of a relational database work, figure 17-6 shows the design of the MMABooks database that I'll use in the programming examples throughout this section. Although this database may seem complicated, its design is actually much simpler than most databases you'll encounter when you work on actual database applications.

The purpose of the MMABooks database is to track invoices for a small book publisher. The top-level table in this database is the Customers table, which contains one row for each of the customers who have purchased books. This table records the name and address for each customer. The primary key for the Customers table is the CustomerID column. This column is an identity column, so SQL Server automatically generates its value whenever a new customer is created.

Information for each invoice is stored in the Invoices table. Like the Customers table, the primary key for this table, InvoiceID, is an identity column. To relate each invoice to a customer, the Invoices table includes a CustomerID column. A *foreign key constraint* is used to enforce this relationship. That way, an invoice can't be added for a customer that doesn't exist. The foreign key constraint also causes deletes to be cascaded from the Customers table to the Invoices table.

The InvoiceLineItems table contains the line item details for each invoice. The primary key for this table is a combination of the InvoiceID and ProductCode columns. The InvoiceID column relates each line item to an invoice, and a foreign key constraint that cascades updates and deletes from the Invoices table is defined to enforce this relationship. The ProductCode column relates each line item to a product in the Products table and gives each line item a unique primary key value.

The Products table records information about the company's products. The primary key for this table is the ProductCode column, which can contain a 10-character code. In addition to the product code, each product row contains a description of the product, the unit price, and the number of units currently on hand.

The Customers table is also related to the States table through its State column. The States table contains the state name and the 2-letter state code for each state. Its primary key is the StateCode column.

The final table in the MMABooks database, OrderOptions, contains information that's used to calculate the sales tax and shipping charges that are applied to each invoice. Because this table consists of a single row, it doesn't have a primary key.

The tables that make up the MMABooks database

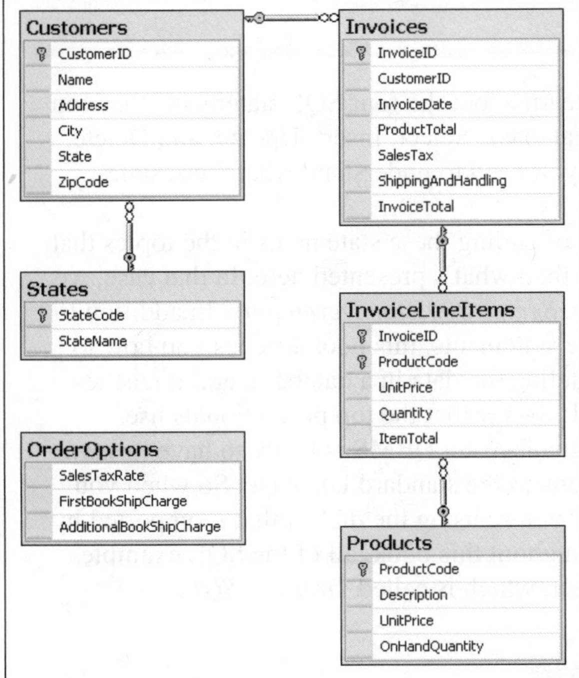

Description

- The Customers table contains a row for each customer. Its primary key is CustomerID, an identity column that's generated automatically when a new customer is created. State is a foreign key that relates each customer to a row in the States table.
- The Invoices table contains a row for each invoice. Its primary key is InvoiceID, an identity column that's generated automatically when a new invoice is created. CustomerID is a foreign key that relates each invoice to a customer.
- The InvoiceLineItems table contains one row for each line item of each invoice. Its primary key is a combination of InvoiceID and ProductCode. InvoiceID is a foreign key that relates each line item to an invoice, and ProductCode is a foreign key that relates each line item to a product.
- The Products table contains a row for each product. Its primary key is ProductCode, a 10-character code that identifies each product.
- The States table contains a row for each state. Its primary key is StateCode.
- The OrderOptions table contains a single row that stores the sales tax and shipping charges used by the application.
- The relationships between the tables in this diagram appear as links, where the endpoints indicate the type of relationship. A key indicates the "one" side of a relationship, and the infinity symbol (∞) indicates the "many" side.

Figure 17-6 The design of the MMABooks database

How to use SQL to work with a relational database

In the topics that follow, you'll learn about the four SQL statements that you can use to manipulate the data in a database: Select, Insert, Update, and Delete. To master the material in this book, you need to understand what these statements do and how they're coded.

Although you'll learn the basics of coding these statements in the topics that follow, you may want to know more than what's presented here. In that case, we recommend our book, *Murach's SQL Server 2005 for Developers*. In addition to the Select, Insert, Update, and Delete statements, this book teaches you how to code the statements that you use to define the data in a database, and it teaches you how to use other features of SQL Server that the top professionals use.

Although SQL is a standard language, each DBMS is likely to have its own *SQL dialect*, which includes extensions to the standard language. So when you use SQL, you need to make sure that you're using the dialect that's supported by your DBMS. In this chapter and throughout this book, all of the SQL examples are for Microsoft SQL Server's dialect, which is called *Transact-SQL*.

How to query a single table

Figure 17-7 shows how to use a Select statement to query a single table in a database. In the syntax summary at the top of this figure, you can see that the Select clause names the columns to be retrieved and the From clause names the table that contains the columns. You can also code a Where clause that gives criteria for the rows to be selected. And you can code an Order By clause that names one or more columns that the results should be sorted by and indicates whether each column should be sorted in ascending or descending sequence.

If you study the Select statement below the syntax summary, you can see how this works. Here, the Select statement retrieves two columns from the Customers table for all customers who live in the state of Washington. It sorts the returned rows by the Name column.

This figure also shows the *result table*, or *result set*, that's returned by the Select statement. A result set is a logical table that's created temporarily within the database. When an application requests data from a database, it receives a result set.

Simplified syntax of the Select statement

```
 Select column-1 [, column-2]...
 From table-1
[Where selection-criteria]
[Order By column-1 [Asc|Desc] [, column-2 [Asc|Desc]]...]
```

A Select statement that retrieves and sorts selected columns and rows from the Customers table

```
Select Name, City
From Customers
Where State = 'WA'
Order By Name
```

The result set defined by the Select statement

Name	City
Allen, Craig	Pullman
Antalocy, S.	Seattle
Cassara, Glenn	Van
Giraka, Eric	Seatle
Hester, Maurice	Kennewickm
Howell, Kim	Renton
Mcmillen, G	Kirkland
Millard, Dwayne	Seattle
Oneil, Ri	Olympia
Seaver, Glenda	Mountlake Terrace
Smith, Lloyd	Pullman
Sundaram, Kelly	Oregon

Concepts

- The result of a Select statement is a *result table*, or *result set*, like the one shown above. A result set is a logical set of rows that consists of all of the columns and rows requested by the Select statement.
- The Select clause lists the columns to be included in the result set. This list can include *calculated columns* that are calculated from other columns.
- The From clause names the table the data will be retrieved from.
- The Where clause provides a condition that specifies which rows should be retrieved. To retrieve all rows from a table, omit the Where clause.
- The Order By clause lists the columns that the results are sorted by and indicates whether each column is sorted in ascending or descending sequence.
- To select all of the columns in a table, you can code an asterisk (*) in place of the column names. For example, this statement will select all of the columns from the Customers table:

```
Select * From Customers
```

Figure 17-7 How to query a single table

How to join data from two or more tables

Figure 17-8 presents the syntax of the Select statement for retrieving data from two tables. This type of operation is called a *join* because the data from the two tables is joined together into a single result set. For example, the Select statement in this figure joins data from the InvoiceLineItems and Products tables into a single result set.

An *inner join* is the most common type of join. When you use an inner join, rows from the two tables in the join are included in the result set only if their related columns match. These matching columns are specified in the From clause of the Select statement. In the Select statement in this figure, for example, rows from the InvoiceLineItems and Products tables are included only if the value of the ProductCode column in the Products table matches the value of the ProductCode column in one or more rows in the InvoiceLineItems table.

Notice that each column in the Select clause is qualified to indicate which table the column is to be retrieved from. For example, the InvoiceID, ProductCode, UnitPrice, and Quantity columns are retrieved from the InvoiceLineItems table, but the Description column comes from the Products table. Qualification is only required for columns that exist in both tables. In this case, only the ProductCode column requires qualification because both the InvoiceLineItems and the Products tables have a column named ProductCode. However, I recommend that you qualify all of the columns just to make it clear which table each column is being retrieved from.

Although this figure shows how to join data from two tables, you should know that you can extend this syntax to join data from additional tables. If, for example, you want to include data from the Invoices table along with the InvoiceLineItems and Products data, you could code a From clause like this:

```
From Invoices
    Inner Join InvoiceLineItems
        On Invoices.InvoiceID = InvoiceLineItems.InvoiceID
    Inner Join Products
        On InvoiceLineItems.ProductCode =
           Products.ProductCode
```

Then, in the column list of the Select statement, you can include any of the columns in the Invoices, InvoiceLineItems, and Products tables.

The syntax of the Select statement for joining two tables

```
Select column-list
From table-1
    [Inner] Join table-2
    On table-1.column-1 {=|<|>|<=|>=|<>} table-2.column-2
[Where selection-criteria]
[Order By column-list]
```

A Select statement that joins data from the InvoiceLineItems and Products tables

```
Select InvoiceLineItems.InvoiceID, InvoiceLineItems.ProductCode,
       Products.Description, InvoiceLineItems.UnitPrice,
       InvoiceLineItems.Quantity
From InvoiceLineItems
    Inner Join Products
        On Products.ProductCode = InvoiceLineItems.ProductCode
Where InvoiceID = 46
```

The result set defined by the Select statement

InvoiceID	ProductCode	Description	UnitPrice	Quantity
46	A2VB	Murach's ASP.N...	62.5000	1
46	DB2R	DB2 for the COB...	45.0000	1
46	MVB5	Murach's Visual ...	52.5000	1
46	SQL5	Murach's SQL Se...	52.5000	1

Concepts

- A *join* lets you combine data from two or more tables into a single result set.
- The most common type of join is an *inner join*. This type of join returns rows from both tables only if their related columns match.

Figure 17-8 How to join data from two or more tables

How to add, update, and delete data in a table

Figure 17-9 presents the basic syntax of the SQL Insert, Update, and Delete statements. You use these statements to add new rows to a table, to update the data in existing rows, and to delete existing rows.

To add a single row to a table, you specify the name of the table you want to add the row to, the names of the columns you're supplying data for, and the values for those columns. The statement in this figure, for example, adds a row to the Products table. If you're going to supply values for all the columns in a table, you can omit the column names. If you do that, though, you must be sure to specify the values in the same order as the columns appear in the table. To avoid errors, I recommend you always code the column list.

Note that if a table includes an identity column, you shouldn't provide a value for that column in an Insert statement. Instead, SQL Server will generate a value for the identity column when it inserts the row.

Also note that you can use single quotes to identify strings. For example, the string for the ProductCode column is enclosed in single quotes. However, if a string value contains a single quote, you can code two single quotes. For example, the string for the Description column uses two single quotes to identify the single quote in *Murach's*.

To change the values of one or more columns in a table, you use the Update statement. On this statement, you specify the name of the table you want to update, expressions that indicate the columns you want to change and how you want to change them, and a condition that identifies the rows you want to change. In the example in this figure, the Update statement changes the UnitPrice column for the product identified by product code MCCP to 54.00.

To delete rows from a table, you use the Delete statement. On this statement, you specify the table you want to delete rows from and a condition that indicates the rows you want to delete. The Delete statement in this figure deletes all the rows from the Customers table for customer 558.

How to add a single row

The syntax of the Insert statement for adding a single row

```
Insert [Into] table-name [(column-list)]
    Values (value-list)
```

A statement that adds a single row to the Products table

```
Insert Into Products (ProductCode, Description, UnitPrice, OnHandQuantity)
    Values ('CS08', 'Murach''s C# 2008', 54.50, 3000)
```

How to update rows

The syntax of the Update statement

```
Update table-name
    Set expression-1 [, expression-2]...
    [Where selection-criteria]
```

A statement that updates the UnitPrice column for a specified product

```
Update Products
    Set UnitPrice = 54.00
    Where ProductCode = 'MCCP'
```

How to delete rows

The syntax of the Delete statement

```
Delete [From] table-name
    [Where selection-criteria]
```

A statement that deletes a specified customer

```
Delete From Customers
    Where CustomerID = 558
```

Description

- You use the Insert, Update, and Delete statements to maintain the data in a database table.
- The Insert statement can be used to add one or more rows to a table. Although the syntax shown above is for adding just one row, there is another syntax for adding more than one row.
- The Update and Delete statements can be used to update or delete one or more rows in a table using the syntax shown above.

Figure 17-9 How to add, update, and delete data in a table

An introduction to ADO.NET

ADO.NET (*ActiveX Data Objects .NET*) is the primary data access API for the .NET Framework. It provides the classes that you use as you develop database applications with C# as well as other .NET languages. These classes can be divided into two categories: the .NET data providers, which provide the classes that you use to access the data in a database, and datasets, which provide the classes that you use to store and work with data in your applications.

The .NET data providers

A *.NET data provider* is a set of classes that enable you to access data that's managed by a particular database server. All .NET data providers must include core classes for creating the four types of objects listed in the first table in figure 17-10. You'll learn more about how these objects work in the topics that follow.

The second table in this figure lists the four data providers that come with the .NET Framework. The SQL Server data provider is designed to provide efficient access to a Microsoft SQL Server database. The OLE DB data provider is a generic data provider that can access any database that supports the industry standard OLE DB interface. Although you can use the OLE DB data provider to access a SQL Server database, you shouldn't do that unless you plan on migrating the data to another database since the SQL Server data provider is optimized for accessing SQL Server data. The ODBC provider lets you access any database that can work with ODBC, another industry standard database interface. The Oracle provider lets you access data stored in Oracle databases.

In addition to the .NET data providers, you should also know that several database vendors have developed .NET data providers that are optimized for use with their databases. For example, .NET data providers are available for the popular MySQL database and for SQL Anywhere. Before you develop an application using the OLE DB or ODBC providers, then, you should check with your database vendor to see if a specialized .NET data provider is available.

The third table in this figure lists the names of the classes you use to create objects using the SQL Server, OLE DB, ODBC, or Oracle providers. Notice that these classes use prefixes ("Sql," "OleDb," "Odbc," and "Oracle") to indicate which provider each class belongs to.

When you develop a C# application that uses ADO.NET, you'll want to add a using statement for the namespace that contains the data provider classes at the beginning of each source file that uses those classes. That way, you won't have to qualify the references to these classes. These namespaces are listed in the second table in this figure.

.NET data provider core objects

Object	Description
Connection	Establishes a connection to a database.
Command	Represents an individual SQL statement that can be executed against the database.
Data reader	Provides read-only, forward-only access to the data in a database.
Data adapter	Provides the link between the command and connection objects and a dataset object.

Data providers included with the .NET Framework

Provider	Namespace	Description
SQL Server	System.Data.SqlClient	Lets you access SQL Server databases.
OLE DB	System.Data.OleDb	Lets you access any database that supports OLE DB.
ODBC	System.Data.Odbc	Lets you access any database that supports ODBC.
Oracle	System.Data.OracleClient	Lets you access Oracle databases.

Class names for the data providers

Object	SQL Server	OLE DB	ODBC	Oracle
Connection	SqlConnection	OleDbConnection	OdbcConnection	OracleConnection
Command	SqlCommand	OleDbCommand	OdbcCommand	OracleCommand
Data reader	SqlDataReader	OleDbDataReader	OdbcDataReader	OracleDataReader
Data adapter	SqlDataAdapter	OleDbDataAdapter	OdbcDataAdapter	OracleDataAdapter

A using statement for the SQL Server data provider namespace

```
using System.Data.SqlClient;
```

Description

- The *.NET data providers* provide the ADO.NET classes that are responsible for working directly with a database. In addition to the core classes shown above, classes are provided for other functions such as passing parameters to commands or working with transactions.
- To use a .NET data provider in a program, you should add a using statement for the appropriate namespace at the beginning of the source file. Otherwise, you'll have to qualify each class you refer to with the SqlClient, OleDb, Odbc, or OracleClient namespace since these namespaces aren't included as references by default.
- The ODBC and Oracle data providers became available with version 1.1 of the .NET Framework, which was included with Visual Studio .NET 2003.
- Other .NET data providers are available to provide efficient access to non-Microsoft databases, such as MySQL and SQL Anywhere.

Figure 17-10 The .NET data providers

How the basic ADO.NET components work

Figure 17-11 shows the primary ADO.NET components you use to work with data in a Windows application. To start, the data used by an application is stored in a *dataset* that contains one or more *data tables*. To retrieve data from the database and load it into a data table, you use a *data adapter*.

The main function of the data adapter is to manage the flow of data between a dataset and a database. To do that, it uses *commands* that define the SQL statements to be issued. The command for retrieving data, for example, typically defines a Select statement. Then, the command connects to the database using a *connection* and passes the Select statement to the database. After the Select statement is executed, the result set it produces is sent back to the data adapter, which stores the results in the data table.

To update the data in a database, the data adapter determines which rows in the data table have been inserted, updated, or deleted. Then, it uses commands that define Insert, Update, and Delete statements for the data table to update the associated rows in the database. Like the command that retrieves data from the database, the commands that update the database use a connection to connect to the database and perform the requested operation.

Although it's not apparent in this figure, the data in a dataset is independent of the database that the data was retrieved from. In fact, the connection to the database is typically closed after the data is retrieved from the database. Then, the connection is opened again when it's needed. Because of that, the application must work with the copy of the data that's stored in the dataset. The architecture that's used to implement this type of data processing is referred to as the *disconnected data architecture*.

Although this approach is more complicated than a connected architecture, it has several advantages. One advantage is that using the disconnected architecture can improve system performance due to the use of fewer system resources for maintaining connections. Another advantage is that it makes ADO.NET compatible with ASP.NET web applications, which are inherently disconnected.

Basic ADO.NET components

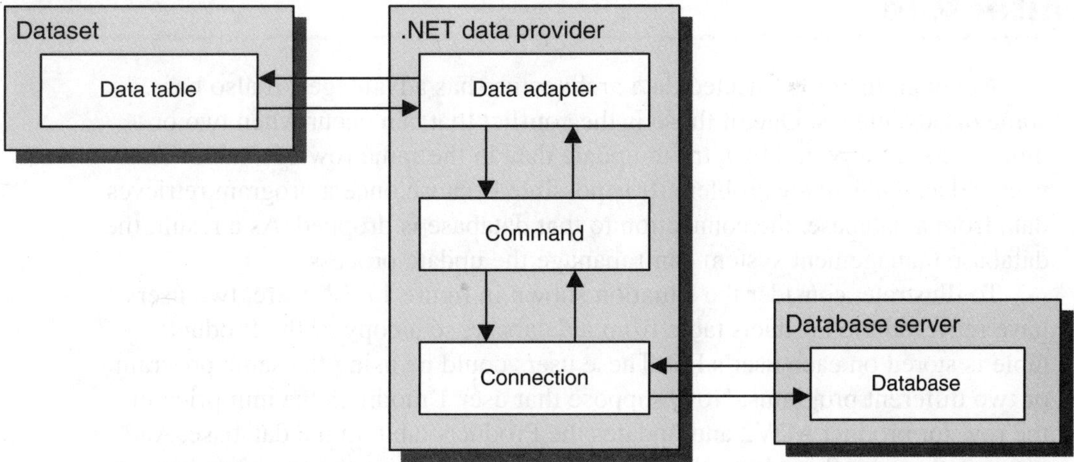

Description

- When you use the .NET data provider objects to retrieve data from a database, you can store the data in an object called a *dataset*.
- A dataset contains one or more *data tables* that store the data from the database. Then, the application can retrieve and work with the data in the data tables, and it can insert, update, and delete rows in the data tables.
- To retrieve data from a database and store it in a data table, a *data adapter* object issues a Select statement that's stored in a *command* object. Next, the command object uses a *connection* object to connect to the database and retrieve the data. Then, the data is passed back to the data adapter, which stores the data in a table within the dataset.
- To update the data in a database based on the data in a data table, the data adapter object issues an Insert, Update, or Delete statement that's stored in a command object. Then, the command object uses a connection to connect to the database and update the data.
- The data provider remains connected to the database only long enough to retrieve or update the specified data. Then, it disconnects from the database and the application works with the data via the dataset object. This is referred to as a *disconnected data architecture*.
- The disconnected data architecture offers improved system performance due to the use of fewer system resources for maintaining connections.

Figure 17-11 How the basic ADO.NET components work

Concurrency and the disconnected data architecture

Although the disconnected data architecture has advantages, it also has some disadvantages. One of those is the conflict that can occur when two or more users retrieve and then try to update data in the same row of a table. This is called a *concurrency* problem. It is possible because once a program retrieves data from a database, the connection to that database is dropped. As a result, the database management system can't manage the update process.

To illustrate, consider the situation shown in figure 17-12. Here, two users have retrieved the Products table from a database, so a copy of the Products table is stored on each user's PC. These users could be using the same program or two different programs. Now, suppose that user 1 modifies the unit price in the row for product ADV2 and updates the Products table in the database. And suppose that user 2 modifies the description in the row for the same product, then tries to update the Products table in the database. What will happen? That depends on the *concurrency control* that's used by the programs.

When you use ADO.NET, you have two choices for concurrency control. By default, a program uses *optimistic concurrency*, which checks whether a row has been changed since it was retrieved. If it has, the update or deletion will be refused and a *concurrency exception* will be thrown. Then, the program should handle the error. For example, it could display an error message that tells the user that the row could not be updated and then retrieve the updated row so the user can make the change again.

In contrast, the "*last in wins*" technique works the way its name implies. Since no checking is done with this technique, the row that's updated by the last user overwrites any changes made to the row by a previous user. For the example above, the row updated by user 2 will overwrite changes made by user 1, which means that the description will be right but the unit price will be wrong. Since errors like this corrupt the data in a database, optimistic concurrency is used by most programs, which means that your programs have to handle the concurrency exceptions that are thrown.

If you know that concurrency will be a problem, you can use a couple of programming techniques to limit concurrency exceptions. If a program uses a dataset, one technique is to update the database frequently so other users can retrieve the current data. The program should also refresh its dataset frequently so it contains the recent changes made by other users.

Another way to avoid concurrency exceptions is to retrieve and work with just one row at a time. That way, it's less likely that two users will update the same row at the same time. In contrast, if two users retrieve the same table, they will of course retrieve the same rows. Then, if they both update the same row in the table, even though it may not be at the same time, a concurrency exception will occur when they try to update the database.

Of course, you will understand and appreciate this more as you learn how to develop your own database applications. As you develop them, though, keep in mind that most applications are multi-user applications. That's why you have to be aware of concurrency problems.

Two users who are working with copies of the same data

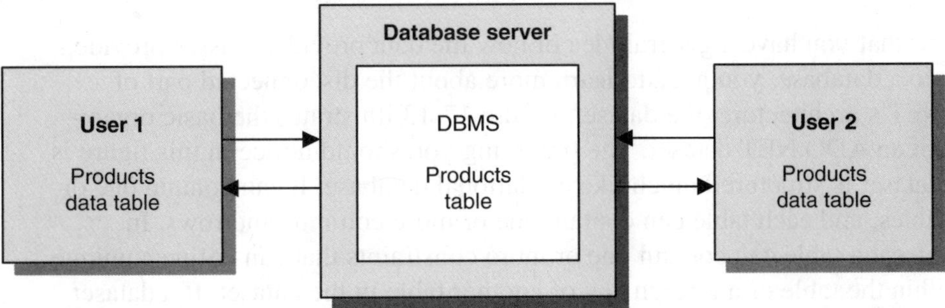

What happens when two users try to update the same row

- When two or more users retrieve the data in the same row of a database table at the same time, it is called *concurrency*. Because ADO.NET uses a disconnected data architecture, the database management system can't prevent this from happening.
- If two users try to update the same row in a database table at the same time, the second user's changes could overwrite the changes made by the first user. Whether or not that happens, though, depends on the *concurrency control* that the programs use.
- By default, ADO.NET uses *optimistic concurrency*. This means that the program checks to see whether the database row that's going to be updated or deleted has been changed since it was retrieved. If it has, a *concurrency exception* occurs and the update or deletion is refused. Then, the program should handle the exception.
- If optimistic concurrency isn't in effect, the program doesn't check to see whether a row has been changed before an update or deletion takes place. Instead, the operation proceeds without throwing an exception. This is referred to as "*last in wins*" because the last update overwrites any previous update. And this can lead to errors in the database.

How to avoid concurrency errors

- For many applications, concurrency errors rarely occur. As a result, optimistic concurrency is adequate because the users will rarely have to resubmit an update or deletion that is refused.
- If concurrency is likely to be a problem, a program that uses a dataset can be designed so it updates the database and refreshes the dataset frequently. That way, concurrency errors are less likely to occur.
- Another way to avoid concurrency errors is to design a program so it retrieves and updates just one row at a time. That way, there's less chance that two users will retrieve and update the same row at the same time.

Figure 17-12 Concurrency and the disconnected data architecture

How a dataset is organized

Now that you have a general idea of how the data provider classes provide access to a database, you need to learn more about the disconnected part of ADO.NET's architecture: the dataset. Figure 17-13 illustrates the basic organization of an ADO.NET dataset. The first thing you should notice in this figure is that a dataset is structured much like a relational database. It can contain one or more tables, and each table can contain one or more columns and rows. In addition, each table can contain one or more constraints that can define a unique key within the table or a foreign key of another table in the dataset. If a dataset contains two or more tables, the dataset can also define the relationships between those tables.

Although a dataset is structured much like a relational database, it's important to realize that each table in a dataset corresponds to the result set that's returned from a Select statement, not necessarily to an actual table in a database. For example, a Select statement may join data from several tables in a database to produce a single result set. In this case, the table in the dataset would represent data from each of the tables involved in the join.

You should also know that each group of objects in the diagram in this figure is stored in a collection. All of the columns in a table, for example, are stored in a collection of columns, and all of the rows are stored in a collection of rows.

The basic dataset object hierarchy

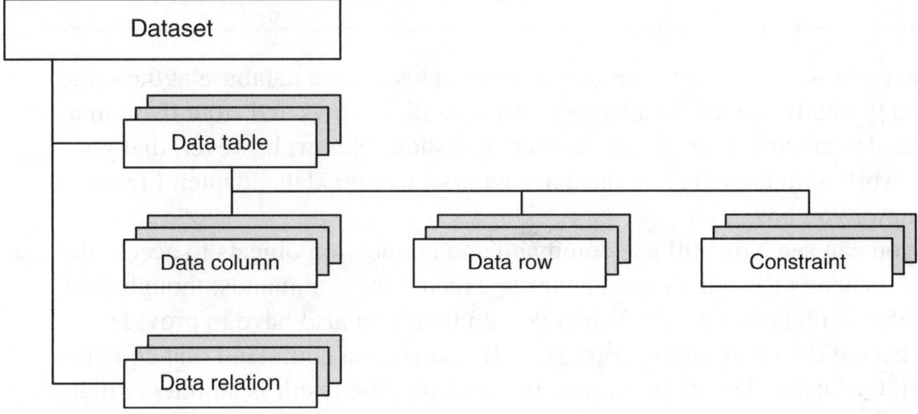

Description

- A dataset object consists of a hierarchy of one or more data table and data relation objects.
- A data table object consists of one or more *data column* objects and one or more *data row* objects. The data column objects define the data in each column of the table, including its name, data type, and so on, and the data row objects contain the data for each row in the table.
- A data table can also contain one or more *constraint* objects that are used to maintain the integrity of the data in the table. A unique key constraint ensures that the values in a column, such as the primary key column, are unique. And a foreign key constraint determines how the rows in one table are affected when corresponding rows in a related table are updated or deleted.
- The data relation objects define how the tables in the dataset are related. They are used to manage constraints and to simplify the navigation between related tables.
- All of the objects in a dataset are stored in collections. For example, the data table objects are stored in a data table collection, and the data row objects are stored in a data row collection. You can refer to these collections through properties of the containing objects.

Figure 17-13 How a dataset is organized

How to work with data without using a data adapter

When you want to work with two or more rows from a database at the same time, you typically use a data adapter to retrieve those rows and store them in a dataset as described earlier in this chapter. You should know, however, that you can also work with the data in a database without using a data adapter. Figure 17-14 shows you how.

As you can see, you still use command and connection objects to access the database. Instead of using a data adapter to execute the commands, though, you execute the commands directly. When you do that, you also have to provide code to handle the result of the command. If you issue a command that contains an Insert, Update, or Delete statement, for example, the result is an integer that indicates the number of rows that were affected by the operation. You can use that information to determine if the operation was successful.

If you execute a command that contains a Select statement, the result is a result set that contains the rows you requested. To read through the rows in the result set, you use a *data reader* object. Although a data reader provides an efficient way of reading the rows in a result set, you can't use it to modify those rows. In addition, it only lets you read rows in a forward direction. Once you read the next row, the previous row is unavailable. Because of that, you typically use a data reader to retrieve and work with a single database row at a time.

ADO.NET components for accessing a database directly

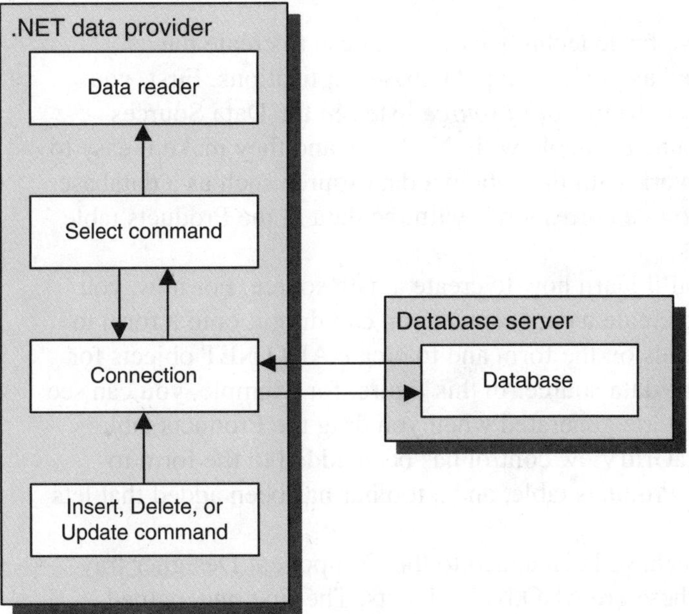

Description

- Instead of using a data adapter to execute commands to retrieve, insert, update, and delete data from a database, you can execute those commands directly.
- To retrieve data from a database, you execute a command object that contains a Select statement. Then, the command object uses a connection to connect to the database and retrieve the data. You can then read the results one row at a time using a *data reader* object.
- To insert, update, or delete data in a database, you execute a command object that contains an Insert, Update, or Delete statement. Then, the command object uses a connection to connect to the database and update the data. You can then check the value that's returned to determine if the operation was successful.
- If you use this technique in an application that maintains the data in a database, you typically work with a single row at a time. Because of that, the chance of a concurrency error is reduced.

Figure 17-14 How to work with data without using a data adapter

Two ways to create ADO.NET objects

Figure 17-15 shows two basic techniques you can use to create the ADO.NET objects you need as you develop database applications. First, you can create ADO.NET objects from a *data source* listed in the Data Sources window. Data sources became available with .NET 2.0, and they make it easy to quickly create forms that work with the data in a data source such as a database. In this example, the data source corresponds with the data in the Products table in the MMABooks database.

In the next chapter, you'll learn how to create a data source. For now, you should know that once you create a data source, you can drag it onto a form to automatically display controls on the form and to create ADO.NET objects for working with the data in the data source. In this figure, for example, you can see the controls and objects that are generated when you drag the Products table onto the form. Here, a DataGridView control has been added to the form to display the products in the Products table, and a toolbar has been added that lets you work with this data.

In addition, five objects have been added to the Component Designer tray below the form. Three of these are ADO.NET objects. The first one, named mMABooksDataSet, defines the dataset for the form. Then, an object named productsTableAdapter defines the table adapter for the Products table. A *table adapter* is similar to a data adapter, but it can only be generated by the designer. You'll learn more about table adapters in the next chapter. Finally, an object named tableAdapterManager makes sure that if two or more related tables are updated by the form, referential integrity is maintained. This is a new feature of Visual Studio 2008, and it's available by default.

The other two objects in the Component Designer tray are used to bind the controls on the form to the data source. The first object, named productsBindingSource, identifies the Products table as the data source for the controls. The second object, named productsBindingNavigator, defines the toolbar that's displayed across the top of the form.

Although you don't usually need to change the properties of the objects in the Component Designer tray, you should know that you can do that using the same technique you use to change the properties of a control on a form. That is, you just select an object to display its properties in the Properties window and then work with them from there.

The second technique for creating ADO.NET objects is to write the code yourself. The code shown in this figure, for example, creates four objects: a connection, a command named selectCommand that contains a Select statement, a data adapter named productsDataAdapter, and a dataset named productsDataSet.

Although creating ADO.NET objects through code is more time-consuming than using data sources, it can result in more compact and efficient code. In addition, creating ADO.NET objects through code lets you encapsulate an application's database processing in specialized database classes. You'll learn how this works in chapter 20.

ADO.NET objects created using the Data Sources window

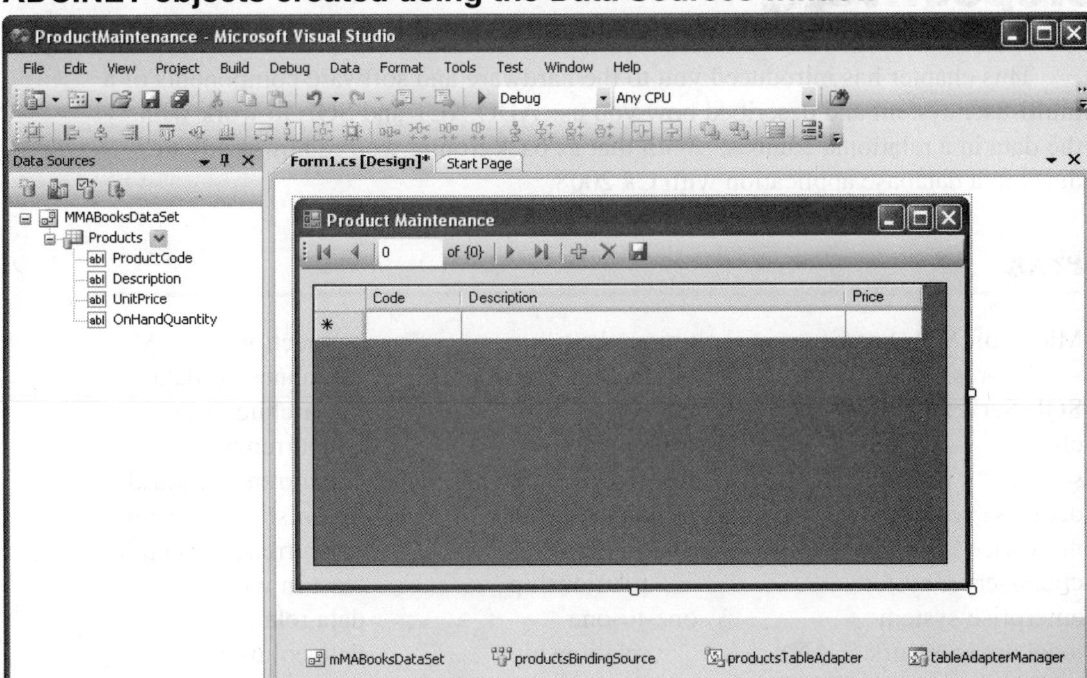

ADO.NET objects created using code

```
string connectionString =
    "Data Source=localhost\\SqlExpress;Initial Catalog=MMABooks;" +
    "Integrated Security=True";
SqlConnection connection = new SqlConnection(connectionString);

string selectStatement = "SELECT * FROM Products ORDER BY ProductCode";
SqlCommand selectCommand = new SqlCommand(selectStatement, connection);

SqlDataAdapter productsDataAdapter = new SqlDataAdapter(selectCommand);

DataSet productsDataSet = new DataSet();
```

Description

- You can use the Data Sources window to create a *data source*. Then, you can drag the data source onto the form to automatically generate a table adapter object and a dataset. A *table adapter* is similar to a data adapter, but it can only be generated by the designer, it has a built-in connection object, and it can contain more than one query. You'll learn how to work with data sources and table adapters in chapter 18.
- To create ADO.NET objects in code, you write a declaration that identifies the class each object is created from. You'll learn how to write code like this in chapter 20.

Figure 17-15 Two ways to work with ADO.NET objects

Perspective

This chapter has introduced you to the hardware and software components of a multi-user system and described how you use ADO.NET and SQL to work with the data in a relational database. With that as background, you're now ready to develop a database application with C# 2008.

Terms

Microsoft SQL Server Express
SQL Server
client
server
database server
network
client/server system
enterprise system
local area network (LAN)
wide area network (WAN)
network operating system
database management system (DBMS)
back-end processing
application software
data source
data access API
application programming interface
front-end processing
SQL query
query
Structured Query Language (SQL)
query results
relational database
table
record
row
field
column
primary key
composite primary key
non-primary key
unique key
unique key constraint
index
foreign key
foreign key table
primary key table
one-to-many relationship
one-to-one relationship
many-to-many relationship
linking table
data type
system data type
null value
default value
identity column
check constraint
foreign key constraint
SQL dialect
Transact-SQL
result table
result set
calculated column
join
inner join
ADO.NET
ActiveX Data Objects .NET
.NET data provider
dataset
data table
data adapter
command
connection
disconnected data architecture
concurrency
concurrency control
optimistic concurrency
concurrency exception
"last in wins"
data relation
data column
data row
constraint
data reader
data source
table adapter

18

How to work with data sources and datasets

In this chapter, you'll learn how to use data sources and datasets to develop database applications. This is the easiest way to generate Windows forms that work with the data in a database. And this is especially useful for developing simple applications or prototyping larger applications.

How to create a data source

As its name implies, a *data source* specifies the source of the data for an application. Since most applications get their data from a database, the next six figures show how to create a data source that gets data from a database.

How to use the Data Sources window

The data sources that are available to a project are listed in the Data Sources window as shown in figure 18-1. Here, the second screen shows a data source for the Products table that's available from the MMABooks database described in the previous chapter. As you can see, this data source includes three columns from the Products table named ProductCode, Description, and UnitPrice.

If no data sources are available to a project, the Data Sources window will display an Add New Data Source link as shown in the first screen. Then, you can click on this link to start the Data Source Configuration Wizard described in figures 18-2 through 18-6. This wizard lets you add a new data source to the project. When you're done, you can drag the data source onto a form to create bound controls as described later in this chapter.

An empty Data Sources window

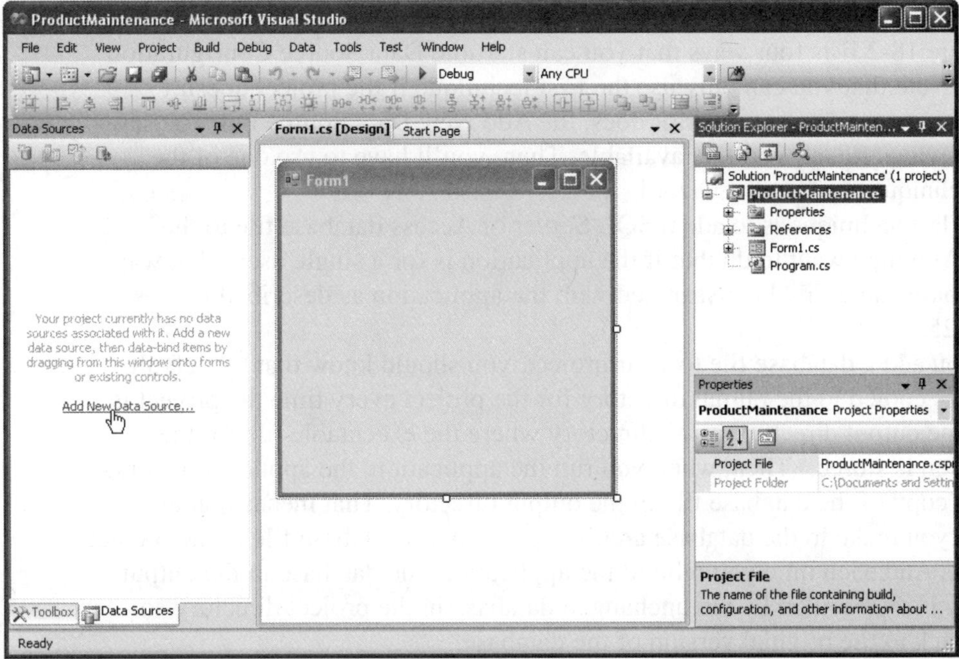

A Data Sources window after a data source has been added

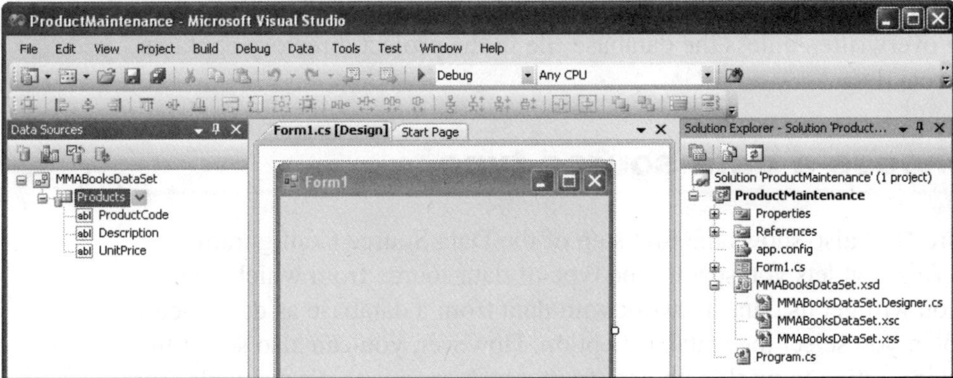

Description

- A *data source* shows all the tables and columns in the dataset that are available to your application.
- You can display the Data Sources window by clicking on the Data Sources tab that's usually at the left edge of the Visual Studio window or by selecting the Show Data Sources command from the Data menu.
- To create a data source, you can click the Add New Data Source link. Then, you can drag the data source to a form to create controls that are bound to the data source.

Figure 18-1 How to use the Data Sources window

How to start the Data Source Configuration Wizard

Figure 18-2 lists four ways that you can start the Data Source Configuration Wizard. Note that you can only use the first technique if the project doesn't already contain a data source. If it does, the Add New Data Source link you saw in the previous figure won't be available. Then, you'll have to use one of the other techniques to start the wizard.

The last technique is to add a SQL Server or Access database file to the project. You may want to do that if the application is for a single user. That way, the database can easily be distributed with the application as described in chapter 25.

If you add a database file to your project, you should know that by default, that file is copied to the output directory for the project every time the project is built. (The output directory is the directory where the executable file for the application is stored.) Then, when you run the application, the application works with the copy of the database file in the output directory. That means that any changes you make to the database aren't applied to the database file in the project directory. And each time you rebuild the application, the database in the output directory is overwritten by the unchanged database in the project directory so you're back to the original version of the database.

If you want to change the way this works, you can select the database file in the Solution Explorer and change its "Copy to Output Directory" property from "Copy always" to "Copy if newer." Then, the database file in the output directory won't be overwritten unless the database file in the project directory contains more current data.

How to choose a data source type

Figure 18-2 also shows the first step of the Data Source Configuration Wizard. This step lets you specify the type of data source from which your application will get its data. To work with data from a database as described in this chapter, you select the Database option. However, you can also select the Web Service option to work with data from a web service that's available from the Internet or from an intranet. Or, you can select the Object option to work with data that's stored in a business object.

The first step of the Data Source Configuration Wizard

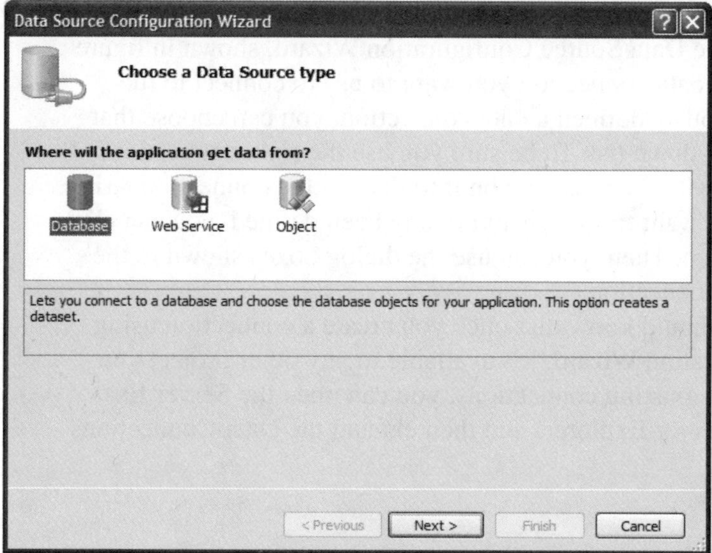

How to start the Data Source Configuration Wizard

- Click on the Add New Data Source link that's available from the Data Sources window when a project doesn't contain any data sources.
- Click on the Add New Data Source button at the top of the Data Sources window.
- Select the Add New Data Source command from Visual Studio's Data menu.
- Add a SQL Server (.mdf) or Access (.mdb) data file to the project using the Project→Add→Existing Item command. Then, the wizard will skip to the step shown in figure 18-6 that lets you choose the database objects you want to include.

How to choose a data source type

- To get your data from a database, select the Database option. This option lets you create applications like the ones described in this chapter.
- To get your data from a web service, select the Web Service option. This option lets you browse the web to select a web service that will supply data to your application.
- To get your data from a business object, select the Object option.

Note

- Before you start this procedure, you need to install your database server software on your own PC or on a network server, and you need to attach your database to it. For more information, please refer to appendix A.

Figure 18-2 How to start the Data Source Configuration Wizard and choose a data source type

How to choose the connection for a data source

The second step of the Data Source Configuration Wizard, shown in figure 18-3, lets you choose the data connection you want to use to connect to the database. If you've previously defined a data connection, you can choose that connection from the drop-down list. To be sure you use the right connection, you can click the button with the plus sign on it to display the connection string.

If the connection you want to use hasn't already been defined, you can click the New Connection button. Then, you can use the dialog boxes shown in the next figure to create the connection.

Before I go on, you should know that once you create a connection using the Data Source Configuration Wizard, it's available to any other project you create. To see a list of the existing connections, you can open the Server Explorer window (View→Server Explorer) and then expand the Data Connections node.

The second step of the Data Source Configuration Wizard

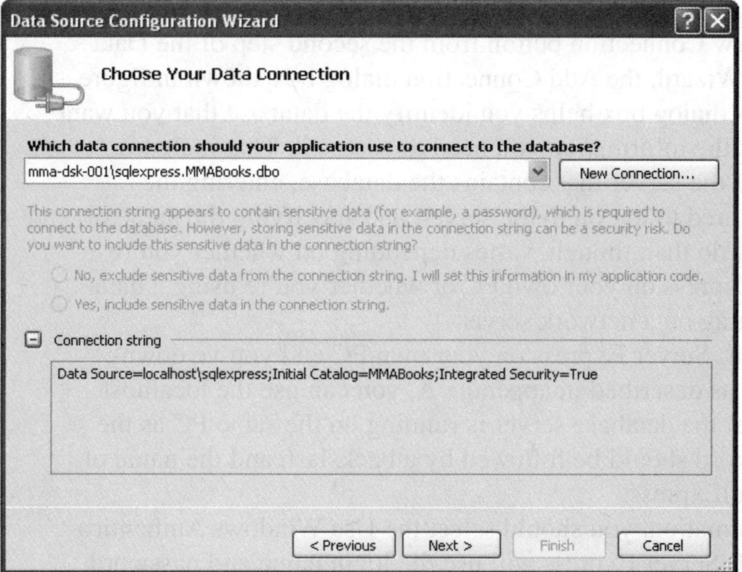

Description

- When you click the Next button in the first step of the Data Source Configuration Wizard, the Choose Your Data Connection step shown above is displayed.
- If you've already established a connection to the database you want to use, you can choose that connection. Otherwise, you can click the New Connection button to display the Add Connection dialog box shown in the next figure.
- To see the connection string for an existing connection, click the button with the plus sign on it.

Figure 18-3 How to choose the connection for a data source

How to create a connection to a database

If you click the New Connection button from the second step of the Data Source Configuration Wizard, the Add Connection dialog box shown in figure 18-4 is displayed. This dialog box helps you identify the database that you want to access and provides the information you need to access it. That includes specifying the name of the server that contains the database, entering the information that's required to log on to the server, and specifying the name of the database. How you do that, though, varies depending on whether you're running SQL Server Express on your own PC or whether you're using a database server that's running on a network server.

If you're using SQL Server Express on your own PC and you've downloaded and installed it as described in appendix A, you can use the localhost keyword to specify that the database server is running on the same PC as the application. This keyword should be followed by a backslash and the name of the database server: SqlExpress.

For the logon information, you should select the Use Windows Authentication option. Then, SQL Server Express will use the login name and password that you use to log in to Windows as the name and password for the database server too. As a result, you won't need to provide a separate user name and password in this dialog box.

Last, you enter or select the name of the database that you want to connect to. In this figure, for example, the connection is for the MMABooks database that's used throughout the chapters in this section of the book. When you're done supplying the information for the connection, you can click the Test Connection button to be sure that the connection works.

In contrast, if you need to connect to a database that's running on a database server that's available through a network, you need to get the connection information from the network or database administrator. This information will include the name of the database server, logon information, and the name of the database. Once you establish a connection to the database, you can use that connection for all of the other applications that use that database.

By default, Visual Studio assumes you want to access a SQL Server database as shown here. This works for SQL Server 7, 2000, and 2005 databases including SQL Server Express databases. If you want to access a different type of database, though, you can click the Change button to display the Change Data Source dialog box. Then, you can select the data source and the data provider you want to use to access that data source. If you want to access an Oracle database, for example, you can select the Oracle Database item in the Data Source list. Then, you can choose the data provider for Oracle or the data provider for OLE DB from the Data Provider drop-down list.

The Add Connection and Change Data Source dialog boxes

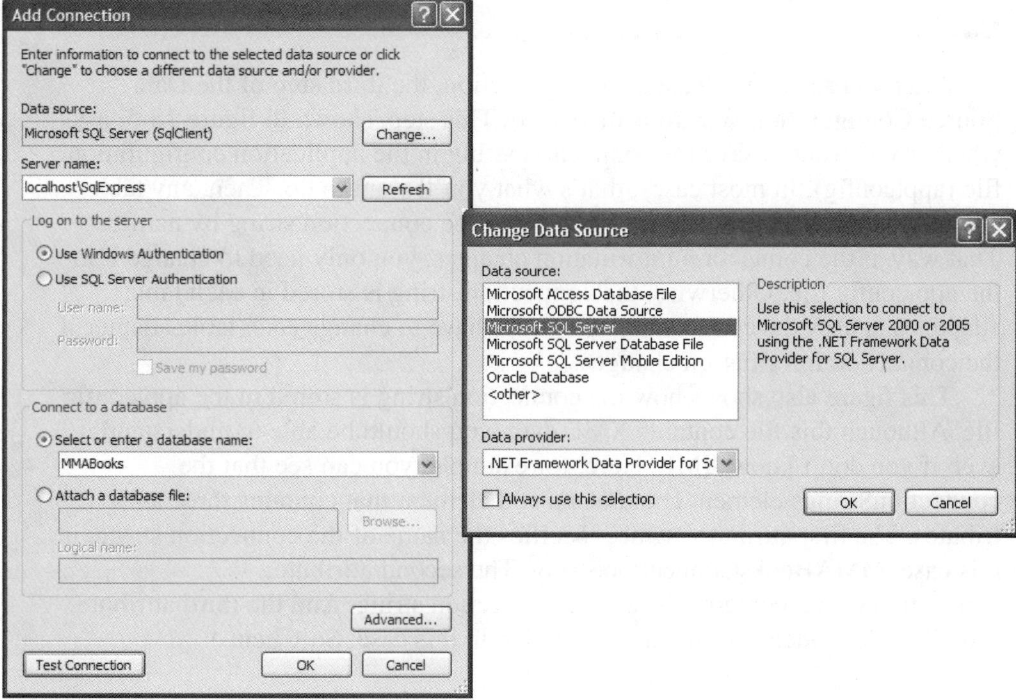

Description

- By default, a connection uses the SQL Server data provider. If that's not what you want, you can click the Change button in the Add Connection dialog box to display the Change Data Source dialog box. Then, you can choose the data source and data provider you want to use.
- To create a connection, specify the name of the server that contains the database, enter the information that's required to log on to the server, and specify the name of the database you want to connect to.
- To be sure that the connection is configured properly, you can click the Test Connection button in the Add Connection dialog box.

Express Edition differences

- The Change Data Source dialog box provides only three options: Microsoft Access Database File, Microsoft SQL Server Compact 3.5, and Microsoft SQL Server Database File. The default is Microsoft SQL Server Compact 3.5, which probably isn't what you want.
- The Add Connection dialog box is simpler, and it includes a Database File Name text box that you use to specify the database. To do that, you click the Browse button to the right of the text box and use the resulting dialog box to point to the data file for the database.

Figure 18-4 How to create a connection to a database

How to save a connection string in the app.config file

After you select or create a data connection, the third step of the Data Source Configuration Wizard is displayed. This step, shown in figure 18-5, asks whether you want to save the connection string in the application configuration file (app.config). In most cases, that's what you'll want to do. Then, any table adapter that uses the connection can refer to the connection string by name. That way, if the connection information changes, you only need to change it in the app.config file. Otherwise, the connection string is stored in each table adapter that uses the connection, and you'll have to change each table adapter if the connection information changes.

This figure also shows how the connection string is stored in the app.config file. Although this file contains XML data, you should be able to understand it even if you don't know XML. Here, for example, you can see that the connectionStrings element contains an add element that contains three attributes. The first attribute, name, specifies the name of the connection string, in this case, MMABooksConnectionString. The second attribute, connectionString, contains the actual connection string. And the third attribute, providerName, identifies the data provider, in this case, SqlClient.

The third step of the Data Source Configuration Wizard

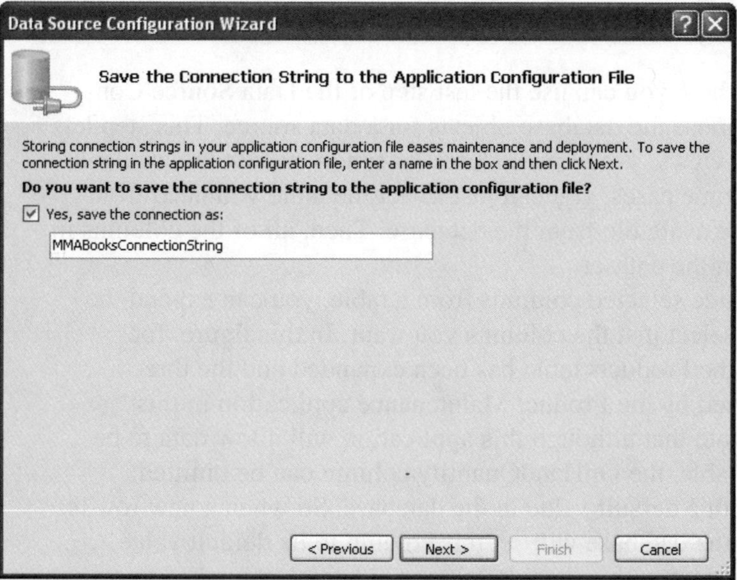

The information that's stored in the app.config file

```
<connectionStrings>
    <add name="ProductMaintenance.My.MySettings.MMABooksConnectionString"
        connectionString="Data Source=localhost\sqlexpress;
                          Initial Catalog=MMABooks;
                          Integrated Security=True"
        providerName="System.Data.SqlClient" />
</connectionStrings>
```

Description

- By default, the connection string is saved in the application configuration file (app.config). If that's not what you want, you can remove the check mark from the Yes option in the third step of the Data Source Configuration Wizard shown above.
- If you don't save the connection string in the app.config file, the string is specified for the connection of each table adapter you create from the data source. Because of that, we recommend you always save the connection string in the app.config file. Then, only the name of the connection string is stored in the connection for each table adapter.
- You can also enter the name you want to use for the connection string in this dialog box. By default, the connection string is given a name that consists of the database name appended with "ConnectionString".

Figure 18-5 How to save a connection string in the app.config file

How to choose database objects for a data source

Figure 18-6 shows how you can use the last step of the Data Source Configuration Wizard to choose the database objects for a data source. This step lets you choose any tables, views, stored procedures, or functions that are available from the database. In some cases, you can just select the table you need from the list of tables that are available from the database. Then, all of the columns in the table are included in the dataset.

If you want to include selected columns from a table, you can expand the node for the table and select just the columns you want. In this figure, for example, the node for the Products table has been expanded and the three columns that will be used by the Product Maintenance application in this chapter are selected. Note that although this application will allow data to be added to the Products table, the OnHandQuantity column can be omitted because it's defined with a default value in the database. So when a new row is added to the database, the database will set this column to its default value.

If you include a column with a default value in a dataset, you need to realize that this value isn't assigned to the column in the dataset, even though the dataset enforces the constraints for that column. For instance, the OnHandQuantity column in the MMABooks database has a default value of zero and doesn't allow nulls. But if you include this column in the dataset, its definition will have a default value of null and won't allow nulls. As a result, an exception will be thrown whenever a new row is added to the dataset with a null value for the OnHandQuantity column.

This means that either the user or the application must provide an acceptable value for the OnHandQuantity column. One way to do that is to provide a way for the user to enter a value for the column. Another way is to use the Dataset Designer to set the DefaultValue property for this column as described in this figure. You'll learn more about working with the Dataset Designer later in this chapter.

In a larger project, you might want to include several tables in the dataset. Then, the dataset will maintain the relationships between those tables whenever that's appropriate. Or, you might want to use views, stored procedures, or functions to work with the data in the database. If you have experience working with views, stored procedures, and functions, you shouldn't have any trouble understanding how this works. Otherwise, you can get another book such as *Murach's SQL Server 2005 for Developers* to learn more about working with these types of objects.

The last step of the Data Source Configuration Wizard

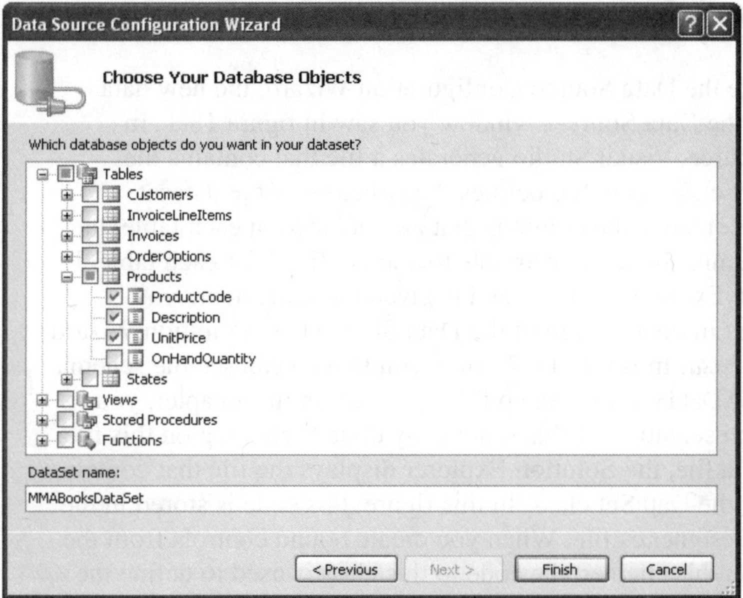

Description

- In the last step of the Data Source Configuration Wizard, you can choose the database objects that you want to include in the dataset for your project.
- In this step, you can choose from any tables, views, stored procedures, or functions that are available from the database. In addition, you can expand the node for any table, view, stored procedure, or function and choose just the columns you want to include in the data source.
- You can also enter the name you want to use for the dataset in this dialog box. By default, the name is the name of the database appended with "DataSet".

How to work with columns that have default values

- If a column in a database has a default value, that value isn't included in the column definition in the dataset. Because of that, you may want to omit columns with default values from the dataset unless they're needed by the application. Then, when a row is added to the table, the default value is taken from the database.
- If you include a column that's defined with a default value, you must provide a value for that column whenever a row is added to the dataset. One way to do that is to let the user enter a value. Another way is to display the Dataset Designer as described in figure 18-16, click on the column, and use the Properties window to set the DefaultValue property.

Figure 18-6 How to choose database objects for a data source

The schema file created by the Data Source Configuration Wizard

After you complete the Data Source Configuration Wizard, the new data source is displayed in the Data Sources window you saw in figure 18-1. In addition to this data source, Visual Studio generates a file that contains the *schema* for the DataSet class. This file defines the structure of the dataset, including the tables it contains, the columns that are included in each table, the data types of each column, and the constraints that are defined for each table. It is listed in the Solution Explorer window and is given the same name you specified for the dataset in the last step of the Data Source Configuration Wizard with a file extension of *xsd*. In figure 18-7, for example, you can see the schema file named MMABooksDataSet.xsd. As you'll learn later in this chapter, you can view a graphic representation of this schema by double-clicking on this file.

Beneath the schema file, the Solution Explorer displays the file that contains the generated code for the DataSet class. In this figure, this code is stored in the MMABooksDataSet.Designer.cs file. When you create bound controls from the data source as shown in this chapter, the code in this class is used to define the DataSet object that the controls are bound to. Although you may want to view this code to see how it works, you shouldn't change it. If you do, the dataset may not work correctly.

By the way, you should know that a dataset that's created from a dataset class like the one shown here is called a *typed dataset*. The code in the dataset class makes it possible for you to refer to the tables, rows, and columns in the typed dataset using the simplified syntax you'll see in this chapter and the next chapter. In contrast, when you use an *untyped dataset*, you have to refer to the tables, columns, and rows through the collections that contain them. In this book, you'll learn only how to create and work with typed datasets.

A project with a dataset defined by a data source

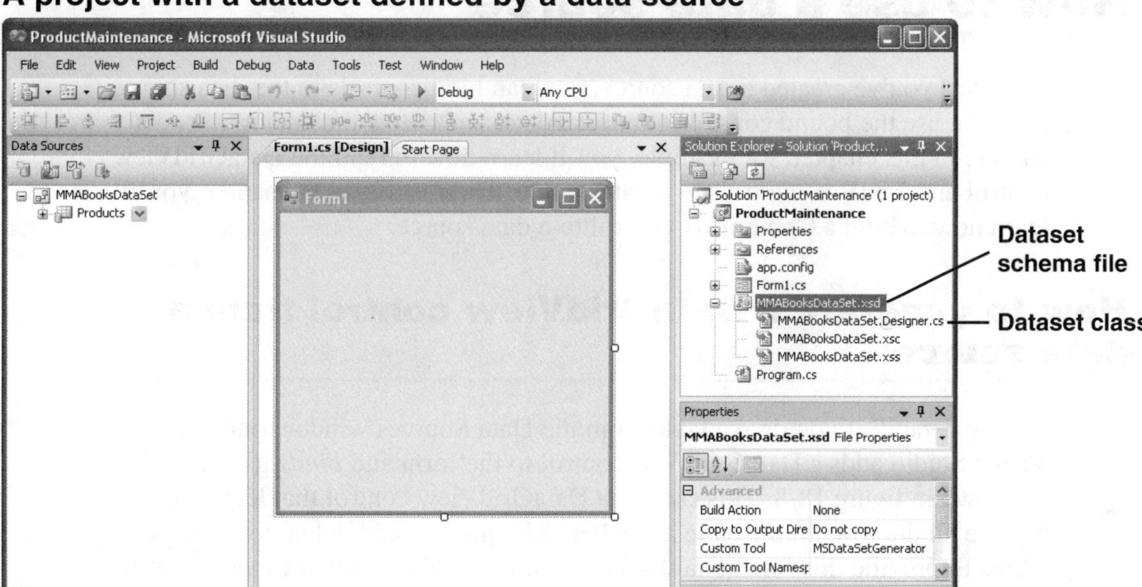

Description

- After you create a data source, it's displayed in the Data Sources window. Then, you can use it to create bound controls as shown in this chapter.
- Visual Studio also generates a file that contains the *schema* for the dataset defined by the data source. This file appears in the Solution Explorer and has a file extension of *xsd*. It defines the structure of the dataset, including the tables it contains, the columns in each table, the data types of each column, and the constraints for each table.
- Subordinate to the schema file is a file that contains the generated code for the dataset class. Visual Studio uses this class to create a dataset object when you add the data source to a form.

Figure 18-7 The schema file created by the Data Source Configuration Wizard

How to use a data source

Once you've created a data source, you can bind controls to the data source and then use the bound controls to add, update, and delete the data in the data source. In this chapter, for example, you'll learn how to bind the DataGridView control and TextBox controls to a data source. Then, in the next chapter, you'll learn how to bind a ComboBox control to a data source.

How to generate a DataGridView control from a data source

By default, if you drag a table from the Data Sources window onto a form, Visual Studio adds a DataGridView control to the form and *binds* it to the table as shown in figure 18-8. This creates a DataGridView control that lets you browse all the rows in the table as well as add, update, and delete rows in the table. To provide this functionality, Visual Studio adds a toolbar to the top of the form that provides navigation buttons along with Add, Delete, and Save buttons.

To bind a DataGridView control to a table, Visual Studio uses a technique called *complex data binding*. This just means that the *bound control* is bound to more than one data element. The DataGridView control in this figure, for example, is bound to all the rows and columns in the Products table.

When you generate a DataGridView control from a data source, Visual Studio also adds five additional objects to the Component Designer tray at the bottom of the Form Designer. First, the DataSet object defines the dataset that contains the Products table. Second, the TableAdapter object provides commands that can be used to work with the Products table in the database. Third, the TableAdapterManager provides for writing the data in two or more related tables to the database so that referential integrity is maintained. Fourth, the BindingSource object specifies the data source (the Products table) that the controls are bound to, and it provides functionality for working with the data source. Finally, the BindingNavigator defines the toolbar that contains the controls for working with the data source.

Before I go on, I want to point out that the TableAdapter object is similar to the DataAdapter object you learned about in the previous chapter. However, it can only be created by a designer. In addition, it has a built-in connection and, as you'll see in the next chapter, it can contain more than one query.

I also want to mention that, in general, you shouldn't have any trouble figuring out how to use the binding navigator toolbar. However, you may want to know that if you click the Add button to add a new row and then decide you don't want to do that, you can click the Delete button to delete the new row. However, there's no way to cancel out of an edit operation. Because of that, you may want to add a button to the toolbar that provides this function. You'll learn how to do that in the next chapter.

A form after the Products table has been dragged onto it

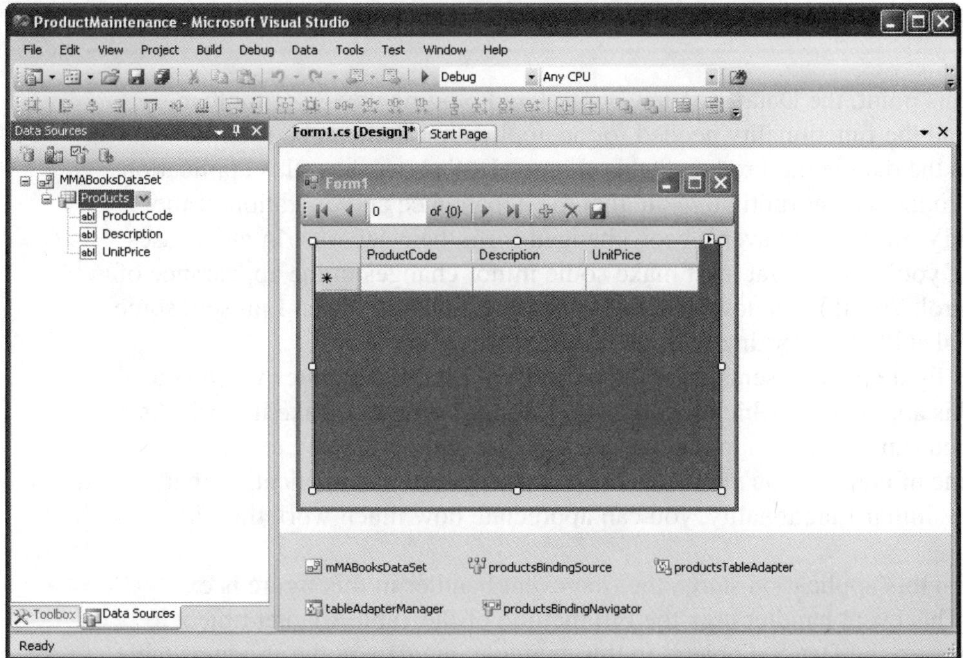

The controls and objects that are created when you drag a data source to a form

Control/object	Description
DataGridView control	Displays the data from the data source in a grid.
BindingNavigator control	Defines the toolbar that can be used to navigate, add, update, and delete rows in the DataGridView control.
BindingSource object	Identifies the data source that the controls on the form are bound to and provides functionality for working with the data source.
DataSet object	Provides access to all of the tables, views, stored procedures, and functions that are available to the project.
TableAdapter object	Provides the commands that are used to read and write data to and from the specified table in the database.
TableAdapterManager object	Provides for writing data in related tables to the database while maintaining referential integrity.

Description

- To *bind* a DataGridView control to a table in a dataset, just drag the table from the Data Sources window onto the form. Then, Visual Studio automatically adds a DataGridView control to the form along with the other controls and objects it needs to work properly. Because the DataGridView control is bound to the table, it can be referred to as a *bound control*.
- To bind a DataGridView control to a data table, Visual Studio uses a technique called *complex data binding*. This means that the control is bound to more than one data element, in this case, all the rows and columns in the table.

Figure 18-8 How to generate a DataGridView control from a data source

A Product Maintenance application that uses a DataGridView control

At this point, the DataGridView control and binding navigator toolbar provide all the functionality needed for an application that can be used to maintain the data in the Products table. Figure 18-9 shows how this application appears to the user at runtime. Note that the appearance and operation of the DataGridView control haven't been changed from their defaults. In most cases, however, you'll want to at least make some minor changes in the appearance of this control. You'll learn how to do that in the next chapter when I present some additional skills for working with the DataGridView control.

This figure also presents the code that Visual Studio generates when you create this application, which includes everything needed to make it work. As a result, you can create an application like this one without having to write a single line of code. If you've ever had to manually write an application that provides similar functionality, you can appreciate how much work this saves you.

When this application starts, the first event handler in this figure is executed. This event handler uses the Fill method of the TableAdapter object to load data into the DataSet object. In this example, the data in the Products table of the MMABooks database is loaded into the Products table of the dataset. Then, because the DataGridView control is bound to this table, the data is displayed in this control and the user can use it to modify the data in the table by adding, updating, or deleting rows.

When the user changes the data in the DataGridView control, those changes are saved to the dataset. However, the changes aren't saved to the database until the user clicks the Save button in the toolbar. Then, the second event handler in this figure is executed. This event handler starts by calling the Validate method of the form, which causes the Validating and Validated events of the control that's losing focus to be fired. Although you probably won't use the Validated event, you may use the Validating event to validate a row that's being added or modified. However, I've found that this event doesn't work well with the binding navigator toolbar, so you won't see it used in this book.

Next, the EndEdit method of the BindingSource object applies any pending changes to the dataset. That's necessary because when you add or update a row, the new or modified row isn't saved until you move to another row.

Finally, the UpdateAll method of the TableAdapterManager object saves the data in the DataSet object to the MMABooks database. When this method is called, it checks each row in each table of the dataset to determine if it's a new row, a modified row, or a row that should be deleted. Then, it causes the appropriate SQL Insert, Update, and Delete statements to be executed for these rows. As a result, the UpdateAll method works efficiently since it only updates the rows that need to be updated. In addition, the Insert, Update, and Delete statements are executed in a sequence that maintains referential integrity.

The user interface for the Product Maintenance application

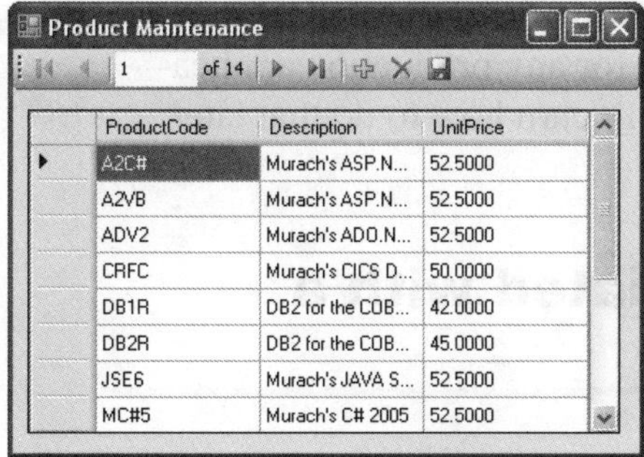

The code that's generated by Visual Studio

```
private void Form1_Load(object sender, EventArgs e)
{
    // TODO: This line of code loads data into the
    // 'mMABooksDataSet.Products' table.
    // You can move, or remove it, as needed.
    this.productsTableAdapter.Fill(this.mMABooksDataSet.Products);
}

private void productsBindingNavigatorSaveItem_Click(
    object sender, EventArgs e)
{
    this.Validate();
    this.productsBindingSource.EndEdit();
    this.tableAdapterManager.UpdateAll(this.mMABooksDataSet);
}
```

The syntax of the Fill method

```
tableAdapter.Fill(dataSet.TableName)
```

The syntax of the UpdateAll method

```
tableAdapterManager.UpdateAll(dataSet)
```

Description

- Visual Studio automatically generates the code shown above and places it in the source code file when you drag a data source onto a form. If necessary, you can edit this code.
- The generated code uses the Fill method of the TableAdapter object that's generated for the table to read data from the database, and it uses the UpdateAll method of the TableAdapterManager object that's generated for the dataset to write data to the database. It also uses the EndEdit method of the BindingSource object to save any changes that have been made to the current row to the dataset.
- The Validate method causes the Validating and Validated events of the control that is losing the focus to be fired. You can use the Validating event to perform any required data validation for the form.
- Users of a DataGridView control can sort the rows by clicking on a column heading and can size columns by dragging the column separators to the left or right. They can also reorder the columns by dragging them if that option is enabled (see figure 19-9).

Figure 18-9 A Product Maintenance application that uses a DataGridView control

Now that you understand this code, you should notice that it doesn't provide for any exceptions that may occur during this processing. Because of that, you need to add the appropriate exception handling code for any production applications that you develop so that they won't crash. You'll learn how to do that later in this chapter.

How to change the controls associated with a data source

If the DataGridView control isn't appropriate for your application, you can bind the columns of a data source to individual controls as shown in figure 18-10. Here, the data source consists of the columns in the Customers table.

To associate the columns in a table with individual controls, you select the Details option from the drop-down list that's available when you select the table in the Data Sources window. This is illustrated in the first screen in this figure. Then, if you drag that table from the Data Sources window onto a form, Visual Studio generates a label and a bound control for each column in the table.

For most string and numeric columns, Visual Studio generates a TextBox control. That's the case for the Customers table, as you'll see in the next figure. If you want to change the type of control that's associated with a column, though, you can select the column in the Data Sources window and then use the drop-down list that's displayed to select a different type of control. You can see the list of controls that are available in the second screen in this figure.

How to change the default control for a data table

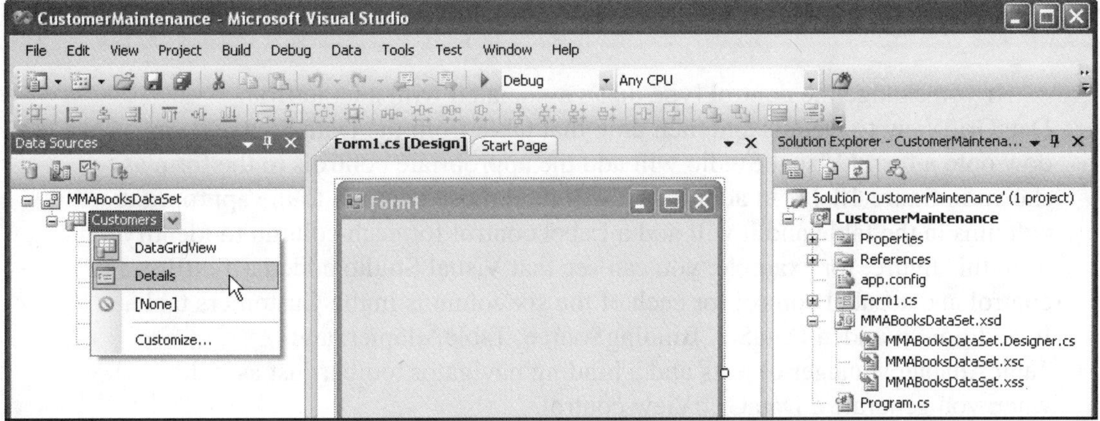

How to change the default control for a column in a data table

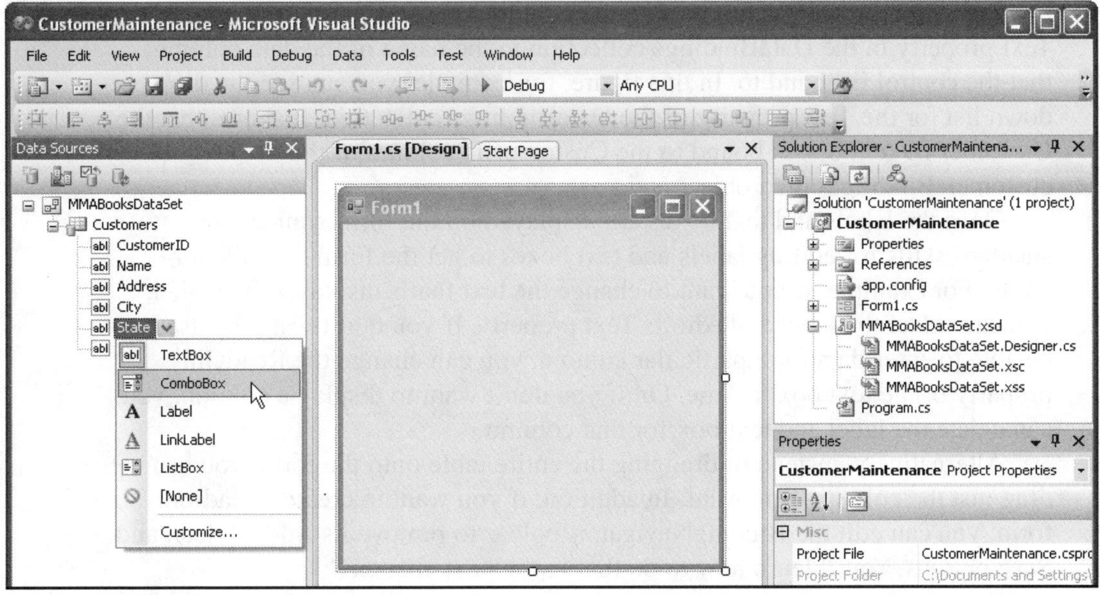

Description

- By default, a data table is associated with a DataGridView control. To change this default so that each column in the table is displayed in a separate control, select the Details option from the drop-down list for the table.
- By default, most string and numeric columns within a data table are associated with the TextBox control. To change this default, select the type of control you want to use from the drop-down list for the column.

Figure 18-10 How to change the controls associated with a data source

How to generate detail controls from a data source

If you change the control type that's associated with a table from DataGridView to Details and then drag that table from the Data Sources window onto a form, Visual Studio will add the appropriate controls to the form as shown in figure 18-11. In addition, it will bind those controls to the appropriate columns in the table and it will add a Label control for each column to identify it. In this figure, for example, you can see that Visual Studio added a TextBox control and a Label control for each of the six columns in the Customers table. In addition, it added DataSet, BindingSource, TableAdapter, and TableAdapterManager objects and a binding navigator toolbar just as it does when you generate a DataGridView control.

Notice that when you use text boxes to work with the data in a table, only one row of the table is displayed at a time. Then Visual Studio uses *simple data binding* to bind each text box to a single column value. To do that, it sets the Text property in the DataBindings collection to the name of the data column that the control is bound to. In this figure, for example, you can see the drop-down list for the Text property of the DataBindings collection. It shows that the Customer ID text box is bound to the CustomerID column of the customersBindingSource object.

Once the labels and text boxes are displayed on the form, you can use standard skills for editing labels and text boxes to get the form to work correctly. For example, if you want to change the text that's displayed in a label, you can select the label and edit its Text property. If you don't want the user to be able to enter data for a particular column, you can change the ReadOnly property of the text box to True. Or, if you don't want to display a column, you can delete the label and text box for that column.

Alternatively, instead of dragging the entire table onto the form, you can drag just the columns you want. In addition, if you want to create a read-only form, you can edit the BindingNavigator toolbar to remove its Add, Delete, and Save buttons. You'll learn how to do that in the next chapter.

A form after the Customers table has been dragged onto it

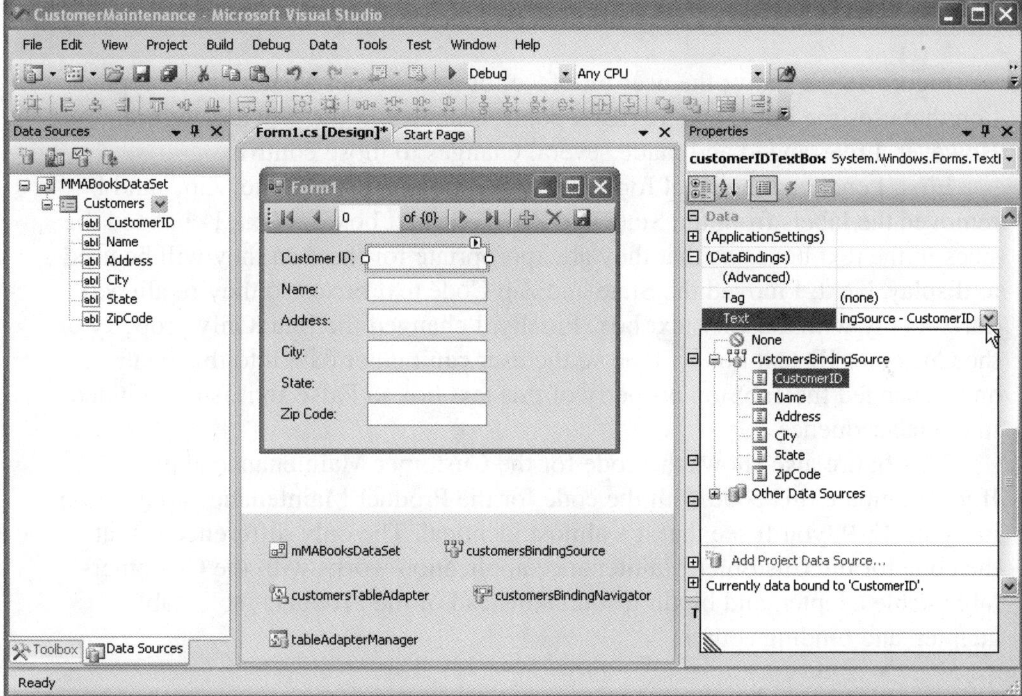

Description

- When you drag a table whose columns are associated with individual controls to a form, Visual Studio automatically adds the controls along with labels that identify the columns. It also adds a binding navigator toolbar and the objects for working with the bound data just as it does for a DataGridView control.
- To display the value of a column in a text box, Visual Studio sets the Text property in the DataBindings collection to the name of the data column. This is known as *simple data binding* because the control is bound to a single column value. To change the binding, you can use the drop-down list for the Text property as shown above.
- To disable the adding, deleting, or updating of rows when you use individual controls, you can remove those buttons from the toolbar. See chapter 19 to learn how to do that.

Note

- When you drag individual controls to a form, don't drop them at the top of the form. If you do, the toolbar will overlay the first label and text box and make them difficult to move.

Figure 18-11 How to generate detail controls from a data source

A Customer Maintenance application that uses TextBox controls

Figure 18-12 shows the user interface for a Customer Maintenance application that uses the Label and TextBox controls shown in the previous figure. However, I rearranged and made several changes to those controls.

First, I changed the label for the City text box to "City, State, Zip:" and I removed the labels from the State and Zip Code text boxes. Next, I changed the sizes of the text boxes so that they are appropriate for the data they will be used to display. Next, I moved the State and Zip Code text boxes so they're aligned horizontally with the City text box. Finally, I changed the ReadOnly property of the Customer ID text box to True so the user can't enter data into this control, and I changed the TabStop property of this text box to False so it isn't included in the tab sequence.

This figure also shows the code for the Customer Maintenance application. If you compare this code with the code for the Product Maintenance application in figure 18-9, you'll see that it's almost identical. The only difference is that the code for the Customer Maintenance application works with the Customers table, table adapter, and binding source instead of the Products table, table adapter, and binding source.

The user interface for the Customer Maintenance application

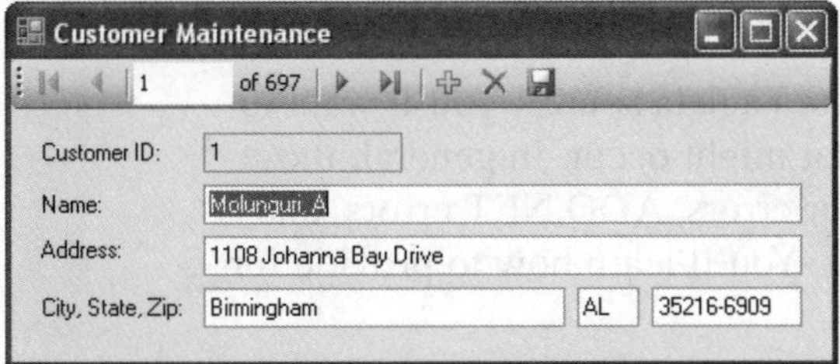

The code for the application

```
private void Form1_Load(object sender, EventArgs e)
{
    // TODO: This line of code loads data into the
    // 'mMABooksDataSet.Customers' table.
    // You can move, or remove it, as needed.
    this.customersTableAdapter.Fill(this.mMABooksDataSet.Customers);
}

private void customersBindingNavigatorSaveItem_Click(
    object sender, EventArgs e)
{
    this.Validate();
    this.customersBindingSource.EndEdit();
    this.tableAdapterManager.UpdateAll(this.mMABooksDataSet);
}
```

Figure 18-12 A Customer Maintenance application that uses TextBox controls

How to handle data errors

When you develop an application that uses a data source, you'll want to provide code that handles any data errors that might occur. In general, those errors fall into three categories: data provider errors, ADO.NET errors, and errors that the DataGridView control detects. You'll learn how to provide for these errors in the topics that follow.

How to handle data provider errors

When you access a database, there is always the possibility that an unrecoverable error might occur. For example, the database server might be shut down when you try to access it, or the network connection to the database server might be broken. Either way, your applications should usually anticipate such problems by catching any database exceptions that might occur.

Figure 18-13 shows the exceptions thrown by the .NET data providers when an unrecoverable error occurs. You can refer to these errors as *data provider errors*. As you can see, each data provider has its own exception class. So, if you're using the SQL Server data provider, you should catch exceptions of the SqlException class. If you're using the Oracle data provider, you should catch exceptions of the OracleException class. And so on.

The code example in this figure shows how you can catch a SqlException that might occur when attempting to fill a dataset using a table adapter. Here, the shaded lines show the code that has been added to the generated code. This code will display an error message when a SqlException occurs, and it uses the Number and Message properties of the SqlException class to display details about the exception. It also uses the GetType method to indicate the type of exception that occurred.

Although it's uncommon, more than one server error can occur as the result of a single database operation. In that case, an error object is created for each error. These objects are stored in a collection that you can access through the Errors property of the exception object. Each error object contains a Number and Message property just like the exception object. However, because the Number and Message properties of the exception object are set to the Number and Message properties of the first error in the Errors collection, you don't usually need to work with the individual error objects.

.NET data provider exception classes

Name	Description
SqlException	Thrown if a server error occurs when accessing a SQL Server database.
OracleException	Thrown if a server error occurs when accessing an Oracle database.
OdbcException	Thrown if a server error occurs when accessing an ODBC database.
OleDbException	Thrown if a server error occurs when accessing an OLE DB database.

Common members of the .NET data provider exception classes

Property	Description
`Number`	An error number that identifies the type of error.
`Message`	A message that describes the error.
`Source`	The name of the provider that generated the error.
`Errors`	A collection of error objects that contain information about the errors that occurred during a database operation.

Method	Description
`GetType()`	Gets the type of the current exception.

Code that catches a SQL exception

```
private void Form1_Load(object sender, EventArgs e)
{
    try
    {
        this.customersTableAdapter.Fill(this.mMABooksDataSet.Customers);
    }
    catch (SqlException ex)
    {
        MessageBox.Show("Database error # " + ex.Number +
            ": " + ex.Message, ex.GetType().ToString());
    }
}
```

Description

- Whenever the data provider (SQL Server, Oracle, ODBC, or OLE DB) encounters a situation it can't handle, a data provider exception is thrown. You can handle these types of exceptions by catching them and displaying appropriate error messages.
- The Number and Message properties pinpoint the specific server error that caused the data provider exception to be thrown.
- The SqlException class is stored in the System.Data.SqlClient namespace.

Figure 18-13 How to handle data provider errors

How to handle ADO.NET errors

When you work with bound controls, *ADO.NET errors* can occur when the data in those controls is saved to the dataset (not the database), or when an Insert, Update, or Delete statement can't be executed against the database. Figure 18-14 presents some of the most common of those errors.

Here, ConstraintException and NoNullAllowedException are subclasses of the DataException class, so you can catch either of these errors by catching DataException errors. In contrast, DBConcurrencyException isn't a subclass of the DataException class, so you must catch DBConcurrencyException errors separately. All of the ADO.NET exception classes are members of the System.Data namespace.

The error-handling code in this figure catches errors caused by the EndEdit method of a binding source and the UpdateAll method of a table adapter manager. The first exception, DBConcurrencyException, occurs if the number of rows that are affected by an insert, update, or delete operation is zero, which typically indicates that concurrency errors have occurred. Then, a message box is used to display an error message, and the Fill method of the table adapter is used to retrieve the current data from the database and load it into the dataset. That will help prevent further concurrency errors from occurring.

Although you might think that a concurrency error would be generated by the database rather than ADO.NET, that's not the case. To understand why, you need to realize that the Update and Delete statements that are generated for a table adapter contain code that checks that a row hasn't changed since it was retrieved. But if the row has changed, the row with the specified criteria won't be found and the SQL statement won't be executed. When the table adapter discovers that the row wasn't updated or deleted, however, it realizes there was a concurrency error and throws an exception.

Like other exception classes provided by the .NET Framework, each ADO.NET exception class has a Message property and a GetType method that you can use to display information about the error. You can see how this property and method are used in the second Catch block, which catches any other ADO.NET exceptions that may occur. This Catch block displays a dialog box that uses the Message property and the GetType method of the DataException object to describe the error. Then, it uses the CancelEdit method of the binding source to cancel the current edit operation.

Incidentally, to test your handling of concurrency exceptions, you can start two instances of Visual Studio and run the same application from both of them. Then, you can access and update the same row from both instances.

Common ADO.NET exception classes

Class	Description
DBConcurrencyException	The exception that's thrown if the number of rows affected by an insert, update, or delete operation is zero. This exception is typically caused by a concurrency violation.
DataException	The general exception that's thrown when an ADO.NET error occurs.
ConstraintException	The exception that's thrown if an operation violates a constraint. This is a subclass of the DataException class.
NoNullAllowedException	The exception that's thrown when an add or update operation attempts to save a null value in a column that doesn't allow nulls. This is a subclass of the DataException class.

Common members of the ADO.NET classes

Property	Description
`Message`	A message that describes the exception.
Method	**Description**
`GetType()`	Gets the type of the current exception.

Code that handles ADO.NET errors

```
try
{
    this.customersBindingSource.EndEdit();
    this.tableAdapterManager.UpdateAll(this.mMABooksDataSet);
}
catch (DBConcurrencyException)
{
    MessageBox.Show("A concurrency error occurred. " +
        "Some rows were not updated.", "Concurrency Exception");
    this.customersTableAdapter.Fill(this.mMABooksDataSet.Customers);
}
catch (DataException ex)
{
    MessageBox.Show(ex.Message, ex.GetType().ToString());
    customersBindingSource.CancelEdit();
}
catch (SqlException ex)
{
    MessageBox.Show("Database error # " + ex.Number +
        ": " + ex.Message, ex.GetType().ToString());
}
```

Description

- An ADO.NET exception is an exception that occurs on any ADO.NET object. All of these exceptions are members of the System.Data namespace.
- In most cases, you'll catch specific types of exceptions if you want to perform special processing when those exceptions occur. Then, you can use the DataException class to catch other ADO.NET exceptions that are represented by its subclasses.

Figure 18-14 How to handle ADO.NET errors

How to handle data errors for a DataGridView control

Because the DataGridView control was designed to work with data sources, it can detect some types of data entry errors before the data is saved to the dataset. If, for example, a user doesn't enter a value for a column that's required by the data source, or if a user tries to add a new row with a primary key that already exists, the DataGridView control will raise the DataError event. Then, you can code an event handler for this event as shown in figure 18-15.

The second parameter that's received by this event handler has properties you can use to display information about the error. The one you'll use most often is the Exception property, which provides access to the exception object that was thrown as a result of the error. Like any other exception object, this object has a Message property that provides a description of the error. You can also use the RowIndex and ColumnIndex properties of the second parameter to identify the row and column that caused the data error.

An event of the DataGridView control

Event	Description
DataError	Raised when the DataGridView control detects a data error such as a value that isn't in the correct format or a null value where a null value isn't valid.

Three properties of the DataGridViewDataErrorEventArgs class

Property	Description
Exception	The exception that was thrown as a result of the error. You can use the Message property of this object to get additional information about the exception.
RowIndex	The index for the row where the error occurred.
ColumnIndex	The index for the column where the error occurred.

Code that handles a data error for a DataGridView control

```
private void productsDataGridView_DataError(
    object sender, DataGridViewDataErrorEventArgs e)
{
    int row = e.RowIndex + 1;
    string errorMessage = "A data error occurred.\n" +
        "Row: " + row + "\n" +
        "Error: " + e.Exception.Message;
    MessageBox.Show(errorMessage, "Data Error");
}
```

Description

- You can code an event handler for the DataError event of the DataGridView control to handle any data errors that occur when working with the DataGridView control.
- You can use the Exception, RowIndex, and ColumnIndex properties of the second parameter of the event handler to display a meaningful error message.

Figure 18-15 How to handle data errors for a DataGridView control

How to use the Dataset Designer

The *Dataset Designer* lets you work with a dataset schema using a graphic interface. In the topics that follow, you'll learn some basic skills for working with the Dataset Designer.

How to view the schema for a dataset

To learn more about a dataset, you can display its schema in the Dataset Designer. In figure 18-16, for example, you can see the schema for the MMABooks dataset used by the Customer Maintenance application. For this simple application, this dataset contains just the Customers table since this is the only table used by the application. The key icon in this table indicates that the CustomerID column is the primary key for the table.

For each table, the dataset schema also includes a table adapter that lists the queries that can be used with the table. Each table adapter includes at least a *main query* named Fill that determines the columns that are used when you drag the table from the Data Sources window. This query is also used to generate the Insert, Update, and Delete statements for the table. In addition, the table adapter includes any other queries you've defined for the table. You'll learn more about defining additional queries in the next chapter.

If you click on a table adapter in the Dataset Designer, you'll see that its properties in the Properties window include the ADO.NET objects that the table adapter defines. That includes a Connection object, as well as SelectCommand, InsertCommand, UpdateCommand, and DeleteCommand objects. If you expand any of these command objects, you can look at the CommandText property that defines the SQL statement it executes. In this figure, for example, you can see the beginning of the Select statement for the SelectCommand object that's used by the Fill query of the table adapter for the Customers table. If you click on the ellipsis button for this property, you can work with the query using the Query Builder as shown in the next figure.

Note that the Dataset Designer also makes it easy to set the properties for a column in a table that's in the dataset. To do that, just select a column and use the Properties window. For instance, you can use this technique to set the DefaultValue property for a column in the dataset, which is something that you often have to do.

The schema displayed in the Dataset Designer

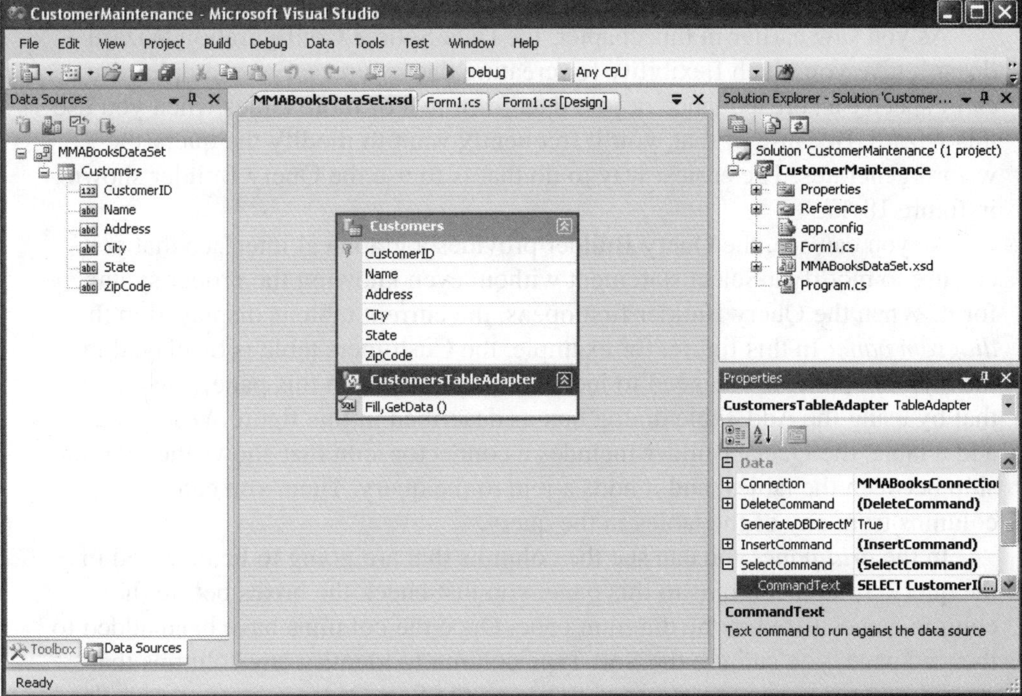

Description

- To view the schema for the dataset of a data source, double-click on the schema file for the dataset (.xsd) in the Solution Explorer, or select the schema file and click the View Designer button at the top of the Solution Explorer. The schema is displayed in the *Dataset Designer*.
- To view the properties for a table adapter in the Properties window, select the table adapter in the Dataset Designer. These properties include the Connection object that's used to connect to the database, and the SelectCommand, InsertCommand, UpdateCommand, and DeleteCommand objects that are used to work with the data in the database.
- To view the properties for a query, select the query in the Dataset Designer.
- For each table adapter, the query named Fill is the *main query*. This query determines the columns that are used when you drag a table from the Data Sources window onto a form. The Insert, Update, and Delete statements for the table are also based on this query.
- To work with the SQL statement in a CommandText property, you can click on the ellipsis button that appears when that property is selected. This displays the statement in the Query Builder, which you'll learn about in the next figure.
- To view and set the properties for a column in a table, select the column. This is an easy way to set the DefaultValue property for a column.

Figure 18-16 How to view the schema for a dataset

How to use the Query Builder

As you saw earlier in this chapter, the Data Source Configuration Wizard doesn't give you much flexibility for creating data sources. For example, you can't specify a sort sequence or join data from two or more tables when you use this wizard. Because of that, you'll frequently want to modify the query the wizard generates. The easiest way to do that is to use the Query Builder shown in figure 18-17.

As you can see, the Query Builder provides a graphical interface that you can use to modify a Select statement without even knowing the proper syntax for it. When the Query Builder first opens, the current table is displayed in the *diagram pane*. In this figure, for example, the Customers table is displayed in the diagram pane. If you need to include related tables in this pane, you can do that by using the Add Table dialog box as described in this figure. When you add a table, the Query Builder includes a connector icon that shows the relationship between the tables, and it adds a join to the query. Then, you can use columns from any of the tables in the query.

In the *grid pane*, you can see the columns that are going to be included in the query. To add columns to this pane, you just check the boxes before the column names listed in the diagram pane. Once the columns have been added to the grid pane, you can use the Sort Type column to identify any columns that should be used to sort the returned rows and the Sort Order column to give the order of precedence for the sort if more than one column is identified. Here, for example, the rows will be sorted in ascending sequence by the Name column.

Similarly, you can use the Filter column to establish the criteria to be used to select the rows that will be retrieved by the query. For example, to retrieve just the customer with a specific ID, you can specify @CustomerID in the Filter column for the CustomerID column. You'll learn more about coding this type of query in the next chapter.

As you create the query, the *SQL pane* shows the resulting Select statement. You can also run this query at any time to display the selected rows in the *results pane*. That way, you can be sure that the query works the way you want it to. To run the query, click the Execute Query button.

When you get the query the way you want it, you can click the OK button to save the query. When you do that, Visual Studio will display a dialog box that asks if you want to regenerate the updating commands based on the new command syntax. In other words, do you want to modify the Insert, Update, and Delete statements so that they match the Select statement. Depending on the changes you made, you may or may not want to do that. If, for example, you simply changed the sort sequence, it's not necessary to update the Insert, Update, and Delete statements. On the other hand, if you added or deleted one or more columns from the original table, you'll want to update the Insert, Update, and Delete statements so that they include the same columns as the Select statement.

The Query Builder

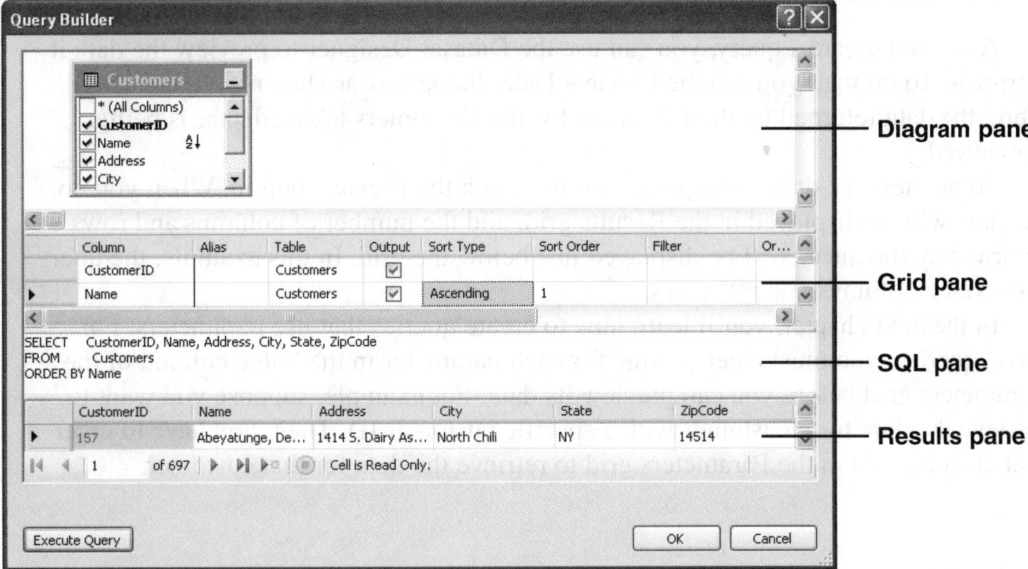

Description

- To display the Query Builder for the main query, select the table adapter that contains the query and then click on the ellipsis to the right of the CommandText property of the SelectCommand object in the Properties window.
- By default, the current table is displayed in the *diagram pane*. To add a related table to this pane, right-click in the pane, select Add Table, and select the table from the dialog box that's displayed. Then, a join is added to the query.
- To include a column in a query, click on the box to its left. Then, that column is added to the *grid pane*. Or, select all the columns by checking the * (All Columns) item.
- To create a calculated column, enter an expression in the Column column and then enter the name you want to use for the column in the Alias column.
- To sort the returned rows by one or more columns, select the Ascending or Descending option from the Sort Type column for those columns in the sequence you want them sorted. You can also use the Sort Order column to set the sort sequence.
- To specify selection criteria (like a specific value that the column must contain to be selected), enter the criteria in the Filter column.
- To use a column for sorting or for specifying criteria without including it in the query results, remove the check mark from the Output column.
- As you select columns and specify sort and selection criteria, the Query Builder builds the SQL statement and displays it in the *SQL pane*.
- To display the results of a query in the *results pane*, click the Execute Query button.
- When you accept the query, a dialog box will be displayed that asks if you want to update the Insert, Update, and Delete queries that are generated from the main query.

Figure 18-17 How to use the Query Builder

How to preview the data for a query

After you create a query, you can use the Dataset Designer to preview the data it retrieves. To do that, you use the Preview Data dialog box as shown in figure 18-18. Here, the data returned by the Fill query for the Customers table adapter is being previewed.

To preview the data for a query, you just click the Preview button. When you do, the data will be displayed in the Results grid, and the number of columns and rows returned by the query will be displayed just below the grid. In this example, the query retrieved 6 columns and 697 rows.

In the next chapter, you'll learn how to create queries that use parameters. For those queries, you must enter a value for each parameter in the Value column of the Parameters grid before you can preview its data. For example, suppose you want to retrieve the data for a customer with a specific customer ID. Then, you have to enter that customer ID in the Parameters grid to retrieve the data for that customer.

The Preview Data dialog box

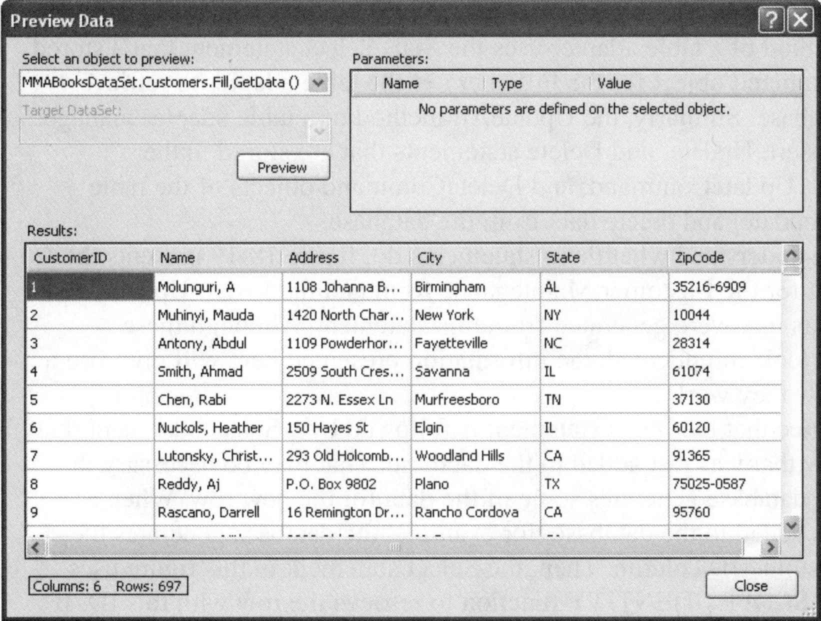

Description

- To display the Preview Data dialog box for a query, right-click on the query in the Dataset Designer and select the Preview Data command, or select the query and then use the Data→Preview Data command.
- To preview the data, click the Preview button. When you do, the data will be displayed in the Results grid, and the number of columns and rows returned by the query will be displayed just below the Results grid.
- If a query requires parameters, you must enter a value for each parameter in the Value column of the Parameters grid. See chapter 19 for more information on query parameters.

Figure 18-18 How to preview the data for a query

How to interpret the generated SQL statements

The Fill method of a table adapter uses the SQL Select statement that's stored in the SelectCommand object for the Fill query of the table adapter to retrieve data from a database. Similarly, the UpdateAll method of a table adapter manager uses the SQL Insert, Update, and Delete statements that are stored in the InsertCommand, UpdateCommand, and DeleteCommand objects of the table adapter to add, update, and delete data from the database.

To help you understand what these statements do, figure 18-19 presents the Select statement for the Customer Maintenance form and the Insert, Update, and Delete statements that were generated from this statement. Although these statements may look complicated, the information presented here will give you a good idea of how they work.

To start, notice that the Insert statement is followed by a Select statement that retrieves the row that was just added to the database. That may be necessary in cases where the database generates some of the data for the new row. When a customer row is added to the database, for example, the database generates the value of the CustomerID column. Then, the Select statement in this figure uses the SQL Server SCOPE_IDENTITY function to retrieve the row with this ID. If the database doesn't generate or calculate any of the column values, however, this Select statement, as well as the one after the Update statement, isn't needed.

Also notice that the Update and Delete statements use optimistic concurrency. Because of that, code is added to the Where clauses of these statements to check whether any of the column values have changed since they were retrieved from the database. This code compares the current value of each column in the database against the original value of the column, which is stored in the dataset. If none of the values have changed, the operation is performed. Otherwise, it's not.

Finally, notice that most of the statements in this figure use one or more parameters. For example, parameters are used in the Values clause of the Insert statement and the Set clause of the Update statement to refer to the current values of the columns in the dataset. Parameters are also used in the Where clauses of the Update and Delete statements to refer to the original values of the columns in the dataset. And one is used in the Where clause of the Select statement after the Update statement to refer to the current row. The wizard inserts these parameters when it creates the command objects for a table adapter. Then, before each statement is executed, Visual Studio substitutes the appropriate value for each variable.

This should give you more perspective on how the dataset is refreshed and how optimistic concurrency is provided when you use ADO.NET. Because of the disconnected data architecture, these features can't be provided by the database management system or by ADO.NET. Instead, they are provided by the SQL statements that are generated by the Data Source Configuration Wizard.

SQL that retrieves customer rows

```
SELECT      CustomerID, Name, Address, City, State, ZipCode
FROM        Customers
```

SQL that inserts a customer row and refreshes the dataset

```
INSERT INTO Customers
             (Name, Address, City, State, ZipCode)
VALUES       (@Name, @Address, @City, @State, @ZipCode);

SELECT      CustomerID, Name, Address, City, State, ZipCode
FROM        Customers
WHERE       (CustomerID = SCOPE_IDENTITY())
```

SQL that updates a customer row and refreshes the dataset

```
UPDATE     Customers
SET        Name = @Name,
           Address = @Address,
           City = @City,
           State = @State,
           ZipCode = @ZipCode
WHERE      (
           (CustomerID = @Original_CustomerID) AND
           (Name = @Original_Name) AND
           (Address = @Original_Address) AND
           (City = @Original_City) AND
           (State = @Original_State) AND
           (ZipCode = @Original_ZipCode)
           );

SELECT      CustomerID, Name, Address, City, State, ZipCode
FROM        Customers
WHERE       (CustomerID = @CustomerID)
```

SQL that deletes a customer row

```
DELETE FROM Customers
WHERE       (CustomerID = @Original_CustomerID) AND
            (Name = @Original_Name) AND
            (Address = @Original_Address) AND
            (City = @Original_City) AND
            (State = @Original_State) AND
            (ZipCode = @Original_ZipCode)
```

Description

- By default, the Data Source Configuration Wizard adds code to the Where clause of the Update and Delete statements that checks that the data hasn't changed since it was retrieved.
- By default, the Data Source Configuration Wizard adds a Select statement after the Insert and Update statements to refresh the new or modified row in the dataset.
- The SQL statements use parameters to identify the new values for an insert or update operation. Parameters are also used for the original column values, which are used to check that a row hasn't changed for an update or delete operation. And one is used in the Where clause of the Select statement after the Update statement to refer to the current row. The values for these parameters are stored in and retrieved from the dataset.

Figure 18-19 How to interpret the generated SQL statements

Perspective

Now that you've completed this chapter, you should be able to use a data source to create simple applications that let you view and maintain the data in one table of a database. That should give you some idea of how quickly and easily you can create applications when you use the data source feature. And in the next chapter, you'll learn how you can use data sources to build more complex applications.

Terms

data source
schema
typed dataset
untyped dataset
binding a control
bound control
complex data binding
simple data binding
parameterized query
data provider error
ADO.NET error
Dataset Designer
main query

Before you do the exercises for this section...

Before you do any of the exercises in this section, be sure to install SQL Server Express and attach the MMABooks database to it as explained in appendix A.

Exercise 18-1 Build a DataGridView application

In this exercise, you'll build the Product Maintenance application shown in figure 18-9. That will show you how to build a simple application with data sources, a dataset, and a DataGridView control.

Build the form and test it with valid data

1. Start a new application named ProductMaintenance in the C:\C# 2008\Chapter 18 directory, and use the techniques in figures 18-1 through 18-8 to create the data source and drag it onto the form. Then, adjust the size of the form and the DataGridView control as needed, but don't change anything else.

2. Test the application with valid data in three phases. First, sort the rows by clicking on a column header, and size one of the columns by dragging its column separator. Second, change the data in one column of a row, and move to another row to see that the data is changed in the dataset. Third, add a new row with valid data in all columns, and move to another row to see that the row has been added. At this point, the changes have been made to the dataset only, not the database. Now, click the Save button in the toolbar to save the changes to the database.

Test the form with invalid data and provide exception handling

3. Test the application with invalid data by deleting the data in the Description column of a row and moving to another row. This should cause a NoNullAllowedException that's automatically handled by the DataGridView control so the application doesn't crash.
4. Add an exception handler for the DataError event of the DataGridView control as shown in figure 18-15. To start the code for that handler, click on the control, click on the Events button in the Properties window, and double-click on the DataError event. Then, write the code for the event, and redo the testing of step 3 to see how your code works.
5. When you're through experimenting, end the application, and close the project.

Exercise 18-2 Build an application with text boxes

In this exercise, you'll build the Customer Maintenance application shown in figure 18-12. That will show you how to use data sources with controls like text boxes.

Build the form and test it with valid data

1. Start a new application named CustomerMaintenance in the C:\C# 2008\Chapter 18 directory, and create a data source for the Customers table. Then, use the techniques in figures 18-10 and 18-11 to drag the data source fields onto the form as text boxes. At this point, the form should look like the one in figure 18-11.
2. Test the application with valid data in three phases. First, use the toolbar to navigate through the rows. Second, change the data in one column of a row (other than the CustomerID column), move to another row, and return to the first row to see that the data has been changed in the dataset. Third, add a new row with valid data in all columns (leave the customer ID at -1), move to another row, and return to the added row to see that the row has been added to the dataset. Now, click the Save button in the toolbar to save the dataset to the database. Notice that the customer ID that was generated by the database is now displayed.

Test the form with invalid data and provide exception handling

3. Add a new row to the dataset, but don't enter anything into the City field. Then, click on the Save button. This should cause a NoNullAllowedException, since City is a required field.
4. Add exception handling code for an ADO.NET DataException as shown in figure 18-14 to catch this type of error. Then, run the application and redo the testing of step 3 to see how this error is handled now.
5. Delete the data in the Name column of a row, which means that the column contains an empty string. Next, move to another row, and return to the first row to see that the row has been accepted into the dataset. Then, click on the Save button and discover that this doesn't throw an exception because an empty string isn't the same as a null value. This indicates that data validation is required because an empty string isn't an acceptable value in the database. In the next chapter, you'll see an enhanced version of the Customer Maintenance application that provides data validation.
6. Adjust the controls on the form and any related properties so the form looks like the one in figure 18-12. This should take just a minute or two.

Use the Dataset Designer

7. Use one of the techniques in figure 18-16 to view the schema for the dataset in the Dataset Designer.
8. Click on the table adapter in the Dataset Designer and review its properties in the Properties window. Then, look at the Select statement that's used for getting the data into the dataset. To do that, click on the plus sign in front of SelectCommand, and click on the ellipsis button for the CommandText property to open up the Query Builder.
9. Use the Query Builder to modify the Select statement so that the rows are sorted in ascending sequence by the Name column as shown in figure 18-17. When you're done, close the Query Builder and click the No button in the dialog box that's displayed.
10. Right-click on the query in the Dataset Designer, and preview the data that will be retrieved by that query as shown in figure 18-18. Note that since you changed the sort sequence, the rows will be displayed in order by the Name column rather than by the CustomerID column.
11. When you're through experimenting, close the Dataset Designer, and close the project.

19

How to work with bound controls and parameterized queries

In the last chapter, you learned the basic skills for developing applications by using data sources and datasets. Now, you'll learn some additional skills for building database applications that way. Specifically, you'll learn how to work with bound controls, how to use parameterized queries, how to customize the generated toolbars, and how to work with a DataGridView control.

How to work with bound text boxes and combo boxes

The topics that follow show you how to work with bound text boxes and combo boxes. First, you'll learn how to format the data that's displayed in text boxes. Second, you'll learn how to bind data to a combo box. And third, you'll learn how to work with the BindingSource object to make sure that the data and controls are synchronized.

How to format the data displayed in a text box

In the last chapter, you learned how to use bound text boxes to work with the data in a Customers table. However, because the columns of that table contain string data, it wasn't necessary to format the data when it was displayed. In many cases, though, you'll want to format the data so it's displayed properly.

Figure 19-1 shows how you can apply standard formatting to the data that's displayed in a bound text box. To do that, you use the Formatting and Advanced Binding dialog box. From this dialog box, you can select the format you want to apply from the Format Type list. Then, you can enter appropriate values for the options that are displayed to the right of this list. In this figure, for example, a currency format is being applied to the text box that's bound to the UnitPrice column of the Products table.

The dialog box that you can use to apply formatting to a column

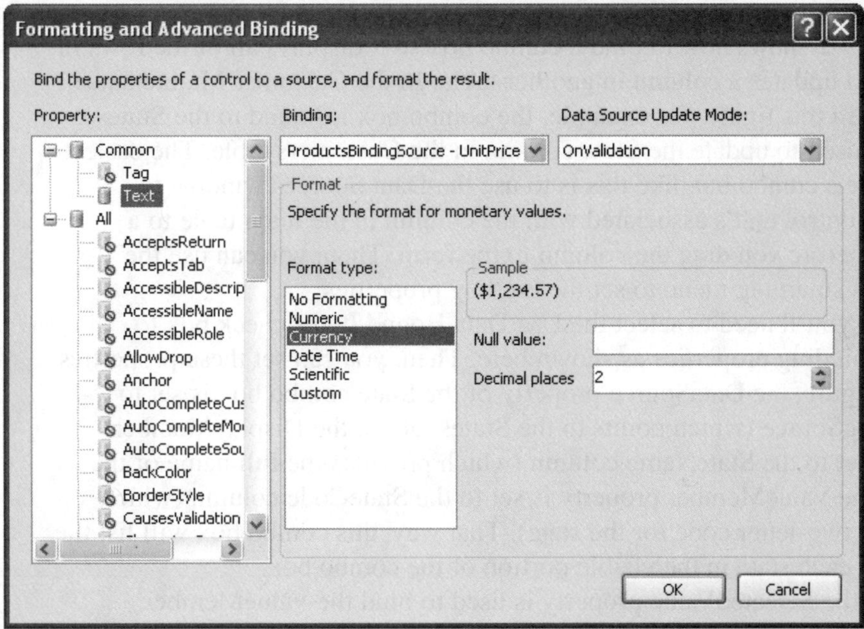

Description

- To display the Formatting and Advanced Binding dialog box, select the text box whose data you want to format, expand the DataBindings group in the Properties window, and then click the ellipsis button that appears when you select the Advanced option.
- To apply a format, select the format you want to use from the Format Type list and enter any additional options that appear to the right of the list. Numeric, Currency, and Scientific let you enter the number of decimal places to be displayed. Date Time lets you select from a number of date and time formats. And Custom lets you enter a custom format.
- Each format also lets you enter the value you want to display in place of a null value. The default is an empty string.
- If you select the Custom format, a note is displayed indicating that the format may not be applied and that you should use the Format or Parse event of the Binding object to apply it instead. See Visual Studio help for more information.

Figure 19-1 How to format the data displayed in a text box

How to bind a combo box to a data source

Figure 19-2 shows how to bind a combo box so it displays all of the rows in one table and updates a column in another table. In the Customer Maintenance form shown in this figure, for example, the combo box is bound to the States table and is used to update the State column in the Customers table. The easiest way to create a combo box like this is to use the Data Sources window to change the control that's associated with the column in the main table to a combo box before you drag the column to the form. Then, you can use the combo box's smart tag menu to set the binding properties.

To start, you'll need to select the Use Data Bound Items check box to display the binding properties as shown here. Then, you can set these properties.

In this figure, the DataSource property of the State combo box is set to statesBindingSource (which points to the States table), the DisplayMember property is set to the StateName column (which provides the full name of the state), and the ValueMember property is set to the StateCode column (which provides the two-letter code for the state). That way, this combo box will list the full name of each state in the visible portion of the combo box.

Finally, the SelectedValue property is used to bind the ValueMember property to a column in another data source. In this case, the SelectedValue property is set to the State column of the customersBindingSource. That way, the StateCode column of the States table is bound to the State column of the Customers table. Then, when the data for a customer is displayed, the state that's selected in the combo box is determined by the State column of the Customers table. Also, if the user selects a different item from the combo box list, the States column in the Customers table is changed to the value selected by the user.

In addition to the four properties in the smart tag menu, you may also need to set a couple of other properties when you bind a combo box. In particular, you can set the DropDownStyle property to DropDownList to prevent the user from entering text into the text portion of the combo box. Then, you can set the Text property in the DataBindings group to None so the application doesn't bind the value stored in this property to the data source. *If this property isn't set correctly, the combo box won't work properly.*

Although you've learned only how to bind combo boxes in this topic, you should realize that you can use similar skills to work with other types of controls. In particular, you can use most of these skills to work with list boxes. If you experiment with this on your own, you shouldn't have any trouble figuring out how it works.

A combo box that's bound to a data source

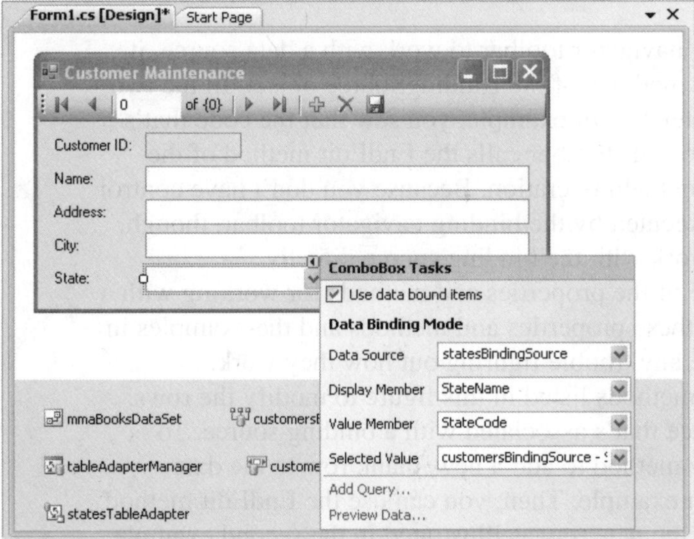

Combo box properties for binding

Property	Description
DataSource	The name of the data table that contains the data displayed in the list.
DisplayMember	The name of the data column whose data is displayed in the list.
ValueMember	The name of the data column whose value is stored in the list. This value is returned by the SelectedValue property of the control.
SelectedValue	Gets the value of the currently selected item. You can use this property to bind the ValueMember property to a column in the data source.

Description

- To access the most common properties for binding a combo box, you can display the smart tag menu for the combo box and select the Use Data Bound Items check box. This will display the properties shown above.
- To set the DataSource property, display the drop-down list; expand the Other Data Sources node, the Project Data Sources node, and the node for the dataset; and select the table you want to use as the data source. This adds BindingSource and TableAdapter objects for the table to the form. Then, you can set the DisplayMember and ValueMember properties to columns in this table.
- The SelectedValue property is typically bound to a column in the main table. That way, if you select a different item from the combo box, the value of this column is set to the value of the ValueMember property for the selected item.
- When you bind a combo box to a data source, you'll typically set the DropDownStyle property of the combo box to DropDownList so the user can only select a value from the list. You'll also want to change the (DataBindings) - Text property to None to remove the binding from the text box portion of the combo box.

Figure 19-2 How to bind a combo box to a data source

How to use code to work with a binding source

When you use the binding navigator toolbar to work with a data source, it works by using properties and methods of the BindingSource object. In the two applications presented in chapter 18, for example, you saw that the code that's generated for the Save button of this toolbar calls the EndEdit method of the binding source to end the current edit operation. Because you don't have control over most of the code that's executed by the binding navigator toolbar, though, you may sometimes want to work with the binding source directly.

Figure 19-3 presents some of the properties and methods for working with a binding source. If you review these properties and methods and the examples in this figure, you shouldn't have any trouble figuring out how they work.

You can use the first four methods listed in this figure to modify the rows that are stored in the data source that's associated with a binding source. To start, you can use the AddNew method to add a new, blank row to the data source as illustrated in the first example. Then, you can use the EndEdit method to save the data you enter into the new row as illustrated in the second example. You can also use this method to save changes you make to an existing row.

If an error occurs when you try to save changes to a row, or if the user decides to cancel an edit operation, you can use the CancelEdit method to cancel the changes as illustrated in the third example. Note, however, that you don't have to explicitly start an edit operation. The binding source takes care of that automatically when you make changes to a row. Finally, you can use the RemoveCurrent method to remove the current row from the data source as illustrated in the fourth example.

You can use the last four methods in this figure to move to the first, previous, next, or last row in a data source. You can also use the Position property to get or set the index of the current row. And you can use the Count property to get the number of rows in the data source.

To illustrate how you might use these properties and methods, the last example in this figure presents an event handler that responds to the Click event of a button. This event handler uses the MoveNext method to move to the next row in the data source. Then, it uses the Position property to get the index of the current row, and it adds one to the result since the index is zero-based. Finally, it uses the Count property to get the total number of rows in the data source, and it displays the position and count in a text box. This is similar to the display that's included in the binding navigator toolbar.

Common properties and methods of the BindingSource class

Property	Description
`Position`	The index of the current row in the data source.
`Count`	The number of rows in the data source.
Method	**Description**
`AddNew()`	Adds a new, blank row to the data source.
`EndEdit()`	Saves changes to the current row.
`CancelEdit()`	Cancels changes to the current row.
`RemoveCurrent()`	Removes the current row from the data source.
`MoveFirst()`	Moves to the first row in the data source.
`MovePrevious()`	Moves to the previous row in the data source, if there is one.
`MoveNext()`	Moves to the next row in the data source, if there is one.
`MoveLast()`	Moves to the last row in the data source.

A statement that adds a new row to a data source

```
this.customersBindingSource.AddNew()
```

A statement that saves the changes to the current row and ends the edit

```
this.customersBindingSource.EndEdit()
```

A statement that cancels the changes to the current row

```
this.customersBindingSource.CancelEdit()
```

A statement that removes the current row from a data source

```
this.customersBindingSource.RemoveCurrent()
```

Code that moves to the next row and displays the position and count

```
private void btnNext_Click(object sender, EventArgs e)
{
    this.customersBindingSource.MoveNext();
    int position = customersBindingSource.Position + 1;
    txtPosition.Text = position + " of " + customersBindingSource.Count;
}
```

Description

- The binding source ensures that all controls that are bound to the same data table are synchronized. That way, when you move to another row, the data-bound controls will display the values in that row.
- If a form provides for updating the rows in a data table, moving from one row to another causes any changes made to the current row to be saved to the data table.
- When you add a new row using the AddNew method, the Position property of the binding source is set to one more than the position of the last row in the data table.
- You can use the EndEdit and CancelEdit methods to save or cancel the changes to an existing row or a new row that was added using the AddNew method.

Figure 19-3 How to use code to work with a binding source

How to work with parameterized queries

In the last chapter, you learned how the Data Source Configuration Wizard uses parameters in the SQL statements it generates. A query like this that contains parameters is called a *parameterized query*. In the topics that follow, you'll learn one way to create parameterized queries for your forms.

How to create a parameterized query

For some applications, such as the Product Maintenance application presented in the previous chapter, it's acceptable (or even preferable) to fill the table in the dataset with every row in the database table. However, if a database table contains many columns and rows, this can have a negative impact on the performance of your application. In addition, for some types of applications, you will only want to allow the user to retrieve certain rows from a table. In either case, the solution is to use a parameterized query.

Fortunately, Visual Studio provides an easy way to create a parameterized query, as shown in figure 19-4. When you use this technique, Visual Studio generates a toolbar that lets the user enter the parameters for the query. It also generates the code that fills the table in the dataset with the results of the query.

To create a parameterized query, you can begin by displaying the smart tag menu for any control that's bound to the data source. Then, you can select the Add Query command from this menu. When you do, Visual Studio will display a Search Criteria Builder dialog box like the one shown here. This dialog box lets you enter the name and parameters for the query.

By default, a query is named FillBy, but you can change it to anything you want. I recommend that you name a query based on the function it performs. In this figure, for example, the query has been named FillByCustomerID because it will be used to retrieve a customer row based on the customer ID.

After you enter the query name, you can modify the Where clause of the query so it includes one or more parameters. In SQL Server, you specify a parameter by coding an @ sign in front of the parameter name. In this figure, for example, the query will return all rows where the value in the CustomerID column equals the value of the @CustomerID parameter.

When you finish specifying the query in the Search Criteria Builder dialog box, Visual Studio automatically adds a toolbar to your form. This toolbar contains one or more text boxes that let the user enter the parameters that are needed by the query and a button that lets the user execute the query. You can see this toolbar in the Customer Maintenance form shown in this figure.

Using this toolbar, the user can retrieve a single row that contains the customer's data by entering the ID for the customer and then clicking the FillByCustomerID button. In this figure, for example, the user has displayed the row for the customer with an ID of 35. That's why the binding navigator toolbar shows that only one row exists in the Customers data table.

The dialog box for creating a parameterized query

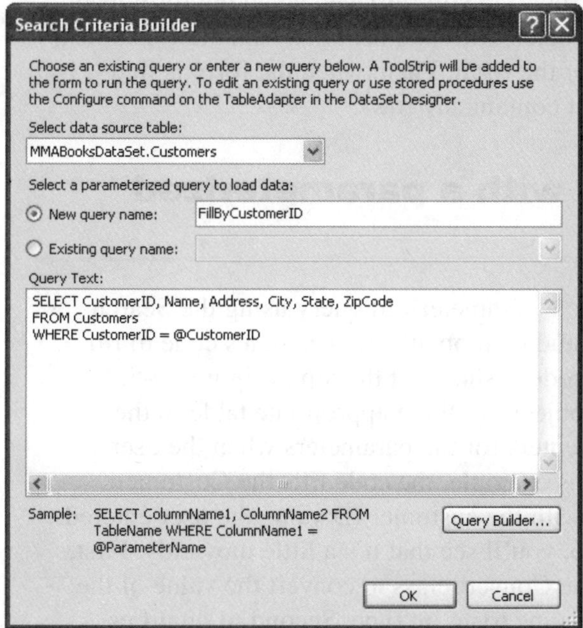

The Customer Maintenance form with a toolbar for the query

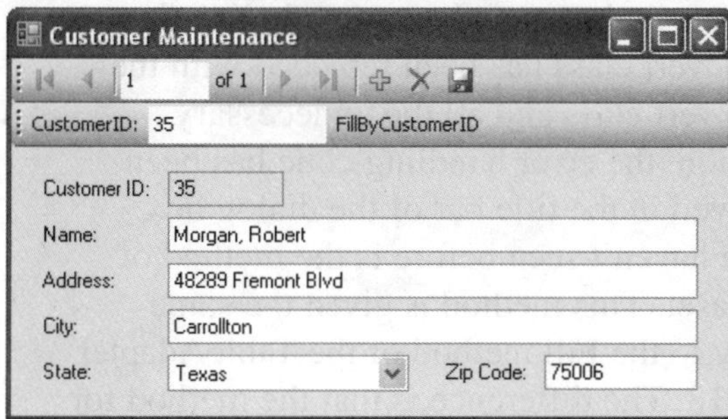

Description

- You can add a *parameterized query* to a data table using the Search Criteria Builder dialog box. To display this dialog box, display the smart tag menu for a control that's bound to the data table and then select the Add Query command.
- When you finish specifying the query in the Search Criteria Builder dialog box, Visual Studio automatically adds a toolbar to your form. This toolbar contains the text boxes that let the user enter the parameters that are needed by the query, and it contains a button that lets the user execute the query.
- You can add more than one parameterized query to a data table using the Search Criteria Builder. Each query you add is displayed in its own toolbar. Because of that, you may want to modify one of the toolbars so that it provides for all the queries.

Figure 19-4 How to create a parameterized query

Although the parameterized query in this example retrieves a single row from the Customers table, all of the rows are still retrieved when the form loads. If that's not what you want, you can delete the statement that fills the Customers table from the Load event handler for the form. Then, when the form is first displayed, the Customers table won't contain any rows.

How to use code to work with a parameterized query

As I mentioned, when you create a parameterized query using the Search Criteria Builder dialog box, Visual Studio automatically generates code to fill the data table using the query. This code is shown at the top of figure 19-5. It calls a method of the TableAdapter object to fill the appropriate table in the dataset based on the values the user enters for the parameters when the user clicks the button in the toolbar. In this example, the code fills the Customers table with the row for the customer with the customer ID value the user entered.

If you review the generated code, you'll see that it's a little unwieldy. First, it uses the ChangeType method of the Convert class to convert the value of the CustomerID parameter from a string type to an int type. Second, it qualifies references to the Convert class, the Forms class, and the MessageBox class even though that's not necessary within the context of this form. To make this code easier to read, you can clean it up as shown in the second example in this figure. Here, the ChangeType method of the Convert class has been replaced with the more concise ToInt32 method of the Convert class and all the unnecessary qualification has been removed. In addition, the error handling code has been enhanced so the exception type is displayed in the title bar of the dialog box.

The only piece of code here that you haven't seen before is the method of the TableAdapter object that fills the dataset. This method is given the same name as the query, and it works similarly to the Fill method of the TableAdapter object that you learned about in chapter 18. The difference is that the method for a parameterized query lets you specify the parameter or parameters that are required by the query. In this figure, for example, the FillByCustomerID method of the customersTableAdapter object requires a single parameter of the int type. To get this parameter, the code gets the string that's entered by the user into the text box on the toolbar, and it converts this string to an int type.

Note that the FillByCustomerID method of the table adapter fills the Customers table of the dataset with only one row. Then, if the user makes any changes to that row, he or she must click the Save button to save those changes to the database. If the user retrieves another row instead, that row fills the dataset and the changes are lost. Similarly, the user must click the Save button to save a deletion before moving to another row. Although this user interface works, it isn't very intuitive. As a result, you'll typically want to modify interfaces like this one.

The generated code for a parameterized query

```
private void fillByCustomerIDToolStripButton_Click(
    object sender, EventArgs e)
{
    try
    {
        this.customersTableAdapter.FillByCustomerID(
            this.mmaBooksDataSet.Customers,
            ((int)(System.Convert.ChangeType(
            customerIDToolStripTextBox.Text, typeof(int)))));
    }
    catch (System.Exception ex)
    {
        System.Windows.Forms.MessageBox.Show(ex.Message);
    }
}
```

The same code after it has been cleaned up and enhanced

```
private void fillByCustomerIDToolStripButton_Click(
    object sender, EventArgs e)
{
    try
    {
        int customerID = Convert.ToInt32(
            customerIDToolStripTextBox.Text);

        this.customersTableAdapter.FillByCustomerID(
            this.mmaBooksDataSet.Customers,
            customerID);
    }
    catch (Exception ex)
    {
        MessageBox.Show(ex.Message, ex.GetType().ToString());
    }
}
```

The syntax of the method for filling a table using a parameterized query

```
tableAdapter.QueryName(dataSet.TableName, param1 [,param2]...)
```

Description

- When you finish specifying a query in the Search Criteria Builder dialog box, Visual Studio automatically generates the code that uses the appropriate method to fill the table in the dataset when the user clicks the button in the toolbar.
- If necessary, you can modify the generated code to make it easier to read or to change the way it works.

Figure 19-5 How to use code to work with a parameterized query

How to work with the ToolStrip control

Although the ToolStrip control Visual Studio generates for a parameterized query works well for simple applications, you may want to modify it as your applications become more complex. For example, you may want to change the text on the button that executes the query. Or, you may want to add additional text boxes and buttons that work with other queries. Fortunately, the ToolStrip control is easy to customize.

Before I go on, you should know that the binding navigator toolbar that gets generated when you drag a data source onto a form is a customized ToolStrip control. As a result, you can work with this toolbar just as you would any other ToolStrip control. If, for example, a form won't provide for inserts, updates, and deletes, you can remove the Add, Delete, and Save buttons from this toolbar. You can also add controls that perform customized functions.

How to use the Items Collection Editor

To work with the items on a ToolStrip control, you use the Items Collection Editor shown in figure 19-6. To start, you can add an item by selecting the type of control you want to add from the combo box in the upper left corner and clicking the Add button. This adds the item to the bottom of the Members list. Then, if necessary, you can move the item using the up and down arrow buttons to the right of the Members list.

You can also use the Items Collection Editor to set the properties for a new or existing item. To do that, just select the item in the Members list and use the Properties list at the right side of the dialog box to set the properties. The table in this figure lists the four properties you're most likely to change. Note that when you add a new Button control, the DisplayStyle property is set to Image by default. If you want to display the text that you specify for the Text property instead of an image, then, you need to change the DisplayStyle property to Text.

Finally, you can use the Items Collection Editor to delete an existing item. To do that, just select the item and click the Delete button to the right of the Members list.

The Items Collection Editor for an enhanced ToolStrip control

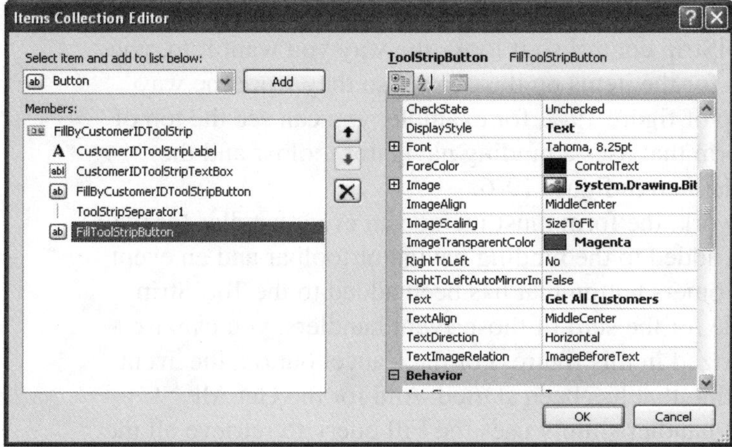

Common properties of ToolStrip items

Property	Description
DisplayStyle	Indicates whether a button displays an image, text, or both an image and text.
Image	The image that's displayed on a button if you select Image or ImageAndText for the DisplayStyle property.
Text	The text that's displayed on a button if you select Text or ImageAndText for the DisplayStyle property.
Width	The width of the item.

Description

- To display the Items Collection Editor dialog box, display the smart tag menu for the ToolStrip and select the Edit Items command.
- To add an item, select the type of control you want to add from the combo box and click the Add button. To add a separator bar, choose Separator. You can also add an item by using the drop-down list that's displayed when the ToolStrip is selected in the Form Designer.
- To move an item, select the item in the Members list and click the up and down arrows to the right of the list.
- To delete an item, select it in the Members list and click the Delete button to the right of the list.
- To set the properties for an item, select the item in the Members list and use the Properties list on the right side of the dialog box to set the properties. You can also set the properties of an item by selecting it in the Form Designer and then using the Properties window.

Note

- Because the BindingNavigator control is a ToolStrip control, you can use the Items Collection Editor to work with the BindingNavigator control.

Figure 19-6 How to use the Items Collection Editor

How to code an event handler for a ToolStrip item

After you modify a ToolStrip control so it looks the way you want it to, you need to code event handlers for the items on the control so they work the way you want them to. At the top of figure 19-7, for example, you can see the top of a Customer Maintenance form that uses a binding navigator toolbar and the ToolStrip control that was defined in figure 19-6.

For this application to work, the form must include an event handler for the Cancel button that has been added to the binding navigator toolbar and an event handler for the Get All Customers button that has been added to the ToolStrip control. To generate the code for the start of those event handlers, you can use the technique that's summarized in this figure. For the Cancel button, the event handler just cancels the editing that has been started. And for the Get All Customers button, the event handler simply uses the Fill query to retrieve all the customer rows.

In addition to the event handlers for the Cancel and Get All Customers buttons, the form also includes the event handler Visual Studio generated when the FillByCustomerID parameterized query was created. You can see an enhanced version of that event handler in this figure. Here, code has been added so that if the customer with the customer ID the user enters isn't found, an error message is displayed. In addition, the single catch block that Visual Studio generated to catch any exception has been replaced by two catch blocks that catch specific exceptions. The first one catches a FormatException, which will occur if the customer ID isn't an int value, and the second one catches a SqlException.

Customized toolbars for a Customer Maintenance application

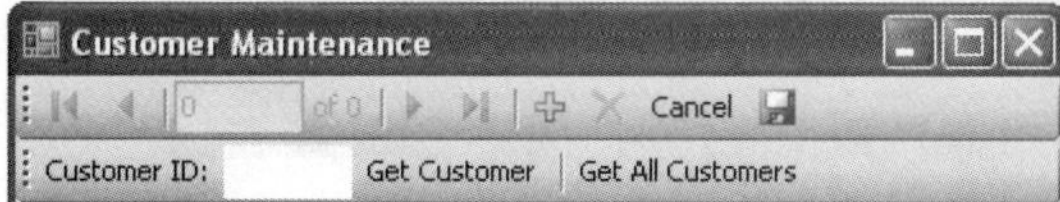

The event handler for the Cancel ToolStrip button

```
private void bindingNavigatorCancelItem_Click(object sender, EventArgs e)
{
    this.customersBindingSource.CancelEdit();
}
```

The event handler for the Get All Customers ToolStrip button

```
private void fillToolStripButton_Click(object sender, EventArgs e)
{
    try
    {
        this.customersTableAdapter.Fill(this.mmaBooksDataSet.Customers);
    }
    catch (SqlException ex)
    {
        MessageBox.Show("Database error # " + ex.Number +
            ": " + ex.Message, ex.GetType().ToString());
    }
}
```

The event handler for the Get Customer ToolStrip button

```
private void fillByCustomerIDToolStripButton_Click(
    object sender, EventArgs e)
{
    try
    {
        int customerID = Convert.ToInt32(customerIDToolStripTextBox.Text);
        this.customersTableAdapter.FillByCustomerID(
            this.mmaBooksDataSet.Customers, customerID);
        if (customersBindingSource.Count == 0)
            MessageBox.Show("No customer found with this ID. "
                + "Please try again.", "Customer Not Found");
    }
    catch (FormatException)
    {
        MessageBox.Show("Customer ID must be an integer.", "Entry Error");
    }
    catch (SqlException ex)
    {
        MessageBox.Show("Database error # " + ex.Number +
            ": " + ex.Message, ex.GetType().ToString());
    }
}
```

Description

- To code an event handler for a ToolStrip item, display the form in the Form Designer, click on the item to select it, and click on the Events button of the Properties window to display the list of events for the item. Then, you can use standard techniques to generate or select an event handler for a specified event.

Figure 19-7 How to code an event handler for a ToolStrip item

An enhanced Customer Maintenance application

To illustrate some of the new skills you've learned so far in this chapter, I'll now present an enhanced version of the Customer Maintenance application that you saw in the last chapter.

The user interface

Figure 19-8 presents the user interface for the Customer Maintenance application. This time, the application uses two queries. The first one retrieves a row from the Customers table based on its customer ID, and the second one retrieves all the rows from the Customers table. In addition, the form uses a combo box that lets the user select a state, and its generated toolbars have been modified.

The code

Figure 19-8 also presents the code for the Customer Maintenance application. Since you've already seen most of this code, you shouldn't have any trouble understanding how it works. So I'll just point out some highlights.

First, the event handler for the Load event of the form doesn't load all the customers into the Customers table. That's because the second toolbar on the form provides a way for the user to do that if necessary. This is more efficient than retrieving all the customers when the form is loaded because the customers are retrieved only if requested.

Second, the event handler for the Click event of the Cancel button contains a single statement that cancels the current edit operation. Since this operation can't cause any exceptions, you don't have to use a try-catch statement with it.

Third, the event handler for the Click event of the Save button starts by checking if the data source contains at least one row. If not, it indicates that the row that was retrieved has been deleted. In that case, the data shouldn't be validated. Instead, the database should just be updated.

If the data source contains at least one row, a function named IsValidData is called. You saw procedures like this in chapter 7. It checks that the user has entered a value into each control on the form by calling another function named IsPresent for each of those controls. Unlike the IsPresent function you saw in chapter 7, this function checks for values in both text boxes and combo boxes. To do that, it uses the GetType method of the control that's passed to the function to get the control type, and it uses the ToString method of that type to get the name of the type. Then, it compares that name with type names that are specified as strings, and it processes the data in the control accordingly.

The user interface for the Customer Maintenance application

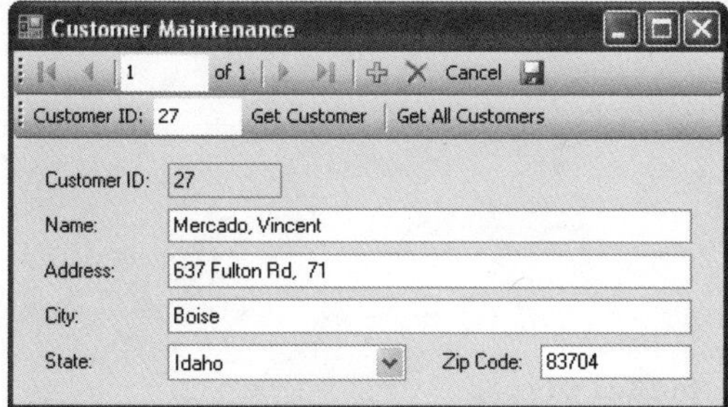

The code for the application **Page 1**

```
private void Form1_Load(object sender, EventArgs e)
{
    try
    {
        this.statesTableAdapter.Fill(this.mmaBooksDataSet.States);
        stateComboBox.SelectedIndex = -1;
    }
    catch (SqlException ex)
    {
        MessageBox.Show("Database error # " + ex.Number +
            ": " + ex.Message, ex.GetType().ToString());
    }
}

private void fillByCustomerIDToolStripButton_Click(object sender, EventArgs e)
{
    try
    {
        int customerID = Convert.ToInt32(customerIDToolStripTextBox.Text);

        this.customersTableAdapter.FillByCustomerID(
            this.mmaBooksDataSet.Customers, customerID);

        if (customersBindingSource.Count == 0)
            MessageBox.Show("No customer found with this ID. "
                + "Please try again.", "Customer Not Found");
    }
    catch (FormatException)
    {
        MessageBox.Show("Customer ID must be an integer.", "Entry Error");
    }
    catch (SqlException ex)
    {
        MessageBox.Show("Database error # " + ex.Number +
            ": " + ex.Message, ex.GetType().ToString());
    }
}

private void bindingNavigatorCancelItem_Click(object sender, EventArgs e)
{
    this.customersBindingSource.CancelEdit();
}
```

Figure 19-8 An enhanced Customer Maintenance application (part 1 of 3)

The code for the application **Page 2**

```
private void customersBindingNavigatorSaveItem_Click(
    object sender, EventArgs e)
{
    if (customersBindingSource.Count > 0)
    {
        if (IsValidData())
        {
            try
            {
                this.customersBindingSource.EndEdit();
                this.tableAdapterManager.UpdateAll(this.mmaBooksDataSet);
            }
            catch (ArgumentException ex)
            {
                MessageBox.Show(ex.Message, "Argument Exception");
                customersBindingSource.CancelEdit();
            }
            catch (DBConcurrencyException)
            {
                MessageBox.Show("A concurrency error occurred. " +
                    "Some rows were not updated.", "Concurrency Exception");
                this.customersTableAdapter.Fill(
                    this.mmaBooksDataSet.Customers);
            }
            catch (DataException ex)
            {
                MessageBox.Show(ex.Message, ex.GetType().ToString());
                customersBindingSource.CancelEdit();
            }
            catch (SqlException ex)
            {
                MessageBox.Show("Database error # " + ex.Number +
                    ": " + ex.Message, ex.GetType().ToString());
            }
        }
    }
    else
    {
        try
        {
            this.tableAdapterManager.UpdateAll(this.mmaBooksDataSet);
        }
        catch (DBConcurrencyException)
        {
            MessageBox.Show("A concurrency error occurred. " +
                "Some rows were not updated.", "Concurrency Exception");
            this.customersTableAdapter.Fill(this.mmaBooksDataSet.Customers);
        }
        catch (SqlException ex)
        {
            MessageBox.Show("Database error # " + ex.Number +
                ": " + ex.Message, ex.GetType().ToString());
        }
    }
}
```

Figure 19-8 An enhanced Customer Maintenance application (part 2 of 3)

The code for the application Page 3

```
public bool IsValidData()
{
    return
        IsPresent(nameTextBox, "Name") &&
        IsPresent(addressTextBox, "Address") &&
        IsPresent(cityTextBox, "City") &&
        IsPresent(stateComboBox, "State") &&
        IsPresent(zipCodeTextBox, "Zip code");
}

public bool IsPresent(Control control, string name)
{
    if (control.GetType().ToString() == "System.Windows.Forms.TextBox")
    {
        TextBox textBox = (TextBox)control;
        if (textBox.Text == "")
        {
            MessageBox.Show(name + " is a required field.", "Entry Error");
            textBox.Focus();
            return false;
        }
    }
    else if (control.GetType().ToString() == "System.Windows.Forms.ComboBox")
    {
        ComboBox comboBox = (ComboBox)control;
        if (comboBox.SelectedIndex == -1)
        {
            MessageBox.Show(name + " is a required field.", "Entry Error");
            comboBox.Focus();
            return false;
        }
    }
    return true;
}

private void fillToolStripButton_Click(object sender, EventArgs e)
{
    try
    {
        this.customersTableAdapter.Fill(this.mmaBooksDataSet.Customers);
    }
    catch (SqlException ex)
    {
        MessageBox.Show("Database error # " + ex.Number +
            ": " + ex.Message, ex.GetType().ToString());
    }
}
```

Figure 19-8 An enhanced Customer Maintenance application (part 3 of 3)

How to work with a DataGridView control

In chapter 18, you saw how easy it is to use a DataGridView control to work with the data in a table of a dataset. Now, you'll learn how to modify a DataGridView control so it looks and functions the way you want. In addition, you'll learn how to use a DataGridView control to create a Master/Detail form.

How to modify the properties of a DataGridView control

When you generate a DataGridView control from a data source, Visual Studio usually sets the properties of this control and the other objects it creates the way you want them. However, if you want to modify any of these properties, you can do that just as you would for any other type of object. In particular, you'll probably want to edit the properties of the DataGridView control to change its appearance and function.

To change the most common properties of a DataGridView control, you can use its smart tag menu as shown in figure 19-9. From this menu, you can create a read-only data grid by removing the check marks from the Enable Adding, Enable Editing, and Enable Deleting check boxes as shown here. Or, you can let a user reorder the columns by checking the Enable Column Reordering check box.

In addition to editing the properties for the grid, you may want to edit the properties for the columns of the grid. For example, you may want to apply currency formatting to a column, or you may want to change the column headings or widths. To do that, you can select the Edit Columns command to display the Edit Columns dialog box shown in the next figure.

By default, when you run an application that uses a DataGridView control, you can sort the rows in a column by clicking in the header at the top of the column. The first time you do this, the rows are sorted in ascending sequence by the values in the column; the next time, in descending sequence. Similarly, you can drag the column separators to change the widths of the columns. Last, if the Enable Column Reordering option is checked, you can reorder the columns by dragging them. These features let the user customize the presentation of the data.

The smart tag menu for a DataGridView control

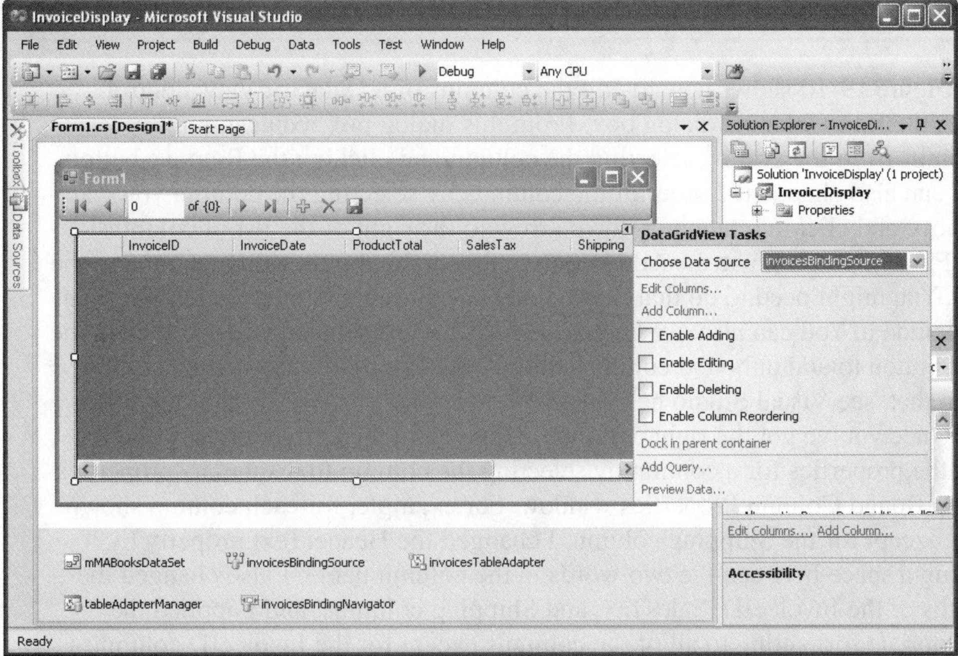

Description

- You can use the smart tag menu of a DataGridView control to edit its most commonly used properties.
- To edit the columns, select the Edit Columns command to display the Edit Columns dialog box. Then, you can edit the columns as described in the next figure.
- To prevent a user from adding, updating, or deleting data that's displayed in the DataGridView control, uncheck the Enable Adding, Enable Editing, or Enable Deleting check boxes.
- To allow a user to reorder the columns in a DataGridView control by dragging them, check the Enable Column Reordering check box.
- You can edit other properties of a DataGridView control by using the Properties window for the control.

Figure 19-9 How to modify the properties of a DataGridView control

How to edit the columns of a DataGridView control

Figure 19-10 shows how to edit the columns of a DataGridView control using the Edit Columns dialog box. From this dialog box, you can remove columns from the grid by selecting the column and clicking the Remove button. You can also change the order of the columns by selecting the column you want to move and clicking the up or down arrow to the right of the list of columns.

Finally, you can use the Add button in this dialog box to add a column to the grid. You might need to do that if you delete a column and then decide you want to include it. You can also use the dialog box that's displayed when you click the Add button to add unbound columns to the grid. For more information on how to do that, see Visual Studio help.

Once you've got the right columns displayed in the correct order, you can edit the properties for a column by selecting the column to display its properties in the Bound Column Properties window. For example, for each column shown here except for the Shipping column, I changed the HeaderText property by adding a space between the two words in the column name. I also changed the widths of the InvoiceID, SalesTax, and Shipping columns, and I applied the appropriate formatting to all of the columns except for the InvoiceID column. You'll see the dialog boxes for formatting data in the next figure.

Another column property you may need to change is the ReadOnly property. This property is useful if a DataGridView control lets the user add or modify rows, but you only want the user to be able to enter data in selected columns. Then, you can set the ReadOnly property of the other columns to True so the user can't enter data into those columns.

The dialog box for editing the columns of a DataGridView control

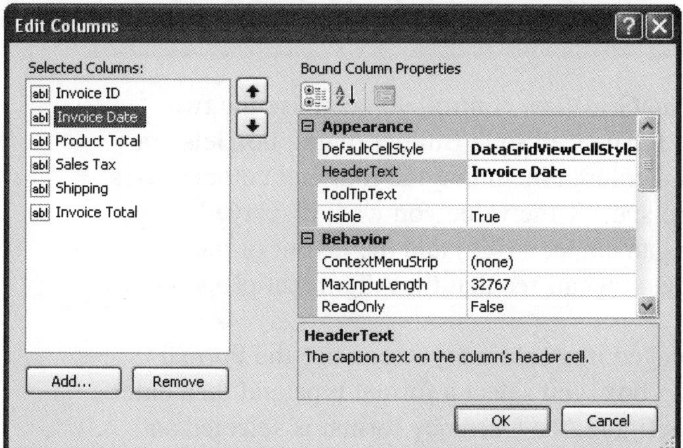

Common properties of a column

Property	Description
HeaderText	The text that's displayed in the column header.
Width	The number of pixels that are used for the width of the column.
DefaultCellStyle	The style that's applied to the cell. You can use dialog boxes to set style elements such as color, format, and alignment.
ReadOnly	Determines if the data in the column can be modified.
SortMode	Determines if the data in the grid can be sorted by the values in the column and how the sorting is performed. The default option is Automatic, which uses the built-in sorting mechanism. To provide for custom sorting, select the Programmatic option. To turn off sorting, select the NotSortable option.

Description

- You can use the Edit Columns dialog box to control which columns are displayed in the grid and to edit the properties of those columns. To display this dialog box, choose the Edit Columns command from the smart tag menu for the control
- To remove columns from the grid, select the column and click the Remove button.
- To add a column to the grid, click the Add button and then complete the dialog box that's displayed. This dialog box lets you add both bound and unbound columns.
- To change the order of the columns, select the column you want to move and click the up or down arrow to the right of the list of columns.
- To edit the properties for a column, select the column and use the Bound Column Properties window to edit the properties.

Figure 19-10 How to edit the columns of a DataGridView control

How to format the data in the columns of a DataGridView control

To format the columns of a DataGridView control, you can use the two dialog boxes shown in figure 19-11. The CellStyle Builder dialog box lets you specify the general appearance of a column including the font and colors it uses. You can also use this dialog box to specify the value you want displayed in place of a null value (the default is an empty string) and the layout of the column. In this figure, for example, you can see that the Alignment property has been set to MiddleRight.

To format the data that's displayed in a column, you can use the Format String dialog box. From this dialog box, you select a format type and then enter any other available options. In this figure, the Currency format is selected and the default number of decimal places (2) is used. When you accept this format, the format code is assigned to the Format property in the CellStyle Builder dialog box as shown here. Of course, if you already know the format code you want to use, you can enter it directly into the CellStyle Builder dialog box.

The dialog boxes for formatting the columns of a DataGridView control

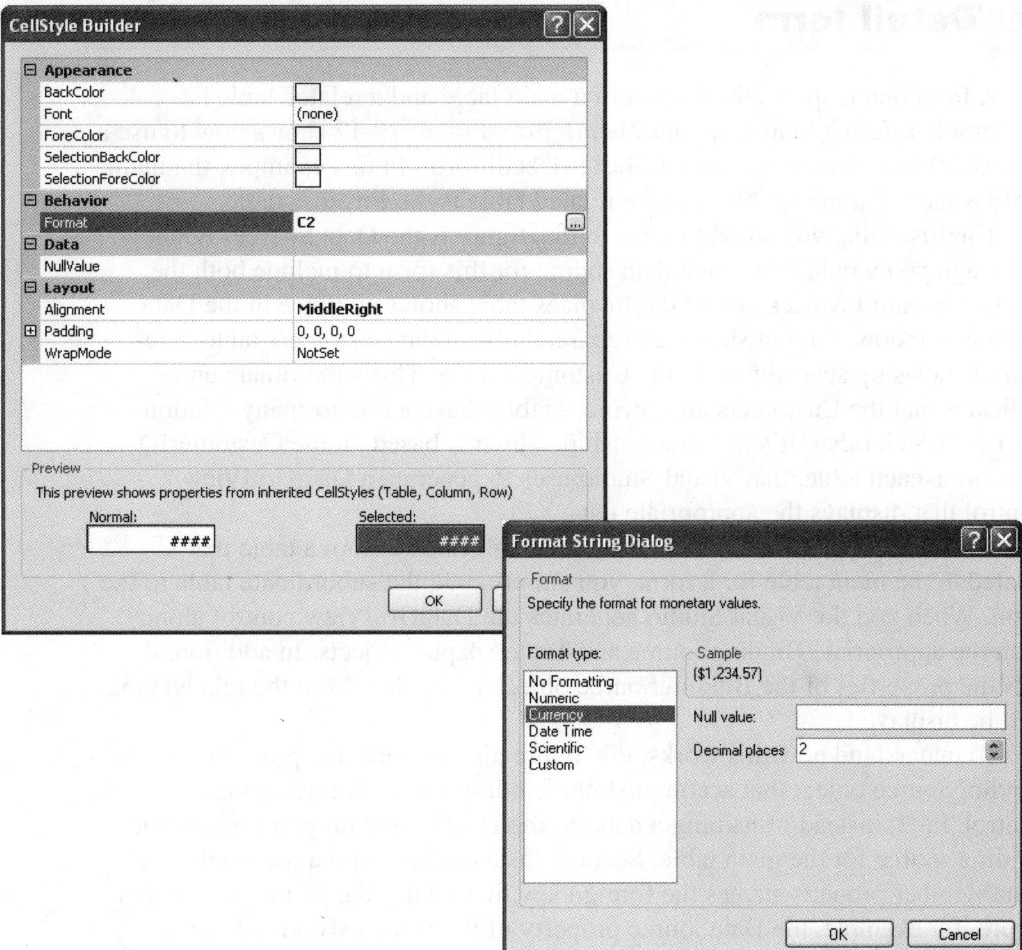

Description

- To display the CellStyle Builder dialog box, click the ellipsis button that appears when you select the DefaultCellStyle property in the Edit Columns dialog box.
- To apply a format to a column, select the Format property and then click the ellipsis button to display the Format String dialog box. Select the format you want to use from the Format Type list and enter any options that appear to the right of the list.

Figure 19-11 How to format the data in the columns of a DataGridView control

How to use a DataGridView control to create a Master/Detail form

A form that displays the data from a main table and a related table is commonly referred to as a *Master/Detail form*. Figure 19-12 shows how to use a DataGridView control to create a Master/Detail form. In this example, the main table is the Customers table, and the related table is the Invoices table.

The first thing you should notice in this figure is the Data Sources window. Although you would expect the data source for this form to include both the Customers and Invoices tables, the Invoices table shows up twice in the Data Sources window. First, it shows up separately from the Customers table. Second, it shows up subordinate to the Customers table. This subordinate entry indicates that the Customers and Invoices tables have a one-to-many relationship with each other. It's this relationship, which is based on the CustomerID column in each table, that Visual Studio uses to generate a DataGridView control that displays the appropriate data.

To create a DataGridView control that displays data from a table that's related to the main table for a form, you simply drag the subordinate table to the form. When you do, Visual Studio generates the DataGridView control along with the appropriate BindingSource and TableAdapter objects. In addition, it sets the properties of the BindingSource object so the data from the related table will be displayed.

To understand how this works, this figure also presents the properties of the BindingSource object that accomplish the binding for the DataGridView control. First, instead of naming a dataset, the DataSource property names the binding source for the main table. Second, instead of naming a data table, the DataMember property names the foreign key that relates the two tables. In this figure, for example, the DataSource property of the invoicesBindingSource object is set to customersBindingSource, and the DataMember property is set to a foreign key named FK_Invoices_Customers.

When you create a Master/Detail form, you should realize that all of the rows are retrieved from the detail table by default. For example, because the Customer Invoices form shown here lets the user display all the invoices for any customer, the invoices for all customers are retrieved when the form is loaded. If the Invoices table contains a large number of rows, that may not be what you want. In that case, you can create a parameterized query to retrieve the invoices just for the customer the user selects. You'll see an example of that in the Customer Invoice Display application that's presented next.

A form that uses a DataGridView control to display data from a related table

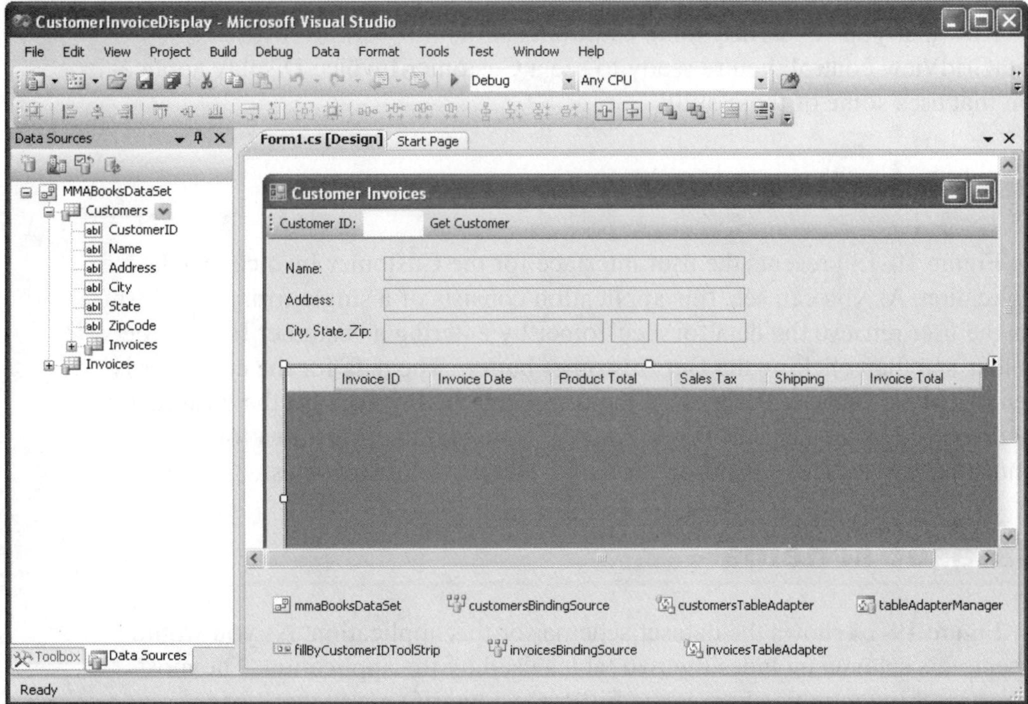

Two BindingSource properties for displaying data from a related table

Property	Description
DataSource	The source of the data for the BindingSource object. To display data from a table that's related to the main table for the form, this property should be set to the BindingSource object for the main table.
DataMember	A sub-list of the data source for the BindingSource object. To display data from a table that's related to the main table for the form, this property should be set to the foreign key that relates the two tables.

The property settings for the invoicesBindingSource object

Property	Setting
DataSource	customersBindingSource
DataMember	FK_Invoices_Customers

Description

- If a table has a one-to-many relationship with another table, that table will appear subordinate to the main table in the Data Sources window. Then, you can drag the subordinate table to a form to create a DataGridView control that displays the rows in the subordinate table that are related to the current row in the main table.

Figure 19-12 How to use a DataGridView control to create a Master/Detail form

A Customer Invoice Display application

Now that you've learned some additional skills for working with a DataGridView control, you're ready to see a Customer Invoice Display application that uses some of those skills.

The user interface

Figure 19-13 presents the user interface for the Customer Invoice Display application. As you can see, this application consists of a single form. This form lets the user retrieve the data for a customer by entering a customer ID into the toolbar and then clicking the Get Customer button. The data for the customer is then displayed in the text boxes on the form, and the invoices for the customer are displayed in the DataGridView control. Note that the properties for this control have been set so the user can't add, edit, or delete invoices.

The dataset schema

Figure 19-14 shows the dataset schema for this application. As you would expect, this schema includes the two tables used by the application. The most important thing to notice here is the FillByCustomerID query that's been created for each table adapter. These queries are used to retrieve the appropriate data based on the customer ID the user enters.

Please note, however, that you don't need the FillByCustomerID query for the Invoices table when you use a Master/Detail form that relates the Customers and Invoices tables. For this application, this FillByCustomerID query will be used just to make the application more efficient. You'll see how this query is used in the code that follows. And you can get some hands-on experience with this by doing exercise 19-2 at the end of this chapter.

The code for the Customer Invoices form

Figure 19-15 presents the code for the Customer Invoices form. The first thing you should notice here is that this form doesn't include a Load event handler. Because of that, no data is loaded into the dataset when the application starts. Instead, when a user enters a customer ID and clicks the Get Customer button, the row for that customer is loaded into the Customers table using the FillByCustomerID query of the Customers table adapter. In addition, any invoices for the customer are loaded into the Invoices table using the FillByCustomerID query of the Invoices table adapter. You can see the code that accomplishes this in the event handler in this figure.

The Customer Invoices form

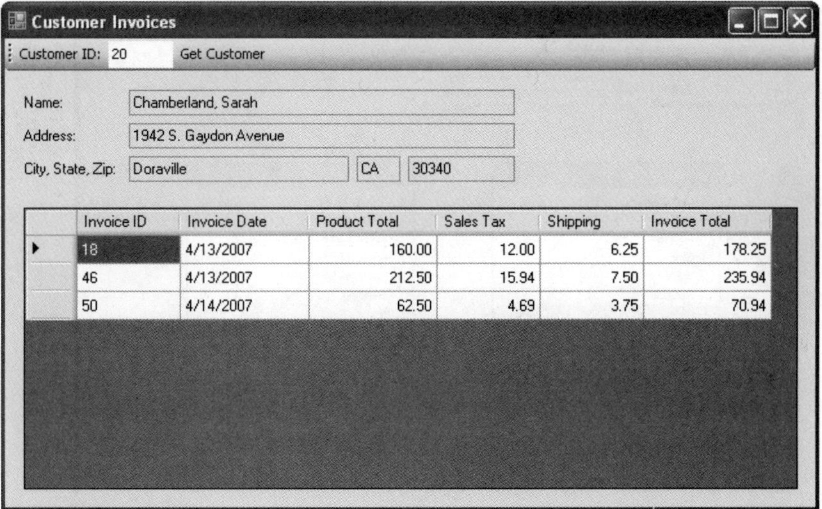

Description

- The Customer Invoices form is a Master/Detail form that displays the Invoices for a selected customer. For efficiency, this form doesn't retrieve any data when the form is loaded. Instead, when the user enters a customer number, the customer and invoice data for that customer is retrieved.
- Because this application doesn't let the user add, modify, or delete invoices, the binding navigator toolbar has been omitted from the Customer Invoices form.

Figure 19-13 The user interface for the Customer Invoice Display application

The dataset schema

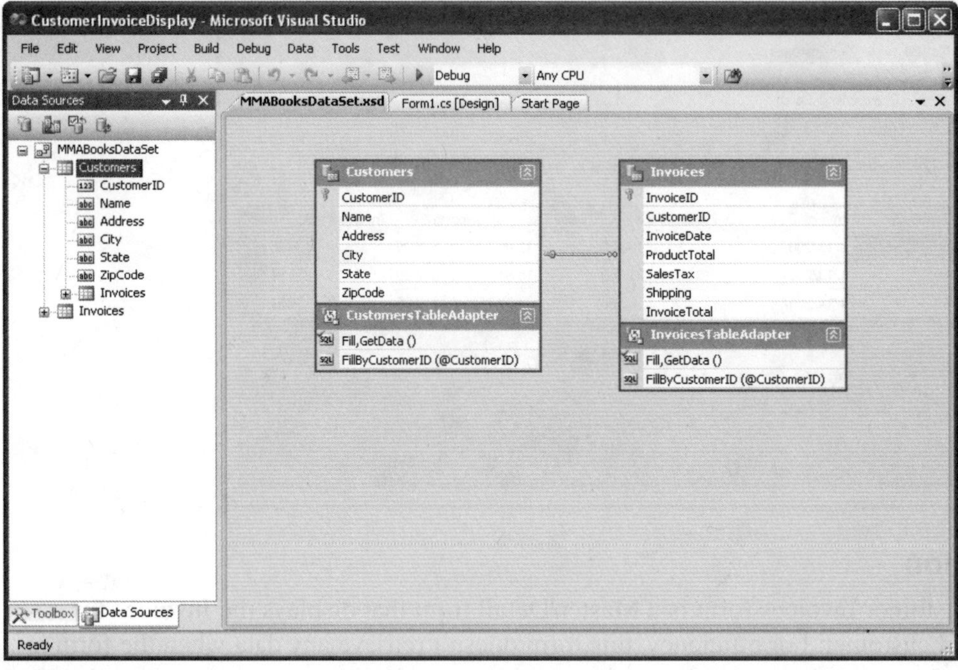

Description

- The MMABooks dataset defines the two tables used by this application: Customers and Invoices.
- The FillByCustomerID query for the Customers table adapter is used to retrieve the customer data that's displayed on the Customer Invoices form. This query is based on the customer ID the user enters into the toolbar on the form.
- The FillByCustomerID query for the Invoices table adapter is used to retrieve the invoice data that's displayed on the Customer Invoices form. This query is also based on the customer ID the user enters into the toolbar on the form.

Figure 19-14 The dataset schema for the Customer Invoice Display application

The code for the Customer Invoices form

```
private void fillByCustomerIDToolStripButton_Click(object sender, EventArgs e)
{
    try
    {
        int customerID = Convert.ToInt32(
            customerIDToolStripTextBox.Text);

        this.customersTableAdapter.FillByCustomerID(
            this.mmaBooksDataSet.Customers, customerID);

        if (customersBindingSource.Count > 0)
            this.invoicesTableAdapter.FillByCustomerID(
                this.mmaBooksDataSet.Invoices, customerID);
        else
            MessageBox.Show("No customer found with this ID. "
                + "Please try again.", "Customer Not Found");
    }
    catch (FormatException)
    {
        MessageBox.Show("Customer ID must be an integer.", "Entry Error");
    }
    catch (SqlException ex)
    {
        MessageBox.Show("Database error # " + ex.Number +
            ": " + ex.Message, ex.GetType().ToString());
    }
}
```

Description

- The only code that's required for this form is the code that retrieves the customer and invoice data. This code is executed when the user enters a customer ID and then presses the Get Customer button on the Customer Invoices form.

Figure 19-15 The code for the Customer Invoice Display application

Perspective

Now that you've completed this chapter, you should be able to use data sources and datasets to develop substantial database applications. You should also realize how quickly you can prototype these applications. But if you do the exercises that follow, which guide you through the development of the chapter applications from scratch, you should start to see that using data sources isn't quite as easy as it may at first appear. Because of that, you may want to use other techniques to develop more complex database applications. In the next chapter, for example, you'll learn the basics of developing applications by writing your own ADO.NET code.

Terms

parameterized query
Master/Detail form

Exercise 19-1 Build the Customer Maintenance application

This exercise will guide you through the development of the application in figure 19-8. You'll learn a lot by doing that.

Build the user interface

1. Start a new project named CustomerMaintenance in the C:\C# 2008\Chapter 19 directory. Then, create a data source that includes all the columns in the Customers and States tables.
2. Change the control that's associated with the State column of the Customers table to a combo box. Then, drag the Customers table onto the form so that detail controls are generated, but leave enough room at the top for two toolbars. Rearrange the controls and change any required properties so those controls look like the ones in figure 19-8.
3. Use the procedure in figure 19-2 to bind the State combo box on the form to the States table in the data source. Then, set the DropDownStyle property for the combo box to DropDownList, and set its (DataBindings) – Text property to None.
4. Test the application to see how this user interface works. If the state that's displayed for the first customer is incorrect, it's because the Customers table is loaded before the States table. That means that the first customer is displayed before the binding defined by the State combo box is applied. To correct this problem, end the application and switch the statements in the Load event handler for the form so that the States table is loaded first.

5. Run the application again to see how this works. Then, use the combo box to change one of the State entries. End the application, and review the other code that has been generated for the form.

Add a parameterized query

6. Use the procedure in figure 19-4 to add a parameterized query named FillByCustomerID that finds the Customer row for a specific customer ID. Then, note the toolbar that has been added to the form. Now, review the code that has been added to the application, and review the schema for the application.
7. Test the application to see how it works. First, use the binding navigator toolbar to move through the rows. Then, enter a customer ID of 9 in the second toolbar and click the FillByCustomerID button. Now, go back to the binding navigator toolbar, and you'll discover that you can't use it to go through the rows any more because the dataset contains only one row.
8. With the application still running, use the second toolbar to go to row 13, and select a new state from the combo box, but don't click the Save button. Then, go to row 10, select a new state, and click the Save button. Now, go to row 13 to see that the state has reverted to what it was originally, and go to row 10 to see that the state has been changed. This shows that you must click the Save button after each change if you want the changes to be made to the database. That's because the dataset consists of only one row at a time.
9. Add a valid row to the dataset and click the Save button. Then, note that the binding navigator toolbar lets you navigate between the previous row and the one you just added because two rows are now in the dataset. As soon as you use the second toolbar to go to a different row, though, the first toolbar shows only one row in the dataset.
10. Delete the row that you added in step 9 by going to that row and clicking the Delete button, which makes the row disappear. Then, click the Save button to apply the deletion to the database. If you don't do that, the row won't be deleted. When you're done, end the application.

Modify the toolbars

11. Use the procedure in figure 19-6 to add a Cancel button to the binding navigator toolbar, to change the text on the FillByCustomerID button in the second toolbar to Get Customer, and to add a separator bar and a second button with the text Get All Customers on it to the second toolbar.
12. Use the procedure in figure 19-7 to start the event handler for the Click event of the Cancel button, and add the one line of code that it requires. Then, start an event handler for the Get All Customers button. This event handler should contain a statement like the one in the Load event handler that loads the Customers table.
13. Test these changes to see how they work. At this point, the application should work like the one in figure 19-8. You just need to enhance the code so that no customer rows are retrieved when the form is loaded and so it provides for data validation and error handling.

Enhance the code

14. Comment out the code for filling the Customers table in the Load event handler, and run the application. As you'll see, only the State combo box has a value when the application starts because no customer has been selected. To fix that, use this statement to set the index for the State combo box to -1:

    ```
    stateComboBox.SelectedIndex = -1;
    ```

    Then, test this change.

15. At this point, you have a prototype of the application. Although you could add the data validation and error handling code that's shown in figure 19-8, that isn't always necessary for a prototype. Just experiment more if you want to, and then end the application.

Add another parameterized query to the form

16. Add a parameterized query named FillByState that gets all the customer rows for a specific state based on the state code. Next, run the application and use the third toolbar to get all of the rows for a specific state code like CA. Note that the binding navigator toolbar lets you navigate through these rows.
17. Add a separator at the right of the controls on the fillByCustomerID ToolStrip, followed by a label, text box, and button that look like the three controls on the fillByState ToolStrip. Then, delete the fillByState ToolStrip.
18. Modify the code for the form so the FillByState button in the fillByCustomerID ToolStrip gets the customer rows by state. Then, test this enhancement. When you've got it working right, close the project.

Exercise 19-2 Build the Customer Invoice Display application

This exercise will guide you through the development of the application in figure 19-13. Here again, you'll learn a lot by doing that.

Build the user interface for the Customer Invoices form

1. Start a new project named CustomerInvoiceDisplay in the C:\C# 2008\Chapter 19 directory. Then, create a data source for the tables and columns shown in the schema in figure 19-14.
2. Drag the columns in the Customers table onto the form as text boxes, and adjust them as shown in figure 19-13. Then, drag the Invoices table that's subordinate to the Customers table onto the form as a DataGridView control.
3. Run the application and use the binding navigator toolbar to scroll through the customer rows. When you come to a row that has related invoice rows, like the row for CustomerID 10, you'll see that the invoice rows are displayed. Now, close the application, and review the code that has been generated for it.

4. Delete the binding navigator toolbar, and comment out the code in the Load event handler for the form that fills the Customers table. Next, use the procedure in figure 19-4 to create a parameterized query named FillByCustomerID that gets the Customer data for a specific CustomerID. Then, run the form and use customer IDs like 10 and 20 to see how the Customer and Invoice data is displayed.
5. Use the procedures in figures 19-9 and 19-10 to disable adding, editing, and deleting rows in the DataGridView control, to delete the CustomerID column, to set the widths of the InvoiceID, SalesTax, and Shipping columns to 80, and to modify the text in the column headings. Then, set the formatting for the InvoiceDate column so it's displayed as shown in figure 19-13. Next, set the formatting for the ProductTotal, SalesTax, Shipping, and InvoiceTotal columns to Numeric with 2 decimal places, and set their Alignment properties to MiddleRight. Now, run the application to make sure that you've got everything right.

Change the way the application gets the invoice data

6. Review the code for the Load event handler for the form. There, you can see that all the rows in the Invoices table are loaded into the dataset when the form is loaded. Then, the data rows for a specific CustomerID are displayed in the DataGridView control each time the CustomerID changes. For some applications, that may be okay, but if there are thousands of invoice rows in the dataset that may be inefficient.
7. To change the way that works, create a parameterized query named FillByCustomerID for the DataGridView control that gets the invoice rows for a specific CustomerID, and delete the ToolStrip and event handler that get generated. Then, modify the code in the event handler for the Click event of the FillByCustomerIDToolStripButton so it looks like the code in figure 19-15 (but don't bother with the error handling code).
8. Delete the Load event handler for this form. Then, test the application again. It should work the same as it did before, but now only the invoice rows for the selected customer are in the Invoices table in the dataset.

Complete the application

9. At this point, you have a prototype of the application, and you should have learned a lot about how building applications with data sources and datasets works. Now, if you want to finish this application, you just need to: (1) add the error handling code for the form and (2) make sure all of the properties for the form and all of the controls are set right.

20

How to use ADO.NET to write your own data access code

In the last two chapters, you learned how to use data sources to develop database applications. When you do that, Visual Studio generates the ADO.NET objects you need. That lets you develop database applications with a minimum of code.

Now, you'll learn how to create and work with ADO.NET objects through code. That lets you separate the data access code from the presentation code by placing the ADO.NET code in database classes. These classes are often reusable and can make your applications easier to read and maintain.

How to work with connections and commands

Before you can access the data in a database, you must create a connection object. Then, you must create one or more command objects that contain the SQL statements you want to execute against the database.

How to create and work with connections

Figure 20-1 shows how you create and use a connection to access a SQL Server database. As you can see from the syntax at the top of this figure, you can specify a connection string when you create the connection. If you do, this string is assigned to the ConnectionString property. That's the case in the code example shown in this figure. If you don't specify a connection string when you create the connection, you have to assign a value to the ConnectionString property after you create the connection object.

Before you can use a command to access a database, you need to open the database connection. And when you're done working with a database, you should close the connection. To open and close a connection, you use the Open and Close methods shown in this figure.

This figure also shows some of the common values that you specify in a connection string for a SQL Server database. The first connection string, for example, specifies the name of the server where the database resides, the name of the database, and the type of security to be used. Notice that this connection string uses the localhost keyword to indicate that the SqlExpress database server is running on the same machine as the application. This should work if you install SQL Server Express on your system as described in appendix A. However, if you're accessing a SQL Server database that resides on a remote server, you'll need to modify this connection string to point to that server.

Because the requirements for each provider differ, you may need to consult the documentation for that provider to determine what values to specify. The second connection string shown in this figure, for example, is for an Access database, which uses the Jet OLE DB provider. As you can see, this connection string includes the name of the provider and the location of the database.

Notice in both the SQL Server and the Jet OLE DB connection strings that you must code two backslash characters (\\) for each backslash you want to include. As you may recall from chapter 4, the backslash identifies an escape sequence when coded within a string. Because of that, you have to code the \\ escape sequence to include a single backslash character.

Before I go on, you should realize that the connection strings for production applications are frequently stored in configuration files outside the application. That way, they can be accessed by any application that needs them, and they can be modified without having to modify and recompile each application. How an application actually retrieves the connection string depends on how it's stored.

Two constructors for the SqlConnection class

```
new SqlConnection()
new SqlConnection(connectionString)
```

Common properties and methods of the SqlConnection class

Property	Description
ConnectionString	Provides information for accessing a SQL Server database.
Method	**Description**
Open()	Opens the connection using the specified connection string.
Close()	Closes the connection.

Common values used in the ConnectionString property for SQL Server

Name	Description
Data source/Server	The name of the instance of SQL Server you want to connect to.
Initial catalog/Database	The name of the database you want to access.
Integrated security	Determines whether the connection is secure. Valid values are True, False, and SSPI. SSPI uses Windows integrated security and is equivalent to True.
User ID	The user ID that's used to log in to SQL Server.
Password/Pwd	The password that's used to log in to SQL Server.
Persist security info	Determines whether sensitive information, such as the password, is returned as part of the connection. The default is False.
Workstation ID	The name of the workstation that's connecting to SQL Server.

A connection string for the SQL Server provider

```
Data Source=localhost\\SqlExpress;Initial Catalog=MMABooks;Integrated
Security=True
```

A connection string for the Jet OLE DB provider

```
Provider=Microsoft.Jet.OLEDB.4.0;Data Source=C:\\Databases\\MMABooks.mdb
```

Code that creates, opens, and closes a SQL connection

```
string connectionString =
    "Data Source=localhost\\SqlExpress;Initial Catalog=MMABooks;" +
    "Integrated Security=True";
SqlConnection connection = new SqlConnection(connectionString);
connection.Open();
...
connection.Close();
```

Description

- You can set the ConnectionString property after you create a connection or as you create it by passing the string to the constructor of the connection class.
- The values you specify for the ConnectionString property depend on the type of database you're connecting to.

Figure 20-1 How to create and work with connections

If it's stored in a text file, for example, the application can use a text reader as shown in chapter 21; if it's stored in an XML file, the application can use an XML reader as shown in chapter 22.

How to create and work with commands

After you define the connection to the database, you create the command objects that contain the SQL statements you want to execute against the database. Figure 20-2 shows three constructors for the SqlCommand class. The first one doesn't require arguments. When you use this constructor, you must set the Connection property to the connection to be used by the command and the CommandText property to the text of the SQL statement before you execute the command.

The second constructor accepts the SQL command text as an argument. Then, you just have to set the Connection property before you can execute the command. The third constructor accepts both the connection and the command text as arguments. The code example in the figure uses this constructor.

Another property you may need to set is the CommandType property. This property determines how the value of the CommandText property is interpreted. The values you can specify for this property are members of the CommandType enumeration that's shown in this figure. The default value is Text, which causes the value of the CommandText property to be interpreted as a SQL statement. If the CommandText property contains the name of a stored procedure, however, you'll need to set this property to StoredProcedure. And if the CommandText property contains the name of a table, you'll need to set this property to TableDirect. Then, all the rows and columns will be retrieved from the table. Note that this setting is only available for the OLE DB data provider.

The last property that's shown in this figure, Parameters, lets you work with the collection of parameters for a command. You'll see how to use this property in the next three topics.

To execute a query that a command contains, you use the Execute methods of the command shown in this figure. To execute a command that returns a result set, you use the ExecuteReader method of the command. In contrast, you use the ExecuteScalar method to execute a query that returns a single value, and you use the ExecuteNonQuery method to execute an action query. You'll learn how to use all three of these methods later in this chapter.

Three constructors for the SqlCommand class

```
new SqlCommand()
new SqlCommand(commandText)
new SqlCommand(commandText, connection)
```

Common properties and methods of the SqlCommand class

Property	Description
Connection	The connection used to connect to the database.
CommandText	A SQL statement or the name of a stored procedure.
CommandType	A member of the CommandType enumeration that determines how the value in the CommandText property is interpreted.
Parameters	The collection of parameters for the command.
Method	**Description**
ExecuteReader()	Executes the query identified by the CommandText property and returns the result as a SqlDataReader object.
ExecuteNonQuery()	Executes the query identified by the CommandText property and returns an integer that indicates the number of rows that were affected.
ExecuteScalar()	Executes the query identified by the CommandText property and returns the first column of the first row of the result set.

CommandType enumeration members

Member	Description
Text	The CommandText property contains a SQL statement. This is the default.
StoredProcedure	The CommandText property contains the name of a stored procedure.
TableDirect	The CommandText property contains the name of a table (OLE DB only).

Code that creates a SqlCommand object that executes a Select statement

```
SqlConnection connection = new SqlConnection(connectionString);
string selectStatement
    = "SELECT CustomerID, Name, Address, City, State, ZipCode "
    + "FROM Customers";
SqlCommand selectCommand = new SqlCommand(selectStatement, connection);
```

Description

- The CommandText and Connection properties are set to the values you pass to the constructor of the command class. If you don't pass these values to the constructor, you must set the CommandText and Connection properties after you create the command object.
- If you set the CommandText property to the name of a stored procedure, you must set the CommandType property to StoredProcedure.

Figure 20-2 How to create and work with commands

How to create and work with parameters

In chapter 19, you learned how to generate a parameterized query from a bound control that was created using a data source. In that case, the parameters were generated for you based on the Select statement you defined. When you work with commands directly, however, you have to create the parameters yourself. You'll learn how to do that in just a minute. But first, you need to know how to use parameters in the SQL statements you code.

How to use parameters in SQL statements

A *parameter* is a variable that's used in a SQL statement. Parameters let you create statements that retrieve or update database data based on variable information. For example, an application that maintains the Customers table can use a parameter in the Where clause of a Select statement to retrieve a specific row from the Customers table based on the value of the CustomerID column. A Select statement that uses parameters in the Where clause is called a *parameterized query*. You can also use parameters in other types of SQL statements, including Insert, Update, and Delete statements.

To use parameters in a SQL statement, you use placeholders as shown in figure 20-3. These placeholders indicate where the parameters should be inserted when the statement is executed. Unfortunately, database management systems don't use a standard syntax for coding placeholders.

For example, the first Select statement in this figure is for SQL Server. As you can see, you use a *named variable* to identify a parameter. Note that the name of the variable must begin with an at sign (@) and is usually given the same name as the column it's associated with. Oracle also uses named variables, but the names must begin with a colon (:) as illustrated in the second Select statement. In contrast, the placeholder for an OLE DB or ODBC parameter is a question mark, as shown in the third Select statement.

The fourth example in this figure shows how you can use parameters in an Insert statement. Here, a row is being inserted into the Customers table. To do that, a variable is included in the Values clause for each required column in the table.

A SQL Server Select statement that uses a parameter

```
SELECT CustomerID, Name, Address, City, State, ZipCode
FROM Customers
WHERE CustomerID = @CustomerID
```

An Oracle Select statement that uses a parameter

```
SELECT CustomerID, Name, Address, City, State, ZipCode
FROM Customers
WHERE CustomerID = :CustomerID
```

An OLE DB or ODBC Select statement that uses a parameter

```
SELECT CustomerID, Name, Address, City, State, ZipCode
FROM Customers
WHERE CustomerID = ?
```

A SQL Server Insert statement that uses parameters

```
INSERT INTO Customers
(Name, Address, City, State, ZipCode)
VALUES (@Name, @Address, @City, @State, @ZipCode)
```

Description

- A *parameter* lets you place variable information into a SQL statement.
- When you use a parameter in the Where clause of a Select statement, the resulting query is often called a *parameterized query* because the results of the query depend on the values of the parameters.
- Parameters are also often used in Insert or Update statements to provide the values for the database row or rows to be inserted or updated. Likewise, you can use parameters in a Delete statement to indicate which row or rows should be deleted.
- To use parameters, you code a SQL statement with placeholders for the parameters. Then, you create a parameter object that defines each parameter, and you add it to the Parameters collection of the command object that contains the SQL statement.
- The placeholder for a parameter in a SQL Server command is a *named variable* whose name begins with an at sign (@). For Oracle, the name of a variable begins with a colon (:). In most cases, you'll give the variable the same name as the column it's associated with.
- If you're using the OLE DB or ODBC provider, you code the placeholder for a parameter as a question mark. The question mark simply indicates the position of the parameter.

Figure 20-3 How to use parameters in SQL statements

How to create parameters

After you define a SQL statement that contains parameters, you create the parameter objects. Figure 20-4 shows you how to do that. Here, you can see four constructors for the SqlParameter class. Although there are others, these are the ones you're most likely to use. You can create a parameter for an OLE DB, ODBC, or Oracle command using similar techniques.

Before you can use a parameter, you must assign a name and value to it. If you don't pass these values as arguments to the constructor when you create the parameter, you can do that using some of the properties shown in this figure.

Note here that you can specify the data type using either the DbType or SqlDbType property for a SQL Server parameter. Because the data type is inferred from the value of the parameter, however, you usually won't set the type. Similarly, you won't usually set the size of a parameter because it can also be inferred from the parameter's value.

The first example in this figure shows how to create a parameter object using the first constructor for the SqlParameter class. This parameter is assigned to a variable named customerIDParm. Then, this variable is used to set the parameter's properties.

The second example shows how to create a parameter using a single statement. This statement uses the second constructor for the SqlParameter class to create a parameter named @CustomerID with the value specified by the customerID variable.

When you assign a name to a SQL Server or Oracle parameter, that name must be the same as the name that's specified in the SQL statement. That's because ADO.NET associates the parameters with the placeholders by name. In contrast, ADO.NET associates OLE DB and ODBC parameters with the placeholders by sequence since the placeholders aren't named.

Four constructors for the SqlParameter class

```
new SqlParameter()
new SqlParameter(name, value)
new SqlParameter(name, type)
new SqlParameter(name, type, size)
```

Common properties of the SqlParameter class

Property	Description
DbType	A member of the DbType enumeration that determines the type of data that the parameter can hold.
ParameterName	The name of the parameter.
Size	The maximum size of the value that the parameter can hold.
SqlDbType	A member of the SqlDbType enumeration that determines the type of data that the parameter can hold. This property is synchronized with the DbType property.
Value	The value of the parameter stored as an Object type.

Code that creates a parameter

```
SqlParameter customerIDParm = new SqlParameter();
customerIDParm.ParameterName = "@CustomerID";
customerIDParm.Value = customerID;
```

Another way to create a parameter

```
SqlParameter customerIDParm = new SqlParameter("@CustomerID", customerID);
```

Description

- When you create a parameter, you can specify the parameter name along with a value, a data type, or a data type and size. If you don't specify the appropriate values, you can set the values of the associated properties after you create the parameter.
- In addition to a name, you must set the value for a parameter before you can use it. However, the type and size can be inferred from the value.
- When you create parameters for a SQL Server or Oracle command, you must give them the same names you used in the SQL statement since ADO.NET refers to them by name.
- Because the parameters for an OLE DB or ODBC command aren't named in the SQL statement, the parameters can be given any name you want.

Figure 20-4 How to create parameters

How to work with parameters

After you create a parameter, you must add it to the Parameters collection of the command that will use the parameter. Because ADO.NET refers to SQL Server and Oracle parameters by name, you can add them to the Parameters collection in any sequence. In contrast, you must add OLE DB and ODBC parameters in the same order that they appear in the SQL statement since ADO.NET refers to them by position.

The first example in figure 20-5 shows how to use the Add method to add a parameter object to the Parameters collection. Here, the Parameters property of the command is used to refer to the Parameters collection. Then, the Add method of that collection is used to add the customerIDParm parameter that was created in the previous figure.

You can also use one of the overloaded Add methods to create a parameter and add it to the Parameters collection in a single statement. These methods let you specify a name and type or a name, type, and size, and they return the parameter that's created. That way, you can store the parameter in a variable so you can refer to it later if you need to.

Another way to create a parameter and add it to the Parameters collection is to use the AddWithValue method. This is illustrated in the second example in this figure, and this is the easiest way to create a parameter if you're not going to change its value. Like the Add methods, the AddWithValue method returns the parameter that's created in case you want to refer to it later.

If you don't create a variable to hold a parameter, you can refer to it through the Parameters collection using either the parameter's name or its position as an indexer. This is illustrated in the third example in this figure. Here, the value of the @CustomerID parameter is set to the value of a variable named customerID.

Common members of the Parameters collection

Indexer	Description
`[parametername]`	Gets the parameter with the specified name from the collection.
`[index]`	Gets the parameter at the specified position from the collection.
Method	**Description**
`Add(parameter)`	Adds the specified parameter to the collection.
`Add(name, type)`	Creates a parameter with the specified name and type and adds it to the collection.
`Add(name, type, size)`	Creates a parameter with the specified name, type, and size and adds it to the collection.
`AddWithValue(name, value)`	Creates a parameter with the specified name and value and adds it to the collection.

A statement that adds a parameter to the Parameters collection

```
selectCommand.Parameters.Add(customerIDParm);
```

A statement that creates a parameter and adds it to the Parameters collection

```
selectCommand.Parameters.AddWithValue("@CustomerID", customerID);
```

A statement that changes the value of an existing parameter

```
selectCommand.Parameters["@CustomerID"].Value = customerID;
```

Description

- To work with the parameters for a command, you use the Parameters property of the command. This property returns a SqlParameterCollection object that contains all the parameters for the command.
- To add an existing parameter to the Parameters collection, you use the Add method. You can also use the Add method to create a parameter with the specified name and type or name, type, and size, and add that parameter to the Parameters collection.
- You can use the AddWithValue method of the Parameters collection to create a parameter with the specified name and value and add that parameter to the collection.
- All the Add methods return the parameter that's created so you can assign it to a variable.
- You can add SQL Server and Oracle parameters to the Parameters in any order you want since ADO.NET refers to the parameters by name. However, you must add OLE DB and ODBC parameters in the same order that they appear in the SQL statement since ADO.NET refers to them by position.

How to execute commands

The method you use to execute the SQL statement associated with a command object depends on the operation the SQL statement performs. The three methods you're most likely to use are ExecuteReader, which lets you retrieve and work with a result set created by a Select statement; ExecuteScalar, which lets you retrieve a single value using a Select statement; and ExecuteNonQuery, which lets you execute an Insert, Update, or Delete statement.

How to create and work with a data reader

To execute a command that contains a Select statement that returns a result set, you use the ExecuteReader method as shown in figure 20-6. This method executes the Select statement and creates a data reader object. Then, you can use the properties and methods of the data reader to work with the result set.

When you execute the ExecuteReader method, you can use the CommandBehavior enumeration to specify a behavior. The most commonly used members of this enumeration are listed in this figure. You can use these members to simplify your code or to improve the efficiency of your application.

After you create a data reader, you use the Read method to retrieve the next row of data in the result set. Note that you must also execute the Read method to retrieve the first row of data. It's not retrieved automatically when the data reader is created.

To access a column from the most recently retrieved row, you can use the column name as an indexer. You can also specify a column by its position in the row by using an integer indexer. For example, since the first column in the States table is named StateCode, you can supply "StateCode" or zero as the indexer for a reader to retrieve the data for that column.

The code example in this figure illustrates how you use a data reader. First, the connection that's used by the SqlCommand object is opened. Although it's not shown here, this command contains a Select statement that retrieves all the data from the States table. Then, the ExecuteReader method is used to retrieve that data and create a data reader that can process the state rows. Because the CloseConnection behavior is included on this method, the connection will be closed automatically when the data reader is closed. The ExecuteReader method also opens the data reader and positions it before the first row in the result set.

Next, a List<> object that can hold State objects is created and a while statement is used to loop through the rows in the result set. The condition on the while statement executes the Read method of the data reader. This works because the Read method returns a Boolean value that indicates whether the result set contains additional rows. As long as this condition is true, the program processes the row that was retrieved. In this case, the program creates a State object for each row in the States table and adds it to the List<> object. After all of the rows have been processed, the data reader is closed.

Two ways to create a SqlDataReader object

```
sqlCommand.ExecuteReader()
sqlCommand.ExecuteReader(behavior)
```

Common CommandBehavior enumeration members

Member	Description
CloseConnection	Closes the connection when the data reader is closed.
Default	Equivalent to specifying no command behavior.
SingleRow	Only a single row is returned.

Common members of the SqlDataReader class

Indexer	Description
[columnname]	Gets the value of the column with the specified name.
[index]	Gets the value of the column at the specified position.
Property	**Description**
IsClosed	Gets a value that indicates if the data reader is closed.
Method	**Description**
Close()	Closes the data reader.
Read()	Retrieves the next row and returns a Boolean value that indicates whether there are additional rows.

Code that uses a data reader to read a list of State objects

```
connection.Open();
SqlDataReader reader =
    selectCommand.ExecuteReader(CommandBehavior.CloseConnection);
List<State> states = new List<State>();
while (reader.Read())
{
    State s = new State();
    s.StateCode = reader["StateCode"].ToString();
    s.StateName = reader["StateName"].ToString();
    states.Add(s);
}
reader.Close();
```

Description

- You must open the connection that's used by the data reader before you execute the ExecuteReader method of the command object.
- The data reader is opened automatically when it's created. While it's open, no other data readers can be opened on the same connection. The exception is if you're using an Oracle data reader, in which case other Oracle data readers can be open at the same time.
- When you first create a data reader, it's positioned before the first row in the result set. To retrieve the first row, you have to execute the Read method.
- You can combine two or more command behavior members using the And (&) operator.

Figure 20-6 How to create and work with a data reader

How to execute queries that return a single value

The first example in figure 20-7 shows you how to execute a command that returns a single value, called a *scalar value*. To do that, you use the ExecuteScalar method of the command. In this case, the command contains a Select statement that retrieves a sum of the invoice totals in the Invoices table. This type of summary value is often called an *aggregate value*. A scalar value can also be the value of a single column, a calculated value, or any other value that can be retrieved from the database.

Since the ExecuteScalar method returns an Object type, you must cast that object to an appropriate data type to get its value. In this example, the object is cast to a decimal value.

Before I go on, you should realize that you can use the ExecuteScalar method with a Select statement that retrieves more than one value. In that case, though, the ExecuteScalar method returns only the first value and the others are discarded.

How to execute action queries

As you know, you can use an Insert, Update, or Delete statement to perform actions against a database. These statements are sometimes referred to as *action queries*. To execute an action query, you use the ExecuteNonQuery method of a command as shown in the second example in figure 20-7.

This example executes a command that contains an Insert statement that adds a row to the Products table. Notice that the ExecuteNonQuery method returns an integer that indicates the number of rows in the database that were affected by the operation. You can use this value to check that the operation was successful. You'll see an example of that in the Customer Maintenance application that follows.

Code that creates and executes a command that returns an aggregate value

```
string selectStatement = "SELECT SUM(InvoiceTotal) FROM Invoices";
SqlCommand selectCommand = new SqlCommand(selectStatement, connection);
connection.Open();
decimal invoiceTotal = (decimal) selectCommand.ExecuteScalar;
connection.Close();
```

Code that creates and executes a command that inserts a row

```
string insertStatement = "INSERT Products "
                       + "(ProductCode, Description, UnitPrice) "
                       + "VALUES (@ProductCode, @Description, @UnitPrice)";
SqlCommand insertCommand = new SqlCommand(insertStatement, connection);
insertCommand.Parameters.AddWithValue("@ProductCode", product.Code);
insertCommand.Parameters.AddWithValue("@Description", product.Description);
insertCommand.Parameters.AddWithValue("@UnitPrice", product.Price);
try
{
    connection.Open();
    int productCount = insertCommand.ExecuteNonQuery();
}
catch (SqlException ex)
{
    MessageBox.Show(ex.Message);
}
finally
{
    connection.Close();
}
```

How to execute queries that return a single value

- You use the ExecuteScalar method of a command object to retrieve a single value, called a *scalar value*.
- The value that's returned can be the value of a single column and row in the database, a calculated value, an *aggregate value* that summarizes data in the database, or any other value that can be retrieved from the database.
- If the Select statement returns more than one column or row, only the value in the first column and row is retrieved by the ExecuteScalar method.

How to execute action queries

- You use the ExecuteNonQuery method of a command object to execute an Insert, Update, or Delete statement, called an *action query*.
- The ExecuteNonQuery method returns an integer that indicates the number of rows that were affected by the query.
- You can also use the ExecuteNonQuery method to execute statements that affect the structure of a database object. For more information, see the documentation for your database management system.

Figure 20-7 How to execute queries that don't return a result set

A Customer Maintenance application that uses commands

In the topics that follow, you'll see another version of the Customer Maintenance application that was first presented in chapter 18. Unlike the application shown in that chapter, this version doesn't use a dataset and a table adapter. Instead, it uses commands to retrieve, insert, update, and delete rows from the Customers table. Although this presentation is lengthy, it's worth taking the time to go through it because it will give you a thorough understanding of how you build applications with commands.

The user interface

Figure 20-8 presents the user interface for the Customer Maintenance application. As you can see, this application consists of two forms. The Customer Maintenance form lets the user select an existing customer and then displays the information for that customer on the form. Then, the user can click the Modify button to modify the information for the customer or the Delete button to delete the customer. The user can also click the Add button to add a new customer.

If the user clicks the Add or Modify button, the Add/Modify Customer form is displayed. Note that the title of this form changes depending on whether a customer is being added or modified. In this case, the user that was selected in the Customer Maintenance form is being modified.

After entering the appropriate values on the Add/Modify Customer form, the user can click the Accept button or press the Enter key to accept the new or modified customer. Alternatively, the user can click the Cancel button or press the Esc key to cancel the operation.

If the user clicks the Delete button, a dialog box like the one shown in this figure is displayed to confirm the delete operation. Then, if the user confirms the operation, the customer is deleted and the form is cleared.

At this point, you may be wondering why I used two forms to implement the Customer Maintenance application. The answer is that, in the real world, most maintenance applications aren't this simple. In many cases, in fact, the maintenance of a table will be combined with other functions. Even if the table maintenance is provided by a separate application, however, it can be easier to implement the application using two forms because it simplifies the program logic.

The Customer Maintenance form

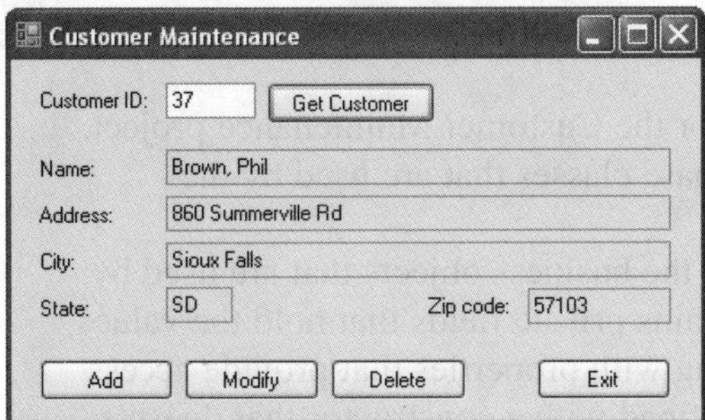

The Add/Modify Customer form

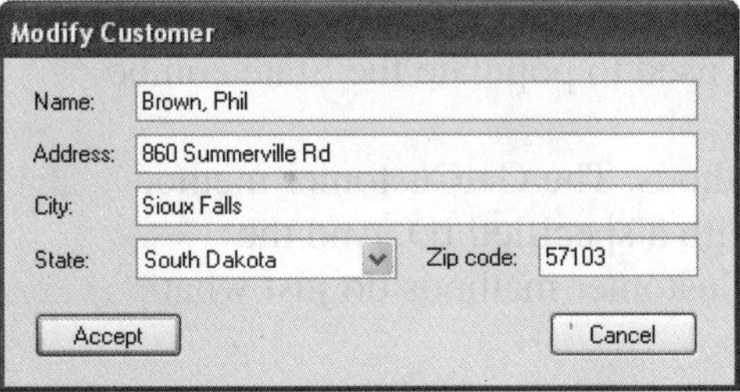

The dialog box that's displayed to confirm a delete operation

Description

- To add a customer, the user clicks the Add button on the Customer Maintenance form to display a blank Add Customer form. Then, the user enters the data for the new customer and clicks the Accept button to return to the Customer Maintenance form.
- To modify the data for an existing customer, the user enters the customer ID and clicks the Get Customer button to display the information for that customer. Then, the user clicks the Modify button to display the Modify Customer form, makes the appropriate modifications, and clicks the Accept button to return to the Customer Maintenance form.
- To delete a customer, the user enters the customer ID and clicks the Get Customer button to display the information for that customer. Then, the user clicks the Delete button and responds to the dialog box that's displayed to confirm the delete operation.

Figure 20-8 The user interface for the Customer Maintenance application

The class diagram for the business and database classes

Figure 20-9 presents a class diagram for the Customer Maintenance project. This diagram shows the business and database classes that are used by the Customer Maintenance application.

The Customer and State classes define the business objects that are used by this application. Each of these classes contains private fields that hold the values of the columns in the associated table, along with properties that provide access to these fields. In addition, each class is defined with a constructor that doesn't accept any parameters.

The CustomerDB and StateDB classes provide methods for working with the tables in the MMABooks database. The StateDB class contains a method for getting a list of State objects. This list is then used to populate the State combo box.

The CustomerDB class contains four methods. The GetCustomer method returns a Customer object for the customer with a specified ID. And the AddCustomer, UpdateCustomer, and DeleteCustomer methods do just what their names imply.

Finally, the MMABooksDB class contains a single method that returns a connection to the MMABooks database. This method is used by the methods in the CustomerDB and StateDB classes.

The class diagram

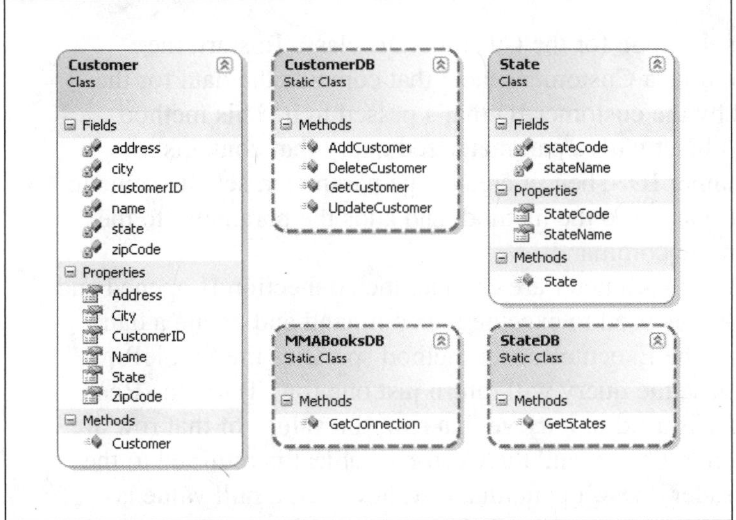

Description

- The Customer Maintenance project contains the classes that define the business objects used by the Customer Maintenance application and the database classes that are used to work with the MMABooks database.
- The business objects are defined by the Customer and State classes. These objects will hold data from the associated tables in the MMABooks database.
- The classes that end with DB, including CustomerDB, StateDB, and MMABooksDB, are the database classes. These classes provide shared methods for working with the MMABooks database.
- The StateDB class provides a public method for getting a list of states from the States table. The CustomerDB class provides public methods for getting the data for a customer and for adding, updating, and deleting a customer. And the MMABooksDB class provides a public method for getting a connection to the MMABooks database.

Figure 20-9 The class diagram for the business and database classes

The code for the CustomerDB class

Figure 20-10 shows the code for the CustomerDB class. To start, the GetCustomer method returns a Customer object that contains the data for the customer row specified by the customer ID that's passed to it. This method creates a SqlCommand object with a parameterized query that contains a placeholder for the customer ID. Then, it creates the parameter, sets its value to the customerID that was passed to the method, and adds the parameter to the Parameters collection of the command.

After the command and parameter are created, the connection is opened and the ExecuteReader method is used to execute the command and create a data reader object. Notice that the ExecuteReader method specifies the SingleRow command behavior because the query will return just one row. Then, the Read method of the data reader is used to retrieve that row, the values of that row are assigned to a new Customer object, and the Customer object is returned to the calling method. If the reader doesn't contain a row, however, a null value is returned to indicate that the customer wasn't found. In either case, the connection is closed, which also closes the data reader.

Notice that the statements that open the connection and data reader and process the rows in the data reader are coded within a try-catch statement. Then, if a SqlException occurs, the catch block throws the exception to the calling method. Because of that, the method that calls this method should catch this exception. Whether or not an exception occurs, the statement that closes the connection is coded within the finally block. That way, if the statement that opens the connection is successful but the statement that executes the command isn't, the connection is still closed.

The AddCustomer method adds a new row to the Customers table. This method receives a Customer object that contains the data for the new row. Then, a command object that contains an Insert statement with a parameter for each column in the row is created. After the command is created, the parameters are created and added to the Parameters collection of the command.

The code for the CustomerDB class **Page 1**

```
public static class CustomerDB
{
    public static Customer GetCustomer(int customerID)
    {
        SqlConnection connection = MMABooksDB.GetConnection();
        string selectStatement
            = "SELECT CustomerID, Name, Address, City, State, ZipCode "
            + "FROM Customers "
            + "WHERE CustomerID = @CustomerID";
        SqlCommand selectCommand =
            new SqlCommand(selectStatement, connection);
        selectCommand.Parameters.AddWithValue("@CustomerID", customerID);
        try
        {
            connection.Open();
            SqlDataReader custReader =
                selectCommand.ExecuteReader(CommandBehavior.SingleRow);
            if (custReader.Read())
            {
                Customer customer = new Customer();
                customer.CustomerID = (int)custReader["CustomerID"];
                customer.Name = custReader["Name"].ToString();
                customer.Address = custReader["Address"].ToString();
                customer.City = custReader["City"].ToString();
                customer.State = custReader["State"].ToString();
                customer.ZipCode = custReader["ZipCode"].ToString();
                return customer;
            }
            else
            {
                return null;
            }
        }
        catch (SqlException ex)
        {
            throw ex;
        }
        finally
        {
            connection.Close();
        }
    }

    public static int AddCustomer(Customer customer)
    {
        SqlConnection connection = MMABooksDB.GetConnection();
        string insertStatement =
            "INSERT Customers " +
            "(Name, Address, City, State, ZipCode) " +
            "VALUES (@Name, @Address, @City, @State, @ZipCode)";
        SqlCommand insertCommand =
            new SqlCommand(insertStatement, connection);
        insertCommand.Parameters.AddWithValue("@Name", customer.Name);
        insertCommand.Parameters.AddWithValue("@Address", customer.Address);
        insertCommand.Parameters.AddWithValue("@City", customer.City);
```

Figure 20-10 The code for the CustomerDB class (part 1 of 3)

Next, the connection is opened and the ExecuteNonQuery method of the command object is executed within a try-catch statement that catches SQL Server exceptions. Then, if an exception occurs, this method throws the exception so it can be handled by the calling method. Otherwise, another command object that contains a Select statement that retrieves the ID of the customer that was just added is created, and this command is executed using the ExecuteScalar method. The customer ID that's returned by this statement is then returned to the calling method.

The UpdateCustomer method receives two arguments: a Customer object named oldCustomer that contains the original data for the customer row to be updated, and another Customer object named newCustomer that supplies the updated values for the customer. The properties of these objects are used to set the values of the parameters defined by the Update statement associated with the command object. Notice that the properties of the oldCustomer object are assigned to parameters in the Where clause of the Update statement. That way, the Update statement will update the row only if none of the customer columns have been changed since the customer was retrieved.

The code for the CustomerDB class Page 2

```
        insertCommand.Parameters.AddWithValue("@State", customer.State);
        insertCommand.Parameters.AddWithValue("@ZipCode", customer.ZipCode);
        try
        {
            connection.Open();
            insertCommand.ExecuteNonQuery();
            string selectStatement =
                "SELECT IDENT_CURRENT('Customers') FROM Customers";
            SqlCommand selectCommand =
                new SqlCommand(selectStatement, connection);
            int customerID = Convert.ToInt32(selectCommand.ExecuteScalar());
            return customerID;
        }
        catch (SqlException ex)
        {
            throw ex;
        }
        finally
        {
            connection.Close();
        }
    }

    public static bool UpdateCustomer(Customer oldCustomer,
        Customer newCustomer)
    {
        SqlConnection connection = MMABooksDB.GetConnection();
        string updateStatement =
            "UPDATE Customers SET " +
            "Name = @NewName, " +
            "Address = @NewAddress, " +
            "City = @NewCity, " +
            "State = @NewState, " +
            "ZipCode = @NewZipCode " +
            "WHERE Name = @OldName " +
            "AND Address = @OldAddress " +
            "AND City = @OldCity " +
            "AND State = @OldState " +
            "AND ZipCode = @OldZipCode";
        SqlCommand updateCommand =
            new SqlCommand(updateStatement, connection);
        updateCommand.Parameters.AddWithValue("@NewName", newCustomer.Name);
        updateCommand.Parameters.AddWithValue(
            "@NewAddress", newCustomer.Address);
        updateCommand.Parameters.AddWithValue("@NewCity", newCustomer.City);
        updateCommand.Parameters.AddWithValue("@NewState", newCustomer.State);
        updateCommand.Parameters.AddWithValue(
            "@NewZipCode", newCustomer.ZipCode);
        updateCommand.Parameters.AddWithValue("@OldName", oldCustomer.Name);
        updateCommand.Parameters.AddWithValue(
            "@OldAddress", oldCustomer.Address);
        updateCommand.Parameters.AddWithValue("@OldCity", oldCustomer.City);
        updateCommand.Parameters.AddWithValue("@OldState", oldCustomer.State);
        updateCommand.Parameters.AddWithValue(
            "@OldZipCode", oldCustomer.ZipCode);
```

Figure 20-10 The code for the CustomerDB class (part 2 of 3)

After the parameter values are set, the UpdateCustomer method uses the ExecuteNonQuery method to execute the Update statement. If no error occurs, the value that's returned by the ExecuteNonQuery method is tested to determine whether the update was successful. If it wasn't, it probably means that the customer has been modified or deleted by another user. In that case, this method returns false to the calling method. Otherwise, it returns true.

The DeleteCustomer method receives a Customer object as an argument. This method implements concurrency checking using the same technique as the UpdateCustomer method. That is, it specifies the value of each of the customer columns in the Where clause of the Delete statement. Then, if the delete operation is unsuccessful due to a concurrency error, the method returns false. Otherwise, it returns true.

Like the AddCustomer and UpdateCustomer methods, the DeleteCustomer method also catches SQL Server errors. Then, if an error occurs, it's thrown to the calling method.

The code for the CustomerDB class — Page 3

```
        try
        {
            connection.Open();
            int count = updateCommand.ExecuteNonQuery();
            if (count > 0)
                return true;
            else
                return false;
        }
        catch (SqlException ex)
        {
            throw ex;
        }
        finally
        {
            connection.Close();
        }
    }

    public static bool DeleteCustomer(Customer customer)
    {
        SqlConnection connection = MMABooksDB.GetConnection();
        string deleteStatement =
            "DELETE FROM Customers " +
            "WHERE Name = @Name " +
            "AND Address = @Address " +
            "AND City = @City " +
            "AND State = @State " +
            "AND ZipCode = @ZipCode";
        SqlCommand deleteCommand =
            new SqlCommand(deleteStatement, connection);
        deleteCommand.Parameters.AddWithValue("@Name", customer.Name);
        deleteCommand.Parameters.AddWithValue("@Address", customer.Address);
        deleteCommand.Parameters.AddWithValue("@City", customer.City);
        deleteCommand.Parameters.AddWithValue("@State", customer.State);
        deleteCommand.Parameters.AddWithValue("@ZipCode", customer.ZipCode);
        try
        {
            connection.Open();
            int count = deleteCommand.ExecuteNonQuery();
            if (count > 0)
                return true;
            else
                return false;
        }
        catch (SqlException ex)
        {
            throw ex;
        }
        finally
        {
            connection.Close();
        }
    }
}
```

Figure 20-10 The code for the CustomerDB class (part 3 of 3)

The code for the StateDB class

Figure 20-11 shows the code for the StateDB class. This class contains a single method named GetStates that returns a generic List<> object that contains one State object for each of the rows in the States table, sorted by state name.

To get this list, the GetStates method creates a SqlCommand object with a Select statement that retrieves the appropriate data. Then, it calls the ExecuteReader method of this command to create a data reader that can be used to read each state. Once the data reader is created, this method uses this reader to read each row in the table, it creates a State object for each row, and it adds each State object to the List<> object. Finally, it closes the data reader and the connection and returns the list of State objects.

The code for the MMABooksDB class

The MMABooksDB class contains a single method named GetConnection that returns a connection to the MMABooks database. As you've already seen, the CustomerDB and StateDB classes call this method to get the connection that's used by the commands they execute. Note that the connection string is hard coded into this method. As I explained earlier, however, the connection string for a production application is typically stored in an external configuration file. Then, the GetConnection method would read the connection string from this file. That way, you could change the location of the database without recompiling the application.

The code for the StateDB class

```
public static class StateDB
{
    public static List<State> GetStates()
    {
        List<State> states = new List<State>();
        SqlConnection connection = MMABooksDB.GetConnection();
        string selectStatement = "SELECT StateCode, StateName "
                               + "FROM States "
                               + "ORDER BY StateName";
        SqlCommand selectCommand =
            new SqlCommand(selectStatement, connection);
        try
        {
            connection.Open();
            SqlDataReader reader = selectCommand.ExecuteReader();
            while (reader.Read())
            {
                State s = new State();
                s.StateCode = reader["StateCode"].ToString();
                s.StateName = reader["StateName"].ToString();
                states.Add(s);
            }
            reader.Close();
        }
        catch (SqlException ex)
        {
            throw ex;
        }
        finally
        {
            connection.Close();
        }
        return states;
    }
}
```

The code for the MMABooksDB class

```
public static class MMABooksDB
{
    public static SqlConnection GetConnection()
    {
        // If necessary, change the following connection string
        // so it works for your system
        string connectionString =
            "Data Source=localhost\\SqlExpress;Initial Catalog=MMABooks;" +
            "Integrated Security=True";
        SqlConnection connection = new SqlConnection(connectionString);
        return connection;
    }
}
```

Figure 20-11 The code for the StateDB and MMABooksDB classes

The code for the Customer Maintenance form

Figure 20-12 shows the code for the Customer Maintenance form. Because this form doesn't contain a Load event handler, no data is displayed when the form is first displayed. Then, the user must enter a customer ID and click the Get Customer button to retrieve the data for a customer or click the Add button to add a new customer.

The event handler for the Click event of the Get Customer button starts by calling the IsPresent and IsInt32 methods in a class named Validator to check that the user entered a customer ID and that the customer ID is an integer. This class contains methods like the ones you saw in the Validator class in chapter 12.

If the customer ID is an integer, this value is passed to a method named GetCustomer. This method calls the GetCustomer method of the CustomerDB class to get the customer with the specified ID. Then, the Customer object that's returned by this method is stored in a class variable named customer.

Notice that the GetCustomer method is coded within a try-catch statement. That's because, if a SQL Server error occurs during the execution of this method, the exception is thrown to the calling method. Then, this method must catch the exception. You'll see this same technique used for all the methods of the database classes that are called by this application.

After it executes the GetCustomer method, the event handler checks if the Customer object contains a null value. If so, a message is displayed indicating that the customer wasn't found, and a method named ClearControls is called. This method assigns empty strings to the text boxes on the form, disables the Modify and Delete buttons, and activates the Customer ID text box so the user can enter another ID.

If the Customer object doesn't contain a null value, a method named DisplayCustomer is called to display the properties of the Customer object in the text boxes on the form. This method also enables the Modify and Delete buttons so the user can modify or delete the selected customer. (These buttons are disabled when the form is first displayed, and they're disabled every time the form is cleared.)

The code for the Customer Maintenance form — Page 1

```
public partial class frmCustomerMaintenance : Form
{
    private Customer customer;

    private void btnGetCustomer_Click(object sender, EventArgs e)
    {
        if (Validator.IsPresent(txtCustomerID) &&
            Validator.IsInt32(txtCustomerID))
        {
            int customerID = Convert.ToInt32(txtCustomerID.Text);
            this.GetCustomer(customerID);
            if (customer == null)
            {
                MessageBox.Show("No customer found with this ID. " +
                    "Please try again.", "Customer Not Found");
                this.ClearControls();
            }
            else
                this.DisplayCustomer();
        }
    }

    private void GetCustomer(int customerID)
    {
        try
        {
            customer = CustomerDB.GetCustomer(customerID);
        }
        catch (Exception ex)
        {
            MessageBox.Show(ex.Message, ex.GetType().ToString());
        }
    }

    private void ClearControls()
    {
        txtCustomerID.Text = "";
        txtName.Text = "";
        txtAddress.Text = "";
        txtCity.Text = "";
        txtState.Text = "";
        txtZipCode.Text = "";
        btnModify.Enabled = false;
        btnDelete.Enabled = false;
        txtCustomerID.Focus();
    }
```

Figure 20-12 The code for the Customer Maintenance form (part 1 of 3)

If the user clicks the Add button, the Click event handler for this button displays the Add/Modify Customer form as a dialog box. But first, it sets the public addCustomer field of this form to true so the form will know that a new customer is being added. If the customer is added successfully, the new customer is retrieved from the Add/Modify Customer form. Then, the data for the new customer is displayed on the form and the Modify and Delete buttons are enabled.

The Click event handler for the Modify button is similar. However, it sets the addCustomer field of the Add/Modify Customer form to false to indicate that a customer is being modified. In addition, it sets the public customer field to the current Customer object. That way, the form can display this data without having to retrieve it from the database again.

If the customer is modified successfully, the updated customer is retrieved from the Add/Modify Customer form and the new data for the customer is displayed on the form. If a concurrency error occurs, however, the result of the Add/Modify Customer form is set to DialogResult.Retry. Then, the GetCustomer method is called to retrieve the customer again.

If the customer is found, it means that the concurrency error was caused by another user modifying the customer. In that case, the updated data for that customer is displayed on the form. If the customer isn't found, however, it means that another user deleted the customer. Then, the ClearControls method is called to clear the text boxes on the form, disable the Modify and Delete buttons, and activate the Customer ID text box.

The code for the Customer Maintenance form **Page 2**

```
private void DisplayCustomer()
{
    txtName.Text = customer.Name;
    txtAddress.Text = customer.Address;
    txtCity.Text = customer.City;
    txtState.Text = customer.State;
    txtZipCode.Text = customer.ZipCode;
    btnModify.Enabled = true;
    btnDelete.Enabled = true;
}

private void btnAdd_Click(object sender, EventArgs e)
{
    frmAddModifyCustomer addCustomerForm = new frmAddModifyCustomer();
    addCustomerForm.addCustomer = true;
    DialogResult result = addCustomerForm.ShowDialog();
    if (result == DialogResult.OK)
    {
        customer = addCustomerForm.customer;
        txtCustomerID.Text = customer.CustomerID.ToString();
        this.DisplayCustomer();
    }
}

private void btnModify_Click(object sender, EventArgs e)
{
    frmAddModifyCustomer modifyCustomerForm = new frmAddModifyCustomer();
    modifyCustomerForm.addCustomer = false;
    modifyCustomerForm.customer = customer;
    DialogResult result = modifyCustomerForm.ShowDialog();
    if (result == DialogResult.OK)
    {
        customer = modifyCustomerForm.customer;
        this.DisplayCustomer();
    }
    else if (result == DialogResult.Retry)
    {
        this.GetCustomer(customer.CustomerID);
        if (customer != null)
            this.DisplayCustomer();
        else
            this.ClearControls();
    }
}
```

Figure 20-12 The code for the Customer Maintenance form (part 2 of 3)

If the user clicks the Delete button, the Click event handler for that button starts by displaying a dialog box to confirm the delete operation. If the operation is confirmed, it calls the DeleteCustomer method of the CustomerDB class to delete the customer. If this method returns false, an error message is displayed indicating that the customer has been updated or deleted and the customer is retrieved again. Then, if the customer is found, the updated data for the customer is displayed. Otherwise, the form is cleared. The form is also cleared if the customer is successfully deleted.

The code for the Customer Maintenance form — Page 3

```
    private void btnDelete_Click(object sender, EventArgs e)
    {
        DialogResult result = MessageBox.Show("Delete " + customer.Name + "?",
            "Confirm Delete", MessageBoxButtons.YesNo,
            MessageBoxIcon.Question);
        if (result == DialogResult.Yes)
        {
            try
            {
                if (!CustomerDB.DeleteCustomer(customer))
                {
                    MessageBox.Show("Another user has updated or deleted " +
                        "that customer.", "Database Error");
                    this.GetCustomer(customer.CustomerID);
                    if (customer != null)
                        this.DisplayCustomer();
                    else
                        this.ClearControls();
                }
                else
                    this.ClearControls();
            }
            catch (Exception ex)
            {
                MessageBox.Show(ex.Message, ex.GetType().ToString());
            }
        }
    }

    private void btnExit_Click(object sender, EventArgs e)
    {
        this.Close();
    }
}
```

Figure 20-12 The code for the Customer Maintenance form (part 3 of 3)

The code for the Add/Modify Customer form

Figure 20-13 shows the code for the Add/Modify Customer form. This form starts by declaring the two public fields that are also used by the Customer Maintenance form.

When the form is first loaded, the Load event handler starts by calling the LoadStateComboBox method. This method uses the GetStates method of the StateDB class to get a generic list that contains State objects. Then, it binds the State combo box on the form to this list.

If a new customer is being added, the Load event handler continues by setting the Text property of the form to "Add Customer" and initializing the State combo box so that no state is selected. Otherwise, it sets the Text property of the form to "Modify Customer" and calls the DisplayCustomerData method. This method displays the current data for the customer on the form. After that, the user can enter the data for a new customer or modify the data for an existing customer.

If the user clicks the Accept button, the Click event handler for this button starts by calling the IsValidData method. This method calls the IsPresent method of the Validator class for each text box to determine if it contains data. It also calls the IsPresent method for the State combo box to be sure that a state is selected.

If the data is valid, the event handler continues by checking whether a customer is being added or modified. If a customer is being added, the customer field is set to a new Customer object and the PutCustomerData method is called. This method sets the properties of the Customer object to the values that the user entered on the form.

Next, the event handler executes the AddCustomer method of the CustomerDB class and assigns the new customer ID that's returned by this method to the CustomerID property of the Customer object. Then, if no SQL Server error occurs, the DialogResult property of the form is set to DialogResult.OK, which causes the form to be closed and control to be returned to the Customer Maintenance form. Otherwise, the exception is caught and an error message is displayed.

If a customer is being modified, this event handler starts by creating a new Customer object and storing it in the newCustomer variable. Then, it sets the CustomerID property of that object to the CustomerID property of the current Customer object since the customer ID can't be changed, and it calls the PutCustomerData method to set the rest of the properties. Next, it calls the UpdateCustomer method of the CustomerDB class and passes it both the old and new Customer objects. If a concurrency error occurs, a value of false is returned. In that case, an error message is displayed and the DialogResult property of the form is set to DialogResult.Retry. Otherwise, the new Customer object is assigned to the original Customer object and the DialogResult property is set to DialogResult.OK. In either case, the form is closed.

The code for the Add/Modify Customer form — Page 1

```
public partial class frmAddModifyCustomer : Form
{
    public bool addCustomer;
    public Customer customer;

    private void frmAddModifyCustomer_Load(object sender, EventArgs e)
    {
        this.LoadStateComboBox();
        if (addCustomer)
        {
            this.Text = "Add Customer";
            cboStates.SelectedIndex = -1;
        }
        else
        {
            this.Text = "Modify Customer";
            this.DisplayCustomer();
        }
    }

    private void LoadStateComboBox()
    {
        List<State> states = new List<State>();
        try
        {
            states = StateDB.GetStates();
            cboStates.DataSource = states;
            cboStates.DisplayMember = "StateName";
            cboStates.ValueMember = "StateCode";
        }
        catch (Exception ex)
        {
            MessageBox.Show(ex.Message, ex.GetType().ToString());
        }
    }

    private void DisplayCustomer()
    {
        txtName.Text = customer.Name;
        txtAddress.Text = customer.Address;
        txtCity.Text = customer.City;
        cboStates.SelectedValue = customer.State;
        txtZipCode.Text = customer.ZipCode;
    }
```

Figure 20-13 The code for the Add/Modify Customer form (part 1 of 3)

The code for the Add/Modify Customer form **Page 2**

```
private void btnAccept_Click(object sender, EventArgs e)
{
    if (IsValidData())
    {
        if (addCustomer)
        {
            customer = new Customer();
            this.PutCustomerData(customer);
            try
            {
                customer.CustomerID = CustomerDB.AddCustomer(customer);
                this.DialogResult = DialogResult.OK;
            }
            catch (Exception ex)
            {
                MessageBox.Show(ex.Message, ex.GetType().ToString());
            }
        }
        else
        {
            Customer newCustomer = new Customer();
            newCustomer.CustomerID = customer.CustomerID;
            this.PutCustomerData(newCustomer);
            try
            {
                if (! CustomerDB.UpdateCustomer(customer, newCustomer))
                {
                    MessageBox.Show("Another user has updated or " +
                        "deleted that customer.", "Database Error");
                    this.DialogResult = DialogResult.Retry;
                }
                else
                {
                    customer = newCustomer;
                    this.DialogResult = DialogResult.OK;
                }
            }
            catch (Exception ex)
            {
                MessageBox.Show(ex.Message, ex.GetType().ToString());
            }
        }
    }
}
```

Figure 20-13 The code for the Add/Modify Customer form (part 2 of 3)

The code for the Add/Modify Customer form — Page 3

```
    private bool IsValidData()
    {
        return
            Validator.IsPresent(txtName) &&
            Validator.IsPresent(txtAddress) &&
            Validator.IsPresent(txtCity) &&
            Validator.IsPresent(cboStates) &&
            Validator.IsPresent(txtZipCode);
    }

    private void PutCustomerData(Customer customer)
    {
        customer.Name = txtName.Text;
        customer.Address = txtAddress.Text;
        customer.City = txtCity.Text;
        customer.State = cboStates.SelectedValue.ToString();
        customer.ZipCode = txtZipCode.Text;
    }
}
```

Figure 20-13 The code for the Add/Modify Customer form (part 3 of 3)

Perspective

In this chapter, you were introduced to another way to develop database applications. Instead of using data sources and datasets, you learned how to use code to create and work with connections, commands, and data readers. When you work this way, your code has to do all of the functions that are done by the table adapter when you use data sources and datasets. This means that you have to write more code, but it also means that you have complete control over how the data is processed.

Although the techniques shown in this chapter are the ones used most often by professional programmers, you should know that there are still other ways to develop database applications. If you want to use a typed dataset, for example, but data sources don't give you enough control over how the data is processed, you can create and work with the dataset and table adapters in code. Or, you can use an untyped dataset (one that's created from the DataSet class rather than a custom class) and a data adapter. To learn more about these and other database programming techniques, you'll want to get a separate book on ADO.NET.

Terms

parameter
parameterized query
named variable
scalar value
aggregate value
action query

Exercise 20-1 Build the Customer Maintenance application

For this exercise, you'll develop the Customer Maintenance application presented in figure 20-8. To make that easier for you to do, we'll give you the two forms for the project as well as the business classes and the Validator class. That way, you'll just need to create the database classes.

Review the application

1. Open the application in the C:\C# 2008\Chapter 20\CustomerMaintenance directory and review the code for the forms and classes. Notice that some of the statements in the forms have been commented out. These are the statements that call the methods of the database classes that you'll create.
2. Run the application, enter 27 in the Customer ID text box, and click the Get Customer button. When you do, an error message will be displayed indicating that the customer wasn't found. That's because the application doesn't include the code to retrieve the customer. Respond to the dialog box and then end the application.

Write the code to retrieve a customer

3. Add a class named MMABooksDB to the project. Then, add a method named GetConnection to this class, and add code like that shown in figure 20-11 to this method. For this to work, you'll also need to add a using statement for the System.Data.SqlClient namespace at the beginning of the class.
4. Add another class named CustomerDB to the project, and add using statements for the System.Data and System.Data.SqlClient namespaces to this class.
5. Add a method named GetCustomer to the CustomerDB class. This method should receive the customer ID of the customer to be retrieved, and it should return a Customer object for that customer. Add the code for this method as shown in part 1 of figure 20-10, but try to do that without looking at this figure.
6. Display the code for the Customer Maintenance form, and remove the comment from the statement in the GetCustomer method that calls the GetCustomer method of the CustomerDB class. Then, run the application and try to display the data for customer number 27. If this doesn't work, modify your code until it does.
7. Click the Modify button to display the Modify Customer form, and notice that no value is displayed in the State combo box. Drop-down the combo box list to see that it doesn't contain any items. That's because you haven't added the code to retrieve the list of states. Click the Cancel button to return to the Customer Maintenance form and then end the application.

Write the code to retrieve the list of states

8. Add a class named StateDB to the project, and add a using statement for the System.Data.SqlClient namespace to this class.
9. Add a method named GetStates to the StateDB class. This method should return a List<> of State objects. Add the code for this method as shown in figure 20-11, but again, try to do that without looking at this figure.
10. Display the code for the Add/Modify Customer form, and remove the comment from the statement in the LoadStateComboBox method that calls the GetStates method. Then, run the application, display the data for customer number 27, and click the Modify button. This time, the correct state should be displayed for the customer and the State combo box should be populated with a list of all the states. However, you still can't modify the data for the customer because you haven't added the code to do that. Cancel out of the Modify Customer form and then end the application.

Write the code to modify a customer

11. Add a method named UpdateCustomer to the CustomerDB class. This method should receive two Customer objects. The first one should contain the original customer data and should be used to provide for optimistic concurrency. The second one should contain the new customer data and should be used to update the customer row. This method should also return a Boolean value that indicates if the update was successful. Add the code for this method using figure 20-10 as a guide if necessary.

12. Display the code for the Add/Modify Customer form, and remove the comments from the if-else statement in the event handler for the Click event of the Accept button. Then, run the application, retrieve customer 27, click the Modify button, and make a change to the data for the customer. Now, click the Accept button. If you coded the UpdateCustomer method correctly, the updated data should now be displayed on the Customer Maintenance form. Otherwise, you'll need to correct the code.

Write the code to add a customer

13. Add a method named AddCustomer to the CustomerDB class. This method should receive a Customer object with the data for the new customer, and it should return an integer with the ID for the new customer. Add the code for this method using figure 20-10 as a guide if necessary.
14. Display the code for the Add/Modify Customer form, and remove the comment from the statement that calls the AddCustomer method. Then, run the application and click the Add button to display the Add Customer form.
15. Enter the data for a new customer. Then, click the Accept button to add the customer to the database and display the customer data on the Customer Maintenance form. Note the customer ID for the new customer. When you have this working correctly, end the application.

Write the code to delete a customer

16. Add a method named DeleteCustomer to the CustomerDB class. This method should receive a Customer object with the data for the customer to be deleted, and it should return a Boolean value that indicates if the delete operation was successful. The Customer object should be used to provide for optimistic concurrency. Add the code for this method using figure 20-10 as a guide if necessary.
17. Display the code for the Customer Maintenance form, and remove the comments from the if-else statement in the event handler for the Click event of the Delete button. Then, run the application and retrieve the customer you added in step 15.
18. Click the Delete button to see the message that's displayed. Then, click the Yes button to delete the customer. If this worked correctly, the data should be cleared from the Customer Maintenance form and the Modify and Delete buttons should be disabled. When you have this working correctly, end the application and close the project.

Section 5

Other skills for C# developers

This section contains four chapters that present some other skills that you may need as you develop Windows applications in C#. Since you won't need them for all your applications, though, you can give these chapters a quick first reading just to find out what skills they offer. Then, you can return to these chapters for reference whenever you need the skills that they present.

In chapter 21, you'll learn how to read and write the data in two of the file types that are supported by .NET: text files and binary files. In chapter 22, you'll learn how to read and write the data in XML files, which will also prepare you for using XML in other contexts. In chapter 23, you'll learn how to use a new feature of C# 2008 called LINQ to work with objects such as arrays and collections. In chapter 24, you'll learn how to enhance a Windows application by using the multi-document interface and by adding features like menus, toolbars, and help to your forms. And in chapter 25, you'll learn about three ways to deploy a Windows application.

21

How to work with files and data streams

In section 4, you learned how to develop applications that store and retrieve data from a database. Because databases provide powerful features for working with data, databases are typically used for the data in most business applications. For some applications, though, you may need to save data in a file on disk and then read that data whenever it's needed. In this chapter, you'll learn how to do that with two different types of files: text and binary.

An introduction to the System.IO classes

The System.IO namespace provides a variety of classes for working with files and for managing directories, files, and paths. You'll be introduced to those classes in the topics that follow. In addition, you'll learn about the types of files and streams supported by the System.IO classes and how they're used to perform file I/O.

The classes for managing directories, files, and paths

Figure 21-1 summarizes the classes in the System.IO namespace that you can use to manage directories, files, and paths. As you can see, you can use the methods of the Directory class to create or delete a directory or determine if a directory exists. And you can use the methods of the File class to copy, delete, or move a file, or to determine if a file exists. Since the methods for both of these classes are static methods, you call them directly from the class.

Before you begin working with any of the classes in the System.IO namespace, you typically code a using statement like the one shown in the first example. Then, you can refer to the classes in this namespace without qualifying each reference with the namespace.

The second example shows how to use some of the methods of the Directory class. This code starts by declaring a string that holds the path to a directory that contains a file to be processed. Then, an if statement uses the Exists method of the Directory class to determine if this directory exists. If it doesn't, it uses the CreateDirectory method to create it.

The third example shows how to use some of the methods of the File class. This code declares a string that will hold the path to a file named Products.txt. Then, the if statement that follows uses the Exists method of the File class to determine if this file exists. If it does, it uses the Delete method to delete it.

System.IO classes used to work with drives and directories

Class	Description
`Directory`	Used to create, edit, delete, or get information on directories (folders).
`File`	Used to create, edit, delete, or get information on files.
`Path`	Used to get path information from a variety of platforms.

Common methods of the Directory class

Method	Description
`Exists(path)`	Returns a Boolean value indicating whether a directory exists.
`CreateDirectory(path)`	Creates the directories in a specified path.
`Delete(path)`	Deletes the directory at the specified path. The directory must be empty.
`Delete(path, recursive)`	Deletes the directory at the specified path. If true is specified for the recursive argument, any subdirectories and files in the directory are deleted. If false is specified, the directory must be empty.

Common methods of the File class

Method	Description
`Exists(path)`	Returns a Boolean value indicating whether a file exists.
`Delete(path)`	Deletes a file.
`Copy(source, dest)`	Copies a file from a source path to a destination path.
`Move(source, dest)`	Moves a file from a source path to a destination path.

A statement that simplifies references to the System.IO classes

```
using System.IO;
```

Code that uses some of the Directory methods

```
string dir = @"C:\C# 2008\Files\";
if (!Directory.Exists(dir))
    Directory.CreateDirectory(dir);
```

Code that uses some of the File methods

```
string path = dir + "Products.txt";
if (File.Exists(path))
    File.Delete(path);
```

Description

- The classes for managing directories, files, and paths are stored in the System.IO namespace.
- To use the classes in the System.IO namespace, you should include a using statement. Otherwise, you have to qualify the references to its classes with System.IO.
- All of the methods of the Directory, File, and Path classes are static methods.

Figure 21-1 The classes for managing directories, files, and paths

How files and streams work

When you use the System.IO classes to do *I/O operations* (or *file I/O*), you can use two different kinds of files: *text files* or *binary files*. To illustrate, figure 21-2 shows the contents of a text file and a binary file as they look when displayed in a text editor. Although both of these files contain the same data, they look quite different.

In a *text file*, all of the data is stored as text characters (or strings). Often, the *fields* in this type of file are separated by delimiters like tabs or pipe characters, and the *records* are separated by end of line characters. Although you can't see the end of line characters in this figure, you know they're there because each record starts at the beginning of a new line.

In contrast, the data in a *binary file* can include text characters as well as data types. Because of that, the data isn't always displayed properly within a text editor. For example, you can't tell what the value of the Price field is in each of these records because this field has a decimal data type. Also, since the records in a binary file don't end with end of line characters, one record isn't displayed on each line in a text editor.

To handle I/O operations with text and binary files, the .NET Framework uses *streams*. You can think of a stream as the flow of data from one location to another. For instance, an *output stream* can flow from the internal memory of an application to a disk file, and an *input stream* can flow from a disk file to internal memory. When you work with a text file, you use a *text stream*. When you work with a binary file, you use a *binary stream*.

To work with streams and files using the System.IO namespace, you use the classes summarized in this figure. To create a stream that connects to a file, for example, you use the FileStream class. Then, to read data from a text stream, you use the StreamReader class. And to read data from a binary stream, you use the BinaryReader class. You'll learn how to use all of these classes later in this chapter.

Since you can store all of the built-in numeric data types in a binary file, this type of file is more efficient for applications that work with numeric data. In contrast, the numeric data in a text file is stored as characters so each field must be converted to a numeric data type before it can be used in arithmetic operations.

When you save a text or binary file, you can use any extension you want for the file name. In this book, though, *txt* is used as the extension for all text files, and *dat* is used for all binary files. For instance, the text file in this figure is named Products.txt, and the binary file is named Products.dat.

A text file displayed in a text editor

A binary file displayed in a text editor

Two types of files

Type	Description
Text	A file that contains text (string) characters. The *fields* in each record are typically delimited by special characters like tab or pipe characters, and the *records* are typically delimited by new line characters.
Binary	A file that can contain a variety of data types.

Two types of streams

Stream	Description
Text	Used to transfer text data.
Binary	Used to transfer binary data.

System.IO classes used to work with files and streams

Class	Description
FileStream	Provides access to input and output files.
StreamReader	Used to read a stream of characters.
StreamWriter	Used to write a stream of characters.
BinaryReader	Used to read a stream of binary data.
BinaryWriter	Used to write a stream of binary data.

Description

- An *input file* is a file that is read by a program; an *output file* is a file that is written by a program. Input and output operations are often referred to as *I/O operations* or *file I/O*.
- A *stream* is the flow of data from one location to another. To write data, you use an *output stream*. To read data, you use an *input stream*. A single stream can also be used for both input and output.
- To read and write text files, you use *text streams*. To read and write binary files, you use *binary streams*.

Figure 21-2 How files and streams work

How to use the FileStream class

To create a stream that connects to a file, you use the FileStream class as shown in figure 21-3. In the syntax at the top of this figure, you can see its arguments. The first two, which specify the path for the file and the mode in which it will be opened, are required. The last two, which specify how the file can be accessed and shared, are optional.

To code the mode, access, and share arguments, you use the FileMode, FileAccess, and FileShare enumerations. If, for example, you want to create a file stream for a file that doesn't exist, you can code the FileMode.Create member for the mode argument and a new file will be created. However, this member causes the file to be overwritten if it already exists. As a result, if you don't want an existing file to be overwritten, you can code the FileMode.CreateNew member for this argument. Then, if the file already exists, an exception is thrown as explained in the next figure.

For the access argument, you can code members that let you read records from the file, write records to the file, or both read and write records. If you omit this argument, the default is to allow both reading and writing of records.

For the share argument, you can code members that let other users read records, write records, or both read and write records at the same time that the first user is accessing the file. Or, you can code the None member to prevent sharing of the file. What you're trying to avoid is two users writing to a file at the same time, which could lead to errors. So if you code the access argument as ReadWrite or Write, you can code the share argument as Read or None. On the other hand, if you code the access argument as Read, you may want to code the share argument as Read or ReadWrite. Then, other applications may be able to write new data to the file while you're using it. However, when you set the share argument, additional permissions may be needed to be able to share this file while it's being used by the current process. In that case, you can use the Close method to close the file when you're done with it to allow other processes to access the file.

The first example shows how to open a file stream for writing. Since this example uses the Write member to specify file access, this file stream can only be used to write the file, not to read it. And since this example uses the Create member for the mode argument, this code will create a new file if the file doesn't exist, or it will overwrite the existing file if the file already does exist. However, if the directory for this file doesn't exist, a DirectoryNotFoundException will be thrown as described in the next figure.

The second example shows how to open a file stream for reading. This works similarly to opening a file stream for writing. However, the Open member is used to specify the mode argument. As a result, if the file doesn't exist, a FileNotFoundException will be thrown as described in the next figure.

The syntax for creating a FileStream object

```
new FileStream(path, mode[, access[, share]])
```

Members in the FileMode enumeration

Member	Description
Append	Opens the file if it exists and seeks to the end of the file. If the file doesn't exist, it's created. This member can only be used with Write file access.
Create	Creates a new file. If the file already exists, it's overwritten.
CreateNew	Creates a new file. If the file already exists, an exception is thrown.
Open	Opens an existing file. If the file doesn't exist, an exception is thrown.
OpenOrCreate	Opens a file if it exists, or creates a new file if it doesn't exist.
Truncate	Opens an existing file and truncates it so its size is zero bytes.

Members in the FileAccess enumeration

Member	Description
Read	Data can be read from the file, but not written to it.
ReadWrite	Data can be read from and written to the file. This is the default.
Write	Data can be written to the file but not read from it.

Members in the FileShare enumeration

Member	Description
None	The file cannot be opened by other applications.
Read	Allows other applications to open the file for reading only. This is the default.
ReadWrite	Allows other applications to open the file for both reading and writing.
Write	Allows other applications to open the file for writing only.

Common method of the FileStream class

Method	Description
`Close()`	Closes the file stream and releases any resources associated with it.

Code that creates a FileStream object for writing

```
string path = @"C:\C# 2008\Files\Products.txt";
FileStream fs = new FileStream(path, FileMode.Create, FileAccess.Write);
```

Code that creates a new FileStream object for reading

```
string path = @"C:\C# 2008\Files\Products.txt";
FileStream fs = new FileStream(path, FileMode.Open, FileAccess.Read);
```

Note

- Operating system level permissions may limit which file access and file share options you can use.

Figure 21-3 How to use the FileStream class

How to use the exception classes for file I/O

In chapter 7, you learned the basic skills for handling exceptions. Now, figure 21-4 summarizes the exceptions that can occur when you perform I/O operations. Most of the time, you can write code so these exceptions are avoided. For example, you can avoid a DirectoryNotFoundException by using the Exists method of the Directory class to be sure that the directory exists before you try to use it in the file path for a new file stream. Similarly, you can avoid a FileNotFoundException by using the Exists method of the File class.

However, I/O exceptions are often serious problems like hardware problems that an application can't do anything about. For example, if an application needs to open a file that's on a network drive that isn't available, an exception will be thrown. In that case, it's common to handle the exception by displaying an error message.

When handling I/O exceptions, it's common to use a finally block. In this block, it's common to use the stream's Close method to close all streams that are open. This frees the resources that are used to access the stream.

The code example shows how to handle some of the most common I/O exceptions. To start, the statement just before the try block declares a variable for the stream. That way, this variable is available to the catch blocks and the finally block. In this case, the stream is a FileStream object, but you'll learn how to work with other types of streams later in this chapter.

Within the try block, the first statement creates an instance of the stream. After this statement, the try block will contain more code that uses the stream to read and write data. Later in this chapter, you'll learn how to write this type of code. For now, you can assume that there is more code in the try block that uses the stream, and you can assume that this code may throw I/O exceptions, such as the exception that occurs when an application attempts to read beyond the end of the stream.

After the try block, the catch blocks are coded starting with the most specific type of exception and moving up the inheritance hierarchy towards the most general type of exception. In this case, both the DirectoryNotFoundException and FileNotFoundException classes inherit the IOException class. As a result, they must be coded before the catch block for the IOException. All three of these catch blocks display a message box that describes the type of exception to the user. This is a common way to handle I/O exceptions. However, in some cases, you may want to create a directory or file, or allow the user to search for a directory or file.

Within the finally block, an if statement is used to determine whether an exception was thrown before the stream was opened. If it was, the variable for the stream will be equal to a null value. As a result, calling the Close method isn't necessary and would throw a NullPointerException. However, if an exception was thrown after the stream was opened, the variable won't be equal to null. In that case, the Close method frees the resources used by the stream.

The exception classes for file I/O

Class	Description
IOException	The base class for exceptions that are thrown during the processing of a stream, file, or directory.
DirectoryNotFoundException	Occurs when part of a directory or file path can't be found.
FileNotFoundException	Occurs when a file can't be found.
EndOfStreamException	Occurs when an application attempts to read beyond the end of a stream.

Code that uses exception classes

```
string dirPath = @"C:\C# 2008\Files\";
string filePath = dirPath + "Products.txt";
FileStream fs = null;
try
{
    fs = new FileStream(filePath, FileMode.Open);
    // code that uses the file stream
    // to read and write data from the file
}
catch(FileNotFoundException)
{
    MessageBox.Show(filePath + " not found.", "File Not Found");
}
catch(DirectoryNotFoundException)
{
    MessageBox.Show(dirPath + " not found.", "Directory Not Found");
}
catch(IOException ex)
{
    MessageBox.Show(ex.Message, "IOException");
}
finally
{
    if (fs != null)
        fs.Close();
}
```

Description

- To catch any I/O exception, you can use the IOException class.
- To catch specific I/O exceptions, you can use the exception classes that inherit the IOException class such as the three shown in this figure.

Figure 21-4 How to use the exception classes for file I/O

How to work with text files

To read and write characters in a text file, you use the StreamReader and StreamWriter classes. When working with text files, you often need to use the techniques you learned in chapters 4 and 9 to build and parse strings.

How to write a text file

Figure 21-5 shows how to use the StreamWriter class to write data to a text file. This class lets you write any data to a text file by using the Write and WriteLine methods. When you use the WriteLine method, a line terminator is automatically added. Typically, a line terminator is used to end each record. However, the fields in a record are typically separated by special characters, such as tab characters or pipe characters, and you have to add those characters through code.

The example shows how this works. This code creates a FileStream object for a file with write-only access and it creates a StreamWriter object for that file stream. Next, it uses a foreach loop to write the three properties for each Product object in the List<> collection named products to the file with pipe characters as separators. (In case you're not familiar with the pipe character, it's available from the same key as the backslash key on your keyboard.) For the last property, the WriteLine method is used to end the record with a line terminator. That way, each record will start on a new line. Finally, after all of the records have been written to the file by the foreach loop, the stream writer and file stream are closed.

Both the Write and WriteLine methods of the StreamWriter class are overloaded to accept any type of data. As a result, if you pass a non-string data type to either of these methods, the method converts the data type to a string that represents the data type and then it writes that string to the stream. To do that, these methods automatically call the ToString method of the data type. In other words, you can write the decimal value that's stored in the Price property of a product to a text file like this:

```
textOut.WriteLine(product.Price);
```

This has the same effect as coding the statement like this:

```
textOut.WriteLine(product.Price.ToString());
```

The basic syntax for creating a StreamWriter object

```
new StreamWriter(stream)
```

Common methods of the StreamWriter class

Method	Description
`Write(data)`	Writes the data to the output stream.
`WriteLine(data)`	Writes the data to the output stream and appends a line terminator (usually a carriage return and a line feed).
`Close()`	Closes the StreamWriter object and the associated FileStream object.

Code that writes data from a collection of Product objects to a text file

```
StreamWriter textOut =
    new StreamWriter(
    new FileStream(path, FileMode.Create, FileAccess.Write));

foreach (Product product in products)
{
    textOut.Write(product.Code + "|");
    textOut.Write(product.Description + "|");
    textOut.WriteLine(product.Price);
}
textOut.Close();
```

Description

- You can use the Write and WriteLine methods of a StreamWriter object to write data to a text file. If the data type that's passed to these methods isn't already a string, these methods will call the ToString method of the data type to convert it to a string before they write the data.
- If the fields that make up a record are stored in individual variables, you need to concatenate these variables to construct each record and you need to add special characters to delimit each field. However, since the WriteLine method adds the line terminator automatically, you can use it to end each record.

Figure 21-5 How to write a text file

How to read a text file

Figure 21-6 shows how to use the StreamReader class to read data from a text file. To create a StreamReader object, you can use a FileStream object as the argument. Then, you can use the methods shown in this figure to work with the StreamReader object.

The three Read methods let you read a single character, a single line of data (a record), or all of the data from the current position to the end of the file. In most cases, though, you'll use the ReadLine method to read one record at a time. You can also use the Peek method to see if there is additional data in the file before you read from it, and you can use the Close method to close the stream reader and file stream when you're done with them.

The example shows how you can use a stream reader to read the data in a file one record at a time. After the file stream and stream reader are created, a while loop is used to read the records in the file. The condition on this loop uses the Peek method to check that there is at least one more character. If there is, the ReadLine method reads the next record in the file into a string and that string is parsed into the individual fields. Then, each field is stored in one of the properties of a Product object, and each Product object is stored in a List<> collection. When all of the records have been read, the Close method of the stream reader is used to close the StreamReader and FileStream objects.

Note in this example that the FileStream object is instantiated in OpenOrCreate mode. Then, if the file exists, it is opened. Otherwise, a new file is created with no records in it. In either case, the code that follows works because it peeks into the file before it tries to read the data. If the file is empty, no records are read.

The basic syntax for creating a StreamReader object

```
new StreamReader(stream)
```

Common methods of the StreamReader class

Method	Description
`Peek()`	Returns the next available character in the input stream without advancing to the next position. If no more characters are available, this method returns –1.
`Read()`	Reads the next character from the input stream.
`ReadLine()`	Reads the next line of characters from the input stream and returns it as a string.
`ReadToEnd()`	Reads the data from the current position in the input stream to the end of the stream and returns it as a string. This is typically used to read the contents of an entire file.
`Close()`	Closes both the StreamReader object and the associated FileStream object.

Code that reads data from a text file into a collection of Product objects

```
StreamReader textIn =
    new StreamReader(
    new FileStream(path, FileMode.OpenOrCreate, FileAccess.Read));

List<Product> products = new List<Product>();
while (textIn.Peek() != -1)
{
    string row = textIn.ReadLine();
    string[] columns = row.Split('|');
    Product product = new Product();
    product.Code = columns[0];
    product.Description = columns[1];
    product.Price = Convert.ToDecimal(columns[2]);
    products.Add(product);
}
textIn.Close();
```

Description

- You use a StreamReader object to read data from a text file. Because the records in most text files end with a line terminator (usually a carriage return and a line feed), you'll typically use the ReadLine method to read one record at a time.
- If the fields in a record are delimited by special characters, you need to parse the fields using the techniques of chapter 9.
- You can use the Peek method to determine if the input stream is positioned at the end of the stream.

A class that works with a text file

In chapter 12, you learned how to develop an application that used a business class named Product. You also learned how to use two static methods in a database class named ProductDB to get the data for Product objects and to save the data for Product objects. However, you didn't learn how to code those database methods.

Now, in figure 21-7, you can see a ProductDB class that implements those methods using a text file. To start, the using statements specify the System.Collections.Generic and System.IO namespaces. That makes it easier to write the code that works with the generic List<> collection that stores the Product objects, and it makes it easier to work with the input and output streams. Then, this class provides two constants that specify the path for the directory and the path for the text file. This makes those constants available to all of the methods in the class.

The GetProducts method reads the product data from the file, stores that data in a List<> of Product objects, and returns the List<> collection. After the StreamReader object and the List<> object are created, the while loop reads the data in the file and stores the Product objects in the List<> collection as described in the previous figure. When the loop ends, the StreamReader and FileStream objects are closed, and the method returns the List<> object. At least that's the way this method works if the file already exists.

Note, however, that the GetProducts method also works if the directory or file doesn't exist when the method is executed. This situation could occur the first time an application is run. In that case, the method creates the directory if the directory doesn't exist, and it creates an empty file if the file doesn't exist. Then, the code that follows will still work, but it won't read any records.

In contrast, the SaveProducts method writes the data in the Product objects that are stored in the List<> collection to the file. To start, this method accepts a List<> of Product objects. Then, this method writes each Product object to the file. Because the FileStream object is instantiated in Create mode, the Product objects will be written to a new file if the file doesn't already exist and they will overwrite the old file if it does exist.

To keep the emphasis on the code for file I/O, this class doesn't include exception handling. In a production application, though, you would probably add exception handling to a class like this. That way, the exceptions can be caught and handled close to their source, which often helps to reduce the amount of exception handling code that's necessary for an application.

A class that works with a text file

```
using System;
using System.IO;
using System.Collections.Generic;

namespace ProductMaintenance
{
    public class ProductDB
    {
        private const string dir = @"C:\C# 2008\Files\";
        private const string path = dir + "Products.txt";

        public static List<Product> GetProducts()
        {
            if (!Directory.Exists(dir))
                Directory.CreateDirectory(dir);

            StreamReader textIn =
                new StreamReader(
                new FileStream(path, FileMode.OpenOrCreate, FileAccess.Read));

            List<Product> products = new List<Product>();
            while (textIn.Peek() != -1)
            {
                string row = textIn.ReadLine();
                string[] columns = row.Split('|');
                Product product = new Product();
                product.Code = columns[0];
                product.Description = columns[1];
                product.Price = Convert.ToDecimal(columns[2]);
                products.Add(product);
            }
            textIn.Close();

            return products;
        }

        public static void SaveProducts(List<Product> products)
        {
            StreamWriter textOut =
                new StreamWriter(
                new FileStream(path, FileMode.Create, FileAccess.Write));

            foreach (Product product in products)
            {
                textOut.Write(product.Code + "|");
                textOut.Write(product.Description + "|");
                textOut.WriteLine(product.Price);
            }
            textOut.Close();
        }
    }
}
```

Figure 21-7 A class that works with a text file

How to work with binary files

To read and write data in a binary file, you use the BinaryReader and BinaryWriter classes. You'll learn how to use these classes in the figures that follow, and you'll see a class that can be used to read and write a binary file.

How to write a binary file

Figure 21-8 shows how to use the BinaryWriter class to write data to a binary file. To start, you create a BinaryWriter object using the syntax at the top of this figure. To do that, you must supply a FileStream object as the argument for the constructor of the BinaryWriter class. This links the stream to the BinaryWriter object so it can be used to write to the file.

Once you create a BinaryWriter object, you can use its Write method to write all types of data. This method begins by figuring out what type of data has been passed to it. Then, it writes that type of data to the file. For example, if you pass a variable that contains a decimal value to the Write method, this method won't convert the decimal value to a string. Instead, it will write the decimal value to the file.

The example shows how this works. Here, a binary writer is created for a file stream that specifies a file that has write-only access. Since the mode argument has been set to Create, this will overwrite the file if it exists, and it will create the file if it doesn't exist. Then, a foreach loop is used to write the elements in the List<> collection named products to the file. Since each element in the List<> collection is an object of the Product class, each field in the Product object is written to the file separately using the Write method. After all of the elements in the List<> collection have been written to the file, the Close method is used to close both the BinaryWriter and the FileStream objects.

The basic syntax for creating a BinaryWriter object

```
new BinaryWriter(stream)
```

Common methods of the BinaryWriter class

Method	Description
`Write(data)`	Writes the specified data to the output stream.
`Close()`	Closes the BinaryWriter object and the associated FileStream object.

Code that writes data from a collection of Product objects to a binary file

```
BinaryWriter binaryOut =
    new BinaryWriter(
    new FileStream(path, FileMode.Create, FileAccess.Write));

foreach (Product product in products)
{
    binaryOut.Write(product.Code);
    binaryOut.Write(product.Description);
    binaryOut.Write(product.Price);
}

binaryOut.Close();
```

Description

- You use a BinaryWriter object to write data to a binary file. In most cases, you'll write one field at a time in a prescribed sequence.
- Unlike the BinaryReader class, which provides several methods for reading fields that contain different types of data, the BinaryWriter class provides a single Write method for writing data to a file. This method determines the type of data being written based on the data types of the variables.

Figure 21-8 How to write a binary file

How to read a binary file

Figure 21-9 shows you how to use the BinaryReader class to read data from a binary file. Like the BinaryWriter class, the argument that you pass to the BinaryReader is the name of the FileStream object that connects the stream to a file.

In a binary file, there's no termination character to indicate where one record ends and another begins. Because of that, you can't read an entire record at once. Instead, you have to read one character or one field at a time. To do that, you use the Read methods of the BinaryReader class that are shown in this figure. When you do, you must use the appropriate method for the data type of the field that you want to read. To read a Boolean field, for example, you use the ReadBoolean method. To read a Decimal field, you use the ReadDecimal method.

The BinaryReader class provides methods to read most of the data types provided by the .NET Framework. However, this figure only shows the most common of these methods. For a complete list of methods, see the online help information for the BinaryReader class.

Before you read the next character or field, you want to be sure that you aren't at the end of the file. To do that, you use the PeekChar method. Then, if there's at least one more character to be read, this method returns that character without advancing the cursor to the next position in the file. If there isn't another character, the PeekChar method returns a value of –1. Then, you can use the Close method to close the binary reader and the associated file stream.

The example shows how you can use some of these methods. Here, a FileStream object is created for a file that will have read-only access. Since the mode argument for the file stream specifies OpenOrCreate, this opens an existing file if one exists or creates a new file that's empty and opens it. Then, a new BinaryReader object is created for that file stream. Finally, the while loop that follows is executed until the PeekChar method returns a value of –1, which means the end of the file has been reached.

Within the while loop, the three fields in each record are read into the Product object. Because the first two fields in each record contain string data, the ReadString method is used to retrieve their contents. Because the third field contains decimal data, the ReadDecimal method is used to retrieve its contents. Then, the Product object is added to the List<> collection. When the while loop ends, the Close method of the BinaryReader object is used to close both the BinaryReader and the FileStream objects.

The basic syntax for creating a BinaryReader object

```
new BinaryReader(stream)
```

Common methods of the BinaryReader class

Method	Description
`PeekChar()`	Returns the next available character in the input stream without advancing to the next position. If no more characters are available, this method returns -1.
`Read()`	Returns the next available character from the input stream and advances to the next position in the file.
`ReadBoolean()`	Returns a Boolean value from the input stream and advances the current position of the stream by one byte.
`ReadByte()`	Returns a byte from the input stream and advances the current position of the stream accordingly.
`ReadChar()`	Returns a character from the input stream and advances the current position of the stream accordingly.
`ReadDecimal()`	Returns a decimal value from the input stream and advances the current position of the stream by 16 bytes.
`ReadInt32()`	Returns a 4-byte signed integer from the input stream and advances the current position of the stream by 4 bytes.
`ReadString()`	Returns a string from the input stream and advances the current position of the stream by the number of characters in the string.
`Close()`	Closes the BinaryReader object and the associated FileStream object.

Code that reads data from a binary file into a collection of Product objects

```
BinaryReader binaryIn =
    new BinaryReader(
    new FileStream(path, FileMode.OpenOrCreate, FileAccess.Read));

List<Product> products = new List<Product>();
while (binaryIn.PeekChar() != -1)
{
    Product product = new Product();
    product.Code = binaryIn.ReadString();
    product.Description = binaryIn.ReadString();
    product.Price = binaryIn.ReadDecimal();
    products.Add(product);
}

binaryIn.Close();
```

Description

- You use a BinaryReader object to read a single character or an entire field from a binary file. To read a single character, you use the Read method. And to read a field, you use the method that indicates the type of data the field contains.
- You can use the PeekChar method to determine if the input stream is positioned at the end of the stream.

A class that works with a binary file

Figure 21-10 presents the code for the ProductDB class that you saw in figure 21-7, but this time it uses a binary file instead of a text file. Because the methods in this class are similar to the ones for the text file, you shouldn't have any trouble understanding how they work.

Note, however, that the signatures for the two methods in this class are the same as the signatures for the methods in the ProductDB class in figure 21-7. As a result, either of these classes can be used with the Product Maintenance application presented in chapter 12. This clearly illustrates the benefit of encapsulation: the calling method doesn't know or care how the method is implemented. As a result, the programmer can change the way these methods are implemented without changing the rest of the application.

A class that works with a binary file

```
using System;
using System.IO;
using System.Collections.Generic;

namespace ProductMaintenance
{
    public class ProductDB
    {
        private const string dir = @"C:\C# 2008\Files\";
        private const string path = dir + "Products.dat";

        public static List<Product> GetProducts()
        {
            if (!Directory.Exists(dir))
                Directory.CreateDirectory(dir);

            BinaryReader binaryIn =
                new BinaryReader(
                new FileStream(path, FileMode.OpenOrCreate, FileAccess.Read));

            List<Product> products = new List<Product>();
            while (binaryIn.PeekChar() != -1)
            {
                Product product = new Product();
                product.Code = binaryIn.ReadString();
                product.Description = binaryIn.ReadString();
                product.Price = binaryIn.ReadDecimal();
                products.Add(product);
            }

            binaryIn.Close();

            return products;
        }

        public static void SaveProducts(List<Product> products)
        {
            BinaryWriter binaryOut =
                new BinaryWriter(
                new FileStream(path, FileMode.Create, FileAccess.Write));

            foreach (Product product in products)
            {
                binaryOut.Write(product.Code);
                binaryOut.Write(product.Description);
                binaryOut.Write(product.Price);
            }

            binaryOut.Close();
        }
    }
}
```

Figure 21-10 A class that works with a binary file

Perspective

In this chapter, you learned how to read and write the data in text and binary files. These files can be used when you need a relatively easy way to store a limited number of records with a limited number of fields. However, when the data requirements for an application are more complex, it usually makes sense to use a database instead of text or binary files.

Terms

input file
output file
I/O operations
file I/O
text file
field
record
binary file
stream
output stream
input stream
text stream
binary stream

Exercise 21-1 Work with a text file

1. Open the project in the C:\C# 2008\Chapter 21\CustomerText directory. This is the Customer Maintenance application that you developed for exercise 12-1, but it doesn't save or retrieve the data.
2. In the CustomerDB class, add code to the GetCustomers and SaveCustomers methods so they use a text file to read and write a List<> of Customer objects. Unless you moved it after downloading and installing the files for this book, the path for this file should be C:\C# 2008\Files\Customers.txt. Then, add code to the methods in the two forms so they use the CustomerDB class to read and write the text file.
3. Test the application by adding and deleting customers. To verify that the data is being saved to disk, stop the application and run it again. Or use a text editor like NotePad to open the file after a test run.

Exercise 21-2 Work with a binary file

1. Use the Windows Explorer to copy the directory named CustomerText that you created for the previous exercise within the Chapter 21 directory. Then, rename that directory CustomerBinary, and open the project in that directory.
2. Modify the CustomerDB class so it uses a binary file named Customers.dat instead of a text file. Also, leave the signatures of the GetCustomers and SaveCustomers methods as they are so you won't need to modify the code in the form class that calls these methods. Then, test the application by adding and deleting customers.

22

How to work with XML files

XML is a standard way of storing data. Although XML is often used to exchange data between applications, particularly web-based applications, it can also be used to store structured data in a file. In this chapter, you'll learn the basics of creating XML documents, and you'll learn how to store those documents in a file.

An introduction to XML

This topic introduces you to the basics of XML. Here, you'll learn what XML is, how it is used, and the rules you must follow to create a simple XML document.

An XML document

XML (*Extensible Markup Language*) is a standard way to structure data by using tags that identify each data element. In some ways, XML is similar to HTML, the markup language that's used to format HTML documents on the World Wide Web. As a result, if you're familiar with HTML, you'll have no trouble learning how to create *XML documents*.

Figure 22-1 shows a simple XML document that contains data for three products. Each product has a code, description, and price. In the next two figures, you'll learn how the tags in this XML document work. But even without knowing those details, you can pick out the code, description, and price for each of the three products represented by this XML document.

XML was designed as a way to structure data that's sent over the World Wide Web. When you use .NET to develop web applications, though, you don't have to deal directly with XML. Instead, the .NET Framework classes handle the XML details for you.

Besides its use for web applications, XML is used internally throughout the .NET Framework to store data and to exchange data between various components of the Framework. In particular, the database features described in section 4 rely on XML. When you retrieve data from a database, for example, the .NET Framework converts the data to XML. However, since this is done automatically, the programmer doesn't have to deal with XML directly.

You can also use XML files as an alternative to the text and binary files described in chapter 21. Later in this chapter, for example, you'll learn how to create a ProductDB class for the Product Maintenance application that uses an XML file.

Data for three products

Code	Description	Price
A3CS	Murach's ASP.NET 3.5 with C# 2008	54.50
JSE6	Murach's Java SE 6	52.50
CS08	Murach's C# 2008	54.50

An XML document that contains the data shown above

```
<?xml version="1.0" encoding="utf-8" ?>
<!--Product data-->
<Products>
  <Product Code="A3CS">
    <Description>Murach's ASP.NET 3.5 with C# 2008</Description>
    <Price>54.50</Price>
  </Product>
  <Product Code="JSE6">
    <Description>Murach's Java SE 6</Description>
    <Price>52.50</Price>
  </Product>
  <Product Code="CS08">
    <Description>Murach's C# 2008</Description>
    <Price>54.50</Price>
  </Product>
</Products>
```

Description

- *XML*, which stands for *Extensible Markup Language*, is a method of structuring data using special *tags*.
- The *XML document* in this figure contains data for three products. Each product has an *attribute* named Code and *elements* named Description and Price, which you'll learn more about in the next two figures.
- XML can be used to exchange data between different systems, especially via the Internet.
- Many .NET classes, particularly the database and web classes, use XML internally to store or exchange data.
- XML documents that are stored in a file can be used as an alternative to binary files, text files, or even database systems for storing data.
- When XML is stored in a file, the file name usually has an extension of xml.
- The .NET Framework includes several classes that let you read and write XML data. These classes are in the System.Xml namespace.

Figure 22-1 An XML document

XML tags, declarations, and comments

Figure 22-2 shows how XML uses tags to structure the data in an XML document. Here, each XML tag begins with the < character and ends with the > character. As a result, the first line in the XML document in this figure contains a complete XML tag. Similarly, the next three lines also contain complete tags. In contrast, the fifth line contains two tags, <Description> and </Description>, with a text value in between.

The first tag in any XML document is an *XML declaration*. This declaration identifies the document as an XML document and indicates which XML version the document conforms to. In this example, the document conforms to XML version 1.0. In addition, the declaration usually identifies the character set that's being used for the document. In this example, the character set is UTF-8, the most common one used for XML documents in English-speaking countries.

An XML document can also contain comments. These are tags that begin with <!-- and end with -->. Between the tags, you can type anything you want. For instance, the second line in this figure is a comment that indicates what type of data is contained in the XML document. It's often a good idea to include similar comments in your own XML documents.

XML elements

Elements are the building blocks of XML. Each element in an XML document represents a single data item and is identified by two tags: a *start tag* and an *end tag*. The start tag marks the beginning of the element and provides the element's name. The end tag marks the end of the element and repeats the name, prefixed by a slash. For example, <Description> is the start tag for an element named Description, and </Description> is the corresponding end tag.

It's important to realize that XML does not provide a pre-defined set of element names the way HTML does. Instead, you create your own element names to describe the contents of each element. Since XML names are case-sensitive, <Product> and <product> are not the same.

A complete element consists of the element's start tag, its end tag, and the *content* between the tags. For example, <Price>54.50</Price> indicates that the content of the Price element is 54.50. And <Description>Murach's C# 2008 </Description> indicates that the content of the Description element is *Murach's C# 2008*.

Besides content, elements can contain other elements, known as *child elements*. This lets you add structure to a *parent element*. For example, a parent Product element can have child elements that provide details about each product, such as the product's description and price. In this figure, for example, you can see that the start tag, end tag, and values for the Description and Price elements are contained between the start and end tags for the Product element. As a result, Description and Price are children of the Product element, and the Product element is the parent of both the Description and Price elements.

An XML document

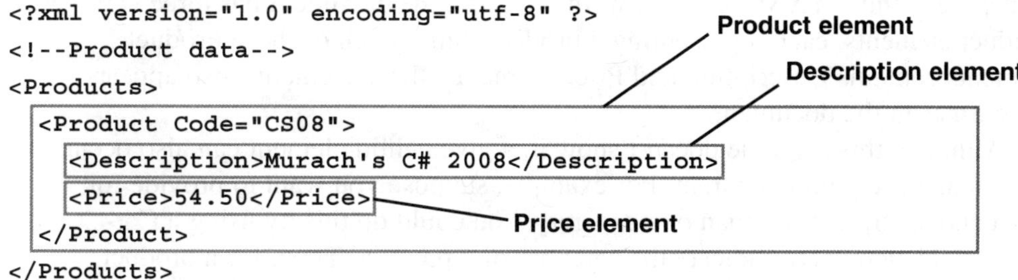

```
<?xml version="1.0" encoding="utf-8" ?>
<!--Product data-->
<Products>
  <Product Code="CS08">
    <Description>Murach's C# 2008</Description>
    <Price>54.50</Price>
  </Product>
</Products>
```


Tags, XML declarations, and comments

- Each XML tag begins with < and ends with >.
- The first line in an XML document is an *XML declaration* that indicates which version of the XML standard is being used for the document. In addition, the declaration usually identifies the standard character set that's being used. For documents in English-speaking countries, UTF-8 is the character set that's commonly used.
- You can use the <!-- and --> tags to include comments in an XML document.

Elements

- An *element* is a unit of XML data that begins with a *start tag* and ends with an *end tag*. The start tag provides the name of the element and contains any attributes assigned to the element (see figure 22-3 for details on attributes). The end tag repeats the name, prefixed with a slash (/). You can use any name you want for an XML element.
- The text between an element's start and end tags is called the element's *content*. For example, <Description>Murach's C# 2008</Description> indicates that the content of the Description element is the string *Murach's C# 2008*.
- Elements can contain other elements. An element that's contained within another element is known as a *child element*. The element that contains a child element is known as the child's *parent element*.
- Child elements can repeat within a parent element. For instance, in the example above, the Products element can contain more than one Product element. Similarly, each Product element could contain repeating child elements. For instance, in the example above, each Product element could contain zero or more Category elements.
- The highest-level parent element in an XML document is known as the *root element*. An XML document can have only one root element.

Figure 22-2 XML tags, declarations, comments, and elements

As the XML document in figure 22-1 shows, an element can occur more than once within an XML document. In this case, the document has three Product elements, each representing a product. Since each of these Product elements contains Description and Price elements, these elements also appear three times in the document.

Although this example doesn't show it, a given child element can also occur more than once within a parent. For example, suppose you want to provide for products that have more than one category. You could do this by using a Category child element to indicate the category of a product. Then, for a product that belongs to multiple categories, you simply include multiple Category child elements within the Product element for that product.

The highest-level parent element in an XML document is known as the *root element*, and an XML document can have only one root element. In the examples in figures 22-1 and 22-2, the root element is Products. For XML documents that contain repeating data, it is common to use a plural name for the root element to indicate that it contains multiple child elements.

XML attributes

As shown in figure 22-3, *attributes* are a concise way to provide data for XML elements. In the products XML document, for example, each Product element has a Code attribute that provides an identifying code for the product. Thus, <Product Code="CS08"> contains an attribute named Code whose value is CS08.

Here again, XML doesn't provide a set of pre-defined attributes. Instead, you create attributes as you need them, using names that describe the content of the attributes. If an element has more than one attribute, you can list the attributes in any order you wish. However, you must separate the attributes from each other with one or more spaces. In addition, each attribute can appear only once within an element.

When you plan the layout of an XML document, you will often need to decide whether to use elements or attributes to represent each data item. In many cases, either one will work. In the products document, for example, I could have used a child element named Code rather than an attribute to represent each product's code. Likewise, I could have used an attribute named Description rather than a child element for the product's description.

Because attributes are more concise than child elements, it's often tempting to use attributes rather than child elements. Keep in mind, though, that an element with more than a few attributes soon becomes unwieldy. As a result, most designers limit their use of attributes to certain types of data, such as identifiers like product codes or customer numbers.

An XML document

```
<?xml version="1.0" encoding="utf-8" ?>
<!--Product data-->
<Products>
  <Product Code="CS08">
    <Description>Murach's C# 2008</Description>
    <Price>54.50</Price>
  </Product>
</Products>
```

Code attribute

Description

- You can include one or more *attributes* in the start tag for an element. An attribute consists of an attribute name, an equal sign, and a string value in quotes.
- If an element has more than one attribute, the order in which the attributes appear doesn't matter, but the attributes must be separated by one or more spaces.

When to use attributes instead of child elements

- When you design an XML document, you can use either child elements or attributes to represent the data for an element. The choice of whether to implement a data item as an attribute or as a separate child element is often a matter of preference.
- Two advantages of attributes are that they can appear in any order and they are more concise because they do not require end tags.
- Two advantages of child elements are that they are easier for people to read and they are more convenient for long string values.

Figure 22-3 XML attributes

How to work with the XML Editor

You can use the XML Editor that comes with Visual Studio to create or edit an XML document. The XML Editor is similar to the Code Editor that you use for working with C# code, but it includes features that make it easier to work with XML.

Of course, since an XML file is really just a text file with XML tags, you can open or create an XML file in any text editor. As a result, if you already have a text editor that you prefer, you can use that editor.

In addition, since XML is a standard format that's used on the web, you can use most web browsers to view an XML document. To do that, you can enter the path for the XML file in the browser's Address text box. Or, on most systems, you can double-click on the file in the Windows Explorer.

How to create a new XML file

To create a new XML file and add it to your project, you can use the Project→Add New Item command as shown in figure 22-4. This adds the file to your project, adds the XML declaration to the top of the file, and opens the file in the XML Editor. In this figure, for example, the XML declaration includes both the XML version attribute and the encoding attribute that indicates which character set the document uses. Unless you're working in a language other than English, you'll want to leave this attribute set to UTF-8.

How to open an existing XML file

To open an existing XML file without adding the file to your project, you can use the File→Open command to open the file. Then, if the file has a common XML extension (such as xml, xsl, or config), or if the file contains XML markup, it is opened in the XML Editor. If this doesn't work, you can right-click on the file in the Solution Explorer, select the Open With command, and select XML Editor from the resulting dialog box.

How to edit an XML file

When you work in the XML Editor, the task of editing XML files is simplified. For example, tags, content, attributes, values, and comments are color-coded so you can easily tell them apart. When you type a start tag, the XML Editor automatically adds the end tag and positions the cursor between the start and end tags so you can enter the content. In addition, the XML Editor makes it easy to work with the indentation of the child elements, and it makes it easy to view data by expanding or collapsing elements. If you work with the XML Editor for a while, you'll quickly see how easy it is to use.

By the way, if you've used a previous version of Visual Basic .NET, you may remember that the XML Editor let you work with the data in an XML document in Data Grid view. Unfortunately, this view has been omitted from Visual Studio 2008. So you can only work with XML data in the view shown here.

An XML document in the XML Editor

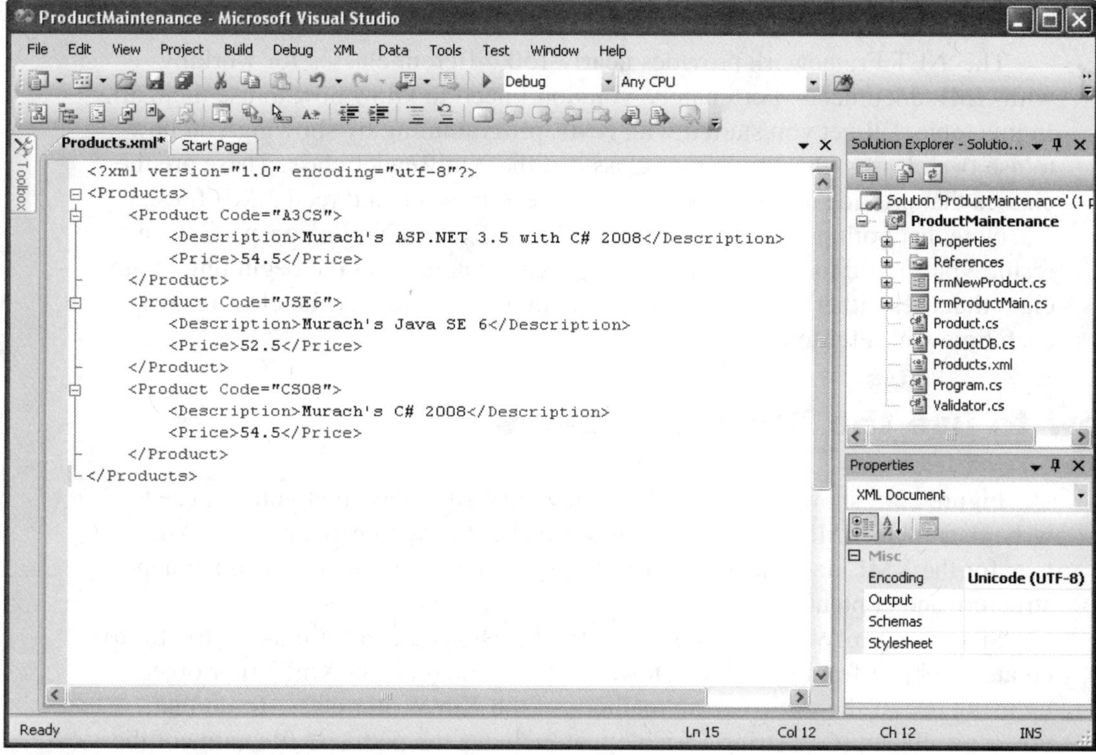

How to add a new XML file to a project

- Choose the Project→Add New Item command. In the Add New Item dialog box, select XML File in the Templates box; type a name for the XML file in the Name text box; and click Open. This adds an XML file to your project, adds the XML declaration for the document, and opens the document in the XML Editor.

How to open an existing XML file

- To open an existing XML file that's stored in the project, double-click on the file.
- To open an existing XML file without adding the file to your project, use the File→Open command.

How to edit an XML file

- When you type a start tag, the XML Editor automatically adds an end tag for the element and positions the insertion point between the start and end tags so you can type the element's content.
- When you type an attribute, the XML Editor automatically adds a pair of quotation marks and positions the insertion point between them so you can type the attribute value.

Figure 22-4 How to work with the XML Editor

How to work with XML

The .NET Framework provides nearly 150 different classes for working with XML documents. Fortunately, you don't need to know how to use them all. In this topic, I'll get you started with XML programming by showing you how to use two classes: the XmlWriter class and the XmlReader class. These are the classes that provide the basic services you need to write and read XML files.

Note that both of these classes reside in the System.Xml namespace. As a result, you should include a using System.Xml statement at the beginning of any class that uses either of them. Otherwise, you have to qualify the class names each time you refer to them.

How to use the XmlWriter class

Figure 22-5 shows the methods of the XmlWriter class that you can use to write data to an XML file. These methods make it easy to generate the XML tags for the XML document. As a result, you can concentrate on the document's structure and content.

Since the XmlWriter class is an abstract class, you can't use a constructor to create an object from this class. However, you can create an XmlWriter object by using one of the static Create methods of the XmlWriter class. To do that, you typically supply a string variable that includes the path and file name of the file. Then, if the file you specify already exists, it's deleted and recreated. As a result, you can't use this technique to add XML to an existing file.

Before you code any statements that write XML to a file, you typically want to change some settings for the XmlWriter object so it uses spaces to indent child elements. This will make your XML files easier to read if they're opened in the XML Editor. To do that, you need to create an XmlWriterSettings object and set its Indent and IndentChars properties. Then, you pass this object to the Create method when you create an XmlWriter object.

To write XML data, you use one of the Write methods of the XmlWriter class. Although this class actually has 28 Write methods, you can create basic XML documents using just the six Write methods in this figure.

When you use these methods, you need to use the WriteStartElement and WriteEndElement methods for elements that have children, such as the Products element. However, you don't need to use a WriteStartElement or WriteEndElement method to create an element that only contains content, such as the Description and Price elements. In this case, you can use the WriteElementString method to automatically write the start tag, the content, and the end tag.

Common properties and methods of the XmlWriter class

Method	Description
`Create(path)`	A static method that creates an XmlWriter object using the specified path or file name.
`Create(path, settings)`	A static method that creates an XmlWriter object using the specified path or file name and the specified XmlWriterSettings object.
`WriteStartDocument()`	Writes an XML declaration line at the beginning of a document.
`WriteComment(comment)`	Writes a comment to the XML document.
`WriteStartElement(elementName)`	Writes a start tag using the element name you provide.
`WriteAttributeString(attributeName, value)`	Adds an attribute to the current element.
`WriteEndElement()`	Writes an end tag for the current element.
`WriteElementString(elementName, content)`	Writes a complete element including a start tag, content, and end tag.
`Close()`	Closes the XmlWriter object.

Common properties of the XmlWriterSettings class

Property	Description
`Indent`	Gets or sets a Boolean value that indicates whether to indent elements.
`IndentChars`	Gets or sets the string to use when indenting.

Description

- The XmlWriter class lets you write XML data to a text file.
- When you create an XmlWriter object, you specify the name or path of the file where you want to write the XML. If the file already exists, it's deleted and then recreated.
- When you create an XmlWriter object, you can also use an XmlWriterSettings object to specify the settings that will be used by the XmlWriter object.
- If you attempt to create an invalid XML document, an XmlException will be thrown. For example, an XmlException will be thrown if you try to write two XML declarations or if you try to write an end tag before you've written a start tag.

Figure 22-5 How to use the XmlWriter class

Code that writes an XML document

Figure 22-6 shows the code that creates an XML document like the one that's in figure 22-1. This code gets its data from a List<> collection of Product objects where each product has three properties: Code, Description, and Price.

To start, this code defines a string variable that points to the Products.xml file that's stored in the C:\C# 2008\Files directory. Then, it creates an XmlWriterSettings object and sets the Indent and IndentChars properties so the XmlWriter object uses four spaces to indent each level of child elements. Finally, this code creates an XmlWriter object by passing the path and settings variables to the static Create method of the XmlWriter class.

After this code creates the XmlWriter object, it uses the WriteStartDocument method to write the XML declaration for the document. In addition, it uses the WriteStartElement method to write the start tag for the root element of the document, which is the Products element.

The heart of this code is the foreach loop that writes a Product element for each Product object in the List<> collection. To write a Product element, the method uses the WriteStartElement method to write the start tag for the Product element, and then uses the WriteAttributeString method to add the Code attribute. Next, two WriteElementString methods are used to write the Description and Price elements. Finally, the WriteEndElement method is used to write the end tag for the Product element.

Since the foreach loop is preceded by a WriteStartElement method that writes the start tag for the document's root element, the foreach loop must be followed by a WriteEndElement method that writes the end tag for the root element. After that, the Close method is used to close the XmlWriter object.

In this code, the path of the XML document is coded as an absolute path like this:

```
string path = @"C:\C# 2008\Files\Products.xml";
```

In this case, the XML file isn't stored in the same directory as the rest of the files for the ProductMaintenance project. However, if you want to use an XML file that's part of the project, you can specify a relative path like this:

```
string path = @"..\..\Products.xml";
```

This works because the exe for the application runs from the bin\Debug subdirectory of the project directory. As a result, you need to navigate back two directories to get to the directory that stores the files for the project.

Code that writes an XML document

```
// create the path variable
string path = @"C:\C# 2008\Files\Products.xml";

// create the XmlWriterSettings object
XmlWriterSettings settings = new XmlWriterSettings();
settings.Indent = true;
settings.IndentChars = ("    ");

// create the XmlWriter object
XmlWriter xmlOut = XmlWriter.Create(path, settings);

// write the start of the document
xmlOut.WriteStartDocument();
xmlOut.WriteStartElement("Products");

// write each Product object to the xml file
foreach (Product product in products)
{
    xmlOut.WriteStartElement("Product");
    xmlOut.WriteAttributeString("Code",
        product.Code);
    xmlOut.WriteElementString("Description",
        product.Description);
    xmlOut.WriteElementString("Price",
        Convert.ToString(product.Price));
    xmlOut.WriteEndElement();
}

// write the end tag for the root element
xmlOut.WriteEndElement();

// close the XmlWriter object
xmlOut.Close();
```

Description

- This example saves a List<> collection of Product objects as an XML document. The resulting XML document will be like the one in figure 22-1.
- To set the path for an XML file in the current project, you can use two dots to refer to the parent directory as in:

  `@"..\..\Products.xml"`

  This works because the current project is run from the bin\Debug subdirectory of the project directory.

Figure 22-6 Code that writes an XML document

How to use the XmlReader class

To read an XML document, you can use the XmlReader class that's summarized in figure 22-7. Like the XmlWriter class, the XmlReader class is an abstract class. As a result, to create an object from this class, you must use the static Create method that's available from the class. When you do that, you must supply the path of the XML file as a string. In addition, you can optionally supply an XmlReaderSettings object that contains any settings that you want to set for the XmlReader object.

For example, you typically want to set the IgnoreWhitespace property of the XmlReaderSettings object to indicate how you want to handle *white space*. White space refers to spaces, tabs, and return characters that affect the appearance but not the meaning of an XML document. To simplify the task of processing XML data, you typically set the IgnoreWhitespace property to true. That way, the XmlReader object will automatically skip white space in the XML document, and you won't have to write code to handle it.

Similarly, you typically want to set the IgnoreComments property of the XmlReaderSettings object to true. That way, the XmlReader object will automatically skip any comments in the XML document, and you won't have to write code to handle them.

To read data from an XML document, you can use the various Read methods of the XmlReader class. This class treats an XML document as a series of *nodes*, and you can use the basic Read method to read the next node from the file. Because the concept of nodes is so important to reading XML data, the next figure describes them in detail and walks you through the process of reading a simple XML document node by node. For now, you just need to know that every tag in an XML document is treated as a separate node, and each element's content is also treated as a separate node. Attributes, however, are not treated as nodes. Instead, an attribute is treated as part of a start tag node.

When you invoke the Read method, the XmlReader gets the next node from the XML document and makes that node the *current node*. Then, you can use the XmlReader's NodeType, Name, or Value property to retrieve the node's type, name, or value. If you read past the last node in the document, the EOF property is set to true. As a result, you can use this property to tell when you have reached the end of the file.

In fact, you can process an entire XML document by using just the Read method to read the document's nodes one at a time, by using the NodeType property to determine what type of node has just been read, and by taking appropriate action based on the node type.

However, the XmlReader has several other methods that simplify the task of parsing an XML document. For example, you can use the ReadToDescendant and ReadToNextSibling elements to read up to the element that you want to process. In addition, you can use the ReadElementContentAsString and ReadElementContentAsDecimal methods to read content from an element that contains content.

Common members of the XmlReader class

Indexer	Description
`[name]`	Gets the value of the specified attribute. If the current element doesn't have the attribute, an empty string is returned.
Property	**Description**
`NodeType`	Returns a member of the XmlNodeType enumeration that indicates the type of the current node.
`Name`	Gets the name of the current node, if the node has a name.
`Value`	Gets the value of the current node, if the node has a value.
`EOF`	Returns a true value if the reader has reached the end of the stream.
Method	**Description**
`Create(path)`	A static method that creates an XmlReader object using the specified path or file name.
`Create(path, settings)`	A static method that creates an XmlReader object using the specified path or file name and the specified XmlReaderSettings object.
`Read()`	Reads the next node.
`ReadStartElement(name)`	Checks that the current node is a start tag with the specified name, then advances to the next node.
`ReadEndElement()`	Checks that the current node is an end tag, then advances to the next node.
`ReadToDescendant(name)`	If the specified descendant element is found, this method advances to it and returns a true value. Otherwise, it advances to the end tag of the current element and returns a false value.
`ReadToNextSibling(name)`	If the specified sibling element is found, this method advances to it and returns a true value. Otherwise, it advances to the end tag of the current element and returns a false value.
`ReadElementContentAsString()`	Reads the current element, returns the content as a string, and moves past the element's end tag.
`ReadElementContentAsDecimal()`	Reads the current element, returns the content as a decimal value, and moves past the element's end tag.
`Close()`	Closes the XmlWriter and release any resources.

Common properties of the XmlReaderSettings class

Property	Description
`IgnoreWhitespace`	Gets or sets a Boolean value that indicates whether to ignore white space. If set to false, white space is treated as a node.
`IgnoreComments`	Gets or sets a Boolean value indicating whether to ignore comments.

Description

- Some of these methods throw an XmlException if they encounter an unexpected situation such as when the next element does not match the specified name.

Figure 22-7 How to use the XmlReader class

The ReadStartElement method starts by confirming that the current node is a start tag. If it is, the method checks to make sure that the name of the start tag matches the name you supply as an argument. If both of these conditions are met, the method then reads the next element. Otherwise, an XmlException is thrown.

The ReadEndElement method is similar, but it checks to make sure the current node is an end tag rather than a start tag, and it doesn't check the element name. If the current node is an end tag, the ReadEndElement method reads the next node. Otherwise, it throws an XmlException.

The ReadElementContentAsString method reads a simple content element (an element that has content but no child elements) and returns its content node as a string. However, if the element contains child elements rather than simple content, an XmlException is thrown. After the element is read, the reader moves past the end element tag so it's positioned to read the next element.

The ReadElementContentAsDecimal method works similarly. However, this method also converts the content that's stored in the element from a string to a decimal value and returns that value. If this method isn't able to convert the content to a decimal value, it throws an XmlException.

To read attributes, you can use the indexer of the XmlReader object. To do that, you code the name of the attribute as a string argument within brackets. Of course, this only works if the current node has an attribute with the specified name.

How the XmlReader class reads nodes

To use the XmlReader class properly, you need to understand exactly how it reads nodes. To help you with that, figure 22-8 presents a simple XML document and lists all of the nodes contained in that document. Even though this document contains just one Product element with two child elements, there are 12 nodes.

By studying this figure, you can see how the methods of the XmlReader class read the nodes. The first node is the XML declaration tag. The second node is the comment. The third node is the start tag for the Products element. And so on.

Notice that when the start tag for the Product element is reached, the Code attribute is available via the indexer. Also notice that the Description and Price child elements each use three nodes: one for the start tag, one for the content, and one for the end tag.

An XML document

```
<?xml version="1.0" encoding="utf-8" ?>
<!--Product data-->
<Products>
  <Product Code="CS08">
    <Description>Murach's C# 2008</Description>
    <Price>54.50</Price>
  </Product>
</Products>
```

The XML nodes in this document

NodeType	Name	Other properties
XmlDeclaration	xml	
Comment		Value = "Product data"
Element	Products	
Element	Product	["Code"] = "CS08"
Element	Description	
Text		Value = "Murach's C# 2008"
EndElement	Description	
Element	Price	
Text		Value = "54.50"
EndElement	Price	
EndElement	Product	
EndElement	Products	

Description

- The XmlReader class lets you read the contents of an XML document one *node* at a time.
- For the XML declaration and each comment, the XmlReader class parses one node.
- For each element without content (usually, a parent element), the XmlReader class parses two nodes: an Element node for the start tag and an EndElement node for the end tag.
- For each element with content, the XmlReader class parses three nodes: an Element node for the element's start tag, a Text node for the element's text value, and an EndElement node for the element's end tag.
- If an element contains an attribute, the attribute is available via the indexer when the Element node is read.

Notes

- This example assumes that the IgnoreWhitespace property of the XmlReaderSettings object has been set to true, so white space is ignored.
- The NodeType, Name, Value, and indexer values shown in the table above correspond to the NodeType, Name, and Value properties and the indexer of the XmlReader class.

Figure 22-8 How the XmlReader class reads nodes

Code that reads an XML document

Figure 22-9 shows code that loads the contents of the Products.xml file into a List<> collection of Product objects. The first statement creates a new List<> collection to store the Product objects. The second statement specifies the path for the Products.xml file, which is in the C:\C# 2008\Files directory. The next three statements create an XmlReaderSettings object and set its IgnoreWhitespace and IgnoreComments properties so the reader will ignore any nodes for whitespace or comments. Then, this code creates an XmlReader object by passing the specified path and settings to the static Create method of the XmlReader class.

After the XmlWriter object has been created, the ReadToDescendant method is used to read past any nodes in the XML file that occur before the first Product element. If this method returns a true value, it indicates that a Product element was found. Then, a do-while loop reads and processes the data for each Product element in the file. This loop begins by using the indexer to retrieve the value of the Code attribute. This works because the do-while loop always begins with the reader positioned at the start tag for the Product element.

After the Code attribute has been retrieved and stored in the Product object, the loop uses the ReadStartElement method to advance to the next node, which is the Description element's start tag. Although it's also possible to use a Read method here, the ReadStartElement ensures that the reader is on the Product element.

After the reader has been positioned at the Description element, the next two statements use the ReadElementContentAsString and ReadElementContentAsDecimal methods to retrieve the contents of the Description and Price elements. Then, the last line adds the Product object to the List<> collection.

Note that the ReadToNextSibling method is coded as the condition at the end of the do-while loop. As a result, if the XML document contains another Product element, this method advances to the start tag for the next Product element and returns a true value so the loop will repeat. However, if the XML document doesn't contain another Product element, this method will return a false value and the loop won't repeat. In that case, the Close method is called to close the reader.

If the Products.xml file doesn't contain an XML document like the one that's expected, one of the Read methods will throw an exception of the XmlException type. To catch this type of exception, you can code a try-catch statement just as you would for any other type of exception.

A class that works with an XML file

Figure 22-10 presents the code for a ProductDB class that works with the data in an XML file. This shows how the code presented in this chapter can be used to implement the database class that's used by the Product Maintenance application that was presented in chapter 12. If you understood the earlier versions of this application, you shouldn't have any trouble understanding how this class works.

Code that reads an XML document

```
// create the list
List<Product> products = new List<Product>();

// create the path variable
string path = @"C:\C# 2008\Files\Products.xml";

// create the XmlReaderSettings object
XmlReaderSettings settings = new XmlReaderSettings();
settings.IgnoreWhitespace = true;
settings.IgnoreComments = true;

// create the XmlReader object
XmlReader xmlIn = XmlReader.Create(path, settings);

// read past all nodes to the first Product node
if (xmlIn.ReadToDescendant("Product"))
{
    // create one Product object for each Product node
    do
    {
        Product product = new Product();
        product.Code = xmlIn["Code"];
        xmlIn.ReadStartElement("Product");
        product.Description =
            xmlIn.ReadElementContentAsString();
        product.Price =
            xmlIn.ReadElementContentAsDecimal();
        products.Add(product);
    }
    while(xmlIn.ReadToNextSibling("Product"));
}

// close the XmlReader object
xmlIn.Close();
```

Description

- This example loads the XML document in figure 22-1 into a List<> collection of Product objects.
- To focus on the code that's used to read an XML file, this code doesn't include any exception handling. However, it's common to code a try-catch block that catches and handles any exceptions that this code might throw. In addition, it's common to include a finally block that frees the resources being used by this code.

Figure 22-9 Code that reads an XML document

A class that works with an XML document **Page 1**

```
using System;
using System.Xml;
using System.Collections.Generic;

namespace ProductMaintenance
{
    public class ProductDB
    {
        private const string path = @"C:\C# 2008\Files\Products.xml";

        public static List<Product> GetProducts()
        {
            // create the list
            List<Product> products = new List<Product>();

            // create the XmlReaderSettings object
            XmlReaderSettings settings = new XmlReaderSettings();
            settings.IgnoreWhitespace = true;
            settings.IgnoreComments = true;

            // create the XmlReader object
            XmlReader xmlIn = XmlReader.Create(path, settings);

            // read past all nodes to the first Product node
            if (xmlIn.ReadToDescendant("Product"))
            {
                // create one Product object for each Product node
                do
                {
                    Product product = new Product();
                    product.Code = xmlIn["Code"];
                    xmlIn.ReadStartElement("Product");
                    product.Description =
                        xmlIn.ReadElementContentAsString();
                    product.Price =
                        xmlIn.ReadElementContentAsDecimal();
                    products.Add(product);
                }
                while(xmlIn.ReadToNextSibling("Product"));
            {

            // close the XmlReader object
            xmlIn.Close();

            return products;
        }
```

Figure 22-10 The code for the ProductDB class (part 1 of 2)

A class that works with an XML document — Page 2

```
        public static void SaveProducts(List<Product> products)
        {
            // create the XmlWriterSettings object
            XmlWriterSettings settings = new XmlWriterSettings();
            settings.Indent = true;
            settings.IndentChars = ("    ");

            // create the XmlWriter object
            XmlWriter xmlOut = XmlWriter.Create(path, settings);

            // write the start of the document
            xmlOut.WriteStartDocument();
            xmlOut.WriteStartElement("Products");

            // write each Product object to the xml file
            foreach (Product product in products)
            {
                xmlOut.WriteStartElement("Product");
                xmlOut.WriteAttributeString("Code",
                    product.Code);
                xmlOut.WriteElementString("Description",
                    product.Description);
                xmlOut.WriteElementString("Price",
                    Convert.ToString(product.Price));
                xmlOut.WriteEndElement();
            }

            // write the end tag for the root element
            xmlOut.WriteEndElement();

            // close the XmlWriter object
            xmlOut.Close();
        }
    }
}
```

Figure 22-10 The code for the ProductDB class (part 2 of 2)

Perspective

In this chapter, you learned the basics of reading and writing XML documents using the XmlReader and XmlWriter classes. With these skills, you should be able to incorporate simple XML documents into your applications. You should also have a better appreciation for the way XML is used internally by the database applications that you learned about in section 4.

However, this chapter is only an introduction to XML that omits some important features. For example, you can use *XML schemas* to define the layout for an XML document. Then, you can use .NET classes to make sure an XML document conforms to its schema. You can also use *DOM*, which stands for *Document Object Model*, to treat an entire XML document as a single XmlDocument object with property collections that represent the XML document's nodes. In short, there's a lot more to learn before you master XML.

Terms

XML (Extensible Markup Language)
tag
XML document
XML declaration
element
start tag
end tag
content
child element
parent element
root element
attribute
white space
node
current node

Exercise 22-1 Work with an XML file

1. Open the project in the C:\C# 2008\Chapter 22\CustomerXML directory. This is the CustomerMaintenance application that you developed for the chapter 12 exercises, but it doesn't save or retrieve the data.
2. Use Visual Studio to open the Customers.xml file that's stored in the C:\C# 2008\Files directory. This should open this file in the XML Editor so you can see how this data is structured.
3. In the CustomerDB class, add code to the GetCustomers and SaveCustomers methods so they read the data from the Customers.xml file into a List<> of Customer objects and write the data from a List<> of Customer objects to the XML file.
4. Test the application by adding and deleting customers. To verify that the data is being saved to disk, you can stop the application and run it again. You can use Visual Studio to view the XML file in the XML Editor. Or you can double-click on the file in the Windows Explorer. On most systems, that will display the XML file in your default web browser.

23

How to use LINQ

In this chapter, you'll learn the basic skills for using a new feature of C# 2008 called LINQ. LINQ provides a way for you to query a data source using constructs that are built into the C# language. That way, you can use the same language to access a variety of data sources.

In this chapter, I'll focus on using LINQ with in-memory data structures such as arrays and generic lists. Keep in mind as you read this chapter, though, that you can also use the same skills to query datasets, relational databases, and XML files.

To give you an idea of how that works, I'll present two applications at the end of this chapter that perform the same function. The first one will use LINQ to query two generic lists, and the second one will use LINQ to query two tables in a typed dataset. Once you see how similar the queries for these applications are, you should begin to understand the real power of using LINQ.

Basic concepts for working with LINQ

As its name implies, *LINQ*, or *Language-Integrated Query*, lets you query a data source using the C# language. Before you learn how to code LINQ queries, you need to learn some concepts related to LINQ, such as how LINQ is implemented and what the three stages of a query operation are. In addition, you'll want to know the advantages you'll get from using LINQ so you can decide for yourself if it's a feature you want to use.

How LINQ is implemented

LINQ is implemented as a set of methods that are defined by the Enumerable class. Because these methods can only be used in a query operation, they're referred to as *query operators*. To make it easy to use the query operators, C# provides keywords that give you access to the operators. The keywords you're most likely to use are listed at the top of figure 23-1.

If you've ever coded a query using SQL, you shouldn't have any trouble understanding what each of these keywords does. For example, you use the *from* keyword to identify the data source for the query. You use the *where* keyword to filter the data that's returned by the query. And you use the *select* keyword to identify the fields you want to be returned by the query. You'll learn how to code queries that use all of these keywords later in this chapter.

Advantages of using LINQ

Figure 23-1 also lists several advantages of LINQ. Probably the biggest advantage is that it lets you query different types of data sources using the same language. As you'll see in this chapter, for example, you can use the same language to query an array and a generic list of objects. Keep in mind as you read this chapter, though, that you can use these same skills to query more sophisticated data sources such as datasets and databases.

The key to making this work is that the query language is integrated into C#. Because of that, you don't have to learn a different query language for each type of data source you want to query. In addition, as you enter your queries, you can take advantage of the IntelliSense features that are provided for the C# language. The compiler can catch errors in the query, such as a field that doesn't exist in the data source, so you don't get errors at runtime. And when a runtime error does occur, you can use the Visual Studio debugging features to determine its cause.

Finally, if you're working with a relational data source such as a SQL Server database, you can use designer tools provided by Visual Studio to develop an *object-relational mapping*. Then, you can use LINQ to query the objects defined by this mapping, and the query will be converted to the form required by the data source. This can make it significantly easier to work with relational data sources.

Some of the C# keywords for working with LINQ

Keyword	Description
from	Identifies the source of data for the query.
where	Provides a condition that specifies which elements are retrieved from the data source.
orderby	Indicates how the elements that are returned by the query are sorted.
select	Specifies the content of the returned elements.
join	Combines data from two data sources.

Advantages of using LINQ

- Makes it easier for you to query a data source by integrating the query language with C#.
- Makes it easier to develop applications that query a data source by providing IntelliSense, compile-time syntax checking, and debugging support.
- Makes it easier for you to query different types of data sources because you use the same basic syntax for each type.
- Makes it easier for you to use objects to work with relational data sources by providing designer tools that create *object-relational mappings*.

Description

- *Language-Integrated Query* (*LINQ*) provides a set of *query operators* that are available as keywords from the C# language. You use these keywords to define a *query expression* that identifies the data you want to retrieve from the data source.
- To use LINQ with a data source, the data source must implement the IEnumerable<T> interface or another interface that implements IEnumerable<T> such as IQueryable<T>. For more information on interfaces, see chapter 15.
- A data source such as an array or an array list that supports the non-generic IEnumerable interface can also be used with LINQ.

Note

- The LINQ operators are implemented as methods of the Enumerable class. Although you can execute these methods directly, you're more likely to use the keywords that are built into the C# language.

Figure 23-1 An introduction to LINQ

The three stages of a query operation

Figure 23-2 presents the three stages of a query operation and illustrates these stages using an array. The first stage is to get the data source. How you do that depends on the type of data source you're working with. For the array shown here, getting the data source means defining an array named numbers and assigning values to its elements. In this case, the array contains five integers with the values 0, 1, 2, 3, and 4.

The second stage is to define the *query expression*. This expression identifies the data source and the data to be retrieved from that data source. The query expression in this figure, for example, retrieves the even integers from the numbers array. It also sorts those integers in descending sequence. (Don't worry if you don't understand the syntax of this query expression. You'll learn how to code query expressions in the topics that follow.)

Notice here that the query expression is stored in a *query variable*. That's necessary because this query isn't executed when it's defined. Also notice that the query variable isn't declared with an explicit type. Instead, it's given a type implicitly based on the type of elements in the data source. In this case, because the data source is an array that contains integers, the query variable is given the type IEnumerable<int>.

For this to work, the data source must implement the IEnumerable or IEnumerable<T> interface. In case you're not familiar with interfaces, they consist of a set of declarations for one or more properties, methods, and events, but they don't provide implementation for those properties, methods, and events. If you want to learn more about interfaces, you can read chapter 15. For the example in this figure, however, all you need to know is that an array implements the IEnumerable interface.

The third stage of a query operation is to execute the query. To do that, you typically use a foreach statement like the one shown in this figure. Here, each element that's returned by the query expression is added to a string variable. Then, after all the elements have been processed, the string is displayed in a message box. As you can see, this message box lists the even numbers from 4 to 0 as defined by the query expression.

When a query is defined and executed separately as shown here, the process is referred to as *deferred execution*. In contrast, queries that are executed when they're defined use *immediate execution*. Immediate execution typically occurs when a method that requires access to the individual elements returned by the query is executed on the query expression. For example, to get a count of the number of elements returned by a query, you can execute the Count method on the query expression. Then, the query will be executed immediately so that the count can be calculated. Although LINQ provides several methods for returning these types of values, you won't learn about them in this book.

The three stages of a query operation

- Get the data source. If the data source is an array, for example, you must declare the array and then assign values to its elements.
- Define the query expression.
- Execute the query to return the results.

A LINQ query that retrieves data from an array

Code that defines the array

```
int[] numbers = new int[6];
for (int i = 0; i < numbers.Length; i++)
    numbers[i] = i;
```

A statement that defines the query expression

```
var numberList = from number in numbers
                 where number % 2 == 0
                 orderby number descending
                 select number;
```

Code that executes the query

```
string numberDisplay = "";
foreach (var number in numberList)
    numberDisplay += number + "\n";
MessageBox.Show(numberDisplay, "Sorted Even Numbers");
```

The resulting dialog box

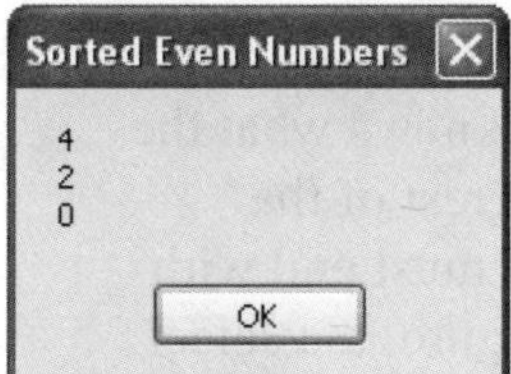

Description

- The process described above is called *deferred execution* because the query isn't executed when it's defined. Instead, it's executed when the application tries to access the individual elements returned by the query, such as when the query is used in a foreach statement.
- If a query isn't executed when it's defined, it's stored in a *query variable*. In that case, the query variable is implicitly typed as IEnumerable<T> where T is the type of each element. In the example above, the numberList variable is assigned the type IEnumerable<int> since the numbers array contains integers.
- If a query requires access to the individual elements identified by the query expression, *immediate execution* occurs. This typically happens when an aggregate value, such as the number of elements in the results, is requested. In that case, the query expression isn't saved in a query variable.

Figure 23-2 The three stages of a query operation

How to code a LINQ query

Now that you have a basic understanding of what a LINQ query is, you need to learn the syntax for coding query expressions. That's what you'll learn in the topics that follow.

How to identify the data source for a query

To identify the source of data for a query, you use the *from* clause shown in figure 23-3. As you can see, this clause declares a *range variable* that will be used to represent each element of the data source, and it names the data source, which must be a collection that implements the IEnumerable or IEnumerable<T> interface. It can also declare a type for the range variable, although the type is usually omitted. If it is omitted, it's determined by the type of elements in the data source.

The first example in this figure shows how to use the from clause with an array of decimals named salesTotals. The first statement in this example declares the array and assigns values to its elements. Then, the second statement defines the query expression, which consists of just the from clause and a select clause. This expression is stored in a query variable named salesList. Finally, a foreach statement loops through the values returned by the query and calculates a sum of those values.

At this point, you should realize that a query expression must always start with a from clause that identifies the data source. That way, C# knows what the source of data for the query is, and it can help you construct the rest of the query based on that data source. In addition, a query expression must end with either a *select* clause or a *group* clause. In the example in this figure, the select clause simply indicates that array elements should be returned by the query. Later in this chapter, however, you'll see that you can use the select clause to return just the fields you want from each element of a data source.

The second example in this figure shows how to use the from clause with a generic list of invoices. Here, you can see that the Invoice class consists simply of a set of public fields. Then, the statement that follows creates a list that's based on this class and loads invoices into it using the GetInvoices method of the InvoiceDB class. Note that it's not important for you to know how this method works. All you need to know is that it returns a List<Invoice> object. This object is then assigned to a variable named invoiceList.

The next statement defines the query expression, which includes a from clause that identifies invoiceList as the data source. This expression is assigned to a query variable named invoices. Then, this variable is used in a foreach statement to calculate a sum of the InvoiceTotal fields in the invoices.

You may have noticed in both of the examples in this figure that the variable that's used in the query expression and the variable that's used in the foreach loop have the same name. That makes sense because they both refer to an element in the data source. However, you should know that you don't have to

The syntax of the from clause

```
from [type] elementName in collectionName
```

An example that uses an array of decimals

A statement that gets the data source

```
decimal[] salesTotals =
    new decimal[4] {1286.45m, 2433.49m, 2893.85m, 2094.53m};
```

A statement that defines the query expression

```
var salesList = from sales in salesTotals
                select sales;
```

Code that executes the query

```
decimal sum = 0;
foreach (var sales in salesList)
    sum += sales;
```

An example that uses a generic list of invoices as the data source

The Invoice class

```
public class Invoice
{
    public int InvoiceID;
    public int CustomerID;
    public DateTime InvoiceDate;
    public decimal ProductTotal;
    public decimal SalesTax;
    public decimal Shipping;
    public decimal InvoiceTotal;
}
```

A statement that gets the data source

```
List<Invoice> invoiceList = InvoiceDB.GetInvoices();
```

A statement that defines the query expression

```
var invoices = from invoice in invoiceList
               select invoice;
```

Code that executes the query

```
decimal sum = 0;
foreach (var invoice in invoices)
    sum += invoice.InvoiceTotal;
```

Description

- The *from* clause identifies the source of data for a query and declares a *range variable* that's used to represent each element of the data source.
- If the range variable you use in a query expression and the iteration variable you use in the foreach statement that executes the query refer to the same type of elements, you should give them the same name for clarity. Otherwise, you should give them different names to indicate the type of elements they refer to.
- The from clause must be the first clause in a query expression. In addition, a query expression must end with a *select* clause or a *group* clause.

Figure 23-3 How to identify the data source for a query

use the same names for these variables. In fact, when you code more sophisticated query expressions, you'll want to use different variable names to indicate the difference between the elements they refer to. That'll make more sense when you see the select clause later in this chapter.

How to filter the results of a query

To filter the results of a query, you use the *where* clause shown in figure 23-4. On this clause, you specify a condition that an element must meet to be returned by the query. The condition is coded as a Boolean expression like the ones you learned about in chapter 5. The two examples in this figure illustrate how this works.

The where clause in the first example specifies that for an element to be returned from the salesTotals array, its value must be greater than 2000. Notice here that the range variable that's declared by the from clause is used in the where clause to refer to the elements that are returned by the query. Then, the code that executes the query adds the returned values to a string, and the string is then displayed in a message box. If you compare the values that are listed in this message box to the values in the array shown in figure 23-3, you'll see that the value that is less than 2000 has been omitted.

The second example is similar, but it uses the generic list of invoices. Here, the where clause indicates that only those invoices with invoice totals greater than 150 should be returned by the query. Notice again that the range variable that's declared by the from clause is used to refer to the elements that are returned by the query. This time, though, because each element is an Invoice object, the condition on the where clause can refer to a member of that object.

The syntax of the where clause

```
where condition
```

An example that filters the salesTotals array

A query expression that returns only sales greater than $2000

```
var salesList = from sales in salesTotals
                where sales > 2000
                select sales;
```

Code that executes the query

```
string salesDisplay = "";
foreach (var sales in salesList)
    salesDisplay += sales.ToString("c") + "\n";
MessageBox.Show(salesDisplay, "Sales Over $2000");
```

The resulting dialog box

An example that filters the generic list of invoices

A query expression that returns invoices with totals over $150

```
var invoices = from invoice in invoiceList
               where invoice.InvoiceTotal > 150
               select invoice;
```

Code that executes the query

```
string invoiceDisplay = "";
foreach (var invoice in invoices)
    invoiceDisplay += invoice.InvoiceTotal.ToString("c") + "\n";
MessageBox.Show(invoiceDisplay, "Invoices Over $150");
```

The resulting dialog box

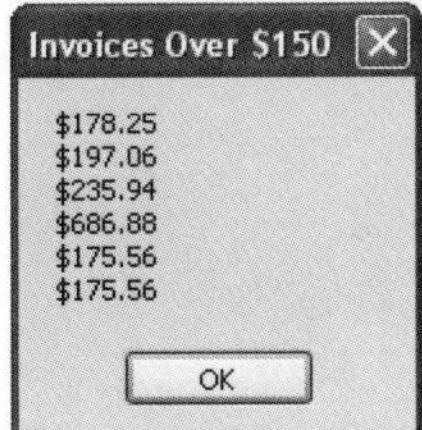

Description

- The *where* clause lets you filter the data in a data source by specifying a condition that the elements of the data source must meet to be returned by the query.
- The condition is coded as a Boolean expression that can contain one or more relational and logical operators.

Figure 23-4 How to filter the results of a query

How to sort the results of a query

If you want the results of a query to be returned in a particular sequence, you can include the *orderby* clause in the query expression. The syntax of this clause is shown at the top of figure 23-5. This syntax indicates that you can sort by one or more expressions in either ascending or descending sequence.

To understand how this works, the first example in this figure shows how you might sort the salesTotals array. Here, the query expression includes an orderby clause that sorts the elements in this array in ascending sequence (the default). To do that, it names the range variable that is declared by the from clause. If you compare the results of this query with the results shown in the previous figure, you'll see how the sequence has changed.

The second example shows how you can sort query results by two expressions. In this case, the query will return invoices from the generic invoice list in descending invoice total sequence within customer ID sequence. If you look at the results of this query, you can see that the customer IDs are in ascending sequence. You can also see that the first two invoices are for the same customer, and the invoice with the largest total is listed first.

The syntax of the orderby clause

```
orderby expression1 [ascending|descending]
    [, expression2 [ascending|descending]]...
```

An example that sorts the salesTotals array

A query expression that sorts the sales in ascending sequence

```
var salesList = from sales in salesTotals
                where sales > 2000
                orderby sales
                select sales;
```

Code that executes the query

```
string salesDisplay = "";
foreach (var sales in salesList)
    salesDisplay += sales.ToString("c") + "\n";
MessageBox.Show(salesDisplay, "Sorted Sales Over $2000");
```

The resulting dialog box

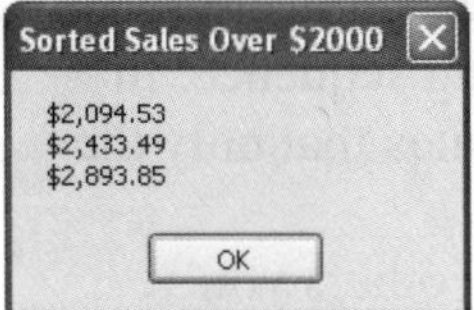

An example that sorts the generic list of invoices

A query expression that sorts the invoices by customer ID and invoice total

```
var invoices = from invoice in invoiceList
               where invoice.InvoiceTotal > 150
               orderby invoice.CustomerID, invoice.InvoiceTotal descending
               select invoice;
```

Code that executes the query

```
string invoiceDisplay = "Cust ID\tInvoice amount\n";
foreach (var invoice in invoices)
    invoiceDisplay += invoice.CustomerID + "\t"
                    + invoice.InvoiceTotal.ToString("c") + "\n";
MessageBox.Show(invoiceDisplay, "Sorted Invoices Over $150");
```

The resulting dialog box

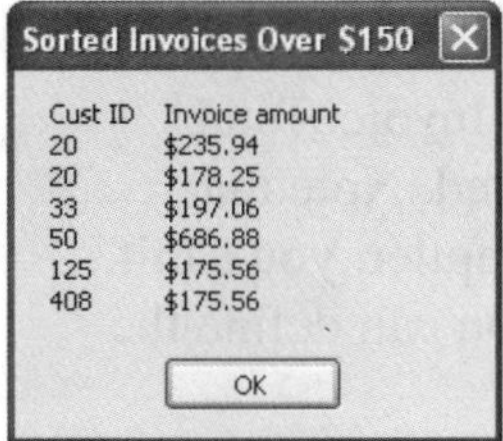

Sorted Invoices Over $150
Cust ID Invoice amount
20 $235.94
20 $178.25
33 $197.06
50 $686.88
125 $175.56
408 $175.56
OK

Description

- The *orderby* clause lets you specify how the results of the query are sorted. You can specify one or more expressions on this clause.

Figure 23-5 How to sort the results of a query

How to select fields from a query

So far, the queries you've seen in this chapter have returned entire elements of a data source. To do that, the select clause simply named the range variable that represents those elements. But you can also return selected fields of the elements. To do that, you code the select clause as shown in figure 23-6. As you can see, the select clause lets you identify one or more fields to be included in the query results. A query that returns something other than entire source elements is called a *projection*.

To illustrate how this works, the first example in this figure uses a sorted list named employeeSales. The keys for this list are employee names, and the values are sales totals. You can see the definition of this list and the data it contains at the beginning of this example.

The query expression that uses this list includes the from, where, and orderby clauses. The where clause indicates that only those elements with values (sales totals) greater than 2000 should be returned, and the orderby clause indicates that the returned elements should be sorted by the values in descending sequence. In addition, this query expression includes a select clause that indicates that only the key field (the employee name) should be returned.

The foreach statement that executes this query works like the others you've seen in this chapter. It creates a string that includes a list of the employee names. Notice, however, that the name of the iteration variable that's used in this statement is different from the name of the range variable used in the query expression. That's because the variable in the query expression refers to an element in the sorted list, but the variable in the foreach statement refers only to the employee names returned from the list by the query.

The second example shows a query expression that returns selected fields from the Invoice objects. Specifically, it returns the CustomerID and InvoiceTotal fields. If you look back at the example in the previous figure, you'll see that these are the only two fields that are used when the query is executed. Because of that, these are the only two fields that need to be retrieved.

Notice that the select clause in this example uses an object initializer to create the objects that are returned by the query. In this case, each object includes a CustomerID property and an InvoiceTotal property. Unlike the object intializers you saw in chapter 12, however, the object initializer shown here doesn't specify a type. That's because a type that includes just CustomerID and InvoiceTotal properties doesn't exist. In that case, an *anonymous type* is created. Note that because the name of an anonymous type is generated by the compiler, you can't refer to it directly. In most cases, that's not a problem. If it is, you can define the type you want to use and then name it on the object initializer.

In addition to the type, the names of the properties have been omitted from the object initializer. Because of that, the properties are given the same names as the fields that are listed in the initializer. If that's not what you want, you can specify the names in the initializer. For example, if I wanted to name the two properties of the type shown here ID and Total, I could have coded the initializer like this:

```
new { ID = invoice.CustomerID, Total = invoice.InvoiceTotal }
```

Two ways to code the select clause

```
select columnExpression
select new [type] { [PropertyName1 =] columnExpression1
                   [, [PropertyName2 =] columnExpression2]... }
```

An example that selects key values from a sorted list

The employee sales sorted list

```
SortedList<string, decimal> employeeSales =
    new SortedList<string,decimal>();
employeeSales.Add("Anderson", 1286.45m);
employeeSales.Add("Menendez", 2433.49m);
employeeSales.Add("Thompson", 2893.85m);
employeeSales.Add("Wilkinson", 2094.53m);
```

A query expression that selects the employee names from the list

```
var employeeList = from sales in employeeSales
                   where sales.Value > 2000
                   orderby sales.Value descending
                   select sales.Key;
```

Code that executes the query

```
string employeeDisplay = "";
foreach (var employee in employeeList)
    employeeDisplay += employee + "\n";
MessageBox.Show(employeeDisplay, "Sorted Employees With Sales Over $2000");
```

The resulting dialog box

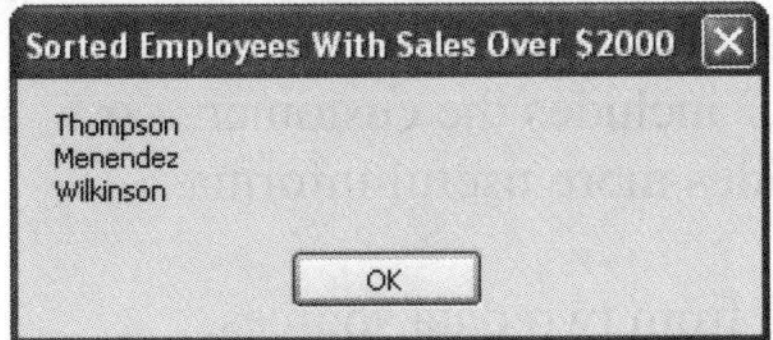

A query expression that creates an anonymous type from the list of invoices

```
var invoices = from invoice in invoiceList
               where invoice.InvoiceTotal > 150
               orderby invoice.CustomerID, invoice.InvoiceTotal descending
               select new { invoice.CustomerID, invoice.InvoiceTotal };
```

Description

- The select clause indicates the data you want to return from each element of the query results.
- A query that returns anything other than entire source elements is called a *projection*. Both examples above illustrate projections.
- To return two or more fields from each element, you code an object initializer within the select clause. If the object initializer doesn't specify a type, an *anonymous type* that contains the specified fields as its properties is created.
- Anonymous types are a new feature of C# that was added to support query expressions.

Figure 23-6 How to select fields from a query

How to join data from two or more data sources

Figure 23-7 shows how you can include data from two or more data sources in a query. To do that, you use the *join* clause shown at the top of this figure. To start, this clause declares a range variable and names a data source just like the from clause does. Then, it indicates how the two data sources are related.

To illustrate, the example in this figure joins data from the list of Invoice objects you've seen in the previous figures with a list of Customer objects. You can see the definition of the Customer class at the beginning of this example, along with the statements that declare and load the two lists. Like the invoice list, the customer list is loaded by calling a method of a database class.

The query expression that follows joins the data in these two lists. To do that, it names the invoice list on the from clause, and it names the customer list on the join clause. Then, the on condition indicates that only customers in the customer list with customer IDs that match customer IDs in the invoice list should be included in the results.

Because both the invoice and customer lists are included as data sources in this query expression, the rest of the query can refer to fields in either data source. For example, the orderby clause in this query expression sorts the results by the InvoiceTotal field in the invoice list within the Name field in the customer list. Similarly, the select clause selects the Name field from the customer list and the InvoiceTotal field from the invoice list.

The remaining code in this example executes the query and creates a list that includes the customer names and invoice totals. This is similar to the list you saw in figure 23-5. Because the list in figure 23-7 includes the customer names instead of the customer IDs, however, it provides more useful information.

Although this figure only shows how to join data from two data sources, you can extend this syntax to join data from additional data sources. For example, suppose you have three data sources named invoiceList, lineItemList, and productList. Then, you could join the data in these lists using code like this:

```
from invoice in invoiceList
join lineItem in lineItemList
  on invoice.InvoiceID equals lineItem.InvoiceID
join product in productList
  on lineItem.ProductCode equals product.ProductCode
```

Once the three tables are joined, you can refer to fields from any of these tables in the query expression.

The basic syntax of the join clause

```
join elementName in collectionName on keyName1 equals keyName2
```

An example that joins data from two generic lists

The Customer class

```
public class Customer
{
    public int CustomerID;
    public string Name;
}
```

Code that gets the two data sources

```
List<Invoice> invoiceList = InvoiceDB.GetInvoices();
List<Customer> customerList = CustomerDB.GetCustomers();
```

A query expression that joins data from the two data sources

```
var invoices = from invoice in invoiceList
               join customer in customerList
               on invoice.CustomerID equals customer.CustomerID
               where invoice.InvoiceTotal > 150
               orderby customer.Name, invoice.InvoiceTotal descending
               select new { customer.Name, invoice.InvoiceTotal };
```

Code that executes the query

```
string invoiceDisplay = "Customer Name\t\tInvoice amount\n";
foreach (var invoice in invoices)
{
    invoiceDisplay += invoice.Name + "\t";
    if (invoice.Name.Length < 17)
        invoiceDisplay += "\t";
    invoiceDisplay += invoice.InvoiceTotal.ToString("c") + "\n";
}
MessageBox.Show(invoiceDisplay, "Joined Customer and Invoice Data");
```

The resulting dialog box

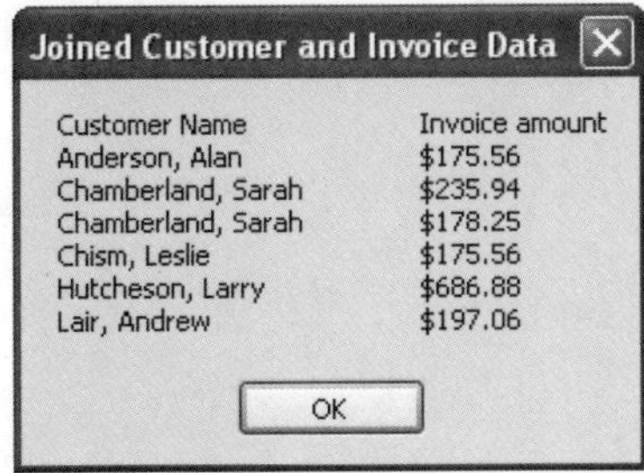

Joined Customer and Invoice Data
Customer Name Invoice amount
Anderson, Alan $175.56
Chamberland, Sarah $235.94
Chamberland, Sarah $178.25
Chism, Leslie $175.56
Hutcheson, Larry $686.88
Lair, Andrew $197.06
OK

Description

- The *join* clause lets you combine data from two or more data sources based on matching key values. The query results will include only those elements that meet the condition specified by the equals operator.

Figure 23-7 How to join data from two or more data sources

A Customer Invoice application that uses generic lists

The next two topics of this chapter present a simple application that uses a query to display customer and invoice information on a form. This will help you see how you can use a query from within a C# application.

The user interface

Figure 23-8 shows the user interface for the Customer Invoice application. As you can see, this interface consists of a single form that lists invoices by customer. This list is sorted by invoice total in descending sequence within customer name.

The list in this form is displayed in a ListView control. If you aren't familiar with this control, you may want to refer to Visual Studio help to find out how it works. For the purposes of this application, though, you just need to set the View property of this control to Details, and you need to define the column headings as described in this figure. In addition, you need to know how to load data into the control as shown in the next figure.

The Customer Invoice form

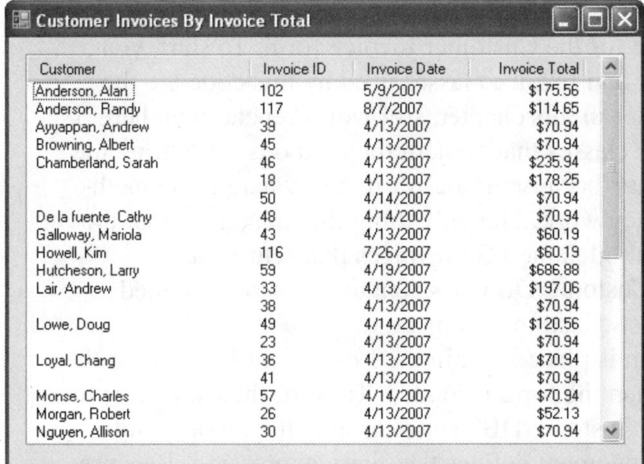

Customer Invoices By Invoice Total

Customer	Invoice ID	Invoice Date	Invoice Total
Anderson, Alan	102	5/9/2007	$175.56
Anderson, Randy	117	8/7/2007	$114.65
Ayyappan, Andrew	39	4/13/2007	$70.94
Browning, Albert	45	4/13/2007	$70.94
Chamberland, Sarah	46	4/13/2007	$235.94
	18	4/13/2007	$178.25
	50	4/14/2007	$70.94
De la fuente, Cathy	48	4/14/2007	$70.94
Galloway, Mariola	43	4/13/2007	$60.19
Howell, Kim	116	7/26/2007	$60.19
Hutcheson, Larry	59	4/19/2007	$686.88
Lair, Andrew	33	4/13/2007	$197.06
	38	4/13/2007	$70.94
Lowe, Doug	49	4/14/2007	$120.56
	23	4/13/2007	$70.94
Loyal, Chang	36	4/13/2007	$70.94
	41	4/13/2007	$70.94
Monse, Charles	57	4/14/2007	$70.94
Morgan, Robert	26	4/13/2007	$52.13
Nguyen, Allison	30	4/13/2007	$70.94

Description

- The Customer Invoice form uses a ListView control to display a list of invoices for each customer. The list is sorted by invoice total in descending sequence within customer name.
- To make this work, the View property of the ListView control is set to Details, which causes the data items to be displayed in columns. In addition, the column headers for the control were added using the ColumnHeader Collection Editor. To display this editor, you can select Edit Columns from the smart tag menu for the control. Then, you can set the Text, TextAlign, and Width properties for each column as necessary.

Figure 23-8 The user interface for the Customer Invoice application

The code for the form

Figure 23-9 shows the code for the Customer Invoice form. To start, you should know that the Customer and Invoice classes used by this code are the same as the classes shown earlier in this chapter, so I won't repeat them here. I also won't present the database classes that contain the methods for getting the customer and invoice data. That's because it doesn't matter where these methods get the data from or how they work. The only thing that matters is that the InvoiceDB class contains a method named GetInvoices that returns a List<Invoice> object, and the CustomerDB class contains a method named GetCustomers that returns a List<Customer> object.

All of the code for this form is placed within the Load event handler for the form so the list is displayed when the form is loaded. To start, this code uses the methods of the InvoiceDB and CustomerDB classes to load the invoice and customer lists. Then, the next statement defines the query expression. Because this expression is similar to others you've seen in this chapter, you shouldn't have any trouble understanding how it works. So I'll just summarize it for you.

First, notice that the query expression joins data from the invoice and customer lists. That's necessary because the customer name will be displayed on the form along with the invoice information. Second, notice that the query expression doesn't include a where clause. Because of that, all of the invoices will be included in the results. Third, the results are sorted by invoice total within customer name so the invoices can be displayed as shown in the previous figure. And fourth, only the fields that are required by the form are included in the results.

To load data into the ListView control, this code uses a foreach statement that loops through the query results. But first, this code initializes two variables. The first one, customerName, will store the name of the current customer. This variable will be used to determine if the customer name is displayed for an invoice. The second variable, i, will be used as an index for the items that are added to the ListView control.

For each element in the query results, the foreach loop starts by checking if the Name field is equal to the customerName variable. If not, the Name field is added to the Items collection of the ListView control, which causes the name to be displayed in the first column of the control. In addition, the customerName variable is set to the Name field so the next element will be processed correctly. On the other hand, if the Name field and the customerName variable are equal, an empty string is added to the Items collection of the ListView control so the name isn't repeated.

The next three statements add the InvoiceID, InvoiceDate, and InvoiceTotal fields as subitems of the item that was just added. This causes these values to be displayed in the columns following the customer name column. Notice that these statements refer to the item by its index. Then, the last statement in the loop increments the index variable.

The code for the Customer Invoice form

```
private void Form1_Load(object sender, EventArgs e)
{
    List<Customer> customerList = CustomerDB.GetCustomers();
    List<Invoice> invoiceList = InvoiceDB.GetInvoices();

    var invoices = from invoice in invoiceList
                   join customer in customerList
                   on invoice.CustomerID equals customer.CustomerID
                   orderby customer.Name, invoice.InvoiceTotal descending
                   select new { customer.Name,
                                invoice.InvoiceID,
                                invoice.InvoiceDate,
                                invoice.InvoiceTotal };

    string customerName = "";
    int i = 0;
    foreach (var invoice in invoices)
    {
        if (invoice.Name != customerName)
        {
            lvInvoices.Items.Add(invoice.Name);
            customerName = invoice.Name;
        }
        else
        {
            lvInvoices.Items.Add("");
        }
        lvInvoices.Items[i].SubItems.Add(invoice.InvoiceID.ToString());
        lvInvoices.Items[i].SubItems.Add(
            Convert.ToDateTime(invoice.InvoiceDate).ToShortDateString());
        lvInvoices.Items[i].SubItems.Add(invoice.InvoiceTotal.ToString("c"));
        i += 1;
    }
}
```

Description

- The LINQ query used by this application makes it easy to include data from two generic lists. Without LINQ, you'd have to code your own procedure to get the customer name from the customer list.
- The LINQ query used by this application also makes it easy to sort the results based on two fields. Although you could sort a list by a single field in ascending sequence by implementing the IComparable<> interface in the class that defines the objects in the list, it would be much more difficult to sort by two fields in one or more lists.

Notes

- The code for the Invoice and Customer classes is the same as shown earlier in this chapter.
- The invoice and customer data for this application is stored in text files. However, it could have been stored in any other type of data source, such as a binary file, an XML file, or a database.

Figure 23-9 The code for the Customer Invoice form that uses generic lists

A Customer Invoice application that uses a typed dataset

Now that you've seen an application that uses LINQ to query generic lists, you might want to compare this application to an application that uses LINQ to query a different type of data source. In the next two topics, then, you'll see an application that uses LINQ to query a typed dataset. If you aren't familiar with typed datasets, you might want to refer to chapter 18 to see how they work.

By the way, the user interface for the application presented here is identical to the interface shown in figure 23-8. So I won't show it again here.

The dataset schema

Figure 23-10 presents the dataset schema for the Customer Invoice application. As you can see, the dataset that this schema defines includes two tables: Customers and Invoices. In addition, the table adapter for each table contains a single query named Fill that can be used to load data into the dataset.

Although you can't tell from this figure, the Fill queries retrieve all the rows and columns from the Customers and Invoices tables in the MMABooks database (see figure 17-6 in chapter 17). To make this application more efficient, you could retrieve just the data it needs. In most cases, though, an application will perform more than just one function.

For example, an order entry application might let you list, select, add, and modify customers, list and add invoices, and so on. An application like that would need to include the data necessary to perform all these functions. So if you think of the function that the Customer Invoice application performs as just one part of a larger application, you can begin to see the power LINQ gives you for working with the data in a dataset.

The dataset schema

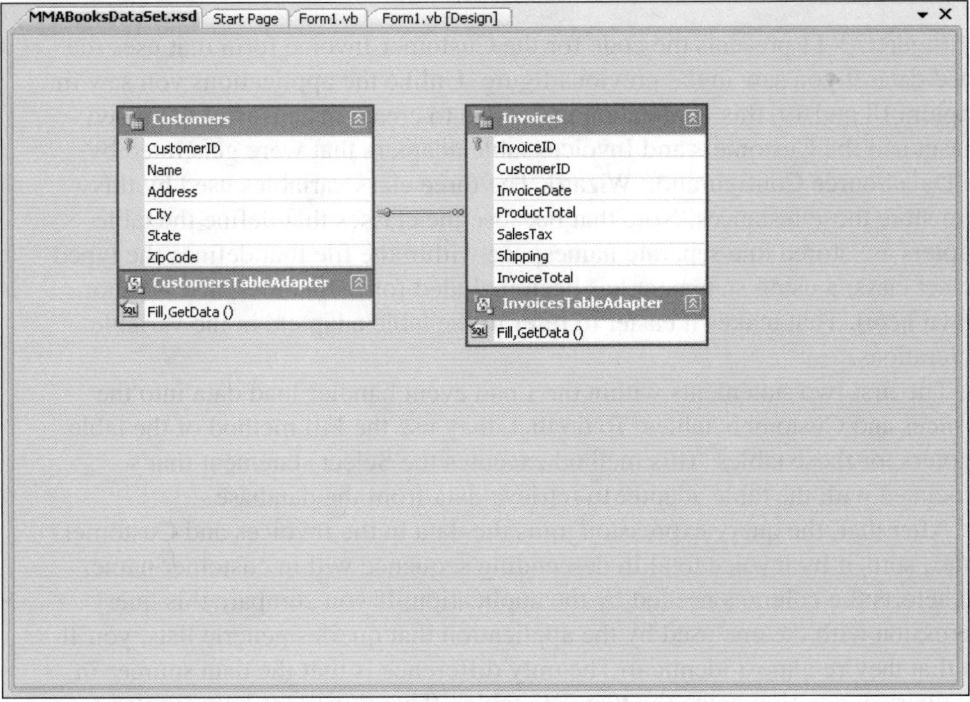

Description

- The dataset for this application includes all the columns from the Customers and Invoices tables in the MMABooks database.
- Because the Customer Invoice application doesn't use all the columns in these tables, the data source could have been defined so that it includes only the required columns. It could also have been defined so that the data is joined into a single table. However, this would give an application that performed additional functions less flexibility.
- The dataset used by this application was generated using the Data Source Configuration Wizard. For information on this wizard, please see chapter 18.

Figure 23-10 The dataset schema for the Customer Invoice application

The code for the form

Figure 23-11 presents the code for the Customer Invoice form that uses the typed dataset you saw in the previous figure. Unlike the applications you saw in chapters 18 and 19, this application uses code to create instances of the typed dataset and the Customers and Invoices table adapters that were generated by the Data Source Configuration Wizard. The three class variables used by this form store these instances. Note that because the classes that define the table adapters are stored in a separate namespace within the file that defines the typed dataset class, a using statement has been included for that namespace (it's not shown here). That makes it easier to refer to the table adapters in the variable declarations.

The first two statements within the Load event handler load data into the Invoices and Customers tables. To do that, they use the Fill method of the table adapters for these tables. This method executes the Select statement that's associated with the table adapter to retrieve data from the database.

After that, the query expression joins the data in the Invoices and Customers tables, sorts it by invoice total in descending sequence within customer name, and selects the columns needed by the application. If you compare this query expression with the one used by the application that queries generic lists, you'll see that they're almost identical. The only difference is that the data sources in this query expression name the two data tables. That illustrates how similar query expressions that work with different data sources can be.

*

Now that you've seen two applications that use LINQ with two types of data sources, you might want to consider how you would accomplish the same thing without using LINQ. If you do, I think you'll see that LINQ makes it quick and easy to select the data you need.

To join data from two generic lists without using LINQ, for example, you could include code that loops through one list looking for the object that's related to the object in the other list. And to join data from two tables of a dataset, you could use a relationship. In contrast, to join data from any two data sources using LINQ, you can simply code a join clause.

Similarly, to sort the data in a generic list without using LINQ, you'd have to write code to implement the sort yourself. If you just needed to sort by a single field in ascending sequence, that would be manageable. If you needed to sort by more than one field, however, or you needed to sort by a field in descending sequence, it would be much more difficult. And if you needed to sort by fields in more than one data source, it would be extremely difficult. To sort the rows in a data table by one or more columns, you could use a data view. However, you couldn't sort by columns in two or more tables. In contrast, to sort by one or more fields using LINQ, you can simply code an orderby clause.

The bottom line is that LINQ provides concise language for querying data. So you should consider using it whenever you need to select data from one or more data sources.

The code for the Customer Invoice form

```
MMABooksDataSet mmaBooksDataSet = new MMABooksDataSet();
InvoicesTableAdapter invoicesTableAdapter = new InvoicesTableAdapter();
CustomersTableAdapter customersTableAdapter = new CustomersTableAdapter();

private void Form1_Load(object sender, EventArgs e)
{
    invoicesTableAdapter.Fill(mmaBooksDataSet.Invoices);
    customersTableAdapter.Fill(mmaBooksDataSet.Customers);

    var invoices = from invoice in mmaBooksDataSet.Invoices
                   join customer in mmaBooksDataSet.Customers
                   on invoice.CustomerID equals customer.CustomerID
                   orderby customer.Name, invoice.InvoiceTotal descending
                   select new { customer.Name,
                                invoice.InvoiceID,
                                invoice.InvoiceDate,
                                invoice.InvoiceTotal };

    string customerName = "";
    int i = 0;
    foreach (var invoice in invoices)
    {
        if (invoice.Name != customerName)
        {
            lvInvoices.Items.Add(invoice.Name);
            customerName = invoice.Name;
        }
        else
        {
            lvInvoices.Items.Add("");
        }
        lvInvoices.Items[i].SubItems.Add(invoice.InvoiceID.ToString());
        lvInvoices.Items[i].SubItems.Add(
            Convert.ToDateTime(invoice.InvoiceDate).ToShortDateString());
        lvInvoices.Items[i].SubItems.Add(invoice.InvoiceTotal.ToString("c"));
        i += 1;
    }
}
```

Description

- The query expression for this application is almost identical to the query expression in figure 23-9 that uses generic lists. The only difference is that the two data sources are tables in the dataset.
- LINQ makes it easy to join and sort the two tables used by this application. Although you can use a data view to filter and sort the data in a single table, and you can use a data relation to get data from a related table, it would involve considerably more code. In addition, you couldn't perform a sort that's based on columns in two tables.
- This application uses code to create an instance of the typed dataset that was generated by the Data Source Configuration Wizard. It also uses code to create instances of the two table adapters that were generated by this wizard.

Figure 23-11 The code for the Customer Invoice form that uses a typed dataset

Perspective

In this chapter, you learned the basic skills for coding and executing LINQ queries in C#. With these skills, you should be able to create simple queries that work with a variety of objects. However, there's a lot more to learn about LINQ than what's presented here.

For example, there are other clauses you can code in a query expression. In addition, there are special techniques you need to learn to use LINQ with other data sources, such as untyped datasets and databases. To learn about these features, you can refer to Visual Studio help, or you can get a separate book on LINQ.

Terms

Language-Integrated Query (LINQ)
object-relational mapping
query operator
query expression
deferred execution
query variable
immediate execution
range variable
projection
anonymous type

Exercise 23-1 Create the Customer Invoice application

In this exercise, you'll develop and test the Customer Invoice application that was presented in this chapter that uses generic lists.

Design the form

1. Open the project that's in the C:\C# 2008\Chapter 23\CustomerInvoices directory. In addition to the Customer Invoice form, this project contains the business and database classes needed by the application.
2. Add a ListView control to the Customer Invoice form, and set the View property of this control to Details.
3. Use the smart tag menu for the ListView control to display the ColumnHeader Collection Editor. Then, define the column headings for this control so they appear like the last three shown in figure 23-8. (You'll add the first column later.)

Add code to display the invoice data

4. Open the Invoice and InvoiceDB classes and review the code that they contain. In particular, notice that the GetInvoices method in the InvoiceDB class gets invoices from a text file named Invoices.txt and returns them in a List<Invoice> object.
5. Add an event handler for the Load event of the form. Then, use the GetInvoices method to get the list of invoices, and store this list in a variable.
6. Define a query expression that returns all the invoices from the invoice list and sorts them by invoice total in descending sequence. Include a select clause in this query expression that selects entire invoices.
7. Use a foreach statement to execute the query and load the results into the ListView control.
8. Run the application to see how it works. Make any necessary corrections, and then end the application.
9. Modify the select clause in the query expression so that the query returns only the fields needed by the form. Then, run the application again to be sure it still works.

Enhance the application to include customer information

10. Open the Customer and CustomerDB classes and review the code they contain. Note that the GetCustomers method in the CustomerDB class gets customers from a text file named CustomersX23.txt and returns them in a List<Customer> object.
11. Add another column at the beginning of the ListView control for displaying the customer name. (To get the column to display before the other columns, you'll need to set its DisplayIndex property to 0.) Then, add a statement to the Load event handler of the form that uses the GetCustomers method of the CustomerDB class to get a list of customers, and store the list in a variable.
12. Modify the query expression so it joins the data in the customer list with the data in the invoice list, so it sorts the results by invoice total within customer name, and so only the fields that are needed by the form are returned by the query.
13. Modify the foreach statement so it adds the customer name to the ListView control, but don't worry about not repeating the customer name.
14. Run the application to make sure it works correctly. When you're done, close the solution.

24

How to enhance the user interface

In this chapter, you'll learn how to modify your applications so they can take advantage of two types of user interfaces. In addition, you'll learn how to add menus, toolbars, and help to your forms. When you're done with this chapter, you should be able to create a professional user interface that allows users to easily and intuitively interact with your application.

Two types of user interfaces

Figure 24-1 shows two versions of the Financial Calculations application that will be presented in this chapter. These applications use the Future Value form that you learned about earlier in this book, and they use a Depreciation form that's new to this chapter. In addition, both of these applications include a third form that provides a way for the user to access the other two forms.

A single-document interface (SDI)

The first version of the Financial Calculations application uses a *single-document interface* (*SDI*). In an SDI application, each form runs in its own application window, and this window is usually shown in the Windows taskbar. Then, you can click on the buttons in the taskbar to switch between the open forms.

When you use this interface, each form can have its own menus and toolbars. In addition, you can include a main form called a *startup form* that provides access to the other forms of the application. In this figure, for example, the startup form includes two buttons that the user can click on to display the Future Value and Depreciation forms.

A multiple-document interface (MDI)

The second version of this application uses a *multiple-document interface* (*MDI*). In an MDI application, a container form called a *parent form* contains one or more *child forms*. Then, the menus and toolbars on the parent form contain the commands that let you open and view the child forms. The main advantage of a multiple-document interface is that the parent form can make it easier to organize and manage multiple instances of the child forms.

Single-document interface (SDI)

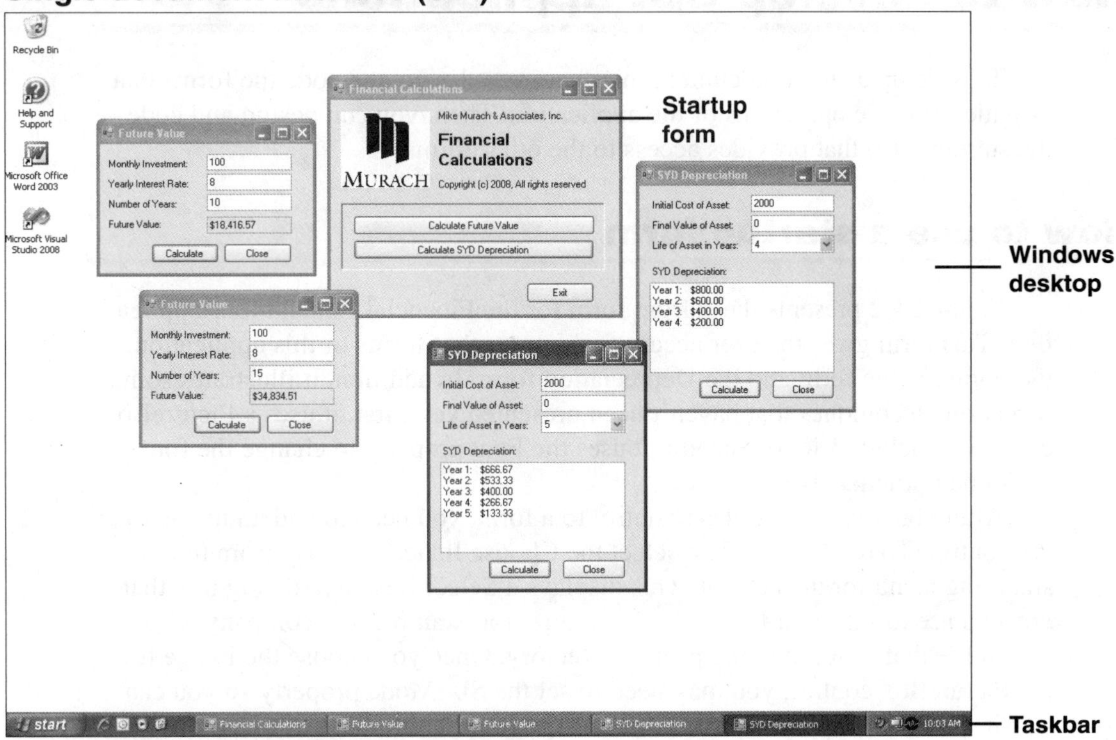

Multiple-document interface (MDI)

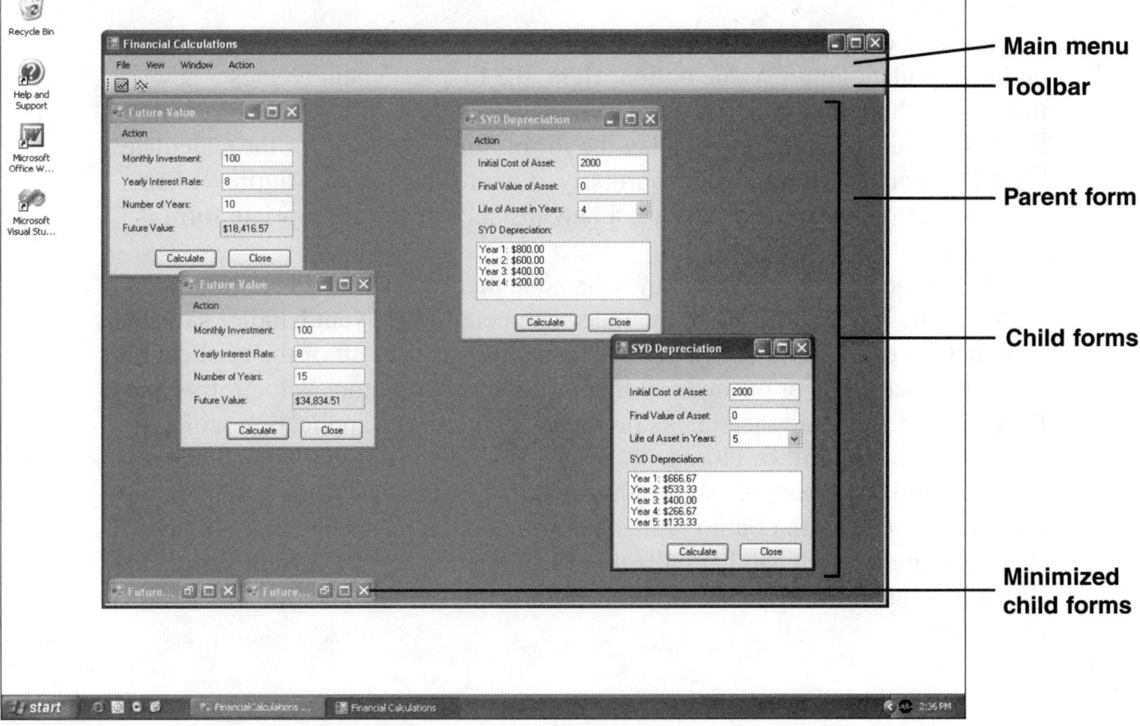

Figure 24-1 Single-document and multiple-document interfaces

How to develop SDI applications

To develop a single-document interface, you design and code the forms that provide the basic operations of the application. Then, you can design and code the startup form that provides access to the other forms.

How to use a startup form

Figure 24-2 presents the startup form for the Financial Calculations application. This form gives the user access to the two other forms of this application: the Future Value form and the Depreciation form. In addition, it illustrates some formatting techniques that haven't been presented yet. First, it uses a PictureBox control to include a logo. Second, it uses the Font property to change the font for some of the labels.

After you add a PictureBox control to a form, you need to add an image to the control. To do that, you can select the Choose Image property from the smart tag menu for the control. This displays a Select Resource dialog box that you can use to select an image. In this figure, for example, the company logo is a bmp file that's stored in the project directory. Once you choose the image for the PictureBox control, you may need to set the SizeMode property so you can size it. If, for example, the image is too large to fit in the PictureBox control, you can set the SizeMode property to Zoom. Then, you can drag the edges of the PictureBox control and the image will automatically be resized to fit within the control.

The first code example shows the code that's executed when the user clicks on the Calculate Future Value button. Here, the first statement creates a new instance of the Future Value form. Then, the Show method of the Future Value form is executed to load and display the form. Since the code for the Calculate SYD Depreciation button works similarly, it isn't shown in this figure. When you click on either of these buttons, a new instance of the appropriate form is displayed.

The second code example shows the code that's executed when the user clicks on the Exit button. Here, the lone statement in the event handler calls the Exit method of the Application class. This method causes all of the application's forms to be closed. For example, if the user opens two Future Value forms and a Depreciation form and then clicks on the Exit button, the application will exit and all four forms will be closed.

The third code example shows the code that's executed when you click on the Close button for the Future Value or Depreciation forms. Here, the lone statement in the event handler calls the Close method for the current form. When this statement is executed, the current form is closed, but the other forms remain open.

A startup form for the Financial Calculations application

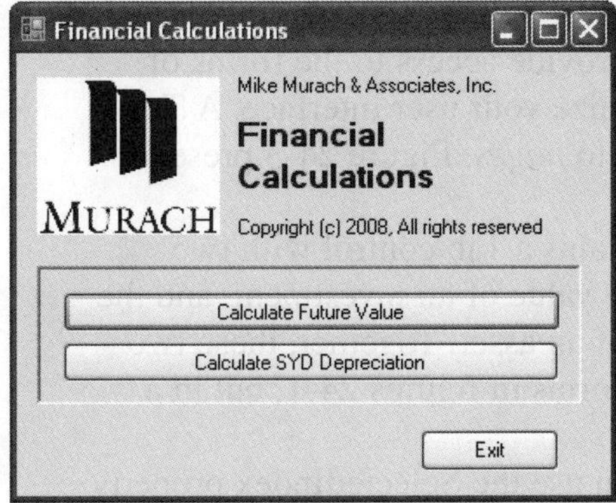

Code that displays a new instance of a form

```
private void btnFutureValue_Click(object sender, System.EventArgs e)
{
    Form newForm = new frmFutureValue();
    newForm.Show();
}
```

Code that exits the application and closes all forms

```
private void btnExit_Click(object sender, System.EventArgs e)
{
    Application.Exit();
}
```

Code that closes the current instance of a form

```
private void btnClose_Click(object sender, System.EventArgs e)
{
    this.Close();
}
```

Description

- An SDI application that consists of more than one form can begin with a *startup form* that directs the user to the other forms of the application.
- You can use the Font property of a control to change the font for the Text property of the control.
- You can use a PictureBox control to display an image on a form. To do that, you add the control to the form and select the Choose Image command from the control's smart tag menu. This opens a Select Resource dialog box that allows you to select the file for the image. In addition, you may need to set the SizeMode property of the PictureBox control to Zoom so you can size the image by dragging the edges of the control.
- A form that's displayed from a startup form should contain a Close button rather than an Exit button to indicate that the button will close the form and not exit the application and close all open forms.

Figure 24-2 How to use a startup form

How to use a Tab control

One alternative to using a startup form to provide access to the forms of your application is to use a Tab control to organize your user interface. A Tab control lets you create *tabs* that provide access to *pages*. Figure 24-3 presents the basic skills for working with Tab controls.

As you can see, the form in this figure contains a Tab control with two pages. The first tab lets you calculate the future value of an investment, and the second tab lets you calculate the depreciation of an asset. Together, these two tabs provide functionality that's similar to the forms in figures 24-1, but in a single form.

When you work with a Tab control, you can use the SelectedIndex property to determine which tab is selected. For instance, when the user clicks the Calculate button, the first code example uses an if-else statement that checks this property to determine which tab is selected. Then, it calls the appropriate method.

The event you'll use most with a Tab control is the SelectedIndexChanged event. This event occurs when the SelectedIndex property of the control changes, which typically happens when a user clicks on another tab. For example, the event handler in the second example in this figure moves the focus to the appropriate control on a tab when that tab becomes the current tab. This method uses the SelectedIndex property to determine which tab is current.

A form that uses a Tab control with two tabs

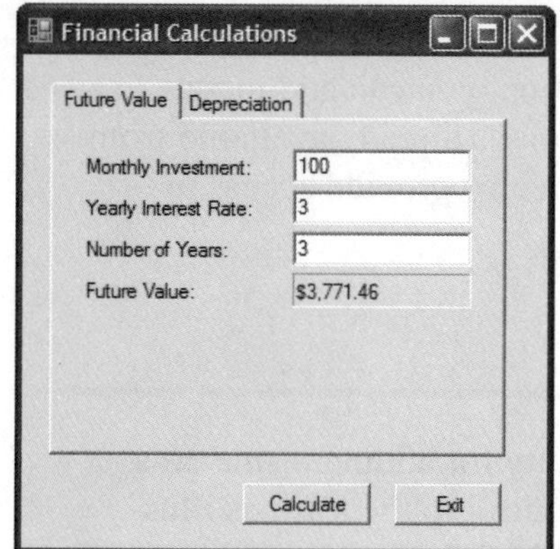

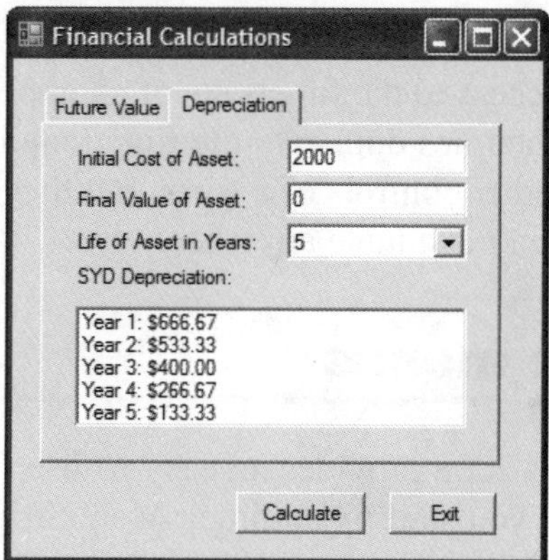

Code that uses the SelectedIndex property of the Tab control

```
private void btnCalculate_Click(object sender, System.EventArgs e)
{
    if (tabCalculations.SelectedIndex == 0)
        DisplayFutureValue();
    else if (tabCalculations.SelectedIndex == 1)
        DisplayDepreciation();
}
```

Code that uses the SelectedIndexChanged event of the Tab control

```
private void tabCalculations_SelectedIndexChanged(object sender,
    System.EventArgs e)
{
    if (tabCalculations.SelectedIndex == 0)
        txtMonthlyInvestment.Focus();
    else if (tabCalculations.SelectedIndex == 1)
        txtInitialCost.Focus();
}
```

Description

- Each Tab control can contain two or more *tabs*. Each tab in a Tab control contains a *page* where you add the controls for the tab.
- To add tabs, right-click on the Tab control and select the Add Tab command from the shortcut menu.
- To set the text that's displayed in a tab, select the page and set the Text property.
- To remove a tab, right-click on the tab's page and select the Delete command from the shortcut menu.
- You can also add and remove tabs by selecting the Tab control and using the TabPages property to display the TabPages Collection Editor.
- You can use the SelectedIndex property of the Tab control to determine which tab is currently selected.
- The SelectedIndexChanged event occurs when another tab is selected.

Figure 24-3 How to use a Tab control

How to add menus to a form

To provide access to the functions of an application, you can add menus to a form. Menus sometimes duplicate the functionality that's already available from the buttons and other controls of a form, but they can also provide access to functions that aren't available anywhere else.

How to create menus

Visual Studio 2008 provides an easy-to-use facility for adding *menus* to a form. To do that, you start by adding a MenuStrip control to the form as illustrated in figure 24-4. When you add this control, the MainMenuStrip property of the form is automatically set to the name of that control but the control isn't displayed on the form. Instead, it's displayed in the Component Designer tray at the bottom of the Form Designer.

After you add the MenuStrip control to the form, the Menu Designer is displayed at the top of the form. Then, you can add menus and *menu items* by typing the text you want to appear in the Menu Designer anywhere it says "Type Here." When you type the text for the first menu, additional areas open up below and to the right of that menu. As a result, it's easy to enter new menus, submenus, and menu items. As with other controls, you can use the ampersand character (&) to provide an access key when you enter the text for the menu item. In addition, you can create a separator bar by using a dash (-) for the menu item's text.

Once you've entered the menus and menu items for your application, you can easily set the Name property for each menu item. To do that, right-click on the name of the menu and select the Edit DropDownItems command from the shortcut menu. This displays the Items Collection Editor dialog box, which makes it easy to edit the names for each menu item or set any of the other properties for a menu item. This dialog box also lets you add, move, and delete menu items.

When setting the names for each menu item, it's a common coding convention to use mnu as the prefix for each name. For example, you might use mnuActionClear as the name for the Clear item of the Action menu. Otherwise, you can accept the default name that's assigned by the Menu Designer. For example, the default name for the Clear item of the Action menu would be clearToolStripMenuItem.

If you need to insert a new item in a menu, you can right-click on a menu item to display a shortcut menu. Then, you can select the MenuItem command from the Insert submenu to insert a new item. Or, you can select the Separator command from the Insert submenu to insert a separator bar. In addition, the shortcut menu for a menu item provides Cut, Copy, Paste, and Delete commands.

The beginning of the menu for the Future Value form

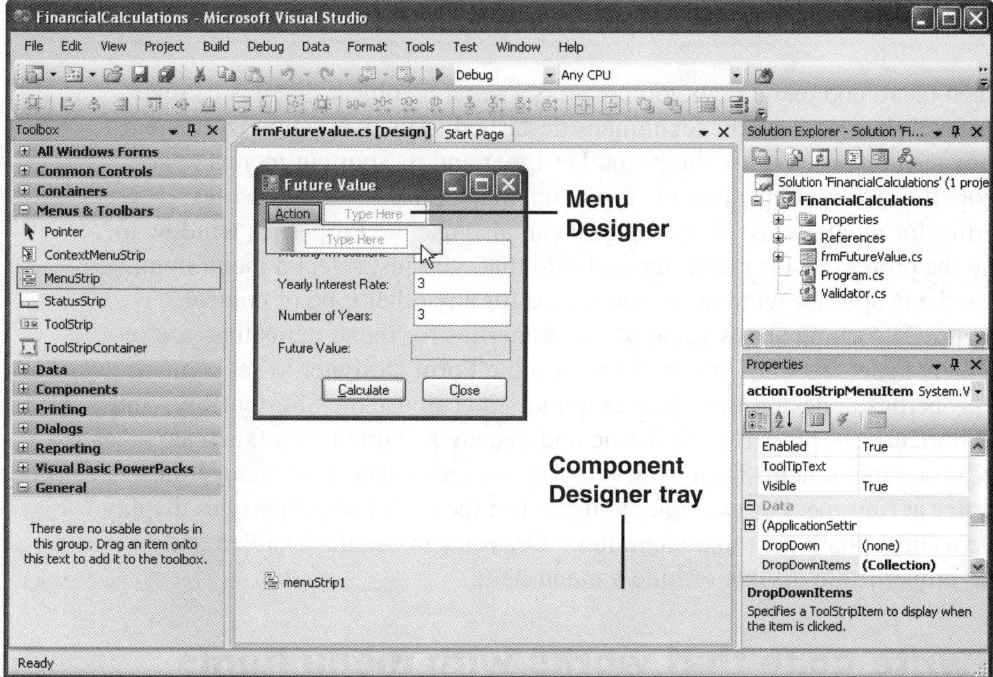

The complete Action menu

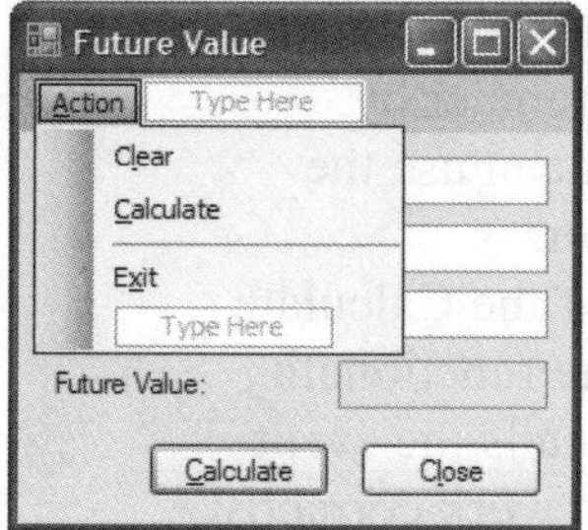

Description

- To add *menus* to a form, add a MenuStrip control to a form. This control will appear in the Component Designer tray at the bottom of the Form Designer window, and the MainMenuStrip property of the form will be set to the name of that control.
- To add items to the menu, click wherever it says "Type Here" in the Menu Designer. Then, type the text of the menu item and press the Enter key. Additional entry areas appear below and to the right of the entry.
- To edit the Name property for each menu item, right-click on the name of the menu and select the Edit DropDownItems command from the shortcut menu. This will display a dialog box that makes it easy to edit the Name property for each item on the menu.
- To insert a new item (including a separator bar), right-click on the menu item to display its shortcut menu and select a command from the Insert submenu.

Figure 24-4 How to create menus

How to set the properties that work with menu items

Each menu and menu item you create is a separate object that has its own properties. When you use the techniques described in the last figure to create a menu or menu item, you use the Menu Designer and its shortcut menus to set the properties for each menu item. Typically, that's the easiest way to set properties for menu items. However, you can also use the Properties window to change the properties for menu items. To do that, you just select a menu item, and use the Properties window as you would for any other type of control.

Figure 24-5 summarizes some of the properties for menu items that you're most likely to set. To start, you typically use the Form Designer to set some of these properties at design-time. For example, you can use the ShortcutKeys and ShowShortcutKeys properties to define and display a shortcut key (such as Ctrl+C) for a menu item. Then, if necessary, you can use code to change these properties at runtime. For example, you can use the Checked property to display or hide a check mark next to a menu item. Or, you can use the Enabled and Visible properties to disable or hide a menu item.

How to write code that works with menu items

The first example in figure 24-5 shows the event handler for the Click event of the Clear item of the Action menu. Since the Click event is the default event for a menu item, you can generate the declaration for the event handler by double-clicking the menu item in the Menu Designer. Then, you can use the Code Editor to enter the code that's executed by the event handler.

The second example shows the handler for the Click event of the Calculate item of the Action menu. Since this menu item provides the same functionality as the Calculate button, the lone statement in this event handler calls the event handler for the Click event of the Calculate button. To get this to work correctly, both of the parameters for the mnuCalculate_Click method are supplied as arguments for the btnCalculate_Click method.

The third example shows another way to handle the Click event for the Calculate item of the Action menu. Here, this event handler calls the PerformClick method of the Calculate button. This causes the event handler for the Click event of the Calculate button to be executed.

Of course, you can handle this situation more elegantly by wiring both events to the same event handler. For example, you could wire the Click event for the Calculate menu item and the Calculate button to an event handler named Calculate_Click. For a refresher course on wiring event handlers, see chapter 6.

Common menu item properties

Property	Description
Text	The text that will appear in the menu for the item. To provide an access key for a menu item, include an ampersand (&) in this property.
Name	The name that's used to refer to the menu item in code.
Checked	Determines if a check mark appears to the left of the menu item when it's selected.
Enabled	Determines if the menu item is available or grayed out. If a menu item is disabled or enabled, all items subordinate to it are disabled or enabled.
Visible	Determines if the menu item is displayed or hidden. If a menu item is hidden or displayed, all items subordinate to it are hidden or displayed.
ShortcutKeys	Specifies the shortcut key associated with the menu item.
ShowShortcutKeys	Determines if the shortcut key is displayed to the right of the menu item.

Code for a menu item that clears four controls

```
private void mnuClear_Click(object sender, System.EventArgs e)
{
    txtMonthlyInvestment.Text = "";
    txtInterestRate.Text = "";
    txtYears.Text = "";
    txtFutureValue.Text = "";
}
```

Code for a menu item that calls another event handler

```
private void mnuCalculate_Click(object sender, System.EventArgs e)
{
    btnCalculate_Click(sender, e);
}
```

Another way to call another event handler

```
private void mnuCalculate_Click(object sender, System.EventArgs e)
{
    btnCalculate.PerformClick();
}
```

Notes

- The Click event is the default event for a menu item. You can code an event handler for this event just as you would for any other Click event.
- If a menu item executes the same code as another event handler, you can call that event handler instead of duplicating its code. You can use the PerformClick method of another button or menu item to cause its event handler to be executed. Or, you can use the Events list in the Properties window to wire the Click event to an existing event handler.

Figure 24-5 How to work with menu items

How to develop MDI applications

If the application you're developing requires multiple instances of one or more forms, you may want to use a multiple-document interface. That way, you can create a parent form that acts as a container for all of the child forms. Then, you can provide a Window menu to make it easier to display and manage the child forms.

How to create parent and child forms

Figure 24-6 shows the design of a parent form for the Financial Calculations application that provides File and Window menus to access its child forms. To create parent and child forms, you begin by adding standard Windows forms to your project. Then, you set the IsMdiContainer property of the parent form to true to identify it as the parent form, and you set the MdiParent property of the child forms to the name of the parent form.

To do that, you can use the Form Designer to set the IsMdiContainer property at design-time, and you can use the Code Editor to write code that sets the MdiParent property at runtime. In the next figure, you'll learn how to write this code, and you'll learn how to write code that uses the ActiveMdiChild property and the LayoutMdi method.

An application with one parent form and two child forms

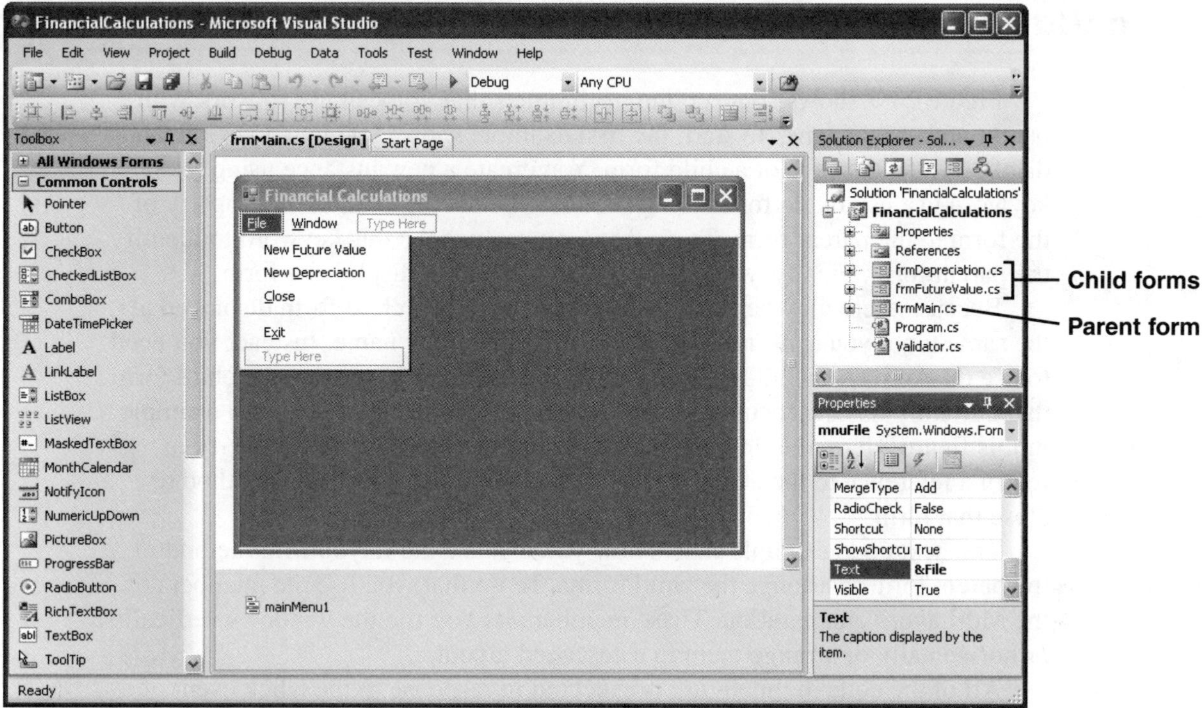

Properties and methods for a parent form

Property/Method	Description
IsMdiContainer	At design-time, you set this property to true to indicate that the form is a parent form.
ActiveMdiChild	At runtime, you can use this property to retrieve a reference to the active child form.
LayoutMdi(mdiLayout)	At runtime, you can use this method to arrange all child forms. To do that, you can specify one of the members of the MdiLayout enumeration: Cascade, TileVertical, TileHorizontal, and so on.

Typical property settings for a child form

Property	Description
MdiParent	At runtime, you can set this property to specify the parent form for a child form.

Note

- An MDI application can also include forms that aren't parent or child forms. These forms are typically modal forms like the ones that you learned about in chapter 10.

Figure 24-6 How to create parent and child forms

How to write code that works with parent and child forms

Figure 24-7 shows some coding techniques that you can use to work with parent and child forms. To start, the first example shows you how to create and display a new instance of a child form. You create a new instance using the new keyword just as you do for any class. Then, you set the MdiParent property of the form to the parent form. To do that, you can use the this keyword to identify the parent form. Finally, you use the Show method to display the form.

Because there may be more than one instance of a child form displayed at the same time, you can't refer to an individual form by name. Instead, you need to use the ActiveMdiChild property of the parent form to refer to the child form that currently has the focus. You can see how this works in the second example in this figure. Here, the first statement uses the ActiveMdiChild property to return a reference to the active child form. Then, it uses the Close method to close that form.

The next code example shows how you can use the LayoutMdi method of the parent form to arrange the child forms. To do that, you use the members of the MdiLayout enumeration. These members let you tile the windows vertically or horizontally or arrange them in a cascaded layout.

All of the code in this figure is executed in response to the Click event of a menu item, which occurs when the user selects the item. For example, the code that creates and displays a new instance of a child form is executed in response to the user selecting the New Future Value item from the File menu. The code that closes the active child form is executed in response to the user selecting the Close item from the File menu. And the code that arranges the child forms is executed in response to the user selecting the Tile Vertical item from the Window menu.

Whenever you need to display and organize the child forms of an MDI application, you can use menus in the parent form to do that. For example, it's common for a parent form to contain a File menu that allows you to display child forms, close the active child form, and exit the application, which closes all open child forms. Similarly, it's common for a parent form to contain a Window menu that allows the user to cascade or tile all child forms. If you set the MdiWindowListItem property of the MenuStrip control to the name of the Window menu, this menu will also display a list of all the open child forms as shown in this figure.

However, when you want to use menus that work directly with a child form, you can add the menus to that child form. If, for example, you want to add a Clear menu item that clears all the text boxes on a child form, you can add that item to a menu on the child form. Then, the menus for the active child form will be displayed to the right of the menus for the parent form. In this figure, for example, the Action menu that's displayed to the right of the Window menu is actually coded in the active child form, the Future Value form. As a result, when you run the Financial Calculations application and select the Future Value child form, this Action menu is automatically appended to the parent form's menus.

An MDI application with three child forms arranged vertically

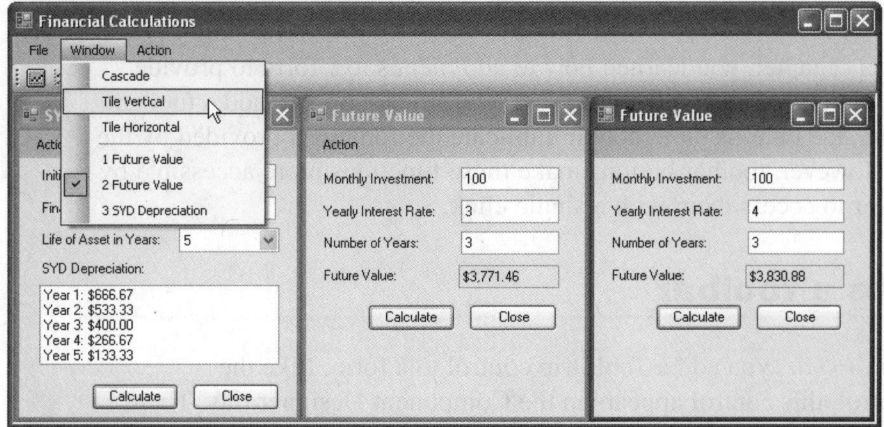

Code that creates and displays a new instance of a child form

```
private void mnuNewFutureValue_Click(object sender, System.EventArgs e)
{
    Form newForm = new frmFutureValue();
    newForm.MdiParent = this;
    newForm.Show();
}
```

Code that refers to the active child form

```
private void mnuClose_Click(object sender, System.EventArgs e)
{
    Form activeForm = this.ActiveMdiChild;
    if (activeForm != null)
        activeForm.Close();
}
```

Code that arranges the child forms vertically

```
private void mnuTileVertical_Click(object sender, System.EventArgs e)
{
    this.LayoutMdi(MdiLayout.TileVertical);
}
```

Code that exits the application and closes all child forms

```
private void mnuExit_Click(object sender, System.EventArgs e)
{
    Application.Exit();
}
```

Description

- You can display a list of the open child forms in a menu by setting the MdiWindowListItem property of the menu strip to the name of the menu. A list like this is typically displayed in the Window menu.
- In this example, the Action menu is stored in the child form. This menu appears in the parent form when a child form that contains it is the active form.

Figure 24-7 How to write code that works with parent and child forms

How to add toolbars to a form

Earlier in this chapter, you learned how to add menus to a form to provide access to the functions of an application. Now, you'll learn how to add a toolbar. Most of the time, the buttons on a toolbar duplicate the functions provided by the menu system. However, toolbar buttons make these functions more accessible by allowing the user to access them with a single click.

How to create a toolbar

To create a *toolbar*, you add a ToolStrip control to a form. Like the MenuStrip control, this control appears in the Component Designer tray. Then, by default, this control is docked at the top of the form below any menus on the form and extends across the full width of the form.

Figure 24-8 presents two examples of toolbars. Here, the first toolbar includes the standard toolbar buttons for functions like Save, Print, Cut, and Paste. You can create a toolbar like this using the Insert Standard Items command in the ToolStrip's smart tag menu. The second toolbar has two custom buttons that let the user display a Future Value or Depreciation form. To add custom buttons, you can use the Items Collection Editor that's shown in this figure.

By default, each button you add to a toolbar displays a graphic image. To specify the image for the button, you can use the Image property of the button to display a dialog box that lets you select the image. In this figure, for example, the two buttons in the second toolbar use images that are stored in bmp files, and these bmp files are stored in the same directory as the form. If you have experience working with computer graphics, you can create your own images. Or, you may be able to find images that you can use on the Internet.

After you've specified an appropriate image for a button, you need to set the Text property for the button. When you set this property, it automatically sets the ToolTipText property, which specifies the text that's displayed when the user places the mouse pointer over the button. This text is known as a *tool tip*, and it's important because it's often hard for a user to determine the function of a button from the button's image alone. Without a tool tip, for example, it's difficult to determine the function of the two custom buttons in the second toolbar. However, if the user points at the first button, it will display a tool tip that says, "Open a new Future Value window," which gives the user a clear idea of what the button does.

By default, the items you add to a toolbar are displayed as standard push buttons. However, you can create other types of toolbar items by selecting a different type of item from the combo box at the top of the Items Collection Editor dialog box. If, for example, you select DropDownButton from this combo box, you can create a menu that drops down from the button. With a little experimentation, you should be able to use this dialog box to add a variety of controls to a toolbar.

A ToolStrip with the standard items

A ToolStrip with two custom buttons

The Items Collection Editor dialog box for a ToolStrip

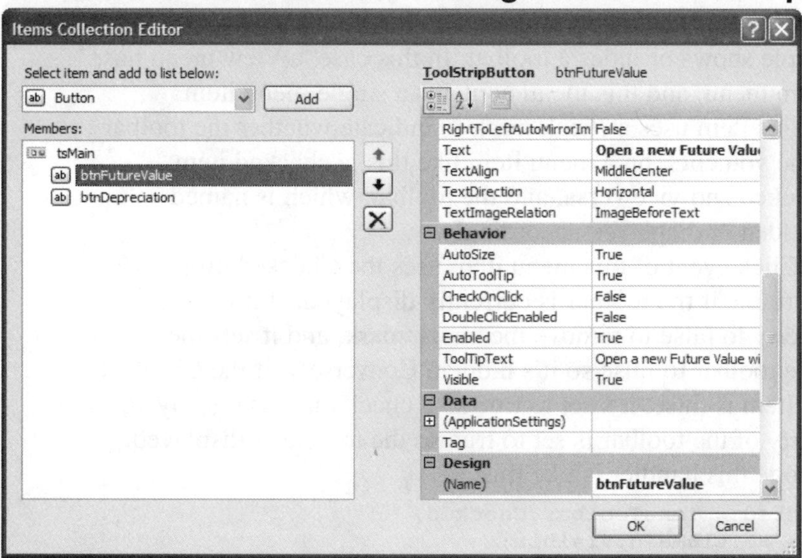

Description

- To create a *toolbar*, add a ToolStrip control to a form. By default, the toolbar is docked at the top of the form below the menus and reaches across the width of the form.
- To insert the standard items shown above, select the Insert Standard Items command from the ToolStrip control's smart tag menu.
- To display the Items Collection Editor dialog box for a toolbar, select the Edit Items command from the smart tag menu for the ToolStrip control. You can use this dialog box to add buttons to the toolbar and to set the properties for those buttons.
- To include an image on a button, you can use the Image property for the button to display a dialog box that let's you specify an image file for the button. This dialog box works with most modern image file formats including gif, jpg, bmp, wmf, and png.
- To specify the text that's displayed when the user points to the button with the mouse (called a *tool tip*), you can enter the text in the Text property for the button. This automatically sets the ToolTipText property for the button.

Figure 24-8 How to create a toolbar

How to write code that works with toolbars

After you create the toolbars for a form, you need to add the code that makes them work. To do that, you can code event handlers like those in figure 24-9.

The first example handles the Click event of the Future Value button on the toolbar. This event handler uses the PerformClick method of the New Future Value menu item to execute that event handler. That way, you don't have to duplicate the code that creates and displays the form.

The second example shows or hides a toolbar. In this case, a View menu has been added to the main menu, and this menu contains a single menu item named mnuToolbar. This item uses a check mark to indicate whether the toolbar is displayed. Each time you click on a menu item like this, a checked item should become unchecked and vice versa, and the toolbar, which is named tlbMain, should be hidden or displayed accordingly.

The code for the Click event of this menu item uses the Checked property of the menu item to determine if the toolbar is currently displayed. If it is, this method sets this property to false to remove the check mark, and it sets the Visible property of the toolbar to false so it's hidden. Conversely, if the Checked property of the menu item is false, it's set to true so a check mark is displayed, and the Visible property of the toolbar is set to true so the toolbar is displayed.

Another way to code this handler is like this:

```
mnuToolbar.Checked = !mnuToolbar.Checked;
tlbMain.Visible = !tlbMain.Visible;
```

Here, the Not operator (!) is used to reverse the values of the menu item's Checked property and the toolbar's Visible property. Although this code isn't as easy to follow as the code in this figure, this type of code is commonly used.

Code for the Click event of a button on a ToolStrip

```
private void btnFutureValue_Click(object sender, EventArgs e)
{
    mnuNewFutureValue.PerformClick();
}
```

A View menu that shows or hides the toolbar

Code that shows or hides a toolbar depending on a menu selection

```
private void mnuToolbar_Click(object sender, System.EventArgs e)
{
    if (mnuToolbar.Checked == true)
    {
        mnuToolbar.Checked = false;
        tlbMain.Visible = false;
    }
    else if (mnuToolbar.Checked == false)
    {
        mnuToolbar.Checked = true;
        tlbMain.Visible = true;
    }
}
```

Description

- You use the Click event of a button in a toolbar to respond to the user clicking on that button.
- You can use the Checked property of a menu item to work with the check mark that's displayed to the left of the item.
- You can use the Visible property of a control to show or hide the control.

Figure 24-9 How to write code that works with toolbars

How to add help information

Because Windows Forms applications use the standard Windows interface, users who are already familiar with other Windows applications should quickly adapt to these applications. In addition, you should try to design and develop each application so it is as easy to use as is practical. Nevertheless, almost all applications can benefit from the addition of at least a minimum amount of help information.

One way to add help information to a form is to add a Help menu. Then, you can add items to that menu for various topics. When the user selects one of these items, you can display a dialog box with the appropriate information. You can also add help information to a form by using tool tips and context-sensitive help.

How to add tool tips

Earlier in this chapter, you learned how to add tool tips to toolbar buttons. In addition, you can add tool tips to each control on a form and to the form itself. Figure 24-10 shows how.

To add tool tips, you add a ToolTip control to the form. Then, a ToolTip property becomes available for the form and each of its controls. This property is listed in the Properties window along with the other properties of the form or control. You can set this property to the text you want displayed when the user places the mouse pointer over the form or control. In this figure, for example, the tool tip for the Initial Cost text box on the Depreciation form describes the value that should be entered.

How to add context-sensitive help

If you want to display help information that's more extensive than what you would normally display in a tool tip, you can use the HelpProvider control. This control lets you provide *context-sensitive help* for a form or control. Then, the user can display the help for the control that has the focus by pressing the F1 key. If help text isn't provided for that control, the help text for the form is displayed if it's provided.

To specify the help text for a form or control, you use the HelpString property that becomes available when you add a HelpProvider control to the form. In this figure, for example, the Depreciation form shows some context-sensitive help that describes the function of the form.

A tool tip

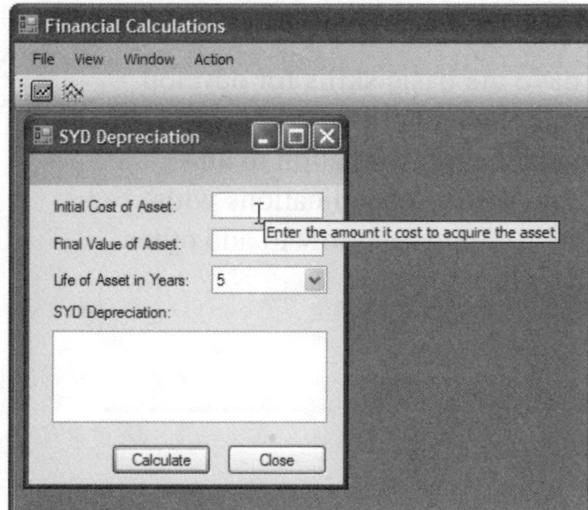

Context-sensitive help

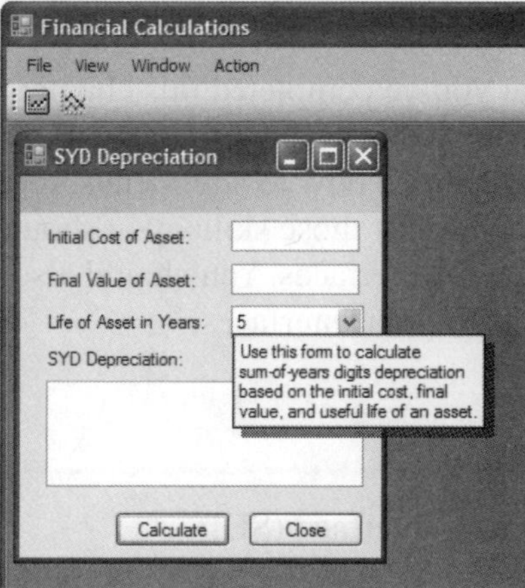

How to work with a tool tip

- A *tool tip* is a brief description of a control that's displayed automatically when you place the mouse pointer over that control.
- To create tool tips for a form, add a ToolTip control to the form. A control named toolTip1 will appear in the Component Designer tray at the bottom of the window.
- The ToolTip control makes a property named "ToolTip on toolTip1" available for each control on the form and for the form itself. You can enter the text for the tool tip in this property.

How to work with context-sensitive help

- To provide *context-sensitive help* for a form or control, add a HelpProvider control to the form. A control named helpProvider1 will appear in the Component Designer tray at the bottom of the window. This control makes several additional properties available for the form and each control it contains.
- To display a text string when the user presses the F1 key for the control that has the focus, enter the text for the "HelpString on helpProvider1" property of the control.
- You can also enter help text for the HelpString property of the form. Then, that text is displayed at the location of the mouse pointer if a help string isn't specified for the control that has the focus.
- When you enter text for the "HelpString on helpProvider1" property, the "ShowHelp on helpProvider1" property automatically changes from false to true.

Figure 24-10 How work with tool tips and context-sensitive help

Perspective

Now that you've completed this chapter, you have the basic skills for developing applications that use single-document or multiple-document interfaces. In addition, you learned how to add menus, toolbars, and help information to an application. With just those skills, you should be able to create applications with professional user interfaces. You should also be able to figure out how to add other enhancements to your interfaces.

Terms

single-document interface (SDI)
startup form
multiple-document interface (MDI)
parent form
child form
tab
page
menu
menu item
toolbar
tool tip
context-sensitive help

Exercise 24-1 Create the SDI application

In this exercise, you'll create the SDI version of the Financial Calculations application that's presented in this chapter.

Open the project and adjust the startup form

1. Open the FinancialCalculations project in the C:\C# 2008\Chapter 24\FinancialCalculationsSDI folder. This project contains the beginning of a startup form named frmMain.
2. Open the Designer window for the startup form, select the PictureBox control, and note how the Image property in the Properties window is set. Then, delete this setting and note that the image in the PictureBox control is gone. To restore this image, select the Choose Image command from the PictureBox's smart tag menu to open the Select Resource dialog box. Then, find the file named Murach logo in the FinancialCalculationsSDI folder, and complete the dialog boxes.
3. Select the text box that contains "Financial Calculations" in a larger than normal font size. Then, click on the plus sign before the Font property in the Properties window, and change the font name to Times New Roman, change the font size to 15, and turn italics on.

Add existing forms and classes from other projects

4. Use the Add Existing Item dialog box to add the frmFutureValue.cs file in the C:\C# 2008\Chapter 24\FutureValue folder to your project.
5. Use the Add Existing Item dialog box to add the class file for the Validator class from the C:\C# 2008\Chapter 24\FutureValue folder to your project.
6. Use the Add Existing Item dialog box to add the frmDepreciation.cs file in the C:\C# 2008\Chapter 24\Depreciation folder to your project.

Add the code for the startup form and fix other coding issues

7. Add code to the startup form that creates instances of the Future Value and Depreciation forms and responds to the Click events of the three buttons.
8. Change the Exit button on the Future Value form to a Close button, and change the handler for the Click event of this button so it closes the form instead of exiting the application.
9. If you were to run the application at this point, you would have build errors because the three forms are in different namespaces. One way to fix this problem is to add using statements at the beginning of the startup form that import the FutureValue and Depreciation namespaces. Do that now.
10. Run and test the application. When the startup form is displayed, use it to display multiple versions of the Future Value and Depreciation forms. Make sure the Close button on each form works properly, and make sure the Exit button on the startup form closes all open forms.
11. Another way to fix the namespace problem is to change the namespaces for the FutureValue and Depreciation forms to FinancialCalculations so all three forms are in the same namespace. To test that, delete the using statements you added in step 9, change the namespaces, and run the application again.
12. Close this version of the Financial Calculations project.

Exercise 24-2 Create the MDI application

In this exercise, you'll create the MDI version of the Financial Calculations application.

Convert the SDI application to an MDI application

1. Create a copy of the FinancialCalculationsSDI folder. Rename this folder FinancialCalculationsMDI and store it in the C:\C# 2008\Chapter 24 folder.
2. Display the form named frmMain in Design view and delete all controls from this form. Then, set the IsMdiContainer property of the Financial Calculations form to true to identify it as the parent form, and resize the form so it's large enough to hold several child forms.

Add the File menu to the parent form

3. Add a MenuStrip control to the form, and note that it's displayed in the Component Designer tray at the bottom of the Form Designer. Also notice that a box with the words "Type Here" appears at the top of the form.
4. Use the Menu Designer to add the File menu with four menu items that will display a new Future Value form, display a new Depreciation form, close the active child form, and exit from the application. Include access keys if you like. Then, use the Menu Designer to name these menu items mnuNewFutureValue, mnuNewDepreciation, mnuClose, and mnuExit, and include a separator bar between the Close and Exit items.

5. Add an event handler for the Click event of each menu item as shown in figure 24-7. Then, delete any code that's left over from the SDI version of the application.
6. Run and test the application. You should be able to display and use multiple versions of either form, you should be able to close the active child form, and you should be able to exit the application, closing all child forms.

Add the Window menu to the parent form

7. Use the Menu Designer to add a Window menu to the right of the File menu. Then, add three items to this menu that will let the user arrange the forms in a cascaded, vertical, or horizontal layout.
8. Right-click in the Window menu and select the Edit DropDownItems command. Then, click on each menu item and enter an appropriate name for it.
9. Code an event handler for the Click event of each of the items in the Window menu. Each event handler should use the LayoutMdi method of the form to arrange the child forms using one of the members of the MdiLayout enumeration as shown in figure 24-7.
10. Set the MdiWindowListItem property of the menu strip to the name of the Window menu.
11. Run the application and display two or more instances of each form. Then, use the items in the Window menu to arrange the open forms and to move from one form to another.

Add the Action menu to one child form

12. Use the Menu Designer to add an Action menu to the Future Value form. Then, add the Clear and Calculate items to this menu.
13. Code the event handlers for these items as described in figure 24-5.
14. Run the application and display two or more instances of each form. Note that the Action menu is only displayed when a Future Value form is the active child form, not when a Depreciation form is the active child form.

Add a toolbar and help

15. Add a ToolStrip control to the main form and add the Future Value and Depreciation buttons as described in figure 24-8. The two icons for the buttons are stored in the C:\C# 2008\Chapter 24 folder.
16. Add a View menu that has a checked Toolbar item. Then, write the code that uses this menu item to display and hide the toolbar as described in figure 24-9, and add the code that handles the Click event of the buttons on the toolbar.
17. Add tool tips and context-sensitive help information for both the Future Value form and the Depreciation form as described in figure 24-10.
18. Run the application and test it to make sure the toolbar and the help are working properly, and the entire interface is "user friendly."

25

How to deploy an application

At some point during the process of developing a Windows application, you need to deploy the application so you can test it on the target system, and ultimately so your users can run it. Since testing an application on the target system may help you discover issues that affect the design of the application, it often pays to deploy and test an application on the target system or systems early in the development process.

In the past, most Windows applications were installed by using a Setup program that was stored on a network share or a CD. In recent years, however, it has become possible for a Windows application to be installed from a web server, which makes it easier to update the application. For example, virus protection software is often installed from a web server. Fortunately, Visual Studio 2008 makes it easy to deploy applications using either method.

An introduction to deploying Windows applications

Figure 25-1 lists three ways to deploy a Windows application. Each of these ways of deploying an application has its advantages and disadvantages.

How XCopy works

The oldest and easiest way to deploy a Windows application is to copy the files that are required by the application to the user's computer. This method of deployment is known as *XCopy deployment* because you can use the DOS XCopy command to copy the files to the user's computer. However, you can also use the Windows Explorer to copy the files to the user's computer.

Although XCopy deployment is adequate for simple applications with just a few users, it doesn't create an icon in the Start menu, it doesn't provide a way to automatically install prerequisite files (such as the .NET Framework 3.5), it doesn't provide an automatic way to update the application, and it doesn't provide a standard way to uninstall the application. As a result, you'll only want to use this type of deployment when you are prepared to copy the files onto the users system and are also prepared to update or delete these files as necessary.

How ClickOnce works

The second way to deploy an application is commonly called *ClickOnce deployment*. This type of deployment lets users install a Windows application by clicking a link from a web page.

Although it requires a little more work to set up ClickOnce deployment, the advantages of ClickOnce deployment are usually worth the effort. This type of deployment creates an icon for the application in the Start menu, lets the user use the Add or Remove Programs dialog box to uninstall the application, and lets the user automatically update the application whenever new versions become available.

How a Setup program works

The third way to deploy an application is to create a *Setup program* for the application. Then, you can run this Setup program from each of the user's computers to install the application. Creating a Setup program requires significantly more work than XCopy or ClickOnce deployment, and it doesn't have the automatic updating feature that's available from ClickOnce. As a result, you'll only want to create a Setup program when ClickOnce isn't adequate for your application. For example, you can use a Setup program if you need to install shared components in the global assembly cache (GAC) or you need to modify the registry.

XCopy

- Installs the application by copying the folder for the application to the user's hard drive.
- Allows the user to start the application by double-clicking on the exe file for the application.
- Allows the user to remove the application by deleting the folder for the application.
- Works as long as all files required by the application are included in the folder for the application.
- Is adequate for some simple applications with just a few users.

ClickOnce

- Allows users to install the application by clicking a link from a web page.
- Was introduced with Visual Studio 2005.
- Creates an icon for the application in the Start menu.
- Allows the application to be uninstalled by using the Add or Remove Programs dialog box that can be accessed from the Control Panel.
- Provides a way to automatically check for and install any files needed by the application.
- Provides a way to automatically distribute updates to the application.
- Is adequate for many types of applications with multiple users.

Setup program

- Allows users to install the application by running a Windows Setup program.
- Allows users to specify the installation directory.
- Creates an icon for the application in the Start menu.
- Allows the application to be uninstalled by using the Add or Remove Programs dialog box that can be accessed from the Control Panel.
- Provides a way to automatically check for and install any files needed by the application.
- Can be used to install shared components in the global assembly cache (GAC).
- Can be used to modify the registry to install COM components.
- Is adequate for all but the most complex applications.

Figure 25-1 Three ways to deploy a Windows Forms application

How to use XCopy

You can use XCopy deployment to install an application just by copying its folder onto the user's hard drive. Then, if the files for all assemblies needed by the application are stored in that folder, the application should run correctly. The advantage of this approach is that no configuration or registration is required.

How to create a release build

Figure 25-2 shows how to use XCopy deployment to deploy an application. Before you begin copying files, you should choose whether you want to create a debug or release version of the application. Because the debug version contains symbolic debugging information that you don't typically need in a production application, and because this version isn't optimized, you'll usually create a release version.

To create a release build, you can select the Release option from the Solution Configurations combo box that's available from the Standard toolbar. Then, you can press F5 to run the project, which will also build the project. By default, this creates a folder named bin\Release in the project's folder.

How to copy the release build to the client machine

Once you've created the Release folder, you can use the XCopy command to copy the Release folder to the user's hard drive. At that time, you can name the folder on the user's computer so it accurately identifies the application.

In this figure, for example, the XCopy command is used to copy all files in the bin\Release folder to a folder on the user's computer named FutureValueV1.0. That way, the user can clearly identify the application and its release number. Here, the first path specifies the source folder, the second path specifies the target folder, and the /S switch indicates that all files in the folders and subfolders of the source folder should be copied to the target location.

If you need to deploy the application to multiple users, you can create a DOS batch file for the XCopy command to automate the deployment. Then, you can run the batch file any time you make changes to the application and want to deploy the updated code. However, even with a batch file, this process isn't as automatic as you would like it to be.

For example, unlike ClickOnce deployment or Setup programs, XCopy deployment doesn't automatically check for dependencies. As a result, if the user's computer doesn't have all of the files required by the application, the application won't be able to run properly. If, for example, the user's computer doesn't have the .NET Framework 3.5 installed on it and the application uses features of this Framework, the application won't be able to run until you install the Framework.

The Build tab of the Project Properties window

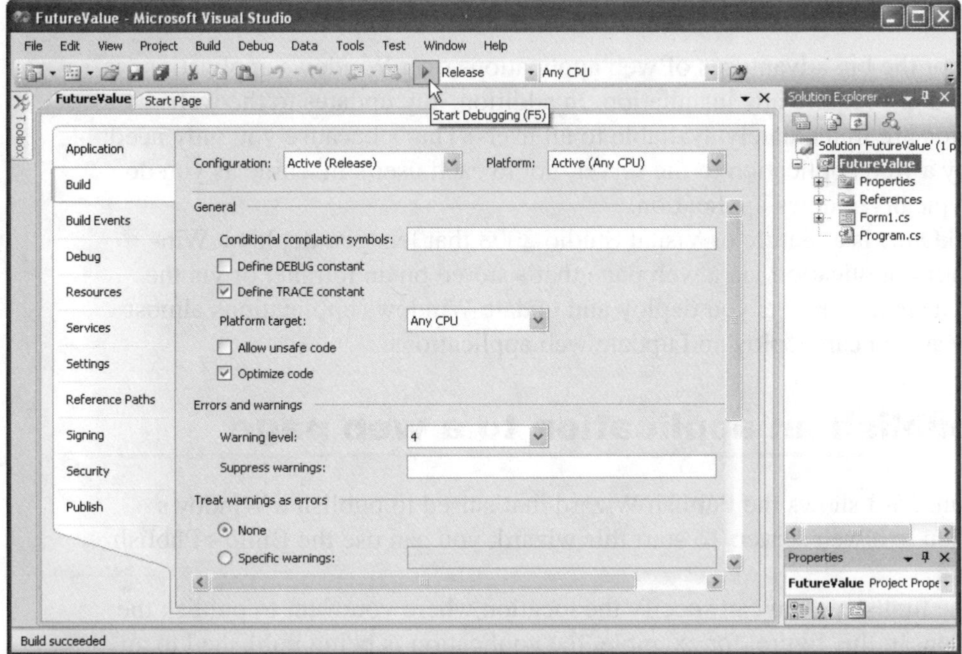

A procedure for using XCopy deployment

1. Select the Release option from the Solution Configurations combo box that's available from the Standard toolbar.
2. Build or run the project to create the bin\Release folder.
3. Use the XCopy command to copy the Release folder to the user's hard drive.

An example of the XCopy command

```
C:\>xcopy "C:\C# 2008\FutureValue\FutureValue\bin\Release\*"
"M:\Murach\FutureValueV1.0\" /S
C:\C# 2008\FutureValue\FutureValue\bin\Release\FutureValue.exe
C:\C# 2008\FutureValue\FutureValue\bin\Release\FutureValue.pdb
C:\C# 2008\FutureValue\FutureValue\bin\Release\FutureValue.vshost.exe
C:\C# 2008\FutureValue\FutureValue\bin\Release\FutureValue.vshost.exe.manifest
4 File(s) copied
```

Description

- If the files for all of the assemblies needed by the application are stored in the Release folder, the application should run correctly. No configuration or registration is required.
- If the application uses features of version 3.0 or 3.5 of the .NET Framework, you need to install that Framework before the user can run the application. Otherwise, only version 2.0 of the Framework is required.
- To automate the deployment, you can create a DOS batch file for the XCopy command. Then, you can run the batch file any time you make changes to the application and want to deploy the updated code.

Figure 25-2 How to use XCopy deployment

How to use ClickOnce

One of the big advantages of web applications over Windows applications is that they don't require any installation. In addition, any updates to the web application are immediately available to all users. That's because you only need to deploy a web application to the server, not to each user's machine as you do with a typical Windows application.

ClickOnce is a feature of Visual Studio 2008 that lets you deploy a Windows Forms application via a web page that's stored on an intranet or via the Internet. This feature lets you deploy and update Windows applications almost as easily as you can deploy and update web applications.

How to publish an application to a web page

Figure 25-3 shows the Publish Wizard that's used to publish a Windows application to a web server. To start this wizard, you can use the Build→Publish command.

In the first step, you can specify the location where you want to publish the application. In this figure, for example, the application is being published to an IIS server that's running on the same computer as Visual Studio. However, it's also common to publish an application to an IIS server that's running on a remote computer. To do that, you can enter the location in the text box or click the Browse button to select the location. For this to work with a remote web site, though, FrontPage Server Extensions must be installed on the web server.

As you can see from this step, it's also possible to publish an application to a directory on your hard disk, to a directory on a network drive, or to a directory on an FTP server. However, it's more common to publish an application to a directory on a web server. As a result, the rest of the examples in this section assume that the application has been published to a web server.

In the second step, you can specify whether the application will be available offline. By default, it will be. In other words, the application will be installed on the user's hard drive, a shortcut will be added to the Start menu, and the application can be uninstalled via the Add or Remove Programs dialog box that's available from the Control Panel.

However, it's also possible to create an application that's only available online. In that case, the application is loaded into memory on the user's computer directly from the web server. As a result, there's no need to create a shortcut for the program in the Start menu or to provide a way to uninstall the application. For this to work, of course, you must be able to establish a connection to the web server each time you run the application. In addition, since you must download the application from the web server before you can run it, the application will start more slowly when the online option is used.

The Publish Wizard dialog box (Step 1)

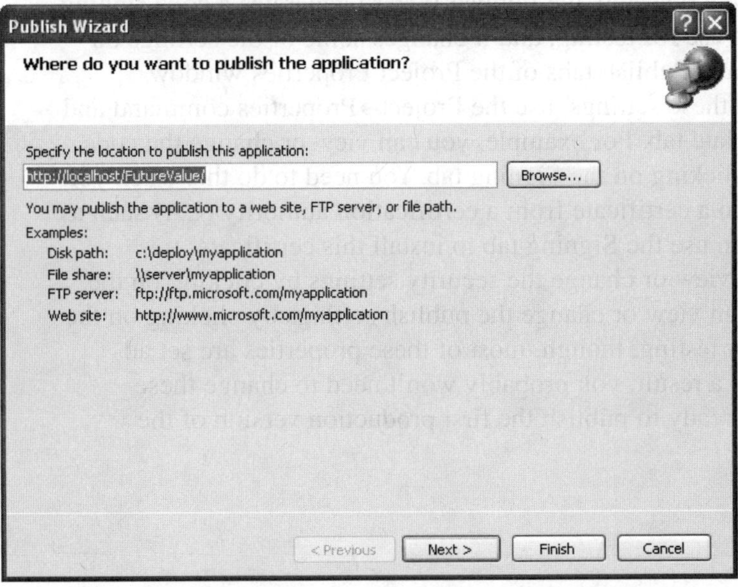

The Publish Wizard dialog box (Step 2)

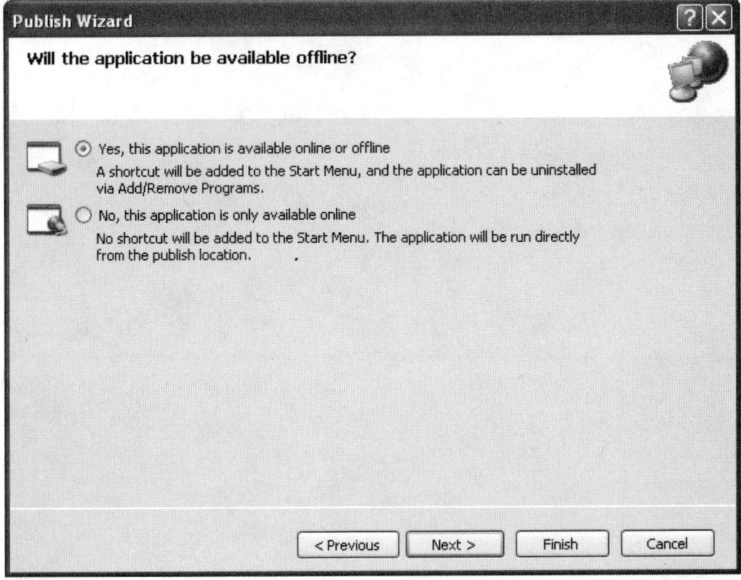

Description

- To start the Publish Wizard, use the Build→Publish command.
- To publish an application to a remote web site, FrontPage Server Extensions must be installed on the web server.

Figure 25-3 How to publish an application to a web page (part 1 of 2)

In the third step, you get a chance to confirm the publication of the application. When you complete this step, the Publish Wizard generates a code signing certificate that you can use for testing, and it changes some of the settings on the Signing, Security, and Publish tabs of the Project Properties window.

To view or change these settings, use the Project→Properties command and then select the appropriate tab. For example, you can view or change the code signing certificate by clicking on the Signing tab. You need to do this when you finish testing and obtain a certificate from a certification authority (CA) such as VeriSign. Then, you can use the Signing tab to install this certificate.

Similarly, you can view or change the security settings by clicking on the Security tab. Or, you can view or change the publish settings by clicking on the Publish tab. At least for testing, though, most of these properties are set adequately by default. As a result, you probably won't need to change these properties until you're ready to publish the first production version of the application.

The Publish Wizard dialog box (Step 3)

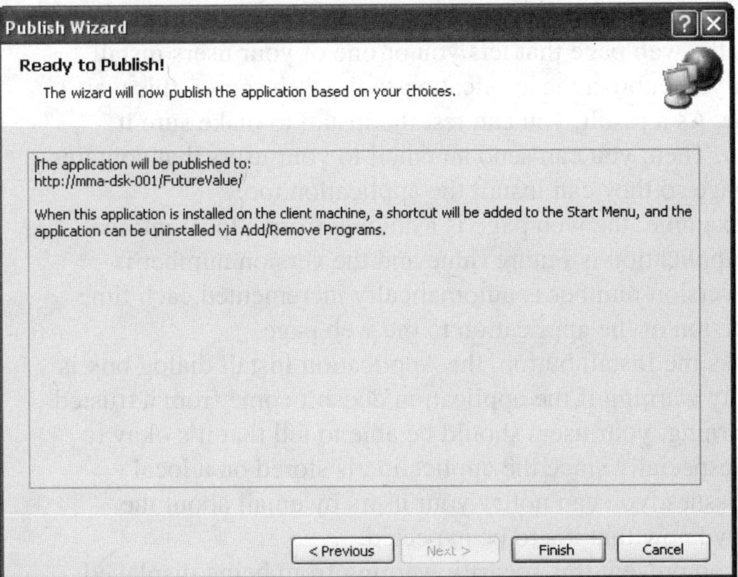

Description

- When you complete the Publish Wizard, it generates a certificate that you can use for testing, and it changes some of the settings on the Signing, Security, and Publish tabs of the Project Properties window.
- To display the Project Properties window, use the Project→Properties command.
- To view or change the certificate, display the Project Properties window and click on the Signing tab.
- To view or change the security settings, display the Project Properties window and click on the Security tab.
- To view or change the publish settings, display the Project Properties window and click on the Publish tab.

Figure 25-3 How to publish an application to a web page (part 2 of 2)

How to install an application from a web page

Figure 25-4 shows the web page that lets you or one of your users install your application. After you publish the application to the web server, this web page becomes available. As a result, you can test the install to make sure it works correctly for you. Then, you can send an email to your users that contains the URL for the web page so they can install the application too.

In this figure, for example, the web page is available from a local intranet. Here, the name of the application is FutureValue and the version number is 1.0.0.0. However, this version number is automatically incremented each time you publish another version of the application to the web page.

When the user clicks the Install button, the Application Install dialog box is displayed with a security warning if the application doesn't come from a trusted source. Despite this warning, your users should be able to tell that it's okay to install the application, especially since the application is stored on a local intranet. If this causes issues, you can notify your users by email about the security warning so they know that it's to be expected.

Alternatively, you can prevent this security warning from being displayed by installing a valid certificate. If the application is published to an intranet, you may be able to use the Microsoft certificate server that can be installed as part of Windows Server 2003. If the application is published to the Internet, you can get a valid certificate from a certification authority such as VeriSign. For more information about certification authorities, you can search the Internet for "certification authorities" and "code signing certificate."

The web page that's created by the Publish Wizard

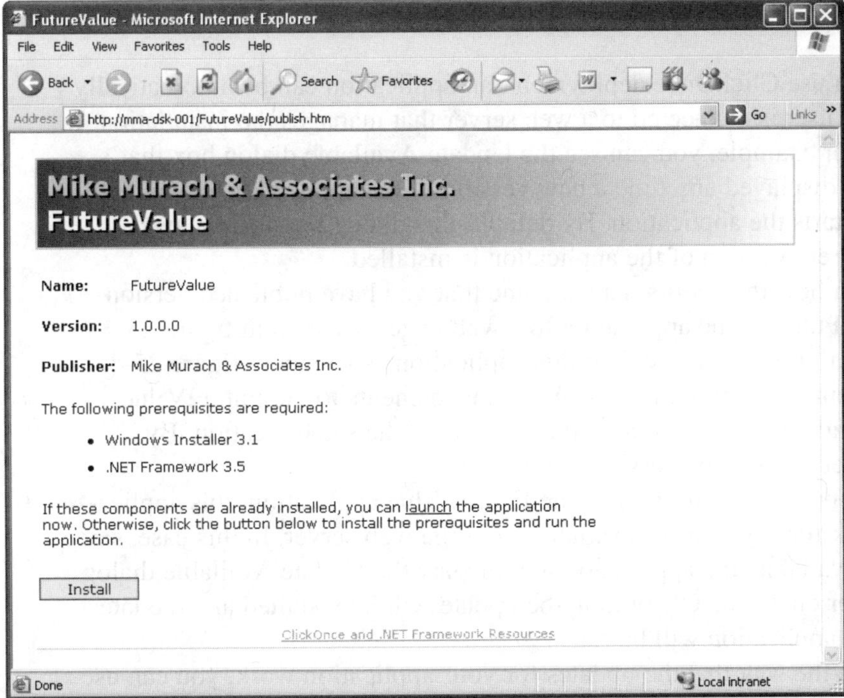

The Application Install dialog box

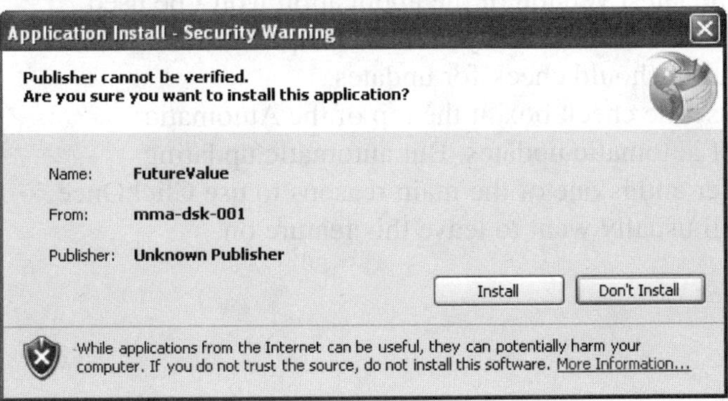

Description

- To install the application, open a web browser and navigate to the publish.htm page that's created when you publish the application. Then, click the Install button.
- If the application doesn't come from a trusted source, a security warning will be displayed. You can click the Install button in this dialog box to install the application.
- To prevent the security warning from being displayed, you must install a valid certificate.
- By default, the version number is incremented each time you update the application and publish it to the web page.

Figure 25-4 How to install an application from a web page

How a ClickOnce application can be automatically updated

When you use ClickOnce deployment, an application can be automatically updated if the user is connected to a web server that manages the installation. In figure 25-5, for example, you can see the Update Available dialog box that's automatically displayed any time a new version of the application is available and the user starts the application. By default, this dialog box is displayed before the current version of the application is installed.

To explain how this works, let's assume that you have published version 1.0.0.0 of the FutureValue application to a web page as shown in figure 25-3 and that several users have installed this application as shown in figure 25-4. Then, let's assume that you made several enhancements to the FutureValue application, and you published a second version to the same location. By default, this version will be version 1.0.0.1.

Then, the next time a user starts the FutureValue application, this application will check for any updates available from the web server. In this case, since an update is available, the application will display the Update Available dialog box. If the user clicks the OK button, the update will be installed and the latest version of the application will be run.

To change the way that the updates for your application work, you can use the Application Updates dialog box that's shown in this figure. If, for example, you want the application to start before the updates are applied, you can click on the first radio button. Then, the latest version of the application won't be used until the next time the application is run. When you use this option, you can also specify how often the application should check for updates.

Of course, you can also use the check box at the top of the Automatic Updates dialog box to turn off automatic updates. But automatic updating makes deployment much easier and is one of the main reasons to use ClickOnce deployment. As a result, you'll usually want to leave this feature on.

The Update Available dialog box

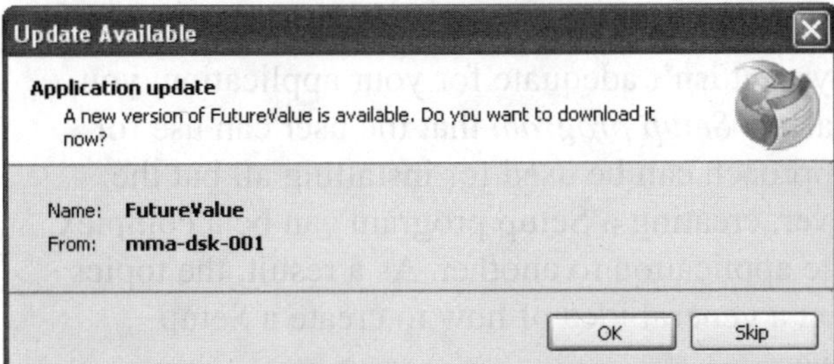

The Application Updates dialog box

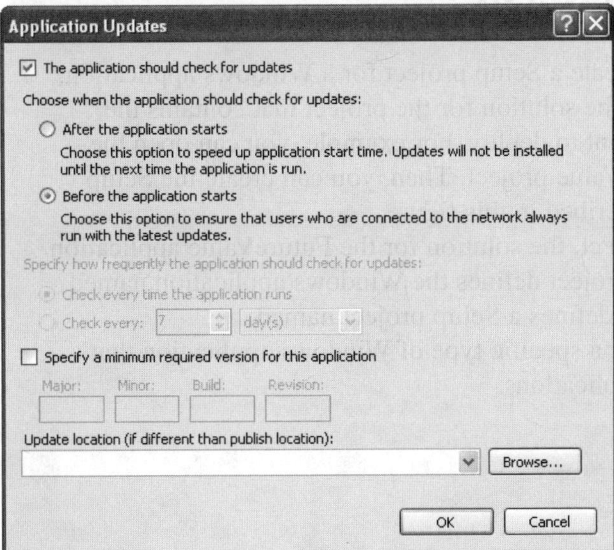

Description

- By default, if the user is connected to the web server that manages the installation, the Update Available dialog box is displayed whenever the user starts an application and a new version of the application is available. Then, the user can click on the OK button to install the updated version.
- To change the update defaults, you can use the Application Updates dialog box. To access this dialog box, use the Project→Properties command, select the Publish tab, and click on the Updates button.

Figure 25-5 How a ClickOnce application can be automatically updated

How to create and use a Setup program

If XCopy or ClickOnce deployment isn't adequate for your application, you can create a *Setup project* that creates a *Setup program* that the user can use for installing your application. This approach can be used for installing all but the most complex applications. However, creating a Setup program can be a complex process that varies widely from one application to another. As a result, the topics that follow are designed to give you a general idea of how to create a Setup program and let you take it from there.

How to create a Setup project

Figure 25-6 shows how to create a Setup project for a Windows application. To do that, you start by opening the solution for the project that contains the Windows application that you want to deploy. For example, you can open the solution that contains the FutureValue project. Then, you can create the Setup project for the application as described in this figure.

After you've created the project, the solution for the FutureValue application contains two projects. The first project defines the Windows application named FutureValue. The second project defines a Setup project named FutureValueSetup. This project is a specific type of Windows application that's used to install other Windows applications.

The New Project dialog box for a Setup project

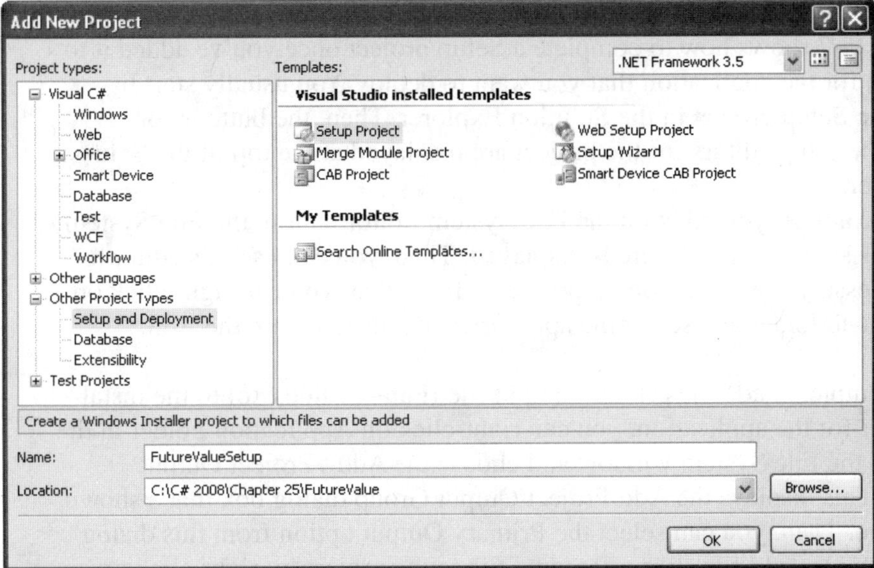

Description

- You use a *Setup project* to create a *Setup program* that installs a Windows application. A Setup program is a type of Windows application that's used to install other Windows applications.
- To create a Setup project, open the solution that contains the Windows application that you want to deploy, and choose the File→Add→New Project command to display the Add New Project dialog box. Then, expand the Other Project Types group, select the Setup and Deployment option, select the Setup Project template, enter a name for the Setup project, and click OK.
- When you create a Setup project, it is added to the solution that contains the Windows project that you want to create the Setup program for.

Express Edition Limitation

- Visual C# 2008 Express Edition doesn't provide for Setup projects.

Figure 25-6 How to create a Setup project

How to complete a Setup project

Figure 25-7 shows how to complete a Setup project once you've added it to the solution for the application that you want to deploy. You usually start by selecting the Setup project in the Solution Explorer. Then, the buttons for accessing the setup editors for the project are displayed at the top of the Solution Explorer.

If, for example, you click on the File System Editor button, the File System Editor that's shown in this figure is displayed. Then, you can use this editor to add the necessary files to the Setup program. To do that, you can right-click on the appropriate folder and select the appropriate command from the Add submenu.

For example, to add the primary output file (FutureValue.exe) to the installation folder for the application, you can right-click on Application Folder in the left pane of the File System window and choose the Add→Project Output command. This displays the Add Project Output Group dialog box that's shown in this figure. Then, you can select the Primary Output option from this dialog box. You can also add files like a Readme file to the project by right-clicking on Application Folder and selecting Add→File.

Similarly, the other editors let you add functions and features to the Setup program. If necessary, for example, you can use the Registry Editor to specify the keys and values that should be added to the registry on the target computer. And you can use the File Types Editor to establish a file association between a file extension and an application on the target computer.

The User Interface Editor lets you customize the dialog boxes that are displayed when you run the Setup program to install an application. For example, you can change the BannerBitMap property of any dialog box to display your company's logo in that dialog box. This editor also lets you change the text that's displayed in the dialog boxes, and it lets you add your own dialog boxes to those that are displayed by the Setup program.

The Custom Actions Editor lets you add actions to those that are performed by the Setup program. For example, you can use a custom action to attach the file for a SQL Server database to the database server when the application is installed. Before you can add a custom action to a Setup project, though, you must first develop a program that implements the action.

Finally, the Launch Conditions Editor lets you set conditions that must be met before the application can be installed. For example, you can use a launch condition to check the operating system version or to see if a particular file exists on the target system. If the condition isn't met, the Setup program aborts the installation.

Besides using the setup editors, you can set the properties of the setup project. Of these properties, the Manufacturer and ProductName properties are two of the most important ones because they're used to construct the path for the default installation folder. In figure 25-8, for example, the path specified in the dialog box starts with the Program Files folder, followed by a folder that

A Setup project displayed in Visual Studio

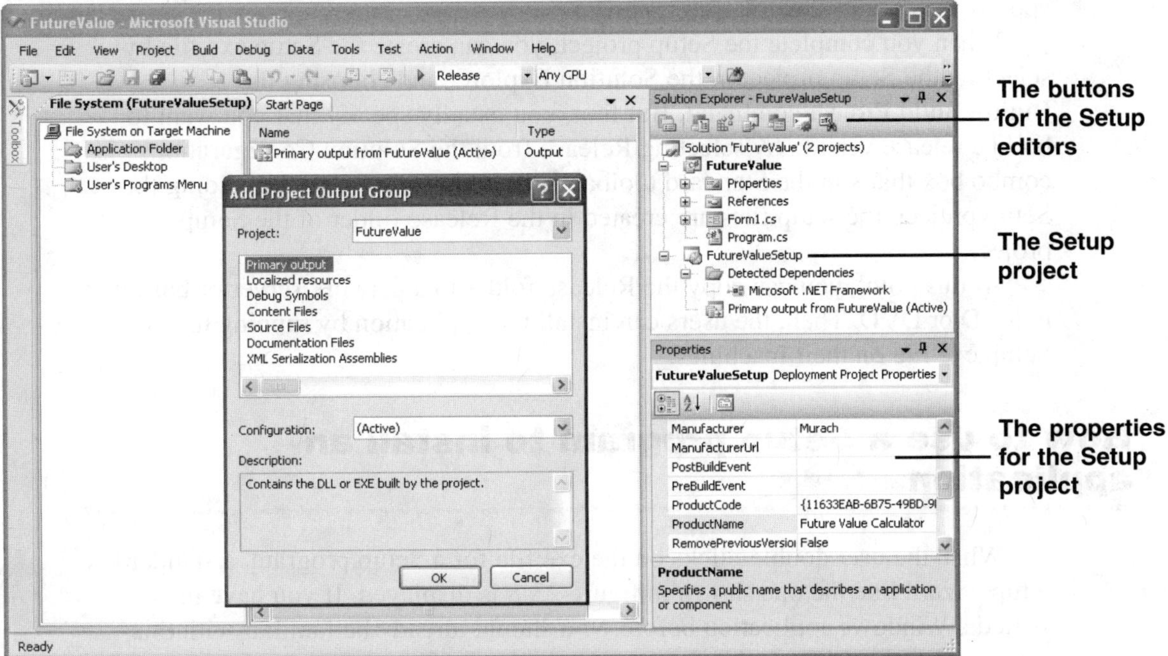

Common properties of the Setup project

Property	Description
Manufacturer	Provides the name of the manufacturer that's used by the Setup program as shown in the next figure.
ProductName	Provides the product name that's used by the Setup program as shown in the next figure.

Description

- To access the setup editors that let you customize the Setup project, select the Setup project in the Solution Explorer, and use the buttons that are displayed at the top of the Solution Explorer.
- To add the necessary files to a Setup project, right-click on the appropriate folder in the File System window, and choose the Add→Project Output command to display the Add Project Output Group dialog box. Then, select the files that you want to add and click OK.
- To create the Setup.exe file, select the Setup project in the Solution Explorer, and choose the Build→Build Project command.

Figure 25-7 How to complete a Setup project

corresponds with the Manufacturer property, followed by a folder that corresponds with the ProductName property.

When you complete the Setup project, you can create the Setup.exe file by selecting the Setup project in the Solution Explorer and choosing the Build→Build Project command. But first, you usually specify that you want to build a release version by selecting Release from the Solution Configurations combo box that's in the Standard toolbar. Then, when you're done building the Setup project, the setup files are created in the Release folder of the Setup project.

At this point, you can copy the Release folder to a network server or burn it to a CD or DVD. Then, the users can install the application by running the Setup.exe file on their machines.

How to use a Setup program to install an application

When the user double-clicks on the exe file for a Setup program, a standard setup wizard like the one shown in figure 25-8 is displayed. If you have installed a Windows application before, you should already be familiar with this type of wizard. Although this figure only shows the first two steps of the setup wizard, these are two of the most important steps.

The first step displays the default welcome message and the default copyright warning. If you want to change the text of either of these, you can use the User Interface Editor. In addition, the ProductName property of the Setup project is displayed in the title bar of this wizard. If you want to change this, you can change the ProductName property of the Setup project.

The second step displays the default installation folder for the application. As I mentioned earlier, this folder is constructed by combining the folder that stores the program files with a folder that has the name of the application's manufacturer and a folder that has the name of the product. However, this is just a suggested folder, so the user can select another folder.

After the user completes these steps, the next three steps let the user confirm the installation, display the progress of the installation, and display a message when the installation has been completed. Although these steps aren't shown in this figure, you've probably seen these steps when you've installed other Windows applications. If necessary, you can use the User Interface Editor to control the appearance of these steps. Or, you can use this editor to add steps such as a step that displays a license agreement or a step that registers a user.

The first step of the Setup program

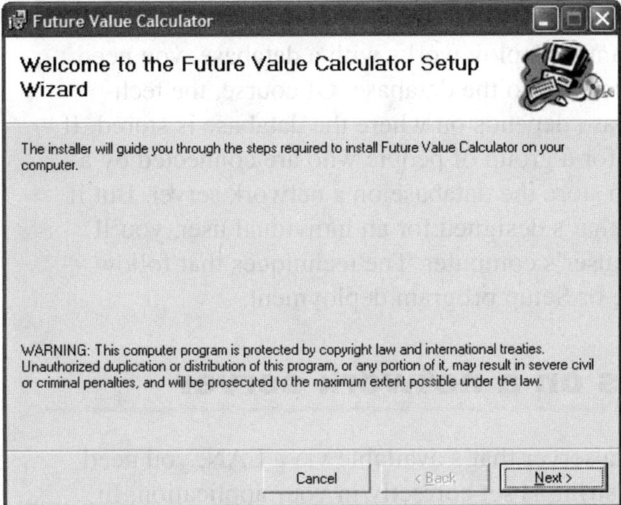

The second step of the Setup program

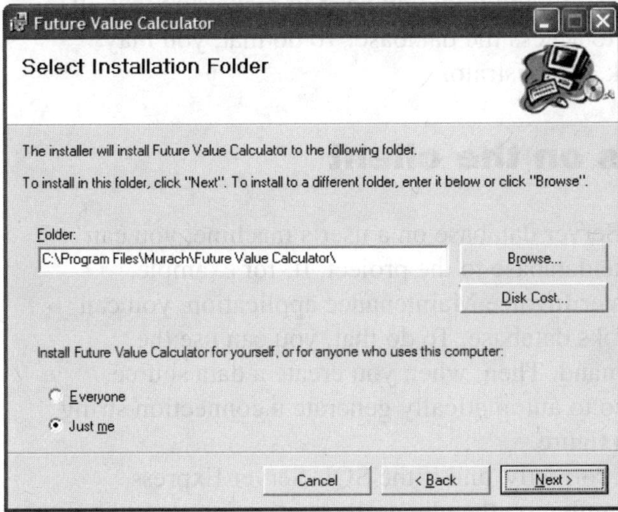

Description

- To start the installation, the user can run the Setup.exe file. This displays a standard setup wizard that's similar to the setup wizard for most Windows applications.

Figure 25-8 How to use a Setup program to install an application

How to deploy database applications

If the application that you want to deploy works with a database, you need to make sure that each user can connect to the database. Of course, the technique for connecting to the database depends on where the database is stored. If you've developed an application for a group of people who are connected by a LAN, for example, you'll want to store the database on a network server. But if you've developed an application that's designed for an individual user, you'll want to store the database on the user's computer. The techniques that follow work whether you use ClickOnce or Setup program deployment.

When the database runs on a network server

If the database is running on a server that's available via a LAN, you need to make sure that the connection string is set correctly in your application. In figure 25-9, for example, the first connection string specifies the MMABooks database that's running under the SQL Server Express database server on a network server named DBSERVER. In addition, you need to make sure that all users have adequate permissions to access the database. To do that, you may need to get help from the network administrator.

When the database runs on the client

If you want to install a SQL Server database on a user's machine, you can start by adding the mdf file for the database to the project. If, for example, you're going to install the Customer Invoice Maintenance application, you can add the mdf file for the MMABooks database. To do that, you can use the Project→Add Existing Item command. Then, when you create a data source, this typically causes Visual Studio to automatically generate a connection string like the second one shown in this figure.

If the connection string is set correctly, and if the SQL Server Express database server is installed and running on the client, the application should be able to access the database. To make sure that the database server is installed on the client, you can use the Prerequisites dialog box as described in figure 25-9. Once you've identified SQL Server 2005 Express as a prerequisite, the installation program will download SQL Server 2005 Express from Microsoft's web site and install it if that's necessary.

When the database runs on a web server

If the database is installed on a remote web site, you can still create a Windows application that will work with it, but you need to use web services to retrieve and update data from the database. Then, the data is passed between the client and the server with standard Internet protocols. That, however, requires different data access techniques than the ones described in this book.

The connection string for a database that's on a network server

```
Data Source=DBSERVER\SqlExpress;Initial Catalog=MMABooks;Integrated
Security=True
```

The connection string for a database that's on the client machine

```
Data Source=.\SQLEXPRESS;AttachDbFilename=|DataDirectory|\MMABooks_Data.MDF;
Integrated Security=True;User Instance=True
```

The Prerequisites dialog box

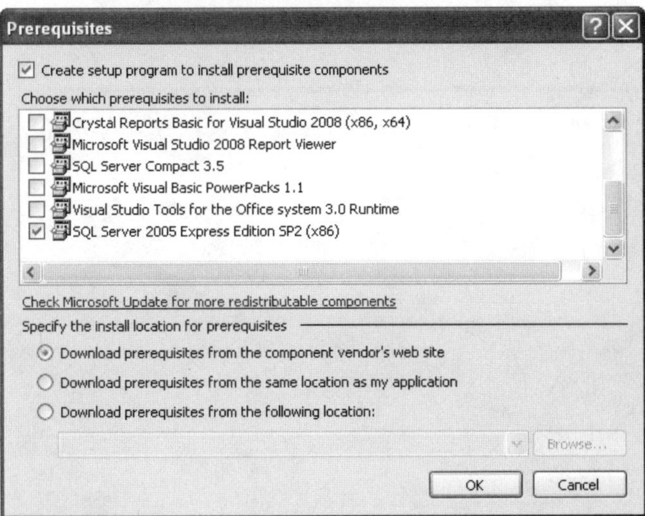

Description

- If the database server is running on a machine that's available via a LAN, you just need to make sure that the connection string is set correctly and that all users have proper security clearance to access the database. To do that, you may need to make the application a full trust application.
- If you want to run the database server on the client computer, you must make sure that the SQL Server Express database server is installed on the client computer. To do that, you can use the Prerequisites dialog box to identify SQL Server 2005 Express Edition as a prerequisite.
- To display the Prerequisites dialog box for ClickOnce deployment, you can display the Property Pages window for the Windows application. Then, you can select the Publish tab and click on the Prerequisites button.
- To display the Prerequisites dialog box for a Setup program, you can display the Property Pages dialog box for the Setup project and click on the Prerequisites button.
- If the database server is running on a web server, you can use web services to interact with the database. However, the techniques for doing that aren't presented in this book.

Figure 25-9 How to deploy database applications

Perspective

You'll probably spend a surprising amount of time developing procedures for deploying even relatively small applications. So for a large application, I recommend that you develop a procedure early in the application's development cycle. Then, you can use this procedure to install the application during testing, and you can use that experience to fine-tune the procedure as you go along. As a side benefit, you may discover installation issues that affect the application's design.

Terms

XCopy deployment
ClickOnce deployment
Setup program
Setup project

Appendix A

How to install and use the software for this book

To develop the applications presented in this book, you need to have Visual Studio 2008 or Visual C# 2008 Express Edition installed on your system. In addition, if you're going to develop database applications that use databases that are stored on your own PC rather than on a remote server, you need to install SQL Server on your PC. The easiest way to do that is to install SQL Server 2005 Express Edition. In fact, this edition of SQL Server is installed by default when you install most editions of Visual Studio 2008.

This appendix describes how to install Visual Studio 2008 or Visual C# 2008 Express Edition. In addition, this appendix describes how to install SQL Server 2005 Express Edition and how to attach the database that's used in this book to this database server. But first, this appendix describes the files for this book that are available for download from our web site and shows you how to download, install, and use them.

How to use the downloadable files

Throughout this book, you'll see complete applications that illustrate the skills that are presented in each chapter. To help you understand how these applications work, you can download these applications from our web site. Then, you can open these applications in Visual Studio, view the source code, and run them.

These applications come in a single download that also includes the starting points for the exercises that are at the end of each chapter. Figure A-1 describes how you can download, install, and use these files. When you download the single setup file and execute it, it will install all of the files for this book in the C:\Murach\C# 2008 directory.

The Book Applications directory contains all of the Windows applications that are presented in this book. If you like, you can use Visual Studio to open these applications. Then, you can view the source code for these applications, and you can run them to see how they work.

The Exercise Starts directory contains all of the starting points for the exercises presented in this book. When you execute the setup file, the subdirectories of this directory are copied to the C:\C# 2008 directory (creating this directory if necessary). This makes it easy to locate the exercise starts as you work through the exercises. For example, you can find the exercise start for chapter 1 in the C:\C# 2008\Chapter 01 directory. In addition, if you make a mistake and want to restore a file to its original state, you can do that by copying it from the directory where it was originally installed.

The Exercise Starts directory also contains a Files subdirectory that's copied to C:\C# 2008. This subdirectory contains all the text, binary, and XML files used by the book applications and exercises.

The Exercise Solutions directory contains the source code for the solutions to the exercises. If you have trouble doing the exercises, you can use Visual Studio to open these applications. Then, you can compare the solution to your application to solve any problems that you encountered while attempting to do the exercises.

The Database and Database Backup directories contain the MMABooks database that's used in section 4 of this book. In addition, the Database directory contains files that you can use to attach this database to a SQL Server Express database server, detach this database from the server, and restore the original database from the Database Backup directory. Figure A-4 describes how to use these files.

What the downloadable files for this book contain

- All of the applications presented in this book
- The starting points for all of the exercises in this book
- The solutions for all of the exercises in this book
- The data files and database for the applications and exercises

How to download and install the files for this book

- Go to www.murach.com, and go to the page for *Murach's C# 2008*.
- Click the link for "FREE download of the book applications." Then, select the "All book files" link and respond to the resulting pages and dialog boxes. This will download a setup file named cs08_allfiles.exe onto your hard drive.
- Use the Windows Explorer to find the setup file on your hard drive. Then, double-click this file and respond to the dialog boxes that follow. This installs the files in directories that start with C:\Murach\C# 2008.

How your system is prepared for doing the exercises

- Some of the exercises have you start from existing projects. The source code for these projects is in the C:\Murach\C# 2008\Exercise Starts directory. After the setup file installs the files in the download, it runs a batch file named exercise_starts_setup.bat that copies all of the subdirectories of the Exercise Starts directory to the C:\C# 2008 directory. Then, you can find all of the starting points for the exercises in directories like C:\C# 2008\Chapter 01 and C:\C# 2008\Chapter 04.

How to view the source code for the applications

- The source code for the applications presented in this book can be found in the C:\Murach\C# 2008\Book Applications directory. You can view this source code by opening the project or solution in the appropriate directory.

How to view the solutions to the exercises

- The exercise solutions can be found in the C:\Murach\C# 2008\Exercise Solutions directory. You can view these applications by opening the project or solution in the appropriate directory.

How to prepare your system for using the database

- To use the database that comes with this book on your PC, you need to make sure that SQL Server 2005 Express is installed as described in figure A-3, and you need to attach the database to SQL Server Express as described in figure A-4.

Figure A-1 How to use the downloadable files for this book

How to install Visual Studio 2008

If you've installed Windows applications before, you shouldn't have any trouble installing Visual Studio 2008. You simply insert the DVD or the first CD and the setup program starts automatically. This setup program will lead you through the steps for installing Visual Studio as summarized in figure A-2.

When you click the Install Visual Studio 2008 link, the setup program starts loading the installation components it needs. Then, after you click the Next button and accept the license agreement, the program lets you select the type of installation. In most cases, you'll perform a default installation so the most commonly used features are installed, including the .NET Framework, Visual Studio, Visual C#, and SQL Server Express.

After you install Visual Studio, you can install the documentation for Visual Studio and all of the products that come with it. To do that, just click the Install Product Documentation link.

If you're going to use the Visual C# 2008 Express Edition, you have to download and install Visual C# 2008 and SQL Server Express separately. But if you follow the directions on the Microsoft web site when you download these products, you shouldn't have any trouble installing them.

The final setup step is to apply any updates that have become available since the product was released. If you don't perform this step, though, you can check for updates from within Visual Studio by using the Help→Check for Updates command. In fact, you should use this command periodically to be sure that Visual Studio is up-to-date.

The Visual Studio 2008 setup program

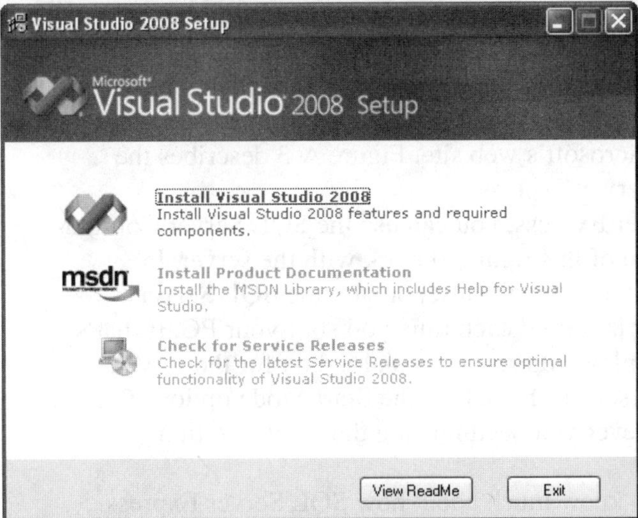

How to install Visual Studio 2008

- Insert the DVD or Disc 1 of the installation CDs. The setup program will start automatically.
- Click the Install Visual Studio 2008 link and follow the instructions. When the Options page is displayed, you can accept the Default option unless you have special requirements.
- To install the documentation for Visual Studio and the related products (Visual C#, ASP.NET, etc.), click the Install Product Documentation link.
- To install any updates that are available, click the Check for Service Releases link.

How to install the Express Edition of Visual C# 2008

1. Go to the page on Microsoft's web site for the download of the Visual Studio 2008 Express Editions and follow the directions to download the setup program for Visual C# 2008.
2. Run the setup program. It works similarly to the setup program for Visual Studio 2008, but fewer options are available.

Description

- The Visual Studio 2008 Setup program installs not only Visual Studio, but also the .NET Framework 3.5, the development web server, and SQL Server 2005 Express.
- The setup program for the Express Edition of Visual C# 2008 does not install the SQL Server 2005 Express Edition. As a result, if you want to use the Express Edition to work with databases, you have to download and install SQL Server 2005 Express Edition separately as described in figure A-3.

Figure A-2 How to install Visual Studio 2008

How to install and use SQL Server 2005 Express

SQL Server 2005 Express Edition is a free, lightweight version of SQL Server 2005 that you can install on your PC to test database applications. If SQL Server Express isn't installed when you install Visual Studio, you can download and install it from Microsoft's web site. Figure A-3 describes the procedure for installing SQL Server Express.

After you install SQL Server Express, you can use the SQL Server Configuration Manager shown at the top of this figure to work with the server. In particular, you can use it to start, continue, pause, or stop the SQL Server engine. By default, SQL Server is started each time you start your PC. If that's not what you want, you can display the Properties dialog box for the server, click the Services tab, and then select Manual for the Start Mode option. Then, you can start SQL Server whenever you need it using the Configuration Manager.

Although you don't need to know much about how SQL Server Express works to use it, you should know that when you run the setup program, it creates a copy of SQL Server with the same name as your computer appended with SQLEXPRESS. For example, the copy of SQL Server on my system is named JOEL2\SQLEXPRESS. After this server is installed and started, you can attach databases to it. Then, you can create connections to those databases that you can use in your C# applications.

The SQL Server Configuration Manager

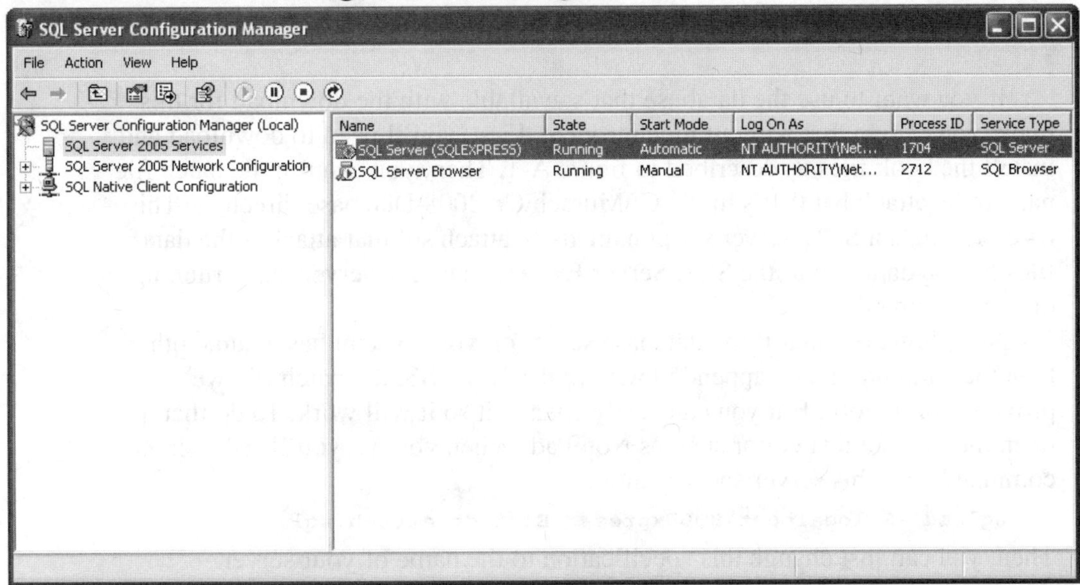

How to install SQL Server 2005 Express

- If you're using Visual Studio 2008, SQL Server 2005 Express is installed when you install Visual Studio as described in figure A-2.
- If you're using Visual C# 2008 Express Edition, you can download the setup file for SQL Server 2005 Express Edition from Microsoft's web site for free. Then, you can run the setup file to install SQL Server Express.

How to use SQL Server Express

- After you install SQL Server Express, it will start automatically each time you start your PC. To start or stop this service or change its start mode, start the SQL Server Configuration Manager (Start→All Programs→Microsoft SQL Server 2005→Configuration Tools→SQL Server Configuration Manager), select the server in the right pane, and use the buttons in the toolbar.
- The setup program creates a copy of SQL Server with a name that consists of your computer name followed by \SqlExpress. You can use this name to define connections to the databases that you use with this server.

Figure A-3 How to install and use SQL Server 2005 Express

How to attach the database for this book to the database server

If you want to use the database that's available with the download for this book, you can do that without much trouble. First, you'll need to download and install the book files as described in figure A-1. Then, you can run the batch file named db_attach.bat that's in the C:\Murach\C# 2008\Database directory. This batch file runs a SQL Server script named db_attach.sql that attaches the data files for the database to the SQL Server Express database server that's running on your computer.

Note, however, that if the database server on your system has a name other than the computer name appended with SQLEXPRESS, the batch file we provide won't work. But you can easily change it so it will work. To do that, just open the file in a text editor such as NotePad. When you do, you'll see a single command with this server specification:

```
sqlcmd -S localhost\SQLExpress -E /i db_attach.sql
```

Then, you can just change this specification to the name of your server.

Another problem can arise if you try to attach the database by running the db_attach.bat file under the Windows Vista operating system. Specifically, you may get an error like this:

```
CREATE DATABASE permission denied in database master
```

This is due to the fact that under Vista, you aren't automatically given administrator privileges even if you're logged on as an administrator, and you need to have administrator privileges to attach the database. Normally, Vista will notify you when administrator privileges are required to perform a task, but this doesn't happen when you run a batch file.

To get around this problem, you'll need to turn off a feature of Vista called User Account Control as described in this figure. Then, after you restart your system, you should be able to attach the database without any problem. Be sure to turn User Account Control back on when you're done as it provides added security for your system.

You'll also need to turn User Account Control off to run the other batch files in the Database directory. These files, along with the associated script files, provide for detaching the database and restoring the original database from the Database Backup directory. Note that if you detach the database and then move the mdf and ldf files, you'll need to use an edited version of the db_attach.sql file to reattach them.

The dialog box for turning User Account Control on and off under Vista

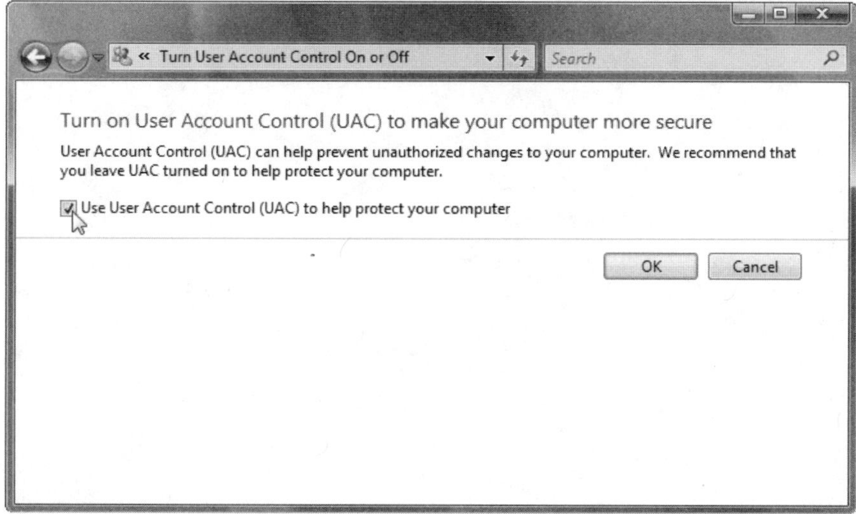

How to attach the database for this book to SQL Server Express

- If you're going to use the MMABooks database that's used by the applications in section 4 of this book on your own PC, you need to attach it to SQL Server Express. To do that, you can use one of the batch files and SQL scripts that are downloaded and installed along with the other files for this book.
- To attach the database to SQL Server Express, run the db_attach.bat file. To do that, you can use the Windows Explorer to navigate to the C:\Murach\C# 2008\Database folder and double-click the db_attach.bat file.

How to detach the database and restore the original database

- To detach the database from the server, run the db_detach.bat file.
- To restore the original database, run the db_restore.bat file. This detaches the database, copies the original database files in the Database Backup directory over the current files in the Database directory, and reattaches the database.

How to work with the database under Windows Vista

- To use the batch files we provide to attach, detach, or restore the MMABooks database under Windows Vista, you will need to temporarily turn a feature of Vista called User Account Control off.
- To access User Account Control, display the Control Panel, switch to Classic View, double-click on User Accounts, and then click on the Turn User Account Control on or off link. Then, remove the check mark from the Use User Account Control option, click the OK button, and restart your system when instructed.

Figure A-4 How to attach the database for this book to the database server

Index

A

B

C

D

E

F

G

H

I

J

K

L

M

N

O

P

Q

R

S

T

U

V

W

X

Y

What software you need for this book

- Any edition of Microsoft Visual Studio 2008 or the Express Edition of Microsoft Visual C# 2008.
- If you want to store databases on your PC, you need to install SQL Server 2005 Express Edition, which is available for free.
- For information about downloading and installing these products, please see appendix A.

The downloadable files for this book

- All of the applications presented in this book including source code and data.
- Starting points and data for the exercises in this book so you can get more practice in less time.
- Solutions for all of the exercises in this book so you can check your work on the exercises.
- The database files for the MMABooks database that's used by this book.

How to download the files for this book

- Go to www.murach.com, and go to the page for ***Murach's C# 2008***.
- Click the link for "FREE download of the book applications." Then, select the "All book files" link and respond to the resulting pages and dialog boxes. This will download a setup file named cs08_allfiles.exe onto your hard drive.
- Use the Windows Explorer to find this exe file on your hard drive. Then, double-click this file and respond to the dialog boxes that follow. This installs the files in directories that start with C:\Murach\C# 2008, and then runs a batch file that copies the subdirectories of the C:\Murach\C# 2008\Exercise Starts directory to the C:\C# 2008 directory.

How to prepare your system for this book

- If you want to attach the MMABooks database that's used by this book to a SQL Server 2005 Express database server that's running on your PC, use the Windows Explorer to navigate to the C:\Murach\C# 2008\Database directory and double-click on the db_attach.bat file.
- For more detailed instructions about preparing your system for this book, please see appendix A.